Ray Tracing from the Ground Up

Ray Tracing
from the Ground Up

Kevin Suffern

CRC Press
Taylor & Francis Group
Boca Raton London New York

CRC Press is an imprint of the
Taylor & Francis Group, an **informa** business

AN A K PETERS BOOK

CRC Press
Taylor & Francis Group
6000 Broken Sound Parkway NW, Suite 300
Boca Raton, FL 33487-2742

© 2007 by Taylor & Francis Group, LLC
CRC Press is an imprint of Taylor & Francis Group, an Informa business

No claim to original U.S. Government works

ISBN-13: 9781568812724

Visit the Taylor & Francis Web site at
http://www.taylorandfrancis.com

and the CRC Press Web site at
http://www.crcpress.com

Library of Congress Cataloging-in-Publication Data

Suffern, Kevin G.
    Ray tracing from the ground up / Kevin G. Suffern.
        p.   cm.
    Includes bibliographical references and index.
    ISBN 978-1-56881-272-4 (alk. paper)
1. Computer graphics.   I. Title.
    T385.S7995 2007
    006.6--dc22
                                                                    2007021706

Printed and bound in Great Britain by
TJ Books Limited, Padstow, Cornwall

Contents

Foreword

Computer graphics involves simulating the distribution of light in a 3D environment. There are only a few fundamentally different algorithms that have survived the test of time. They can be loosely classified into projective algorithms and image-space algorithms. The former class projects each geometric primitive onto the image plane, with local shading taking care of the appearance of objects. This class of algorithm is still widely used because it is amenable to pipeline processing and therefore to hardware implementation as evidenced by all modern graphics cards.

Image-space algorithms compute the color of each pixel by figuring out where the light came from for that pixel. Here, the basic operation is to determine the nearest object along a line of sight. Following light back along a line has given this basic operation and the associated image-synthesis algorithm their name: ray tracing.

In 1980, ray tracing was at the forefront of science. The quality of the images that can be computed with ray tracing was an eye opener, as it naturally includes light paths such as specular reflection and transmission, which are difficult to compute with projective algorithms. Some shapes are easier to intersect rays with than others, and in those early days, spheres featured heavily in ray-traced images. Hence, old images often contained shiny spheres to demonstrate the power of ray tracing.

A vast amount of research was then expended to make ray tracing both more tractable and to include more features. Variants were introduced, for instance, that compute diffuse inter-reflection, caustics, and/or participating media. To speed up image generation, many data structures were developed that spatially sort the 3D geometry. Spatial subdivision algorithms allow a very substantial reduction of the candidate set of objects that need to be intersected to find the nearest object for each ray. Ray tracing is also amenable to parallel processing and has therefore attracted a substantial amount of research in that area.

All of this work moved ray tracing from being barely tractable, to just about doable for those who had state-of-the-art computers and plenty of time to kill. High-quality rendering tends to take a whole night to complete, mostly because this allows artists to start a new rendering before going home, to find the finished image ready when they arrive at work the next day. This, by the way, still holds true. For many practical applications, hardware and algorithmic improvements are used for rendering larger environments, or to include more advanced shading, rather than to reduce the computation time.

On the other hand, more than 25 years after its introduction, ray tracing has found a new lease on life in the form of interactive and real-time implementations. Such rendering speeds are obtained by using a combination of super-fast modern hardware, parallel processing, state-of-the-art algorithms, and a healthy dose of old-fashioned low-level engineering. Recent advances have enabled ray tracing to be a useful alternative for real-time rendering of animated scenes, as well as huge scenes that do not fit into main memory. In addition, there is a trend towards the development of dedicated hardware for ray tracing.

All of this research has helped to push ray tracing from an interesting esoteric technique for image synthesis to a seriously viable algorithm for practical applications. If necessary, ray tracing can operate in real time. If desired, ray tracing can be physically based and can therefore be used in predictive lighting simulations. As a result, ray tracing is now used in earnest in the movie industry, but also, for instance, in the automotive industry and in scientific visualization. In addition, it forms the basis for several other graphics algorithms, including radiosity and photon mapping.

The practical importance of ray tracing as a lighting-simulation technique means that ray tracing needs to be taught to students, as well as to practitioners in industry. In addition, ray tracing is sufficiently multifaceted that teaching students all aspects of the algorithm will give them all manner of additional benefits: 3D modeling skills, mathematics skills, software engineering skills (writing a ray tracer is for many students the first time that they will have to manage a sizeable chunk of code), hands-on experience in object-oriented programming, and deeper insights into the physics of light, as well as knowledge of the behavior of materials.

It would be ideal to present a ray-tracing course to students at the undergraduate level for all of the above reasons, but also because a deep understanding of ray tracing will make it easier to grasp other image-synthesis algorithms.

For this, a book is required that explains all facets of ray tracing at the right pace, assuming only a very moderate amount of background knowledge.

I'm positively delighted that such a book now exists. *Ray Tracing from the Ground Up* not only covers all aspects of ray tracing, but does so at a level that allows both undergraduate and graduate students to appreciate the beauty and algorithmic elegance of ray tracing. At the same time, this book goes into more than sufficient detail to deserve a place on the bookshelves of many professionals as a reference work.

Kevin was gracious enough to let me read early drafts of several chapters when I was teaching a graduate-level ray-tracing course at the University of Central Florida. This has certainly taught me many of the lesser-known intricacies of ray tracing. Kevin himself has taught ray tracing to undergraduate students for many years, and it shows. This book, which grew out of his course notes, is remarkably easy to follow, especially given the complexity of the subject matter.

As such, I can heartily recommend this book to both professionals as well as students and teachers. Whether you are only interested in rendering a collection of shiny spheres or want to create stunning images of highly complicated and realistic environments, this book will show you how. Whether its intended use is as a ray-tracing reference or as the basis of a course on ray tracing, this book is essential reading.

Erik Reinhard
University of Bristol
University of Central Florida

Preface

Where Did This Book Come From?

Since the early 1990s, I have had the privilege of teaching an introductory ray-tracing course at the University of Technology, Sydney, Australia. This book is the outcome of all of those years in the classroom. The ray tracer presented here has been developed and taught over the years, during which time my students have provided invaluable feedback, bug reports, ideas, and wonderful images. The book's manuscript has evolved from the teaching notes for the course and has been written (and re-written) chapter by chapter as the ray tracer, and my teaching of it, have developed. Writing in a teaching context with the feedback provided by students has helped me produce a book that is, I hope, much more understandable than it would have been had I written it in isolation. I like to call the iterative processes of programming, writing, and teaching ray tracing the *ray-tracing circle*.

What Is Ray Tracing?

Ray tracing is a computer-graphics technique that creates images by shooting rays. It's illustrated in Figure 1, which shows a camera, a window with pixels, two rays, and two objects. The rays go through pixels and are tested for intersection with the objects. When a ray hits an object, the ray tracer works out how much light is reflected back along the ray to determine the color of the pixel. By using enough pixels, the ray tracer can produce an image of the objects. If the objects are reflective, the rays can bounce off of them and hit other objects.

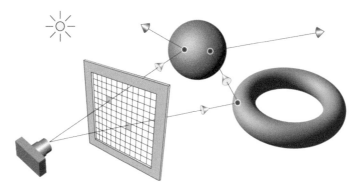

Figure 1. The ray-tracing process.

This process is conceptually simple, elegant, and powerful. For example, it allows ray tracing to accurately render reflections, transparent objects, shadows, and global illumination. Ray tracing can also render large triangle meshes more efficiently than other rendering techniques.

Why Is Ray Tracing Important?

The production of ever more realistic images is a trend of long standing in 3D computer graphics. This is a task at which ray tracing excels. A major application of ray tracing is the film industry, not just for visual effects, but for rendering whole movies. For example, the animated films *Ice Age*, *Ice Age 2*, and *Robots* were fully ray traced, as were the short films *Bunny* and *The Cathedral* (a.k.a. *Katedra*). *Ice Age* was nominated for the Academy Award for Best Animated Feature in 2002, *Bunny* won the Academy Award for Animated Short Film in 1998, and *The Cathedral* was nominated for the Academy Award for Animated Short Film in 2002. Ray tracing was also used in *Happy Feet* to render the penguins with ambient occlusion, and for reflection and refraction with the ocean surface (see Chapters 17, 27, and 28). *Happy Feet* won the Academy Award for Best Animated Feature in 2006.

The major software packages used in the visual-effects industry have built-in ray tracers, and there are numerous state-of-the art ray tracers available as plug-ins or stand-alone applications. These include Brazil (http://www.splutterfish.com/), Mental Ray (http://www.mentalimages.com/), finalRender (http://www.finalrender.com/), and Maxwell Render (http://www.maxwell-render.com/). Cinema 4D (http://www.maxon.net/) also has a state-of-the art ray tracer.

Real-time 3D computer games also have an increasing demand for realism. Although current PCs are not fast enough for real-time ray-traced games, this is likely to change in the next few years. The introduction of chips with specialized graphics processors on multiple cores that can be programmed using existing programming tools will make this possible. Because each ray can be traced independently, ray tracing can trivially use as many processors as are available. In fact, ray tracing has been described as being "embarrassingly parallelizable."[1] These hardware advances should also result in ray tracing being used more frequently in the visual-effects industry.

All this means that ray tracing has a great future, and within a few years you should be able to use the techniques you will learn in this book to write real-time ray-tracing applications such as games.

Graphics education also benefits greatly. My experience has been that getting students to write a ray tracer is the best way for them to understand how rendering algorithms work. Ray tracing's flexibility and ease of programming is the primary reason for this.

In a more general context, ray tracing helps us understand the appearance of the world around us. Because it simulates geometric optics, ray tracing can be used to render many familiar optical phenomena. The appearance of the fish and bubbles on the front cover is an example.

Book Features

This book provides a detailed explanation of how ray tracing works, a task that's accomplished with a combination of text, code samples, about 600 ray-traced images, and over 300 illustrations. Full color is used throughout. Almost all of the ray-traced images were produced with the software discussed here. The book also showcases the work of about 25 students. You can develop the ray tracer chapter by chapter.

Most chapters have questions and exercises at the end. The questions often ask you to think about ray-traced images; the exercises cover the implementation of the ray tracer and suggest ways to extend it. There are almost 400 questions and exercises.

Shading is described rigorously as solutions to the rendering equation and is specified in radiometric terms such as radiance (see Chapter 13).

---

1. Alan Norton, circa 1984, personal communication.

The book's website (http://www.raytracegroundup.com) contains several animations that demonstrate effects and processes that are difficult or impossible to see with static images.

 ## Pathways through This Book

You don't have to read the chapters in order, or read all of the material in every chapter, or read all of the chapters. For example, Chapters 2 and 20 cover some of the mathematics you need for ray tracing, and you may already be familiar with this; you can read Chapter 19 on ray-object intersections, or parts of it, when you need to.

Chapters 1–4, 9, and 13–16 cover ray-tracing fundamentals, perspective viewing with a pinhole camera, theoretical foundations, and basic shading. Chapter 13 is heavy going mathematically but provides the essential theoretical foundations for the following chapters on shading. The good news is that you don't have to master all of the material in Chapter 13. Most of the complicated integrals in this and the following chapters can be expressed in a few simple lines of code, which are in the book.

Chapter 24 covers mirror reflection, Chapters 27 and 28 cover transparency, and Chapters 29–31 cover texturing. Although You will find many interesting things to explore here, and you can read the texturing chapters first, if you want to.

If you read the sampling chapters, Chapters 5–7, you will have the background to understand the different camera models in Chapters 10–12, ambient occlusion in Chapter 17, area lights in Chapter 18, glossy reflection in Chapter 25, and global illumination in Chapter 26.

Chapter 21 explains how to ray trace transformed objects, and Chapter 22 covers grid acceleration, which is the tool for ray tracing triangle meshes in Chapter 23.

 ## What Knowledge and Skills Do You Need?

Because the ray tracer is written in C++, you should be reasonably proficient at C++ programming. A first course in C++ should be sufficient preparation, but there is a heavy emphasis on inheritance, dynamic binding, and polymorphism right from the start. That's a critical design element, as I'll explain in Chapter 1.

You should also be familiar with coordinate geometry, elementary trigonometry, and elementary vector and matrix algebra. Although there is some calculus in the book, I usually just quote the results and give you the relevant code.

You don't need previous studies in computer graphics because the book is self-contained in this regard. Chapters 3, 8, and 13 cover the necessary graphics background material. As far as graphics output is concerned, ray tracing is a simple as possible—you just draw pixels into a window on your computer screen.

 ## Intended Audience

The book is intended for computer-graphics students who have had at least an introductory course in C++. The book is suitable for both undergraduate and graduate courses.

It's also intended for anyone with the required background who wants to write a ray tracer or who wants find out how ray tracing works. This includes people working in the computer-graphics industry.

 ## Online Resources

The book's website is at http://www.raytracegroundup.com, where you will find:

- the skeleton ray tracer described in Chapter 1;
- sample code;
- triangle mesh files in PLY format;
- image files in PPM format;
- the ray-traced images in JPEG format;
- additional images;
- C++ code for constructing scenes;
- animations;
- a place where you can post errata;
- useful links.

 ## Topics Not Covered

Due to time and space constraints, here are some of the many topics that I have not discussed: high dynamic range (HDR) imaging with local tone-mapping operators; comparisons between grid acceleration and other acceleration schemes such as bounding volume hierarchies; an efficient global illumination algorithm; an efficient technique for rendering caustics; sub-surface scattering; bump mapping; the volumetric rendering of participating media. Although HDR imaging would require some serious retrofitting, the other topics could be implemented as add-ons. Any of these could be student assignments or projects.

Acknowledgments

It's traditional for authors to start by thanking their long-suffering families. This is not a tradition I'm about to break. First, my thanks go to my wife, Eileen, without whose support this book would not have been written. Eileen read the whole book about three times, and then the proofs, corrected innumerable grammar mistakes, improved my writing, and did a lot of work on the index. She did all the cooking and housework through this period, while completing her own diploma studies, and watched in despair as the number of urgent repair jobs on the house grew and grew. As a result, I probably have about a year's work of repairs awaiting me.

My son Chris provided expert help with Adobe Illustrator and did all the curves in the figures. Chris also did the photography and graphic design for Figure 29.26. I'm very grateful for Chris's help. My son Tim checked the references, for which I am also very grateful. And finally, my four-year-old grandson Broden gave me permission to use his photograph in Figure 29.26.

Paul Perry, a friend of 40 years, provided on more than one occasion advice and a quiet refuge in Melbourne for writing.

I would like to thank Erik Rienhard, who acted as my reviewer. Erik read the whole manuscript, found many mistakes, and made many suggestions that have improved this book. I'm honored that he also wrote the foreword. Frequent phone conversations with him were very helpful.

I would also like to thank Pete Shirley, who has helped and inspired me in several ways. For example, Pete suggested that I use orthonormal bases and use instances for ray tracing transformed objects. There is a lot of Pete's work in this book, and it is the better for it.

The following people trialed early versions of the manuscript in their ray-tracing courses: Dave Breen at Drexel University, Bob Futrelle at Northeastern University, Steve Parker at the University of Utah, Erik Reinhard at the University of Central Florida, and Pete Shirley at the University of Utah. I wish to thank all of them.

Special thanks must go to Alice Peters at A K Peters, who believed in this book, right from the start, was amazingly patient during interminable delays on my part, and worked extremely hard to get it published for SIGGRAPH 2007. I particularly wish to thank Kevin Jackson-Mead, Senior Editor at A K Peters, who expertly edited the manuscript. This was a huge job. I also thank the typesetter, Erica Schultz, for an expert job.

Thanks go to Darren Wotherspoon at Skye Design for the beautiful cover design.

Richard Raban also deserves special thanks. Richard, as my Department Head at the University of Technology, Sydney, gave me a lot of support and a working environment that made writing easier. Chris W. Johnson and Helen Lu at UTS also read several chapters and pointed out mistakes.

The following students graciously provided permission to use their ray-traced images: Steve Agland, Nathan Andrews, John Avery, Peter Brownlow, David Gardner, Peter Georges, Mark Howard, Tania Humphreys, Daniel Kaestli, Adeel Khan, Mark Langsworth, Lisa Lönroth, Alistair McKinley, Jimmy Nguyen, Riley Perry, Duy Tran, and Ving Wong. Thank you all for your beautiful images, which have enhanced this book.

Thanks also go to Tania Humphreys for modeling and rendering the Mirage 2000 device by Opti-Gone Associates, to Alistair McKinley for implementing the ray-visualization software that made Figure 27.24(b) possible, and to Jimmy Nguyen for performing a number of file conversions.

The following students pointed out errors in the manuscript: Deepak Chaudhary, Tim Cooper, Ronnie Sunde, Ksenia Szeweva, and Mark White.

I must thank Naomi Hatchman for allowing me to use her penguin model in Chapters 23 and 29 and for a lot of work in supplying files in various formats and triangle resolutions.

I also thank James McNess for permission to use his goldfish model, shown on the cover and in Chapters 23 and 28.

There are two critical pieces of software associated with this book. One is the skeleton ray tracer. I'd like to thank Peter Kohout and James McGregor for producing early versions. I particularly thank Sverre Kvåle for writing the current version. Sverre also converted all the code files to PC format and tested the sample code. I am most grateful for all his work and his great programming skills.

The other is the website, built by HwaLeon (Ayo) Lee. Thank you, Ayo, for your generosity and professional development skills.

Ayo, James McGregor, Naomi, Peter, and Sverre have been students of mine; James McNess has been a student of Naomi.

Another student, Hong Son Nguyen, kindly produced a number of computer animations for the book and allowed me to put these on the website. Thank you, Hong.

My students, Naomi Hatchman, André Mazzone, Glen Sharah, Rangi Sutton, and the "UTS Amigos": Steve Agland, Peter Brownlow, Chris Cooper, Peter Georges, Justen Marshall, Adrian Paul, and Brian Smith, have inspired me by earning credits on Academy Award winning films for their outstanding visual-effects work. The films include *Happy Feet*, *The Lord of the Rings: The Return of the King*, and *The Matrix*.

I have also benefited greatly from discussions with Paul Bourke about nonlinear projections and stereoscopy. Paul read Chapters 11 and 12, and as a result of his feedback, these chapters are now more relevant to real-world applications. He also permitted me to use material in these chapters from his website at http://local.wasp.uwa.edu.au/~pbourke/. I thank Paul for all his help.

I also thank Paul Debevec for permission to use the Uffizi probe image from his website at http://www.debevec.org/Probes/ and for providing advice on light-probe mappings.

Henrik Jensen provided advice on various aspects of ray tracing.

The following people and organizations allowed me to use various information. Stephen Addleman from Cyberware: images of the horse, Isis, and Ganesh models from http://www.cyberware.com/; James Hastings-Trew: Earth images in Chapter 29 from his website at http://planetpixelemporium.com/planets.html; Phillipe Hurbain: sky images from http://www.philohome.com/ in Chapters 11 and 12; Michael Levin from Opti-Gone International: material from http://www.optigone.com/ about the Mirage 2000 in Chapter 12; Ric Lopez-Fabrega at Lopez-Fabrega Design: sky images from http://www.lfgrafix.com in Chapter 29; Morgan Kaufmann Publishers: images and code in Chapter 31; Steve Parker at the University of Utah: the Cornell-box image in Chapter 26; Greg Turk: PLY code and various PLY models of the Stanford bunny at http://www.cc.gatech.edu/projects/large_models/index.html. I thank you all.

Finally, I wish to thank Eric Haines and Pete Shirley for graciously providing endorsements for the book.

1

Ray Tracer Design and Programming

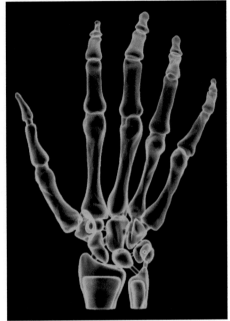

Image courtesy of Jimmy Nguyen
Skeleton model from Clemson University

A ray tracer with any reasonable set of features is a large and complex software system that must be designed carefully and developed in a systematic manner. This chapter gives you guidelines for the design and programming of a ray tracer. You can also find information on these topics in Glassner (1989), Wilt (1994), Shirley (2002), Shirley and Morley (2003), and Pharr and Humphreys (2004).

 ## 1.1 General Approaches

It's best to develop your ray tracer using object-oriented (OO) techniques for several reasons. The first is size and complexity. Object-oriented techniques are best for handling the design and implementation of large and complex systems, and ray tracers can certainly be large and complex. One of the largest was the Kilauea ray tracer, which consisted of about 700,000 lines of C++ code (Kato et al., 2001, Kato, 2002). Although the ray tracer I discuss here is

1

not nearly this large, it is large and complex enough for OO techniques to be essential for its development.

The second reason is extensibility, which is not really separate from the first, because large and complex software systems are developed by extending simpler systems. Ray tracers can be extended in many ways, for example, by adding new types of geometric objects. You should design your ray tracer so that adding new types of objects is as simple as possible. OO techniques allow you to do this without altering the existing code that renders the objects. Your ray tracer will also have to deal with different types of cameras, samplers, lights, BRDFs, materials, mappings, textures, noises, and bump maps. Adding a new type of any of these things should also be as simple as possible.

Let's look at how OO techniques facilitate these processes. The code that performs the ray-object intersections should not have to know the type of objects it deals with. Why? Because it would then have to explicitly identify the type of each object, and intersect it in a case or switch statement. This makes it more work to program because you must provide an identifier for each type, and add a new clause to the switch statement. To make matters worse, the switch statement may have to appear in more than one place in the ray tracer. It's far better for objects to be *anonymous* in the intersection part of the ray tracer. To do this you define a *uniform public interface* for the intersection (hit) functions, so that they are called the same way for all objects. The ray tracer, which can still identify the type of each object at run time, will then call the correct hit function.

You should also apply the same process to lights, materials, textures, etc. Except for build functions and `#include` statements, your ray tracer should not have to explicitly identify the type of anything that it deals with. From a design and development perspective, this is the most important aspect of your ray tracer code.

Kirk and Arvo (1988) discussed the above issues for the first time in a ray tracing context, including the use of a common user interface for all objects. This was the first paper on object oriented ray tracing; it contains many good ideas.

1.2 Inheritance

The best way to implement the above processes is to use *inheritance*. Figure 1.1 shows a sample geometric object inheritance chart. Provided you implement the objects correctly, *dynamic binding* guarantees that the correct hit functions are called. This is called *polymorphism*.

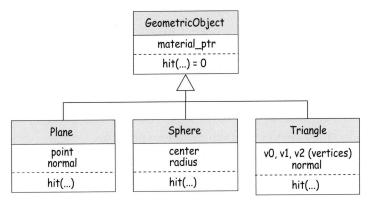

Figure 1.1 A sample object inheritance chart.

Code re-use is another benefit of inheritance. The fact that derived classes can use all the code in their base classes means that you only have to write the new parts when you add derived classes. For example, the code to handle the material only has to be written once in the GeometricObject class.

1.3 Language

The sample code in this book is C++ because it's the mainstream ray tracing language. The reasons are: its OO facilities, the ability to mix C and C++ code in the same program, and its computational efficiency. State of the art commercial ray tracers such as Brazil, Mental Ray, finalRender, and Maxwell Render are written in C++. Also, many major commercial rendering and animation packages, which were originally written in C, were re-written from the ground up in C++ during the 1990s. RenderMan plug-ins can also be written in C++.

Computational efficiency is important for ray tracers because of their extensive use of floating point calculations. C++ programs can be written efficiently because of the C heritage of C++, and the fact that they are fully compiled. If you are not careful, however, you can write inefficient C++ programs. The books by Meyers (1996, 2001, 2005), Lippman et al. (2005), and Bulka and Mayhew (2000) discuss computational efficiency in C++. Writing efficient code is, however, not as important as writing code that's easy to read, easy to maintain, and easy to extend. In other words, efficiency is not as important as good design. Fortunately, the two can go hand in hand in C++. Also, efficiency is not as important as using language features that make your job as a programmer easier. For example, there can be a cost penalty with inheritance in C++

because of the extra indirection of virtual function calls, and because dynamic binding prevents the inlining of virtual functions, but this is far outweighed by the benefits.

C++ can also use the Standard C library functions, and has excellent library facilities of its own, particularly the Standard Template Library (STL). See Lippman et al. (2005), Meyers (2001), and Ford and Topp (2001). C++ also has operator overloading that allows the code for many vector and matrix operations to be written in mathematical-like notation.

Public domain C code, such as code for solving cubic and quartic polynomial equations (Schwarze, 1990), can be simply incorporated into C++ programs, as can the efficient C macros for generating lattice noises by Peachey (2003). C++ also has an ANSI ISO standard that is platform independent.

Finally, there are good integrated development environments (IDEs) for C++ on all common computer platforms, but you should make sure that the code is compiled.

1.4 Building Scenes

Ray tracers render *scenes*. Before a scene can be rendered, the ray tracer needs everything to be specified: all the parameters for the camera, geometric objects, lights, materials, textures, etc. The most common way to do this is with a *scene description file*, but another way uses a *build function*. Each approach has its advantages and disadvantages.

Scene description files require a *scene description language* in which the files are written and a parser for the language. This can require a lot of programming. There are also limits to the type of scenes for which you can easily hand-craft a parser. Parsers that can handle control structures such as loops, branches, and recursive function calls are best written with lex and yacc, or Bison and Flex (Levine et al., 1992).

Build functions written in C++ don't require scene description files or parsing, and can exploit the full power of C++. They are functions that are included in your ray tracer code, and although they make it simpler and quicker to add new features, they require your ray tracer to always run in a development environment, at least in the simple approach that I've adopted.[1]

---

1. The executable produced by the development environment will, of course, run as a stand-alone application, but it can only render a single scene.

This is because the build function also has to be re-compiled each time you change the scene. This isn't a serious problem, for two reasons. First, C++ compilation is fast, and second, you will have to run your ray tracer this way while you are developing it. Your ray tracer would only need to run as a stand-alone program if you wanted to sell it, or distribute it. You could also run it as a stand-alone application if you finished it, but has anyone ever finished a ray tracer?

My experience from teaching both approaches is that build functions allow students more time to concentrate on the ray tracing itself. I therefore use build functions exclusively in this book, starting in Chapter 3. Wilt (1994) was the first ray-tracing book to use this approach.

Your ray tracer will still need to read some information from files. Examples include triangle mesh data and texture images, but I provide code for this.

1.5 The User Interface

This book is about writing the *engine* part of a ray tracer, because graphical user interface elements such as windows, dialogues, and menus, are operating system dependent. Technically, the only "user interface" your ray tracer needs is a command line—it can write the image out to a file, and you can use third-party software to look at it. You can use a command-line interface with Linux, Unix, and Mac OS X, but there's a potential problem. Although most of the scenes I discuss should only take seconds or minutes to render, scenes can take hours or more; in fact, there's no upper limit to ray tracer rendering times.[2] You don't want to wait hours, only to find out that you incorrectly typed one of the viewing parameters in the build function. You should therefore use image-viewing software that allows you to view partially rendered scenes.

From my perspective however, there's a more serious problem with this approach. If your ray tracer doesn't open a window and display the image as it's being rendered, you will miss out on one of life's great pleasures—watching scenes being ray traced. If you haven't done any ray tracing, you will just have to take my word on this for now.

---

2. Steven Parker has an image on his website (http://www.cs.utah.edu/~sparker) that took two CPU years to ray trace on an eight-processor Silicon Graphics machine. This figure is reproduced in Chapter 26.

1.6 Skeleton Ray Tracer

To help you get started, there's a skeleton ray tracer on the book's website. This runs under Windows and has the following useful features:

- It renders the scene into a window, which can be of arbitrary size.
- It displays the rendering time.
- It can save images in a variety of file formats.
- As it's multi-threaded, it doesn't tie up the computer while it's rendering.

 ## 1.7 Developing the Ray Tracer

The following chapters will take you step by step through the process of developing a ray tracer in C++. Chapter 3, *Bare Bones Ray Tracing*, starts with the simplest possible ray tracer: one that only ray traces a single sphere and then adds multiple objects. In later chapters you can add facilities such as antialiasing, samplers, cameras, lights, materials, shadows, reflections, transparency, other types of objects, affine transformations, an acceleration scheme, triangle meshes, and textures. Each chapter is designed to allow you to add new capabilities to the existing ray tracer.

In the early chapters, certain classes are presented in simplified versions, because a lot of the data members and functions are not required until later chapters. An example is the ShadeRec class, which I'll be adding data members to throughout the book. To present the complete classes from the beginning would make them too complex. I've therefore employed code that, with few exceptions, uses only the facilities that you need at the time. Because of the fine-grained design of the ray tracer, and the layers of abstraction present, changes will involve additions to existing classes and adding new classes. In particular, the user interfaces of all member functions are frozen from the start, even though some parameters may not be required until later chapters. Examples are the Plane:hit and Sphere:hit functions discussed in Chapter 3. About the only change you will have to make to an existing function is one line in the main function.

The code samples I'll present and discuss in each chapter will be restricted to simplified class declarations and key functions, but numerous complete classes are on the book's website. The exercises ask you to add the features discussed in each chapter and implement additional features.

The most important thing here is that I'll provide you with a ray-tracer design that has the three principal objectives of extensibility, efficiency, and readability. Design is generally more difficult than programming.

1.8 Floats or Doubles

Doubles provide more numerical precision than floats, but they have twice the memory footprint. As suggested by Peter Shirley, I use doubles for all ray-object intersection calculations, where numerical accuracy is critical, and floats for shading calculations. This involves storing geometric object data members, and the components of all the utility classes as doubles. If you define a global type `typedef float FLOAT;` you can easily change between floats and doubles by changing a single word.

 ## 1.9 Efficiency Issues

Efficiency is critical to a ray tracer, as there's no upper limit to rendering times, even for simple scenes when we use sophisticated shading techniques. For example, the opening image in Chapter 26 took 2 CPU years to render! Below are a few relevant issues, mainly at the coding level. I'll discuss broader issues, such as acceleration schemes, in Chapters 22 and 23.

1.9.1 Small is Beautiful

I use a "small is beautiful" design philosophy applied to object sizes and executed code size. This involves a multitude of specialized inheritance hierarchies, objects, materials, lights, functions, etc.; each one designed for a specific task, and individually kept as small, simple, and efficient as possible. Here's an example. I use two hit functions for each object.[3] The first is the ordinary ray-object hit function discussed above, which returns the ray parameter at the nearest hit point, as well as other information required for shading. The second is for shadow rays, which doesn't return the shading information because we don't need it for shadow testing. This approach increases the size of the ray-tracer executable, but that rarely affects the speed of execution. We gain efficiencies by minimizing the code that's actually executed and the size of stored objects. This approach also creates more compilation units, but that's not a problem as most of your builds will be incremental.

The ideal is to be able to add new features with zero impact on the speed of the existing code, but that's often not possible. Instead, I try to add new features in such a way that they have minimum impact.

---

3. This example is common practice in ray tracing.

1.9.2 Data Storage

The geometric objects, lights, and sample points need to be stored in linear data structures. The STL `vector` class is the most suitable for this purpose because of its speed, see Bulka and Mayhew (2000), and because the collections of objects are usually static. When we know how many objects we are going to store in a `vector`, we can reserve the memory, which speeds up the construction since the underlying C array doesn't have to be resized. This applies to the sample points.

There's also the notational convenience of being able to access a vector element with array notation [ ], which allows a vector to be traversed with code like the following:

```
int  num_objects = objects.size();
for (int j = 0; j < num_objects; j++) {
    if (objects[j]->hit(ray, t, sr) && (t < tmin))
        ...
}
```

where `objects` is a `vector` of `GeometricObject` pointers. There's a small speed penalty for using this notation compared with using iterators.

We also need 2D and 3D data structures in ray tracing: images and sample points (Chapters 5–7) use 2D data structures, regular grids (Chapter 22) and lattice noises (Chapter 31) use 3D data structures. I store these in 1D arrays and use indexing to simulate the 2D and 3D structures. This is also common practice. An exception is the `Matrix` class which uses a 2D C array: `float m[4][4]`, to store the elements.

1.9.3 Pass by Reference

You should pass all compound objects into functions with references or constant references to avoid the construction and destruction of temporary objects. The following triangle constructor declaration is an example:

```
Triangle::Triangle(const Point3D & v1, const Point3D & v2,
    const Point3D & v3);
```

1.9.4 Don't Return by Reference

Don't use a reference to a complex class as the return type of function to try and save a temporary. As an example, the following is a `Matrix` member function for multiplying two matrices.

```
Matrix&
Matrix::operator* (const Matrix& mat) const {
      Matrix product;
      // compute the product ...
      return (product);
}
```

At best, this will cause memory leak, and at worst, the function won't work. Instead, use

```
Matrix
Matrix::operator* (const Matrix& mat) const
```

and let your compiler return the matrix in the most efficient way it can. See Meyers (2005), Item 23. Exceptions include the assignment operators = and *=, and /= that we require for a variety of structured data types.

1.9.5 Avoid Floating-Point Divides

Because a floating-point division requires many more machine cycles on Intel chips than a floating multiplication, it's best to avoid them when you can. One way is to define constants such as `const double invPI = 0.31830988618379067154;`, which avoids having to divide by π.

1.9.6 Use Inlining Judiciously

The judicious use of inlining can help your ray tracer run faster, but it can also have the opposite effect, and actually make it run slower, as well as make debugging difficult. Only inline small functions, don't inline constructors, destructors, or virtual functions, and remember that inlining is only a suggestion to your compiler. You usually have to place inline functions in a header file; see Meyers (2005), Item 33.

1.9.7 Utility Classes

Your ray tracer will need a number of utility classes such as `Vector3D`, `Point3D`, `Normal`, `Matrix`, `RGBColor`, and `ShadeRec`. Because of their ubiquitous use in the ray tracer, it's important that these classes are written as efficiently as possible. The code for these classes is on the book's website.

1.10 Coding Style

I've kept the C++ code as elementary as possible, consistent with getting the job done. Most of the C++ you require should therefore be covered in a first course, but you will have to know how to construct an inheritance hierarchy where the classes allocate memory dynamically. I've only used single inheritance. All code samples are ANSI Standard C++, and some ANSI Standard C.

1.10.1 Identifiers

Class names, data member names, and member function names use the following style, but with some exceptions.

- *Class names* start with upper case, all words in multi-word names start with upper case.
  Examples: `Sphere`, `PointLight`, `GeometricObject`.

- *Member function and data member names* are lower case with the second and subsequent words in multi-word names separated by underscores.
  Examples: `Sphere::center`, `World::add_object(...)`, `ShadeRec::local_hit_point`.

- *Pointer names* end with `_ptr` as in `Sphere* sphere_ptr = new Sphere;`, unless the identifier would be too long. Thus, `glossy_specular_brdf_ptr` is `glossy_specular_brdf`.

- *The names of functions that set or compute data members* usually contain the data-member name after an underscore, or indicate what is being set or computed.
  Examples: `Matte:set_cd()`, where `cd` is the name of the data member, `Camera::compute_uvw(void)`, where uvw stands for three data members called u, v, and w.

1.10.2 Concrete Data Types

One of the rules for writing correct C++ code is that classes that allocate memory dynamically must have their own copy constructor, assignment operator, and destructor; see, for example, Meyers (2005). To save space, the class declarations in the text usually don't list these functions, but they are in the electronic versions on the book's website. To provide a uniform class style, I've written most classes as concrete data types even when they don't allocate memory dynamically; see, for example, the Ray class declaration in Listing 3.1. Of course, you don't have to use this style.

1.10.3 Encapsulation

Class data members are generally private or protected, but there are exceptions based on their frequency of access. All data members of the following classes are public: BBox, Matrix, Normal, Point3D, Ray, RGBColor, ShadeRec, Vector3D, ViewPlane, and World.

1.10.4 Function Signatures

The way you write function signatures can affect the amount of typing you have to do in build functions and the efficiency of scene construction. As an example, consider the function that sets the diffuse color of a Matte material and has the following signature:

```
void
Matte::set_cd(const RGBColor& c);
```

This is nice and object-oriented, but every time you call it in a build function, you will have to write something like the following:

```
mattePtr->set_cd(RGBColor(r, g, b));
```

On the other hand, if you use the less object-oriented signature

```
void
MattePtr::set_cd(const float r, const float g, const float b);
```

you can write

```
mattePtr->set_cd(r, g, b);
```

This will not only save you a lot of typing over a lifetime of writing build functions, it's more efficient because it saves an RGBColor temporary. If all components of the color are the same, you can use a third version that takes a single float argument. This is particularly useful for setting colors to black, white, and grays. For most set functions of this type, it's best to write all three versions.

1.10.5 Changing a Function Signature

Yes, it may happen that you have to change the signature of a function that's called on a lot of objects with dynamic binding. It's happened to me several times, the worst one being the ray-object hit function. Here's how you can do it with minimum disruption. Define the new function as a virtual (not pure virtual) function in the base class, and add it to the class you want to test it with. Then, add it to the other objects as you need to. When you've added it to all of the objects, you can make it pure virtual in the base class and get rid of the original version. This technique allows you to test the new function with one object type at a time.

1.10.6 Pure Virtual and Virtual Functions

If a member function has to be defined for every derived class in an inheritance hierarchy, you should declare it as pure virtual in the base class. The example is the function GeometricObject::hit(...). If a function doesn't have to be defined for every derived class, you can declare it as virtual in the base class, and also define it there, to either do nothing, or return a default value. That will keep the C++ compiler happy, even if you don't define it in any derived class. An example is the function GeometricObject::pdf(...), which I have only defined for two geometric objects out of about 30 in my ray tracer. The version in the base just returns 1.0, which is the default value.

1.10.7 File Structure

You should put each class declaration in a header file, such as **Sphere.h**, and prevent it from being #included more than once in each compilation unit (see Listing 1.1).

You should put the class definition in a separate file, such as **Sphere. cpp**.

```
#ifndef __SPHERE__
#define __SPHERE__

#include "GeometricObject.h"
class Sphere: public GeometricObject {
    // data member and member function declarations ...
};

// inlined functions ...
#endif
```

Listing 1.1. Code fragment from the file **Sphere.h**.

1.10.8 Project Structure

I put classes of each type such as geometric objects, materials, and lights, into separate groups, and I include all .h files in my IDE project for ease of access. This doubles the number of files in the project, but it's worth it.

 # 1.11 Debugging

As debugging your ray tracer is something you will definitely have to do at some stage, here are a few tips.

1.11.1 Get to Know Your Debugger

First, make sure you are familiar with the debugger in your development environment. This should allow you to set break points, examine variables and the call stack, step through the program, and step into and out of functions.

1.11.2 Ray Trace Single-Pixel Images

Ray tracing has the following nice feature that often simplifies the debugging process: you can ray trace single pixel images. Here's an example. One of my students was implementing an axis-aligned box whose outline was correct, but whose shading was only ambient. This indicated that the hit function was correct but the normal was wrong. He debugged this by using a default box centered on the world origin, placing the camera on the z_w-axis, looking at the origin, and ray tracing a one pixel image with a breakpoint in the material's shade function. The box normal at the hit point should have been $(0, 0, 1)$, but was $(0, 0, -1)$ because he had made a mistake when he typed in the Box:: get_normal function in Chapter 19.

1.11.3 Keep Track of Pixel Coordinates

Maintain two global variables, say ph and pv, that store the coordinates of the current pixel being rendered. If you find a problem with your image, for example a black dot, you can find the pixel coordinates using an image viewer, and then insert a statement if (row == ph && column == pv) ... at a relevant point in the code. Inside the if statement, you can place a dummy executable statement that you can put a debugger break point on or print out variables. This technique was also suggested by Erik Reinhard.

1.11.4 Use `cout`

It's often easiest to debug code in loops with `cout` statements. For example, you might be debugging a new sampling technique with 25 rays per pixel and need to look at the sample points for a single pixel. It's a lot quicker and more useful to see them all displayed in a window than having to manually step through the debugger 25 times.

1.11.5 Watch Out for Unallocated Memory

The most common error I get is an *unallocated memory* error caused by trying to access a pointer-based object that has not been constructed or allocated. This is known as sucking vacuum. A way to avoid this is to always check that a pointer is not null before accessing it, but this would slow down your ray tracer too much. I therefore don't do this, and instead live dangerously, but always run with the debugger on when I'm implementing anything new, which is almost all the time.

1.11.6 Simplify

When debugging, it's often best to simplify things as much as possible. Suppose you have just added a new type of object to an existing scene, and it's not working. It's easy to temporarily remove all the other objects by commenting out their `add_object` statements in the build function. You don't have to comment out any of their other code.

1.11.7 Transparency

Transparency code is often difficult to debug because you need recursion depths of at least three to correctly ray trace transparent objects, and the reflected and transmitted rays result in a binary tree of stack frames. It's particularly difficult if there are random errors, where only some pixels are incorrect. The only general guideline I can give you is to use single-pixel images, but fortunately, I've been through all this. As a result, I'm confident that the transparency code and images in Section 7 of the book are correct.

1.11.8 Use the Images Here

How do you know when an image is correct? Although there are no general answers, the hundreds of ray traced images in this book and on the book's website are here to help you.

Further Reading

There are many excellent books that cover C++ design and programming issues. The *C++ Primer*, Fourth Edition (2005) by Lippman, Lajoie, and Moo is comprehensive. *Object-Oriented Programming in C++*, Second Edition (2000) by Johnsonbaugh and Kalin is an excellent introductory book on C++ that emphasizes an object-oriented approach from the start.

If you already know some C++, you owe it to yourself to read Scott Meyers' three books on C++: *Effective C++*, Third Edition (2005), *More Effective C++* (1996), and *Effective STL* (2001). There's nothing quite like these books for their collective insights and wisdom. These books can also help you avoid some of the common mistakes that can make your ray tracers inefficient.

Efficient C++ by Bulka and Mayhew (2000) discusses the relative performance of the vector and list container classes and is an excellent book on writing efficient C++ programs.

Extreme Programming Explained (2004) by Kent Beck was written by the inventor of the methodology. Although extreme programming is a holistic and integrated set of practices for software development by small teams, it has a number of practices that are applicable to software development by individuals. For example, no matter how large your final application is going to be, you start with the smallest application that does something sensible and build incrementally from there. That's the approach I adopt here for ray-tracer development. In Chapter 3, you will start with the simplest ray tracer that actually does something and then add features to it. Beck's book is well worth a read. Extreme programming is now one of the *agile computing* methodologies.

Brian Kernighan has written two classic books on programming: *The C Programming Language* (1988) with Dennis Ritchie, the developer of C, and *The Unix Programming Environment* (1984) with Rob Pike. The *Practice of Programming* (1999) by Kernighan and Pike discusses many important aspects of programming, and is well worth reading.

An Introduction to Ray Tracing (1989), edited by Andrew Glassner, was the first book on ray tracing. Chapter 7 by Paul Heckbert is called *Writing a Ray Tracer* and discusses features, design issues, advocates an OO approach, and has sample code in C. *Object-Oriented Ray Tracing in C++* (1994) by Nicholas Wilt presents a ray tracer in C++. There are a lot of good ideas and code in this book. *Realistic Ray Tracing*, Second Edition (2003) by Shirley and Morley discusses how to write a modern ray tracer and includes C++ code. Although this book is small, it covers a lot of ground, including Monte Carlo ray tracing, to which Shirley has made significant contributions. *Fundamentals of Computer Graphics,* Second Edition (Shirley et al., 2005), has a number of chapters on ray tracing and covers a lot of other material that's relevant to ray tracing.

Pharr and Humphreys (2004) discuss a ray tracer using Knuth's literate programming style. This is an excellent book, but the ray tracer is more advanced than the one presented here and is not designed to be implemented step by step by the readers.

2 Some Essential Mathematics

Image courtesy of Lisa Lönroth

 Objectives

By the end of this chapter you should:

- be familiar with some of the mathematics you need for ray tracing;
- understand the difference between vectors, points, and normals;
- understand how to construct an orthonormal frame.

Ray tracing uses a lot of mathematics, from elementary coordinate geometry to multi-dimensional calculus. Fortunately, there are excellent books on all of these topics (see the Further Reading section). I'll present here the mathematical notation used in this book and a number of mathematical topics from a ray-tracing perspective. For example, I'll discuss three-dimensional coordinate systems defined the way we use them in ray tracing, and the difference between vectors, points, and normals. These topics are used throughout the book. Other topics such as barycentric coordinates, which are only used for ray tracing triangles, will be discussed in Chapter 19, where they are used. Except for the presentation of some integrals in Section 2.10, I won't discuss calculus, which is used in Chapter 13 and the subsequent shading chapters. I also won't discuss matrices, which are used in Chapters 20 and 21. Monte Carlo integration will be covered briefly in Chapter 13.

To keep this book to a reasonable size, I've had to draw the line on mathematics somewhere. Most of the topics in this chapter are therefore only covered briefly.

 2.1 Sets

2.1.1 Definition and Notation

Definition 2.1. A *set* is an unordered collection of objects of the same type, with a rule for determining if a given object is in the set.

The objects in a set are known as its *elements*. Although the objects can be of any type, in ray tracing, we usually deal with sets of real (floating-point) numbers. Here are some common sets, all of which have an infinite number of elements:

- $\mathbb{R}$: the set of all real numbers. This is also known as the real number line and contains all real numbers from $-\infty$ to $+\infty$.
- $\mathbb{R}^+$: the set of non-negative real numbers, which includes zero.
- $\mathbb{R}^2$: the set of all points on the (x, y) plane.
- $\mathbb{R}^3$: the set of all points (x, y, z) in 3D space.

If s is an element of a set S, we use the notation $s \in S$, where $\in$ means *belongs to*. We also use a notation called *predicate form* to define sets, which is best explained with an example. The definition of $\mathbb{R}^+$ can be written as

$$\mathbb{R}^+ = \{x : x \in \mathbb{R} \text{ and } x \geq 0\}.$$

This can be read as follows: $\mathbb{R}^+$ is the set of all numbers x such that x is real and greater than or equal to zero. Here, the symbol ":" is read as *such that*. I'll use this notation to define intervals in the following section, because it's the most compact way for doing this.

2.1.2 Subsets

We often need to use sets whose elements belong to some larger set, which leads to the concept of *subsets*.

Definition 2.2. A set A is a *subset* of a set B if every element of A also belongs to B. Symbolically, we write this as $A \subseteq B$.

From the above examples, $\mathbb{R}^+ \subseteq \mathbb{R}$. As another example, consider the square S centered on the origin, where $S = \{(x, y) : -1 \leq x \leq 1, -1 \leq y \leq 1\}$. $S \subseteq \mathbb{R}^2$. Also, the set of integers $\mathbb{Z} = \{0, \pm1, \pm2, ...\} \subseteq \mathbb{R}$.

2.1.3 Ordered Pairs and the Cartesian Product of Sets

An *ordered pair* (x, y) of elements is a sequence of two elements in a definite order. A common example is a point on the (x, y) plane, where we always write the x-coordinate first, followed by the y-coordinate.

Definition 2.3. For two sets A and B, the set of all ordered pairs of elements (x, y) where $x \in A$ and $y \in B$ is known as the *Cartesian product* of the sets A and B, and is denoted by $A \times B$.

For example, the (x, y) plane is the Cartesian product of the real line with itself, that is, $\mathbb{R}^2 = \mathbb{R} \times \mathbb{R}$. Another example is $\mathbb{R}^3 = \mathbb{R} \times \mathbb{R} \times \mathbb{R}$.

 ## 2.2 Intervals

Definition 2.4. An *interval* is a subset of the real line that contains at least two numbers, and contains all of the real numbers lying between any two of its elements.

Intervals are represented geometrically by segments of the real line, and can be finite, semi-infinite, or infinite. Finite intervals have two endpoints that are finite numbers, while infinite intervals have *at most* one finite endpoint and stretch to infinity in one or both directions. In addition, intervals are said to be *open* if neither endpoint is included, *half-open* (or *half-closed*) if one of the endpoints is included, and *closed* if both endpoints are included. We use square brackets [ ] if the endpoints are included in the interval, and parentheses ( ) if they're not included. Infinite intervals can't be closed because no real number is equal to infinity. A standard notation is used for all the types of intervals, as shown in Table 2.1. This is re-written from Thomas and Finney (1996), p. 3.

Type of Interval		Notation	Set Definition	Endpoints
Finite	open	(a, b)	$\{ x : a < x < b \}$	a and b are not in the interval
	closed	$[a, b]$	$\{ x : a \leq x \leq b \}$	a and b are both in the interval
	half-open	$[a, b)$	$\{ x : a \leq x < b \}$	a is in the interval, b is not
	half-open	$(a, b]$	$\{ x : a < x \leq b \}$	a is not in the interval, b is
Infinite	open	(a, ∞)	$\{ x : x > a \}$	a is not in the interval
	half-open	$[a, \infty)$	$\{ x : x \geq a \}$	a is in the interval
	open	$(-\infty, b)$	$\{ x : x < b \}$	b is not in the interval
	half-open	$(-\infty, b]$	$\{ x : x \leq b \}$	b is in the interval
	open	$(-\infty, \infty)$	$\{ x : -\infty < x < \infty \}$	there are no endpoints

Table 2.1. Interval types, notation, and definitions.

I'll use interval notation extensively in the following chapters to specify the range of numbers that variables can take, for example, $x \in [-1, 1]$, $r \in [0, \infty)$.

The empty interval. The empty interval has no numbers that belong to it, and is denoted by $\emptyset$.

Intersection of intervals. The intersection of two intervals A and B is the set of numbers that belong to both intervals, and is denoted by $A \cap B$. Geometrically, the intersection is the part of the real line where the intervals overlap. For example, if $A = [0, 10]$, $B = [8, 15]$, $A \cap B = [8, 10]$, but if $A = [0, 10]$, $B = [11, 15]$, $A \cap B = \emptyset$.

Cartesian products of intervals. Since intervals are sets, their Cartesian product is defined the same way that it is for sets. The Cartesian product can be used to define finite and infinite planar areas. Here are some examples: the real plane is $\mathbb{R} \times \mathbb{R} = (-\infty, \infty) \times (-\infty, \infty)$; a rectangle is $[0, 1] \times [0, 2]$. When both intervals are the same, I'll often use the notation $A \times A = A^2$. For example, the generic unit square is $[-1, 1] \times [-1, 1] = [-1, 1]^2$.

 ## 2.3 Angles

2.3.1 Measurement

In 2D (x, y) coordinates, positive angles are measured from the positive x-axis, in a *counterclockwise* direction, and negative angles are measured *clockwise* from the positive x-axis (see Figure 2.1).

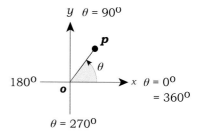

Figure 2.1. Angle definition.

Figure 2.1 also shows the values of the angle θ in degrees and radians along the positive and negative x- and y-axes. There are 360 degrees in a circle, and so along the positive x-axis, $\theta = 0$ degrees, but also $\theta = 360$ degrees. However, angles are not restricted to the range $0 \leq \theta \leq 2\pi$, because the line op can be rotated any number of times about the origin in the positive or negative direction.

2.3.2 Degrees and Radians

Angles can be specified in degrees or radians.

Definition 2.5. A radian is the angle subtended at the center of circle by an arc around the circumference whose length is equal to the radius.

Since there are 2π radians and 360 degrees in a circle,

$$1 \text{ radian} = 180° / \pi = 57.29577...°.$$

When specifying angles, most people find it easier to use degrees because these are the common everyday measurement of angles. For example, saying that we want to cut a piece of wood at 45° to its sides is more meaningful than saying that we want to cut it at 0.79 radians. It's important to realize, however, that the angle θ in the definitions of the trigonometric functions is *always* in radians. Consequently, you must convert into radians any angles specified in degrees, with the formula

$$\text{radians} = (180 / \pi) \text{ degrees}$$

before using the angles in trigonometric functions. Angles often have to be specified for ray-tracing purposes. For example, the viewing angles for fish-eye and panoramic cameras in Chapter 11, the stereo separation angles in Chapter 12, and in Chapter 19, several part objects will be defined in terms of angles. The user interface in each case will use degrees, while the code inside will convert the degrees to radians.

2.4 Trigonometry

Because trigonometry is used so extensively in ray tracing, I'll present here some of its definitions and relevant formulae.

2.4.1 Definitions

Consider the right-angled triangle in Figure 2.2. The trigonometric functions sine, cosine, and tangent of the angle θ are defined as

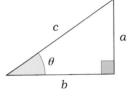

Figure 2.2. A right-angled triangle.

$$\sin \theta = a / c,$$
$$\cos \theta = b / c,$$
$$\tan \theta = a / b = \sin \theta / \cos \theta.$$

Pythagoras' theorem for the right-angled triangle is

$$c^2 = a^2 + b^2.$$

2.4.2 Relations

$$\sin^2\theta + \cos^2\theta = 1,$$
$$\sin(\theta \pm \phi) = \sin\theta\cos\phi \pm \cos\theta\sin\phi,$$
$$\cos(\theta \pm \phi) = \cos\theta\cos\phi \mp \sin\theta\sin\phi.$$

(2.1)

When $\phi = \pi/2$, Equations (2.1) become

$$\sin(\theta \pm \pi/2) = \pm\cos\theta,$$
$$\cos(\theta \pm \pi/2) = \mp\cos\theta.$$

 ## 2.5 Coordinate Systems

Ray tracing uses the following 2D and 3D coordinate systems:

- world coordinates (3D);
- viewing coordinates (3D);
- object coordinates (2D and 3D);
- local shading coordinates (3D);
- view-plane coordinates (2D);
- texture coordinates (2D and 3D).

In later chapters, I'll discuss each of these coordinate systems and how to use them. Below, I'll just discuss the mathematical definitions of some common 3D coordinate systems in the way that we use them in ray tracing.

2.5.1 3D Cartesian Coordinates

Figure 2.3(a) illustrates 3D Cartesian coordinates, where we use an *ordered triple*[1] of real numbers (x, y, z) to specify the location of a point in 3D space. These coordinates are the perpendicular distances of the point along the three coordinate axes, measured from the origin. Cartesian coordinates are used to specify the location of points in infinite 3D space. Each pair of coordinate axes defines a *coordinate plane*, of which there are three: the (x, y) plane defined by the x- and y-axes, and the (x, z) and (y, z) planes.

---

1. An ordered triple is a sequence of three numbers in a definite order.

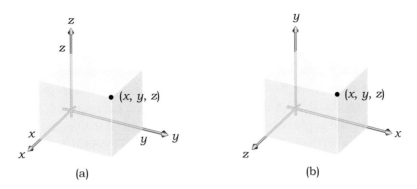

Figure 2.3. 3D Cartesian coordinates (a) as drawn in fields other than computer graphics; (b) as drawn in computer graphics.

If your background is in a field other than computing, for example, science or engineering, you are probably used to drawing the x-, y-, and z-axes as shown in Figure 2.3(a), with the z-axis pointing up. This is the convention in most fields, where the (x, y)-plane is horizontal. In 3D computer graphics, a different convention has been adopted for *world coordinates*, as shown in Figure 2.3(b), where the y-axis points up and the (x, z)-plane is horizontal.[2] It's important to realize that this is just a *drawing* convention; the coordinates in Figure 2.3(b) are still the same as in part (a).

Computer graphics also uses *right-handed* and *left-handed* coordinate systems, but I'll only use right-handed systems, as illustrated in Figure 2.3. The right-handedness of a coordinate system or set of basis vectors will come up later on, starting with orthonormal bases and frames in Section 2.12.

2.5.2 Cylindrical Coordinates

Cylindrical coordinates are based on Cartesian coordinates, but instead of using the x-, y-, and z-coordinates directly, we use a straight-line distance r, an angle ϕ, and the y-coordinate (see Figure 2.4). Because I'll use cylindrical coordinates to define circular cylinders in Chapter 19 with a vertical central

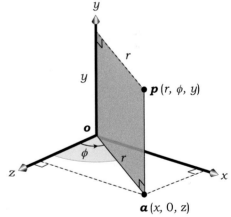

Figure 2.4. Definition of cylindrical coordinates.

---

2. This is also the convention adopted by the 3D rendering APIs OpenGL and RenderMan and the major 3D rendering and animation packages such as Maya, Houdini, and SoftImage.

axis in world coordinates, the Cartesian coordinates in Figure 2.4 also have the y-axis up.

The first coordinate r is the perpendicular distance between the point $p(r, \theta, \phi)$ and the y-axis. Its value lies in the interval $r \in [0, \infty)$. To define the second coordinate ϕ, we first project p onto the (x, z) plane to get the point $a = (x, 0, z)$. This also defines the orange vertical plane in Figure 2.4. The angle ϕ is defined to be the angle between the positive z-axis and the line oa, measured counterclockwise in the (x, z) plane. Its value lies in the interval $\phi \in [0, 2\pi)$. This is known as the *azimuth angle*. The third coordinate is simply the y-coordinate.

With these definitions, it follows that the Cartesian coordinates of p can be expressed in terms of r, ϕ, and y as follows:

$$x = r \sin \phi,$$
$$y = y, \tag{2.2}$$
$$z = r \cos \phi.$$

2.5.3 Spherical Coordinates

Spherical coordinates are also based on Cartesian coordinates, but here, we specify locations with a distance r and two angles θ and ϕ, as shown in Figure 2.5. The coordinate r is now the straight-line distance from the origin o of the Cartesian coordinates to the point $p(r, \theta, \phi)$. Again, its value lies in the interval $r \in [0, \infty)$. The second coordinate θ is the angle between the positive y-axis and the line op. It's measured from the y-axis in the vertical plane defined by (o, p, a), where a is again the projection of p onto the (x, z) plane, and its value lies in the interval $\theta \in [0, \pi]$. This is known as the *polar angle*. The third coordinate ϕ is the same azimuth angle as in cylindrical coordinates.

With these definitions, it follows that the Cartesian coordinates of p can be expressed in terms of r, θ, and ϕ as follows:

$$x = r \sin \theta \sin \phi,$$
$$y = r \cos \theta, \tag{2.3}$$
$$z = r \sin \theta \cos \phi.$$

Spherical coordinates have a number of uses in ray tracing. Examples include the distribution of sample points on a hemisphere (Chapter 7), which has numerous shading applications, integration over a solid angle

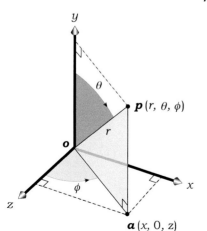

Figure 2.5. Definition of spherical coordinates.

(Section 2.10), and an intimate involvement with the theoretical foundations of ray tracing (Chapter 13).

 ## 2.6 Vectors

2.6.1 Definition and Representation

I'll present here some basic information about vectors, because we need this before I discuss points and normals in the following two sections. Vectors are used to represent many things in ray tracing, including ray directions, directions from hit points to light sources, reflection models, and orthonormal bases.

A vector is a *directed line segment*, as Figure 2.6 illustrates in 2D. A vector is defined by its length and direction, but not by its location in space. All vectors in Figure 2.6(a) are the same, while those in Figure 2.6(b) are all different, although they have the same lengths. We can represent a 3D vector by three floating-point numbers that are its projections onto the Cartesian (x, y, z) coordinate axes. See Figure 2.6(c) for a 2D representation, where the vector starts at the origin. These are the *components* of the vector, which are independent of the vector's location.

We denote a vector by a bold italic letter, for example, u, and use the same letter for its components: u_x, u_y, and u_z. The *magnitude* of a vector is the length of its line segment, and is denoted by $\|u\|$.

Vectors are represented by the class `Vector3D`, which stores the components as three doubles: x, y, and z.

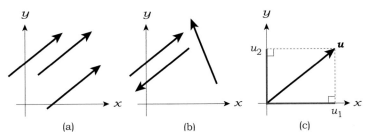

Figure 2.6. (a) Identical vectors defined by the same directed line segment; (b) different vectors defined by different line segments; (c) a vector's components are its projections (red) onto the coordinate axes.

2.6.2 Operations

Let

$$u = (u_x, u_y, u_z),$$
$$v = (v_x, v_y, v_z),$$

be two vectors. We need the following operations:

Operation	Definition	Return Type
$u + v$	$(u_x + v_x, u_y + v_y, u_z + v_z)$	vector
$u - v$	$(u_x - v_x, u_y - v_y, u_z - v_z)$	vector
au	(au_x, au_y, au_z)	vector
ua	(au_x, au_y, au_z)	vector
u / a	$(u_x/a, u_y/a, u_z/a)$	vector
$u = v$	(v_x, v_y, v_z)	vector reference
$\|u\|$	$(u_x^2 + u_y^2 + u_z^2)^{1/2}$	double
$\|u\|^2$	$u_x^2 + u_y^2 + u_z^2$	double

where a is a double. We also need the dot and cross products of two vectors, defined by

$u \bullet v$	$u_x v_x + u_y v_y + u_z v_z$	double	(2.4)
$u \times v$	$(u_y v_z - u_z v_y, u_z v_x - u_x v_z, u_x v_y - u_y v_x)$	vector	

Other useful operations are

$-u$	$(-u_x, -u_y, -u_z)$	vector
$u \mathrel{+}= v$	$(u_x + v_x, u_y + v_y, u_z + v_z)$	vector reference

The dot product in Equation (2.4) can also be written as

$$u \bullet v = \|u\| \, \|v\| \, \cos \theta,$$

where θ is the angle between u and v. Although we won't use this to compute the value of $u \bullet v$, it's valuable for mathematical calculations. For example, if u and $u \bullet v$ are perpendicular, $\theta = \pi/2$, and $u \bullet v = 0$, since $\cos \pi/2 = 0$. I'll use this fact to write down Equation (2.6) for a plane in Section 2.9.1

We can use C++ operator overloading for many of the above operations, including *, which can be multiply overloaded for $u \bullet v$, au, and ua. I use the operator ∧ for the cross product, because the *outer product* of two n-dimensional vectors is denoted by $u \wedge v$, and this reduces to the cross product in 3D.

We also need to be able to *normalize* the vector. This converts it into a *unit vector*, which has length one. This is an important operation, as nearly all of the vectors used in ray tracing must be normalized at some stage. There are a couple of ways this can be written. One way doesn't return a value and has to be called in its own statement, such as `u.normalize();`, while the other returns a vector and can be called in expressions such as `u * v.hat()`. The second function is called `hat` because the common mathematical notation for unit vectors is to write them as $\hat{u}$.

We must also be able to multiply a vector by a 4 × 4 matrix m on the left, to produce a new vector: $u' = mu$. Matrices are used to implement *affine transformations* on vectors, points, and normals, each of which transforms in a different way. For example, translation doesn't affect vectors. The details are in Chapters 20 and 21.

 ## 2.7 Points

Points represent locations in space, as indicated in Figure 2.7 for the point *a*. Although each 3D point has a *location vector* with components (x, y, z) associated with it, and can be represented in the same way as vectors, points and vectors are not the same. For example, the dot and cross products don't make sense for points, neither does the magnitude of a point, and we can't add points. We can, however, add a vector to a point, which gives a new point displaced from the original by the components of the vector (see Figure 2.7(a)). We can also subtract points, because the result is the vector that joins them, as Figure 2.7(b) illustrates. The distance between two points makes sense, but it doesn't make sense for vectors.

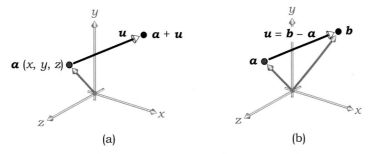

(a)   (b)

Figure 2.7. Each point has a location vector associated with it, as indicated by the red arrows. (a) Adding the vector *u* to the point *a* defines the new point *b* = *a* + *u*; (b) subtracting *b* from *a* defines the vector *b* − *a* that joins them.

Let

$$a = (a_x, a_y, a_z)$$
$$b = (b_x, b_y, b_z),$$

be two points, $u = (u_1, u_2, u_3)$ be a vector, and c be a double. We need the following operations:

Operation	Definition	Return Type
$a + u$	$a_x + u_x, a_y + u_y, a_z + u_z)$	point
$a - u$	$(a_x - u_x, a_y - u_y, a_z - u_z)$	point
$a - b$	$(a_x - b_x, a_y - b_y, a_z - b_z)$	vector
$\|a - b\|^2$	$(a_x - b_x)^2 + (a_y - b_y)^2 + (a_z - b_z)^2$	double
$\|a - b\|$	$[(a_x - b_x)^2 + (a_y - b_y)^2 + (a_z - b_z)^2]^{1/2}$	double
$a = b$	(b_x, b_y, b_z)	point reference
ca	(ca_x, ca_y, ca_z)	double
ac	(ca_x, ca_y, ca_z)	double

We also need a function that multiplies a point by a 4×4 matrix m on the left to return a new point, $a' = ma$. Finally, we need functions that return the distance and the square of the distance between two points.

 ## 2.8 Normals

Normals are also directed line segments and are therefore like vectors, but they behave differently. Because normals are always perpendicular to object surfaces, they must remain perpendicular when the objects are transformed. See Figure 2.8, which shows a sphere that's scaled to become an ellipsoid. This

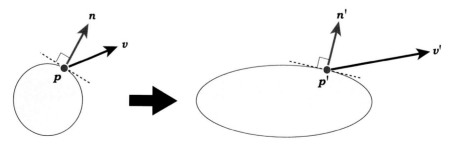

Figure 2.8. A vector, a point, and a normal are transformed differently when an object is transformed.

constraint is the reason that normals transform differently from vectors and points under affine transformations.

Because smooth surfaces have only a single (outward-pointing) normal at each point, it doesn't make sense to take the dot or cross products of normals with themselves, or subtract them. We also can't add a normal and a point. We must, however, be able to add normals, take the dot product of a normal and a vector, in either order, multiply a normal on the left or right by a scalar, and add a vector and a normal to give a vector. We must also be able to normalize a normal, and, you guessed it, multiply a normal on the left by a matrix to produce a transformed normal.

Consider two normals $n = (n_x, n_y, n_z)$, $m = (m_x, m_y, m_z)$, and a vector $u = (u_x, u_y, u_z)$. We need the following operations:

Operation	Definition	Return Type
$-n$	$(-n_x, -n_y, -n_z)$	normal
$n + m$	$(n_x + m_x, n_y + m_y, n_z + m_z)$	normal
$n \bullet u$	$n_x u_x + n_y u_y + n_z u_z$	double
$u \bullet n$	$n_x u_x + n_y u_y + n_z u_z$	double
an	(an_x, an_y, an_z)	normal
na	(an_x, an_y, an_z)	normal
$n + u$	$(n_x + u_x, n_y + u_y, n_z + u_z)$	vector
$u + n$	$(u_x + n_x, u_y + n_y, u_z + n_z)$	vector
$n = m$	(m_x, m_y, m_z)	normal reference
$n += m$	$(n_x + m_x, n_y + m_y, n_z + m_z)$	normal reference

At various places, we will have to make assignments between vectors, points, and normals. There are two ways that these can be programmed. The proper way is to use constructors, for example, v = Vector(n), where a vector is constructed from a normal. For simplicity and efficiency, however, I've used straight assignment functions, where the above example is just v = n. Technically, this is bad programming practice, and the assignment operators can't test for self assignment.

The book's website contains the complete code for the classes Vector3D, Point3D, Normal, and Matrix. As these are important utility classes, I would rather you spent your time creating nice images, than implementing these. You will, however, have to implement a class that represents 2D points, as these are used in Chapters 5–7 to store sample points. This is considerably simpler than the Point3D class because the code doesn't involve vectors, normals, or matrices.

2.9 Mathematical Surfaces

We use mathematical definitions of surfaces to define the objects we ray trace. There are two basic ways of doing this: with implicit equations (which result in implicit surfaces) and with parametric equations (which result in parametric surfaces).

The objects we ray trace directly are all defined by implicit surfaces, because simple implicit surfaces are easy to ray trace (see Chapters 3 and 19). In contrast, even simple parametric surfaces are *difficult* to ray trace, because there's no easy way to calculate where a ray hits a parametric surface. Parametric surfaces are, however, an essential modeling tool in commercial rendering and animation packages (see the Further Reading section). For rendering purposes, the software packages convert the parametric surfaces to triangle meshes, a process known as *polygonization* or *tessellation*. Fortunately we *can* ray trace triangles and triangle meshes, as I'll discuss in Chapters 19 and 23.

All of the objects we ray trace can also be expressed as parametric surfaces, which is fortunate, because these have a number of uses that include ray tracing part objects and texture mapping.

2.9.1 Implicit Surfaces

An implicit surface is defined by an equation of the form

$$f(x, y, z) = 0, \tag{2.5}$$

where f is some arbitrary function of x, y, and z. We can express an implicit surface using set notation as $\{(x, y, z) : f(x, y, z) = 0\}$.

Implicit surfaces divide 3D space into two regions, where $f(x, y, z) < 0$ on one side of the surface, $f(x, y, z) > 0$ on the other side, and $f(x, y, z) = 0$ on the surface. Implicit surfaces are either *open* or *closed*, where an open surface extends to infinity, while a closed surface is finite in extent and has an inside and an outside. For example, planes and hyperboloids are open, while spheres and tori are closed. Implicit surfaces can also consist of a number of disconnected pieces. Figure 2.9 shows a cross section of a closed surface with the inside shaded. The inside can, however, be the region $f(x, y, z) < 0$ or $f(x, y, z) > 0$, depending on how the surface is defined.

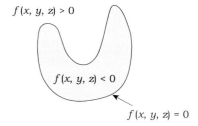

Figure 2.9. A closed implicit surface divides space into regions that are inside and outside the surface.

I'll illustrate implicit surfaces with a couple of simple examples that we'll ray trace in the following chapter.

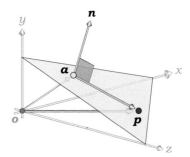

Figure 2.10. A plane is defined by a point a, which determines where it is, and a normal n, which determines its orientation.

Planes. A plane is an infinite flat sheet and is the simplest open surface. We define a plane by specifying a point a that lies on the plane, and a normal n to the plane. This defines the plane uniquely, because there is only one plane that passes through a given point and has the orientation specified by the normal. Since a plane is flat, all points on the surface have the same normal. Figure 2.10 shows a plane defined this way, where p is an arbitrary point on the plane, and I have only drawn the part of the plane that's in the first octant of the world coordinates (infinite planes are difficult to draw!).

The vector from a to p is $p - a$, and since this lies in the plane, it's perpendicular to the normal n. We can therefore express the equation of a plane in terms of the dot product of $p - a$ and n as

$$(p - a) \bullet n = 0. \tag{2.6}$$

If we write the points and normal in Equation (2.6) in component form ($p = (x, y, z)$, $a = (a_x, a_y, a_z)$, and $n = (n_x, n_y, n_z)$) and use the component expression (2.4) for the dot product, we can express this equation as

$$Ax + By + Cz + D = 0. \tag{2.7}$$

This is the implicit equation of an arbitrary plane. Here, the coefficients $A = n_x$, $B = n_y$, and $C = n_z$ are the components of the normal, and $D = -a \bullet n = -a_x n_x - a_y n_y - a_z n_z$. An example is the (x, z) plane, whose implicit equation is as simple as we can get: $y = 0$.

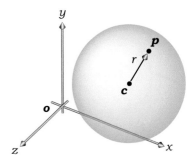

Figure 2.11. Sphere definition. The point p is on the surface of the sphere.

Spheres. A sphere is the set of points that's within a constant specified distance r from a given point c. Formally, a sphere $= \{p : |p - c| \leq r\}$, where c is the center of the sphere, and r is the radius (see Figure 2.11). The surface of the sphere, which is the part we're interested in for ray tracing, is defined by $\{p : |p - c| = r\}$; that is, it's the set of points at distance r from c. Technically, this is a *spherical shell*, but I'll refer to it as a sphere.

If $c = (c_x, c_y, c_z)$, and $p = (x, y, z)$ is a point on the surface of the sphere, the implicit equation of the surface can be written by inspection, since the square of the distance between p and

c is equal to the square of the radius. The implicit equation is therefore

$$(x - c_x)^2 + (y - c_y)^2 + (z - c_z)^2 - r^2 = 0, \qquad (2.8)$$

using Pythagoras' theorem in 3D. An example is a unit sphere (radius $r = 1$) centered on the origin, for which Equation (2.8) simplifies to

$$x^2 + y^2 + z^2 - 1 = 0.$$

2.9.2 Parametric Surfaces

A point on a parametric surface is expressed in the form

$$\boldsymbol{p}\,(u, v) = [f\,(u, v), g\,(u, v), h\,(u, v)], \qquad (2.9)$$

where $f\,(u, v)$, $g\,(u, v)$, and $h\,(u, v)$ are explicit functions of the two parameters u and v. Since these three functions are really the (x, y, z) coordinates of $\boldsymbol{p}$, we usually write Equation (2.9) in the form

$$\boldsymbol{p}\,(u, v) = [x\,(u, v), y\,(u, v), z\,(u, v)].$$

For given values of u and v, the expressions for x, y, and z can be evaluated to give the location of $\boldsymbol{p}$. In modeling for graphics applications, including computer-aided design, x, y, and z are usually polynomials in u and v, or the ratio of two polynomials. The parameters are also restricted to a certain range, typically $(u, v) \in [0, 1] \times [0, 1]$. This defines a *parametric surface patch*, which is finite in extent (see the Further Reading section).

I'll illustrate parametric surfaces with circular cylinders and spheres. Why not planes? As it turns out, these are more complex to write in parametric form than cylinders and spheres, and since we only need their parametric representation to ray trace triangles, I'll discuss that in Chapter 19.

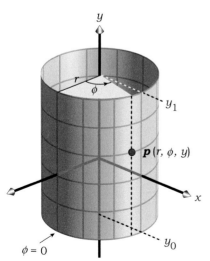

Circular cylinders. A circular cylinder centered on the y-axis with radius r and finite extent in the y-direction is defined by $\{(x, y, z): x^2 + z^2 = r^2 \text{ and } y \in [y_0, y_1]\}$, as Figure 2.12 illustrates.

Figure 2.12. A circular cylinder centered on the y-axis with radius r and finite extent in the y-direction.

The parametric representation of the cylinder is the same as Equations (2.1) for cylindrical coordinates,

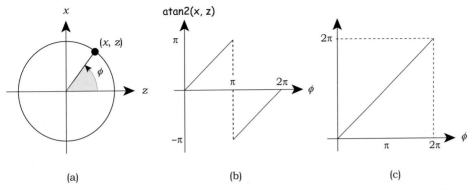

Figure 2.13. (a) Point (x, z) that defines an angle ϕ; (b) plot of atan2(x, z), which is discontinuous at $\phi = \pi$; (c) plot of adjusted function that returns an angle $\phi \in [0, 2\pi]$.

where r is the specified radius of the cylinder and y is confined to the interval $[y_0, y_1]$. The parameters are ϕ and y, as these vary over the surface. We need to calculate the (ϕ, y)-values from the (x, y, z)-coordinates of a point on the cylinder. As there's nothing to calculate for y, that only leaves ϕ to deal with. From Equation (2.1), we have

$$\phi = \tan^{-1}(x / z). \tag{2.10}$$

The Standard C Library function double atan2(double x, double z) is the most convenient way to compute ϕ, because it returns the angle whose tangent is x / z, in the full 2π angular range $[-\pi, +\pi]$ radians. However, we need an angle in the range $[0, 2\pi]$, not $[-\pi, +\pi]$. Imagine a point with coordinates (x, z) that moves around a circle centered on the origin, as in Figure 2.13(a). Figure 2.13(b) shows the value of atan2(x, z) as a function of the angle ϕ. When $x \geq 0$, atan2 = ϕ, but when $x < 0$, atan2 = $\phi - 2\pi$, to give the angular range $[-\pi, +\pi]$. Since we want an angle in the interval $[0, 2\pi]$, we have to check if atan2(x, z) < 0, and when that's true, add 2π to the value. This gives the graph in Figure 2.13(c).

This can be coded as in Listing 2.1.

```
double phi = atan2(x, z);
if (phi < 0.0)
    phi += TWO_PI;
```

Listing 2.1. Code to evaluate ϕ.

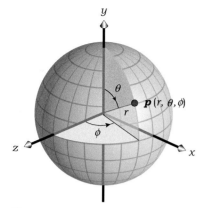

Figure 2.14. A sphere of radius r centered at the world origin.

Spheres. I'll only consider the parametric representation of spheres that are centered on the world origin. Although it's simple to generalize the parametric equations to spheres with arbitrary centers, I'll use *affine transformations* (Chapters 20 and 21) to construct parametric spheres that are not centered at the origin.

The parametric equations of a sphere are the same as Equations (2.2) for spherical coordinates, where r is now the radius of the sphere, and the two spherical-coordinate angles θ and ϕ are the parameters. These are illustrated in Figure 2.14. Note that θ is measured from the top of the sphere.

Given a point p (x, y, z) on the surface of the sphere, we need to calculate θ and ϕ. The calculation of ϕ is the same as it is for cylinders, and θ is simple to calculate. It follows from Equation (2.3) that

$$\theta = \cos^{-1}(y/r).$$

We can use the Standard C library function `double acos(double x)` to compute θ, because this returns $\theta \in [0, \pi]$ for $x = y / r \in [-1, +1]$.

2.9.3 Tangent Planes

At every point p on a surface where we can define the normal, we can also define a *tangent plane*. This is a plane that's perpendicular to the normal and just touches the surface at the given point (see Figure 2.15.) Although we won't have to compute the equation of the tangent plane, or use it in the ray-tracer code, I'll often refer to it in the shading chapters.

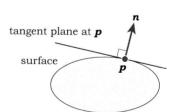

Figure 2.15. Cross section of a tangent plane at a surface point p.

 ## 2.10 Solid Angles

2.10.1 Definition

Solid angles are the 2D generalization of 1D angles. To see how these are defined, let's consider an object that's visible from a point p, as shown in Figure 2.16(a). First, place a sphere around the point and centered on it. Next, draw

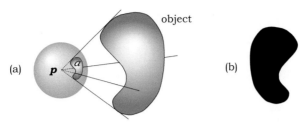

object

(a) p

(b)

Figure 2.16. (a) Definition of solid angle; (b) silhouette of the object as seen from p.

a line from p to some point on the outline of the object as seen from p. This outline is the edge of the object's silhouette as seen from p (see Figure 2.16(b)). Finally, run the line completely around the outline and draw the curve (red) traced on the surface of the sphere where the line intersects it. This curve will enclose a certain area a (cyan) on the sphere's surface. The *ratio* of this area to the total surface area of the sphere is the *solid angle* subtended at p by the object. Solid angles are measured in *steradians* and are usually denoted by ω.

If the sphere has radius 1, its surface area is 4π, and the solid angle is $\omega = a \,/\, 4\pi$ steradians. This definition does not depend on the radius of the sphere. The maximum value of a solid angle is 4π steradians, which is the solid angle subtended at a point by an object that completely surrounds it.

Figure 2.17 shows a differential surface element dA, oriented so that its normal makes an angle θ with the line that joins it and the center of a unit sphere. If dA is distance d from the center of the sphere, its differential solid angle $d\omega$ is given by

$$d\omega = \frac{\cos\theta \, dA}{d^2}. \tag{2.11}$$

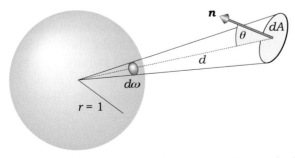

n

θ

dA

d

$d\omega$

$r = 1$

Figure 2.17. A differential surface element dA and its differential solid angle $d\omega$.

2.10.2 Solid Angles in Spherical Coordinates

The radiometric quantities and the definitions of reflectance in Chapter 13 require solid angles to be computed on the surface of a unit hemisphere. For this, we need to start with an expression for the differential solid angle $d\omega$ in spherical coordinates. Figure 2.18 shows how to use the definition of spherical coordinates to compute $d\omega$.

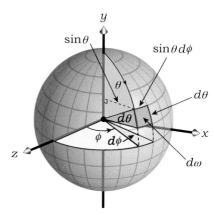

Figure 2.18. Differential solid angle $d\omega$ on the surface of a unit sphere.

Calculating the second-order differential yields

$$d\omega = \sin\theta \; d\theta \; d\phi.$$

A simple application is to compute the surface area of the unit sphere:

$$area = \int_0^{2\pi} \int_0^{\pi} \sin\theta \; d\theta \; d\phi = 4\pi,$$

as expected.

2.10.3 Integrals Over a Hemisphere

In later chapters, we'll need to use integrals of various functions $f(\theta, \phi)$ over the top hemisphere of the unit sphere: $(\theta, \phi) \in [0, \pi/2] \; [0, 2\pi]$. Although most of the integrands will be too complex to evaluate analytically, we can evaluate some of them exactly. The general integral is

$$I = \int_\omega f(\theta,\phi)\cos\theta \; d\omega,$$

where there are a few things to notice. First, it's written as a single integral over a solid angle, which is a shorthand notation for the double integral over θ and ϕ. Second, the ω on the integral sign denotes the solid-angle domain over which the integral is evaluated: $\omega \in [0, 2\pi]$ steradians, where $\omega = 2\pi$ is the whole hemisphere. Third, $\cos\theta$ is present in the integrand. This is a geometric factor that's present in all hemisphere integrands, as I'll explain in Chapter 13. The quantity $\cos\theta \; d\omega$ is known as the *projected solid angle*, because it's the projection of the differential solid angle $d\omega$ onto the (x, z) plane.

We will frequently need integrals with $f(\theta, \phi) = \cos^{n-1}\theta$, where n is an integer. In this case,

$$I = \int\limits_{2\pi} \cos^n\theta \, d\omega = \int\limits_0^{2\pi} \int\limits_0^{\pi/2} \cos^n\theta \sin\theta \, d\theta \, d\phi.$$

Fortunately, these integrals can be evaluated exactly. A major factor is that the integrand is separable, allowing I to be written as the product of two 1D integrals:

$$I = \int\limits_0^{2\pi} d\phi \int\limits_0^{\pi/2} \cos^n\theta \sin\theta \, d\theta = 2\pi \int\limits_0^{\pi/2} \cos^n\theta \sin\theta \, d\theta.$$

We can evaluate the θ integral with the change of variable $u = \cos\theta$, so that $du = -\sin\theta \, d\theta$, $u = 1$ when $\theta = 0$, and $u = 0$ when $\theta = \pi/2$. This gives

$$I = 2\pi \int\limits_0^1 u^n du = \left[\frac{u^{n+1}}{n+1} \right]_0^1 = \frac{2\pi}{n+1}. \tag{2.12}$$

 ## 2.11 Random Numbers

Ray tracing makes extensive use of random numbers because many ray-tracing effects are based on them. Most of the sampling techniques covered in Chapters 5–7 are based on random numbers, and these are used for antialiasing, depth of field, ambient occlusion, area lights, global illumination, and glossy reflection. The noise-based textures in Chapter 33 are also based on random numbers. It's therefore worthwhile to discuss informally what they are and how we can generate them.

If we had a function that returned a true random number every time it was called, it would always return a different number, and there would be no way we could predict what the number was going to be. Because computers are deterministic devices, the common random-number-generation algorithms don't return true random numbers; instead, they return *pseudorandom numbers*, which we call PRNs. To see what this means, suppose we have a program that generates n PRNs. Each time we run the program, we'll get the same numbers, but that's actually what we want. Let's say you are modeling a scene that contains a noise-based texture such as marble. If the numbers were truly random, you would get a slightly different marble texture each time you ran the program. This could make it difficult to debug your program and design the exact scene you want. It would be even worse for animation, where each frame would show a different texture.

We use PRNs that are in the range [0, 1] and are *uniformly distributed* in that range. To see what this means, we need to look at the numbers from a

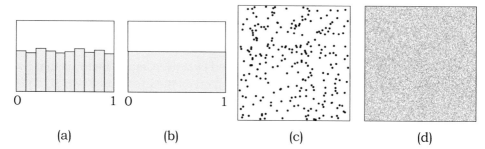

Figure 2.19. (a) Random numbers in 10 bins; (b) uniform distribution; (c) 256 random points; (d) 100,000 random points.

statistical point of view. Therefore, let's divide the interval [0, 1] into 10 sub-intervals [0.0, 0.1] ... [0.9, 1.0], called *bins*, and generate n =1000 PRNs. If these are uniformly distributed in [0, 1], there will be approximately 100 of them in each bin. Because the numbers won't be exactly the same, we will get a *frequency histogram*, something like that shown in Figure 2.19(a). Here, the height of each bar represents the number of PRNs in the bin. If we now increase n, the *fractional* difference between the numbers should decrease, and in the limit $n \to \infty$, this difference should approach zero. In this limit we could also have an infinite number of infinitely small bins, and the frequency histogram will look like Figure 2.19(b), a horizontal line. An exact uniform distribution only exists in the limit $n \to \infty$. Back in the real world, where we can only generate a finite number of PRNs, they will only be approximately uniformly distributed, as in Figure 2.19(a). This can create problems if we don't use enough of them, but that's best illustrated in two dimensions.

We'll often need to generate pairs of PRNs r_1 and r_2, where $(r_1, r_2) \in$ [0, 1] × [0, 1]. Figure 2.19(c) shows the locations of 256 = 16 × 16 random pairs in a unit square and illustrates a problem with using low numbers. Here, the distribution of points is not particularly uniform because we have only generated 16 PRNs in each direction. As a result, there are clumps and gaps in the distribution. Because we'll often use even lower numbers, for example, 4 × 4 or 5 × 5, we need a way of making the pairs more uniformly distributed but still random. In Chapter 5, I'll discuss a number of ways to achieve this. We could also solve the problem by using very large numbers, as in Figure 2.19(d), where there are 100,000 random pairs. This is a nice uniform distribution but, of course, completely impractical.

We can generate pseudorandom numbers with the Standard C library function rand, which returns an integer uniformly distributed in the interval [0, RAND_MAX]. Here, RAND_MAX is system-dependent. Depending on your sys-

```
inline int
rand_int(void) {
    return (rand());
}
```

Listing 2.2. The function rand_int.

```
inline float
rand_float(void) {
    return ((float)rand() / (float)RAND_MAX);
}
```

Listing 2.3. The function rand_float.

```
inline void
set_rand_seed(const int seed) {
    srand(seed);
}
```

Listing 2.4. The function set_rand_seed.

tem, there may be other random-number generators that you can use. To make it as simple as possible for you to use another random-number generator, I've wrapped rand inside the function rand_int as in Listing 2.2.

It's simple to convert the output of rand to floating-point numbers in the interval [0, 1] by dividing it by RAND_MAX. In fact, it's also convenient to define the wrapper function rand_float, as Listing 2.3 indicates.

Another convenient wrapper function is set_rand_seed, in Listing 2.4, which just calls srand. This has two essential uses, the first of which is for scene construction. For example, one of the scenes used in Chapter 11 has random boxes. If the build function didn't call set_rand_seed before constructing the boxes, their sizes, shapes, and colors would depend on how many samples were used for antialiasing. The reason is that the antialiasing samples also use rand. The second use is for setting up noise values for texture synthesis in Chapter 31, to guarantee that the textures are the same for every time that we render them.

As rand_int, rand_float, and set_rand_seed are the only functions that call rand and srand, it's easy to use another random-number generator. For example, if you want to use random in rand_float, it can return (float)random() / (float) 0x80000000U.

2.12 Orthonormal Bases and Frames

2.12.1 Definition

Definition 2.6. Three vectors u, v, and w form an *orthonormal basis* (ONB) if they are mutually perpendicular, they are all unit vectors, and they form a right-handed system where $w = u \times v$.

The *ortho* in the name is short for orthogonal, and *normal* is there because the vectors are unit vectors. The word *basis* is there because when we have three non-parallel vectors that are not in the same plane, we can express any other 3D vector as a linear combination of them. Because it's most convenient to work with mutually orthogonal unit vectors, most of the common coordinate systems such as Cartesian and spherical coordinates have mutually orthogonal axes, and mutually orthogonal unit basis vectors.[3] In the case of Cartesian coordinates, the unit vectors (i, j, k) form an orthonormal basis.

Orthonormal bases are an important construct in ray tracing because we use them whenever we need to set up a local coordinate system, a task we often have to do. Here's a list of the situations where we need an ONB:

- cameras (Chapters 9–12)
- ambient occlusion (Chapter 17)
- area-light shading (Chapter 18)
- rotation about an arbitrary line (Chapter 20)
- glossy reflection (Chapter 25)
- global illumination (Chapter 26)

2.12.2 Construction

We can construct an orthonormal basis from two arbitrary vectors, for example, the vectors a and b in Figure 2.20(a). These don't have to be unit vectors or be orthogonal. If a and b are defined in world coordinates, u, v, and w will also be defined in world coordinates when we construct them. That's what we always need.

We can construct the orthonormal basis vectors in the order w, u, v by taking w to be parallel to a and then using cross products. First, make w a unit vector in the direction of a:

$$w = a \,/\, \|a\|,$$

---

3. Barycentric coordinates, which we use to ray trace triangles, are an exception: these are non-orthogonal.

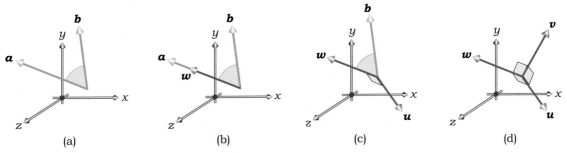

Figure 2.20. Construction of an orthonormal basis from two given vectors.

as in Figure 2.20(b). Next, construct u as the cross product of b and w, normalized to a unit vector:

$$u = (b \times w) / \|b \times w\|,$$

as in Figure 2.02(c). Finally, construct v as the cross product of w and u to form a right-handed system:

$$v = w \times u,$$

as in Figure 2.20(d). This is a unit vector by construction.

Where do a and b come from? In practice, we only have a single predefined direction, for example, the view direction for a camera or the surface normal at a point being shaded. The normal, of course, isn't even a vector. Given a, I arbitrarily use $b = (0, 1, 0)$, which is vertically up in world coordinates and results in u being horizontal. There is, however, a potential problem when a is also vertical and therefore parallel to b. This will be the situation if a is the normal to a horizontal surface. In this case, the construction above for u and v will fail. There are a couple of solutions, the simplest being to set b to a vector like

$$b = (0.00424, 1, 0.00764),$$

as this is slightly offset from vertically up. This situation also arises when the camera is looking vertically up or down in world coordinates, but there, I'll use a different technique (see Chapter 9).

2.12.3 Orthonormal Frames

An orthonormal basis and a point o where the unit vectors meet is an *orthonormal frame*. This defines a coordinate system with o as the origin. A common example consists of the (*i*, *j*, *k*) basis vectors and the origin in 3D Cartesian coordinates. In shading applications, the origin of the (*u*, *v*, *w*) frame is a ray-object hit point, and the orthonormal frame defines a local coordinate system centered on the hit point.

2.12.4 Using an Orthonormal Frame

Typically, we need to calculate a ray direction in a local coordinate system *and* specify the direction in world coordinates. This is because rays are always defined in world coordinates. Suppose we have calculated a ray direction $d = (d_u, d_v, d_w)$ with respect to an orthonormal frame. We can express *d* as

$$d = d_u u + d_v v + d_w w. \tag{2.13}$$

In case you are puzzled by this formula, it's helpful to remember that Equation (2.13) is no different from writing an arbitrary vector *e* in Cartesian coordinates as

$$e = e_x i + e_y j + e_z k.$$

The critical thing to note about Equation (2.13) is that since (*u*, *v*, *w*) are defined in world coordinates, it also expresses *d* in world coordinates.

Setting up an orthonormal frame only takes a few lines of code, and using it typically consists of calculating (d_u, d_v, d_w). I've included several examples of how to carry out this process, with sample code. The first is in Chapter 9 for a pinhole camera.

 ## 2.13 Geometric Series

A *geometric series* is a sum of *n* terms of the form

$$s_n = a + ar + ar^2 + \ldots + ar^{n-1}, \tag{2.14}$$

$$= \sum_{j=0}^{n-1} ar^n, \tag{2.15}$$

where, for our purposes, *a* and *r* are floating-point numbers. The number *a* is the *scale factor*, and *r* is the *ratio*, because the ratio of successive terms is always the same: $ar^n/ar^{n-1} = r$. If $r = 1$, the sum (2.15) is

$$s_n = an. \tag{2.16}$$

If $r \neq 1$, we can write the sum (2.15) as

$$s_n = \frac{a(1 - r^n)}{1 - r}.$$ (2.17)

An *infinite geometric series* is of the form (2.14), but where the number of terms is infinite. Provided $r \in (-1, +1)$, that is, $|r| < 1$, $r^n \to 0$ as $n \to \infty$, and Equation (2.17) becomes

$$s = \frac{a}{1 - r}.$$ (2.18)

I'll use the expressions (2.15)–(2.18) in Chapters 28 and 31.

 ## 2.14 The Dirac Delta Function

The Dirac delta function $\delta(x)$ is defined as the function with the following properties:

$$\delta(x) = 0 \text{ if } x \neq 0,$$

$$\int_{-\infty}^{\infty} \delta(x)\, dx = 1,$$

$$\int_{a}^{b} \delta(x - c) f(x)\, dx = f(c), \text{ provided } c \in [a, b].$$ (2.19)

This is not an ordinary function; it's zero everywhere except the origin, where it's infinite. Notice from Equation (2.19) that when an integrand contains a delta function, the integral collapses to $f(c)$. This happens with multi-dimensional integrals as well as one-dimensional integrals, a property that will make it simple for us to evaluate certain radiometric integrals in the shading chapters. When the distribution of incoming radiance at a surface point is confined to a single direction, it can be represented by a delta function (see Chapters 14, 24, and 27). I'll define radiometry and radiance in Chapter 13.

 ## Notes and Discussion

Because vectors, normals, and points all store an ordered triple of floating-point numbers, you can represent all three in a single class as vectors, instead of using separate classes for each. Opinion in the ray-tracing community is divided as to which is the best approach. Certainly, using a single class is simpler and saves code, but it's incorrect modeling. With separate classes, the application code shows explicitly the types of all of the relevant variables and is therefore more readable. My experience in the classroom is that it's also easier to teach affine transformations when there are separate classes.

Where should you put the functions `rand_int` and `rand_float` introduced in Section 2.9? As you develop your ray tracer, you will write or use numerous mathematical utility functions. It's most convenient to keep these in a separate compilation unit called, say, **Maths.cpp** or **Utilities.cpp**. You should put their prototypes in a corresponding header file that you can `#include` as required. These functions don't have to be class members, and the shorter ones can be inlined.

 ## Further Reading

There are many excellent books on the mathematics discussed in this chapter, and the mathematics not discussed, such as calculus and matrices. Here are some examples. Vince and Morris (1990) discusses sets. The calculus text Thomas and Finney (1996) covers intervals, coordinate systems, vectors, geometric series, and of course, calculus. Anton (2004) covers systems of linear equations, matrices, determinants, and vectors. Mortenson (1999) is on mathematics for computer graphics and discusses vectors and points. Rogers (2001) is an introduction to parametric curves and surfaces with code. Hill and Kelley (2006) also discusses curves and surfaces. Bloomenthal (1997) is an introduction to implicit surfaces.

 ## Questions

2.1. In Figure 2.16, why doesn't the solid angle subtended at p by the object depend on the radius of the sphere?
2.2. When we construct an orthonormal basis with the procedure described in Section 2.12.2, why is v a unit vector by construction?
2.3. Why does the construction of u and v in an orthonormal basis fail when a and b are parallel?

 ## Exercises

2.1. Use Equations (2.4) and (2.6) to derive the plane equation (2.7).
2.2. Prove that when b is vertical, the orthonormal basis vector u is horizontal.

3 Bare-Bones Ray Tracing

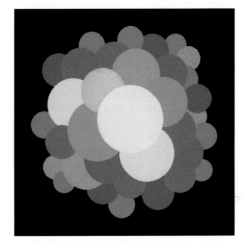

Objectives

By the end of this chapter, you should:

- understand how ray casting works;
- know how rays are defined;
- know how to intersect a ray with a plane and a sphere;
- understand the structure of a simple ray tracer;
- have implemented a ray tracer that can render orthographic views of an arbitrary number of planes and spheres.

The purpose of this chapter is to explain how a number of ray-tracing processes work in a simplified context. I'll discuss here how ray tracing generates images, how rays are defined, how ray-object intersections work, the classes required for a simple ray tracer, and how to ray trace an arbitrary number of spheres and planes. To make things as simple as possible, I've left out a lot of important processes such as antialiasing, perspective viewing with a pinhole camera, and shading. By doing this, the resulting ray tracer is as simple as possible, although, as you'll see, it still has a degree of complexity. This is also a long chapter because it covers a lot of material.

This chapter differs from the following chapters in that the skeleton ray tracer on the book's website does everything in the chapter. Hopefully, this will have you quickly ray tracing multiple planes and spheres.

3.1 How Ray Tracing Works

A simple ray tracer works by performing the following operations:

```
define some objects
specify a material for each object
define some light sources
define a window whose surface is covered with pixels

for each pixel
    shoot a ray towards the objects from the center
        of the pixel
    compute the nearest hit point of the ray with the
        objects (if any)

    if the ray hits an object
        use the object's material and the lights to
        compute the pixel color
    else
        set the pixel color to black
```

This is known as *ray casting*. Figure 3.1 illustrates some of the above processes for a sphere, a triangle, and a box, illuminated by a single light. The gray rectangles on the left are the pixels, and the white arrows are the rays, which start at the center of each pixel. Although there is one ray for each pixel, Figure 3.1 only shows a few rays. The red dots show where the rays hit the objects. The rays used in ray tracing differ from real light rays (or photons) in two ways. First, they travel in the opposite direction of real rays. This is best appreciated when we use a pinhole camera (Chapter 9), because there the rays start at the pinhole, which is infinitely small. If the rays started at the lights, none of them would pass through the pinhole, and we wouldn't have any images. Starting the rays from the camera (or pixels, in this chapter) is the only practical way to render images with ray tracing. The second difference is that we let the rays pass through the objects, even if they are opaque. We have to do this because the ray tracer needs to intersect each ray with each object to find the hit point that's closest to the start of the ray.

In Figure 3.1, one ray doesn't hit any objects, two rays hit one object, and one ray hits two objects. The hit points are always on the surfaces of the objects, which we treat as empty shells. As a result, rays hit the sphere and the box in two places and the triangle in one place.

The pixels are on a plane called the *view plane*, which is perpendicular to the rays. I'll sometimes refer to these as view-plane pixels. The rays are paral-

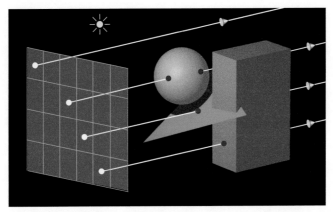

Figure 3.1. Rays shot from pixels into a scene that consists of three objects and a single light source.

lel to each other and produce an *orthographic projection* of the objects. When a ray hits an object, the color of its pixel is computed from the way the object's material reflects light, a process that's known as *shading*. Although the pixels on the view plane are just mathematical abstractions, like everything else in the ray tracer, each one is associated with a real pixel in a window on a computer screen. This is how you view the ray-traced image.

The process of working out where a ray hits an object is known as the *ray-object intersection calculation*. This is a fundamental process in ray tracing and usually takes most of the time. The intersection calculation is different for each type of object; some objects are easy to intersect, while others are difficult. All intersection calculations require some mathematics.

In Figure 3.1, there are 24 pixels arranged in four rows of six pixels, and in this case we say the image has a *pixel resolution* of 6 × 4. What would these objects look like if we ray traced them at this resolution? The result is in Figure 3.2(a), which gives no indication of what we are looking at. So, how can we get a meaningful image of these objects? The answer is simple: just increase the number of pixels. The other parts of Figure 3.2 show the objects ray traced at increasing pixel resolutions. With 24 × 16 pixels, we have some idea of what the objects are, and with 150 × 100 pixels, the image is quite good.

The above example was just to illustrate how ray tracing works with multiple objects, a light source, and shading. We'll start with something much simpler in Section 3.6: a single sphere with no lights, no material, and no shading, but first you need to learn how a basic ray tracer is organized and works.

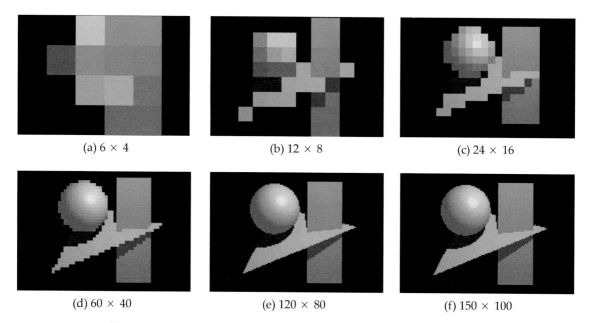

(a) 6 × 4   (b) 12 × 8   (c) 24 × 16

(d) 60 × 40   (e) 120 × 80   (f) 150 × 100

Figure 3.2. The objects in Figure 3.1 ray traced at different pixel resolutions.

 ## 3.2 The World

Ray tracers render *scenes* that contain the geometric objects, lights, a camera, a view plane, a tracer, and a background color. In the ray tracer described in this book, these objects are all stored in a *world* object. For now, the world will only store the objects and view plane. The locations and orientations of all scene elements are specified in *world coordinates,* which is a 3D Cartesian coordinate system, as described in Chapter 2. I'll denote world coordinates by (x_w, y_w, z_w), or just (x, y, z) when the context is clear.

World coordinates are known as *absolute coordinates* because their origin and orientation are not defined, but that's not a problem. The only task of the ray tracer is to compute the color of each pixel, and the pixels are also defined in world coordinates. I'll discuss the world class in Section 3.6.

 ## 3.3 Rays

A ray is an infinite straight line that's defined by a point *o*, called the *origin*, and a unit vector *d*, called the *direction*. A ray is parametrized with the *ray param-*

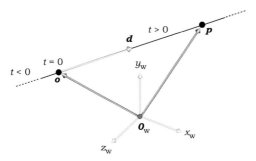

Figure 3.3. Ray definition in world coordinates.

eter t, where $t = 0$ at the ray origin, so that an arbitrary point p on a ray can be expressed as

$$p = o + t\,d. \tag{3.1}$$

Figure 3.3 is a schematic diagram of a ray. The direction d defines an intrinsic direction for the ray along the line, where the value of the parameter t increases in the direction d. Since d is a unit vector, t measures distance along the ray from the origin. Although we regard a ray as starting at its origin, we allow t to lie in the infinite interval $t \in (-\infty, +\infty)$ so that Equation (3.1) generates an infinite straight line. As we'll see later, it's essential to consider values of $t \in (-\infty, +\infty)$ in ray-object intersections. The origin and direction are always expressed in world coordinates before the ray is intersected with the objects.

Ray tracing uses the following types of rays:

- primary rays;
- secondary rays;
- shadow rays;
- light rays.

Primary rays start at the centers of the pixels for parallel viewing, and at the camera location for perspective viewing. Secondary rays are reflected and transmitted rays that start on object surfaces. Shadow rays are used for shading and start at object surfaces. Light rays start at the lights and are used to simulate certain aspects of global illumination, such as caustics. I'll only discuss primary rays in this chapter.

You should have a Ray class that stores the origin and direction, as in Listing 3.1. Because of their frequent use, all data members are public. In my shading architecture, there's no need to store the ray parameter in the ray. The code in Listing 3.1 will go in the header file **Ray.h**. Note the pre-compiler

```
#ifndef __RAY__
#define __RAY__

#include "Point3D.h"
#include "Vector3D.h"

class Ray {
    public:

            Point3D     o;                      // origin
            Vector3D    d;                      // direction

            Ray(void);                          // default constructor

            Ray(const Point3D& origin, const Vector3D& dir); // constructor

            Ray(const Ray& ray);                // copy constructor

            Ray&                                // assignment operator
            operator= (const Ray& rhs);

            ~Ray(void);                         // destructor
};

#endif
```

Listing 3.1. The **Ray.h** file.

directives #ifndef __RAY__, etc., to prevent multiple inclusion. These should go in every header file, but to save space, I won't quote them with other class declarations. You should also #inlcude header files for any classes that the current class requires: Point.h and Vector3D in this case. Again, to save space, I'll leave these out except for the world class in Section 3.6.1.

3.4 Ray-Object Intersections

3.4.1 General Points

The basic operation we perform with a ray is to intersect it with all geometric objects in the scene. This finds the nearest hit point, if any, along the ray from *o* in the direction *d*. We look for the hit point with the smallest value of *t* in the interval $t \in [\varepsilon, +\infty)$ where ε is a small positive number, say $\varepsilon = 10^{-6}$. Why don't

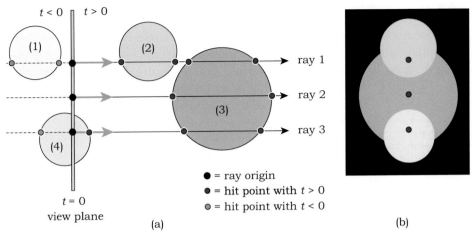

Figure 3.4. (a) Rays and their intersections with spheres; (b) ray-traced image of the spheres.

we use $\varepsilon = 0$? We could get away with this here, but it would create problems when we use shadows (Chapter 16), reflections (Chapters 24–26), and transparency (Chapters 27 and 28). I'll discuss what the problem is in Chapter 16. By using $\varepsilon > 0$ in this chapter, we won't have to change the plane and sphere hit functions in later chapters.

Because a ray origin can be anywhere in the scene, including inside objects and on their surfaces, ray-object hit points can occur for positive, negative, and zero values of t. This is why we need to treat rays as infinite straight lines instead of semi-infinite lines that start at o. Figure 3.4(a) shows a number of spheres that are behind, straddling, and in front of the view plane, with three rays.

The spheres in Figure 3.4(a) will be rendered (or not) in the following ways:

- Sphere (1) is behind the origin of all rays that intersect it ($t < 0$) and will not appear in the image.
- Sphere (2) will be rendered with ray 1 and with all rays that hit it.
- Sphere (3) will only be rendered with rays like ray 2 that don't hit any other spheres.
- Sphere (4) will only be rendered with rays like ray 3 that start inside it.

Figure 3.4(b) shows how the spheres would look if we ray traced them with no shading and if their centers were all in the vertical plane that contains the three rays. The nearest hit points of these rays are indicated in the figure.

3.4.2 Rays and Implicit Surfaces

As I discussed in the previous chapter, the objects we ray trace are defined by implicit surfaces. A ray can hit an implicit surface any number of times, depending on how complex the surface is (see Figure 3.5). If the surface is closed, rays that start outside the surface will have an even number of hit points for $t > \varepsilon$ (rays 1 and 2). In principal, a ray that starts outside can have an odd number of hit points, including a single hit point, if it hits the surface tangentially (rays 3 and 5). In practice, this rarely happens (see Question 3.1). When the ray starts inside the surface, it will have an odd number of hit points for $t > \varepsilon$ (ray 4).

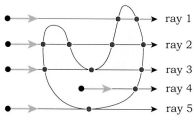

Figure 3.5. (a) Ray intersections with a closed implicit surface.

To intersect a ray with an implicit surface, we can re-write Equation (2.5), $f(x, y, z) = 0$, as

$$f(\boldsymbol{p}) = 0, \tag{3.2}$$

because the x, y, and z variables in $f(x, y, z)$ define a 3D point $\boldsymbol{p} = (x, y, z)$.

To find the hit points, we have to find the values of the ray parameter t that correspond to them. How do we do this? Here's the key point: *Hit points satisfy both the ray equation (3.1) and the implicit surface equation (3.2)*. We can therefore substitute (3.1) into (3.2) to get

$$f(\boldsymbol{o} + t\,\boldsymbol{d}) = 0 \tag{3.3}$$

as the equation to solve for t. Since Equation (3.3) is symbolic, we can't do anything with it unless we specify $f(x, y, z)$. For a given ray and a given implicit surface, the only unknown in Equation (3.3) is t. After we have found the values of t, we substitute the smallest $t > \varepsilon$ value into Equation (3.1) to find the coordinates of the nearest hit point. If all this seems confusing, don't worry, because I'm going to illustrate it for planes and spheres. For these objects, we can solve Equation (3.3) exactly.

3.4.3 Geometric Objects

All geometric objects belong to an inheritance structure with class `GeometricObject` as the base class. This is by far the largest inheritance structure in the ray tracer, with approximately 40 objects, but in this chapter we'll use a simplified structure consisting of `GeometricObject`, `Plane`, and `Sphere`, as shown on the left of Figure 1.1.

```
class GeometricObject {
    public:

        ...

        virtual bool
        hit(const Ray& ray, double& tmin, ShadeRec& sr)
        const = 0;

    protected:

        RGBColor color;    // only used in this chapter
};
```

Listing 3.2. Partial declaration of the GeometricObject class.

Listing 3.2 shows part of the GeometricObject class declaration that stores an RBGColor for use in Section 3.6. I'll replace this with a material pointer when I discuss shading in Chapter 14. This listing also doesn't show other functions that

```
class ShadeRec {
    public:

        bool        hit_an_object;    // did the ray hit an object?
        Point3D     local_hit_point;  // world coordinates of hit point
        Normal      normal;           // normal at hit point
        RGBColor    color;            // used in Chapter 3 only
        World&      w;                // world reference for shading

        ShadeRec(World& wr);              // constructor
        ShadeRec(const ShadeRec& sr);     // copy constructor
        ~ShadeRec(void);                  // destructor

        ShadeRec&                         // assignment operator
        operator= (const ShadeRec& rhs);
};

ShadeRec::ShadeRec(World& wr)                    // constructor
    :     hit_an_object(false),
          local_hit_point(),
          normal(),
          color(black),
          w(wr)
{}
```

Listing 3.3. Declaration of the ShadeRec class.

this class must have in order to operate as the base class of the geometric objects hierarchy, but it does show the declaration of the pure virtual function `hit`.

The `ShadeRec` object in the parameter list of the hit function is a utility class that stores all of the information that the ray tracer needs to *shade* a ray-object hit point. Briefly, shading is the process of computing the color that's reflected back along the ray, a process that most of this book is about. The `ShadeRec` object plays a critical role in the ray tracer's shading procedures, as this chapter starts to illustrate in a simplified context. Listing 3.3 shows a declaration of the `ShadeRec` class with the data members that we need here. Note that one data member is a world reference. Although this is only used for shading, I've included it here, as it prevents the `ShadeRec` class from having a default constructor; the reference must always be initialized when a `ShadeRec` object is constructed (Listings 3.14 and 3.16) or copy constructed (Listing 3.17). Listing 3.3 includes the `ShadeRec` constructor code (see also the Notes and Discussion section). I haven't included an assignment operator, as the ray tracer is written in such a way that it's not required. For example, no class has a `ShadeRec` object as a data member.

3.4.4 Planes

Planes are the best geometric objects to discuss first because they are the easiest to intersect. To do this, we first substitute Equation (3.1) into the plane equation (2.6),

$$(p - a) \bullet n = 0,$$

to get

$$(o + t\,d - a) \bullet n = 0.$$

This is a *linear equation* in the ray parameter t whose solution is

$$t = (a - o)\ n\,/\,(d \bullet n). \tag{3.4}$$

A linear equation has the form

$$at + b = 0,$$

where a and b are constants, and t is an unknown variable. The solution is

$$t = -b\,/\,a.$$

See Exercise 3.10.

Because linear equations have a single solution, Equation (3.4) tells us that a ray can only hit a plane once. We could now substitute the expression (3.4) for t into Equation (3.1) to get a symbolic expression for the hit-point coordinates, but we don't do this for two reasons. First, we don't need the hit-

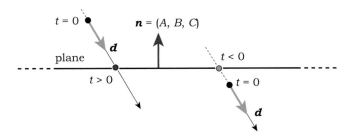

Figure 3.6. Ray-plane intersections.

point coordinates until we shade the point, and we only do that for the closest point to the ray origin. We won't know what that point will be until we've intersected the ray with all of the objects. Second, it's more efficient to calculate the *numerical* value of t from Equation (3.4) and substitute that into (3.1) to get *numerical* values for the coordinates. This applies to all geometric objects. The ray tracer must have numerical values for shading.

Figure 3.6 shows an edge-on view of a plane with two rays. The ray on the left hits the plane with $t > \varepsilon$, but the ray on the right hits it with $t < 0$. We must check that the value of t in Equation (3.4) satisfies $t > \varepsilon$ before recording that an intersection has occurred. In this context, it doesn't matter whether the normal to the plane points up or down in Figure 3.6, as this will only affect the shading.

```
class Plane: public GeometricObject {
    public:

        Plane(void);

        Plane(const Point3D p, const Normal& n);
        ...

        virtual bool
        hit(const Ray& ray, double& t, ShadeRec& s) const;

    private:

        Point3D                point;       // point through which
                                            //    plane passes
        Normal                 normal;      // normal to the plane
        static const double    kEpsilon;    // see Chapter 16
};
```

Listing 3.4. The Plane::hit function.

```
bool
Plane::hit(const Ray& ray, double& tmin, ShadeRec& sr) const {
    double t = (point - ray.o) * normal / (ray.d * normal);

    if (t > kEpsilon) {
        tmin = t;
        sr.normal              = normal;
        sr.local_hit_point     = ray.o + t * ray.d;

        return (true);
    }
    else
        return (false);
}
```

Listing 3.5. The `Plane::hit` function.

What happens if the ray is parallel to the plane? In this case, $d \bullet n = 0$, and the value of the expression (3.4) is infinity. Is this a problem? Not if you are programming in C++, because floating-point calculations in this language satisfy the IEEE floating-point standard, where division by zero returns the legal number INF (infinity). As a result, there's no need to check for $d \bullet n = 0$ as a special case; your ray tracer will not crash if it divides by zero.

The class Plane stores the point and the normal. Its declaration appears in Listing 3.4 with two constructors; each class should have a default constructor, and other constructors as required.

Listing 3.5 shows the ray-plane hit function. Ray-object hit functions don't come any simpler than this.

All object hit functions compute and return information in three ways: their return type is a bool that indicates if the ray hits the object; they return the ray parameter for the nearest hit point (if any) through the parameter tmin; they return information required for shading with the ShadeRec parameter. We won't need the normal until shading in Chapter 14, and we won't need the hit point local_hit_point until texturing in Chapter 29. By including them now, we won't have to change this hit function later on.

3.4.5 Spheres

Equation (2.8) for a sphere can be written in vector form as

$$(p - c) \bullet (p - c) - r^2 = 0 \qquad (3.5)$$

(see Exercise 3.11). To intersect a ray with a sphere, we substitute Equation (3.1) into (3.5) to get

$$(o + t\,d - c) \bullet (o + t\,d - c) - r^2 = 0. \tag{3.6}$$

Expanding Equation (3.6) gives

$$(d \bullet d)t^2 + [2(o - c) \bullet d]t + (o - c) \bullet (o - c) - r^2 = 0. \tag{3.7}$$

Equation (3.7) is a *quadratic equation* for t, which we can write as

$$at^2 + bt + c = 0, \tag{3.8}$$

where[1]

$$a = d \bullet d,$$
$$b = 2(o - c) \bullet d, \tag{3.9}$$
$$c = (o - c) \bullet (o - c) - r^2.$$

The solution to Equation (3.8) is given by the standard expression

$$t = \frac{-b \pm (b^2 - 4ac)^{1/2}}{2a}.$$

Quadratic equations can have zero, one, or two real roots, depending on the value of the discriminant

$$d = b^2 - 4ac.$$

This is reflected in the fact that a ray can hit a sphere zero, one, or two times (see Figure 3.7). Here, ray 1 does not hit the sphere ($d < 0$), ray 2 has one hit

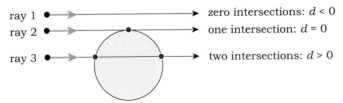

ray 1   zero intersections: $d < 0$
ray 2   one intersection: $d = 0$
ray 3   two intersections: $d > 0$

Figure 3.7. Ray-sphere intersections.

---

1. In Equation (3.8), c is not $\|c\|$.

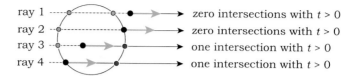

Figure 3.8. Further ray-sphere intersections.

```
bool
Sphere::hit(const Ray& ray, double& tmin, ShadeRec& sr) const {
    double    t;
    Vector3D  temp    = ray.o - center;
    double    a       = ray.d * ray.d;
    double    b       = 2.0 * temp * ray.d;
    double    c       = temp * temp - radius * radius;
    double    disc    = b * b - 4.0 * a * c;

    if (disc < 0.0)
        return(false);
    else {
        double e = sqrt(disc);
        double denom = 2.0 * a;
        t = (-b - e) / denom;       // smaller root

        if (t > kEpsilon) {
            tmin = t;
            sr.normal = (temp + t * ray.d) / radius;
            sr.local_hit_point = ray.o + t * ray.d;
            return (true);
        }

        t = (-b + e) / denom;       // larger root

        if (t > kEpsilon) {
            tmin = t;
            sr.normal = (temp + t * ray.d) / radius;
            sr.local_hit_point = ray.o + t * ray.d;
            return (true);
        }
    }

    return (false);
}
```

Listing 3.6. Ray-sphere hit function.

point with $t \in [\varepsilon, +\infty)$ ($d = 0$) because it hits the sphere tangentially, and ray 3 has two hit points with $t \in [\varepsilon, +\infty)$ ($d > 0$).

Although we only need the situations shown in Figure 3.7 in this chapter, the ray-sphere hit function must also give correct answers for the situations shown in Figure 3.8. Since ray 1 in this figure only hits the sphere with $t < 0$, this ray has zero intersections with the sphere. Because ray 2 starts on the surface of the sphere and d points out of the sphere, one hit point has $t = 0$ (at least in theory), and the other has $t < 0$. Therefore, this ray also has zero intersections. Ray 3 starts inside the sphere and has one hit point with $t > 0$ and one with $t < 0$, and therefore has one intersection. Finally, ray 4 also starts on the surface, but d points into the sphere. This ray, therefore, has one intersection. Rays 2 and 4 could be reflected, transmitted, or shadow rays, and as we'll see in later chapters, it's critical that these rays *do not* record an intersection at their origins.

The ray-sphere hit function in Listing 3.6 correctly handles all of the above situations, but note that we don't test for tangential intersection when $d = 0$ (see Question 3.2).

 ## 3.5 Representing Colors

As ray tracing is all about computing the color of each pixel, we need a way to represent and store colors. One of the most remarkable aspects of our perception of color is that it's three dimensional. We can therefore specify colors in 3D *color spaces*. There are a number of these in common use, but the one that's most aligned to graphics monitors is called RGB, which is short for red, green, and blue.

What does the RGB color space look like? First, there are three axes (r, g, b) defined by the red, green, and blue colors. These form a right-handed coordinate system, except that there are no negative values, and $(r, g, b) \in [0, 1]^3$. The RGB color space, the set of all legal values of r, g, and b, is therefore a unit cube with one vertex at the (r, g, b) origin (see Figure 3.9). It's therefore called the *RGB color cube*.

Pure red, green, and blue are known as the *additive primary colors* and are represented by $r = (1, 0, 0)$, $g = (0, 1, 0)$, and $b = (0, 0, 1)$. They have the following properties (see Figure 3.10):

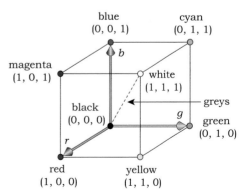

Figure 3.9. The RGB color cube.

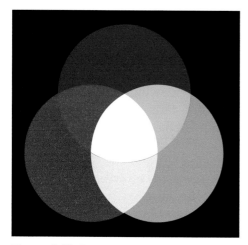

Figure 3.10. Properties of the three additive primary colors red, green, and blue.

$$red + green + blue = white,$$
$$red + blue = (1, 0, 1) = magenta,$$
$$red + green = (1, 1, 0) = yellow,$$
$$green + blue = (0, 1, 1) = cyan.$$

Figure 3.11 shows some views of the RGB color cube. Yellow, cyan, and magenta are known as *secondary colors* and are at the three cube vertices that lie in the (r, g, b) coordinate planes, as indicated in Figure 3.11(a). These are also the CMY *subtractive primary colors*, used for printing (see Figure 28.8).

Figure 3.11(b) is the surface of the cube that lies in the (r, g) plane, and it shows all combinations of red and green with no blue. For example, the orange color $(1, 0.5, 0)$ is half way along the right boundary of the square. Colors along the red axis are $(r, 0, 0)$, with $r \in [0, 1]$, and range from black to pure red. Similarly, all combinations of red and blue are on the surface of the cube in the (r, b) plane, and all combinations of green and blue are on the surface in the (g, b) plane.

Figure 3.11(c) shows the cube sliced in two by a plane that contains the blue axis and that passes through $(1, 1, 1)$. Grays lie along the diagonal dashed line from black to white, but it's not possible to see them in this figure, as the line from $(0, 0, 0)$ to $(1, 1, 1)$ is, of course, infinitely thin. Grays have all compo-

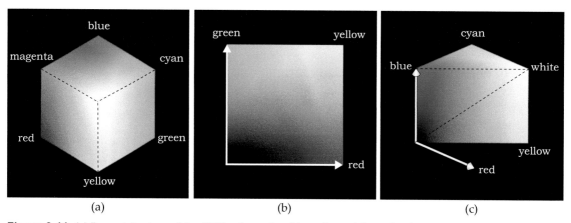

(a)   (b)   (c)

Figure 3.11. (a) Isometric view of the RGB color cube; (b) surface of the cube that's in the (r, g) plane; (c) the cube sliced in half by a plane through the blue axis.

nents the same; that is, gray = (a, a, a), where $a \in (0, 1)$. For example, a medium gray is $(0.5, 0.5, 0.5)$.

I'll store RGB colors in the RGBColor class, which represents the components with an ordered triple of floating-point numbers r, g, b. Let

$$c = (r, g, b),$$
$$c_1 = (r_1, g_1, b_1),$$
$$c_2 = (r_2, g_2, b_2)$$

be three colors, and let a and p be floating-point numbers. We will need the following operations:

Operation	Definition	Return Type
$c_1 + c_2$	$(r_1 + r_2, g_1 + g_2, b_1 + b_2)$	RGB color
ac	(ar, ag, ab)	RGB color
ca	(ar, ag, ab)	RGB color
c / a	$(r / a, g / a, b / a)$	RGB color
$c_1 = c_2$	$(r_1 = r_2, g_1 = g_2, b_1 = b_2)$	RGB color reference
$c_1 * c_2$	$(r_1 r_2, g_1 g_2, b_1 b_2)$	RGB color
c^p	(r^p, g^p, b^p)	RGB color
$c_1 \mathrel{+}= c_2$	$(r_1 \mathrel{+}= r_2, g_1 \mathrel{+}= g_2, b_1 \mathrel{+}= b_2)$	RGB color reference

The operator $c_1 * c_2$ is component-wise multiplication of two colors; it's used for color mixing. For convenience, I've defined black, white, and red as constants in the **Constants.h** file.

The ray tracer will compute an RGB color for each pixel, but before you can display these on your computer screen, they must be converted to the representation that your computer uses for display purposes. This process is platform-dependent and can involve arcane code. You don't have to worry about this, as the skeleton program does the conversion for Windows machines. I will discuss some display issues in Section 3.8, but we also have to be able to handle color values that are outside the color cube. As these can occur during shading operations, I'll discuss that in Section 14.9. The skeleton program also allows you to save the images in various file formats, such as JPEG and TIFF.

3.6 A Bare-Bones Ray Tracer

It's now time to do some ray tracing. With all the preceding mathematics and theory, you may be feeling a little intimidated. If that's the case, don't

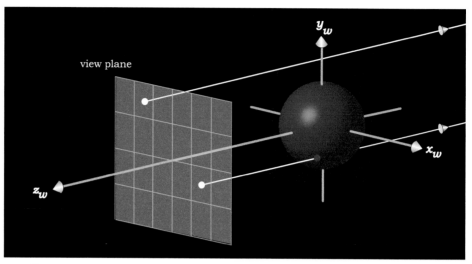

Figure 3.12. The view plane, sphere, and world coordinate axes, with two rays.

worry, because we are going to start with the simplest possible bare-bones ray tracer. This ray traces an orthographic view of a single sphere centered on the origin of the world coordinates. If a ray hits the sphere we color the pixel red, otherwise we color it black. As the skeleton ray tracer does this, you don't have to program it unless you want to; you only have to get it running.

Figure 3.12 shows how the view plane, the world coordinate axes, and the sphere are arranged. This also shows a ray that hits the sphere and a ray that misses it.

3.6.1 Required Classes

Just to ray trace this simple scene, we need the following 12 classes:

Geometric Objects	Tracers	Utility	World
GeometricObject Sphere	Tracer SingleSphere	Normal Point3D Ray RGBColor ShadeRec Vector3D	ViewPlane World

These are in the skeleton program. The World, ViewPlane, ShadeRec, and GeometricObject classes are in simplified form at this stage.

Listing 3.7 shows the declaration of a simple `world` class that's in the file **World.h**. This version contains all of the data members and member functions that we need at present. The sphere is a temporary measure for this section only. All data members of `world` are public. The background color is the color returned by rays that don't hit any geometric objects. Its default color is black, which is also the default color of an `RGBColor` object.

Listing 3.8 shows part of the `world` class definition in the file **World.cpp**. An important thing to note here are the `#include` statements. The **World.cpp** file should contain the header files for all classes used in the ray tracer, except those #included in **World.h**; by doing this, there shouldn't be any unknown classes during compilation. I also #include the build functions here, as a simple way to manage them. The code for each build function is in a separate file and

```
#include "ViewPlane.h"
#include "RGBColor.h"
#include "Sphere.h"
#include "Tracer.h"

class World {
    public:

            ViewPlane    vp;
            RGBColor     background_color;
            Sphere       sphere;
            Tracer*      tracer_ptr;

            World(void);

            void
            build(void);

            void
            render_scene(void) const;

            void
            open_window(const int hres, const int vres) const;

            void
            display_pixel(const int row,
                    const int column,
                    const RGBColor& pixel_color) const;
};
```

Listing 3.7. A simple `world` class declaration.

```
#include "Constants.h"  // contains kEpsilon and kHugeValue

// utilities

#include "Vector3D.h"
#include "Point3D.h"
#include "Normal.h"

#include "Ray.h"

#include "World.h"

// build functions

#include "BuildRedSphere.cpp"  // builds the red sphere

// World member function definitions ...
```

Listing 3.8. Part of the **World.cpp** file that contains the #include statements.

#included in **World.cpp** after all the classes have been #included. All build functions are commented out except for the one currently running. Depending on which development environment you use, you may also need to #include various system header files.

3.6.2 The Main Function

In a pure C++ ray tracer with no user interface, the build function would be called from the main function, as shown in Listing 3.9. Depending on your development environment, there may not be a main function as such, but the code that's in Listing 3.9 will have to appear somewhere.

```
int
main(void) {
    World w;            // construct a default world object
    w.build();
    w.render_scene();

    return(0);
}
```

Listing 3.9. The main function.

```
class ViewPlane {
    public:

        int         hres;          // horizontal image resolution
        int         vres;          // vertical image resolution
        float       s;             // pixel size
        float       gamma;         // monitor gamma factor
        float       inv_gamma;     // one over gamma

        ...

};
```

Listing 3.10. The ViewPlane class.

3.6.3 The View Plane

The ViewPlane class stores the number of pixels in the horizontal and vertical directions, along with their size (see Listing 3.10). I'll discuss the gamma data member in Section 3.8. In later chapters, we'll store additional data members in this class.

The view plane contains the pixels that form a window through which the scene is rendered. In this chapter, the view plane is perpendicular to the z_w-axis, the pixels are arranged in horizontal rows, and the window is centered on the z_w-axis. Figure 3.13 is a schematic diagram of the pixels for an 8×6 window. Here, the z_w-axis would stick out of the paper through the middle of the window (the center dot). The window can also cut the z_w-axis at any suitable

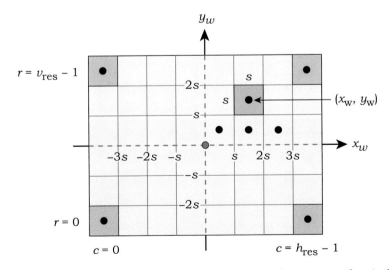

Figure 3.13. Schematic diagram of a view plane window and ray origins, for pixels of size $s \times s$.

location. Notice how the rows and columns of pixels are parallel to the x_w- and y_w-axes, which can be behind or in front of the view plane.

Here, a single ray starts at the center of each pixel, as indicated by the black circles on some pixels. We specify the z_w-coordinate for the ray origins, which are all the same, but we have to calculate the x_w- and y_w-coordinates. As each pixel is a square of size $s \times s$, these coordinates are proportional to s. We number the pixel rows from 0 to $v_{res} - 1$, from bottom to top, and the columns from 0 to $h_{res} - 1$, from left to right, as indicated in Figure 3.13. The values of h_{res} and v_{res} are always even, so that the z_w-axis goes through the corners of the four center pixels.

Given the above conditions, the expressions for the (x_w, y_w)-coordinates of the ray origins are

$$x_w = s(c - h_{res} / 2 + 0.5), \tag{3.10}$$

$$y_w = s(r - v_{res} / 2 + 0.5).$$

These are simple to derive (see Exercise 3.13).

The ray directions are all $\boldsymbol{d} = (0, 0, -1)$ because the rays travel in the negative z_w-direction.

3.6.4 Pixels and Pictures

In a general viewing situation, the part of the scene that's visible through the window is known as the *field of view*. In the arrangement here, the field of view depends only on the number of pixels in the horizontal and vertical directions, and their size, because these factors determine the physical dimensions of the window: width sh_{res}, and height sv_{res}. They also determine where the rays are and, hence, where the scene is sampled. Let me illustrate this with the objects in Figure 3.2. Figure 3.14 shows these objects with three different windows

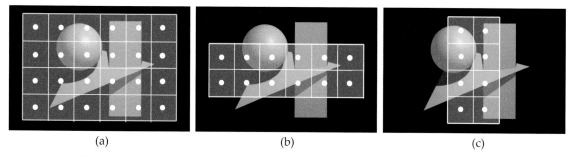

| (a) | (b) | (c) |

Figure 3.14. Windows with different pixel resolutions superimposed on a scene: (a) 6 × 4; (b) 6 × 2; (c) 2 × 4. The white dots are the ray origins and indicate where the scene is sampled.

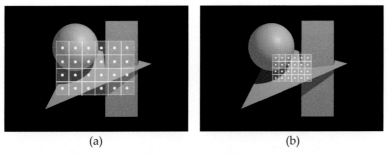

(a)   (b)

Figure 3.15. The windows that result when we reduce the size of the pixels: (a) *s* is one-half the size it is in Figure 3.14(a); (b) *s* is one-quarter the size.

superimposed. Here, the pixels are the same size in each window, but their numbers are different. If we change h_{res} or v_{res}, or both, the shape and size of the window changes accordingly. In each case, the only part of the scene that will be rendered is the part that's projected through the window. If we rendered the scene in Figure 3.14(a), the result would be the same as Figure 3.2 (a).

In contrast, Figure 3.15 shows the 6×4 pixel window in Figure 3.14(a) with pixels of different size. In Figure 3.15(a), the pixel size *s* has been reduced by a factor of 2, and in Figure 3.15(b), it's been reduced by another factor of 2. This results in a most useful process, but see if you can think what it is before reading further.

Because the part of the scene projected through the window decreases as the pixel size gets smaller, decreasing *s* *zooms* into the view. For fixed values of h_{res} and v_{res}, this is the only way we can zoom with an orthographic projection. The process is analogous to zooming with a real camera.

Let's look now at a different process. Suppose the window you are using gives a good view of a scene, but you aren't using enough pixels. Figure 3.14(a) might be an example. You can increase the number of pixels, and keep the window the same size, by making the pixels smaller by a corresponding amount. An example is to increase the horizontal and vertical resolutions by two and to make the pixel size half as big. Figure 3.16 shows the window from Figure 3.14(a) with $h_{\text{res}} = 24$ and $v_{\text{res}} = 16$. I've used this process to render the images in Figure 3.2.

Of course, the size of the view-plane pixels doesn't affect the size of the image on your computer screen. When you display the image, each

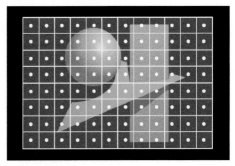

Figure 3.16. The window in Figure 3.14(a) with a pixel resolution of 12×8. This results in Figure 3.2(b).

| (a) | (b) |

Figure 3.17. Zoomed views of the objects in Figure 3.2. The pixel size in (a) is 0.26, and in (b) it's 0.13.

view-plane pixel is still associated with a real pixel on your screen, regardless of the value of s. The only thing that affects the physical size of the image is the pixel resolution $h_{res} \times v_{res}$ and the physical size of the screen pixels.

To illustrate the zooming process, Figure 3.17 shows the views though the two windows in Figure 3.15, rendered at a pixel resolution of 660×440, but with view-plane pixels of different size. These images will be the same physical size on your computer screen.

3.6.5 The Build Function

Listing 3.11 shows the `build` function that I'll use first, which sets parameters for the view plane and the sphere. Notice that although the data members of

```
void
World::build(void) {
    vp.set_hres(200);
    vp.set_vres(200);
    vp.set_pixel_size(1.0);
    vp.set_gamma(1.0);

    background_color = black;
    tracer_ptr = new SingleSphere(this);

    sphere.set_center(0.0);
    sphere.set_radius(85.0);
}
```

Listing 3.11. The `World::build` function.

the view plane are public, I've used set functions to specify the image resolution and pixel size. This allows a uniform notation for constructing objects; some "set" functions require more than a simple assignment statement to perform their tasks. A simple example is the set_gamma function, which also sets inv_gamma.

3.6.6 Rendering the Scene

The function world::render_scene is responsible for rendering the scene.[2] Its code appears in Listing 3.12. After storing the image resolution in local variables, it opens a window on the computer screen by calling the function open_window. The main work in render_scene is carried out in the for loops, where the color of each pixel is computed. In this example, the view plane is located at $z_w = 100$, which is hard-wired in. This is, of course, bad programming, but it's a temporary measure for this chapter. The scene is rendered row-by-row, starting at the bottom-left of the window. Although the render_scene function in the skeleton ray tracer looks the same as Listing 3.12, it writes the pixel colors to an off-screen array and buffers the output.

```
void
World::render_scene(void) const {
    RGBColor  pixel_color;
    Ray       ray;
    double    zw           = 100.0;                      // hard wired in
    double    x, y;

    open_window(vp.hres, vp.vres);
    ray.d = Vector3D(0, 0, -1);

    for (int r = 0; r < vp.vres; r++)                    // up
        for (int c = 0; c <= vp.hres; c++) {            // across
            x = vp.s * (c - 0.5 * (vp.hres - 1.0));
            y = vp.s * (r - 0.5 * (vp.vres - 1.0));
            ray.o = Point3D(x, y, zw);
            pixel_color = tracer_ptr->trace_ray(ray);
            display_pixel(r, c, pixel_color);
        }
}
```

Listing 3.12. The world::render_scene function.

---

2. From Chapter 9 onwards, cameras will be responsible for rendering the scenes.

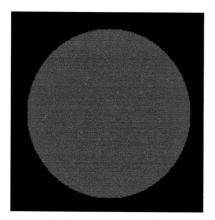

Figure 3.18. A red sphere at the origin.

After the ray's origin and direction have been computed, the function `trace_ray` is called. This is a key function in the ray tracer because it controls how rays are traced through the scene and returns the color for each pixel. But instead of being called directly, this function is called through a `Tracer` object called `tracer_ptr`. See Listing 3.7 and the following section. The last thing the loops do is display the pixel in the window using the `display_pixel` function. This converts the `RGBColor` to the display format used by the computer.

OK, that's enough theory, code, and discussion. Let's ray trace the sphere and look at the result in Figure 3.18. This is an impressive image when you consider how many things have to work together to produce it.

 ## 3.7 Tracers

Tracers allow us to implement different types of ray tracing with different versions of the function `trace_ray`, without altering the existing code. They thus provide a critical layer of abstraction between the `render_scene` function, which computes the origin and direction of each ray, and the code that determines what happens to the rays. The tracers are organized in an inheritance structure, as shown in Figure 3.19.

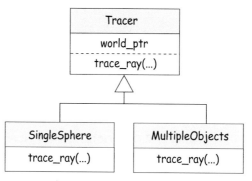

Figure 3.19. The `Tracer` inheritance chart for the two tracers used in this chapter.

```
class Tracer {
    public:

        Tracer(void);

        Tracer(World* w_ptr);

        virtual RGBColor
        trace_ray(const Ray& ray) const;

    protected:

        World* world_ptr;
};

Tracer::Tracer(void)
    : world_ptr(NULL) {}

Tracer::Tracer(World* w_ptr)
    : world_ptr(w_ptr) {}

RGBColor
Tracer::trace_ray(const Ray& ray) const {
    return (black);
}
```

Listing 3.13. The base class `Tracer`.

The code for the `Tracer` base class appears in Listing 3.13 in the simplified form we need for this chapter. This contains a pointer to the world
because tracers need access to the geometric objects and the background
color. The classes derived from `Tracer` have to redefine the function `trace_`
`ray`, which is not pure virtual in the base class because the version with
this signature (`const Ray&`) is only used by the tracers `SingleSphere` and
`MultipleObjects`.

Listing 3.14 shows how `trace_ray` is redefined in the derived class
`SingleSphere`. This ray traces a single red sphere whose center and radius
were set in the build function in Listing 3.11.

In later chapters I'll use tracers called `RayCast`, `Whitted`, `AreaLighting`,
and `PathTrace` to simulate a variety of optical effects. The type of tracer to use
for each scene is specified in the build function.

```
RGBColor
SingleSphere::trace_ray(const Ray& ray) const {
    ShadeRec  sr(*world_ptr);              // not used
    double    t;                           // not used

    if (world_ptr->sphere.hit(ray, t, sr))
        return (red);
    else
        return (black);
}
```

Listing 3.14. The `SingleSphere::trace_ray` function where the ray is tested for intersection against the single sphere stored in the world.

 ## 3.8 Color Display

The function `display_pixel` converts the color computed for each pixel to a color that the computer monitor can display, a process that involves three steps: *tone mapping, gamma correction,* and an *integer mapping.*

It will help to explain why we need tone mapping if we look at the integer mapping first, even though that's the last step. Each monitor can only display a finite number of colors, known as the *gamut* of the monitor, where, typically, there are 256 integer values for the red, green, and blue color components in the range [0, 255]. The real-valued (r, g, b) color components computed by the ray tracer therefore have to be mapped to [0, 255] (or some other integer range) before they can be displayed. However, there's a problem. The (r, g, b) color components can have any positive values, and we don't know before-hand how large they are going to be. In order to sensibly map these to [0, 255], they need to be in a fixed range: the RGB color cube $(r, g, b) \in [0, 1]^3$, so that (0, 0, 0) can be mapped to (0, 0, 0), and (1, 1, 1) can be mapped to (255, 255, 255). Colors outside the color cube can't be mapped to a displayable color and are known as *out-of-gamut colors*. Tone mapping is the process of mapping all color components into the range [0, 1], and it is a complex field. I'll discuss two simple tone-mapping techniques in Section 14.9, as these are best explained in the context of shading. They are implemented in the skeleton ray tracer.

Gamma correction is necessary because the brightness of monitors is generally a nonlinear function of the applied voltages. It can be modeled with a power law of the form

$$\text{brightness} = v^{\gamma},$$

where v is the voltage and γ is the *gamma value* of the monitor. Most PCs have $\gamma = 2.2$, and Macs have $\gamma = 1.8$. Because of these gamma values, the color (255, 255, 255), will appear more than twice as bright as (125, 125, 125), and by a significant amount. The process of gamma correction adjusts the (r, g, b) colors, after tone mapping, by raising them to the inverse power of γ:

$$(r, g, b) \ (r^{1/\gamma}, g^{1/\gamma}, b^{1/\gamma}),$$

which cancels the γ power to produce a linear brightness function. Gamma correction is also implemented in the skeleton ray tracer, but it's only applied when $\gamma \neq 1.0$. If the gamma value and its inverse are stored in the view plane, it's simple to apply gamma correction with the following code, where the RGBColor member function powc raises the (r, g, b) components to the specified power:

```
if (vp.gamma != 1.0)
        color = color.powc(vp.inv_gamma);
```

This code is in the function world::display_pixel. Because γ varies between computer platforms and monitors, I've rendered all of the ray-traced images in this book with $\gamma = 1.0$.

 ## 3.9 Ray Tracing Multiple Objects

If you got the skeleton program working as described in the previous section, that's good work on your part, but of course, a ray tracer that can only render a single sphere isn't much use. We now need to add the ability to ray trace an arbitrary number of geometric objects of different types, and to do this we'll have to add some code to the world class. Specifically, we need a data structure to store the geometric objects, a function to add an object to the scene, and a function to intersect a ray with all of the objects. The revised world declaration appears in Listing 3.15, with the new code in blue. Note that we store the objects in an array of geometric object pointers, as discussed in Chapter 1. The function add_object adds a new object to the array.

The function hit_bare_bones_objects in Listing 3.16 intersects the ray with all of the objects in the scene and returns a ShadeRec object. Because the code doesn't use specific geometric object types, it will work for any type of object that belongs to the geometric objects inheritance hierarchy and has the correct public interface for the hit function. With multiple objects, we need a different color for each object, as stored in the GeometricObject class in

```
#include <vector>

#include "ViewPlane.h"
#include "RGBColor.h"
#include "Tracer.h"
#include "GeometricObject.h"
#include "Ray.h"

class World {
    public:

        ViewPlane                      vp;
        RGBColor                       background_color;
        Tracer*                        tracer_ptr;
        vector<GeometricObject*>       objects;

        ...
        void

        build(void);

        void
        add_object(GeometricObject* object_ptr);

        ShadeRec
        hit_bare_bones_objects(const Ray& ray) const;

        void

        render_scene(void) const;
};

inline void
World::add_object(GeometricObject* object_ptr) {
    objects.push_back(object_ptr);
}
```

Listing 3.15. World class for ray tracing an arbitrary number of objects.

Listing 3.2. The `hit_bare_bones_objects` function shows how the color of the nearest object hit by the ray is stored in the ShadeRec object.

This function is called from the `trace_ray` function defined in the tracer MultipleObjects. The code in Listing 3.17 illustrates how the nearest object's color is returned (to the `render_scene` function) when the ray hits an object.

```
ShadeRec
World::hit_bare_bones_objects(const Ray& ray) const {
     ShadeRec  sr(*this);
     double    t;
     double    tmin           = kHugeValue;
     int       num_objects    = objects.size();

     for (int j = 0; j < num_objects; j++)
          if (objects[j]->hit(ray, t, sr) && (t < tmin)) {
               sr.hit_an_object    = true;
               tmin                = t;
               sr.color            = objects[j]->get_color();
          }

     return (sr)
}
```

Listing 3.16. The `World::hit_bare_bones_objects` function.

```
RGBColor
MultipleObjects::trace_ray(const Ray& ray) const {
     ShadeRec sr(world_ptr->hit_bare_bones_objects(ray));

     if (sr.hit_an_object)
          return (sr.color);
     else
          return (world_ptr->background_color);
}
```

Listing 3.17. The function `MultipleObjects::trace_Ray`.

You should study these two functions carefully to make sure you understand how they work together.

A simple example of multiple objects consists of two intersecting spheres and a plane. The resulting image is in Figure 3.20(a), where the bottom sphere (red) doesn't look much like a sphere because the plane cuts through it (see Figure 3.20(b)). Shading and shadows would make Figure 3.20(a) a lot more meaningful.

The `build` function for this scene in Listing 3.18 illustrates how to set object parameters with access functions and constructors. You can mix and match these techniques as you please. In general, an object can have as many

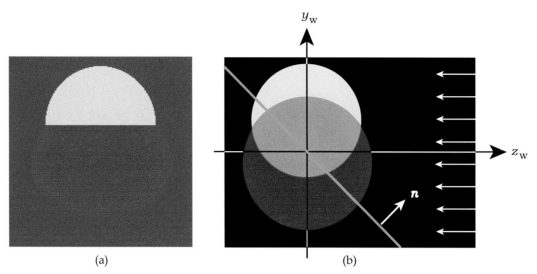

(a)   (b)

Figure 3.20. (a) Ray-traced image of two spheres and a plane; (b) side view of the spheres and plane, looking towards the origin, along the negative x_w axis, with some rays.

constructors, with different signatures, as you need. I haven't set the pixel size in Listing 3.18 because this scene uses its default value of 1.0, initialized in the ViewPlane default constructor. The same applies to the value of gamma. As most scenes use $s = 1.0$, and all scenes use $\gamma = 1.0$, there's not much point in setting these in each build function.

 ## Notes and Discussion

Why do we render images from the bottom left instead of from the top left? The reason is symmetry. Rendering from the bottom allows the World:: render_scene code in Listing 3.12 to be written symmetrically in x and y. This will also apply to the antialiasing and filtering code in Chapter 4, and the render_scene functions for the cameras in Chapters 9–11, which will include the use of stored sample points.

Why is a world pointer stored in the tracers, but a world reference stored in the ShadeRec objects? Why not store a pointer or a reference in both? The reason is notational convenience. We have to specify a tracer in every build function, and if we used a reference, we would have to de-reference the pointer this. Using the example from Listing 3.11, the code would be tracer_ptr = new SingleSphere(*this); instead of tracer_ptr = new SingleSphere(this);,

```
void
World::build(void) {
    vp.set_hres(200);
    vp.set_vres(200);

    background_color = black;
    tracer_ptr = new MultipleObjects(this);

    // use access functions to set sphere center and radius

    Sphere* sphere_ptr = new Sphere;
    sphere_ptr->set_center(0, -25, 0);
    sphere_ptr->set_radius(80);
    sphere_ptr->set_color(1, 0, 0);              // red
    add_object(sphere_ptr);

    // use constructor to set sphere center and radius

    sphere_ptr = new Sphere(Point3D(0, 30, 0), 60);
    sphere_ptr->set_color(1, 1, 0);              // yellow
    add_object(sphere_ptr);

    Plane* plane_ptr = new Plane(Point3D(0, 0, 0), Normal(0, 1, 1));
    plane_ptr->set_color(0.0, 0.3, 0.0);         // dark green
    add_object(plane_ptr);
}
```

Listing 3.18. The build function for two spheres and a plane.

a small point perhaps, but this could be a lifetime of having an extra thing to remember to do in every build function.

The ShadeRec object stores a reference to simplify the shading code syntax. The world is necessary for accessing the lights, and with a reference, the code will be sr.w.lights ..., compared with sr.w->lights ..., using a pointer. Again, this may seem a small point, but this syntax will be used a large number of times in the shading chapters, starting with Chapter 14. Every time you implement a new shader, you will have to use this. A reference is also marginally faster than a pointer because we save an indirection.

Another way to organize the build functions is to put all of their #includes in a separate file called, say, **BuildFunctions.cpp**, and #include this in the **World.cpp** file.

All class data members have default values to which they are initialized in the class default constructors. As a general rule, build functions don't have to set default values, but sometimes they will, to emphasize the value or to emphasize that something needs to be there. An example is setting the background color to black, although that's the default. Pointer data members are always initialized to the zero pointer NULL (see Exercise 3.9).

Alvy Ray Smith (1995) has argued forcefully that a pixel is not a little square. In spite of this, the model of a pixel as a square of dimension $s \times s$ is the right one for our purposes. The reason is clarity of exposition. In this chapter, this model provides the best framework for explaining the field of view and computing where the rays start from; in the sampling chapters, it provides the best framework for explaining how we distribute multiple rays (that is, sample points) over a pixel; in perspective viewing, it again provides the best way for explaining the field of view and the ray directions.

 ## Further Reading

A number of books discuss the elementary aspects of ray tracing that this chapter covers, but in their own ways. Shirley and Morley (2003) is the closest in approach to this chapter, because this also starts with a simple ray tracer that's similar to the bare-bones ray tracer. These authors also discuss properties of the IEEE floating-point arithmetic in a lot more detail than I have here. Glassner (1989) covers elementary ray tracing concepts, and ray-object intersections. Shirley et al. (2005) and Hill and Kelley (2006) contain a chapter on ray tracing.

 ## Questions

3.1   Why is it unlikely that a ray will hit a curved implicit surface tangentially?

3.2   Why don't we need to test for $d = 0$ in the Sphere::hit function (Listing 3.6)?

3.3   What is the maximum radius of a sphere centered at the origin that will just fit into Figure 3.18?

3.4   The build functions in Listings 3.11 and 3.18 illustrate how the world pointer is set in the tracer object by calling a tracer constructor with the pointer this as the argument. The world is incomplete at this stage because the geometric objects haven't been constructed or added to it, but this doesn't matter. Do you know why?

3.5 Why does the intersection of the two spheres in Figure 3.20(a) appear as a straight line?

3.6 Figure 3.21 is the same as Figure 3.20(a) but rendered at 300 × 300 pixels instead of 200 × 200. Can you explain what has happened at the bottom of the image where you can just see the bottom of the red sphere?

 **Exercises**

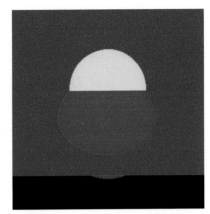

Figure 3.21. Two spheres and a plane.

3.1 The first thing to do is to get the skeleton program running on your computer, assuming you want to use it. You can, of course, write everything yourself from scratch. The program should reproduce Figures 3.18 and 3.20(a) by using the appropriate build functions.

3.2 Change the z_w-coordinate of the view plane from $z_w = 100.0$ in Listing 3.11 to a value that makes the view plane cut through the sphere in Figure 3.18. Can you explain the results?

3.3 Change the center, radius, and color of the sphere.

3.4 Experiment with different view-plane pixel sizes to zoom into and out of the sphere. Also experiment with different pixel resolutions for the image.

3.5 By comparing Figure 3.2(a) with Figure 3.14(a), and Figure 3.2(b) with Figure 3.16, make sure you understand how the images in Figure 3.2 were formed.

3.6 Study the code in the skeleton ray tracer and make sure you understand how the ray-tracing part of the program works. Because you will make extensions to the program throughout this book, it's essential that you understand this.

3.7 Render Figure 3.20(a) and experiment with different numbers of spheres and planes.

3.8 Render the image on the first page of this chapter, which consists of 35 spheres.

3.9 Here's a check that you can make in the `main` function in Listing 3.9. After the scene has been constructed, but before it's rendered, check that the world's `tracer_ptr` data member is not NULL. If it is NULL, bail out of the program with an appropriate error message. This will prevent your ray tracer from crashing if you forget to set the tracer in a build function.

The following are some pencil-and-paper exercises:

3.10 Derive Equation (3.4).

3.11 Derive Equation (3.5) from Equation (2.8).

3.12 Derive Equations (3.8) and (3.9) from Equation (3.7).

3.13 Derive Equation (3.10) for the ray origins. *Hint*: Let $x_w = a\, h_{res} + b$ and $y_w = c\, v_{res} + d$, where a, b, c, and d are unknown constants that can be determined by the values of x_w and y_w at the corner pixels in Figure 3.13.

4 Antialiasing

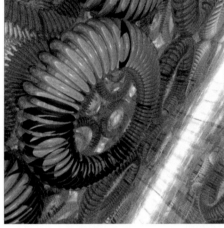

Image courtesy of Peter Brownlow

 ## Objectives

By the end of this chapter you should:

- understand what aliasing is and what causes it in ray tracing;
- understand why you can't completely eliminate aliasing in all ray-traced images;
- have implemented antialiasing in the bare-bones ray tracer with uniform, random, and jittered sampling patterns.

Computers are discrete devices that display a finite number of pixels, work with a finite number of colors, and in the case of ray tracing, sample scenes at a finite number of discrete points. As such, most ray-traced images are subject to *aliasing*, where an alias means a *substitute*. Here, the images are substitutes for the real scenes we are trying to render. The most obvious effects of aliasing are *jaggies*, which are the staircase appearance of sharp edges. Other aliasing effects include the incorrect rendering of small details, particularly in textures, moiré patterns, and color banding if insufficient colors are used. Small objects can also be missed.

I'll discuss here some simple techniques for reducing the amount of aliasing in ray-traced images. The general process is known as *antialiasing*. In most cases, we can't eliminate the aliasing completely, but we can reduce it to acceptable levels, or replace it with noise.

The antialiasing techniques I'll discuss here involve sampling pixels with multiple rays. You can easily implement antialiasing by hard-wiring simple sampling patterns into the `world::render_scene` function. Although this is an ad hoc approach, its great advantage is that each pattern only requires a few lines of code and is therefore quickly implemented.

In Chapter 5, I'll discuss more sophisticated sampling techniques in a broader context.

4.1 Aliasing Effects

Many of the aliasing effects visible in ray-traced images are caused by the fact that ray tracing is a *point-sampling* process, where we sample scenes with infinitesimally thin rays. Although each sample point is infinitely small, it represents a finite area of a surface, which is projected onto a pixel.

Because the bare-bones ray tracer shoots a single ray through the center of each pixel, the rays are on a regular grid. To see how this produces aliasing, look at Figure 4.1. Figure 4.1 (a) shows a sharp edge, and Figure 4.1 (b) shows the results of ray tracing this through the center of each pixel at a resolution of 7 × 5 pixels. This results in staircase jaggies where the color of each pixel is either yellow or gray, depending on whether its ray hits a yellow area or a gray area. The colors should, however, be a *weighted average* of yellow and gray that represents the relative areas of these colors in each pixel. The lower the image resolution, the worse the aliasing effects are, as Figure 3.2 demonstrates.

Scenes with smoothly varying intensities are also subject to aliasing when their rendered resolutions are too low to reproduce the smallest details. Figure 4.2(a) shows the function

$$f(x,y) = \frac{1}{2}(1 + \sin(x^2 y^2)),   \tag{4.1}$$

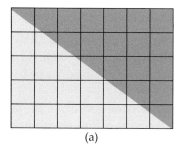 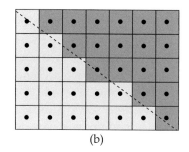

(a)   (b)

Figure 4.1. (a) Sharp edge; (b) ray traced at 7 × 5 pixels with rays through the black dots.

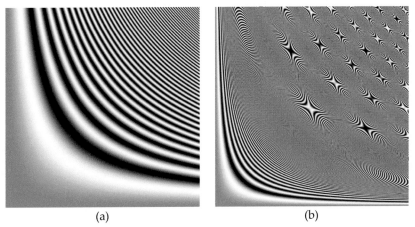

(a)   (b)

Figure 4.2. The sinusoid function (4.1) rendered at 512×512 pixels over two regions of the (x, y) plane.

rendered in the range $(x, y) \in [0, 3.79]^2$ at 512×512 pixels. With one ray per pixel, there's little visible aliasing because the bands are all more than two pixels wide. Here, the narrowest bands at the top right are about 5 pixels wide. Figure 4.2(b) shows the same function rendered over the larger area $(x, y) \in [0, 10.83]^2$. In this image, most of the bands have been replaced by moiré patterns, although their widths have only decreased by a factor of 2.85. See the Further Reading section for information on moiré patterns.

 ## 4.2 Remedies

In ray tracing, the only remedy for the aliasing problem is to increase the sampling density. As this always involves shooting more rays, the result is longer rendering times. I discuss here several simple antialiasing techniques and discuss descriptively why some are better than others. There are a lot of theoretical and mathematical underpinnings for these techniques, but we needn't be concerned with them here. If you are interested, the references discussed in the Further Reading section discuss them in detail.

4.2.1 Increase the Image Resolution

The simplest antialiasing technique is to render the scene at a higher pixel resolution, because that requires no additional programming. Of course, you will need to decrease the pixel size, according to the discussion in Section 3.6.4.

However, this technique has the following problem: it doesn't eliminate the aliasing. For example, the pixels in Figure 4.1 would still be yellow or gray, no matter how many there are, and the jaggies would still be there. Fortunately, due to the limited angular resolving power of our eyes, there are limits to how high the resolution has to be before we can't *see* any aliasing. There are, however many variables involved, including whether we look at the image on a computer screen or as a printed image, the lighting conditions, viewing distance, etc.

I'll therefore concentrate on techniques that reduce aliasing without increasing the pixel resolution. These techniques all involve shooting more than one ray per pixel.

4.2.2 Regular Sampling

With regular sampling, we shoot rays on a regular grid inside each pixel, as shown in Figure 4.3(a), where the outer square is a single pixel boundary. This allows us to get a more accurate estimate of the color for the pixel, and the more rays we shoot, the more accurate the estimate becomes. All we have to do is shoot the extra rays and average the color. Figure 4.3(b) shows the top-left pixel from Figure 4.1(b), sampled with 25 rays. Here, 16 samples are yellow, and 9 are gray, resulting in a rendered color of (16/25) × (1, 1, 0) + (9/25) × (0.5, 0.5. 0.5) = (0.82, 0.82, 0.18), as in Figure 4.3(c). This is still not exact, but it's much better than rendering it yellow or gray.

Regular sampling is simple to program, as Listing 4.1 shows. This is a modified version of Listing 3.12, where the new code is in blue. Note that we now store the number of samples per pixel in the view plane. The regular sampling patterns I'll use have the same number of rows and columns of samples,

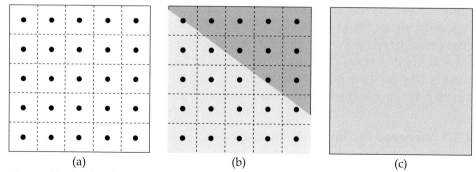

(a)   (b)   (c)

Figure 4.3. (a) Regular sampling on a 5 × 5 grid in a single pixel; (b) regular sampling of the top-left pixel in Figure 4.1; (c) rendered color of top-left pixel.

```
void
World::render_scene(void) const {
    RGBColor pixel_color;
    Ray ray;
    float zw = 100.0;
    int n = (int)sqrt((float)vp.num_samples);
    Point2D pp;                    // sample point on a pixel

    open_window(vp.hres, vp.vres);
    ray.d = Vector3D(0, 0, -1);

    for (int r = 0; r < vp.vres; r++)                   // up
        for (int c = 0; c <= vp.hres; c++) {            // across
            pixel_color = black;

            for (int p = 0; p < n; p++)                 // up pixel
                for (int q = 0; q < n; q++) {           // across pixel
                    pp.x = vp.s * (c - 0.5 * vp.hres + (q + 0.5) / n);
                    pp.y = vp.s * (r - 0.5 * vp.vres + (p + 0.5) / n);
                    ray.o = Point3D(pp.x, pp.y, zw);
                    pixel_color += tracer_ptr->trace_ray(ray);
            }

            pixel_color /= vp.num_samples;   // average the colors
            display_pixel(r, c, pixel_color);
        }
}
```

Listing 4.1. World::render_scene function that samples each pixel on a regular grid.

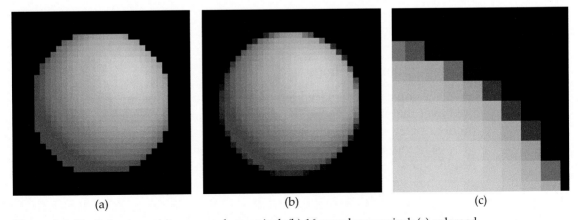

(a)   (b)   (c)

Figure 4.4. Shaded sphere: (a) one sample per pixel; (b) 16 samples per pixel; (c) enlarged
view of top-right section of (b).

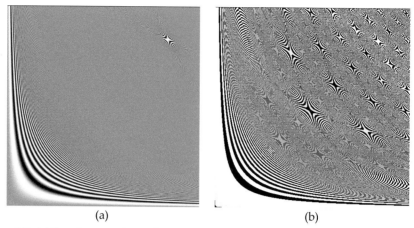

(a)   (b)

Figure 4.5. (a) Regular sampling of Figure 4.2(b) does not eliminate the moiré patterns; (b) contrast-enhanced version of (a).

and therefore the number of samples per pixel has to be a perfect square; that is, num_samples = $n \times n$ for some integer n.

Figure 4.4 demonstrates how regular sampling works in a low-resolution image of a shaded sphere.

A problem with regular sampling is that aliasing is still present and often shows up as regular artifacts such as the moiré patterns in Figure 4.2(b). Although these may look nice, they are not an accurate representation of the function. Figure 4.5(a) is the same as Figure 4.2(b), but rendered with uniform sampling using 25 samples per pixel. It looks like most of the moiré patterns are gone, but in fact, most of the image is still covered with them, as the contrast-enhanced version in Figure 4.5(b) demonstrates.

4.2.3 Random Sampling

Most aliasing can be replaced by *noise* if we use rays that are *randomly* distributed over the pixel surfaces. Now, what is noise in this context? Noise is just random pixel colors. To illustrate, let's render Figure 4.5(a) with 16 samples per pixel randomly distributed over the pixel surface. Figure 4.6(a) shows the results where most of the aliasing artifacts have been replaced by noise. Figure 4.6(b) shows a (contrast-enhanced) 16×16 pixel section of the noise.

For most images, noise is better than aliasing because we more readily notice regular aliasing artifacts than noise, and we are able to tolerate surprisingly large amounts of noise in images (Glassner, 1995). Images with noise

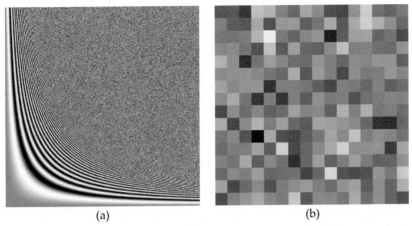

(a)   (b)

Figure 4.6. (a) Random sampling replaces aliasing artifacts with noise; (b) random pixel values in an enlarged section of (a).

can therefore look better than aliased images, even though the noise may not represent the underlying scene any more accurately than the aliasing. On the other hand, noisy images can also look worse, because noise can look quite unpleasant at low image resolutions. See Figure 5.22 for an example. To generate random samples, we simply replace the inner loops in Listing 4.1 with the code in Listing 4.2. In this case, the number of samples doesn't have to be a perfect square.

```
for (int p = 0; p < vp.num_samples; p++) {
        pp.x = vp.s * (c - 0.5 * vp.hres + rand_float());
        pp.y = vp.s * (r - 0.5 * vp.vres + rand_float());
        ray.o = Point3D(pp.x, pp.y, zw);
        pixel_color += tracer_ptr->trace_ray(ray);
}
```

Listing 4.2. Code for random sampling.

4.2.4 Jittered Sampling

Random sampling is not the best way to distribute rays over the pixel because the samples can clump together and leave gaps (see Figure 4.7(a)). A better strategy is to force a more even distribution of the samples over the pixel, while still maintaining the randomness. We can achieve this by dividing the pixel into a uniform grid of $n \times n$ cells and generating one random point in

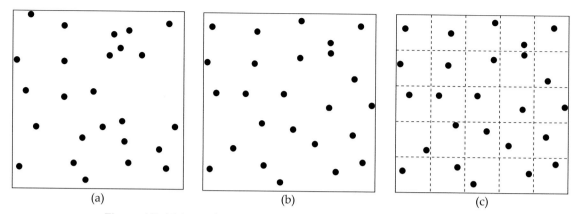

Figure 4.7. (a) 25 random samples in a pixel; (b) 25 jittered samples; (c) same as (b) but with sub-grid lines shown.

each cell. If you look at Figure 4.7(b), the points are still random, but as Figure 4.7(c) shows, there is one point in each of the 25 cells. This technique is called *jittered* sampling. The sample points can still clump and leave gaps, but the problem is not as severe as in random sampling.

To program jittered sampling, all you have to do is replace the expressions q + 0.5 and p + 0.5 in Listing 4.1 with q + rand_float() and p + rand_float(), respectively.

Once you have implemented a sampling technique, it's simple to specify the degree of antialiasing in the build function. Because we store the number of samples per pixel in the view plane, you can specify this with code such as vp->set_num_samples(25).

 ## 4.3 Antialiasing Fine Detail

Textures are often difficult to antialias because they can contain fine detail. In fact, some images contain texture detail that is infinitely small. Figure 4.8 is an example. This shows a perspective view of a plane with a checker texture. In Figure 4.8(a), the scene is ray traced with one ray per pixel, and you can see how the checkers break up as they approach the horizon. This happens because the area of the plane covered by each pixel increases without limit as the horizon is approached. Any pixels that the horizon passes through cover an infinite area. Figure 4.8(b) is rendered with 64 jittered samples per pixel, which improves the image, but the checkers still break up near the horizon. No

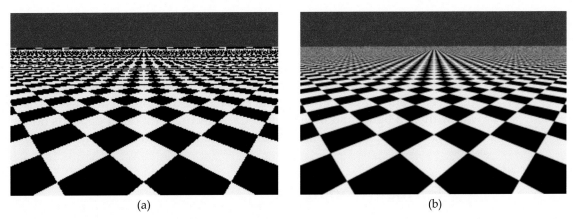

Figure 4.8. Checkerboard plane rendered at 300×200 pixels with one sample per pixel (a) and 64 jittered samples per pixel (b).

antialiasing technique can prevent this from happening, because the projected sizes of the checkers become infinitely small at the horizon.

4.4 Filtering

Many computer graphics textbooks discuss antialiasing in the context of *filtering*. In ray tracing, filtering involves computing a pixel color by using rays that are outside the pixel boundary, as well as inside. See Figure 4.9, where the rays are distributed over an area of four pixels. In this figure, the dark-gray square in the center is the pixel being anti-aliased, and the filter area is the pixel area plus the surrounding light-gray area.

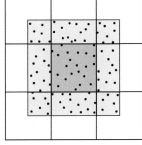

We can use various types of filters that differ in the way the ray colors are weighted in the final pixel color. If all rays are weighted equally, as in Listings 4.1 and 4.2, we have a *box filter*, which is essentially what we use in Section 4.2, but for a single pixel. However, box filters that extend over more than one pixel are crude and will usually just blur your images. We can get better results by decreasing the weights as the rays move away from the center of the pixel, with the weights going to zero at the boundary of the filter. If the decrease is linear, we have a *tent filter*; if it decreases as a cubic polynomial, we have a *cubic filter*; if it decreases exponentially, we have a *Gaussian filter*.

Figure 4.9. A filter of width two pixels is used to compute the color of the center pixel by distributing rays over the light-gray area.

For the sampling techniques presented in this chapter and the following chapter, filtering doesn't seem to produce significantly better results for antialiasing than the single-pixel sampling techniques described in Section 4.2. Blinn (1989a and 1989b) are classic articles on filtering and antialiasing. These are reprinted in Blinn (1998). For other sampling techniques, filtering can produce better antialiasing. Filtering can also reduce the noise in images for shading with area lights and other Monte Carlo techniques, but it depends on the type of filter and the sampling technique. See Pharr and Humphreys (2004).

 Further Reading

Glassner (1995) discusses in detail the mathematical theory of antialiasing in terms of sampling and reconstruction theory. Foley et al. (1995) and Watt (2000) also discuss the mathematical theory of antialiasing.

Shirley (2002), Shirley and Morley (2003), and Pharr and Humphreys (2004) discuss antialiasing in ray tracing. Cook et al. (1984) introduced random sampling as one of the applications of distribution ray tracing.

Moiré patterns are interference patterns that can occur in many situations. An example is where two regular patterns are superimposed with one rotated with respect to the other, or with a different size. There is a large literature on these with a good place to start being the Wikipedia article at http://en.wikipedia.org/wiki/Moire_effect. Figure 16.15 shows moiré patterns that result from regularly spaced circular holes.

If you are interested in filtering, Shirley and Morley (2003) and Pharr and Humphreys (2004) discuss a number of filtering techniques with C++ code.

 Questions

4.1   How do you "ray trace" a function of x and y, such as the function (4.1)?

 Exercises

4.1   Ray trace the function (4.1) and experiment with different image resolutions, areas of the function (range of x and y), and sampling techniques. Compare the results.

4.2   Ray trace a sphere similar to that in Figure 4.4. You don't have to do any shading; just return a constant color as in Chapter 3. Use different sampling techniques and compare the pixels around the edge of the sphere. To do this, you will need to use third-party software to enlarge the images as in Figure 4.4(c).

4.3   Ray trace the sphere with one random ray per pixel. The sampling code in Listing 4.2 will do this when `num_samples` = 1. What do you think of the results?

5 Sampling Techniques

Image courtesy of Duy Tran

 Objectives

By the end of this chapter you should:

- understand why sampling is important in ray tracing;
- understand how several common sampling techniques are implemented;
- know the characteristics of good sampling techniques;
- have at your disposal a flexible sampling architecture.

In the previous chapter, I hard-wired a few simple sampling patterns into the world::render_scene function to perform antialiasing. There is, however, a lot more to sampling than antialiasing, because all of ray tracing is essentially an exercise in sampling and reconstruction. It's not only pixels that have to be sampled. If you want to render scenes with depth of field, you have to use a camera with a finite-area lens and sample the lens. If you want to render scenes with area lights and soft shadows, you have to sample the light surfaces. If you want to implement global illumination, or render glossy reflection and transmission, you have to sample BRDFs and BTDFs. In other words, if you want to get away from the sharp-edged, clinically clean, traditional ray-traced images, you will have to do a lot more sampling than what's required for antialiasing.

Because we need to compare a number of different sampling methods, and be able to mix and match different techniques in the same scene, we require a sampling architecture that allows application code to use sample points without having to know how they were generated. I discuss such an architecture here and also discuss the *n*-rooks, multi-jittered, and Hammersley sampling patterns. The sampling architecture is as simple as I'll make it, consistent with it providing samples that result in artifact-free images for all of the applications in the following chapters. Some of the discussion of random and jittered sampling overlaps that from the previous chapter, but I've included it here for comparison with the other sampling techniques.

5.1 A Sampling Architecture

Figure 5.1 shows the inheritance chart for the sampler classes. The base class `Sampler` has a number of data members and a member function `sample_unit_square` that returns sample points in a unit square. The only difference between the derived classes is the way they generate these sample points, by defining the function `generate_samples`. At this stage, the `Sampler` class is not complete, because it will also need to return samples on a unit disk and a hemisphere. I'll discuss these in the following two chapters. Because sampling is a fundamental tool for ray tracing, I've included the code for the `Sampler` classes on the book's website.

Listing 5.1 shows a partial declaration of the base class `Sampler`, whose member function `sample_unit_square` is called from objects that need to sup-

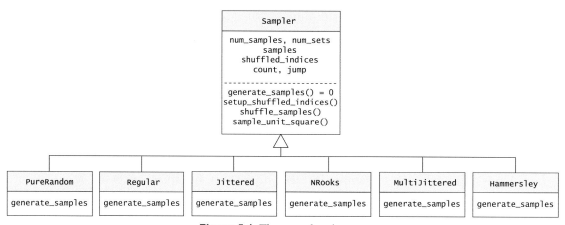

Figure 5.1. The sampler classes.

```
class Sampler {
    public:

        // constructors, access functions, etc.

        virtual void      // generate sample patterns in a unit square
        generate_samples(void) = 0;

        void              // set up the randomly shuffled indices
        setup_shuffled_indices(void);

        void              // randomly shuffle the samples in each pattern
        shuffle_samples(void);

        Point2D           // get next sample on unit square
        sample_unit_square(void);

    protected:

        int num_samples;  // the number of sample points in a pattern
        int num_sets;     // the number of sample sets (patterns) stored
        vector<Point2D> samples  // sample points on a unit square
        vector<int> shuffled_indices;  // shuffled samples array indices
        unsigned long count;     // the current number of sample points used
        int jump;                // random index jump
};
```

Listing 5.1. The Sampler class.

ply sample points on squares. For example, the view plane will do this for every scene. You will need to store a pointer to one of the derived sampler class objects in each such object.

A feature of the derived sampler classes is that they compute and store all of the required sample points while the scene is constructed. Not only is this more efficient than computing them during the ray tracing, but for certain sampling techniques, it's essential. Although the samples for PureRandom, Regular, and Jittered sampling can be computed as we need them, that's not possible for NRooks and MultiJittered sampling.[1] I'll discuss the code for these methods later in this chapter, where the reasons should become clear.

There's also another reason to store the sample points—we need more than one set of them. For most sampling applications, it's important to use

---

1. I can't compile a class called Random on my system because it's probably used in the operating system. You may be able to do so.

```
class Jittered: public Sampler {
    ...
    private:

        virtual void

        generate_samples(void);
};

void
Jittered::generate_samples(void) {
    int n = (int) sqrt(num_samples);

    for (int p = 0; p < num_sets; p++)
        for (int j = 0; j < n; j++)
            for (int k = 0; k < n; k++) {
                Point2D sp((k + rand_float()) / n, (j + rand_float()) / n);
                samples.push_back(sp);
            }
}
```

Listing 5.2. Jittered class code.

different sets with adjacent pixels. If we don't do this, the results can be aliasing artifacts that are far worse than the jaggies. See Figure 5.5(a) for an example.

It's easiest to explain how the sampler classes work with an example. To do this, I'll use the Jittered class, whose relevant code is in Listing 5.2. Although the function generate_samples generates the samples in a unit square, it's simplest to store them in a 1D array and use indexing to access them. All of the derived classes are simple because they only have to define this single function, which they call from their constructors.

The view plane provides the samples for antialiasing and therefore needs to store a pointer to a sampler object, the number of samples, and functions to set these that can be called from the build functions. I've implemented two access functions for this: set_sampler and set_samples, both of which set the sampler pointer and the number of samples. The set_sampler function in Listing 5.3 takes a sampler pointer as an argument. It allows us to use any type of sampler that we want to for antialiasing. A build function fragment that uses jittered sampling is in Listing 5.4.

I use the function set_samples much more frequently than set_sampler, because it specifies multi-jittered sampling (Section 5.3.4) by default, and when the number of samples is one, it specifies regular sampling. This puts a single

```
void
ViewPlane::set_sampler(Sampler* sp) {
     if (sampler_ptr) {
          delete sampler_ptr;
          sampler_ptr = NULL;
     }

     num_samples = sp->get_num_samples();
     sampler_ptr = sp;
}
```

Listing 5.3. The function Viewplane::set_sampler.

```
void
World::build(void) {

     int num_samples = 25;

     vp.set_hres(400);
     vp.set_vres(400);
     vp.set_sampler(new Jittered(num_samples));
     ...
}
```

Listing 5.4. Build function fragment.

```
void
ViewPlane::set_samples(const int n) {
     num_samples = n;

     if (sampler_ptr) {
          delete sampler_ptr;
          sampler_ptr = NULL;
     }

     if (num_samples > 1)
          sampler_ptr = new MultiJittered(num_samples);
     else
          sampler_ptr = new Regular(1);
}
```

Listing 5.5. The function ViewPlane::setSamples.

sample point in the center of each pixel, according to Listing 4.1, to avoid ugly images like Figure 5.22(a). The code appears in Listing 5.5.

In Chapter 4, the samples were generated directly in the `world::render_scene` function, and the code was specific for each sampling technique (see Listings 4.1 and 4.2). The new version of this function, which applies to all sampling techniques, is in Listing 5.6. Here, the code that refers to the sample points is in blue.

The function `Sampler::sample_unit_square` returns the *next* sample point that's stored in the sampler object. Listing 5.7 shows a preliminary version of this function. Simple, isn't it? As it turns out, it's a bit too simple, but more on that later. The `Sampler` data member `count` is initialized to zero when a `Sampler` object is constructed. Because `count` is incremented by one each time `sample_unit_square` is called, its value at the end of each function call is the total number of samples returned at the time. The % operator ensures that the array index is always in the correct range [0, `num_samples` * `num_sets` - 1].

```
void
World::render_scene(void) const {
    RGBColor pixel_color;
    Ray ray;
    float zw = 100.0;
    Point2D sp;              // sample point in [0, 1] x [0, 1]
    Point2D pp;              // sample point on a pixel

    open_window(vp.hres, vp.vres);
    ray.d = Vector3D(0, 0, -1);

    for (int r = 0; r < vp.vres; r++)                    // up
        for (int c = 0; c <= vp.hres; c++) {             // across
            pixel_color = black;

            for (int j = 0; j < vp.num_samples; j++) {
                sp = vp.sampler_ptr->sample_unit_square();
                pp.x = vp.s * (c - 0.5 * vp.hres + sp.x);
                pp.y = vp.s * (r - 0.5 * vp.vres + sp.y);
                ray.o = Point3D(pp.x, pp.y, zw);
                pixel_color += tracer_ptr->trace_ray(ray);
            }

            pixel_color /= vp.num_samples;   // average the colors
            display_pixel(r, c, pixel_color);
        }
}
```

Listing 5.6. The `world::render_scene` function that uses a sampler object.

```
Point2D
Sampler::sample_unit_square(void) {

    return (samples[count++ % (num_samples * num_sets)]);
}
```

Listing 5.7. The function `Sampler::sample_unit_square`.

There are no parameters because this function is called from many places in the ray tracer, and its interface has to be as simple as possible.

There is, however, a subtle but critical interaction between `sample_unit_square` and the rest of the ray tracer. To illustrate this, Figure 5.2 shows a pixel that's sampled with four jittered samples, and where each ray hits a surface that's shaded with an area light. For each ray, we send a single shadow ray to a sample point on the light surface. We therefore use four sample points per pixel on the light, which could be generated by a different sampling technique to those on the pixel. When the ray tracer has finished sampling a pixel, the value of `count` in Listing 5.7 will be pointing to the first sample of the next pixel in *both* the view plane and the light `samples` arrays. For example, the two values of `count` will be 4 after the first pixel has been rendered (see Figure 5.3).

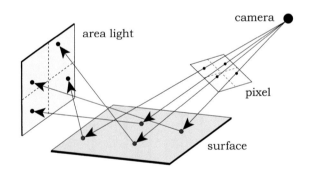

Figure 5.2. Shading a surface with an area light and four samples per pixel.

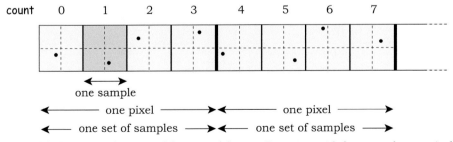

Figure 5.3. Schematic diagram of the start of the `samples` array with four samples per pixel.

pixel samples

light samples

Figure 5.4. Four jittered pixel samples (left) and nine jittered light samples, where only the four samples in the dark squares have been used (right).

For most sampling techniques, it's important to keep the two indices in step, because if they get out of step, we can end up with bad sampling. Figure 5.4 illustrates how we could artificially set up a misalignment. The left part shows four jittered pixel samples, and the right shows what could happen if we used 16 jittered samples per pixel for the light. The resulting subset of samples used (the dark squares) does not represent a complete jittered sample pattern and in this case are all in the bottom row. For each successive pixel, a new row is used, with a complete set used for every four pixels.

This can produce aliasing artifacts, as Figure 5.5 demonstrates. Figure 5.5(a) shows a glossy reflector plane rendered with four jittered samples per pixel for both antialiasing and sampling the surface BRDF.[2] The result is just a noisy image. Figure 5.5(b) still uses four samples per pixel for antialiasing but uses 25 samples per pixel to sample the surface. The resulting aliasing effects are striking. The moral here is that your build functions should specify a single variable `num_samples` that specifies the *same* number of samples for everything. Even so, the sampling can still get out of step (see Question 5.3). Fortunately, index shuffling, described in Section 5.4, will allow us to avoid serious aliasing problems when this happens.

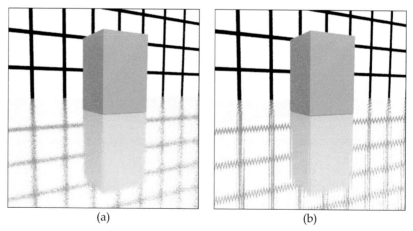

(a)   (b)

Figure 5.5. (a) Glossy reflector surface rendered with four jittered samples per pixel for everything; (b) the result of using 25 jittered samples per pixel to sample the glossy reflector surface.

---

2. I'll explain how to model glossy reflection in Chapter 25.

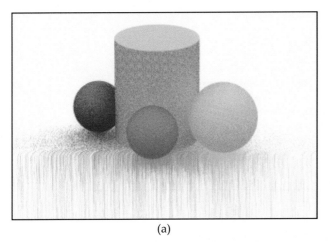

(a) (b)

Figure 5.6. Global illumination images that exhibit bad aliasing caused by using the same samples in vertical columns (a) and in a regular horizontal displacement (b).

There's another problem with the function `sample_unit_square`. Aliasing effects can also occur when we use the same set of sample points for each pixel. To avoid this happening, I store by default 83 separate sets of samples in the `samples` array. There's nothing magical about the number 83; it's just a prime number that seems to be large enough for most applications. It prevents adjacent pixels in rows from using the same pattern, but we also have to prevent this from happening in columns. Look at the bad aliasing in Figure 5.6(a), particularly the vertical lines in the lower part of the image. This is a simulation of diffuse-diffuse global illumination, as discussed in Chapter 26. It's rendered here with random sampling and 16 samples per pixel, and the important thing is the horizontal resolution of the image: it's 332 pixels, which is 4×83. As a result, pixels in the same columns use the same set of samples, at least until the scan lines hit the spheres (see Question 5.4). Aliasing can also occur at other horizontal resolutions, as Figure 5.6(b) shows. This is 260 pixels wide, which has no direct relation to 83.

To eliminate this problem, we must ensure that we use different sets of samples vertically, as well as horizontally. A common way to achieve this is to use a 2D array of sample sets. I've implemented this, and it works fine, but since `sample_unit_square` has no parameters, the code to traverse the 2D array is terrible. It's also unnecessary. All we have to do is introduce a random jump in `sample_unit_square` so that the sets are accessed randomly, instead of in sequence. Listing 5.8 shows the revised code, where the `sampler` data member `jump` is initialized to zero when a sampler object is constructed. Because

```
Point2D
Sampler::sample_unit_square(void) {

    if (count % num_samples == 0)          // start of a new pixel
        jump = (rand_int() % num_sets) * num_samples;

    return (samples[jump + count++ % num_samples]);
}
```

Listing 5.8. Revised function `Sampler::sample_unit_square`.

Figure 5.7. The scene in Figure 5.6 rendered with 16 random samples per pixel using the revised `sample_unit_square` function.

`count` is also initialized to zero, there is a random jump the first time this function is called.

This simple technique isn't perfect, because it doesn't systematically use all of the sets, but it does work. Figure 5.7 shows the results for the scene in Figure 5.6, which is now just a noisy image because of the low number of samples per pixel. We are, however, not finished with this function, because there's still one more problem, which I'll discuss in Section 5.4.

5.2 Characteristics of Good Sampling

Good 2D sampling techniques have a number of characteristics. First, the points are uniformly distributed over the 2D unit square, so that clumping and gaps are minimized. Second, if we project the points in the x- and y-directions, the 1D projections are also uniformly distributed. Uneven distributions can result in parts of scenes being undersampled or oversampled, and this can increase aliasing. A third characteristic is some minimum distance between sample points, for the same reasons. Sample patterns that have these characteristics are called *well-distributed*. Of the sampling techniques I discuss here, only Hammersley samples have all three characteristics, but they have other characteristics that can result in aliasing. For example, although we want *uniformly* distributed samples, we don't want samples that have *regular* spacing, where the distance between sample points in the x- or y-directions is exactly the same. Hammersley samples are regularly spaced in the x- and y-directions.

I'll examine here a number of sampling techniques to see how the points are distributed. One of the "bottom lines" for sampling is that if we use enough samples per pixel, most sampling techniques produce similar results. This is particularly true for methods based on random numbers. See, for example, the results with 256 samples per pixel in Figures 5.19–5.21. The issues are as follows: how many samples do we need for *satisfactory* results, and what do we mean by satisfactory? This latter issue is subjective, of course, but for most shading applications, we can take it to mean that the amounts of aliasing and noise in the images are acceptable. Figures 5.5(a) and 5.7, for example, have unacceptable amounts of noise.

Compared with the best sampling techniques, the worst techniques can require three times as many samples per pixel to reduce noise to an acceptable level. For example, glossy reflection, discussed in Chapter 25, can require over 600 samples per pixel with random sampling but only 256 with multi-jittered sampling, for similar results. The reason is that the stratification in multi-jittered sampling distributes the points more evenly than random sampling does in 2D and the 1D projections. It's therefore worthwhile to look at a number of different sampling patterns, because the saving in rendering times that they provide can be considerable. Since we may still need hundreds of samples per pixel, or thousands with path tracing, even with the best techniques, rendering times will always be long, and any saving is important.

5.3 Sampling Patterns

5.3.1 Random Sampling

Random sampling fails on all three of the above characteristics because the points can clump and leave gaps in 2D (see Figure 5.8(a)). This behavior also leaves the separate 1D projections badly distributed, as shown at the bottom

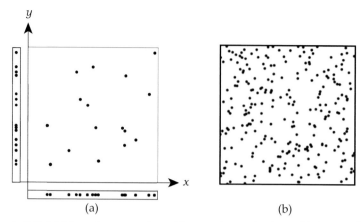

Figure 5.8. (a) 16 random samples with x- and y-projections; (b) 256 random samples.

and left of Figure 5.8(a). Figure 5.8(b) shows 256 random samples for comparison with the other sampling techniques.

5.3.2 Jittered Sampling

Jittered samples are better distributed than random samples because they are *stratified*. To stratify a domain, we divide it into a number of regions that cover the domain without gaps or overlapping. Each region is known as a *stratum*. We then place a single sample in each stratum. The domain being sampled here is the unit square where the strata are the cells in the $n \times n$ sub-grid. Figure 5.9(a) shows 16 jittered samples with the 1D projections. The 1D and 2D distributions are better than the random distributions, where all 16 samples could end up in one of the strata. Figure 5.9(b) shows 256 jittered samples.

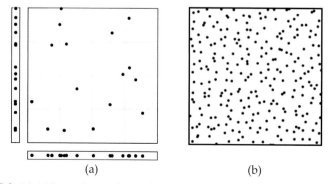

Figure 5.9. (a) 16 jittered samples with x- and y-projections; (b) 256 jittered samples.

5.3.3 *n*-Rooks Sampling

We can achieve a more even distribution in 1D by using *n-rooks* sampling, as developed by Shirley (1991). In this technique, we place *n* samples in an *n* × *n* grid, so that there's exactly one sample in each row and column. This is where the name *n*-rooks comes from. If we place *n* rooks on an *n* × *n* chess board with one rook in each row and column, they can't capture each other.

There's a major difference between jittered and *n*-rooks sampling. With jittered sampling on an *n* × *n* grid, we have n^2 samples. In other words, there's one sample per grid cell, and the number of samples has to be a perfect square. With *n*-rooks sampling, we only have *n* samples on an *n* x *n* grid, and the number of samples doesn't have to be a perfect square.

Figure 5.10(a) shows 16 *n*-rooks samples along a main diagonal of a 16 × 16 grid, where each sample is randomly placed in its cell. This is how we initially generate the samples. We then randomly shuffle the *x*- and *y*-coordinates while maintaining the *n*-rooks condition, producing the 2D distribution in Figure 5.10(b). Although the 1D projections are good, the 2D distribution is bad. Figure 5.10(c) shows 256 samples where 2D clumping and gaps are still evident. In fact, these look no better than the 256 random samples in Figure 5.8(b). This is a general characteristic of *n*-rooks sampling: the 2D distributions are no better than random sampling and therefore are worse than jittered sampling.

Listing 5.9 shows the code for generating the *n*-rooks samples.

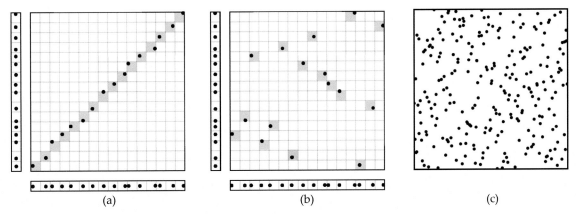

(a)   (b)   (c)

Figure 5.10. (a) 16 *n*-rooks samples in their initial positions; (b) the same samples shuffled in the *x*- and *y*-directions; (c) 256 samples.

```
void
NRooks::generate_samples(void) {

    // generate samples along main diagonal

    for (int p = 0; p < num_sets; p++)
        for (int j = 0; j < num_samples; j++) {
            Point2D pv;
            pv.x = (j + rand_float()) / num_samples;
            pv.y = (j + rand_float()) / num_samples;
            samples.push_back(pv);
        }

    shuffle_x_coordinates();
    shuffle_y_coordinates();

}
```

Listing 5.9. Code to generate *n*-rooks samples.

The code for shuffling the *x*-coordinates of the sample points is in Listing 5.10. The code for shuffling the *y*-coordinates is similar.

```
void
NRooks::shuffle_x_coordinates(void) {
    for (int p = 0; p < num_sets; p++)
        for (int i = 0; i < num_samples - 1; i++) {
            int target = rand_int() % num_samples + p * num_samples;
            float temp = samples[i + p * num_samples + 1].x;
            samples[i + p * num_samples + 1].x = samples[target].x;
            samples[target].x = temp;
        }

}
```

Listing 5.10. The function `NRooks::shuffle_x_coordinates`.

5.3.4 Multi-Jittered Sampling

Multi-jittered sampling was developed by Chiu et al. (1994) to improve the 2D distribution of the samples in *n*-rooks sampling, while preserving the even 1D projections. In essence, this technique combines jittering and *n*-rooks sampling, where we use a two-level grid. Let me explain this with 16 samples. We

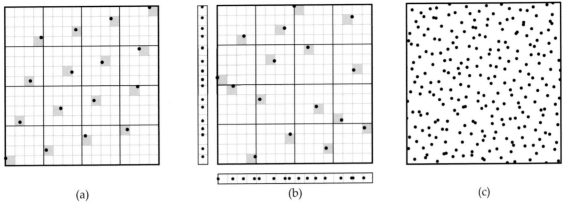

Figure 5.11. (a) 16 multi-jittered samples in the initial distribution; (b) after shuffling in the *x*- and *y*-directions; (c) 256 multi-jittered samples.

still use a 16 × 16 grid, which I'll refer to here as the *sub-grid*, but we superimpose on this a 4 × 4 grid. These grids are illustrated in Figure 5.11. We initially generate a single sample in each of the 4 × 4 grid cells, in the pattern shown in Figure 5.11(a). Here, each sample is generated randomly within its sub-grid cell. This is a jittered distribution with respect to the 4 × 4 grid, but it also satisfies the *n*-rooks condition on the sub-grid. We then shuffle the samples in such a way that the *n*-rooks condition is maintained on the sub-grid. The results are in Figure 5.11(b). The *n*-rooks condition gives good 1D projections, while the 4 × 4 jittering results in a better 2D distribution than with *n*-rooks. Figure 5.11(c) shows 256 multi-jittered samples. Compared with the 256 random, jittered, and *n*-rooks samples, the 2D distribution here is more even. Multi-jittering is an excellent sampling technique.

In the general case of *n* samples, where *n* must be a perfect square, multi-jittered samples are jittered on a $\sqrt{n} \times \sqrt{n}$ grid, and *n*-rooks on an *n* × *n* sub-grid. Due to its length and the fact that it uses two auxiliary functions, I won't reproduce the code for `MultiJittered::generate_samples` here. It's on the book's website.

5.3.5 Hammersley Sampling

Hammersley sampling was developed in the 1960s, and as such, it's a lot older than jittered, *n*-rooks, and multi-jittered sampling (see Hammersley and Hanscomb (1964)). Hammersley sampling points are not random because they are based on the computer representation of numbers in various prime number bases.

I'll only discuss binary number representations here, as these give the best sampling distributions, but this does involve some binary arithmetic. Let's start with the binary representation of an integer i:

$$i_2 = \sum_{j=0}^{n} a_j(i)2^j = a_0(i)2^0 + a_1(i)2^1 + a_2(i)2^2 + \ldots,$$

where the coefficients $a_j(i)$ are the binary digits 0 and 1, and n is the number of terms required to represent the maximum integer. The Hammersley sequence involves the *radical inverse function* of the integer i to base 2: $\Phi_2(i) \in [0, 1)$. This takes the sequence of binary digits of i, reflects them around the decimal point, and evaluates the resulting number in floating-point form. Here's an example: the binary representation of 6 is $6_2 = 110_2$, or $110._2$, after including the decimal point. We then have $\Phi_2(6) = .011_2 = 0/2 + 1/4 + 1/8 = 0.325$, as a decimal number. Notice how the binary digits 110 are written in reverse order after the decimal point. The definition of $\Phi_2(i)$ is

$$\Phi_2(i) = \sum_{j=0}^{n} a_j(i)2^{-j-1} = a_0(i)\frac{1}{2} + a_1(i)\frac{1}{4} + a_2(i)\frac{1}{8} + \ldots.$$

To help you understand this better, Table 5.1 shows the binary representations and radical inverse functions for the integers 1–8.

i			Reflection around the Decimal Point			$\Phi_2(i)$ (base 2)
1	=	1_2	$.1_2$	=	1/2	0.5
2	=	10_2	$.01_2$	=	1/4	0.25
3	=	11_2	$.11_2$	=	1/2 + 1/4	0.75
4	=	100_2	$.001_2$	=	1/8	0.125
5	=	101_2	$.101_2$	=	1/2 + 1/8	0.635
6	=	110_2	$.011_2$	=	1/4 + 1/8	0.325
7	=	111_2	$.111_2$	=	1/2 + 1/4 + 1/8	0.875
8	=	1000_2	$.0001_2$	=	1/16	0.0625

Table 5.1. Binary representations and radical inverse functions for the integers 1–8.

The *Hammersley sequence* of n 2D samples is the set of n points p_i in the unit square defined by

$$p_i = (x_i, y_i) = [1/n, \Phi_2(i)]. \tag{5.1}$$

Figure 5.12 shows Hammersley sequences of 16, 64, and 256 samples. From Figure 5.12(a), you can see that all samples are on an $n \times n$ grid in the unit

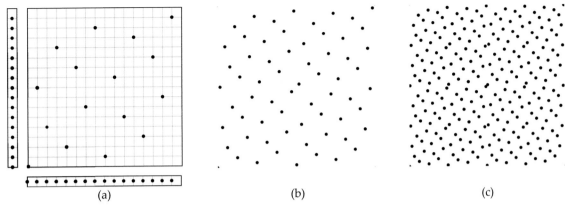

Figure 5.12. (a) 16 Hammersley samples with 1D projections; (b) 64 Hammersley samples; (c) 256 Hammersley samples.

square. The 1D projections are therefore regularly spaced.[3] This can lead to aliasing, as we'll see in Section 5.5 and in later chapters. On the plus side, the sample points are well-distributed in 2D, with a minimum distance between the samples. That's something that none of the other sampling patterns discussed here have. Unfortunately, though, there's another problem. For a given n, there is only one Hammersley sequence, a fact that can also lead to aliasing, as discussed in Section 5.1.

If you look carefully at Figure 5.12, you can see numerous repeating patterns and symmetries in the samples. For example, they are all symmetric

```
double
phi (int j) {
    double x = 0.0;
    double f = 0.5;

    while (j) {
        x += f * (double) (!j & 1);
        j /= 2;
        f *= 0.5;
    }

    return (x);
}
```

Listing 5.11. The radical inverse function for base 2.

---

3. This also follows from Equation (5.1).

about the main diagonal from (0, 0) to (1, 1). Rotating the page through 45° can make these more obvious.

Listing 5.11 shows the code for computing the radical inverse function with base 2 for the integer j. The code for generating the Hammersley samples from Equation (5.1) is then simple, and is left as an exercise.

 ## 5.4 Shuffling the Indices

There's one more thing that we have to cover. Consider a scene where the view plane and a rectangular area light use sample points. Each object will have a pointer to its own sampler object, and let's suppose that the sampling is multi-jittered. Each pixel whose rays hit an object that is shaded with the light will use samples from both sampling objects. According to `sample_unit_square` in Listing 5.8, the samples will be accessed in the same order in both objects. For a stratified sampling technique such as multi-jittered, this means row-by-row in the $n \times n$ sub-grid, starting from the bottom left and ending at the top right. This correlation can produce ugly shading artifacts, as shown in Figure 5.13(a). The scene here consists of a reflective sphere and a plane illuminated by a rectangular light, rendered with 16 multi-jittered samples. Notice the horizontal streaks on the lower surface of the sphere.

To eliminate these streaks, we have to break this correlation. A possible solution would be to access the samples randomly in each set with code analo-

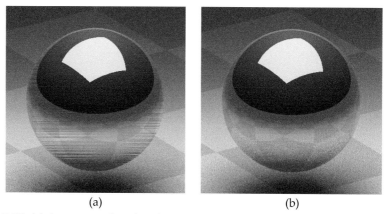

(a)   (b)

Figure 5.13. (a) A scene rendered with 16 correlated view-plane and area-light samples; (b) the same scene rendered with uncorrelated samples, which eliminates the artifacts in (a).

```
#include <algorithm>   // required for random_shuffle

void
Sampler::setup_shuffled_indices(void) {
    shuffled_indices.reserve(num_samples * num_sets);
    vector<int> indices;

    for (int j = 0; j < num_samples; j++)
        indices.push_back(j);

    for (int p = 0; p < num_sets; p++) {
        random_shuffle(indices.begin(), indices.end());

        for (int j = 0; j < num_samples; j++)
            shuffled_indices.push_back(indices[j]);
    }
}
```

Listing 5.12. The function `Sampler::setup_shuffled_indices`.

gous to the jump variable in Listing 5.8, but this doesn't guarantee that all of the samples will be used. Another possibility is to use a final shuffle on the samples in each set, but this destroys the *n*-rooks condition for *n*-rooks and multi-jittered samples. The best way is to randomly shuffle the indices used in `sample_unit_square`, for each set, but guarantee that all samples are used. This is where the `Sampler::shuffled_indices` array is used (see Listing 5.12). Here, `random_shuffle` is a C++ generic algorithm and requires the system `algorithm` header file to be #included. All `Sampler` class constructors call the function `setup_shuffled_indices`.

With the `shuffled_indices` array set up, the modification to `sample_unit_square` is simple, as Listing 5.13 indicates. The result of shuffling the indices can be seen in Figure 5.13(b).

```
Point2D
Sampler::sample_unit_square(void) {

    if (count % num_samples == 0)
        jump = (rand_int() % num_sets) * num_samples;

    return (samples[jump + shuffled_indices[jump + count++
        % num_samples]]);
}
```

Listing 5.13. The final version of `Sampler::sample_unit_square`.

Figure 5.14. This is Figure 5.5(b) re-rendered with shuffled indices.

As it turns out, shuffling the indices also eliminates the aliasing in Figure 5.5(b) (see Figure 5.14). This is similar to Figure 5.5(a) because four samples per pixel randomly selected from 25 jittered samples are similar to four pure random samples. Because this example has a deliberate mismatch in the number of samples, it indicates that index shuffling can also allow us to avoid serious aliasing problems when the sampling gets out of step (see Question 5.3).

That's the end of the modifications to `Sampler::sample_unit_square`. The code is still simple, it can be used with all of the sampling techniques I've discussed, and it handles all of the aliasing problems I've encountered in the following chapters. However, it's not perfect, as you will see when you read the Notes and Discussion section in Chapter 26.

 ## 5.5 Some Results

As antialiasing is the simplest application of sampling, let's look at how the different sampling techniques can antialias a couple of simple scenes. The first is a plane with horizontal and vertical lines, as illustrated in Figure 5.15(a). I'll render these lines with an orthographic projection, where the lines' thickness is slightly smaller than a pixel, as Figure 5.15(b) indicates.

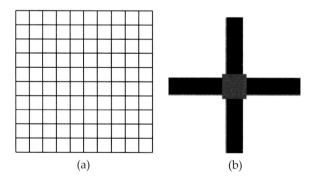

(a)   (b)

Figure 5.15. (a) The sets of parallel lines rendered in Figures 5.16–5.18; (b) the magnified intersection of two lines to show their thickness relative to the size of a pixel (the red square).

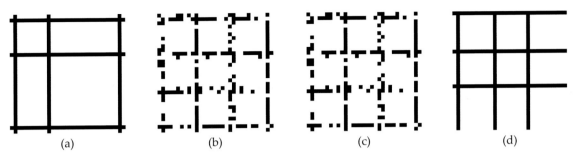

Figure 5.16. A section of the lines in Figure 5.15 rendered at 31 × 31 pixels and one sample per pixel with regular (a), random (b), multi-jittered (c), and Hammersley (d) sampling.

Figure 5.16 shows a section of these lines rendered at 31 × 31 pixels with four of the sampling techniques, and with one sample per pixel. Note that regular sampling misses some of the lines, and so does Hammersley, but this misses different lines because its samples are at the lower-left corners of the pixels. Because jittered, *n*-rooks, and multi-jittered sampling all reduce to random sampling for one sample per pixel, the results for random and multi-jittered sampling in Figures 5.16(b) and (c) are the same.

No lines are missed when we use 16 samples per pixel in Figure 5.17, but some lines are double thickness where they have been sampled in adjacent pixels. Also, because of color averaging, none of the lines are black, which is their correct color.

Figure 5.18 shows the results of using 100 samples per pixel. Although the sampling patterns produce similar results, none of them is correct. In fact, it's impossible to render these lines correctly no matter how many samples we use, because they are thinner than a pixel (see Question 5.4).

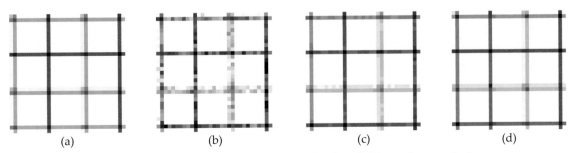

Figure 5.17. This figure is the same as Figure 5.16 but rendered with 16 samples per pixel.

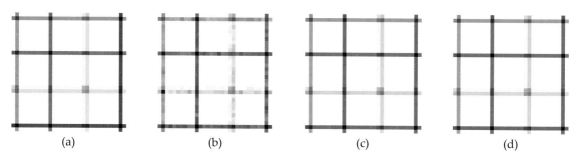

        (a)   (b)   (c)   (d)

Figure 5.18. This figure is the same as Figure 5.16 but rendered with 100 samples per pixel.

     As another example, Figures 5.19–5.21 show a reflective sphere and a plane with a grid of thin lines. These were rendered with the pinhole camera that I'll discuss in Chapter 9, using one and 256 samples per pixel, for each sampling technique. There are a few things to notice in these images. First, there's the reflection of the plane on the sphere, particularly near the horizon. Here, the reflections of the lines become infinitely thin, and no sampling technique can render them. This is the same situation that arose with the checkers on the plane in Figure 4.8. Second, none of the sampling techniques correctly render the horizontal lines near the tops of the images, where they become thinner than a pixel. Third, the sampling techniques all produce results that look essentially the same when 256 samples are used. There are subtle differences, but you have to look at the images on the book's website to see them. In general, we only need about 16–25 samples per pixel for antialiasing. If this number can't resolve fine detail, using more samples usually doesn't improve things much.

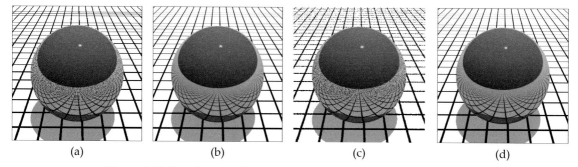

        (a)   (b)   (c)   (d)

Figure 5.19. Regular sampling with one sample per pixel (a) and 256 samples per pixel (b); random sampling with one sample per pixel (c) and 256 samples per pixel(d).

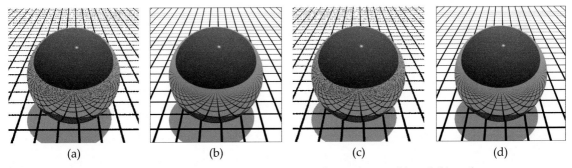

(a)   (b)   (c)   (d)

Figure 5.20. This is the same as Figure 5.19 but with jittered sampling in (a) and (b) and *n*-rooks sampling in (c) and (d).

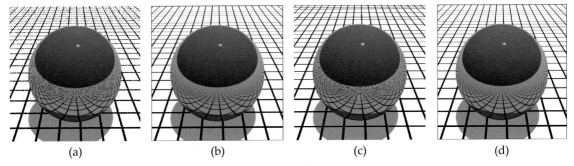

(a)   (b)   (c)   (d)

Figure 5.21. This is the same as Figure 5.19 but with multi-jittered sampling in (a) and (b) and Hammersley sampling in (c) and (d).

The final thing to notice is that the random, jittered, *n*-rooks, and multi-jittered images with one sample per pixel are unattractive because a single random sample per pixel renders sharp edges with a ragged appearance (see Figure 5.22(a)). In contrast, regular sampling "only" produces jaggies, as in Figure 5.22(b), as would Hammersley sampling.

For this reason, my ray tracer uses regular sampling by default when there is one sample per pixel. This applies to most of the images I render, because most of the time, I'm implementing new features, which always involves some debugging, or rendering new scenes, which always involves many test images before I'm happy with the results. Using one sample per pixel is obviously the quickest way to render new images. I use multi-jittered sampling by default when the number of samples is greater than one because it's the best of the techniques I discuss for most applications.

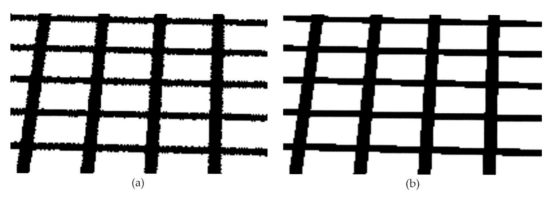

(a)   (b)

Figure 5.22. Grid lines rendered with one random sample per pixel (a) and one regular sample through the center of each pixel (b).

 ## Notes and Discussion

Because we can leave the number of sample sets the same for most scenes, the `Sampler` class constructor sets the number to 83 by default. There is an access function for changing the number.

Antialiasing is the weakest way to test sampling techniques. To really stress-test them and expose their flaws, you need to use them for depth-of-field simulation (Chapter 10), ambient occlusion (Chapter 17), shading with area lights, particularly environment lights (Chapter 18), glossy reflection (Chapter 25), and diffuse-diffuse light transport (Chapter 26). These are tougher tests because these techniques spread the rays through wide angles—up to a whole hemisphere instead of confining them to narrow angles over pixel surfaces, as in antialiasing. You will have plenty of opportunities to experiment in these chapters.

The amount of noise in images can often be subtly reduced when a single sampling object is shared by the view plane, lights, materials, etc. See Exercise 5.2.

I wish I could say that I just wrote down the version of `sample_unit_square` in Listing 5.13 in one go, but it didn't happen like that. I started with the version in Listing 5.7 and then changed it to the second version in Listing 5.8 to fix the aliasing in Figure 5.5, Figure 5.6, and similar images. The aliasing in Figure 5.13(a) was more difficult to fix because there was no obvious cause (at least to me), and I couldn't use any of the debugging techniques from Chapter 1. You can't see a streak on a one-pixel image, and they didn't appear on small (10 × 10) images. I had originally used code for shuffling the sample points but commented it out when it didn't seem to make any differences to the images. Fortunately, this removed the streaks from Figure 5.13(a), and I then changed it to shuffling the indices. The whole process took about 2 years.

 # Further Reading

The business of sampling and reconstruction of images has a long history, a huge literature, and many applications. Glassner (1995) contains an in-depth and very well-written discussion of this subject in the area of digital image synthesis.

The material in this chapter comes from a variety of sources. Jittered sampling was introduced in the pioneering paper by Cooke et al. (1984). Shirley (1991) developed n-rooks sampling and discusses it in Shirley and Morley (2003). The code in Listings 5.9 and 5.10 is based on code in Shirley and Morley (2003).

Multi-jittered sampling was developed by Chiu et al. (1994), and my description of multi-jittering borrows heavily from this article.

Heinrich and Keller (1994(a), 1994 (b)) introduced Hammersley sampling to computer graphics, and Keller introduced jittered Hammersley sampling (not discussed here) in Keller (1997). The radical inverse function was first published by Halton and Weller (1964). The code for this function in Listing 5.11 is from Keller (1997). Table 5.1 is based in part on Table 3.1 in Dutré et al. (2006). A recent article on Hammersley sampling is Wong et al. (1997), who displayed images of 2D Hammersley distributions for bases other than 2. They also discussed how to map Hammersley points onto a sphere.

Questions

5.1 Which sampling techniques don't require index shuffling?

5.2 For certain pixels, sets of samples can be incompletely sampled, which breaks the synchronization between the traversal of pixels and the sample sets in the `samples` array. Can you think of any circumstances where this can happen? *Hint:* It happens in most images.

5.3 In Figure 5.6(a), why do the vertical lines on the plane start to disappear when the scan lines (which are rendered from the bottom) hit the other objects?

5.4 Suppose we were able to render Figure 5.18 with an infinite number of samples per pixel. Why would the result still be incorrect? What would be wrong with the image?

🎱 Exercises

5.1   Implement multi-jittered sampling with the `Sampler` and `MultiJittered` classes on the book's website, or from your own code, and test it with antialiasing. You can use the scenes from Chapter 3 and the sinusoid functions from Chapter 4.

5.2   In a scene that requires more than one object to provide samples, each object can have its own sampler, they can all share the same sampler, or any there can be any combination of shared and individual samplers. How does sampling work when two or more objects share a sampler? To help you understand this, draw some diagrams like Figure 5.3.

5.3   Implement the other sampling techniques so that you can compare their results with antialiasing and with other applications in later chapters.

5.4   When you have implemented shading effects that require large numbers of samples, such as ambient occlusion, area lights, and diffuse-diffuse light transport, experiment with different numbers of sample sets.

6 Mapping Samples to a Disk

6.1   Rejection Sampling
6.2   The Concentric Map

Objectives

By the end of this chapter you should:

- understand the requirements for a good mapping technique from a square to a disk;
- understand how the concentric map is implemented.

We require sample points distributed on a unit disk for the simulation of depth of field with a circular camera lens in Chapter 10 and for shading with disk lights in Chapter 18. As we can already generate samples on a unit square, it's natural to generate these as before and then map them to a unit disk. Although a number of techniques can be used for this task, some are better than others.

The basic requirement for a good mapping technique is that if the sample points are well-distributed on the unit square, they will also be well-distributed on the disk. In other words, the map should not introduce significant amounts of distortion. As it turns out, this is not trivial to achieve. Another requirement is that the map fits in well with the shading architecture described in the previous chapter.

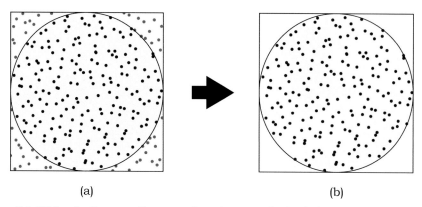

(a)   (b)

Figure 6.1. With rejection sampling, sample points outside the disk, which are colored red in (a), are rejected, leaving the disk samples in (b).

 ## 6.1 Rejection Sampling

Rejection sampling is a technique for generating sample points that satisfy specified geometric conditions. To use rejection sampling to produce samples on a disk, we generate samples on a square that just contains the disk but only keep those samples that are on the disk. Figure 6.1 illustrates this technique with 256 multi-jittered samples.

The best aspect of rejection sampling is that there's no distortion, but a technical problem is that only a subset of the original samples are kept. This raises the question of what can happen if you only use a subset of a sampling pattern. This question also arose in the previous chapter, but the answer depends on the sampling technique. Although subsets of uniform, random, and jittered pattern are still uniform, random, and jittered patterns, respectively, this does not apply to n-rooks, multi-jittered, or Hammersley sampling. For example, if we used n-rooks to generate the samples on the square, the samples on the disk would not satisfy the n-rooks condition. Although the index shuffling should allow us to avoid serious aliasing problems, it's far from ideal to have different numbers of samples in different sampler objects. Rejection sampling therefore does not fit in well with my shading architecture.

 ## 6.2 The Concentric Map

It's better to generate the samples on a unit square, where we can specify their exact number and then map all of them to a unit disk. Although there are a

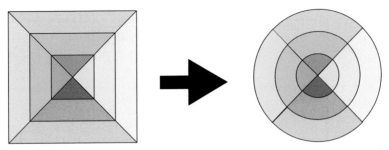

Figure 6.2. Visualization of the concentric map from a unit square to a unit disk.

couple of simple maps that do this, they significantly distort the samples. The best technique is Shirley's concentric map, visualized in Figure 6.2, which maps concentric squares to concentric circles and has low distortion. It therefore keeps points that are close together on the square close together on the disk.

We first map the samples to the square $[-1, 1]^2$, where each triangular quarter has to be considered separately. These are the four colored triangles numbered 1–4 in Figure 6.3(a), defined by the lines $x = y$ and $x = -y$. They are mapped to the corresponding colored sectors of the disk shown in Figure 6.3(b). Although the mapping technique is the same in each quarter, we have to consider these separately because we can't write the complete map as a single set of equations.

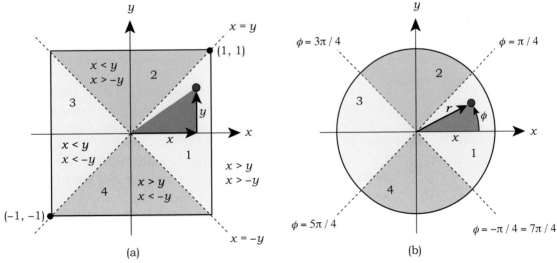

(a)   (b)

Figure 6.3. (a) The square $[-1, 1]^2$ with a sample point (x, y) in the first quarter; (b) the result of applying the concentric map to the square in (a).

Quarter	x and y Inequalities	Angular Range	Map Equations
1	$x > y$ $x > -y$	$\theta \in [-\pi/4, \pi/4]$	$r = x$ $\phi = \dfrac{\pi}{4} \dfrac{y}{x}$
2	$x < y$ $x > -y$	$\theta \in [\pi/4, 3\pi/4]$	$r = y$ $\phi = \dfrac{\pi}{4}\left(2 - \dfrac{x}{y}\right)$
3	$x < y$ $x < -y$	$\theta \in [3\pi/4, 5\pi/4]$	$r = -x$ $\phi = \dfrac{\pi}{4}\left(4 + \dfrac{y}{x}\right)$
4	$x > y$ $x < -y$	$\theta \in [5\pi/4, 7\pi/4]$	$r = -y$ $\phi = \dfrac{\pi}{4}\left(6 - \dfrac{x}{y}\right)$

Table 6.1. The x and y inequalities, the angular range of the sectors, and the concentric map equations for each quarter of the square.

For each quarter of the square, Table 6.1 gives the x and y inequalities defined by the lines $x = y$ and $x = -y$, the angular range of the corresponding sector, and the map equations.

To implement the map, we add an array disk_samples to the Sampler class to hold the new samples. We also need to add a function map_samples_to_unit_disk to perform the map. This is a member function of the Sampler class because the map is independent of the sampling technique. Listing 6.1 shows the code.

The function map_samples_to_unit_disk is called when we construct an object that has to supply samples on a disk. The object's set_sampler function is the appropriate place to call this. See Listing 10.2 for an example.

Figure 6.4 shows the samples in Figure 6.1(a) after they have been mapped to the unit disk. The red samples were originally outside the disk.

Finally, the Sampler class requires the function sample_unit_disk, but as this is identical to sample_unit_square except for the name of the samples array, I won't reproduce the code here. It's in the file **Sampler.cpp** on the book's website. Listing 10.4 shows an example of where this function is called.

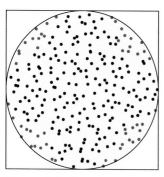

Figure 6.4. Samples mapped to a unit disk with the concentric map.

```
void
Sampler::map_samples_to_unit_disk(void) {

    int size = samples.size();
    float r, phi;                           // polar coordinates
    Point2D sp;                             // sample point on unit
    disk

    disk_samples.reserve(size);

    for (int j = 0; j < size; j++) {
        // map sample point to [-1, 1]   [-1,1]

        sp.x = 2.0 * samples[j].x - 1.0;
        sp.y = 2.0 * samples[j].y - 1.0;

        if (sp.x > -sp.y) {                 // sectors 1 and 2
            if (sp.x > sp.y) {              // sector 1
                r = sp.x;
                phi = sp.y / sp.x;
            }
            else {                          // sector 2
                r = sp.y;
                phi = 2 - sp.x / sp.y;
            }
        }
        else {                              // sectors 3 and 4
            if (sp.x < sp.y) {              // sector 3
                r = -sp.x;
                phi = 4 + sp.y / sp.x;
            }
            else {                          // sector 4
                r = -sp.y;
                if (sp.y != 0.0)            // avoid division by zero
                at origin
                    phi = 6 - sp.x / sp.y;
                else
                    phi = 0.0;
            }
        }

        phi *= pi / 4.0;

        disk_samples[j].x = r * cos(phi);
        disk_samples[j].y = r * sin(phi);
    }
}
```

Listing 6.1. The function Sampler::map_samples_to_unit_disk.

Further Reading

The concentric map was developed by Shirley in the early 1990s, but the most accessible reference is Shirley and Chiu (1997). Listing 6.1 is based on code in this reference.

Pharr and Humphreys (2004) also discusses maps from squares to disks. In addition to the concentric map, they discuss two maps that distort the distribution of points. One of these is the *polar map* $(r, \theta) = (\sqrt{r_1}, 2\pi r_2)$.

 Questions

6.1. It's simple to generate a specified number of samples on a disk with rejection sampling using one of the sampling techniques discussed in Chapter 5. Which technique is this?

6.2. Suppose we used rejection sampling as in Figure 6.1(a) with n uniformly distributed samples in the square. In the limit $n \rightarrow \infty$, what fraction of the samples will be on the disk?

 Exercises

6.1. Examine Figure 6.3, Table 6.1, and the code in Listing 6.1 for the concentric map. Make sure you understand the x and y inequalities for each quarter of the square and how the formulae are implemented in the code.

7

Mapping Samples
to a Hemisphere

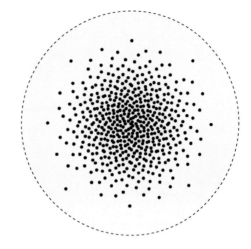

Objectives

By the end of this chapter you should:

- understand how to map sample points from a square to a hemisphere with a cosine power density distribution;
- have the sampling tools available to model a number of direct and indirect illumination effects.

A number of shading applications in later chapters require sample points distributed over the surface of a unit hemisphere. These samples need to have a density that varies as a cosine power of the polar angle measured from the top of the hemisphere. The reason is a cosine factor in the rendering equation (Chapter 13) and because some of the BRDFs describe the reflection of light in terms of cosine powers. To use the samples, we will center the hemisphere on a ray-object hit point and then shoot a ray from the hit point through each sample. The rays can be shadow rays, reflected rays, or transmitted rays, depending on the application. I'll use these samples to simulate ambient occlusion in Chapter 17, environment lights in Chapters 28 and 29, glossy reflection in Chapter 25, and diffuse-diffuse light transport in Chapter 26. They can also be used to simulate glossy transmission. Collectively, these form an important part of the shading effects to be described in this book.

125

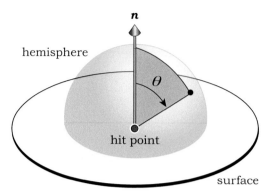

Figure 7.1. Unit hemisphere at a hit point with the surface normal and polar angle.

 ## 7.1 Cosine Distributions

The polar angle θ is measured from the top of the hemisphere, which can be oriented about the surface normal at a hit point or about a reflected or transmitted ray. In Figure 7.1, the normal goes through the top of the hemisphere, and θ is measured from the normal.

The surface density d of the samples varies with θ according to

$$d = \cos^e\theta, \tag{7.1}$$

where the power $e \in [0, \infty)$. We can use e to control how rapidly d decreases as θ increases: the larger e is, the more rapid the decrease (see Figure 7.2).

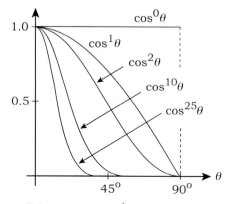

Figure 7.2. Graphs of $\cos^e\theta$ for various values of e.

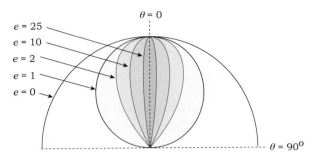

Figure 7.3. Polar graphs of the cosine power curves in Figure 7.2.

Alternatively, we can use *polar graphs* to plot the cosine powers, as shown in Figure 7.3, where the curves have been mirrored across the vertical axis. As Figures 7.2. and 7.3 show essentially the same information, why show both? There are two reasons. The first is that Figure 7.3 makes a connection with *Phong lobes*, which are used to model specular reflection (see Chapter 15). To model the reflection of light in 3D, we can rotate the curves about the $\theta = 0$ line to produce surfaces of revolution. These are the Phong lobes. The $e = 0$ lobe is the unit hemisphere itself, the $e = 1$ lobe is a sphere of radius 0.5, and as e increases from 1, lobes become progressively thinner. The second reason is that the curves in Figure 7.3 provide a different way to visualize how the cosine power density of the samples decreases with increasing θ.

It may appear from the curves in Figures 7.2 and 7.3 that for $e > 1$, the density can go to zero for some value of $\theta < \pi/2$, but that's not the case. From Equation (7.1), $d > 0$ for $\theta \in [0, \pi/2)$, and $e \geq 0$. This means that the bottoms of the Phong lobes in Figure 7.3 are all horizontal.[1] It also means that for any value of e, sample points can be generated at any place on the hemisphere.

7.2 Mapping Theory

There exist simple formulae for mapping sample points that are uniformly distributed on the unit square $[0, 1]^2$ onto a unit hemisphere with the density distribution (7.1) in the polar angle. I'll just quote the results here, because the derivation requires an understanding of probability density distributions and the evaluation of a multi-dimensional integral. There are also good references available that cover their derivation, as discussed in the Further Reading

---

1. The figure would have to be drawn to a much larger scale to make this visible.

section. Given two random numbers $(r_1, r_2) \in [0, 1]^2$, their azimuth and polar angles (ϕ, θ) on the hemisphere are

$$\phi = 2\pi r_1,$$
$$\theta = \cos^{-1}[(1 - r_2)^{1/(e+1)}]. \qquad (7.2)$$

To tie this in with the sampling techniques in Chapter 5, (r_1, r_2) are the (x, y)-coordinates of a sample point in the unit square. A given sampling distribution on the unit square results in the same distribution on the hemisphere but warped into a cosine power distribution in the θ-direction. For example, multi-jittered samples on the unit square are mapped to warped multi-jittered samples on the hemisphere. The good and bad characteristics of each sampling technique are therefore preserved. If the samples have uniform 1D distributions in x and y, they will have a uniform distribution in the ϕ-direction and a cosine power distribution in the θ-direction. Similarly, if the samples satisfy the n-rooks condition in x and y, they will still satisfy it in θ and ϕ.

Because we'll use the samples to define ray directions, we need to associate the angles (ϕ, θ) in Equations (7.2) with a 3D point on the hemisphere. To do this, the application code needs to define a local orthonormal basis in which to orient the hemisphere and compute the directions. Figure 7.4 shows an example where w is through the top of the hemisphere and, in this case, parallel to the normal. The orientation of u and v don't matter because the density is always symmetric about the $\theta = 0$ axis. I'll explain how to set up the (u, v, w) vectors in the chapters that use cosine distributions, starting with ambient occlusion in Chapter 17. From the spherical coordinate Equations (2.3) with $r = 1$, we can express a hemisphere sample point p in terms of (u, v, w) as follows:

$$p = \sin \theta \cos \phi \, u + \sin \theta \sin \phi \, v + \cos \theta \, w. \qquad (7.3)$$

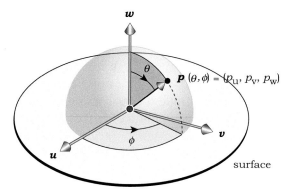

Figure 7.4. Local orthonormal basis at hit point.

7.3 Implementation

To implement the mapping, I've added an array `hemisphere_samples` to the `Sampler` class to hold the 3D points, and a function `map_samples_to_hemisphere` to perform the mapping. Since Equation (7.3) only involves the sine and cosine of θ, there's no need to compute the inverse cosine function in Equations (7.2). Listing 7.1 shows the code for `map_samples_to_hemisphere`.

```
void
Sampler::map_samples_to_hemisphere(const float e) {
    int size = samples.size();
    hemisphere_samples.reserve(num_samples * num_sets);

    for (int j = 0; j < size; j++) {
        float cos_phi = cos(2.0 * PI * samples[j].x);
        float sin_phi = sin(2.0 * PI * samples[j].x);
        float cos_theta = pow((1.0 - samples[j].y), 1.0 / (e + 1.0));
        float sin_theta = sqrt (1.0 - cos_theta * cos_theta);
        float pu = sin_theta * cos_phi;
        float pv = sin_theta * sin_phi;
        float pw = cos_theta;

        hemisphere_samples.push_back(Point3D(pu, pv, pw));
    }
}
```

Listing 7.1. The function `Sampler::map_samples_to_hemisphere`.

The function `map_samples_to_hemisphere` is called when we construct an object that has to supply samples on a hemisphere. The object's `set_sampler` function is again the appropriate place to call this from; see Listing 17.2 for an example. The `Sampler` class also requires a function `sample_hemisphere` that returns the next sample on the hemisphere, but the code for this is identical to the code in `sample_unit_square`, and `sample_unit_disk`, except for the name of the array.

 ## 7.4 Results

Figure 7.5 shows Hammersley samples mapped to three cosine power distributions and rendered with an orthographic view perpendicular to the

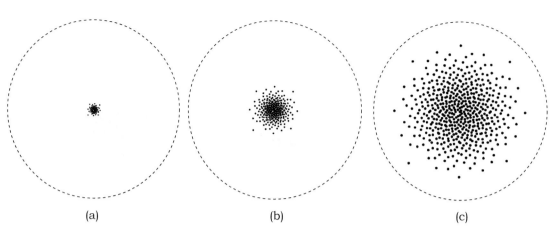

Figure 7.5. Cosine power distributions of Hammersley samples: (a) 64 samples with $e = 1000$; (b) 256 samples with $e = 100$; (c) 512 samples with $e = 10$; The dashed circles indicate the circumference of the hemisphere.

circumference of the hemisphere. Notice how the samples spread out over the hemisphere as e decreases.

As the samples spread towards the circumference, the foreshortening in these orthographic views gives a false impression about their distribution on the hemisphere. Figure 7.6(a) shows a cosine ($e = 1$) distribution that appears to be uniform when viewed from the top, but it's not uniform, as the side view in Figure 7.6(b) shows. Figure 7.6(c) shows a $e = 0$ distribution where the samples are uniformly distributed in *solid angle* around the center of the hemisphere,

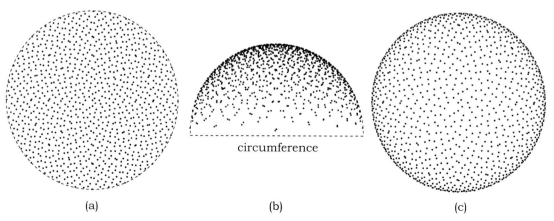

Figure 7.6. Cosine power distributions of Hammersley samples: (a) 1024 samples with $e = 1$; (b) side view of the hemisphere in (a); (c) 1024 samples with $e = 0$.

but these appear denser towards the circumference due to foreshortening. I'll use the $e = 1$ distribution in Chapters 17, 18, 26, and 29. The noise code on the book's website uses the $e = 0$ distribution to construct a vector noise function.

Further Reading

The calculus textbook Thomas and Finney (1996) discusses polar graphs. Shirley and Morley (2003) discusses the derivation of the formulae (7.2) with a good discussion of the background material that you need to understand them. Shirley's earlier article (Shirley, 1992) discusses mappings to other surfaces. The mappings were originally used for Monte Carlo integration (Screider, 1966).

Exercises

7.1. Using Equations (7.2), calculate the angles (θ, ϕ) that correspond to the four corners of the unit square $(r_1, r_2) = (0, 0)$, $(1, 0)$, $(1, 1)$, $(0, 1)$, and its center $(0.5, 0.5)$. Doing this will help you understand some of the figures in Chapter 17.

8   Perspective Viewing

 Objectives

By the end of this chapter, you should:

- understand how perspective viewing is defined;
- understand the difference between computer viewing and how our eyes see the world around us;
- understand how perspective distortion arises;
- understand the properties of perspective projections;
- have examined a number of ray-traced perspective images.

Perspective viewing produces more realistic images than orthographic viewing because it corresponds more closely to the way our eyes work. I'll present here the definitions and properties of perspective projections and then discuss *axis-aligned perspective viewing*. This is simple to implement and will allow you to explore most of the properties of perspective projections. I'll also present several ray-traced images that illustrate how 3D computer perspective viewing works, and I'll discuss perspective distortion. This chapter is mainly descriptive.

If you are familiar with 3D viewing and perspective projections, you can skip Sections 8.1 and 8.2. If you want to go straight to the implementation of a virtual camera in the following chapter, you can also skip Sections 8.3 and 8.4.

You should, however, look at the ray-traced images in Sections 8.5 and 8.6. As most of the ray-traced figures in this book are rendered using perspective viewing, it's important that you understand how this works.

8.1 Definitions

In the context of computer graphics, a *projection* transforms points in 3D space onto a flat 2D surface called the *view plane*.[1] The points are transformed along straight lines called *projectors,* and in a perspective projection, these all converge to a point called the *center of projection* (see Figure 8.1).

As in orthographic projection, we define a window on the view plane that's covered with pixels. The amount of a scene that's visible through the window depends on the location of the center of projection, the relative location and orientation of the window with respect to the center of projection, and the widow's size. These define the *view volume*: an infinite four-sided pyramid whose apex is at the center of projection (see Figure 8.2(a)). The faces of the view volume are planes through the edges of the window that meet at the center of projection.

In a general perspective viewing system, the location of the center of projection, the location of the window, and the orientation of the window are arbitrary, but I'll use the following special case. This is the symmetric arrangement in Figure 8.2(b), where the center of projection is on a line that passes through the center of the window (the green circle) and is perpendicular to the window. This line is called the *view direction*, and here, the view volume is a symmetric infinite four-sided pyramid.[2] Most of the ray-traced images in this

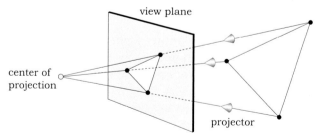

Figure 8.1. Perspective projection of a triangle.

---

1. This is also called the *film plane* or *projection plane*.
2. The view direction is also known as the *gaze direction*.

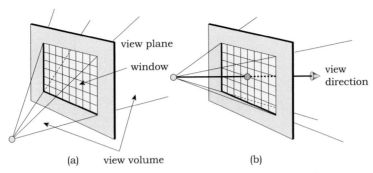

Figure 8.2. The window on the view plane and the view volume: (a) arbitrary arrangement; (b) symmetric arrangement.

book are produced with this arrangement, the exception being the stereo pairs discussed in Chapter 12.

General computer graphics textbooks such as Hearn and Baker (2004) and Shirley et al. (2005) discuss the clipping of objects that are outside the view volume, but in ray tracing, primary rays can only intersect objects or parts of objects that are inside the view volume (see Questions 8.1 and 8.2). We can also define a *view frustum* with near and far *clipping planes* parallel to the view plane.[3] In ray tracing, only clipping against the clipping planes is relevant, but I'll leave this as an exercise. None of the ray-traced images in this book use clipping.

Another viewing quantity is the *field of view*. For the viewing arrangement in Figure 8.2(b), this is the angle subtended at the center of projection by the top and bottom edges of the window. It's illustrated in Figure 8.3. What about the angle subtended by the left and right sides of the window? We can define this in terms of the field of view and the *aspect ratio* of the window, which is the window's width divided by its height (Shreiner et al., 2005).

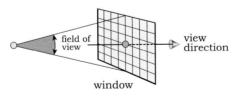

Figure 8.3. The field of view.

3. A frustum is a finite section of a pyramid (or cone) bounded by two parallel planes.

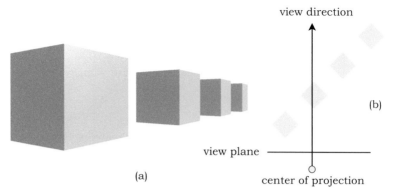

Figure 8.4. (a) Perspective view of four cubes; (b) top-down view of the cubes and the view plane.

8.2 Properties of Perspective Projections

Perspective projections have a number of properties, and although I'll discuss these separately, it's important to realize that they operate simultaneously.

Property 1. The perspective projection of an object becomes smaller as the object gets farther away from the center of projection.

This is the most obvious property of perspective projections and is the main reason they are more realistic than parallel projections; after all, objects in the real world look smaller as they get farther away. As an example, Figure 8.4(a) shows four identical cubes at different distances from the center of projection, with their relative distances indicated in Figure 8.4(b). The exact relationship between projected sizes and distances is not simple, because of *perspective distortion*, which I'll discuss in Section 8.6.

Property 2. As an object is rotated, its projected width becomes smaller. This is known as foreshortening.

Figure 8.5 shows three perspective views of a rectangular box, seen face-on to its wide face in Figure 8.5(a) and rotated in Figure 8.5(b) and (c). As the box rotates, the projected width of the wide face becomes smaller due to foreshortening. Because foreshortening works on all faces, we see that the projected width of one of its end faces, which comes into view in Figure 8.5(b) and (c), becomes larger. Of course, part of this increase in size is due to Property 1; the end gets closer to the view point as the box rotates. Property 1 also affects the projected height of the box, which is constant in Figure 8.5(a) but varies with distance along the box in Figure 8.5(b) and (c).

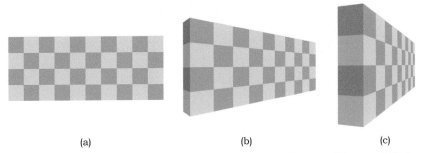

(a) (b) (c)

Figure 8.5. Three perspective views of a rectangular box: (a) face-on; (b) rotated 45 degrees; (c) rotated 75 degrees.

Property 3. Perspective projections preserve straight lines.

Figures 8.4 and 8.5 also illustrate this property, where the cubes' edges and the checker outlines remain straight after projection.

Property 4. Sets of parallel lines that are parallel to the view plane remain parallel when projected onto the view plane.

Figure 8.6(a) illustrates this property, where the horizontal (red) and vertical (green) edges of the two cubes are parallel to the view plane. Figure 8.6(b) illustrates where the center of projection and view direction are located in relation to the cubes.

Property 5. Sets of parallel lines that are not parallel to the view plane converge to a vanishing point on the view plane.

Consider a set of parallel lines that are not parallel to the view plane. Their projections become closer together as their distances from the view plane

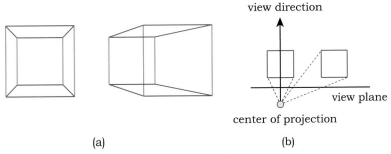

(a) (b)

Figure 8.6. (a) Two wireframe cubes in perspective, (b) location of the center of projection and the view direction.

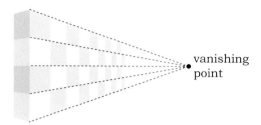

Figure 8.7. Parallel lines converge to a vanishing point.

increase. This is illustrated in Figures 8.4 and 8.5. If we extend these lines to an infinite distance, their projections all converge to a point, called a *vanishing point*, as shown in Figure 8.7.

Before we look at more figures with vanishing points, I need to discuss ground planes and horizons. A *ground plane* is parallel to the (x_w, z_w) plane and is therefore horizontal. In a perspective projection, a plane can have a horizon (see Figure 8.8). This figure shows a vertical cross section of a view volume, its window, and a ground plane that's parallel to the view direction and therefore perpendicular to the window. I'll assume that the window's top and bottom boundaries are horizontal.

Rays that go through the upper half of the window don't hit the ground plane, but those that go through the bottom half do hit it. The horizon is formed by those rays that are parallel to the plane, and can therefore be considered to hit the plane at an infinite distance from the center of projection. In this configuration, the horizon will be a horizontal line in the image (see Question 8.3 and Exercise 8.4).

Figure 8.9 shows the two cubes in Figure 8.6(a) with the vanishing point defined by extending the blue edges of each cube until they meet. Since these are the only set of parallel lines that are not parallel to the view plane, there is a single vanishing point. The gray area is the ground plane, and the important thing to notice is the location of the vanishing point, which is on the hori-

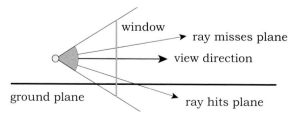

Figure 8.8. Viewing geometry in which a plane has a horizon.

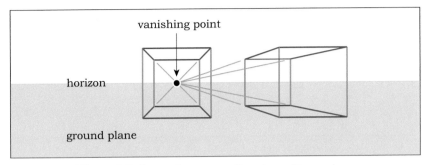

Figure 8.9. One-point perspective view of two cubes.

zon. In fact, *the vanishing points of horizontal lines are always on the horizon*. This is because the "real" vanishing points in 3D space are at an infinite distance away, as is the horizon. Although the plane is drawn below the cubes, the location of the horizon is independent of its vertical position. In Figure 8.9, the blue edges also happen to be perpendicular to the view plane, but that's not necessary for the formation of the vanishing point.

We classify perspective views by their number of vanishing points, from one to three. They are known as *one-point*, *two-point*, and *three-point* perspective views, respectively. Figure 8.9 is therefore a one-point perspective view of the cubes because it has a single vanishing point.

If we rotate the view plane in Figure 8.9 so that it's no longer parallel to the red edges of the cubes, but still vertical, we get the perspective view in Figure 8.10(a). The orientation of the view plane in this case is shown in Figure 8.10(b). As only the vertical (green) lines are still parallel to the view plane, the result is a two-point perspective view. The vanishing points are shown in Figure 8.11. Architectural drawings commonly use two-point perspective.

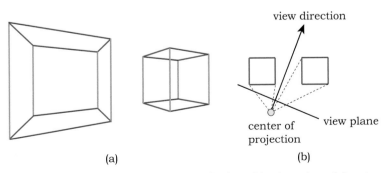

Figure 8.10. (a) Two-point perspective view of cubes; (b) orientation of the view plane.

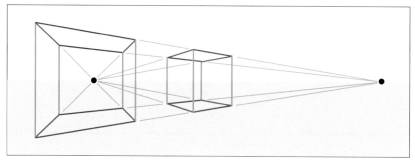

Figure 8.11. Two-point perspective view of cubes with vanishing points.

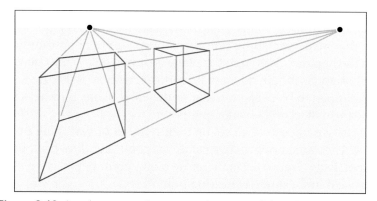

Figure 8.12. Another two-point perspective view of the cubes in Figure 8.6.

Figure 8.12 shows the cubes from Figure 8.11 with the center of projection moved above the cubes but with the view plane still vertical.

Finally, we can change the center of projection again and orient the view plane so that it's not parallel to any cube edges. The result is a three-point perspective view, as shown in Figure 8.13(a) for a single cube. Here, the vanishing point for the vertical lines is an infinite distance below the ground plane.

Property 6. If a set of parallel lines is parallel to a world coordinate axis, its vanishing point is on the axis and is known as a principal vanishing point.

Figure 8.13(b) shows the principal vanishing points for an *axis-aligned cube*. This is a cube whose edges are parallel to the world coordinate axes. The number of principal vanishing points is related to the number of world coordinate planes (or axes) that the view plane cuts. Can you work out the relationship?

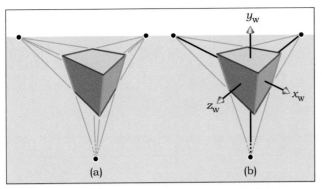

Figure 8.13. (a) Three-point perspective view of a cube; (b) axis-aligned cube with three principal vanishing points.

 ## 8.3 Axis-Aligned Perspective Viewing

Here's the simplest way for you to set-up perspective viewing in your existing ray tracer. You specify the center of projection somewhere on the z_w-axis at $z_w = e$. This is called the *eye point*, as illustrated in Figure 8.14.[4] The window is still perpendicular to the z_w-axis, and the pixels are still in horizontal rows. The rays now all start at the eye point but still go through the center of each pixel. This fanning out of the rays from the eye point creates the perspective projection; the rays travel along the projectors but in the opposite direction of the arrows in Figure 8.1.

In ray tracing, there is no need to perform the explicit perspective projection that 3D graphics APIs, such as OpenGL, require.

Figure 8.14 shows two rays with a 6 × 4 pixel window. You should compare this figure with Figure 3.1. This is called *axis-aligned perspective viewing* because the view direction is parallel to the z_w-axis. The situation shown in Figure 8.1 is a special case of general perspective viewing, where the view direction is actually *along* the z_w-axis and points in the negative z_w-direction. The differences between orthographic and perspective projection in ray tracing are as follows:

- in orthographic projection, the rays have the same direction but have different origins;
- in perspective projection, the rays have the same origin (the eye point) but have different directions.

---

4. This is also called the *view point*.

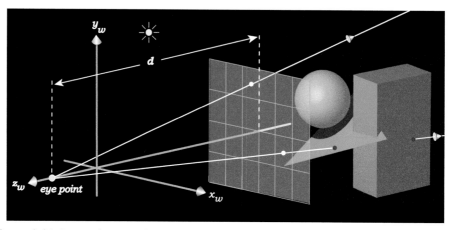

Figure 8.14. Set-up for axis-aligned perspective viewing with the eye point and two rays going through pixel centers.

We also need to specify where the view plane cuts the z_w-axis, which I do by specifying the perpendicular distance d between the eye point and the view plane. This is also illustrated in Figure 8.14. I call this the *view-plane distance*; it will form part of the user interface of the virtual camera in Chapter 9.

For given image resolutions h_{res} and v_{res} and pixel size s, we can easily compute the ray directions using Equations (3.10). In world coordinates, the direction of the ray that goes through the center of the pixel in row r and column c is

$$d = (s(c - h_{res}/2 + 0.5),\ s(r - v_{res}/2 + 0.5),\ -d) \qquad (8.1)$$

(see Exercise 8.1). As this is not a unit vector, you must normalize it before tracing the ray.

 ## 8.4 Implementation

Axis-aligned perspective projection can be implemented with the `World::render_perspective` function in Listing 8.1. This can be called in the `main` function in place of the `render_scene` function. The eye point e and view-plane distance d also have to be stored somewhere. As a temporary measure, you can store these directly in the world, so that you can specify their values in build functions. You can also use the `MultipleObjects` tracer.

```
void
World::render_perspective(void) const {
    RGBColor  pixel_color;
    Ray       ray;

    open_window(hres, vres);
    ray.o = Point3D(0.0, 0.0, eye);

    for (int r = 0; r < vp.vres; r++)              // up
        for (int c = 0; c <= vp.hres; c++) {  // across
            ray.d = Vector3D(s * (c - 0.5 * (hres - 1.0)),
                s * (r - 0.5 * (vres - 1.0)), -d);
            ray.d.normalize();
            pixel_color = tracer_ptr->trace_ray(ray);
            display_pixel(r, c, pixel_color);
        }
}
```

Listing 8.1. `world::renderScene` function for axis-aligned perspective viewing using a single ray through the center of each pixel.

The ray-traced images in Sections 8.5 and 8.6 were all rendered using axis-aligned perspective viewing but with a pinhole camera, antialising, and shading.

 ## 8.5 Processes and Results

We'll now look at some perspective images and examine what happens when the viewing parameters e and d are changed. Let's start by fixing e and varying d. In Figure 8.15, d increases from (a) to (c), while the pixel size and image resolutions stay the same. As d *increases*, the field of view *decreases*, as does the amount of the scene that's visible through the window. Increasing d therefore

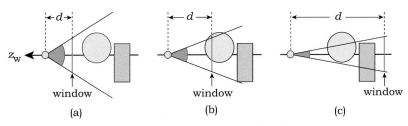

Figure 8.15. Increasing d acts like using a telephoto lens on a camera.

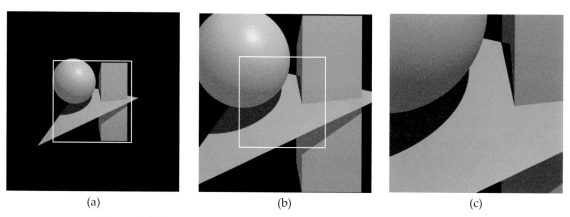

(a)   (b)   (c)

Figure 8.16. The scene in Figure 3.2 rendered with the eye point at (0, 0, 500) and $d = 200$ (a), $d = 400$ (b), and $d = 1000$ (c).

acts like using a telephoto lens on a camera and allows us to zoom into a scene.

To illustrate this zoom effect, Figure 8.16 shows the objects in Figure 3.2 rendered with the eye point at (0, 0, 500) and three different values of d. The white squares show the successive zoom areas.

As Figure 8.15 demonstrates, the window can be located anywhere on the z_w-axis to the right of the eye point, including locations where it cuts through objects. When the view plane is between the center of projection and an object, the object's projection is smaller than its real size, as in Figure 8.1, but the opposite is true when an object is between the center of projection and the view plane. Here, the projection is larger than the object, as Figure 8.17 illustrates.

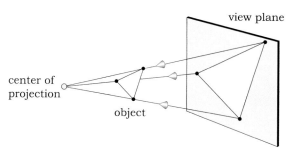

Figure 8.17. When an object is between the center of projection and the view plane, the object's projection is larger than the object itself.

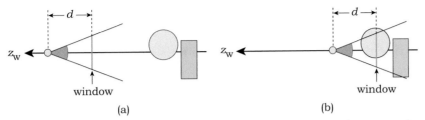

Figure 8.18. Changing the eye point while keeping d fixed changes the perspective projection.

Recall from Chapter 3 that orthographic projections are zoomed by changing the pixel size. Can we do that in perspective projection? Yes we can, but see Question 8.5.

Now, let's see what happens when we keep d fixed and change e, as in Figure 8.18. With d fixed, the field of view stays the same, but as the eye point gets closer to the objects, they appear larger, because less of the scene is visible in the window. Some results are shown in Figure 8.19, but unlike Figure 8.16, this is no longer a simple zoom. Because the center of perspective changes, the objects change shape, a fact that's particularly apparent for the sphere. Here, it no longer looks like a sphere as a result of *perspective distortion*. Many people who are new to ray tracing are puzzled by this, but it's correct behavior for computer perspective viewing, as I'll discuss in Section 8.6.

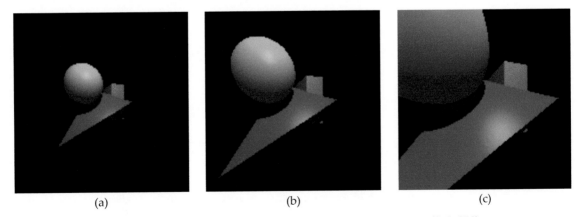

Figure 8.19. The scene in Figure 8.16 rendered with $d = 50$ and the eye point at $(0, 0, 200)$ (a), $(0, 0, 150)$ (b), and $(0, 0, 100)$(c).

8.6 Perspective Distortion

Perspective distortion in computer viewing is caused by the fact that the view plane is flat. In contrast, we don't see this type of distortion in real life, because our retinas are spherical. Figure 8.20 illustrates how perspective distortion arises. In this figure, we are looking in the negative y_w-direction at three spheres whose centers are the same distance from the view plane but have different values of x_w. The middle sphere has its center on the z_w-axis, and the outline of its projection on the view plane is circular. As the spheres move away from the z_w-axis, their projections become progressively elongated in the x_w-direction, creating the perspective distortion. The amount of distortion increases with their distance from the z_w-axis. The projected shapes are shown on the x_w-axis.

Figure 8.21 illustrates perspective distortion far better than Figure 8.20 because the distortion is really two-dimensional over the view plane. This figure shows a ray-traced grid of spheres with their centers in the (x_w, y_w) plane, and rendered with the indicated values of e and d. The center sphere is at the world origin, and its outline is always circular. As the spheres get farther from the z_w-axis, their projections become progressively elongated in radial directions away from the z_w-axis. These directions are indicated by the red arrows in Figure 8.21(b). The distortion ranges from mild in Figure 8.21(a) to extreme in Figure 8.21(c), where the center of projection is close to the spheres. I've adjusted the values of d so that the spheres just fit into the window for each value of e. To help visualize the distortion, the spheres are shaded with a 3D checker texture.[5] The animation **Spheres.avi** shows the distortion in action.

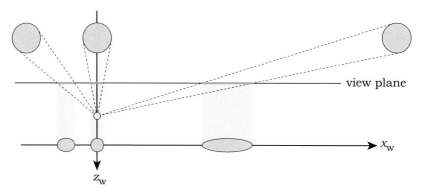

Figure 8.20. Perspective distortion of spheres in the x_w-direction.

---

5. The 3D checker texture is covered in Chapter 30.

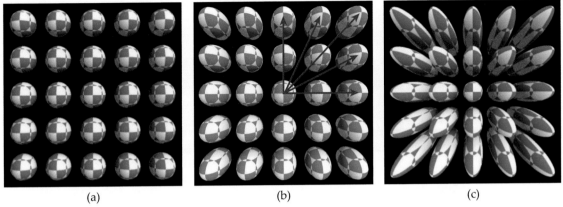

(a)   (b)   (c)

Figure 8.21. Perspective distortion of a grid of spheres in the (x_w, y_w) plane with radius 0.75 and $e = 15$, $d = 875$ (a), $e = 5$, $d = 140$ (b), and $e = 2$, $d = 85$ (c).

Do other objects suffer perspective distortion? Yes, perspective distortion applies to all objects; for example, the cubes illustrated in Section 8.2 are also distorted. The distortion is usually not as obvious for cubes and other polyhedra as it is for spheres, because their projected edges remain straight (Property 3). Therefore, polyhedra still look like polyhedra, and buildings still look like buildings.

Later chapters contain many ray-traced images that use perspective viewing. The following figures are therefore just a few one-point perspective images of wireframe and solid cubes. Figure 8.22 shows an axis-aligned wireframe cube centered on the origin, and Figure 8.23 shows four solid cubes symmetrically placed about the z_w-axis. The exercises ask you to examine and think about these images.

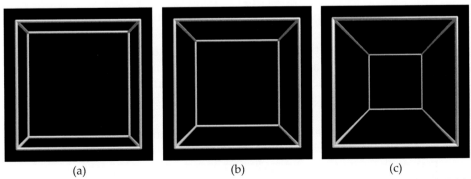

(a)   (b)   (c)

Figure 8.22. Perspective views of a wireframe cube of edge length 2 with $e = 10$, $d = 1687$ (a), $e = 5$, $d = 750$ (b), and $e = 2.5$, $d = 280$ (c).

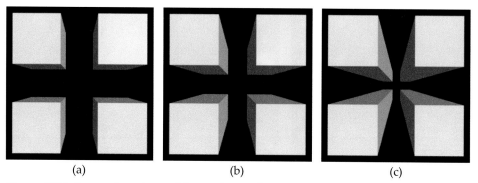

(a)   (b)   (c)

Figure 8.23. Perspective views of four cubes with $e = 5$, $d = 500$ (a), $e = 2$, $d = 200$ (b), and $e = 0.5$, $d = 50$ (c).

 Further Reading

Most general textbooks on computer graphics discuss perspective projections and 3D viewing. See, for example, Hearn and Baker (2004) and Shirley et al. (2005). The most comprehensive treatment is Foley et al. (1995), Chapter 6. The book on OpenGL by Shreiner et al. (2005) also discusses perspective viewing.

 Questions

8.1. Why don't we have to clip rays against the faces of the view volume in ray tracing?

8.2. Does foreshortening happen in parallel projection?

8.3. Must the plane in Figure 8.8 cut the window for its horizon to appear in the image?

8.4. Suppose d was negative in Figure 8.15; that is, the view plane is to the left of the eye point. What would the objects in Figure 8.16 look like if you ray traced them? The short answer is that they wouldn't appear in the image because all the ray intersection t values would be negative. So, let's allow negative roots.

8.5. To zoom into a scene by a factor of two using an orthographic projection, you make the pixels half as big. To zoom into a scene by a factor of two in perspective projection, what do you have to do to d?

8.6. For the axis-aligned perspective viewing discussed here, where can you place a sphere so that its outline on the view plane is circular?

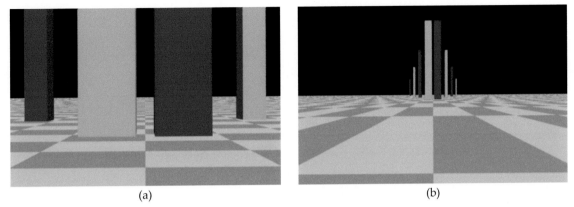

(a)   (b)

Figure 8.24. Perspective views of boxes and a plane: (a) close-up view; (b) wide-angle view.

8.7. Do spheres with circular outlines look spherical when ray traced?

8.8. Can you explain the directions and relative lengths of the edges of the wireframe cube in Figure 8.22? For example, why does the back of the cube get smaller as the eye point gets closer to the cube?

8.9. Can you explain the projected shapes of the cubes in Figure 8.23?

8.10. Can a plane that's not parallel to the view direction have a horizon?

8.11. How can you simulate an orthographic projection with a perspective projection?

8.12. Figure 8.24(a) shows a plane with a checker texture and some rectangular boxes. Although the checkers are square, the perspective projection makes them appear foreshortened in the view direction, which is parallel to the plane. In Figure 8.24(b), the value of d has been decreased to widen the field of view and show the tops of the boxes, but now, the foreground checkers are *elongated* in the view direction. Can you explain this?

Exercises

8.1. Derive Equation (8.1) for the un-normalized ray direction.

8.2. When an object is centered on the view direction (the z_w-axis, in this chapter), we can sometimes derive an exact expression for its projected size on the view plane as a function of its distance from the eye point. This makes explicit the relationship between projected size and distance in Property 1 of perspective projections.

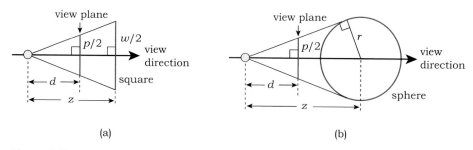

Figure 8.25. (a) Perspective projection of a square; (b) perspective projection of a sphere.

Figure 8.25(a) shows a square of size w at distance s from the eye point. It's perpendicular to the view direction. Prove that the square's projected size p on the view plane is

$$p = d(w/s),$$

which is inversely proportional to s. Note that $p \to \infty$ as $s \to 0$.

Figure 8.25(b) shows a sphere of radius r whose center is distance s along the view direction. Prove that the sphere's projected diameter on the view plane is

$$p = dr/(s^2 - r^2)^{1/2},$$

which is not inversely proportional to s. What values does this expression approach as $s \to r$ and $s \to 0$? Does this expression make sense when $s < r$? Write an approximate expression for p that is valid when $s \gg r$. Compare this with the expression for the square.

8.3. Implement axis-aligned perspective viewing as discussed in this chapter. Render Figure 3.20 and the image on the first page of Chapter 3 using different values of e and d. These won't require any shading. When you have implemented shading, reproduce some of the images in Sections 8.5 and 8.6.

Alternatively, you can use the pinhole camera in Chapter 9 to reproduce the images in this chapter by placing the camera's eye point on the z_w-axis and using a view direction that's in the negative z_w-direction.

8.4. Ray trace a horizontal plane and vary its y_w-value. Keep everything else the same. Notice what happens to the horizon in the image. Can you explain this?

9 A Practical Viewing System

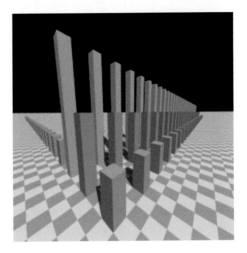

 Objectives

By the end of this chapter, you should:

- understand how a practical perspective viewing system works;
- understand the differences between virtual and real cameras;
- have implemented a virtual pinhole camera.

The axis-aligned perspective viewing I discussed in Chapter 8 is too restrictive to use in a practical ray tracer. I'll remove the restrictions in this chapter by discussing a *virtual pinhole camera* with all of the degrees of freedom we'll need for the following chapters.

 9.1 Description

The virtual pinhole camera implements perspective viewing with the following features:

- an arbitrary eye point;
- an arbitrary view direction;
- an arbitrary orientation about the view direction;
- an arbitrary distance between the eye point and the view plane.

151

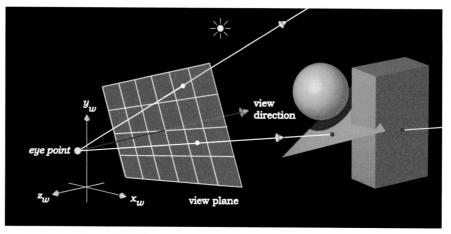

Figure 9.1. The virtual pinhole-camera viewing system.

This viewing system is illustrated in Figure 9.1. Here, the window is still centered on and perpendicular to the view direction, the view plane distance d is still specified along the view direction from the eye point, and the eye point is still the center of projection.

 The feature of the viewing system that Figure 9.1 doesn't illustrate is that we can rotate the window around the view direction, provided it stays perpendicular to it. With this operation included, we have all of the degrees of freedom we need for a practical viewing system. In spite of the new features, this new viewing system works fundamentally the same way as axis-aligned perspective viewing.

 Viewing systems such as this are often referred to as *virtual cameras*. Our system models a pinhole camera where the eye point corresponds to the pinhole. There is, however, an important difference between real and virtual

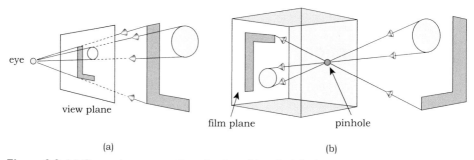

Figure 9.2. (a) Computer perspective viewing; (b) real pinhole camera, where the image on the film plane is inverted.

pinhole cameras. Figure 9.2(a) shows a virtual pinhole camera where the view plane is between the eye point and the objects. In contrast, Figure 9.2(b) shows a real pinhole camera, where the pinhole is between the objects and the film plane. Here, the image projected onto the film plane is inverted about a line through the pinhole and perpendicular to the film plane. This inversion makes the image upside-down and back-to-front, a process that does not happen with the virtual camera (see Question 9.1).

 ## 9.2 The User Interface

The *user interface* of a viewing system refers to the parameters that a user has to specify in order to uniquely set up the system. In my ray tracer, the viewing system consists of the camera and view plane, with the following parameters:

- the eye point *e*;
- the look-at point *l*;
- the up vector *up*;
- the view-plane distance *d*.

It's important to realize that you have to specify all parameters in world coordinates, as this is essential for computing the camera rays in world coordinates (see Section 9.4). However, the camera also requires its own *viewing coordinates*, denoted by (x_v, y_v, z_v) and illustrated in Figure 9.3.[1] These form a right-handed Cartesian coordinate system attached to the camera, which we need to compute the camera-ray directions.

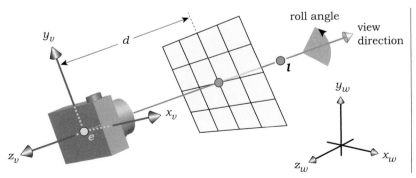

Figure 9.3. Components of the virtual camera, shown with the viewing coordinate system.

1. Viewing coordinates are also called *camera coordinates*.

The eye and look-at points define the view direction for the camera, which is $l - e$. You could, of course, specify this directly, but I've always found it more useful in perspective viewing to specify l. This allows us to specify explicitly how each scene is centered in the image.

The up vector up allows us to orient the camera and view plane about the z_v-axis. In graphics APIs such as OpenGL, users can also specify the camera's field of view, but that's not part of the pinhole camera's user interface. Although it's defined by the view-plane distance, the image resolution, and the pixel size, the code doesn't use the field of view.

Of course, the user interface is a matter of personal choice, so feel free to implement other interfaces (see Exercises 9.3–9.5).

9.3 Viewing Coordinates

To define the viewing coordinates, we use an orthonormal basis (u, v, w), which needs to be defined from two vectors, as explained in Section 2.12. The first is the view direction $l - e$, but I define w to point in the opposite direction of this (see Figure 9.4). I'll explain why below. We therefore have

$$w = (e - l)/\|e - l\|. \tag{9.1}$$

The second vector is the up vector, which I take by default to be the unit vector in the y_w-direction: $up = (0, 1, 0)^2$ (see Figure 9.5(a)). I use this to calculate u as

$$u = up \times w/\|up \times w\|, \tag{9.2}$$

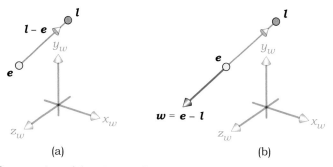

(a)   (b)

Figure 9.4. Construction of the viewing ONB: (a) the view direction is $l - e$; (b) $w = e - l$ is in the opposite direction to the view direction.

---

2. This is also the OpenGL default up vector (Shreiner et al., 2005).

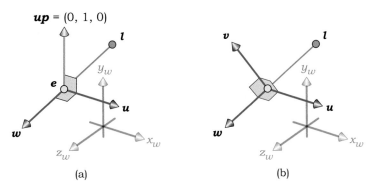

Figure 9.5. (a) u is perpendicular to up and w; (b) v is perpendicular to u and w.

as Figure 9.6(a) also illustrates. Note that since up is vertical, u is horizontal by construction; that is, it's parallel to the (x_w, z_w)-plane.

The third vector v of the ONB is then defined by

$$v = w \times u \qquad (9.3)$$

and is a unit vector by construction (see Figure 9.5(b)). The v vector lies in the vertical plane defined by up and w and points out of the top of the camera along the y_v-axis in Figure 9.3. The u, v, and w vectors are the unit basis vectors for the viewing coordinate system (x_v, y_v, z_v) illustrated in Figure 9.3. Of course, a coordinate system needs an origin, and that's the eye point e. Adding this to (u, v, w) defines the viewing orthonormal frame.

As Figure 9.6(a) shows, u and v are parallel to the view plane, as this is also perpendicular to the view direction. We orient the pixels so that the rows are parallel to u and the columns are parallel to v. As a result, rows of pixels are horizontal in world coordinates. Although the view direction can be tilted up

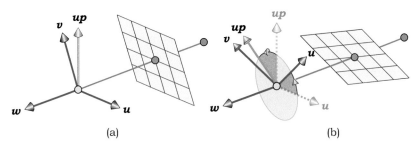

Figure 9.6. (a) The u, v, and w vectors with the default up vector $up = (0, 1, 0)$; (b) u, v, and up rotated through the roll angle.

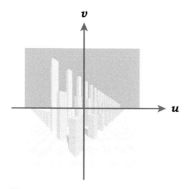

v

u

Figure 9.7. From the camera's point of view, which looks in the negative w-direction, u is horizontal, and v is vertical.

or down, this orientation corresponds to the way we usually view the world, with our eyes horizontal, and the way we usually take photographs. If you rendered a horizontal plane with this camera orientation, its horizon would be horizontal in the image. These geometric relations explain why this orientation is so useful and should suffice for the majority of images you ray trace.

There is, however, a final degree of freedom for the camera. We can rotate it around the view direction by using an up vector that's not vertical (see Figure 9.6(b)). Here, the camera is rotated through a *roll angle*. Roll is an aeronautical term, as are pitch and yaw. Because this has some difficulties from a user-interface perspective, I'll discuss how to do this another way in Section 9.8.

Now, here's why w points in the opposite direction of the viewing direction. Let's pretend we're the camera looking at a scene. We want u to point horizontally to the right and v to point vertically up, as shown superimposed on an image in Figure 9.7. Why? Because we use these to calculate the primary-ray directions, and this arrangement conveniently leaves u parallel to the pixel rows, pointing left to right, and v parallel to the columns, pointing up. This simplifies the calculations. If w pointed in the viewing direction, this arrangement would leave the viewing coordinate system left-handed instead of right-handed and therefore not representable by an ONB.[3] This may not make much difference in practice, because you could always fiddle with Equations (9.1)–(9.3) and (9.5) to get u and v pointing the right way, but this construction would be inconsistent with the way we will construct ONBs in later chapters.

 9.4 Primary-Ray Calculation

We need an expression for the primary rays in world coordinates, a situation where the ONB really pays off. The eye point e, which is the origin of all primary rays, is specified in world coordinates as part of the camera's user interface. It's the ray directions we have to compute. The (x_v, y_v) coordinates of a sample point p on the pixel in row r and column c are

$$x_v = s(c - h_{res}/2 + p_x),$$
$$y_v = s(r - v_{res}/2 + p_y).$$

(9.4)

---

3. An ONB is by definition right-handed, as discussed in Section 2.12.

The nice thing about an ONB is that we can express any vector as a linear combination of its basis vectors. We can therefore write the primary-ray direction *d* as

$$d = x_v\, u + y_v\, v - d\, w,$$
(9.5)

where x_v, y_v, and $-d$ are the components of *d* in the *u*-, *v*-, and *w*-directions, respectively. Since *u*, *v*, and *w* are constructed in world coordinates with Equations (9.1)–(9.3), Equation (9.5) expresses *d* in world coordinates. That's all there is to it! Of course, you will need to normalize *d* before you use it as the ray direction.

9.5 Implementation

Because I'll define a number of camera types in this and the following chapters, these need to be organized in an inheritance hierarchy (see Figure 9.8). These cameras will give you the ability to implement a variety of projection methods and create interesting images.

Because each camera type renders the scene in a different way, the cameras, not the world, must now be responsible for the rendering. I store a camera pointer in the world to allow the build functions to specify the type of camera. Listing 9.1 shows the new `main` function. Note that we pass the world into `render_scene` to allow this function to access the view plane, the tracer, and the member functions `open_window` and `draw_pixel`.

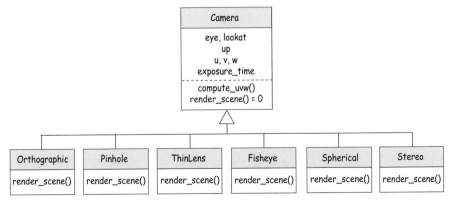

Figure 9.8. The camera classes.

```
main {
     World world;
     world.build();
     world.camera_ptr->render_scene(world);
}
```

Listing 9.1. The new `main` function that uses the camera to do the rendering.

The data members common to all cameras represent the eye point, look-at point, up vector, orthonormal basis vectors, and exposure time, as indicated in Figure 9.8. I'll explain why the `exposure_time` data member is necessary in Chapter 28; for now, it will have the default value of 1.0, set in the `Camera` default constructor.

There are two common member functions: `compute_uvw`, defined in the `Camera` base class, and `render_scene`, defined in each derived class. Listing 9.2 shows a partial declaration of the `Camera` class.

Listing 9.3 shows the function `compute_uvw`, but see Section 9.9, as there's more to it than this listing shows.

The `PinHole` camera class adds the view-plane distance d and `zoom` factor (Section 9.7), defines the `render_scene` function (Listing 9.5), and adds a func-

```
class Camera {
     public:

          // constructors, access functions, etc.

          void
          compute_uvw(void);

          virtual void
          render_scene(World& w) = 0;

     protected:

          Point3D eye;
          Point3D lookat;
          Vector3D up;
          Vector3D u, v, w;
          float exposure_time;
};
```

Listing 9.2. Camera base class.

```
void
Camera::compute_uvw(void) {
    w = eye - lookat;
    w.normalize();
    u = up ^ w;
    u.normalize();
    v = w ^ u;
}
```

Listing 9.3. The function `Camera::compute_uvw`.

tion `ray_direction` to compute the ray direction according to Equation (9.5) (see Listings 9.4–9.6).

In the `render_scene` function, I've called the color that's computed for each pixel L because L is the symbol for *radiance,* and radiance is the quantity that a ray tracer computes for each ray. The details are in Chapter 13.

The additional argument `depth` in the `trace_ray` function is there to provide a uniform interface for these functions in all types of shading (see Section 14.5).

Although you can set any default values you like for the camera parameters, you will have to set eye, lookat, and d in each build function. In contrast, the parameters up, exposure_time, and zoom can be left as their default values, because only a few images will use non-default values for these.

```
class Pinhole: public Camera {
    public:

        // constructors, etc.

        Vector3D
        ray_direction(const Point2D& p) const;

        virtual void
        render_scene(World& w);

    private:

        float d;        // view-plane distance
        float zoom;     // zoom factor
};
```

Listing 9.4. Part declaration of the `Pinhole` class.

```
void
Pinhole::render_scene(World& w) {
    RGBColor  L;
    ViewPlane vp(w.vp);
    Ray ray;
    int depth = 0;              // recursion depth
    Point2D sp;                 // sample point in [0, 1] x [0, 1]
    Point2D pp;                 // sample point on a pixel

    w.open_window(vp.hres, vp.vres);
    vp.s /= zoom;
    ray.o = eye;

    for (int r = 0; r < vp.vres; r++)            // up
        for (int c = 0; c < vp.hres; c++) {   // across
            L = black;

            for (int j = 0; j < vp.num_samples; j++) {
                sp = vp.sampler_ptr->sample_unit_square();
                pp.x = vp.s * (c - 0.5 * vp.hres + sp.x);
                pp.y = vp.s * (r - 0.5 * vp.vres + sp.y);
                ray.d = ray_direction(pp);
                L += w.tracer_ptr->trace_ray(ray, depth);
            }

            L /= vp.num_samples;
            L *= exposure_time;
            w.display_pixel(r, c, L);
        }
}
```

Listing 9.5. The `Pinhole::render_scene` function.

```
Vector3D
Pinhole::ray_direction(const Point2D& p) const {
    Vector3D dir = p.x * u + p.y * v - d * w;
    dir.normalize();
    return(dir);
}
```

Listing 9.6. The `Pinhole::ray_direction` function.

9.6 Examples

We can now look at some images rendered with the pinhole camera, starting with Figure 9.9. This shows the objects in Figures 8.16 and 8.19 with a checker

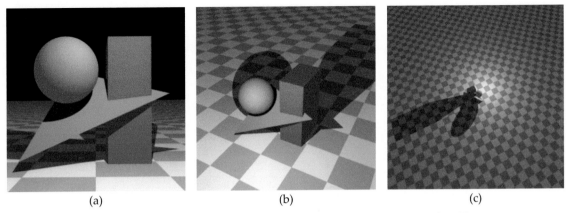

Figure 9.9. (a) $e = (0, 0, 500)$, $l = (0, 0, 0)$, $d = 500$; (b) $e = (300, 400, 500)$, $l = (0, 0, -50)$, $d = 400$; (c), $e = (-1000, 2000, -500)$, $l = (0, -100, 0)$, $d = 250$.

plane added. Figure 9.9 shows three views rendered with the indicated camera parameters. It's nice to be able to place the camera anywhere and be able to look anywhere. Part of the build function for Figure 9.9(b) is in Listing 9.7 to illustrate how to set up the camera. Note that compute_uvw is called *after* all of the camera parameters have been specified. You have to call this explicitly in each build function because the ray tracer has no way of knowing when you have finished defining the camera. I often end up with a number of cameras, all but one of which are commented out, and a single call to compute_uvw just before the camera is stored in the world. This is a convenient way of providing different views of a scene in a single build function.

```
void
World::build(void) {
    ...
    Pinhole* pinhole_ptr = new Pinhole;
    pinhole_ptr->set_eye(300, 400, 500);
    pinhole_ptr->set_lookat(0, 0, -50);
    pinhole_ptr->set_view_distance(400);// set d
    pinhole_ptr->compute_uvw();
    set_camera(pinhole_ptr);

}
```

Listing 9.7. Build function code fragment that shows the camera set-up code for Figure 9.9(b).

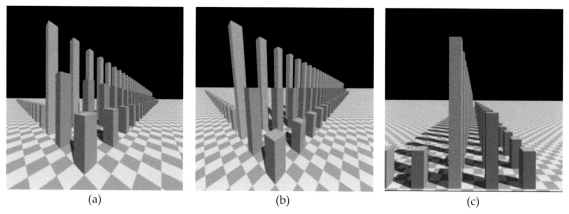

(a)   (b)   (c)

Figure 9.10. Perspective views of boxes with different camera parameters.

Figure 9.10 shows 157 axis-aligned boxes, where all boxes of the same color have the same height. There are some questions about these images at the end of the chapter.

 ## 9.7 Zooming

The simple mechanism for zooming from Chapter 8 allows us to zoom with the pinhole camera by changing the view-plane distance. There are, however, situations where we will need a zoom technique that's independent of the view-plane distance. One situation is where the pinhole camera is used for stereo viewing (Chapter 12), and the other is the thin-lens camera in Chapter 10, which also uses perspective viewing.

From Section 3.6.4, we know that changing the pixel size performs zooming for orthographic projections. Fortunately, this also works for perspective viewing, and it's independent of d. We can therefore zoom by changing the pixel size with the view plane's `set_pixel_size` function, or alternatively, we can use the `zoom` data member, which performs the same task (Listing 9.5) but with a more initiative user interface. Because increasing `zoom` decreases the pixel size and zooms into the scene, it's more intuitive to use `pinhole_ptr ->set_zoom(2.0)` to zoom in by a factor of two than to halve the pixel size in `vp.set_pixel_size`. The zoom factor isn't a data member of the `Camera` class because it doesn't work for the fisheye and panoramic cameras in Chapter 11; we zoom these with a completely different mechanism.

9.8 The Roll Angle

Sometimes, we need to rotate the camera around the view direction. An example is simulating an aircraft flying over terrain that has to be banked for a turn. To see how to do this with the up vector, let's start with Figure 9.9(a) and rotate the camera 45 degrees clockwise, while keeping the view direction horizontal. It's easy to see that an un-normalized up vector that accomplishes this is (1, 1, 0). Figure 9.11(a) shows the result, where you should notice that the image has been rotated 45 degrees *counterclockwise*. That's because the image always rotates in the opposite direction of the camera. Next, let's put the camera at (500, 0, 0) and rotate it 45 degrees clockwise to get Figure 9.11(b). What's the up vector in this case? It's not too difficult to see that (0, 1, −1), un-normalized again, will do the job, but you have to think about it first. Finally, let's make e = (300, 400, 500), l = (−20, −30, −50), and rotate the camera 145 degrees to get Figure 9.11(c). Now quickly, what's the up vector? Not so easy this time, is it? In fact, the exact value may not matter, as you could adjust the up vector until you have the approximate orientation you want, but there's another way. I rotate the camera with an explicit roll angle for the simple reason that I hate having to think, and this doesn't require any thinking. It's therefore a more convenient user interface. An example of the API is `camera_ptr-> set_roll_angle(45)`.

How do we implement the roll angle? The mechanism is a rotation of the camera about an arbitrary line, the view direction in this case (see Section 20.6). I've left the implementation of the roll angle as an exercise.

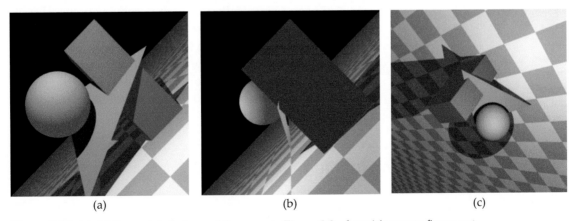

| (a) | (b) | (c) |

Figure 9.11. (a), (b) Two rotated views of the scene in Figure 9.9 where it's easy to figure out the up vector; (c) a rotated view rendered with the roll angle.

9.9 The Singularity

Here's a fact of life: viewing systems have a singularity, and ours is no exception. A singularity in this context means that there are certain viewing parameters for which the construction of u and v in Equations (9.2) and (9.3) breaks down. This happens when the view direction is parallel or anti-parallel to the up vector, in which case u will be the zero vector divided by zero, according to Equation (9.2). As my default up vector is $(0, 1, 0)$, this will happen when the camera is looking vertically up or down.

It's best if the ray tracer detects this automatically and treats it as a special case, where you can then specify the directions of u and v. Here's one way to do it. In the function `compute_uvw`, test if the camera is looking exactly down; that is,

$$e_x = l_x, \; e_z = l_z, \tag{9.6}$$

to machine precision, and $l_y < e_y$. When these conditions are satisfied, set u, v, and w to

$$u = (0, 0, 1), \; v = (1, 0, 0), \; w = (0, 1, 0). \tag{9.7}$$

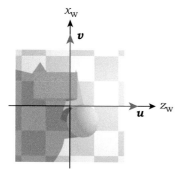

Figure 9.12. The vectors u, v, w in Equation (9.7) result in x_w pointing up and z_w pointing to the right when the roll angle is zero.

An example is where the camera is looking straight down the y_w-axis: $e = (0, 1000, 0)$, $l = (0, 0, 0)$. The conditions (9.6) will be satisfied to machine precision when you use whole numbers, but also see Question 9.6. Equations (9.7) result in x_w pointing up and z_w pointing to the right in the images when the roll angle is zero (see Figure 9.12). Although the up vector isn't useful in this case, the roll-angle mechanism still works.

You need to be familiar with this singularity because it's an intrinsic part of viewing systems, and several images in later chapters have the camera looking vertically down. I treat the case when the camera is looking vertically up in a similar manner. The complete code for `compute_uvw` is on the book's website. A possible alternative way to handle the singularity is covered in Exercise 9.9.

Further Reading

Several books discuss pinhole cameras similar to the one discussed here. See, for example, Shirley and Morley (2003), Shirley et al. (2005), Hill and Kelley (2006), and Shreiner et al. (2005).

Questions

9.1. If the image on the film of a real camera is inverted, as described in Section 9.1, why are photographic prints not inverted?

9.2. It's possible to get the inversion with the Pinhole camera by setting one of the viewing parameters appropriately. Which parameter is this, and what is the range of its values?

9.3. How many vanishing points are there in each part of Figure 9.10? Given that the checkers are axis-aligned, are these principal vanishing points?

9.4. In each part of Figure 9.10, does the view direction point up or down, or is it horizontal? How can you tell when it's horizontal?

9.5. In Figure 9.10(b), what is the value of e_y in relation to the height of the cyan boxes?

9.6. What type of numbers can you use for the x_w- and y_w-components of e and l and have the conditions (9.7) return true?

Exercises

9.1. Prove that for an arbitrary vector w, the vector u in Equation (9.2) is parallel to the (x_w, z_w) plane.

9.2. Implement a pinhole camera and use the images in this chapter for testing purposes. Hit functions for axis-aligned boxes and triangles are in Chapter 19. The checkerboard texture is discussed in Chapter 30, but you don't need that for testing.

9.3. Allow the user to specify an arbitrary up vector.

9.4. Allow the user to specify a view direction.

9.5. Allow the user to specify the field of view of the camera in degrees.

9.6. When we change the image resolution, the current camera implementation alters the field of view because the window size changes. Implement an option on the pinhole camera that keeps the field of view the same by altering the size of the pixels. For example, if you change a 300 × 200 pixel image to 600 × 400 pixels, you can keep the field of view the same by making the pixels half as big. This example does, however, keep the aspect ratio of the images the same. Does this process make sense if you change the aspect ratio, say from 300 × 200 pixels to 200 × 300?

9.7. Implement the roll angle as described in Sections 9.8 and 20.6.

9.8. Implement functions that rotate the viewing ONB about the u and v vectors and translate it in the u-, v-, and w-directions. This will allow you to translate the camera and perform yaw and pitch operations on it in addition to roll.

9.9. A possible solution to the singularity is to use a default up vector that's not quite vertical, for example, *up* = (0.000679879, 1, 0.00967967), but there's a problem with this approach. See if you can work out what it is.

10   Depth of Field

Image courtesy of Tania Humphreys

Objectives

By the end of this chapter, you should:

- understand how depth of field is simulated in ray tracing;
- have implemented a thin-lens camera.

The *depth of field* of a camera is the range of distances over which objects appear to be in focus on the film. A photographer can set the depth of field of a real camera by adjusting the camera lens. In contrast, everything is in focus with the pinhole camera we modeled in Chapter 9 because the "lens" is infinitely small. Real cameras have finite-aperture lenses that only focus perfectly at a single distance called the *focal distance*. I'll present here a virtual camera that simulates depth of field with a finite-radius circular lens.

167

10.1 Thin-Lens Theory

We first need to cover some classic *thin-lens theory* from optics. Figure 10.1 shows the cross section of a thin lens composed of two spherical surfaces, and some rays that go through the lens. A magnifying glass is a good model for this.[1] Thin-lens theory is an approximation that applies when the thickness of the lens is negligible compared to its radius. In this case, the lens has a number of simple and useful optical properties. Consider a plane that's perpendicular to the lens axis, for example, the plane labeled the *focal plane* in Figure 10.1. As there's nothing special about this, it doesn't matter where it's located. A thin lens will focus points on this plane onto another plane on the other side of the lens. This is the *image plane* in Figure 10.1. Every point p on the focal plane has a corresponding image p' on the image plane. For an ideal thin lens, every ray from p that hits the lens goes through the point p'. If this lens were in a real camera and the film were on the image plane, the focal plane would be in focus, but everything else would be out of focus to varying degrees.

Each focal plane and image plane exist as a matched pair. They are also interchangeable because light can travel either direction, a fact that I'll use in Section 10.2. In Figure 10.2, I've added a second pair of focal and image planes to the configuration shown in Figure 10.1. The important thing to notice here is that different rays from q hit the image plane of p' at different places. For rays that only make a small angle with the lens axis, the area they cover is roughly circular and is known as the *circle of confusion*. If we placed a film on this image plane in Figure 10.2, q would be out of focus. The further q gets from the focal

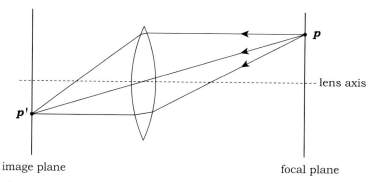

Figure 10.1. Cross section through a thin lens showing a focal plane and its corresponding image plane.

---

1. After reading Chapters 19 and 27, you should be able to model and render a magnifying glass.

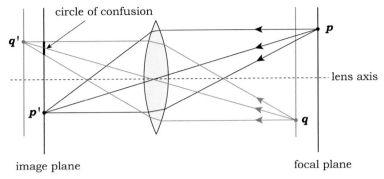

Figure 10.2. Rays starting a point q go through the image plane of p at different locations, with the result that q will appear out of focus.

plane of p (on either side), the larger the circle of confusion becomes, and the more out of focus q becomes.

The *depth of field* of a camera is the range of distances parallel to the lens axis in which the scene is in focus. By this definition, a camera made with the above thin lens would have zero depth of field. In contrast, photographs taken with traditional film cameras can appear in focus over finite distances, or off to infinity, because of the finite size of the film grains. In ray tracing and digital cameras, the image can appear in focus over the range of distances where the circle of confusion is smaller than a pixel.

Figures 10.1 and 10.2 also illustrate another property of a thin lens: a ray that goes through the center of the lens is not refracted. I'll also use this in Section 10.2.

10.2 Simulation

To simulate depth of field, we have to simulate the optical properties of the thin lens discussed above. Although to do this exactly would be a complex process, it turns out that we can make a couple of simplifications and still get convincing results. First, we represent the lens with a disk. Because the disk has zero thickness, we are not quite simulating a real thin lens, which always has finite thickness. The disk is centered on the eye point of the camera and is perpendicular to the view direction, as Figure 10.3 illustrates. Second, we don't calculate exactly how the light is refracted as it passes through the lens.

The simulation usually requires a large number of rays per pixel whose origins are distributed over the surface of the lens. We can use the concentric

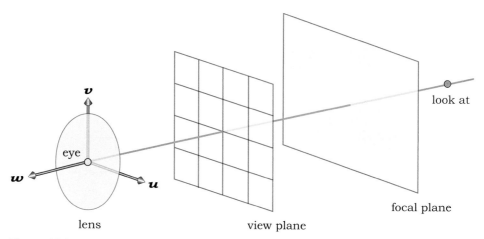

Figure 10.3. A thin-lens camera consists of a disk for the lens, a view plane (as usual), and a focal plane, all perpendicular to the view direction.

map from Chapter 6 to perform the distribution. Figure 10.4 shows two light paths that join corresponding points on the focal and image planes,[2] where one is the straight line through the center of the lens and the other is through a sample point on the lens. For each path, we start a primary ray on the lens.

The center ray starts at the eye point at the center of the lens and goes through a sample point on a pixel. In common with the pinhole camera, the

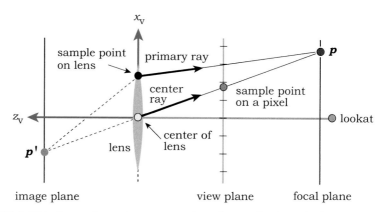

Figure 10.4. This figure shows two rays projected onto the (x_v, z_v)-plane. The center ray starts at the center of the lens and hits the focal plane at p. The primary ray starts at a sample point on the lens and also hits the focal plane at p.

2. In this and other 2D figures, I've drawn the lens with a finite thickness to make it visible.

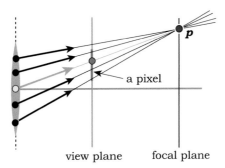

view plane   focal plane

Figure 10.5. If all of the primary rays for a given pixel hit the focal plane at the same point, it will be in perfect focus but will not be antialiased.

thin lens camera has the view plane on the opposite side of the lens as the image plane, but this doesn't invalidate the simulation. The primary ray starts on a sample point on the lens. To simulate depth of field we perform the following three tasks:

1. compute the point p where the center ray hits the focal plane;
2. use p and the sample point on the lens to compute the direction of the primary ray so that this ray also goes through p;
3. ray trace the primary ray into the scene.

There are a couple of things to note about this procedure. First, the center ray doesn't contribute any color to the pixel; we only use it to find out where p is. It's the primary rays that form the image. The second thing to notice is that the process does take refraction through the lens into account. The two paths from p' to p are thin-lens paths for an infinitely thin lens, but we don't start the rays at p' and refract them through the lens. Instead, we start the primary rays on the lens but make sure they point in the correct direction.

   The above process produces good results, but if we used a single center ray for each pixel, all primary rays for a given pixel would hit the focal plane at the same point p, as Figure 10.5 illustrates. This will result in the focal plane being perfectly in focus but with no antialiasing.

   Although the blurring effects of depth of field can obliterate aliasing artifacts as hit points move away from the focal plane, it's still best to use antialiasing, because this improves the appearance of the scene that's near the focal plane. We can easily accomplish this by using a different center ray for each primary ray. See Figure 10.6, where four center rays go through different sample points on the pixel and therefore hit the focal plane at different locations.

   Figure 10.7 shows four primary rays that start at sample points on the lens and hit the focal plane at the four points shown in Figure 10.6. Notice that

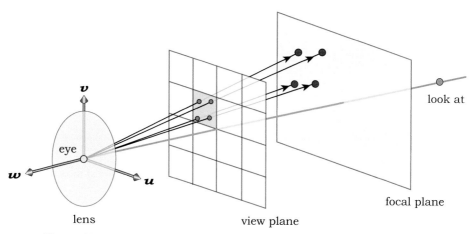

Figure 10.6. Four center rays go through different sample points on a pixel.

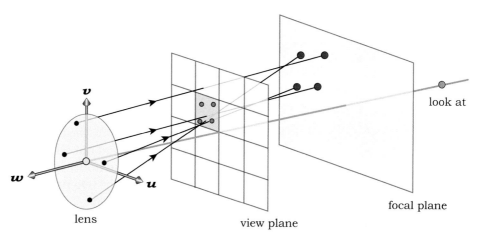

Figure 10.7. Four primary rays that start at sample points on the lens and hit the focal plane at the same points that the center rays in Figure 10.6 hit it.

the top ray does *not* go through the pixel that's being sampled, but that's all right because there's no geometric requirement for that to happen with thin-lens primary rays.

This technique fits in well with the sampling architecture from Chapter 5, where for each pixel, we use the same number of samples for antialiasing and sampling the lens. We can also use different sampling techniques for each, if we want to.

We don't have to trace the center rays to find out where they hit the focal plane. Instead, we can use similar triangles as indicated in Figure 10.8. This

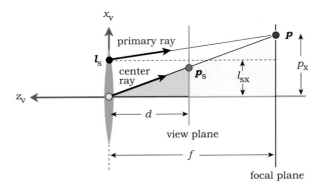

Figure 10.8. Geometry for computing p. The two shaded triangles are similar.

is a projection of the rays and points onto the (x_v, z_v) plane, where the three relevant points are a pixel sample point p_s on the view plane, a sample point l_s on the lens, and the point p on the focal plane. The viewing coordinates of these points are

$$p = (p_x, p_y, -f),$$
$$p_s = (p_{sx}, p_{sy}, -d),$$
$$l_s = (l_{sx}, l_{sy}, 0),$$

where f is the *focal length* of the camera, because this is the distance along the view direction that's in focus, and d is the view-plane distance. These will be user-specified parameters for the thin-lens camera described in Section 10.3.

The x- and y-components of p_s are known quantities, given by Equations (9.4). The x- and y-components of l_s are also known because the sampler object stored in the thin-lens camera returns a sample point on a unit disk, and the x- and y-components are then multiplied by the lens radius (see Listing 10.4). It follows from similar triangles that

$$p_x = p_{sx} \ (f/d) \tag{10.1}$$

and

$$p_y = p_{sy} (f/d). \tag{10.2}$$

The direction of the primary ray is then

$$d_r = p - l_s$$
$$= (p_x - l_{sx})u + (p_y - l_{sy})v - fw. \tag{10.3}$$

As this is not a unit direction, you will have to normalize it before tracing the ray.

10.3 Implementation

The ThinLens camera class is declared in Listing 10.1. Although this has a number of new data members, we don't need to store the number of lens samples because these are accessed in lockstep with the pixel samples.

```
class ThinLens: public Camera {
    public:

        // constructors, access functions, etc

        void
        set_sampler(Sampler* sp);

        Vector3D
        ray_direction(const Point2D& pixel_point, const Point2D&
            lens_point) const;

        virtual void
        render_scene(World& w);

    private:

        float lens_radius;          // lens radius
        float d;                    // view plane distance
        float f;                    // focal plane distance
        float zoom;                 // zoom factor
        Sampler* sampler_ptr;       // sampler object
};
```

Listing 10.1. Declaration of the class ThinLens.

```
void
ThinLens::set_sampler(Sampler* sp) {
    if (sampler_ptr) {
        delete sampler_ptr;
        sampler_ptr = NULL;
    }

    sampler_ptr = sp;
    sampler_ptr->map_samples_to_unit_disk();
}
```

Listing 10.2. The function ThinLens::set_sampler.

```
Vector3D
ThinLens::ray_direction(const Point2D& pixel_point, const Point2D& lens_point)
    const {
        Point2D p;                          // hit point on focal plane
        p.x = pixel_point.x * f / d;
        p.y = pixel_point.y * f / d;

        Vector3D dir = (p.x - lens_point.x) * u + (p.y - lens_point.y) * v - f * w;
        dir.normalize();

        return (dir);
}
```

Listing 10.3. The function `ThinLens::ray_direction`.

In contrast to the function `ViewPlane::set_sampler` in Listing 5.3, the `ThinLens::set_sampler` function in Listing 10.2 doesn't use regular sampling when the number of samples per pixel is one. Instead, their distribution will be determined by the type of sampling object used. The ray origins will be randomly distributed over the surface of the lens when we use random, jittered, and multi-jittered sampling. As a result, the images will become progressively noisier as the lens radius increases. This will, however, quickly show you the depth-of-field effects. See Figure 10.9(b) for an example. Note that `ThinLens::set_sampler` also maps the sample points to the unit disk.

The function `ray_direction` in Listing 10.3 follows directly from Equations (10.1)–(10.3).

Finally, the `ThinLens::render_scene` function in Listing 10.4 illustrates how the pixel and lens sampling work together.

10.4 Results

Listing 10.5 shows part of the build function for the following images. Notice that the pixel size is 0.05, which is much smaller than the default value of 1.0. This is so that we use a view-plane distance (40) that's less than the focal distances used in the images below. All this does, however, is make the camera configuration consistent with the figures in Section 10.2. You need to look at Questions 10.1 and 10.2 and do Exercise 10.2.

Figures 10.9 and 10.10 show three boxes and a plane with checker textures. Figure 10.9(a) shows the scene with everything in focus by using a lens radius of zero. Figure 10.9(b) shows the noisy type of image that results from

```
void
ThinLens::render_scene(World& w) {
    RGBColor L;
    Ray ray;
    ViewPlane vp(w.vp);
    int depth = 0;

    Point2D sp;              // sample point in [0, 1] x [0, 1]
    Point2D pp;              // sample point on a pixel
    Point2D dp;              // sample point on unit disk
    Point2D lp;              // sample point on lens

    w.open_window(vp.hres, vp.vres);
    vp.s /= zoom;

    for (int r = 0; r < vp.vres - 1; r++)              // up
        for (int c = 0; c < vp.hres - 1; c++) {        // across
            L = black;

            for (int n = 0; n < vp.num_samples; n++) {
                sp = vp.sampler_ptr->sample_unit_square();
                pp.x = vp.s * (c - vp.hres / 2.0 + sp.x);
                pp.y = vp.s * (r - vp.vres / 2.0 + sp.y);

                dp = sampler_ptr->sample_unit_disk();
                lp = dp * lens_radius;

                ray.o = eye + lp.x * u + lp.y * v;
                ray.d = ray_direction(pp, lp);
                L += w.tracer_ptr->trace_ray(ray, depth);
            }

            L /= vp.num_samples;
            L *= exposure_time;
            w.display_pixel(r, c, L);
        }
}
```

Listing 10.4. The function ThinLens::render_scene.

using a single multi-jittered sample per pixel and a lens radius of one. Here, the front face of the far box is on the focal plane and is therefore in focus.

Figure 10.10 shows the scene where the camera is focused on the front face of each of the three blocks in turn. Notice how your attention is drawn to the block that's in focus. These images were rendered with a lens size of 1.0. Although the 100 samples per pixel used here is adequate for most parts of these images, there's still noise near the horizon.

```
void
World::build(void) {
    int num_samples = 100;

    vp.set_hres(400);
    vp.set_vres(300);
    vp.set_pixel_size(0.05);
    vp.set_sampler(new MultiJittered(num_samples));
    vp.set_max_depth(0);

    tracer_ptr = new RayCast(this);      // see Section 14.5
    background_color = white;

    Ambient* ambient_ptr = new Ambient;
    ambient_ptr->scale_radiance(0.5);
    set_ambient_light(ambient_ptr);

    ThinLens* thin_lens_ptr = new ThinLens;
    thin_lens_ptr->set_sampler(new MultiJittered(num_samples));
    thin_lens_ptr->set_eye(0, 6, 50);
    thin_lens_ptr->set_lookat(0, 6, 0);
    thin_lens_ptr->set_view_distance(40.0);
    thin_lens_ptr->set_focal_distance(74.0);
    thin_lens_ptr->set_lens_radius(1.0);
    thin_lens_ptr->compute_uvw();
    set_camera(thin_lens_ptr);
    ...
}
```

Listing 10.5. Part of a build function that demonstrates how to construct a thin-lens camera.

(a)   (b)

Figure 10.9. (a) When the lens radius is zero, the image is the same as a pinhole-camera image with everything in focus; (b) noisy image from using one random sample per pixel.

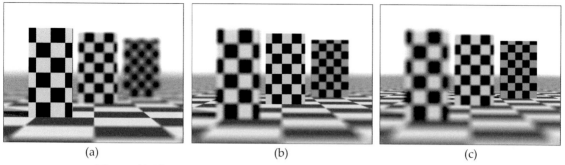

(a)   (b)   (c)

Figure 10.10. Each of these images shows the camera focused on the front face of one of the boxes, where the view plane distance is 40 and the focal distance is 50 (a), 74 (b), and 98 (c).

As the lens size increases, the amount of blurriness in the images increases because the radius of the circle of confusion at a given distance from the focal plane is proportional to the lens radius. The effective depth of field also decreases because the radius of confusion becomes larger than a pixel at a smaller distance from the focal plane. These effects are demonstrated in Figure 10.11(a), which is the same as Figure 10.10(c) but rendered with a lens radius of 3.0. To keep noise to an acceptable level, we usually need to use more samples per pixel as the radius increases.

In Figure 10.11(b), the focal distance is 100000, which is essentially infinity, and as a result, the horizon is the only part of the scene in focus. In this image, the lens diameter is 0.25.

(a)   (b)

Figure 10.11. (a) As the lens radius increases, the image becomes more out of focus, the depth of field decreases, and we require more samples per pixel. This image was also rendered with 100 samples per pixel and is quite noisy; (b) a large value for the focal distance results in the whole image being out of focus except the horizon.

Further Reading

As thin-lens theory is a part of classic geometric optics, most optics textbooks discuss it. See, for example, Hecht (1997).

The landmark paper by Cook et al. (1984) was the first paper to simulate depth of field in ray tracing. This paper also introduced motion blur, soft shadows, glossy reflection, and glossy transmission!

Kolb et al. (1995) used a physically based camera model with a finite-aperture, multi-element thick lens for ray tracing. This is a much more sophisticated camera model than the one discussed here.

Questions

10.1. Is the simulation in Section 10.2 still applicable when the view plane is farther from the lens than the focal plane?

10.2. How do you zoom with a thin-lens camera?

10.3. Figure 10.12 shows a thin box with a mirror material, sitting on a ground plane. The focal plane, which I've added to the scene and rendered in red to make it visible, cuts the ground plane behind the box. The part of the plane that's reflected in the box is therefore not only in front of the focal plane but is actually farther away from it than the box . Why, then, is part of the reflected plane in focus?

Figure 10.12. Mirrored surface.

Figure 10.13. Boxes scene rendered with a lens radius of 1.0 and a single regular sample per pixel.

10.4. Figure 10.13 is the same as Figure 10.9(b), except that it's rendered with one *regular* sample per pixel. Can you explain the result?

 Exercises

10.1. Implement a thin-lens camera as described here and test it with the images in Section 10.4.

10.2. Experiment with different values for the view-plane distance, focal distance, lens radius, and number of samples per pixel. In particular, render some images when the view-plane distance is larger than the focal distance.

10.3. Experiment with different sampling patterns on the lens, including Hammersley sampling.

11   Nonlinear Projections

11.1   **Fisheye Projection**
11.2   **Spherical Panoramic Projection**

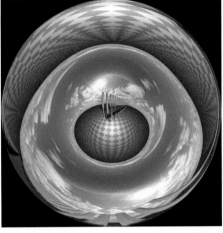

Clouds image courtesy of Phillipe Hurbain

 **Objectives**

By the end of this chapter, you should:

- understand how angular fisheye projection works;
- have implemented a fisheye camera;
- understand how spherical panoramic projection works;
- have implemented a spherical panoramic camera;
- have the tools to produce interesting images using nonlinear projections.

    This chapter highlights one of the many advantages that ray tracing has over other graphics algorithms: it's simple to implement projections that are different from the orthographic and perspective projections discussed in previous chapters. In these projections, the field of view is determined by shooting rays from the eye point through points on the view plane. They are known as linear projections because the projectors are straight lines.

    There are, however, an infinite number of other ways that we can define ray directions at the eye point from sample points on the view plane. These are *nonlinear* projections in which the rays do not go through the view-plane sample points. Provided we can define the ray directions, we can implement a camera based on them.

181

I'll present here two nonlinear projections: a *fisheye* projection and a *spherical panoramic* projection. These both allow us to render the whole scene that surrounds the eye point, a feat that's not possible with perspective or orthographic projections. The resulting images can be surreal and wonderful. But these projections also have important practical applications. For example, fisheye projections are used in planetariums and other immersive viewing environments (see the Further Reading section). Another projection technique that's used for immersive environments is a *cylindrical panoramic* projection, but I've left that as an exercise. Most of the applications of these projections involve real-time animated immersive displays, for which the images in this chapter can't do justice. This chapter will, however, give you an understanding of how two types of nonlinear projections are implemented in ray tracing.

 ## 11.1 Fisheye Projection

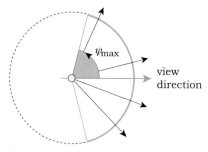

11.1.1 Theory

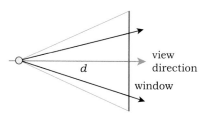

Figure 11.1. Cross section of a fisheye projection with some sample rays.

A fisheye projection uses a view volume that's an infinite circular cone with apex at the eye point and centered on the view direction. Figure 11.1 shows a cross section of part of a view volume that's inside a unit sphere centered on the eye point. The half angle of the cone $\psi_{max} \in [0, 180°]$ defines the field of view (*fov*), where the value $\psi_{max} = 180°$ provides the full 360° field of view around the eye point.[1] Within the cone, rays can be shot in any direction. In other words, we can regard the rays as being shot through the surface of a sphere.

For comparison, Figure 11.2 shows a perspective projection in cross section where the field of view is determined by the size of the window and its distance from the eye point. Rays are shot through the window.

A fisheye projection differs from this in two ways. First, only pixels in a circular disk centered on the window have rays associated with them. Second, the field of view is independent of the location and size of the window.

Figure 11.2. In perspective projection, the field of view is determined by the window size and its distance from the eye point.

---

1. This is a 4π steradian view in solid angle.

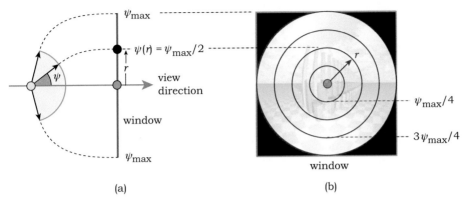

Figure 11.3. (a) In a fisheye projection, the field of view is independent of the size of the window and its distance from the eye point; (b) only pixels in a disk centered on the window have rays traced.

Figure 11.3(a) shows a cross section of a fisheye projection and a window. For a given point on the window, we compute the angle ψ that its ray makes with the viewing direction. This will only be a function of the straight-line distance r between the point and the center of the window. As a result, concentric circles around the center of the window map to constant values of ψ (see Figure 11.3(b)). The value ψ is 0 in the middle of the window, and the edge of the disk is mapped to ψ_{max}. We therefore only render square images and only trace rays for pixels in the disk, but see Exercise 11.10. The viewing geometry is rotationally symmetric about the view direction. The key point here is that the ray directions are not constrained by the straight-line geometry that connects the eye and pixel points in linear projections; instead, rays are only associated with pixel points by a mathematical expression that we devise.

Although we can specify how ψ varies with r any way we want to, the fisheye projection I'll discuss here has ψ proportional to r, as this is the simplest technique (see Equation (11.3)). Figure 11.4 shows two special cases of this fisheye projection in cross section. Figure 11.4(a) shows a 180° ($\psi_{max} = 90°$) projection, while Figure 11.4(b) shows a 360° ($\psi_{max} = 180°$) projection. The dashed lines simply associate points on the window with ray directions; their shapes don't mean anything.

For each sample point on the view plane, we perform the following tasks:

- compute the distance r;
- if the pixel is inside the disk, compute $\psi(r)$;
- compute the ray direction in world coordinates.

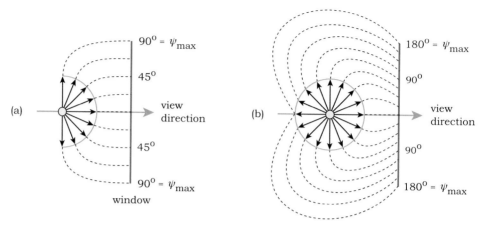

Figure 11.4. Schematic relationship between points on the view-plane window and fisheye-camera ray directions: (a) 180° view; (b) 360° view.

To carry out these tasks, we first transform the view-plane coordinates of a sample point $(x_p, y_p) \in [-sh_{res}/2, -sv_{res}/2] \times [sh_{res}/2, sv_{res}/2]$ to *normalized device coordinates*, $(x_n, y_n) \in [-1, +1] \times [-1, +1]$.[2] (see Figure 11.5). I've drawn Figure 11.5(a) with $h_{res} \neq v_{res}$, because a variation of the fisheye projection allows us to render rectangular images, and so does spherical panoramic projection. Both projection techniques use the transformation to normalized device coordinates. The transformation equations are

$$x_n = \frac{2}{sh_{res}} x_p,$$
$$y_n = \frac{2}{sv_{res}} y_p. \tag{11.1}$$

See Exercise 11.1. We next check that the square of the distance from the origin satisfies

$$r^2 = x_n^2 + y_n^2 \leq 1.0, \tag{11.2}$$

and if this is satisfied, we compute ψ with

$$\psi(r) = r\psi_{max}. \tag{11.3}$$

To compute the ray direction in world coordinates, we use Equations (11.1) and (11.3), with the orthonormal basis of the fisheye camera. Although the

---

2. Normalized device coordinates can also be defined as $(x_n, y°) \times [0, 1]^2$.

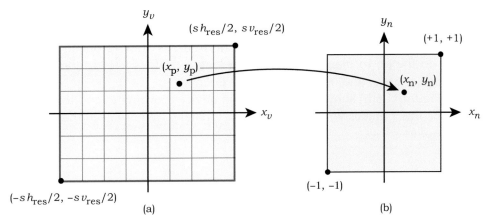

Figure 11.5. (a) View-plane coordinates; (b) normalized device coordinates.

$(\mathbf{u}, \mathbf{v}, \mathbf{w})$ vectors have the same orientation as a pinhole camera, the calculation of the ray direction is quite different. This is because we don't have the coordinates $(x_p, y_p, -d)$ to work with as in perspective projection; instead, we have to work with angles. The angles are also different from the standard spherical coordinate angles discussed in Chapter 2. For example, ψ is measured from the view direction $(-\mathbf{w})$.

I've illustrated how to compute the ray direction $\mathbf{d}$ with three 2D diagrams in Figure 11.6. I've also made the ray direction a unit vector from the

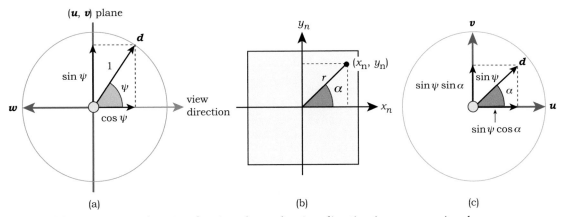

Figure 11.6. (a) A unit ray direction $\mathbf{d}$ projected onto the view direction (orange arrow) and onto the $(\mathbf{u}, \mathbf{v})$ plane (the vertical cyan line); (b) the (x_n, y_n)-coordinates determine the angle α that r makes with the $\mathbf{u}$-direction when it's projected onto the $(\mathbf{u}, \mathbf{v})$-plane; (c) the projections of $\mathbf{d}$ onto the $\mathbf{u}$- and $\mathbf{v}$-directions.

start to simplify the calculations. This places the vector ends on a unit sphere centered on the eye point. Figure 11.6(a) shows the projections of the ray onto the view direction and the (u, v) plane. This figure is drawn from an arbitrary point on the (u, v) plane. The projected length of the vector in the viewing direction is $\cos \psi$, and on the (u, v) plane is $\sin \psi$.

Figure 11.6(b) shows the normalized device coordinates and the angle α that the line r makes with the x_n-axis. Fortunately, we only need the sine and cosine of α:

$$\sin \alpha = y_n/r,$$
$$\cos \alpha = x_n/r.$$

Figure 11.6(c) shows the projections of d onto the (u, v) plane, where from Figure 11.6(a), the vector's length is foreshortened to $\sin \psi$. We can now write the expression for d:

$$d = \sin \psi \cos \alpha \, u + \sin \psi \sin \alpha \, v - \cos \psi \, w. \tag{11.4}$$

Note that this is a unit vector by construction (see Exercise 11.7).

11.1.2 Implementation

The fisheye projection is implemented with a Fisheye camera, whose class declaration appears in Listing 11.1. The only new data member is psi_max.
The FishEye::render_scene function appears in Listing 11.2.

```
class Fisheye: public Camera {
    public:

        // constructors, etc.

        Vector3D
        ray_direction(const Point2D& p, const int hres,
            const int vres, const float s, float& r) const;

        virtual void
        render_scene(World& w);

    private:

        float psi_max;              // in degrees
};
```

Listing 11.1. Declaration of the camera class FishEye.

```
void
FishEye::render_scene(World& wr) {
    RGBColor L;
    ViewPlane vp(wr.vp);
    int hres = vp.hres;
    int vres = vp.vres;
    float s = vp.s;
    Ray ray;
    int depth = 0;
    Point2D sp;              // sample point in [0, 1] x [0, 1]
    Point2D pp;              // sample point on the pixel
    float r_squared;         // sum of squares of normalized device
    coordinates

    wr.open_window(vp.hres, vp.vres);
    ray.o = eye;

    for (int r = 0; r < vres; r++)           // up
        for (int c = 0; c < hres; c++) {     // across
            L = black;

            for (int j = 0; j < vp.num_samples; j++) {
                sp = vp.sampler_ptr->sample_unit_square();
                pp.x = s * (c - 0.5 * hres + sp.x);
                pp.y = s * (r - 0.5 * vres + sp.y);
                ray.d = ray_direction(pp, hres, vres, s, r_squared);

                if (r_squared <= 1.0)
                    L += wr.tracer_ptr->trace_ray(ray, depth);
            }

            L /= vp.num_samples;
            L *= exposure_time;
            wr.display_pixel(r, c, L);
        }
}
```

Listing 11.2. The function FishEye::render_scene.

The function ray_direction in Listing 11.3 computes the ray direction according to the theory presented in Section 11.1.1. Note that this function also returns the square of the normalized device coordinates and that the render_scene function only traces the ray when Equation (11.2) is satisfied.

The user interface of the fisheye camera doesn't specify ψ_{max} directly but instead allows users to specify a field of view = $2\psi_{max}$. This is more intuitive because, for example, if we want to render a 360° view, we can specify the field of view as 360° in the build function.

```
Vector3D
FishEye::ray_direction( const Point2D& pp, const int hres, const int
                        vres, const float s, float& r_squared) const {

    // compute the normalized device coordinates

    Point2D pn(2.0 / (s * hres) * pp.x, 2.0 / (s * vres) * pp.y);
    r_squared = pn.x * pn.x + pn.y * pn.y;

    if (r_squared <= 1.0) {
        float r          = sqrt(r_squared);
        float psi        = r * psi_max * PI_ON_180;
        float sin_psi    = sin(psi);
        float cos_psi    = cos(psi);
        float sin_alpha  = pn.y / r;
        float cos_alpha  = pn.x / r;
        Vector3D dir     = sin_psi * cos_alpha * u +  sin_psi
                              * sin_alpha * v - cos_psi * w;

        return (dir);
    }
    else
        return (Vector3D(0.0));
}
```

Listing 11.3. The function `FishEye::ray_direction`.

11.1.3 Results

Now we can have some fun. Figure 11.7(a) shows a perspective view of the boxes from Chapter 9 with the green boxes increased in height, and a sky-dome with clouds.[3] The scene is rendered with a pinhole camera looking horizontally.

Figure 11.7(b)–(d) show the scene rendered with a fisheye camera that has the same eye and look-at points as the pinhole camera. The angle ψ_{max} ranges from 60° in Figure 11.7(b) to 180° in Figure 11.7(d), which is the 360° view. An obvious fact from these images is that the fisheye projection doesn't preserve straight lines, although some of the lines are straight (see Question 11.3).

Figure 11.7(e) shows another 360° view, this time with the camera looking in a downwards direction. Finally, Figure 11.7(f) shows the sky with the

---

3. The clouds result from a spherical projection of an image onto a large sphere (radius 1000000), but it's not a light source (see Chapter 29).

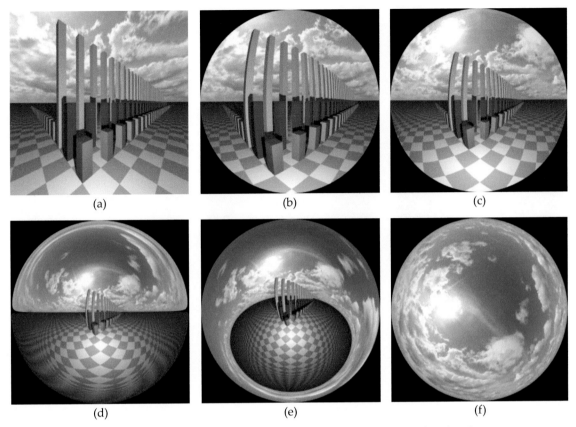

Figure 11.7. Various views of rectangular boxes, a checker plane, and clouds rendered with a pinhole camera (a) and a fisheye camera in (b)–(e). The fisheye camera uses the following values for the *fov*: (b) 120°; (c) 180°; (d) 360°; (e) 360°; (f) 180°.

camera looking vertically up, $\psi_{\max} = 90°$, and no boxes. Real cameras with circular fisheye lenses can take photographs like this.

Figure 11.8 shows three views of the Uffizi Gallery buildings in Florence, Italy. Here, the only object in the scene is the cloud sphere in Figure 11.7 with the clouds replaced by the Uffizi image. This is based on one of Paul Debevec's high dynamic light probe images at http://www.debevec.org/Probes, with a light probe mapping to render the scene. The camera is near the center of the sphere. I'll discuss the light probe mapping in Chapter 29.

As an example of how fisheye projections can be used for scientific visualization, Figure 11.9 shows photographs of an immersive dome that uses fisheye projections. This is in the Western Austalian Supercomputer Program (WASP) at the University of Western Australia.

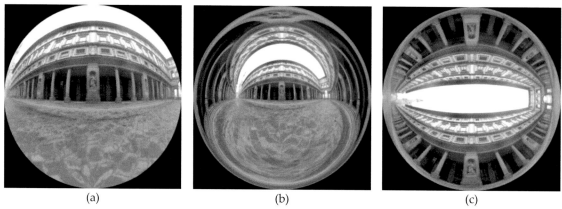

Figure 11.8. Three views of the Uffizi Gallery buildings: (a) *fov* = 180°; (b) *fov* = 360°; (c) looking up, *fov* = 100°. The Uffizi Gallery image is courtesy of Paul Debevec.

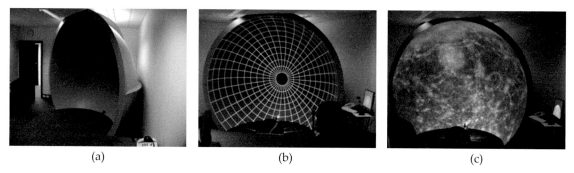

Figure 11.9. Immersive dome: (a) angle view; (b) grid test image; (c) cosmological simulation by Paul Burke. These images are from the website http://local.wasp.uwa.edu.au/~pbourke/exhibition/domeinstall/. Photographs courtesy of Paul Burke.

11.2 Spherical Panoramic Projection

11.2.1 Theory

A spherical panoramic projection is similar to a fisheye projection, but it has one major difference. We use the normalized device coordinates of a pixel point to define separate angles λ in the azimuth direction and ψ in the polar direction instead of a single radial angle. Figure 11.9 illustrates these angles, which are used to define the primary ray directions. The angle λ is in the (u, w) plane, and is measured *counterclockwise* from the view direction. The angle ψ is measured *up* from the (u, w) plane in a vertical plane. As such, λ and ψ have a simple relationship with the standard spherical coordinate angles θ and ϕ, also shown in Figure 11.10. The expressions are

$$\phi = \pi - \lambda \,,$$

$$\theta = \pi/2 - \psi.$$
(11.5)

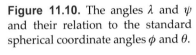

We define ψ and λ as linear functions of the normalized device coordinates x_n and y_n as follows:

$$\lambda = x_n \, \lambda_{max} ,$$

$$\psi = y_n \, \psi_{max} .$$

Figure 11.10. The angles λ and ψ and their relation to the standard spherical coordinate angles ϕ and θ.

These result in $(\lambda, \psi) \in [-\lambda_{max}, \lambda_{max}] \times [-\psi_{max}, \psi_{max}]$, where $\lambda_{max} = 180°$ and $\psi_{max} = 90°$ give the full $360° \times 180°$ field of view. The general *fov* is defined as $2\lambda_{max} \times 2\psi_{max}$.

By relating λ and ψ to the standard spherical coordinate angles in Equation (11.5), we can use Equations (2.3) with $r = 1$ to write the ray direction as

$$d = \sin \theta \sin \phi \, u + \cos \theta \, v + \sin \theta \cos \phi \, w. \qquad (11.6)$$

This is a unit vector by construction.

11.2.2 Implementation

The camera class that implements the spherical panoramic projection is just called `Spherical`. Listing 11.4 shows the implementation of the function `Spherical::ray_direction`. I won't reproduce the spherical camera's `render_scene` function here, as the only difference between it and the fisheye's function is the absence of the r^2 factor.

The user interface of the `Spherical` camera allows the user to specify the horizontal and vertical *fov* angles separately.

11.2.3 Results

Images rendered with a spherical camera must have their aspect ratio equal to λ_{max}/ψ_{max}, otherwise the images will be distorted. Figure 11.11(a) shows a city modeled with random axis-aligned boxes and rendered with an *fov* of $84° \times 56°$ at a pixel resolution of 600×400. Figure 11.11(b) is rendered with a view that shows the horizon.

```
Vector3D
Spherical::ray_direction(    const Point2D&  pp,
                             const int       hres,
                             const int       vres,
                             const float     s   ) const {

    // compute the normalized device coordinates

    Point2D pn( 2.0 / (s * hres) * pp.x, 2.0 / (s * vres) * pp.y);

    // compute the angles lambda and phi in radians

    float lambda = pn.x * lambda_max * PI_ON_180;
    float psi = pn.y * psi_max * PI_ON_180;

    // compute the spherical azimuth and polar angles

    float phi       = PI - lambda;
    float theta     = 0.5 * PI - psi;

    float sin_phi   = sin(phi);
    float cos_phi   = cos(phi);
    float sin_theta = sin(theta);
    float cos_theta = cos(theta);

    Vector3D dir    = sin_theta * sin_phi * u +  cos_theta* v
                    + sin_theta * cos_phi * w;

    return (dir);
}
```

Listing 11.4. The function Spherical::ray_direction.

Figure 11.12 shows two views of the city with the camera above the central park and looking horizontally. Note that in these images, the vertical building edges are vertical straight lines, and the horizon is horizontal. This is a property of spherical projection images, but only when the camera looks horizontally. You should compare these images with Figure 11.11. In Figure 11.12(a), the *fov* = 180° × 120°. Figure 11.12(b) is rendered with the full view in each direction, *fov* = 360° × 180°. Such images must be rendered with an aspect ratio of 2.0.

Figure 11.13 shows the Uffizi buildings rendered with *fov* = 360° × 180°.

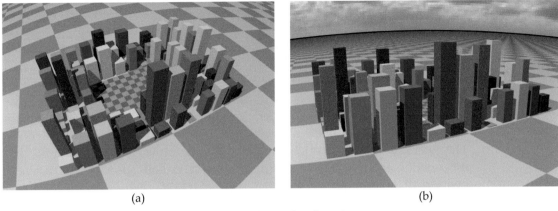

Figure 11.11. Two views of a random box city.

Figure 11.12. Camera above the park rendered with $fov = 180° \times 120°$ (a) and $fov = 360° \times 180°$ (b).

Figure 11.13. Full $360° \times 180°$ spherical projection view of the Uffizi Gallery buildings with the view direction horizontal. The Uffizi Gallery image is courtesy of Paul Debevec.

Further Reading

The best place to read about the material in this chapter is Paul Burke's wonderful website at http://local.wasp.uwa.edu.au/~pbourke/. Section 11.1.1 is based on material in http://local.wasp.uwa.edu.au/~pbourke/projection/fisheye/. This website also discusses different types of projections. The website http://local.wasp.uwa.edu.au/~pbourke/exhibition/domeinstall/ has photographs of numerous spherical dome installations that use fisheye projections. The website http://www.icinema.unsw.edu.au/projects/infra_avie.html has information about a state-of-the-art immersive visualization system that uses cylindrical panoramic projection.

Paul Debevec's website at http://www.debevec.org/ and the links on this site have a large amount of information on high dynamic range imagery and light probes. The clouds image can be found on Phillipe Hurbain's website at http://www.philohome.com/skycollec.htm.

 Questions

11.1. Can you have a 180° field of view with perspective projection? If you could, would it be useful?

11.2. How do you zoom with the fisheye camera?

11.3. Which straight lines are preserved in fisheye projections?

11.4. How do you zoom with the spherical panoramic camera? Is it different from zooming with the fisheye camera?

 Exercises

11.1. Verify that Equations (11.1) are correct.

11.2. Implement the fisheye camera as described in this chapter.

11.3. Reproduce images similar to those in Figure 11.7. I've stored the boxes in a regular grid acceleration scheme (Chapter 22), but you can use fewer boxes, a matte material on the plane, and a non-black background color instead of the clouds. Experiment with different view directions, for example, with the camera angled up and looking straight down.

11.4. Implement a view direction as part of the user interface for the fisheye and spherical panoramic cameras. For wide-angle views, you may find this more useful than specifying a look-at point.

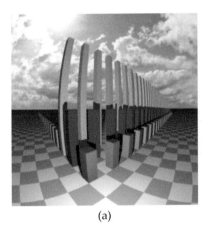
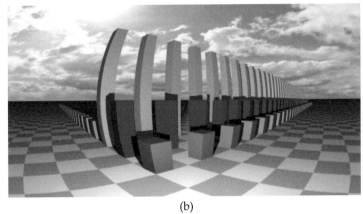

(a)   (b)

Figure 11.14. (a) Square fisheye image; (b) distorted rectangular fisheye image.

11.5.   Experiment with other functions $\psi(r)$.

11.6.   Because this is ray tracing, the *fov* for the fisheye camera is not restricted to the range *fov* $\in [0, 360°]$; we can set any limits on the *fov* that we like. Experiment with values outside this range; in particular, try *fov* = $n \times 360°$, with $n = 2, 3, 4, ...$

11.7.   Prove that the ray direction in Equation (11.4) is a unit vector.

11.8.   Take one of the square fisheye images, which have all been rendered at 600×600 pixels, and render it with a different pixel resolution. Notice what happens to the image. The images have also been rendered with a pixel size of one, so vary that too and see what happens. Can you explain the results?

11.9.   Prove that the ray direction in Equation (11.6) is a unit vector.

11.10. You can render square fisheye images by rendering all of the pixels. To do this, you just ignore the $r^2 < 1.0$ inequality (11.2) in the render_scene and ray_direction functions. Figure 11.14(a) shows the scene in Figure 11.7(b) rendered in this manner, but you have to be careful with wide-angled views. If $\psi_{\max} > 180/\sqrt{2}$, ψ will exceed 360° towards the corners of the square. You will also have to be careful with rectangular images. Figure 11.14(b) shows what will happen if you render the same scene with a pixel resolution of 600×300 pixels. Notice how everything is squashed in the vertical direction.

Figure 11.15 shows how Figure 11.14(b) should look. See if you can get the fisheye camera to render rectangular images without the distortion. *Hint*: one way to do this is to map the normalized device coordinates to

Figure 11.15. Undistorted rectangular fisheye image.

a rectangle that has the same aspect ratio as the image and just fits into the disk in Figure 11.3(b).

11.11. Implement the Spherical camera and use Figures 11.11 and 11.12 for testing it. The boxes in this scene are randomly generated, and although I've seeded rand() in the build function, you may get different boxes, even with the same seed.

11.12. Render Figure 11.12 with the camera angled up or down and observe what happens to the vertical box edges.

11.13. Render spherical panoramic images with the horizontal *fov* > 360° and the vertical *fov* > 180°.

11.14. Implement a camera that renders cylindrical panoramic projections. This type of projection has a limited *fov* in the vertical direction but allows a 360° horizontal *fov*. In contrast to spherical panoramic projections, these have wide applications in immersive cylindrical viewing environments (see the Further Reading section).

12 Stereoscopy

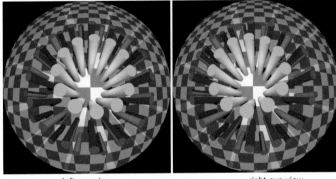

left-eye view   right-eye view

 Objectives

By the end of this chapter, you should:

- understand what stereoscopy is;
- understand how we can produce stereo pairs with ray tracing;
- have implemented a stereo camera.

This is a fun chapter whose material is not strictly necessary for the following chapters. Most readers will need a stereoscope to view the images in this chapter, but not everyone can see in stereo.

Stereoscopy is the phenomenon of seeing in three dimensions. It exists because our left and right eyes see slightly different views of the world around us, which leads to *binocular disparity*. This is the difference between the images projected onto our left and right retinas, and it's responsible for the stereo effect when our visual cortex fuses the two views into a single image. The stereo effect is one of our strongest depth cues, although not everyone can see in stereo. Stereoscopy is also of major benefit in many areas of visualization because the stereo effect provides depth information that is often not present in single images.

I'll discuss here the use of *stereo pairs* for creating stereoscopic images, where a stereo pair consists of the left and right images displayed on a flat surface. These are viewed in such a way that our visual cortex can fuse them into a single acceptable stereo image. This is not an ideal way to present stereo images, because it differs from the way we view the real world. In real viewing, we use a combination of visual clues for depth perception. These include perspective viewing, object occlusion, shadows, lighting, and the relative motion of objects when we move our heads. An additional clue is *accommodation*, where we change the focal length of our eyes in order to focus at a particular depth. Another clue is *convergence*, where we rotate each eye so that it's facing the focal point. If any of these cues are inconsistent, the images may be uncomfortable and tiring to view, or we may not be able to fuse them. With stereo pairs, binocular disparity and convergence are consistent, but the accommodation is inconsistent, because both images are flat. As it turns out, we can tolerate a certain amount of inconsistency and still get good stereo images, provided we're careful about how we generate the stereo pairs (see Section 12.2).

In this chapter, I'll explain how ray tracing can generate the left- and right-eye views of scenes and display the resulting images side-by-side for viewing with a stereoscope. The images can be rendered using pinhole, thin-lens, fisheye, spherical-panoramic, and cylindrical-panoramic cameras. In Chapters 24 and 28, I'll use stereo pairs to help explain certain properties of reflections and transparency that are difficult to see without stereoscopy.

12.1 Parallax

To generate stereo pairs, we need left and right cameras separated by a distance called the *camera separation*.[1] When a point is projected onto a view plane with both cameras, its two projections are displaced from each other in the direction of the line that joins the cameras. This is known as *parallax* and can be positive, negative, or zero, depending on where the point is located relative to the cameras and the view plane. As you'll see below, parallax is an important quantity for the formation of stereo images.

To help explain the processes involved in stereo-pair production, Figures 12.1–12.5, 12.7, and 12.10 are top-down views of the camera locations and the view plane.

Figure 12.1 illustrates the case where the point is behind the view plane relative to the cameras. Here, the left projection is on the left, and the right projection is on the right, if we are looking towards the view plane from the

---

1. For our eyes, this is known as the *interocular distance*.

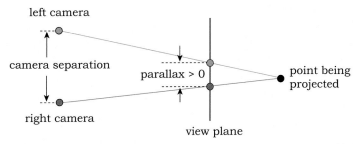

Figure 12.1. When a point being projected is behind the view plane, the parallax is positive.

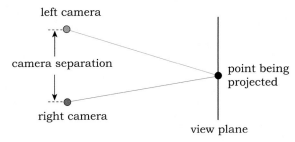

Figure 12.2. When a point being projected is on the view plane, the parallax is zero.

cameras' side. In this case, the parallax is positive. When rendered, all points with positive parallax will appear behind the screen.

Figure 12.2 shows a point being projected that's on the view plane, where the parallax is zero. In stereo viewing, the view plane is also called the *plane of zero parallax*. When rendered, points on this plane will appear at screen depth.

Figure 12.3 shows a point that's in front of the view plane. Here, the left projection is on the right, the right projection is on the left, and the parallax is

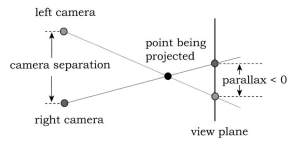

Figure 12.3. When a point is in front of the view plane, the parallax is negative.

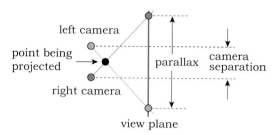

Figure 12.4. As the point moves closer to the camera's line, the parallax increases without limit.

negative. When rendered, all points with negative parallax will appear in front of the screen.

Unlike positive parallax, which is always finite (see Question 12.1), negative parallax becomes unlimited as the projected point approaches the cameras. Figure 12.4 shows an example of negative parallax that's larger than the camera separation.

Parallax is the flat-surface version of the 3D binocular disparity and therefore creates the stereo effect when we fuse the stereo pairs. Its sign and size determines the apparent distance of objects from our eyes in the resulting stereo image. When we look at a stereo pair on a computer screen, the view plane is on the screen because that's where the pixels are. Objects that pop out from the screen produce a more dramatic stereo effect but can be more tiring to look at and difficult to fuse. For perspective stereoscopic viewing, we can use the view-plane distance to control which part of a scene will appear at screen depth, because this determines the location of the view plane. When we look at printed stereo pairs, the paper takes the place of the computer screen.

12.2 Camera Arrangements

How do we set up the two cameras for stereo viewing? There are a number of arrangements that produce stereo pairs, but not all of them are strictly correct. Because of convergence, you might think that using the same look-at point for each camera would give good results. After all, that's the way our eyes work. Figure 12.5 shows this arrangement, which is known as *toe-in*. This figure also shows the symmetric view frustum for each camera, where the window is centered on the view direction. This is the same type of frustum that the pinhole camera uses. Each camera has distinct view planes (and windows).

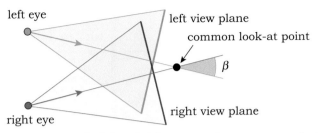

Figure 12.5. With toe-in, the left and right cameras have a common look-at point.

Let's consider an object that's centered on the common look-at point and think about how the left and right cameras will render it. The only way the views will differ is that the object will appear to be rotated through the angle β shown in Figure 12.5. The apparent rotation is about a line through the look-at point and perpendicular to the plane defined by the eye points and the look-at point. Figure 12.6 shows perspective views of a vertical triangle that's rotated about the y_w-axis. Because of the properties of perspective projection, two things happen to the triangle as it rotates. The projected length of the vertical edge changes, and therefore the angle that the other two edges make with the horizontal also changes. These introduce *vertical parallax* in the images. This is something to avoid, because it can make the stereo pairs difficult to fuse, particularly for non-vertical lines.

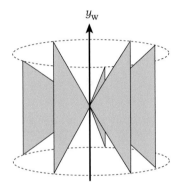

Figure 12.6. In perspective viewing, the projected height of a vertical triangle varies as it rotates about the y_w-axis.

Figure 12.7 illustrates a better way to render stereo pairs for perspective viewing, where the camera arrangements are as follows:

- Each camera has its own look-at point, arranged so that the view directions are parallel. The look-at points are therefore the same distance apart as the eye points.[2]
- The two view planes are coincident.
- The two windows are also coincident, which requires the cameras to use *asymmetric* view frustums.

With an asymmetric view frustum, the z_v-axis does not go through the center of the window. As a result, the frustum defined by the eye and the four corners of the window is no longer symmetric. A physical model for changing

---

2. This makes the eye points and look-at points coplanar.

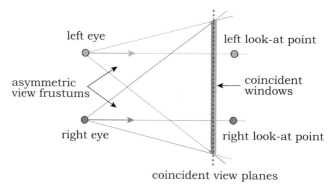

Figure 12.7. Correct camera arrangement for rendering stereo pairs with two look-at points, parallel view directions, coincident view planes and windows, and asymmetric view frustums.

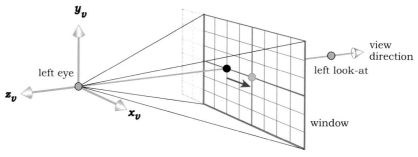

Figure 12.8. The window used by the left camera is translated in the positive x_v-direction, as indicated by the red arrow.

a symmetric frustum to an asymmetric frustum is to translate the window over the view plane. To produce stereo pairs, we only need a special case of this, where we translate the view plane in the x_v-direction. For the left camera, as shown in Figure 12.8, the translation is in the *positive* x_v-direction by half the camera separation. For the right camera, the translation is in the *negative* x_v-direction by the same amount (see Exercise 12.3).

These camera arrangements are for pinhole and thin-lens cameras. The fisheye and panoramic cameras use separate look-at points as above but use symmetric view frustums (see Section 12.6).

Photographic stereo pairs are captured in exactly the same way as described here, using one or two cameras with a toe-in or a parallel setup. Figure 12.11 is an example from a single translated camera with parallel viewing.

12.3 The Stereo Camera

My stereo camera inherits from the Camera class and therefore has its own eye point and look-at point, as well as sharing the other Camera data members. The difference is that the stereo camera also encapsulates the left- and right-eye cameras, which do the actual rendering. I use the stereo camera's eye and look-at points and its **up** vector to construct its (u, v, w) orthonormal basis in the usual way. I then use these vectors and the camera separation to construct the left- and right-eye cameras (see Figure 12.9 and the code in Section 12.5). In this arrangement, the left- and right-eye cameras are displaced in the stereo camera's x_v-direction, and their corresponding u, v, and w basis vectors are parallel.

When rendering stereo pairs, I normally use the default up vector (and a zero roll angle) so that the line through the left- and right-camera eye points is horizontal. Stereo pairs produced with a nonzero roll angle can be difficult to fuse (see Exercise 12.5).

Of course, the left and right eye points aren't defined until we specify the camera separation, but instead of specifying this as a distance, I use the *stereo separation angle β*, as illustrated in Figure 12.10. Here, $β$ is the angle subtended at the stereo camera's look-at point by the left- and right-camera eye points.

In Figure 12.10, x is half the camera separation, and the distance r between e and l is

$$r = \|e - l\|.$$

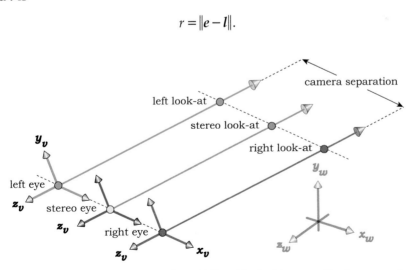

Figure 12.9. The stereo camera is in the middle with the blue coordinate axes and orange view direction. The left and right eye points are displaced along the stereo camera's x_v-axis, which is horizontal.

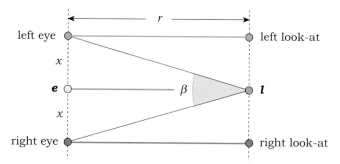

Figure 12.10. The stereo separation angle β is defined by the left and right eye points and the look-at point.

It follows from simple trigonometry that

$$x = r \tan (\beta/2).$$

 ## 12.4 Stereo-Pair Display and Viewing

There are numerous techniques for displaying computer-sourced stereo pairs. These all employ a mechanism that presents the correct image to each eye. One technique alternates the left and right images on a computer screen, and the viewer wears glasses with synchronized left- and right-eye shutters. A disadvantage of this technique is that the glasses must be connected to the computer, which limits the number of people who can view the imagery and where they can view it from. Another technique projects the left and right images simultaneously onto a screen that preserves the polarization. The projectors have polarizing filters fitted, and the viewers wear passive polarized glasses. This technique can be used for projection onto flat screens using perspective projection, spherical domes using fisheye projections, and cylinders using cylindrical panoramic projections. It's also used in movie theatres. Because the glasses are not connected to the computer, large numbers of people can be accommodated. A disadvantage of these techniques is the requirement for special hardware and viewing setups. The Further Reading section has references about these and other techniques.

The simplest technique, however, is to just display them side-by-side on your computer screen, or print them side-by-side. There are also several ways that they can be fused. In principle, the simplest way is unassisted, where each eye focuses on the correct image. In practice, few people can do this. Most

| (a) left-eye view | (b) right-eye view | (c) left-eye view |

Figure 12.11. Stereo pair arranged for parallel viewing in (a) and (b) and transverse viewing in (b) and (c). Photographs by Kevin Suffern.

people need some form of assistance, for example, a stereoscope. The great advantage that this has over other techniques is that it requires no specialized computer hardware and is therefore inexpensive.

In unassisted viewing, the stereo pairs can be viewed in two ways. One is called *parallel viewing*, where the left-eye image is displayed on the left and the right-eye image on the right. Figure 12.11(a) and (b) is an example. The other way is *transverse viewing*, where the left-eye image is on the right and the right-eye image is on the left. This is illustrated with Figure 12.11(b) and (c).

Size matters for parallel viewing, where in general, the images should be no larger than about 5 cm across for unassisted viewing. If they are larger than this, they can be difficult or impossible to fuse. There are no such size restrictions for transverse viewing. Stereoscopes use parallel viewing, where the particular stereoscope model determines the maximum size of the images. All stereo pairs in this chapter will be displayed as left-right-left images.

12.5 Implementation

Although a stereo camera isn't difficult to implement, there are a couple of things that you need to be careful with. Listing 12.1 shows the declaration of the StereoCamera class in which the left and right cameras are pointers. This allows us to use any type of cameras and provides much flexibility for rendering stereo pairs. The data member viewing allows us to specify parallel or transverse viewing when the ray tracer displays the images. You will see how this and the pixel_gap data member work in the following listings.

```
typedef enum {
    parallel,
    transverse
} ViewingType;

class StereoCamera: public Camera {
    public:

        // constructors, etc.

        void
        setup_cameras(void);

        virtual void
        render_scene(World& w);

    private:

        ViewingType viewing;             // specifies type of viewing
        int pixel_gap;                   // gap in pixels between images
        float beta;                      // stereo separation angle
        Camera* left_camera_ptr;         // left eye camera
        Camera* right_camera_ptr;        // right eye camera
};
```

Listing 12.1. The StereoCamera class declaration.

To demonstrate how to construct a stereo camera that uses pinhole cameras, Listing 12.2 displays part of the build function for the images in Figure 12.12.

Although it's the stereo camera's responsibility to set up the left- and right-eye cameras using the setup_cameras function shown in Listing 12.3, this function can only set parameters that are common to all camera types. This is why the build function in Listing 12.2 has to specify the view-plane distance for the left and right pinhole cameras; orthographic, fisheye, and panoramic cameras don't have a view-plane distance. Because we have set up the stereo camera's (u, v, w) basis vectors before we call the function setup_cameras, it's simple for this function to compute the locations of the left and right eye points and look-at points.

The stereo camera's render_scene function differs in a number of ways from the render_scene functions of the other cameras:

- The window it opens must be wide enough to display the left and right images plus the pixel gap that separates them. This gap is helpful when you

```
...
float vpd = 100;          // view-plane distance

Pinhole* left_camera_ptr = new Pinhole;
left_camera_ptr->set_view_distance(vpd);

Pinhole* right_camera_ptr = new Pinhole;
right_camera_ptr->set_view_distance(vpd);

StereoCamera* stereo_ptr = new StereoCamera;
stereo_ptr->set_left_camera(left_camera_ptr);
stereo_ptr->set_right_camera(right_camera_ptr);
stereo_ptr->use_parallel_viewing();
//stereo_ptr->use_transverse_viewing();
stereo_ptr->set_pixel_gap(5);          // in pixels
stereo_ptr->set_eye(5, 0, 100);
stereo_ptr->set_lookat(0);
stereo_ptr->compute_uvw();
stereo_ptr->set_stereo_angle(0.75); // in degrees
stereo_ptr->setup_cameras();
set_camera(stereo_ptr);
...
```

Listing 12.2. Part of the build function for Figure 12.12.

```
void
StereoCamera::setup_cameras(void) {
    double r = eye.distance(lookat);
    double x = r * tan(0.5 * beta * PI_ON_180);   // half the camera
                                                  // separation

    left_camera_ptr->set_eye(eye - x * u);
    left_camera_ptr->set_lookat(lookat - x * u);
    left_camera_ptr->compute_uvw();

    right_camera_ptr->set_eye(eye + x * u);
    right_camera_ptr->set_lookat(lookat + x * u);
    right_camera_ptr->compute_uvw();
}
```

Listing 12.3. The function `StereoCamera::setup_cameras`.

are trying to fuse the images because it visibly separates them. Although the stereo-pair figures in this chapter show two copies of the left-camera view, the stereo camera only renders a single view for each camera.

- It calculates half the camera separation for setting up the asymmetric view frustums.
- It decides whether to display the images for parallel or transverse viewing.
- It gets the left and right cameras to do the actual rendering but *not* by calling their render_scene functions. These functions won't work here because they also open a window, and they use symmetric view frustums. Instead, it calls a new virtual function render_stereo, defined for each type of camera that we want use for stereo-pair production.

Listing 12.4 shows the stereo camera's render_scene function.

The render_stereo functions differ from the render_scene functions in three ways:

- They don't open a window.
- They use an asymmetric view frustum.
- They offset the pixels when they draw the image that's in the right half of the window.

```
void
StereoCamera::render_scene(World& w) {
    ViewPlane vp = w.vp;
    int hres = vp.hres;
    int vres = vp.vres;

    w.open_window(2 * hres + pixel_gap, vres);

    double r = eye.distance(lookat);
    double x = r * tan(0.5 * beta * PI_ON_180);

    if (viewing == parallel) {
        // left view on left
        left_camera_ptr->render_stereo(w, x, 0);
        // right view on right
        right_camera_ptr->render_stereo(w, -x, hres + pixel_gap);
    }

    if (viewing == transverse) {
        // right view on left
        right_camera_ptr->render_stereo(w, -x, 0);
        // left view on right
        left_camera_ptr->render_stereo(w, x, hres + pixel_gap);
    }
}
```

Listing 12.4. The function StereoCamera::render_scene.

Recall from Section 12.2 that the windows are displaced by half the camera separation. The stereo camera's render_scene function recomputes this distance and passes the correct signed value into the render_stereo functions through the second argument. Listing 12.5 shows how this is used. The pixel offset for the right-hand image (which can be either the left- or right-eye view, depending on the type of viewing) is the horizontal image resolution plus the pixel gap.

Listing 12.5 shows the render_stereo function for the pinhole camera. The differences between this and Pinhole::renderScene are in blue. Because it's so easy to use the asymmetric frustum, it's also easy to miss the code. It's just the addition of x to the x_v-coordinate of the pixel sample point.

```cpp
void
Pinhole::render_stereo(World& w, float x, int offset) {
    RGBColor L;
    Ray ray;
    ViewPlane vp = w.vp;
    int depth = 0;
    Point2D sp;                 // sample point in [0, 1] x [0, 1]
    Point2D pp;                 // sample point on the pixel

    vp.s /= zoom;
    ray.o = eye;

    for (int r = 0; r < vp.vres; r++)           // up
        for (int c = 0; c < vp.hres; c++) {     // across
            L = black;

            for (int j = 0; j < vp.num_samples; j++) {
                sp = vp.sampler_ptr->sample_unit_square();
                pp.x = vp.s * (c - 0.5 * vp.hres + sp.x) + x;
                pp.y = vp.s * (r - 0.5 * vp.vres + sp.y);
                ray.d = ray_direction(pp);
                L += w.tracer_ptr->trace_ray(ray, depth);
            }

            L /= vp.num_samples;
            L *= exposure_time;
            w.display_pixel(r, c + offset, L);
        }
}
```

Listing 12.5. The function Pinhole::render_stereo.

I've left the `render_stereo` functions for the other camera types as exercises.

 ## 12.6 Results

Let's start with pinhole cameras. Figure 12.12 shows a scene that consists of three spheres, where the view plane goes through the center of the brown sphere. When you view these in stereo, the silhouette of this sphere should have zero depth, the cyan sphere should appear in front of the paper, and yellow sphere behind. This stereo pair was rendered with $\beta = 0.75°$, and although it's a simulated image, it still shares some stereo properties with the real world. First, notice how you can focus your eyes on each sphere in turn, just like you do when you look at a real scene. Second, if you focus on the brown sphere, you will see that the other spheres are not fused. This also corresponds to the way we see the real world. If you put an object close to your eyes and focus on a distant object, you will see two distinct images of the close object. However, we have to be careful with the interpretation of the depth. The apparent depth between objects is proportional to the angle β, and when $\beta = 0$, there is no depth.

Figure 12.13 shows two-point perspective views of a "wireframe" cube rendered with pinhole cameras and $\beta = 5°$. The whole cube should appear to stick out of the paper because the view plane is behind it. Figure 12.14 shows three-point perspective views of the same cube.

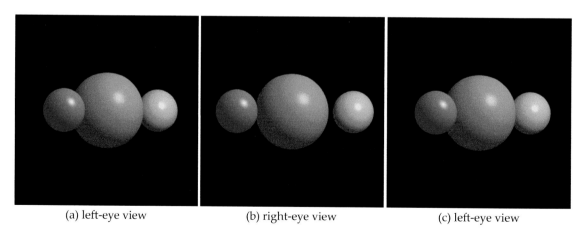

(a) left-eye view   (b) right-eye view   (c) left-eye view

Figure 12.12. A scene with three spheres displayed for parallel viewing in (a) and (b) and transverse viewing in (b) and (c).

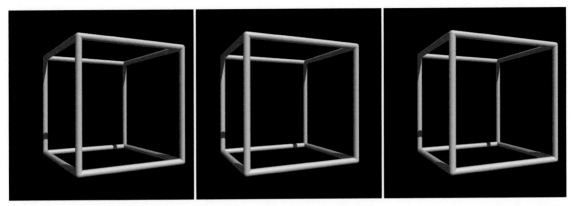

Figure 12.13. Two-point perspective views of a cube.

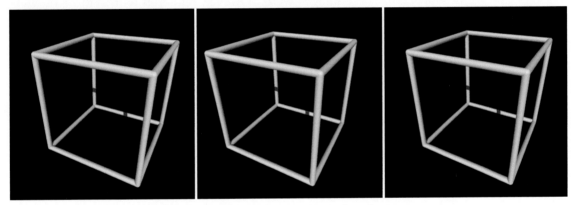

Figure 12.14. Three-point perspective views of a cube.

Figure 12.15 shows a stereo version of Figure 10.10 rendered with two thin-lens cameras and $\beta = 2°$. Here, the focal plane is on the front face of the middle box, as in Chapter 10, but the view plane is on the front face of the right box. This box should therefore appear with zero depth, with the other two boxes in front of the paper. The plane is a problem, because it cuts the frame of the image, which has zero depth. This creates an inconsistency. For example, the bottom "edge" of the plane, where it cuts the frame, should stick out of the paper, but it doesn't. In fact, the stereo-depth effect only works in the interior of this image.

Figure 12.16 shows rows of boxes and a checker plane rendered with fisheye cameras and $\beta = 5°$. The interesting thing here is the strong stereo effect, where the whole image, and in particular the boxes, sticks out of the paper.

Figure 12.15. The boxes and checker plane from Chapter 10.

This happens even though the fisheye camera does not have a view plane (see Question 12.5). These images were, however, rendered with symmetric view frustums. The reason is that the fisheye camera is only set up for rendering square images where the circular viewing area just touches the sides of the image. Asymmetric frustums displace these areas horizontally so that they are cropped. You don't have to change the stereo camera to use symmetric frustums; the `FishEye::render_stereo` function can just ignore the parameter x.

Although this stereo pair and the pair on the first page of this chapter have the strongest stereo effect, they are unrealistic. The real-world applications of fisheye stereo imagery are in immersive domes, such as the dome in Figure 11.9. When stereo pairs are projected onto the inner surface of this dome, the stereo effect is correct only for the view that's directly into the dome. The effect essentially disappears towards the edges, and you can't stand in the dome, look anywhere at its surface, and see stereo. Also, it's unlikely that the strong stereo

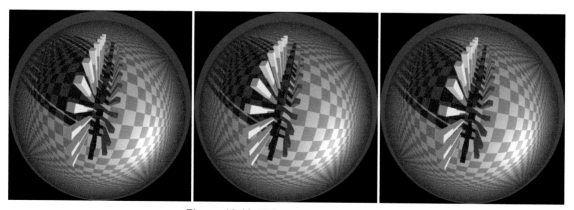

Figure 12.16. Fisheye-camera view of boxes and a plane.

Figure 12.17. Spherical panoramic views of the city scene from Chapter 11.

effect in Figure 12.16 would be achievable or fusible. In contrast, the flat surface in Figure 12.16 helps the stereo effect. The stereo fisheye camera can, however, render stereo pairs from anywhere in a scene and from any direction.

Finally, Figure 12.17 shows the city scene from Chapter 11 rendered with spherical panoramic cameras and $\beta = 5°$. These are 180° × 180° views, and to make them a bit more realistic-looking, they have been rendered with ambient occlusion (Chapter 17). Notice the large differences in the checkers at the bottom of the images due to their close proximity to the cameras.

This stereo pair is, however, only here to demonstrate that stereoscopy works with spherical panoramic projections. The practical applications of stereoscopic panoramic projections are immersive cylindrical viewing environments, and for these, *cylindrical* panoramic projections are used to provide the stereo content instead of spherical projections. In addition, the left- and right-eye views are constructed by rendering many images instead of just two. For example, 360 tall and narrow images, each 1° wide, can be rendered for each of the left and the right eyes and then stitched into the two images. This provides stereo imagery that can be viewed from anywhere inside the cylinder. The details can be found at http://local.wasp.uwa.edu.au/~pbourke/projection/stereopanoramic/.

 Notes and Discussion

There are many stereoscope models for sale that are designed for viewing printed stereo pairs. Inexpensive models with plastic lenses can be purchased for a few dollars and can also be used for viewing images on your computer screen. Some stereoscopes are designed specifically for viewing stereo pairs on a computer screen. You can purchase many models online.

 Further Reading

Again, the best place to read about the material in this chapter is Paul Burke's website at http://local.wasp.uwa.edu.au/~pbourke/. Sections 12.1 and 12.2 are based on material in http://local.wasp.uwa.edu.au/~pbourke/projection/stereorender/. There is also a lot of other information about stereo rendering on this site.

   Hodges and McAllister (1985) discusses the use of parallel view directions to avoid vertical parallax in stereo pairs.

 Questions

12.1. In Figure 12.1, what is the maximum positive parallax, and where does the point being projected have to be located for this value to occur?

12.2. Suppose a point being projected is on a plane that's parallel to the view plane and halfway between the eye points and the view plane. What is the parallax for this point? Does the parallax depend on the location of the point on the plane?

12.3. An alternate implementation of the stereo camera involves using the view-plane distance, instead of the distance to the look-at point, to define the stereo angle. Can you see why I didn't use this?

12.4. Does stereo work for orthographic viewing?

12.5. Why does the stereo effect work for fisheye and panoramic cameras, which don't have a view plane and therefore don't have a plane of zero parallax?

 Exercises

12.1. Implement the stereo camera as described here and reproduce the pinhole-camera images in Section 12.6. For each stereo pair, experiment with different viewing parameters, including the stereo separation angle.

12.2. Implement stereo viewing for any other camera types that you have implemented and reproduce the corresponding images in Section 12.6. Again, experiment with different viewing parameters.

12.3. This is a pencil-and-paper exercise on asymmetric view frustums. By drawing a diagram, convince yourself that the correct distance to translate the left- and right-camera windows in the x_v-direction is half the camera separation.

12.4. Ray trace Figure 12.15 with a zero radius for the lenses (or with pinhole cameras) so that everything is in focus. Does this make any difference to the apparent lack of stereo effect around the frame of the image?

12.5. Experiment with nonzero roll angles or up vectors different from $(0, 1, 0)$ and see how this affects the stereo images and your ability to fuse them. The left, right, and stereo cameras should all have the same roll angles and up vectors.

12.6. Experiment with toe-in. How much difference does this make to the images? Does it affect your ability to fuse them?

12.7. Use *symmetric* view frustums with the pinhole and thin-lens cameras and see how this affects the images, particularly when there are objects in front of the view plane (keep the look-at points distinct).

12.8. Make some nice stereo images of your own.

13

Theoretical Foundations

Image courtesy of Peter Georges

 ## Objectives

By the end of this chapter, you should:

- understand how radiometric quantities are defined;
- understand how bidirectional reflectance distribution functions (BRDFs) are defined;
- understand how a perfect diffuse BRDF is implemented;
- know what the rendering equation is;
- have seen a solution of the rendering equation;
- have been exposed to basic Monte Carlo concepts and processes.

I'll discuss here the radiometric theory that underpins ray tracing. This will establish a firm theoretical foundation for the shading material in the following chapters. Please note that this chapter uses differential and integral calculus, including multi-dimensional integrals, because calculus is the only rigorous way to discuss radiometry and the rendering equation. If you are not familiar with calculus, don't worry! Most of the theoretical material in this book, which can often be long and complicated, can be represented as simple pieces of code. The BRDFs, one of the central features of this chapter, are no exception. For example, the perfect diffuse BRDF functions f and rho in Listings 13.3 and 13.4 have a lot of theory behind them but only contain a single line of code. Certainly, things will become more complicated in later chapters, but most of the heavy calculus is in this chapter.

You should read Section 2.10 before you read this chapter, as that covers solid angles, some of the integrals, and establishes some of the notation. An additional piece of notation in this chapter is that I'll use an ω with various subscripts to indicate directions.

13.1 Radiometric Quantities

Radiometry deals with the measurement of radiation throughout the electro-magnetic spectrum. Below are the definitions of radiometric quantities with their units of measurement in square brackets. The most important of these for ray tracing is radiance, but since its definition depends on other radiometric quantities, I'll define it last.

Radiant energy Q. Radiant energy is the basic unit of electromagnetic energy, measured in *joules* with symbol J. Its units are therefore [J]. The radiant energy carried by each photon is $Q = hc/\lambda$, where $h = 6.62620 \times 10^{-34}$ joules-seconds is Planck's constant, $c = 2.998 \times 10^8$ meters/second is the speed of light, and λ is the wavelength of the photon in meters.

Radiant flux Φ. Radiant flux is the amount of radiant energy that passes through a surface or region of space per second: $\Phi = dQ/dt$. It has units of joules per second [J · s^{-1}], but since one joule per second is called a *watt* with symbol W, the units are also written as [W]. Radiant flux is also the amount of radiant energy that a light source emits per second and is also called *radiant power*. Another way of looking at this is that flux is a restriction of Q in time.

Radiant flux density. Radiant flux density is the radiant flux per unit surface area: $d\Phi/dA$, where dA is a differential area. Its units are watts per square meter [W · m^{-2}]. As the definition isn't restricted to real surfaces, it can be applied to an imaginary surface in space where it specifies the total amount of radiant energy that passes through a unit area of the surface per second, from both sides. Flux density is therefore a restriction of Q in time and space.

Irradiance E. Irradiance is the flux density that *arrives* at a surface. Its units are [W · m^{-2}], and it's denoted by

$$E = d\Phi/dA. \tag{13.1}$$

Radiant exitance M. Radiant exitance is the flux density that *leaves* a surface [W · m^{-2}]. It's also called the *radiosity B*.

Radiant intensity *I*. Radiant intensity is the flux density per unit solid angle: $I = d\Phi/d\omega$. It has units $[\text{W} \cdot \text{m}^{-2} \cdot \text{sr}^{-1}]$, where sr^{-1} stands for inverse steradians, but it's only meaningful for point light sources. Radiant intensity is a restriction of Q in time and direction.

Radiance *L*. Radiance is the flux per unit projected area per unit solid angle. Its units are the same as for radiant intensity: $[\text{W} \cdot \text{m}^{-2} \cdot \text{sr}^{-1}]$, but it's different. Radiance measures the flux at an arbitrary point in space, coming from a specific direction, and measured per unit area on an imaginary surface perpendicular to the direction. To illustrate this, Figure 13.1(a) shows a direction ω and a surface element $dA^{\perp}$ that's perpendicular to ω. This is the projected area. This figure also shows a differential cone of incident directions $d\omega$ centered on ω. A good way to describe radiance is in terms of photons. The radiance measures the radiant flux from photons traveling down the cone $d\omega$. In the limit where $d\omega$ and dA both approach zero, the photons are confined to a single direction, as shown in Figure 13.1(b). Radiance is a restriction of Q in time, space, and direction.

Radiance is defined as

$$L = \frac{d^2\Phi}{dA^{\perp}d\omega}. \tag{13.2}$$

Since rays are infinitely thin lines, radiance is the natural quantity to compute for them. Radiance also has a number of useful properties for ray tracing:

- Radiance is constant along rays that travel through empty space and is also the same in both directions along the ray.[1] See, for example, Dutré et al. (2006).

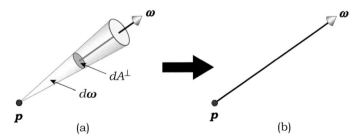

(a)   (b)

Figure 13.1. (a) Radiant flux in a cone of incident angles $d\omega$ passing through a surface element $dA^{\perp}$. (b) In the limit $d\omega \rightarrow 0$ and $dA \rightarrow 0$, the radiance is defined as coming from a single direction ω. The point p can be an arbitrary point in space.

---

1. Although the rays will also travel through transparent materials in Chapters 27 and 28, it's only when we use color filtering in Chapter 28 that the radiance will vary along the rays.

- As radiance can be defined at any point in space, not just on surfaces, it can be defined at the eye point of a pinhole camera or a point on a pixel.
- If the point is on a surface, the radiance doesn't depend on whether the flux is arriving at or leaving the surface. In fact, it doesn't matter if the flux is reflected, transmitted, emitted, or scattered (Akenine-Möller and Haines, 2002).

Radiance that hits a surface is called *incident radiance*; radiance that leaves a surface is called *exitant radiance*, but I'll often use the colloquial terms incoming and reflected radiance, and *light* for irradiance, radiant intensity, and radiance.

 ## 13.2 Angular Dependence of Irradiance

When the point p is on a real surface, it's more convenient to represent the radiance using an area element on the surface instead of $dA^\perp$ as in Equation (13.2). Consider irradiance E that hits a surface with normal incidence, as shown in Figure 13.2(a). If the irradiance is in a beam with cross section $dA^\perp$, the area dA of the surface that receives it will also have area $dA^\perp$. Figure 13.2(b) shows a beam that hits the surface with incidence angle θ measured from the normal. This beam hits the surface over the larger area $dA^\perp/\cos\theta$ (see Figure 13.2(c)). Irradiance is therefore proportional to the cosine of the incidence angle. This is known as *Lambert's law*. Figures 7.2 and 7.3 show plots of $\cos\theta$ for $\theta \in [0, \pi/2]$, which demonstrate how the irradiance goes to zero as the light becomes parallel to the surface.

We thus have the following relation between projected area and surface area:

$$dA^\perp = \cos\theta \, dA. \tag{13.3}$$

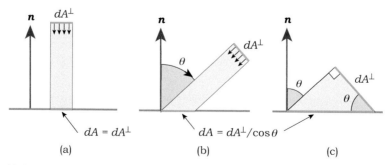

Figure 13.2. (a) and (b) Irradiance spreads out over a larger area as the incidence angle θ increases. (c) An enlarged view of the incident beam.

For incident radiance at a surface point, we can substitute the relation (13.3) into Equation (13.2) to get

$$L = \frac{d^2\Phi}{dA\cos\theta d\omega}.$$

(13.4)

Here, $\cos\theta\, d\omega$ is called the *projected solid angle* because it's the projection of the differential solid angle $d\omega$ onto the (x, z) plane (see Exercise (13.2)).

13.3 Notation and Directions

A large part of this chapter is concerned with specifying how light is reflected at a surface point p, a process that requires directions to be specified for the incoming and reflected light. I'll use the commonly used notation of ω_i for the incoming direction and ω_o for the reflected direction. By convention, these are both specified by unit vectors that point away from p and are on the same side of the surface as the normal. See Figure 13.3, which also shows their spherical coordinate angles (θ_i, ϕ_i) and (θ_o, ϕ_o).

For shading purposes, ω_o will be the direction from which a ray hits the surface at p. The incoming ray direction will therefore be $-\omega_o$.

We ultimately want to compute the reflected radiance along ω_o as a function of the total incoming radiance at p from all directions in the hemisphere above p, but there are actually two hemispheres: one on each side of the surface, as Figure 13.4 illustrates. Because rays can hit the inside or outside surfaces of objects, the ray tracer has to be able to correctly shade both sides of surfaces. I'll

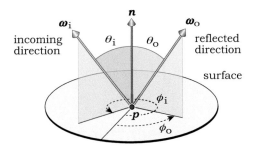

Figure 13.3. The incoming direction ω_i and reflected direction ω_o point away from the surface and are on the same side of the surface as the normal. Each direction is defined by its polar and azimuth angles (θ, ϕ). These are arbitrary directions; for perfect mirror reflection, $\phi_o = \phi_i \pm \pi$, as illustrated in Figure 24.2(b).

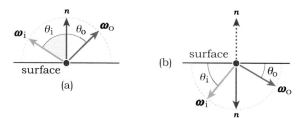

Figure 13.4. (a) ω_o is on the same side of the surface as the normal; (b) ω_o is on the opposite side of the surface to the normal, which is then reversed for shading purposes. This schematic figure does not mean to imply that ω_i, ω_o, and n are coplanar; they may or may not be coplanar, depending on the shading application.

discuss the shading aspects of this in Chapter 14 and the intersection aspects in Chapter 19. In Figure 13.4(a), the ray hits the surface on the same side as the normal, and ω_i, ω_o, and n are the same side of the surface. In Figure 13.4(b), the ray hits the surface on the opposite side to the normal, which is then reversed so that ω_i, ω_o, and n are still on the same side of the surface.

 ## 13.4 Radiance and Irradiance

We can now establish the relationship between incident radiance and irradiance. It follows from Equations (13.1) and (13.4) that

$$dE_i(p, \omega_i) = L_i(p, \omega_i) \cos \theta_i \, d\omega_i, \tag{13.5}$$

where $L_i(p, \omega_i)$ is the incident radiance at p from direction ω_i and $dE_i(p, \omega_i)$ is the irradiance in a cone with differential solid angle $d\omega_i$ centered on ω_i. The irradiance at p from a *finite* solid angle Ω_i is obtained by integrating dE over Ω_i:

$$E_i(p) = \int_{\Omega_i} L_i(p, \omega_i) \cos \theta_i d\omega_i. \tag{13.6}$$

 ## 13.5 Spectral Representation

The radiometric quantities all depend on the wavelength of the light, and often in complex ways. We can specify these at a particular wavelength λ, where the names are prefixed by the word *spectral*. An example is the spectral radiance

$L_\lambda(p, \omega_i, \lambda)$, which has units of $[\text{W} \cdot \text{m}^{-2} \cdot \text{sr}^{-1} \cdot \text{nm}^{-1}]$.[2] Integrating over wavelength, the radiance is

$$L(p, \omega_i) = \int_0^\infty L_\lambda(p, \omega_i, \lambda) d\lambda,$$

but we need a way to represent this in the ray tracer. As you can probably guess from the previous chapters, beginning with Chapter 3, I'll represent radiance with an RGBColor. This essentially uses three wavelengths: one in each of the red, the green, and the blue parts of the visible spectrum, but the actual wavelengths in nanometers aren't specified. I'll use the same representation for the BRDFs and reflectance, to be discussed in the Sections 13.6 and 13.7.

 ## 13.6 BRDFs

13.6.1 Definition

It's common practice in ray tracing to represent the reflective properties of surfaces with *materials*, but to do this, we need a way to precisely describe how light is reflected at surfaces. The *bidirectional reflectance distribution function* (BRDF) provides this precise description. Consider a differential amount of irradiance $dE_i(p, \omega_i)$ at a point p that's arriving in an element of solid angle $d\omega_i$ centered on the direction ω_i (see Figure 13.5). The BRDF specifies the contribution of this irradiance to the reflected radiance in the direction ω_o. This is a differential amount of radiance $dL_o(p, \omega_o)$.

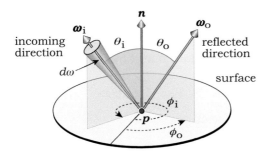

Figure 13.5. At a surface point p, a BRDF relates reflected radiance in one direction ω_o to irradiance centered on another direction ω_i.

---

2. To be consistent with the other units, the wavelength should be specified in meters, but nanometers are commonly used because they have a different symbol (nm) from the meters area measurement (m).

In ray tracing, a ray will hit p from the direction ω_o, and it's the reflected radiance along this ray that we have to compute. Because ω_o points away from p, the incoming ray direction is opposite of ω_o.

Because the optical properties of materials are linear, the irradiance and radiance elements are proportional. For example, if the irradiance were doubled, the reflected radiance would also double. Hence,

$$dL_o(p, \omega_o) \propto dE_i(p, \omega_i),$$

where the BRDF $f_r(p, \omega_i, \omega_o)$ is simply the constant of proportionality:

$$dL_o(p, \omega_o) = f_r(p, \omega_i, \omega_o)\, dE_i(p, \omega_i).$$

Equation (13.5) allows us to express $dL_o(p, \omega_o)$ in terms of the incoming radiance:

$$dL_o(p, \omega_o) = f_r(p, \omega_i, \omega_o)L_i(p, \omega_i) \cos \theta_i\, d\omega_i, \tag{13.7}$$

and solving Equation (13.7) for $f_r(p, \omega_i, \omega_o)$ gives

$$f_r(p, \omega_i, \omega_o) = \frac{dL_o(p, \omega_o)}{L_i(p, \omega_i)\cos\theta_i d\omega_i}. \tag{13.8}$$

A BRDF has units of inverse steradians $[\text{sr}^{-1}]$ because of the solid angle in the denominator. Note that the BRDF is only a function of p and the two directions. It can range in value from zero to infinity. An example of an infinite BRDF occurs with mirror reflection, where it has to be represented by a delta function (see Chapter 24).

Spatial variance and invariance. BRDFs that vary over object surfaces are known as *spatially variant*, as indicated by the hit point p in their arguments. The textured materials described in Chapters 29–31 contain spatially variant BRDFs. BRDFs that are constant over object surfaces are known as *spatially invariant*.

13.6.2 Reflected Radiance

The reflected radiance in the ω_o direction that results from irradiance in a finite solid angle Ω_i is obtained by integrating Equation (13.7) over Ω_i:

$$L_o(p, \omega_o) = \int_{\Omega_i} f_r(p, \omega_i, \omega_o)L_i(p, \omega_i)\cos\theta_i d\omega_i. \tag{13.9}$$

By integrating the irradiance over the whole hemisphere above p, indicated by $2\pi^+$, we get the total reflected radiance in the ω_o direction:

$$L_o(p,\omega_o) = \int_{2\pi^+} f_r(p,\omega_i,\omega_o)L_i(p,\omega_i)\cos\theta_i d\omega_i. \qquad (13.10)$$

This is known as the *reflection equation*. It plays a pivotal role in ray tracing because the value of the integral on the right-hand side is the quantity that ray tracers have to compute at each hit point, at least for purely reflective materials that are not light sources.

13.6.3 Properties

BRDFs have a number of useful properties.

Reciprocity. BRDFs have a property called *reciprocity*: when we swap ω_i and ω_o, the value of the BRDF stays the same; that is,

$$f_r(p, \omega_i, \omega_o) = f_r(p, \omega_o, \omega_i)$$

for all ω_i and ω_o. If we therefore change the direction in which the light travels, the reflected radiance stays the same. This is an important property for *bidirectional ray tracing*, where some rays are traced from the light sources (see Jensen (2001)).

Linearity. Materials often need multiple BRDFs to model their reflective properties. In this case, the total reflected radiance at a surface point will simply be the sum of the reflected radiance from each BRDF. A common example involves diffuse and specular reflection, which will be modeled by different BRDFs.

Conservation of energy. This is specified in terms of reflectance in Section 13.7.

 ## 13.7 Reflectance

Reflectance is defined as the ratio of reflected flux to incident flux (or equivalently, reflected power to incident power). The radiant flux that's incident on a differential surface element dA through the solid angle Ω_i is

$$d\Phi_i = dA \int_{\Omega_i} L_i(p,\omega_i)\cos\theta_i d\omega_i. \qquad (13.11)$$

The reflected flux from the same surface element, in the solid angle Ω_o is

$$d\Phi_o = dA \int_{\Omega_o} L_o(p,\omega_o)\cos\theta_o d\omega_o. \tag{13.12}$$

We can substitute Equation (13.9) into (13.12) to get

$$d\Phi_o = dA \int_{\Omega_o}\int_{\Omega_i} f_r(p,\omega_i,\omega_o)L_i(p,\omega_i)\cos\theta_i \cos\theta_o d\omega_i d\omega_o. \tag{13.13}$$

The reflectance $\rho(p, \Omega_i, \Omega_o)$ is defined by

$$\rho(p, \Omega_i, \Omega_o) = d\Phi_o/d\Phi_i$$

$$= \frac{\int_{\Omega_o}\int_{\Omega_i} f_r(p,\omega_i,\omega_o)L_i(p,\omega_i)\cos\theta_i \cos\theta_o d\omega_i d\omega_o}{\int_{\Omega_i} L_i(p,\omega_i)\cos\theta_i d\omega_i}, \tag{13.14}$$

where the dAs have canceled. This is a general expression that makes no assumptions about the solid angles, the BRDF, or the angular distribution of incidence radiance in the hemisphere above p. The reflectance is dimensionless.

Conservation of energy. No real materials reflect all of the light that hits them; some is absorbed and then re-radiated, often as heat. As a result, the value of $\rho(p, 2\pi^+, 2\pi^+)$ satisfies

$$\rho(p, 2\pi^+, 2\pi^+) < 1$$

when the integration is over the whole hemisphere at p. This inequality states that the surface element dA reflects less light in all directions than it receives from all directions.

13.8 The Perfect Diffuse BRDF

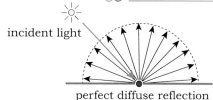

incident light

perfect diffuse reflection

Figure 13.6. Light being scattered from a perfectly diffuse surface.

It should help to clarify some of the above theory by discussing one of the simplest BRDFs. This represents perfect diffuse reflection, where incident radiance is scattered equally in all directions. Figure 13.6 illustrates this for a point light. Perfect diffuse reflection is also called *Lambertian reflection*. Although no real materials behave exactly like this, perfect diffuse reflection is an important part of direct and indirect illumination models because it's a good approximation for dull, matte materials, such as paper and completely flat paint.

For Lambertian surfaces, the reflected radiance $L_o(p, \omega_o) = L_{r,d}(p)$ is independent of ω_o. From Equation (13.9), this is only possible when the BRDF is independent of ω_i and ω_o, so I'll denote this by $f_{r,d}(p)$ and take it out of the integral. This gives, with Equation (13.6),

$$L_{r,d}(p) = f_{r,d}(p) \int_{\Omega_i} L_i(p,\omega_i)\cos\theta_i d\omega_i = f_{r,d}(p)E_i(p). \qquad (13.15)$$

From Equation (13.15), we have

$$f_{r,d}(p) = L_{r,d}(p)/E_i(p). \qquad (13.16)$$

We want to now express $f_{r,d}$ in terms of the *perfect diffuse reflectance* ρ_d, defined as the fraction of the total incident flux that's reflected into the full hemisphere above the surface element dA when the BRDF is independent of ω_i and ω_o. In this case, Equation (13.12) becomes

$$d\Phi_o = dA\, L_{r,d}(p) \int_{2\pi^+} \cos\theta_o d\omega_o = dA\, L_{r,d}(p)\pi.$$

From Equation (13.11),

$$d\Phi_i = dA \int_{2\pi^+} L_i(p,\omega_i)\cos\theta_i d\omega_i = dA\, E_i(p) ,$$

where now $E_i(p)$ is the total irradiance from the hemisphere above dA. Dividing these expressions, and using Equation (13.16), the reflectance (13.14) becomes

$$\rho_d(p) = d\Phi_o / d\Phi_i = L_{r,d}(p)\, \pi/E_i(p) = f_{r,d}(p)\, \pi.$$

It then follows that

$$f_{r,d}(p) = \rho_d(p)/\pi. \qquad (13.17)$$

To model ambient illumination (see Chapter 14) for perfectly diffuse surfaces, we need to use the *bihemispherical reflectance*, denoted by ρ_{hh}.[3] This is the fraction of the total incident flux from the full hemisphere that's reflected into the full hemisphere when the incident radiance is isotropic and spatially invariant. In plain English, it means that the incoming radiance is the same

---

3. Another name for this is the *hemispherical-hemispherical reflectance*.

from all directions and doesn't vary with position; that is, $L_i(p, \omega_i) = L_i$ is a constant. The fraction reflected should also be spatially invariant (Nicodemus et al., 1977), but I'm going to let it vary with position so that I can also use ρ_{hh} for textured surfaces.

With the above assumptions, we can take $L_i(p)$ out of both integrals in Equation (13.14), where it cancels, as well as taking $f_{r,d}(p)$ out of the top integral, to leave

$$\rho_{hh}(p) = \frac{f_{r,d}(p)}{\pi} \int_{2\pi^+} \int_{2\pi^+} \cos\theta_i \cos\theta_o d\omega_i d\omega_o = \pi f_{r,d}(p) = \rho_d(p). \quad (13.18)$$

 ## 13.9 The BRDF Classes

13.9.1 Organization and Member Functions

The BRDF classes are organized in an inheritance hierarchy, as illustrated in Figure 13.7.

As BRDF objects implement the basic reflection mechanisms that give materials their appearances, each material will contain at least one BRDF. Figure 13.7 shows the BRDFs `Lambertian`, `PerfectSpecular`, and `GlossySpecular`, which are spatially invariant. Each BRDF class defines three functions: `f`, `sample_f`, and `rho`, which return an RGB color. The declaration of the base class `BRDF` appears in Listing 13.1.

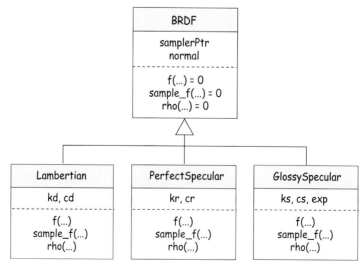

Figure 13.7. Inheritance chart for the BRDF classes.

```
class BRDF {
    public:
        ...

            virtual RGBColor
            f(const ShadeRec& sr, const Vector3D& wi, const Vector3D& wo)
                const = 0;

            virtual RGBColor
            sample_f(const ShadeRec& sr, Vector3D& wi, const Vector3D& wo)
                const = 0;

            virtual RGBColor
            rho(const ShadeRec& sr, const Vector3D& wo) const = 0;

    protected:

        Sampler* sampler_ptr;
};
```

Listing 13.1. Part of the base class BRDF.

The function f returns the BRDF itself, unless it contains a delta function (Chapter 2). The function sample_f is used to compute the direction of reflected rays for simulating reflective materials and diffuse-diffuse light transport. Note that the ω_i parameter of sample_f is not constant, as this is used to return the direction ω_i. As the name implies, the directions are computed by sampling the BRDF. That's why the base class BRDF contains a pointer to a sampler object. The function rho returns the bihemispherical reflectance ρ_{hh}.

As a quick summary, Table 13.1 lists the information that these three functions return for the Lambertian, PerfectSpecular, and GlossySpecular

BRDF	Lambertian	PerfectSpecular	GlossySpecular
f	ρ_d/π this chapter	black	$\rho_s(\mathbf{r} \bullet \omega_o)^e$ Chapter 15
sample_f	ω_i $\rho_d/(\mathbf{n} \bullet \omega_i)$ Chapter 26	ω_i $\rho_s/(\mathbf{n} \bullet \omega_i)$ Chapter 24	ω_i $\rho_s(\mathbf{r} \bullet \omega_o)^e$ Chapter 25
rho	ρ_d this chapter	black	black

Table 13.1. Return values for the functions f, sample_f, and rho.

BRDFs, along with the chapters where they are discussed. In this table, ρ_s is the specular reflectance, and e is the specular exponent (Chapter 15). The ω_i directions returned by the sample_f functions are as follows:

- For the Lambertian BRDF, ω_i is determined by a cosine-weighted sample point on the hemisphere above p.
- For the PerfectSpecular BRDF, ω_i is the direction of mirror reflection at p.
- For the GlossySpecular BRDF, ω_i is determined by a cosine-power-weighted sample point on the hemisphere that's oriented around the direction r of mirror reflection at p.

13.9.2 Lambertian **class implementation**

Since ρ_d is an RGB color, I'll express it as

$$\rho_d = k_d c_d,$$

where $k_d \in [0, 1]$ is the *diffuse reflection coefficient* and c_d is the diffuse color. This is a programming convenience that allows us to change the fraction of light reflected by an object and keep its hue the same by changing a single number.

```
class Lambertian: public BRDF {
     public:

          // constructors, etc.
          // access functions for kd and cd
          ...
          virtual RGBColor
          f(const ShadeRec& sr, const Vector3D& wi, const Vector3D& wo) const;

          virtual RGBColor
          sample_f(const ShadeRec& sr, Vector3D& wi, const Vector3D& wo) const;

          virtual RGBColor
          rho(const ShadeRec& sr, const Vector3D& wo) const;

     private:

          float kd;
          RGBColor cd;
};
```

Listing 13.2. Partial declaration of the class Lambertian.

```
RGBColor
Lambertian::f(const ShadeRec& sr, const Vector3D& wi, const Vector3D& wo) const {
    return (kd * cd * invPI);
}
```

Listing 13.3. The function `Lambertian::f`.

```
RGBColor
Lambertian::rho(const ShadeRec& sr, const Vector3D& wo) const {
    return (kd * cd);
}
```

Listing 13.4. The function `Lambertian::rho`.

Without it, we would have to change three numbers to alter ρ_d, with the same end result. From Equation (13.17), the BRDF is

$$f_{r,d} = k_d c_d / \pi. \tag{13.19}$$

Listing 13.2 shows the declaration of the `Lambertian` class, which stores k_d and c_d.

The code for `Lambertian::f` in Listing 13.3 follows directly from Equation (13.19).

The function `Lambertian::rho` returns

$$\rho_{hh} = k_d c_d \tag{13.20}$$

from Equation (13.18). The code is in Listing 13.4.

 # 13.10 The Rendering Equation

13.10.1 Hemisphere Form

The *rendering equation* expresses the steady-state radiative energy balance in a scene.[4] The reflection equation (13.10) is part of the rendering equation, as it expresses the reflective energy balance between surfaces. All we have to do is

---

4. Alternate names for the rendering equation are the *radiosity equation* and the *light transport equation*.

add the light sources to this equation to get the rendering equation for reflective surfaces.

The surface of a light source emits light and is known as an *emissive* surface. We can allow for self-emission in Equation (13.10) by adding a term $L_e(p, \omega_o)$ on the right-hand side for the *emitted radiance* in the direction ω_o:

$$L_o(p,\omega_o) = L_e(p,\omega_o) + \int_{2\pi^+} f_r(p,\omega_i,\omega_o)L_i(p,\omega_i)\cos\theta_i d\omega_i. \qquad (13.21)$$

This is the rendering equation expressed in its *hemisphere form*, where the integration is in terms of solid angle over the hemisphere at the point p. Equation (13.21) states that the exitant radiance is the sum of the emitted and reflected radiance.

Rendering algorithms, including ray tracing and radiosity, are just ways of computing approximate solutions to the rendering equation. This process does, however, present us with a dilemma. The exitant radiance that we wish to compute depends on the incoming radiance, which in turn depends on the exitant radiance from other surfaces. So, how do we compute this for arbitrary scenes? Fortunately, ray tracing provides a powerful technique for solving the rendering equation, where a key fact is that the incident radiance $L_i(p, \omega_i)$ in Equation (13.21) can be computed by tracing a ray from the point p. We define the *ray-casting operator* $r_c(p, \omega_i)$ to be the nearest hit point along the ray in the direction ω_i. Because radiance is constant along each ray and the same in each direction, $L_i(p, \omega_i)$ can be written as

$$L_i(p, \omega_i) = L_o(r_c(p, \omega_i), -\omega_i) \qquad (13.22)$$

(see Figure 13.8). Here, the incident radiance at p is the same as the exitant radiance at $p' = r_c(p, \omega_i)$. In an enclosed environment, the ray will always hit

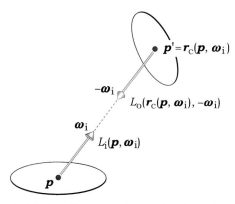

Figure 13.8. The incident radiance at p is equal to the exitant radiance at p'.

something, but if the environment is open, it may not. In this case, the radiance brought back to p will be the background color, which can be black. If the scene contains directional and point lights, the ray can also bring back their radiance without hitting any objects (see Chapter 14).

Substituting Equation (13.22) into (13.21) gives

$$L_o(p,\omega_o) = L_e(p,\omega_o) + \int_{2\pi^+} f_r(p,\omega_i,\omega_o) L_o(r_c(p,\omega_i), -\omega_i) \cos\theta_i d\omega_i. \quad (13.23)$$

A critical advantage of writing the rendering equation this way is that the exitant radiance L_o is now the only unknown, but this doesn't mean that the equation is easy to solve. Far from it, in fact. Equation (13.23) is an example of a *Fredholm integral equation of the second kind* because it contains an integral with constant integration limits, the unknown L_o appears on the left- and right-hand sides, and L_o is inside the integral. These equations can be difficult to solve in general, but to make matters worse in our case, Equation (13.23) is recursive in L_o. That's because the expression for $L_o(r_c(p, \omega_i), - \omega_i)$ in the integral is an identical expression for $L_o(p, \omega_o)$ but evaluated at p'. The depth of the recursion depends on how many times each ray is reflected, but that's the topic of Chapters 24–26.

13.10.2 Area Form

An alternate formulation of the rendering equation expresses it as an integral over all surface areas in a scene. This is known as the *area form*, where sample points are generated on all scene surfaces, and these determine the directions of the rays that start at p. As in the hemisphere form, the incident radiance at p is equal to the exitance radiance at p', but in this case, p' is a sample point on a surface, and the incident radiance at p will only be nonzero when p and p' can see each other. If A is the set of all surfaces in a scene, we can define a *visibility function* $V(p,p')$ as

$$\forall(p,p') \in A : V(p,p') = \begin{cases} 1 & \text{if } p \text{ and } p' \text{ can see each other,} \\ 0 & \text{if } p \text{ and } p' \text{ cannot see each other.} \end{cases} \quad (13.24)$$

The points p and p' can only see each other when no objects block the straight line between them.

We also have to re-cast the solid angle $d\omega_i$ to use a surface-area measure. If the differential surface element at a sample point p' is dA, it follows from Equation (2.11) that

$$d\omega_i = \cos\theta' dA / \|p' - p\|^2,$$

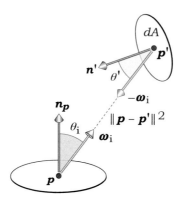

Figure 13.9. In the area form of the rendering equation, p and p' are sample points on surfaces. It's necessary to work out if they are mutually visible and to compute the square of the distance between them.

where

$$\cos\theta' = n' \bullet (-\omega_i)$$

and n' is the normal to dA (see Figure 13.9).

We can now write the rendering equation in its area form as

$$L_o(p,\omega_o) = L_e(p,\omega_o) + \int_A f_r(p,\omega_i,\omega_o) L_o(p',-\omega_i) V(p,p') G(p,p') \, dA, \quad (13.25)$$

where

$$G(p,p') = \cos\theta_i \cos\theta' / \|p'-p\|^2 \quad (13.26)$$

is known as the *geometry term*.

It's useful to compare the two forms. For example, why is there no visibility term in Equation (13.23)? We obtain estimates of the exitant radiance in both versions by shooting rays into the hemisphere above the point p, but the ray directions are chosen differently in each form. In the hemisphere form, the directions are determined by the BRDF at p, and by construction, p' is the nearest hit point (if any) along each ray. This is illustrated in Figure 13.10(a). Because each ray brings back the exitant radiance at p' or the background color, there's no need for a visibility term.

Things are quite different in the area form, where the ray directions are determined by the locations of sample points p' on object surfaces. That is,

$$\omega_i = (p'-p)/\|p'-p\|. \quad (13.27)$$

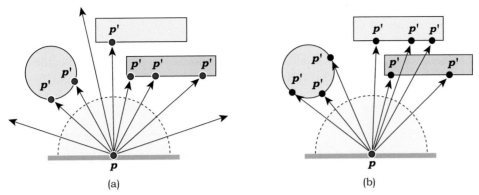

Figure 13.10. (a) Ray directions are independent of the objects in the scene. (b) Ray directions are determined by sample points on object surfaces. Here, two of the samples on the top object are not visible from *p*.

These points may or may not be visible from *p*, as Figure 13.10(b) illustrates. If a point is not visible, its ray returns zero radiance at *p* because only the nearest surface along each ray can return any radiance.

Both forms are useful for ray tracing. I'll use the area form for direct illumination from area lights, where we only have to generate sample points on the light surfaces. That's a lot more practical than trying to generate points on all surfaces. I'll use the hemisphere form for everything else. Some scenes can be rendered with both forms.

13.10.3 Solutions

As complex as the rendering equation is, it can be solved, at least approximately. In this chapter I'll look at a general solution that will form the basis of the shading techniques in the following chapters. The technique is as follows. To solve an equation numerically, we can often start with an initial estimate of the solution and substitute it into the equation. This gives a revised estimate that's (hopefully) closer to the real solution. We then substitute this into the equation to get another revised estimate and repeat the process. This technique is known as *successive substitution*, and if all goes well, these estimates will converge to the real solution.

Successive substitution can be used to solve the rendering equation in the following way. We first define the *linear integral operator*

$$K \circ L_o = \int_{2\pi^+} f_r(p, \omega_i, \omega_o) L_o(r_c(p, \omega_i), -\omega_i) \cos \theta_i d\omega_i \qquad (13.28)$$

using the integral on the right-hand side of Equation (13.23).[5] There's nothing mysterious about Equation (13.28). For a given L_o, which is an exitant radiance distribution in solid angle at p, the operator $K \circ L_o$ just converts L_o into another radiance distribution. It's analogous to the process of multiplying a vector by a matrix to change the vector into another vector. Since K is linear, it satisfies

$$K \circ (L_1 + L_2) = K \circ L_1 + K \circ L_2,$$
$$K \circ (\alpha L) = \alpha K \circ L,$$

where α is a constant or a function that can be taken outside the integral. Using Equation (13.28) and dropping the arguments, we can write the rendering equation as

$$L_o = L_e + K \circ L_o.$$

The right-hand side $L_e + K \circ L_o$ can now be taken as the first approximation for the solution, and so we substitute that into the right-hand side to get the second approximation:

$$L_o = L_e + K \circ (L_e + K \circ L_o)$$
$$= L_e + K \circ L_e + K^2 \circ L_o,$$

where $K^2 \circ L_o = K \circ K \circ L_o$. Repeating this process gives

$$L_o = L_e + K \circ L_e + K^2 \circ (L_e + K \circ L_o)$$
$$= L_e + K \circ L_e + K^2 \circ L_e + K^3 \circ L_o.$$

Notice how we are getting more terms on the right that only involve L_e and K. These are quantities that are known or can be computed, at least in theory. They are defined by the objects in a scene, their materials, and the light sources. If we keep repeating this process, it can be proved that the approximations do get closer to the real solution of the rendering equation, and after an infinite number of repetitions, the sum

$$L_o = \sum_{j=0}^{\infty} K^j \circ L_e, \tag{13.29}$$

where $K^0 \circ L_e = L_e$, is the real solution. That's a beautiful result. However, the simple appearance hides a huge amount of complexity in the individual terms, where $K^j \circ L_o$ for $j > 0$, is a $2j$-dimensional integral over the hemisphere at p.

---

5. We could also use the integral on the right-hand side of Equation (13.25) because this technique works for both forms of the rendering equation.

To compute exact solutions of the rendering equation, we would have to simulate all light paths in a scene, a task that's not possible, but fortunately, we don't need exact solutions. Here are five pieces of good news about solving the rendering equation:

1. Ray casting only requires the first two terms.
2. Because real materials don't reflect all of the light that hits them, the more times light bounces between surfaces, the less effect it has on images. Combine this fact with the finite representation of colors on computers, and after a finite number of bounces, the contribution of reflected rays will drop below the threshold of 1/255 for each color component, and we can stop adding terms.
3. For shading with point and directional lights and simulating perfect specular reflection and transmission, the integrals reduce to small sums of simple expressions that we can evaluate exactly. This Whitted-style ray tracing, named after Whitted (1980), is the focus of Chapters 24, 27, and 28.
4. For shading with area lights and simulating diffuse-diffuse light transport, we can use Monte Carlo techniques to numerically evaluate the multi-dimensional integrals.
5. The series (13.29) corresponds to path tracing (Chapter 26).

The shading techniques that I'll discuss in the following chapters can all be expressed as approximations of the rendering equation or variations of it to include transparency and shadows. The best places to discuss these approximations are in the context of the various shading techniques in the relevant chapters.

13.11 Monte Carlo Integration

This section is a short introduction to *Monte Carlo integration*, which is a large topic. To fully appreciate the material here, you should be familiar with elementary probability theory, continuous random variables, and one-dimensional calculus. Fortunately, these topics are covered in much greater detail in the references cited in the Further Reading section. I'll mainly just quote some results here, without derivation.

13.11.1 The Basic Technique

The integrals involved in the rendering equation are multi-dimensional, and for arbitrary incident radiance distributions, they can't be solved exactly. We

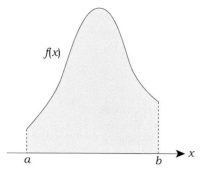

Figure 13.11. The definite integral of a function $f(x)$ over the interval $x \in$ [a, b] is the shaded area between $f(x)$ and the x-axis.

therefore need to be able to compute numerical estimates of their values. Fortunately, Monte Carlo integration is ideally suited for evaluating these integrals because it's an efficient technique for estimating the values of multi-dimensional integrals. To keep things simple, I'll illustrate how Monte Carlo integration works for one-dimensional integrals.

Consider the definite integral

$$I = \int_a^b f(x)dx \tag{13.30}$$

of some function $f(x)$, as shown in Figure 13.11. The interpretation of this integral is that its value is the area between $f(x)$ and the x-axis for the interval $x \in [a, b]$.

In Monte Carlo integration, we can estimate the value of this integral by evaluating $f(x)$ at n uniformly distributed random values of x in the interval [a, b] (see Figure 13.12(a)). The *Monte Carlo estimator* for the integral I, denoted by $\langle I \rangle$, is

$$\langle I \rangle = \frac{b-a}{n} \sum_{j=1}^{n} f(x_j). \tag{13.31}$$

We can gain some intuition into the estimator (13.31) by looking at Figure 13.12(b), where the yellow rectangle has the same area as the integral. The height of the rectangle, $\overline{f(x)}$, is the average (or mean) value of $f(x)$ in the interval [a, b]. We thus have

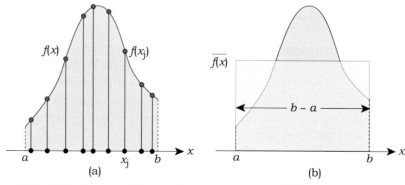

Figure 13.12. (a) Uniformly distributed random samples of $f(x)$ for Monte Carlo integration. The black dots are random values $x_j \in [a, b]$ of x; the cyan dots are the corresponding values $f(x_j)$ of $f(x)$. (b) The yellow rectangle has the same area as the grey area under $f(x)$.

$$I = (b - a)\,\overline{f(x)}. \tag{13.32}$$

Now, an estimate for $\overline{f(x)}$ is simply the average value of the samples $f(x_j)$:

$$\overline{f(x)} \approx \frac{1}{n} \sum_{j=1}^{n} f(x_j). \tag{13.33}$$

Combining (13.32) and (13.33) gives the estimator (13.31). In the limit $n \to \infty$, $\langle I \rangle = I$, but for any finite value of n, there's always an error in the estimator.

13.11.2 Variance

We need a way of being able to quantify this error. Fortunately, a quantity called *variance* is a standard measure of the error in random functions. In a ray-tracing context, variance is a measure of the error in images rendered using Monte Carlo techniques. For the integral (13.30) and the estimator (13.31), the variance V can be written as

$$V = \frac{1}{n-1} \sum_{j=1}^{n} \left[f(x_j) - \langle I \rangle \right]^2 \tag{13.34}$$

Admittedly, this formula is not particularly informative, but variance is defined and discussed in detail in the references.

Another quantity is the *standard deviation* $\sigma = \sqrt{V}$, also known as the root mean square (RMS) error. It can be shown that the RMS error σ behaves as

$$\sigma \propto 1/\sqrt{n}, \tag{13.35}$$

(see, for example, Dutré et al. (2006)). As a result, if we wanted to halve the error, we would have to use four times as many samples. This is a problem with Monte Carlo integration, but that's more than compensated for by its advantages. Although there exist more efficient *numerical quadrature* techniques for evaluating 1D integrals, the error involved in these increases exponentially with the dimension of the integrals. In contrast, the error behavior (13.35) for Monte Carlo integration is independent of the integral's dimension. That makes it by far the best technique for evaluating the integrals in ray tracing, which can have arbitrarily high effective dimensions.

The variance in images shows up as noise; Figure 26.7(b) is an example.

13.11.2 Importance Sampling

There are a number of techniques that we can use to reduce the variance with Monte Carlo integration. Instead of using uniformly distributed samples, we

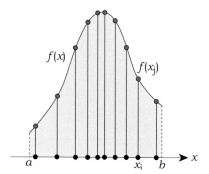

Figure 13.13. In importance sampling, we try to use sample points with a density that matches the shape of the function as closely as we can.

can try to use a sample density that has a similar shape to $f(x)$. This is called *importance sampling* (Figure 13.13). The logic behind importance sampling is that areas where the function is large contribute more to the integral than areas where it's small and are therefore more *important*. We can therefore get a better estimate of the integral by using a higher sampling density in these areas.

The density of the samples is specified by a *probability density function* $p(x)$, or pdf for short. The reason for this name is that the sample points will be generated using random numbers, where the probability P of a sample being generated in an interval $[x_0, x_1]$ is

$$P(x_0 \le x \le x_1) = \int_{x_o}^{x_1} p(x)\,dx.$$

For the integral (13.30), the pdf will have the following properties:

$$p(x) \ge 0 \; \forall \; x \in [a, b], \tag{13.36}$$

$$\int_a^b p(x)\,dx = 1. \tag{13.37}$$

The property (13.36) states that probabilities can't be negative. The property (13.37) is a normalization condition that states that all the sample points will be in the interval $[a, b]$, or in other words, the probability of a given sample being in the interval is one.

It can be shown that the Monte Carlo estimator in this situation is

$$\langle I \rangle = \frac{1}{n} \sum_{j=1}^{n} \frac{f(x_j)}{p(x_j)}. \tag{13.38}$$

This is not valid if any zero values of $p(x_j)$ occur where $f(x_j)$ is not zero.

For a uniform distribution of samples, $p(x) = c$ for some constant c. Substituting this into Equation (13.37) gives

$$c \int_a^b dx = c(b - a) = 1 \Rightarrow c = \frac{1}{b - a}. \tag{13.39}$$

Substituting (13.39) into (13.38) gives the estimator (13.31), as expected.

For a multi-dimensional integral

$$I = \int_D f(\mathbf{x})\,d\mathbf{x}$$

over some m-dimensional domain D, the Monte Carlo estimator is

$$\langle I \rangle = \frac{1}{n} \sum_{j=1}^{n} \frac{f(x_j)}{p(x_j)}, \tag{13.40}$$

where x_j is an m-dimensional sample point.

The optimal pdf for the estimator (13.40) is $p(x) = f(x)/I$, where the variance is zero, but we usually can't use this, because $f(x)$ is often unknown. For pdfs that don't exactly match the function, the estimator (13.40) has the same $1/\sqrt{n}$ error as the 1D case in Equation (13.35).

I'll use (13.40) to evaluate the integrals in the hemisphere and area forms of the rendering equation. In the hemisphere form (13.21), the integral will be over the hemisphere above a hit point, with an angular domain of 2π steradians. This is a 2D integral. In the area form (13.25), the integral will be over the surfaces of area lights, again a 2D integral. However, these integrals may have to be evaluated recursively, so that the effective dimension can be much larger than two. In fact, Equation (13.29) involves infinite-dimensional integrals.

For the rectangular area lights to be discussed in Chapter 18, I'll use samples uniformly distributed over the surface of the lights. In this case, the pdfs will be constant, and the normalization condition over the surface area A_l of the light will be

$$\int_{A_l} p(x)dA = 1.$$

This gives $p(x) = 1/A_l$ (Section 18.3).

In the hemisphere form, the incident radiance distribution $L_i(p, \omega_i)$ is usually unknown, but we can still make the pdf proportional to $\cos \theta_i$, which is always present in the integral, or proportional to the product of the BRDF and $\cos \theta_i$. These are known quantities. Doing this can dramatically reduce the variance compared with a uniform distribution for the same number of samples.

From the sampling chapters (Chapters 5–7), the samples will always be generated with a uniform distribution on a unit square and then mapped onto a rectangle, a disk, or a hemisphere with a cosine distribution, depending on the shading application.

I'll also use multi-jittered sampling, which is stratified, for all shading applications. Stratification can also be used as a variance-reduction technique because the variance over the individual strata is often smaller than the variance of the whole integration domain. A property of the variance is that stratification never increases it. My experience is that multi-jittered sampling always produces images with less variance than random samples do with the same number of samples per pixel. Refer to the discussion in Section 5.2.

Further Reading

Johann Lambert (1728–1777) carried out pioneering work on photometry.[6] Some of this work was recently translated into English by DiLaura (Lambert, 1760).

The monograph by Nicodemus et al. (1977) sets out the notation and formal specification of reflectance. In particular, this is where the name BRDF comes from. This is well worth reading for its comprehensive coverage of reflectance, and it is available online. I've drawn heavily on material in this monograph for Sections 13.6 and 13.7.

In his seminal paper, Kajiya (1986) derived the rendering equation in a different form from that used here, as he formulated it in terms of intensity instead of radiance. Kajiya also solved the equation using a series expansion analogous to Equation (13.23) and demonstrated how a number of existing rendering algorithms at the time were approximate solutions of it. These were hidden-surface removal, Whitted ray tracing, distribution ray tracing (Cooke et al., 1984), and radiosity (Goral et al., 1984).[7]

A number of graphics textbooks provide good coverage of some or all of the material presented here. These include Akenine-Möller and Haines (2002), Dutré et al. (2006), Glassner (1995), Jensen (2001), Pharr and Humphreys (2004), Shirley and Morley (2003), and Shirley et al. (2005). Glassner also has a nice introduction to integral equations and their solution. The notation varies somewhat from book to book. There is also Dutré's excellent *Global Illumination Compendium*, which is available online (Dutré, 2003).

Although I'll only discuss a few simple BRDFs in this book, most of the above books discuss other BRDFs, including different models for glossy specular reflection, and anisotropic reflection models.

Monte Carlo techniques were first discussed by Kelvin (1901), and then independently rediscovered by Enrico Fermi, John von Neumann, and Stanislaw Ulam in the 1940s. See the book by Hammersley and Handscomb (1964), which is also a good introduction to the subject. Other classic books include Schreider (1966) and Rubenstein (1981). Graphics textbooks that discuss the topics in Section 13.11 include Dutré et al. (2003), Glassner (1995),

---

6. Photometry is like radiometry except that it's restricted to the visible spectrum by weighting all of the radiometric quantities by the sensitivity of the human eye (see, for example, Akenine-Möller and Haines (2002)).

7. In Cook et al. (1984), distribution ray tracing is called *distributed* ray tracing.

Jensen (2001), Pharr and Humphreys (2004), Shirley and Morley (2003), and Shirley et al. (2005).

 Exercises

13.1.   With the help of the references cited in the Further Reading section, try to understand as much of this chapter as you can.

13.2.   Prove that the projected solid element $\cos \theta \, d\omega$ is the projection of $d\omega$ onto the (x, z) plane.

13.3.   If you are familiar with integral calculus, verify that Equation (13.18) is correct.

14   **Lights and Materials**

 Objectives

By the end of this chapter, you should:

- know the difference between direct and indirect illumination;
- understand how directional lights and point lights are defined;
- understand how ambient and diffuse shading work;
- have implemented ambient and diffuse shading with directional and point lights and a matte material.

In this chapter, I'll start to discuss shading, the process that gives visual appearance to objects. Without shading, we can only render objects with constant colors, as in Chapter 3, where all of the objects look flat. Shading results from the interaction of light with the surfaces of objects, as described by the BRDFs introduced in Chapter 13. Light sources provide emitted radiance, which becomes incident radiance at object surfaces. Materials encapsulate the BRDFs, and at least one material is stored with each geometric object. Shading is the most complex part of the ray tracer because of the large number of light paths that have to be simulated, the complex ways that light can interact with materials, and the number of classes involved in even simple shading operations: the world, the camera, tracers, materials, BRDFs, lights, and the `ShadeRec` object. A robust, flexible, and extensible shading architecture is therefore critical.

This chapter describes how to use ray casting to shade perfectly diffuse materials with ambient, directional, and point lights, but in the process, it also describes the shading architecture and how it works. To help you understand how the various objects interact, Figure 14.1 shows the classes and member functions involved in this type of shading. It also lists the information that's passed to and returned from the functions. Arrows on the left and top indicate function calls, while arrows on the right and bottom indicate return values.[1]

The following is a brief description of how these processes work, some of which you have seen before. The main function constructs the scene by calling the `World::build` function, and then it calls the `render_scene` function

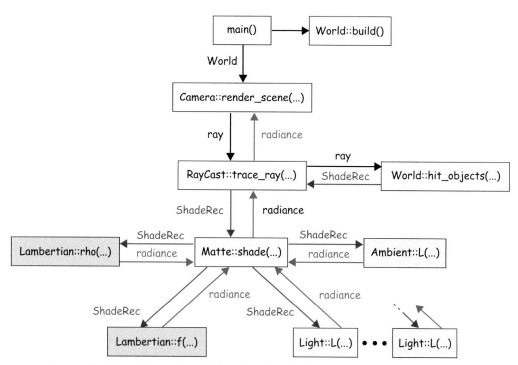

Figure 14.1. Function calls and data flow for shading with a `Matte` material. The BRDFs (mauve) are on the left of the matte material, and the lights (lemon) are on the right. The ellipsis (• • •) at the lower right indicates that there can be any number of lights involved in the shading.

---

1. I've left out some of the information that's transferred between functions because the BRDF functions rho and f also have ω_i and ω_o as parameters, but they aren't used for Lambertian BRDFs.

for a particular camera type with the world as an argument. See, for example `Pinhole::render_scene` in Listing 9.5.

The `render_scene` function constructs a primary ray and calls the `trace_ray` function for a particular tracer with the ray as an argument. In this case, we use a `RayCast` tracer. The first task of `RayCast::trace_ray` in Listing 14.10 is to call the world `hit_objects` function, which constructs a `ShadeRec` object and returns it to `trace_ray`. If the ray has hit an object, the `ShadeRec` object will contain a pointer to the nearest object's `Matte` material, whose `shade` function is then called.

The Matte::shade function in Listing 14.14 uses two `Lambertian` BRDFs and the lights to compute the reflected radiance back along the ray. The reflected radiance is returned to the `trace_ray` function and then to the `render_scene` function, where it contributes to the pixel's color.

What this example doesn't illustrate is the extensive information flow contained in the `ShadeRec` object, which is passed to all BRDFs and lights. `Lambertian` BRDFs and directional lights are too simple to need the `ShadeRec` object, although the `Matte::shade` function does use it (see Listing 14.14).

14.1 Illumination and Reflection

The *illumination* in a scene is a general term for the light that originates at the light sources and arrives at object surfaces. *Direct illumination* is light that hits a surface by traveling directly from a light source (see Figure 14.2(a)). In

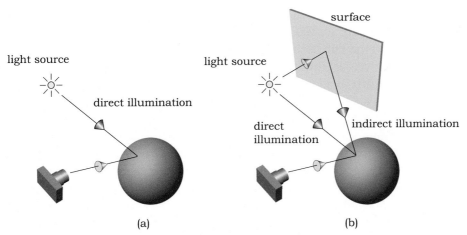

(a)   (b)

Figure 14.2. (a) Direct illumination hits the surface of an object directly from a light source; (b) indirect illumination hits a surface after being reflected from at least one other surface.

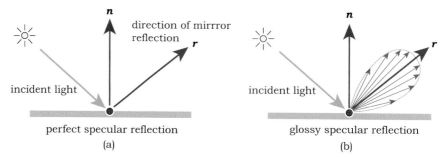

Figure 14.3. (a) Perfect specular reflection; (b) glossy specular reflection.

contrast, *indirect illumination*, as illustrated in Figure 14.2(b), hits a surface after being reflected from at least one other surface. Here, the sphere receives both direct and indirect illumination from the light source. Another common naming convention is to call direct illumination *local illumination* and to call indirect illumination *global illumination*.

The way that light is reflected from surfaces can be quite complex, but computer graphics has traditionally modeled this using a combination of specular and diffuse reflection. At one extreme, there's *perfect specular reflection*, where the light is reflected in the single direction r of mirror reflection (see Figure 14.3(a)). The other extreme is perfect diffuse reflection as illustrated in Figure 13.6, where the light is scattered equally in all directions. In between these extremes, there's *glossy specular reflection*, where the light is concentrated around the direction of mirror reflection but is also scattered. This is illustrated in Figure 14.3(b). Although these are the only reflection models I'll use, they don't fully capture the reflection properties of many real materials (see Chapter 13 and the Further Reading section).

Perfect specular reflection is used to render mirrors, and transparent materials such as glass, with indirect illumination. Mirrors can be modeled by tracing a single reflected ray at each hit point (see Figure 14.4(a) and Chapter 24). In contrast, glossy specular reflection is used for both direct and indirect illumination. First, it's a component of the Phong reflection model, where it's used to give materials a shiny appearance without rendering reflections (see Chapter 15). Second, it can be used to render glossy reflections, a process that's more complex than rendering mirror reflections because many rays per pixel have to be traced to produce accurate results (see Figure 14.4(b) and Chapter 25). Perfect diffuse reflection is also used for direct and indirect illumination where it's a direct-reflection component of matte materials (see Section 14.6). For indirect illumination, it can be used to model diffuse-diffuse

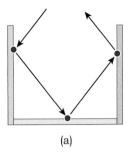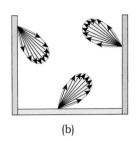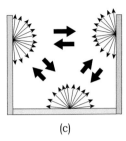

(a)   (b)   (c)

Figure 14.4. (a) Mirror reflection can be modeled by tracing a single reflected ray at each hit point; (b) modeling glossy specular light transport between surfaces requires many rays to be traced per pixel; (c) modeling perfect diffuse light transport between surfaces also requires many rays to be traced per pixel.

light transport (see Figure 14.4(c) and Chapter 26). This also requires many rays per pixel for accurate results.

14.2 Lights

The light types I'll define are ambient, ambient occluder, directional, point, area, and environment, which will all be handled polymorphically by the ray tracer. The directional and point lights are simple to shade with but are non-physical. Lights should be defined in terms of their power (radiant flux), but that's difficult to define for directional lights and not necessary in my shading architecture. Instead, the lights I'll discuss in this chapter, ambient, directional, and point lights, are specified by a color c_l and a radiance scaling factor l_s, where $l_s \in [0, \infty)$. This is appropriate because lights deliver radiance proportional to $l_s c_l$ along rays to the hit points. By changing l_s, which is a convenience feature like k_d, we can change the brightness of the lights by changing a single number that multiplies the color. Although brightness is a perceptual quantity, the lights are still defined using radiometric quantities.

14.2.1 The Ambient Light

Because of the difficulties in simulating indirect diffuse illumination, a common practice is to assume that this illumination is constant throughout the scene, where it's called *ambient illumination*. Although this is of course not even approximately correct for real scenes, it's better than doing nothing. It provides some illumination to those parts of objects that receive no direct illumination.

Without ambient illumination, these would be rendered black, which is not realistic. In real scenes, just about all surfaces receive some light.

Ambient illumination corresponds to the first term in the rendering equation solution (13.29). This is L_e but from a volume light that provides all surface points with the same amount of incident radiance. Essentially, we model the ambient illumination as an isotropic 3D radiance field. The ambient light that implements this provides part of the reflected radiance for all materials that contain a diffuse-reflection component. Images rendered with only ambient illumination show all surfaces with constant colors, but each material can have a different diffuse color and reflect a different fraction of the ambient illumination.

The incident radiance $L_i(p, \omega_i)$ from the ambient light is

$$L_i = l_s\, c_l,\tag{14.1}$$

which is independent of p and ω_i.

The reflected ambient radiance is

$$L_o(p, \omega_o) = \rho_{hh}(p) * l_s\, c_l,$$

where $\rho_{hh}(p)$ is given by Equation (13.18) and the $*$ operator is component-wise muliplication of two RGB colors as defined in Equation (3.10). Figure 14.5

Figure 14.5. Two spheres, a cylinder, an axis-aligned box, and a plane, rendered with ambient illumination only.

shows a number of objects rendered with ambient illumination. This is a good candidate for the most boring image in the book.

14.2.2 Directional Lights

Light rays from a directional light are parallel, as Figure 14.6(a) illustrates, and they therefore come from a single direction. In addition, their incidence radiance doesn't vary with position. The Sun is a good approximation of a directional light source because its rays on the surface of the Earth are essentially parallel, but directional lights are mathematical abstractions that don't exist in nature. For example, the Sun is really a spherical light source, about $0.5°$ across in the sky.

A directional light is specified by the direction l from which the light is coming. This is *opposite* to the direction of the incoming light. Direct illumination at a point p from a directional light is represented by the integral (13.10)

$$L_o(p,\omega_o) = \int_{2\pi^+} f_r(p,\omega_i,\omega_o)L_i(p,\omega_i)\cos\theta_i d\omega_i, \tag{14.2}$$

where the incident radiance comes from the single direction $\omega_i = l$. This is independent of p, as illustrated in Figure 14.6(b). We can express ω_i in terms of the azimuth and polar angles oriented around the normal at p:

$$\omega_i = (\sin\theta_l \sin\phi_l, \cos\theta_l, \sin\theta_l \cos\phi_l). \tag{14.3}$$

These are illustrated in Figure 13.3, where $\phi_i = \phi_l$, and $\theta_i = \theta_l$.

The reflected radiance is

$$L_o(p, \omega_o) = f_r (p, l, \omega_o) * l_s c_l \cos\theta_l. \tag{14.4}$$

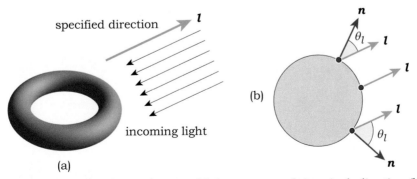

(a)   (b)

Figure 14.6. (a) The light from a directional light source travels in a single direction; (b) the light direction l is the same for all hit points.

Since we know the expression for $L_o(p, \omega_o)$, we can work backwards and *design* an incident radiance distribution $L_i(p, \omega_i)$ that gives the expression (14.4) when it's substituted into the integral (14.2). The distribution has to be zero for all incoming directions except l, where it has to be infinite. $L_i(p, \omega_i)$ is therefore represented by a *delta function* (Section 2.14), but how do we write it? The answer is

$$L_i(p, \omega_i) = l_s\, c_l\, \delta(\cos\theta_i - \cos\theta_l)\delta(\phi_i - \phi_l), \qquad (14.5)$$

because this gives the right answer (see Exercise 14.9). If you don't understand this, don't worry. It's only here to demonstrate how illumination from a directional light is represented in the rendering equation. The important practical things are Equation (14.4), which I'll use in diffuse materials to compute $L_o(p, \omega_o)$, and the BRDF function f_r. Also, the expression (14.3) for ω_i is only used in Equation (14.5). In the shading code, we will only need l in world coordinates. For example, $l = (0, 1, 0)$ is for a directional light coming straight down.

Figure 14.7 shows the objects in Figure 14.5 illuminated with a single directional light. Notice that the color of the ground plane is constant (see also Figure 14.11(c)).

For n directional lights, the reflected radiance can be written as the sum

$$L_o(p, \omega_o) = \sum_{j=1}^{n} f_r(p, l_j, \omega_o) * l_{s,j} c_{l,j} \cos\theta_{l,j}. \qquad (14.6)$$

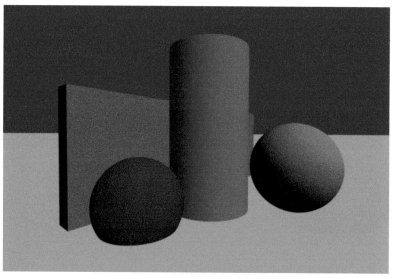

Figure 14.7. The scene in Figure 14.5 illuminated with a directional light.

14.2.3 Point Lights

Light from a point light radiates from a specified point in world coordinates, as illustrated in Figure 14.8(a). In the simplest type of point light, the light is emitted isotropically.

If the radiant intensity of the light is I, its flux Φ is obtained by integrating I over the surface of a unit sphere centered on the light:

$$\Phi = \int_{4\pi} I d\omega = 4\pi I. \tag{14.7}$$

Now consider another sphere of radius r that surrounds the light, as in Figure 14.8(b). The flux through this sphere must be the same, but because the surface area is $4\pi r^2$, the irradiance at every point on its surface is

$$E = \Phi/(4\pi r^2) = I/r^2,$$

from Equation (14.7). This equation expresses the fact that irradiance from a point light decreases as the inverse square of the distance from the light. In physics, this is called the *inverse square law*; in computer graphics, it's referred to as *distance attenuation*.

Point lights are also mathematical abstractions that can't exist in nature; a point can't emit light because it has zero surface area. In contrast, all real light sources have finite surface area. Nonetheless, point lights are useful for lighting scenes because of the simple expression for their irradiance.

If we let $I = l_s\, c_l$, the reflected radiance at a surface point is

$$L_o(p, \omega_o) = f_r(p, l(p), \omega_o) * l_s\, c_l/(r^2) \cos\theta_l, \tag{14.8}$$

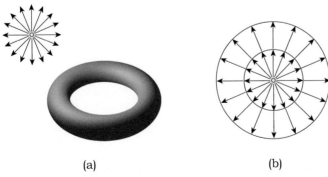

(a)   (b)

Figure 14.8. (a) The light radiates from a single point from a point light. (b) A point light with two imaginary spheres centered on it. Although the total flux for each sphere is the same, the flux per unit area is inversely proportional to the square of the radius.

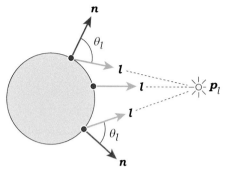

Figure 14.9. The incoming light direction for a point light always points towards the light.

where $r = \|p_l - p\|$ is the distance between p and the location of the light p_l. In contrast to a directional light, the light direction l does vary with p because it always points towards the light location (see Figure 14.9).

In analogy to Equation (14.5), the incident radiance distribution is

$$L_i(p, \omega_i) = l_s \, c_l/(r^2) \, \delta(\cos \theta_i - \cos \theta_l) \delta(\phi_i - \phi_l).$$

For n point lights, there's also an analogous expression to Equation (14.6). Figure 14.10 shows the scene in Figure 14.5 rendered with a point light. Notice how the shading of the plane reduces to ambient illumination towards the horizon. This is due to two factors. The first is the distance attenuation, but the second is the $\cos \theta_l$ term in Equation (14.8), which approaches zero as the hit points approach the horizon.

It's useful to compare the shading under a number of lighting conditions. Figure 14.11(a) shows the scene rendered with the point light in Figure 14.10 but with the camera farther from the objects. Notice how the light reflected from the plane is concentrated under the point light (the white dot). Figure 14.11(b) shows the shading with distance attenuation turned off so that

$$L_o(p, \omega_o) = f_r(p, l(p), \omega_o) * l_s \, c_l \cos \theta_l.$$

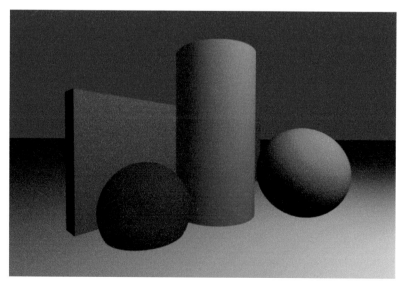

Figure 14.10. The scene from Figure 14.5 rendered with a point light.

(a)

(b)

Figure 14.11. (a) Shading with a point light with distance attenuation; (b) shading with a point light with no distance attenuation; (c) shading with a directional light.

(c)

The reflected light is more spread out but still decreases with distance due to the $\cos \theta_l$ term in L_o. Figure 14.11(c) shows the shading with the directional light, where the shading on the plane is constant.

In my experience, there are three practical problems with using distance attenuation. The first is that the drop-off in irradiance is too sharp; it certainly doesn't accurately model real indoor or outdoor lighting situations. The second problem is that the lighting is extremely sensitive to the size of the objects in the scene. For large scenes, it's difficult to get adequate (or any) shading far from the light without the shading significantly overflowing near the light. I'll discuss how to handle overflow in Section 14.9. The third problem is the issue of scaling the radiance. Although the objects on the plane are not huge (the cylinder is 8.5 units high) and the light is at world coordinates (15, 15, 2.5), the value of l_s for the point light in Figure 14.11(a) is 300 times that of Figure 14.11(b) and for the directional light in Figure 14.11(c). If all dimensions were scaled by a factor of 10, it would have to be 30,000 times larger.

For these reasons, I don't normally use distance attenuation, although it can be an option in the PointLight class. The cosine factor provides adequate drop-off for most applications, and the required value of l_s is not sensitive to the scale of the scene. Commercial renderers often allow users to specify the attenuation as an arbitrary power of the distance (see Exercise 14.4).

An advantage of point lights over directional lights is that they can provide localized illumination, a property that's particularly useful in enclosed environments. Figures 24.19–24.22 are examples.

14.3 Light Classes

Figure 14.12 shows a simplified Light inheritance chart with the three light types introduced in Section 14.2. I'll discuss the shadows data member in Chapter 16. Each derived class defines the following two functions: get_direction, which returns the direction of the incoming light at a hit point, and L, which returns the incident radiance at a hit point.

Listing 14.1 shows part of the declaration of the Light base class. The data members common to the three derived classes are ls and color. You will need access functions for these, but since the vast majority of images in the book

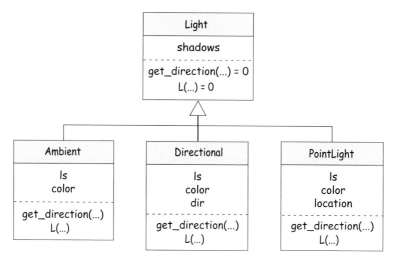

Figure 14.12. Simplified Light inheritance chart.

```
class Light {
    public:

        ...

        virtual Vector3D
        get_direction(ShadeRec& sr) = 0;

        virtual RGBColor
        L(ShadeRec& sr) = 0;

    protected:

        bool shadows;
};
```

Listing 14.1. Partial declaration of the Light base class.

```
class Ambient: public Light {
    public:

        ...

        virtual Vector3D
        get_direction(ShadeRec& sr);

        virtual RGBColor
        L(ShadeRec& sr);

    private:
        float       ls;
        RGBColor    color;

};

Ambient::Ambient(void)        // default constructor
    : Light(),
    ls(1.0),
    color(1.0)                // white
{}

Vector3D
Ambient::get_direction(ShadeRec& sr) {
    return (Vector3D(0.0));
}

RGBColor
Ambient::L(ShadeRec& sr) {
    return (ls * color);
}
```

Listing 14.2. Code for the Ambient light class.

have white lights, I've set white as the default color in the Light constructor.
The build functions therefore only have to set the color if it's not white.

The ls data member is not in the base class because, for area and environment lights, ls is in the *emissive material* that they use (see Chapter 18). The color data member is not in the base class because area lights can have a textured material where the color varies with position (see Chapter 29).

Ambient is the simplest light class because there's no direction involved. Listing 14.2 shows part of the code for this class where the L function just returns $l_s\, c_l$. The get_direction function returns the zero vector because it's not called anywhere.

Listing 14.3 contains code for the PointLight class. Notice how the get_direction function returns a unit vector that points away from the hit point and uses the hit-point coordinates stored in the ShadeRec object. Also notice that the L function, without distance attenuation, is the same as Ambient::L.

I won't reproduce the directional-light code here, because it's similar to the point light.

```
class PointLight: public Light {
    public:

        ...
        virtual Vector3D
        get_direction(ShadeRec& sr);

        virtual RGBColor
        L(ShadeRec& sr);

    private:

        float ls;
        RGBColor color;
        Vector3D location;
};

Vector3D
PointLight::get_direction(ShadeRec& sr) {
    return((location - sr.hitPoint).hat());
}

RGBColor
PointLight::L(const ShadeRec& sr) const {
    return (ls * color);
}
```

Listing 14.3. Part of the code for the PointLight class.

14.4 The World and ShadeRec Classes

To perform shading operations, we need to include additional data members and member functions in the World and ShadeRec classes introduced in Chapter 3.

14.4.1 The World

Listing 14.4 shows how we store the ambient light and other lights in the World class, where the new code is blue. The ambient light is stored directly in the

```cpp
class World {
    public:

            ViewPlane vp;
            Camera* camera_ptr;
            Tracer* tracer_ptr;
            RGBColor background_color;
            Light* ambient_ptr;
            vector<GeometricObject*> objects;
            vector<Light*> lights;

    public:

            // constructors, etc.

            void
            add_object(Object* object_ptr);

            void
            add_light(Light* light_ptr);

            void
            build(void);

            void
            display_pixel(const int row, const int col, RGBColor& pc) const;

            void
            open_window(const int hres, const int vres) const;

            ShadeRec
            hit_objects(const Ray& ray, float& tmin) const;

};
```

Listing 14.4. World declaration that includes the lights.

```
World::World(void)
    : camera_ptr(NULL),
    background_color(black),
    tracer_ptr(NULL),
    ambient_ptr(new Ambient)
{}
```

Listing 14.5. The world default constructor.

world because its illumination is handled separately from the direct illumination by the other lights. The ambient pointer is a `Light` pointer instead of a pointer to `Ambient` so that it can be assigned different types of ambient lights. I'll also use it for ambient occlusion in Chapter 17.

In the world default constructor (Listing 14.5), I've initialized the ambient pointer to a default `Ambient` object instead of the null pointer. The default is all we need for the majority of scenes, because we can specify k_a independently for each material. As a result, we only have to specify the ambient light in build functions when we need an l_s or a color that's different from their default values in Listing 14.2.

14.4.2 The `ShadeRec` Class

Listing 14.6 shows in blue the additional `ShadeRec` data members that we need for shading. As a reminder, the world reference was included in Listing 3.3.

One of the shading problems that the `ShadeRec` object solves is the following. The shade functions for each material have to work with the lights to compute the reflected radiance, but materials have no direct access to the lights. The `ShadeRec` object provides this access through the `world` reference data member. Refer to the Chapter 3 Notes and Discussion section. The `ShadeRec` object is the glue that holds the whole shading architecture together. You can see how it flows between the shading objects in Figure 14.1. Listing 14.7 shows the `ShadeRec` constructor and copy constructor.

Listing 14.8 shows the function `World::hit_objects`, whose first line constructs a `ShadeRec` object using the world reference. It then stores in it all of the information required for shading the nearest hit point. Note that the loop maintains the normal and the local hit-point coordinates in local variables. Why, then, are these stored back in the `ShadeRec` object after the loop has finished? It's because these are set in every `hit` function where the ray hits an object. Suppose the nearest hit point occurs on the next-to-last object in the objects list and that the ray hits the last object. When the loop terminates, the values for the normal and the local hit-point coordinates stored in

```
class ShadeRec {
    public:

            bool hit_an_object;          // did the ray hit an object?
            Material* material_ptr;      // nearest object's material
            Point3D hit_point;           // world coordinates of hit point
            Point3D local_hit_point;  // for attaching textures to objects
            Normal normal;               // normal at hit point
            RGBColor color;              // only used in Chapter 3
            Ray ray;                     // for specular highlights
            int depth;                   // recursion depth
            Vector3D dir;                // for area lights
            World& w;                    // world reference

            ShadeRec(World& wr);         // constructor
            ShadeRec(const ShadeRec& sr);  // copy constructor

};
```

Listing 14.6. The class ShadeRec.

```
ShadeRec::ShadeRec(World& wr)
    : hit_an_object(false),
    material_ptr(NULL),
    hit_point(), local_hit_point(), normal(),
    ray(), depth(0), dir(),
    w(wr)                             // initialize world reference
{}

ShadeRec::ShadeRec(const ShadeRec& sr)
    : hit_an_object(sr.hit_an_object),
    material_ptr(sr.material_ptr),         // just copy pointer
    hit_point(sr.hit_point), local_hit_point(sr.local_hit_point),
    normal(sr.normal),
    ray(sr.ray), depth(sr.depth), dir(sr.dir),
    w(sr.w)
{}
```

Listing 14.7. The ShadeRec constructor and copy constructor.

the ShadeRec object will be for the last object, not for the nearest hit point. In contrast, the material pointer is only stored in the ShadeRec object when there's a nearer hit, and the loop always terminates with the correct material pointer. You may be wondering what the difference is between the hit_point

```
World::hit_objects(const Ray& ray) const {
    ShadeRec sr(*this);   // constructor
    float t;
    Normal normal;
    Point3D local_hit_point;
    float tmin = kHugeValue;
    int num_objects = objects.size();

    for (int j = 0; j < num_objects; j++)
        if (objects[j]->hit(ray, t, sr) && (t < tmin)) {
            sr.hit_an_object = true;
            tmin = t;
            sr.material_ptr = objects[j]->get_material();
            sr.hit_point = ray.o + t * ray.d;
            normal = sr.normal;
            local_hit_point = sr.local_hit_point;
        }

    if (sr.hit_an_object) {
        sr.t = tmin;
        sr.normal = normal;
        sr.local_hit_point = local_hit_point;
    }

    return (sr);
}
```

Listing 14.8. The function `World::hit_objects`.

and `local_hit_point` coordinates. These are the same unless the object has been transformed, as I'll explain in Chapter 21.

14.5 Tracers

The tracer classes, which were also introduced in Chapter 3, are a critical component of the shading architecture. They provide the flexibility to implement different shading algorithms without having to change the cameras' `render_scene` functions. The `trace_ray` functions implement the shading algorithms by calling a particular shade function for each material in a scene. This should be clear after you have read Section 14.7 on materials.

Figure 14.13 shows the inheritance chart for the tracers, where I've left out the simple tracers from Chapter 3. I've also simplified the member func-

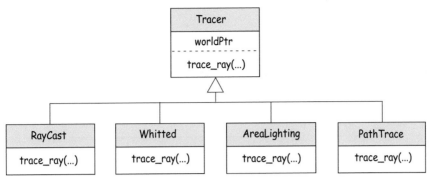

Figure 14.13. The Tracer inheritance chart.

tions because the base class actually defines three trace_ray functions with different signatures. These are shown in Listing 14.9, with the new functions in blue.

I won't reproduce the Tracer class definition here because the only difference between it and the code in Listing 3.13 are the two new trace_ray functions, which return black. The version with tmin as a parameter is only used to implement color filtering with the Dielectric material in Chapter 28.

```
class Tracer {
    public:

        Tracer(void);

        Tracer(World* _world_ptr);

        virtual RGBColor
        trace_ray(const Ray& ray) const;

        virtual RGBColor
        trace_ray(const Ray ray, const int depth) const;

        virtual RGBColor
        trace_ray(const Ray ray, float& tmin, const int depth) const;

    protected:

        World* world_ptr;
};
```

Listing 14.9. The base class Tracer.

```
RGBColor
RayCast::trace_ray(const Ray ray, const int depth) const {
    ShadeRec sr(world_ptr->hit_objects(ray));     // copy constructor

    if (sr.hitAnObject) {
        sr.ray = ray;                 // for specular reflection (Chapter 15)
        return (sr.material_ptr->shade(sr));
    }
    else
        return (world_ptr->background_color);
}
```

Listing 14.10. The function RayCast::trace_ray.

The depth parameter is used to simulate reflections and transparency in Chapters 24–28.

This chapter is concerned with ray casting, as originally described in Chapter 3 for axis-aligned orthographic projection. The RayCast tracer handles ray casting, where its trace_ray function in Listing 14.10 ignores the depth parameter.[2] Notice that the local ShadeRec object is copy constructed using the return value from the World::hit_objects function. You may have also noticed that the ShadeRec copy constructor in Listing 14.7 only copies the material pointer. That's because, in this context, there's no need to clone it.[3]

14.6 Diffuse Shading

14.6.1 Basic Expressions

The reflected radiance from a material that implements diffuse reflection will generally have ambient and direct illumination components. The ambient component is given by the product of ρ_{hh} in Equation (13.20) and the incident ambient radiance in Equation (14.1):

$$L_o(p, \omega_o) = \rho_{hh} * L_i(p, \omega_i)$$
$$= k_a\, c_d * (l_s\, c_l), \tag{14.9}$$

---

2. Putting the depth parameter in this trace_ray function for all the tracers is necessary to give them a common signature.

3. My compiler also copy constructs the ShadeRec object in the return statement in World::hit_objects in Listing 14.8.

where $k_a \in [0, 1]$ is the *ambient reflection coefficient* of the material. This should be the same as the diffuse coefficient k_d introduced in Equation (13.20) because ambient reflection *is* diffuse reflection, but allowing these to be different gives us more shading flexibility.

Since I'm not using distance attenuation for point lights, the reflected radiance from a number of directional and point lights is the sum (14.6) with the BRDF $f_{r,d}$ given by Equation (13.19). This is added to the ambient reflection to give

$$L_o(\boldsymbol{p}, \boldsymbol{\omega}_o) = k_a\, \boldsymbol{c}_d * (l_s\, \boldsymbol{c}_l) + \sum_{j=1}^{n}(k_d\, \boldsymbol{c}_d / \pi) * (l_{s,j}\, \boldsymbol{c}_{l,j})\, (\boldsymbol{n} \bullet \boldsymbol{l}_j) \qquad (14.10)$$

for the total reflected radiance at p, where $\boldsymbol{n} \bullet \boldsymbol{l}_j = \cos\theta_j$.

This is, however, not the end of the story. To shade closed objects such as spheres and axis-aligned boxes from the outside, we have to check if each hit point is visible to the light source. Figure 14.14 shows a single convex object where surface points that receive light have $\boldsymbol{n} \bullet \boldsymbol{l} \geq 0$ ($\theta \in [0, \pi/2]$). Here, point a is visible to the light with $\boldsymbol{n} \bullet \boldsymbol{l} > 0$, point b is on the terminator with $\boldsymbol{n} \bullet \boldsymbol{l} = 0$, but point c can't be seen by the light because the object is in the way, with $\boldsymbol{n} \bullet \boldsymbol{l} < 0$. Materials therefore need to check the value of $\boldsymbol{n} \bullet \boldsymbol{l}$ at each hit point and only shade the point with ambient illumination if $\boldsymbol{n} \bullet \boldsymbol{l} < 0$.

For points with $\boldsymbol{n} \bullet \boldsymbol{l} > 0$, the light could also be blocked by other objects and the object itself, if it's not convex, but that's where shadows come in (see Chapter 16).

Figure 4.15 shows 25 spheres shaded with ambient illumination with $l_s = 1.0$ and a single directional light with $l_s = 3.0$. This illustrates how the shading varies as k_a and k_d are changed. As you can see, we can get a wider variety

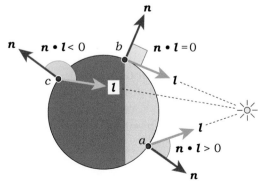

Figure 14.14. Points on the surface of an object that can and can't be seen by a light source are determined by the sign of $\boldsymbol{n} \bullet \boldsymbol{l}$, where $\boldsymbol{n}$ is the outward-pointing normal.

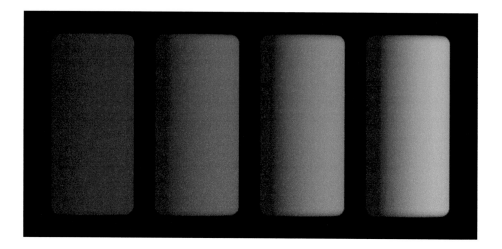

Figure 14.15. Cylinders rendered with ambient and diffuse illumination. All cylinders have k_a =0.25, and from left to right: k_d = 0.1, 0.5, 0.75, 1.0.

of shading results with $(k_a, k_d) \in [0, 1]^2$ than by restricting their values to $k_a = k_d$ for consistency and to $k_a + k_d < 1.0$ for energy conservation.

Of course, the brightness of the spheres also depends on how bright the ambient light and the directional lights are.

14.6.2 Shading Both Sides of Surfaces

The surfaces of all the geometric objects are infinitely thin shells, and the ray tracer has to be able to correctly shade both sides of these surfaces. For open cylinders and partial objects, both sides will often be visible in the same image. For planar objects, either side can be visible.[4] We can also put the camera and lights inside closed objects such as spheres and tori.

There are two aspects to getting the shading correct, the first being to make sure that the normal points in the right direction at each hit point. This is the responsibility of the hit functions. As an example, Figure 14.16 shows an open cylinder with ambient and diffuse shading from a single point light. Although the outside surface is shaded correctly, the shading on the inside surface is incorrect; most of it is ambient only, and on the right, it looks as if the light is shining through the surface.

---

4. This sentence only applies to ray casting. Reflection and transparency can completely change the visibility of surfaces; for example, both sides of planar objects can be visible.

The problem is that the normal to the cylinder points outwards. This results in $n \bullet l < 0$ for *some* hit points on the inside surface, where the shaders will use ambient illumination only. For other hit points, we have $n \bullet l > 0$, which results in full shading. This is where the light seems to be shining through the cylinder, on the right.

To fix this, we have to reverse the direction of the normal when the ray hits the inside surface. Fortunately, this situation is simple to detect, as the condition is $n \bullet \omega_o < 0$ (see Figure 14.17). The responsibility for reversing the normal lies with the hit functions.

Figure 14.18 illustrates the four shading situations where a ray can hit an object from the inside or the outside, *after* the hit function has reversed the normal when the ray hits the inside surface.

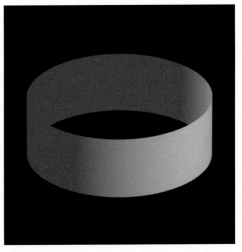

Figure 14.16. An open cylinder with incorrect shading on the inside surface.

Figure 14.19 shows the correct shading of the open cylinder in Figure 14.16 where four example hit points are labeled with the corresponding part of Figure 14.18.

You can decide which objects to render with full illumination on both sides, but you need to know that reversing the normal in the hit functions will create problems with transparent objects, where rays can also hit the inside surfaces. As you'll see in Chapter 27, the transparent material shading code also reverses the normal in this case, and if the hit function reverses it, these would cancel. As a result, the transparency code would not work. The solution I've adopted is to implement three versions of certain open and planer objects, as discussed in Section 19.7.

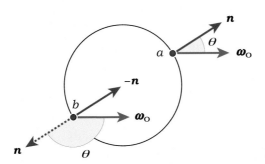

Figure 14.17. When a ray hits the outside surface of an object as at point a, $n \bullet \omega_o > 0$; when it hits the inside surface as at b, $n \bullet \omega_o < 0$.

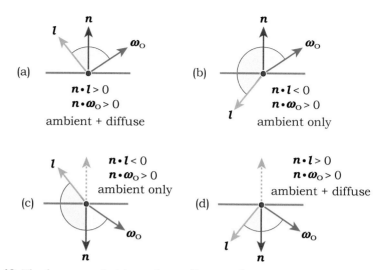

Figure 14.18. The four ways that incoming radiance and a ray can hit a surface if the hit function has reversed the normal when the ray hits the inside surface. This has happened in (c) and (d). Each part lists the type of shading that results.

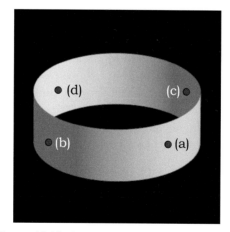

Figure 14.19. Correct shading of an open cylinder.

14.7 Materials

Materials and their associated BRDFs are the final link in the shading chain. The simplified Material inheritance chart in Figure 14.20 only shows two derived classes: Matte and Phong. I'll discuss Matte here and Phong in Chapter 15. Each material stores the required BRDFs and defines a number

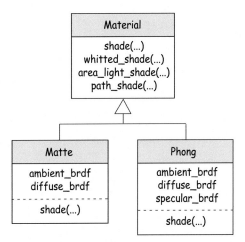

Figure 14.20. Simplified material inheritance chart.

of shading functions. There is a shading function for each derived tracer type in Figure 14.13, whose names reflect the type of shading involved: `whitted_shade`, `area_light_shade`, and `path_shade`. The exception is for ray casting, where the name is just `shade` instead of `ray_cast_shade`, as this is used in several chapters and is shorter. An important point about the `shade` functions is that they only handle directional and point lights. The purpose of each shading function is to compute the exitant radiance at the hit point in the ω_o direction.

Listing 14.11 shows the declaration for the `Material` base class, which is simple because, at this stage, it has no data members.

The shade functions are not pure virtual so that we don't have to define all of them in every material; in fact, we can start with just `shade` in `Matte` and `Phong`. As the shade functions just return black in the `Material` class, I won't reproduce their code here.

```
class Material {
    ...
    virtual RGBColor
    shade(ShadeRec& sr);

    virtual RGBColor area_light_shade(ShadeRec& sr);

    virtual RGBColor
    path_shade(ShadeRec& sr);
};
```

Listing 14.11. The class `Material`.

```
class Matte: public Material {

    public:

        Matte(void);
            ...

        void
        set_ka(const float k);

        void
        set_kd(const float k);

        void
        set_cd(const RGBColor& c);

        virtual RGBColor
        shade(ShadeRec& sr);

    private:

        Lambertian*  ambient_brdf;
        Lambertian*  diffuse_brdf;
};
```

Listing 14.12. Part of the Matte class declaration. Although the ambient and diffuse BRDFs are pointers, their names don't end with _ptr due to length.

The simplest material is Matte, which models perfect diffuse reflection with ambient and diffuse shading. The Matte class declaration appears in Listing 14.12.

From the discussion in Section 14.6.1, we specify a matte material with an ambient reflection coefficient k_a, a diffuse reflection coefficient k_d, and a diffuse color c_d. These quantities are specified in the build functions. Although they comprise the user interface of matte materials, they are stored in the BRDFs instead of the materials. Note from Listing 14.12 that the Matte class contains pointers to two Lambertian BRDFs. That's because k_a and k_d can be different, although they both represent perfect diffuse reflection. Listing 14.13 shows the default Matte constructor, which initializes the BRDF pointers to default BRDF objects instead of null pointers so that they are ready to store the parameters. Listing 14.13 also shows the access functions for k_a, k_d, and c_d, which simply pass these through to the BRDFs. See Listing 14.15 for an example of how these work in a build function.

```
Matte::Matte (void)
    : Material(),
    ambient_brdf(new Lambertian),
    diffuse_brdf(new Lambertian)
{}

void
Matte::set_ka(const float ka) {
    ambient_brdf->set_kd(ka);
}

void
Matte::set_kd (const float kd) {
    diffuse_brdf->set_kd(kd);
}

void
Matte::set_cd(const RGBColor c) {
    ambient_brdf->set_cd(c);
    diffuse_brdf->set_cd(c);
}
```

Listing 14.13. The `Matte` default constructor and access functions for setting the ambient and diffuse shading parameters.

```
RGBColor
Matte::shade(ShadeRec& sr) {
    Vector3D wo      = -sr.ray.d;
    RGBColor L = ambient_brdf->rho(sr, wo) * sr.w.ambient_ptr->L(sr);
    int numLights = sr.w.lights.size();

    for (int j = 0; j < numLights; j++) {
        Vector3D wi = sr.w.lights[j]->get_direction(sr);
        float ndotwi = sr.normal * wi;

        if (ndotwi > 0.0)
            L += diffuse_brdf->f(sr, wo, wi) * sr.w.lights[j]->L(sr) * ndotwi;
    }

    return (L);
}
```

Listing 14.14. The function `Matte::shade`.

The `Matte::shade` function in Listing 14.14 computes the ambient illumination and then loops over the lights to compute the direct diffuse illumination. Notice the BRDF function calls in red where the ambient BRDF calls rho and the diffuse BRDF calls f. See Listings 13.4 and 13.3, respectively, for the radiance values returned by these functions. The Matte::shade function is called from RayCast::trace_ray in Listing 14.10.

14.8 An Example

Figure 14.21 shows a simple scene with two spheres and a plane. The partial build function in Listing 14.15 demonstrates how to construct a ray-cast tracer, an ambient light, a point light, and the matte material for the yellow sphere.

Figure 14.21. The scene rendered from the build function in Listing 14.15.

14.9 Out-of-Gamut Colors

Section 3.8 explained how the RGB color computed for each pixel is mapped to a dispayable color, provided its components are all in the range [0, 1]. The *gamut* of a display device is the set of colors that it can display. Colors that are not in the range $(r, g, b) \in [0, 1]^3$ are called out-of-gamut colors because they don't map to displayable colors, at least not without artifacts. Many computer systems will wrap these colors into the displayable range, but this usually causes spurious colors and banding. Colors are also said to *overflow* when they are out-of-gamut. As the computed colors can easily overflow, we have to do something about them. The best technique is to render all scenes as *high dynamic range* images and apply a *local tone-mapping operator* to the image to bring the colors into gamut. This would require major modifications to the ray tracer, but Reinhard et al. (2005) discusses high dynamic range imaging in detail.

Here are a number of simpler approaches. One is to keep the lights dim enough, and k_a and k_d small enough, so that all computed colors are in gamut. Figure 14.22(a) shows a shaded version of the figure on the first page of this chapter, with no overflow. This approach isn't particularly satisfactory because it places too many restrictions on the scenes and the resulting images, which can be dull and lifeless. There are many things that can cause overflow: bright lights, highly reflective materials, specular highlights, and reflections, for

```
void
World::build(void) {

        vp.set_hres(400);
        vp.set_vres(400);
        vp.set_pixel_size(1.0);
        vp.set_samples(16);

        background_color = black;
        tracer_ptr = new RayCast(this);

        Ambient* ambient_ptr = new Ambient;
        ambient_ptr->scale_radiance(1.0);        // default
        set_ambient_light(ambient_ptr);

        Pinhole* pinhole_ptr = new Pinhole;
        pinhole_ptr->set_eye(0, 0, 500);
        pinhole_ptr->set_lookat(-5, 0, 0);
        pinhole_ptr->set_vpd(850.0);
        pinhole_ptr->compute_uvw();
        set_camera(pinhole_ptr);

        PointLight* light_ptr2 = new PointLight;
        light_ptr2->set_location(100, 50, 150);
        light_ptr2->scale_radiance(3.0);
        add_light(light_ptr2);

        Matte* matte_ptr1 = new Matte;
        matte_ptr1->set_ka(0.25);
        matte_ptr1->set_kd(0.65);
        matte_ptr1->set_cd(1, 1, 0);                  // yellow
        Sphere* sphere_ptr1 = new Sphere(Point3D(10, -5, 0), 27);
        sphere_ptr1->set_material(matte_ptr1);
        add_object(sphere_ptr1);
                       ...
}
```

Listing 14.15. Build function for two spheres and a plane rendered with ambient and diffuse shading.

example. In Figure 14.22(b), the light is twice as bright as in Figure 14.22(a), and the resulting overflow on about half the spheres has caused anomalous shading. Exactly what happens in this situation is system-dependent.

A better approach is to map the out-of-gamut colors into the displayable range with a global tone-mapping operator called max_to_one. It works as

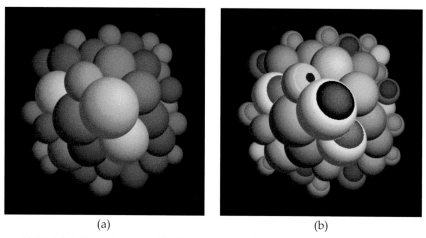

(a)   (b)

Figure 14.22. (a) Spheres image with all computed colors in gamut; (b) out-of-gamut colors have been wrapped back into the displayable range, resulting in anomalous shading.

follows: if any component of a pixel color is greater than one, all components are divided by that value. This preserves the hue and leaves the maximum component as 1.0. Here's an example where the green component is 2.0: (0.7, 2.0, 0.2) → (0.7/2.0, 2.0/2.0, 0.2/2.0) = (0.35, 1.0, 0.1). This process is also called *clamping* and is a crude technique. I've currently implemented this as a `World` member function as shown in Listing 14.16. Here, the function `max` returns the maximum of its two arguments. The code is in **Maths.h**.

Figure 14.23(a) shows the results of applying this operator to Figure 14.22(b). As you can see, this certainly improves the appearance, but the out-of-gamut areas are still obvious because they have constant colors. You should therefore try to ensure that overflow is kept to a minimum. You can call `max_to_one` at the start of the function `World::display_pixel`.

```
RGBColor
World::max_to_one(const RGBColor& c) const {
    float max_value = max(c.r, max(c.g, c.b));

    if (max_value > 1.0)
        return (c / max_value);
    else
        return (c);
}
```

Listing 14.16. The tone mapping operator `max_to_one`.

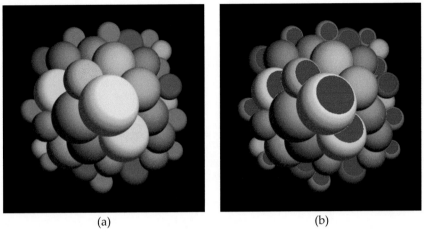

(a)   (b)

Figure 14.23. (a) The colors in Figure 14.22(b) have been clamped so that their maximum component is 1.0; (b) computed out-of-gamut colors are displayed in red.

```
RGBColor
World::clamp_to_color(const RGBColor& raw_color) const {
    RGBColor c(raw_color);

    if (raw_color.r > 1.0 || raw_color.g > 1.0 || raw_color.b > 1.0) {
        c.r = 1.0; c.g = 0.0; c.b = 0.0;
    }

    return (c);
}
```

Listing 14.17. The tone-mapping operator clamp_to_color.

Figure 14.23(b) shows the results of applying another operator, clamp_to_color, which maps all out-of-gamut colors to a specified color, red in this case. This can make it easier for you to see where overflow has occurred. The code for clamp_to_color is in Listing 14.17.

Finally, Listing 14.18 shows how these tone-mapping operators are called from the World::display_pixel function and how gamma correction is performed. Note that the view plane's clamp_to_color data member determines which tone-mapping operator is used. This allows you to specify the tone-mapping operator in the build functions, but see Exercise 14.12. The code that actually displays the pixel is system-dependent.

```
void
World::display_pixel(const int row, const int column, const RGBColor&
                      raw_color) const {
    RGBColor mapped_color;

    if (vp.show_out_of_gamut)
        mapped_color = clamp_to_color(raw_color);
    else
        mapped_color = max_to_one(raw_color);

    if (vp.gamma != 1.0)
        mapped_color = mapped_color.powc(vp.inv_gamma);

    // display the pixel - system-dependent
}
```

Listing 14.18. The function `world::display_pixel`.

 ## Further Reading

Shading with ambient, point, and directional lights is discussed in many general computer-graphics textbooks, for example Akenine-Möller and Haines (2002), Foley et al. (1994), Hearn and Baker (2004), Hill and Kelley (2006), and Shirley et al. (2005). Glassner (1995) discusses diffuse reflection in terms of BRDFs; Pharr and Humphreys (2004) discusses ray tracing with diffuse reflection, BRDFs, and directional and point lights. Several of these books discuss a variety of reflection models other than the three discussed in Section 14.1. The original inspiration for the shading architecture presented here was RenderMan, as discussed in Apodaca and Gritz (2000), but the original (and only) paper on RenderMan is Hanrahan and Lawson (1990).

The books Pharr and Humphreys (2004) and Reinhard et al. (2005) discuss *local* tone-mapping operators that operate on the whole image. These produce far better results than the simple global operators discussed here.

 ## Questions

14.1. Why is the right-hand side of Equation (14.4) the correct expression for the reflected radiance from a point light?

14.2. Figure 14.24(a) shows four spheres colored red, orange, yellow, and green, shaded with a white light. The spheres have no ambient illu-

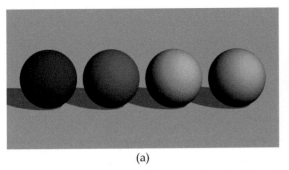 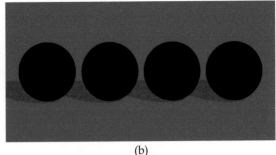

(a)   (b)

Figure 14.24. Four spheres rendered with a white light (a) and a blue light (b).

mination and are sitting on a white plane. In Figure 14.24(b), the scene is illuminated with a pure blue light with color $c_l = (0, 0, 1)$. Why are the spheres black?

14.3. Figure 14.25 shows the results of rendering the figure on the first page of this chapter with the statement `sr.normal = normal;` commented out in the function `world::hit_objects` (see Listing 14.8). Can you explain what has happened?

 Exercises

14.1. Implement ambient and diffuse shading as described in this chapter with directional and point lights. The example in Section 14.8 is the simplest way to test your implementation.

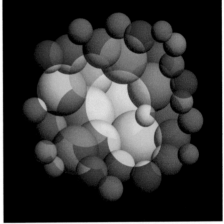

Figure 14.25. Incorrect rendering of the figure on the first page of this chapter.

14.2. Reproduce the figure on the first page of this chapter.

14.3. Reproduce Figures 14.5, 14.7, and 14.10.

14.4. Implement distance attenuation as a user-specified option for point lights and use this in the scenes in Exercises 14.1–14.3.

14.5. For point lights, allow the user to specify the distance attenuation with

$$L = b c_l / \left\| \boldsymbol{p}_l - \boldsymbol{p} \right\|^p ,$$

where $p \in [0, \infty)$ controls how fast the attenuation operates, and $p = 2$ is the inverse square law. Experiment with different values of p. What happens when $p = 0$?

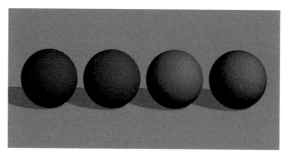

Figure 14.26. The scene in Figure 14.24(a) rendered with an orange light.

14.6. Experiment with different `Matte` parameters. In particular, render some of your images with $k_a = 0$ for all materials. What do you think of the results?

14.7. Experiment with colored ambient, directional, and point lights. You will find that colored lights can have dramatic effects on the images. Figure 14.24(b) is an extreme example. Less extreme is the scene in Figure 14.24(a) rendered with an orange light with color $c_l = (1.0, 0.5, 1.0)$ (see Figure 14.26).

14.8. The `Matte` material has a single diffuse color c_d for the ambient and diffuse illumination components. Experiment with a material that has an ambient color c_a that's different from c_d.

14.9. Show that the expression (14.4) for $L_o(p, \omega_o)$ results when you substitute the expression (14.5) into Equation (14.2). Evaluate the integral. *Hint:* Change the θ_i integration variable to $u = \cos\theta_i$ and be careful with the integration limits.

14.10. Amend the main function to check that the tracer, etc. have been defined.

14.11. Allow the user to specify the overflow color in the `clamp_to_color` tone mapper in Listing 14.17.

14.12. Instead of implementing the tone-mapping operators as member functions of the `world` class, implement an inheritance hierarchy for them. This is better design.

15 Specular Reflection

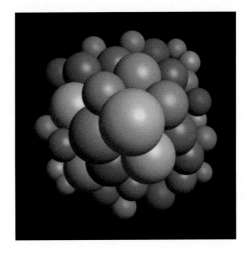

 Objectives

By the end of this chapter, you should:

- understand how glossy specular reflection is modeled in direct illumination;
- have implemented a material that includes glossy specular reflection;
- understand the difference between viewer-dependent and viewer-independent shading.

We can make materials look shiny by allowing them to reflect light that's concentrated around the direction of mirror-reflection. This glossy specular reflection results in specular highlights on surfaces, which are the smeared-out reflections of light sources. In fact, this is the only way we can make point and directional lights visible. I'll discuss here a simple model of specular reflection for direct illumination. This is the third component of the Phong direct illumination model (Phong, 1975), and it gives materials the appearance of shiny plastic. The specular highlights, if they are bright enough, are the same color as the lights, which are usually white. I'll also discuss a simple extension of the Phong model that allows us to render colored highlights with white lights.

15.1 Modeling

To model specular reflection, we need an expression for the unit vector r in the direction of mirror reflection at a hit point p, given an incoming light direction l and the normal n. These two vectors and the normal are all in the same plane, called the *plane of incidence* (see Figure 15.1). Three or more vectors and normals in the same plane are known as *coplanar*. This figure also shows the angle of incidence θ_i and the angle of reflection θ_r between the reflected direction and the normal. According to the *law of reflection* (Hecht, 1997), these angles are equal, and I'll therefore use θ_i for both. In Figure 15.1, r is not necessarily the same as the viewing direction ω_o, which also doesn't have to be in the plane of incidence. For example, these are different vectors in Figure 15.3 but the same vector in Figure 15.9.

To derive the expression for r, we note that because l, r, and n are coplanar, r must be a linear combination of l and n:

$$r = al + bn, \tag{15.1}$$

where a and b are numbers. We need two equations to determine a and b. The first equation comes from noticing that the projections of r and l onto n are the same, as Figure 15.2 shows. Taking the dot product of both sides of Equation (15.1) with n gives

$$r \bullet n = al \bullet n + bn \bullet n,$$

so that

$$(1 - a)\, l \bullet n = b. \tag{15.2}$$

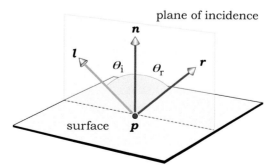

Figure 15.1. The incident-radiance direction l, surface normal n, and mirror-reflection direction r lie in the plane of incidence, with $\theta_r = \theta_i$.

Figure 15.2 also shows the unit direction $n^\perp$ that's perpendicular to n and lies in the plane of incidence. This is known as the *perp* of n (Hill, 1994), where n and $n^\perp$ form a 2D orthonormal basis in this plane. The projections of r and l onto $n^\perp$ are the negatives of each other, and taking the dot product of Equation (15.1) with $n^\perp$:

$$r \bullet n^\perp = a l \bullet n^\perp + b n \bullet n^\perp,$$

leads to

$$a = -1. \qquad (15.3)$$

Equations (15.1)–(15.3) then give the following expression for r:

$$r = -l + 2(n \bullet l)\, n \qquad (15.4)$$

(see Exercise 15.4). This is a unit vector by construction. In deriving Equations (15.2) and (15.3), I've simply projected l and r onto the 2D orthonormal basis directions n and $n^\perp$.

Since glossy specular reflection is concentrated around r, we need a way to model how the reflected radiance decreases as the angle α between r and ω_o increases. See Figure 15.3, which illustrates how ω_o can be arbitrarily oriented around r.

Phong modeled this decrease with the expression $(\cos \alpha)^e = (r \bullet \omega_o)^e$, where the *Phong exponent e* is a number that satisfies $e \geq 0$. Figure 15.4 shows $(\cos \alpha)^e$ plotted for various values of e. Since $\cos \alpha \in [0, 1]$ for $\alpha \in [0, \pi/2]$, raising $\cos \alpha$ to a power $e > 0$ makes it decrease more rapidly as α increases, a process that allows us to control the size of the specular highlights.[1]

Using Phong's original model for specular reflection, the reflected radiance from a single directional light is

$$L_o(p, \omega_o) = k_s (r \bullet \omega_o)^e\, l_s c_l, \qquad (15.5)$$

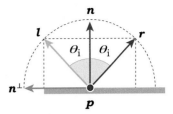

Figure 15.2. The direction of mirror reflection can be computed by projecting r onto a 2D orthonormal basis in the plane of incidence.

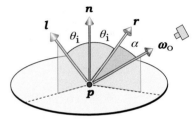

Figure 15.3. The viewing direction ω_o makes an angle α with r.

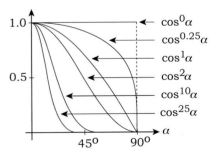

Figure 15.4. Plots of $(\cos \alpha)^e$ for various values of e.

---

1. Figure 15.4 is based on Figure 7.2 but has the $\cos^{0.25}\alpha$ curve added and different notation, and α is measured from r instead of from the top of the hemisphere.

where $k_s \in [0,1]$ is the *coefficient of specular reflection*. This is an empirical model that's not reciprocal and doesn't conserve energy, but due to the work of Lewis (1994), the reciprocity and energy-conservation problems can be fixed. One of the problems with Equation (15.5) is that there is no $\cos \theta_l = n \bullet l$ term present, although that's always in the rendering equation (13.21) and hence also in Equation (14.4) for the reflected radiance from a directional light. A reciprocal glossy specular BRDF is of the form

$$f_{r,s}(l, \omega_o) = k_s(r \bullet \omega_o)^e \qquad (15.6)$$

(Lewis, 1994). This satisfies the reciprocity condition

$$f_{r,s}(l, \omega_o) = f_{r,s}(\omega_o, l)$$

for all l and ω_o. With the BRDF (15.6), the reflected specular radiance is, from Equation (14.4),

$$L_o(p, \omega_o) = k_s(r \bullet \omega_o)^e l_s c_l (n \bullet l), \qquad (15.7)$$

which has the $n \bullet l$ term present.

We can make the BRDF energy conserving by enforcing the condition $k_d + k_s < 1.0$. The reason is that although k_d and k_s specify different types of reflection, they are for the same light source. The following expression is the sum of the ambient, diffuse, and specular reflection for n point and directional lights:

$$L_o(p, \omega_o) = k_a c_d * (l_s c_l)$$

$$+ \sum_{j=1}^{n} (k_d \, c_d \, / \, \pi) * (l_{s,j} \, c_{l,j}) \, (n \bullet l_j) \; + \sum_{j=1}^{n} k_s (r_j \bullet \omega_o)^e \, (l_{s,j} \, c_{l,j}) \, (n \bullet l_j). \quad (15.8)$$

Figure 15.5(a) shows the distribution of reflected radiance about r as a polar diagram (Phong lobe) for $e = 20$ (see also Figure 7.3). Figure 15.5(b) shows the Phong lobe for $e = 2$. Notice how this lobe penetrates the surface. In fact, for grazing incidence, half the lobe will be below the surface. That's not a problem for direct illumination, where we just evaluate the reflected radiance with $(r \bullet \omega_o)^e$, but it would be a problem for indirect illumination, unless we do something about it (see Chapter 26).

An issue with direct illumination is that the angle between r and ω_o can be greater than $\pi/2$, as also shown in Figure 15.5(b). Because this results in a negative value of $r \bullet \omega_o$, we must clamp $r \bullet \omega_o$ to positive values in Equation (15.9).

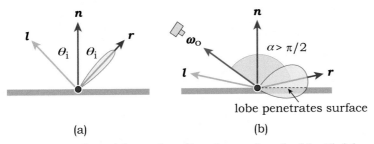

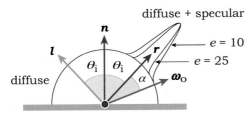

(a)   (b)

Figure 15.5. (a) Narrow Phong lobe produced by a large value of e; (b) wide lobe produced by a small value of e. This figure also illustrates how α can satisfy $\alpha > \pi/2$.

Figure 15.6. The addition of diffuse and specular reflection.

Figure 15.6 shows how specular reflection, when it's added to diffuse reflection, produces a spike in the total reflected radiance in the direction of r.

 ## 15.2 Implementation

The BRDF GlossySpecular introduced in Chapter 13 stores k_s and e (in the data member exp) and implements glossy specular reflection. The function GlossySpecular::f in Listing 15.1 returns the clamped version of Equation (15.7). Notice that, in contrast to Lambertian::f, this function makes use of all three of its parameters: it uses the normal stored in sr and wi to compute the reflected direction r and then uses wo to compute $r \cdot \omega_o$.

I've incorporated specular reflection in a material called Phong. This inherits directly from Material instead of from Matte, because a matte material does not reflect light in a specular manner. The Phong class, whose declaration appears in Listing 15.2, includes a GlossySpecular BRDF. The default constructor sets all BRDFs to their default objects.

```
RGBColor
GlossySpecular::f(const ShadeRec& sr, const Vector3D& wo, const Vector3D&
                  wi) const {

    RGBColor L;
    float ndotwi = sr.normal * wi;
    Vector3D r(-wi + 2.0 * sr.normal * ndotwi);
    float rdotwo = r * wo;

    if (rdotwo > 0.0)
        L = ks * pow(rdotwo, exp);

    return (L);
}
```

Listing 15.1. The BRDF function `GlossySpecular::f`.

```
class Phong: public Material {
        public:

                Phong(void);

                virtual RGBColor
                shade(ShadeRec& s);

        protected:

                Lambertian* ambient_brdf;
                Lambertian* diffuse_brdf;
                GlossySpecular* specular_brdf;
};
```

Listing 15.2. The `Phong` class declaration.

Listing 15.3 shows the function `Phong::shade`. The only difference between this and `Matte::shade` in Listing 14.14 is the addition of the specular term (in red).

Figure 15.7 shows a number of spheres with specular highlights, where the spheres are shaded with a single directional light. As e increases, the highlights become smaller, and the spheres look more shiny. The specular reflection coefficient k_s controls how bright the specular highlight is.

```
RGBColor
Phong::shade(ShadeRec& sr) {
    Vector3D  wo -sr.ray.d;
    RGBColor L = ambient_brdf->rho(sr, wo) * sr.w.ambient_ptr->L(sr);
    int num_lights = sr.w.lights.size();

    for (int j = 0; j < num_lights; j++) {
        Vector3D wi = sr.w.lights[j]->get_direction(sr);
        float ndotwi = sr.normal * wi;

        if (ndotwi > 0.0)
            L += (          diffuse_brdf->f(sr, wo, wi) +
            specular_brdf->f(sr, wo, wi)) * sr.w.lights[j]->L(sr) * ndotwi;
    }

    return (L);
}
```

Listing 15.3. The `Phong::shade` function.

According to Equation (15.9), the light reflected from any point on the spheres has an ambient, a diffuse, and a specular component. In practice, however, outside the specular highlights, there's essentially no visible contribution from the specular reflection (see Question 15.4).

Figure 15.8(a) shows the scene in Figure 14.7 rendered with Phong materials on all objects except the plane. The exponents range from $e = 4$ on the cylinder to $e = 500$ on the orange sphere. For comparison, Figure 15.8(b) shows the scene in Figure 14.10 rendered with the Phong materials.

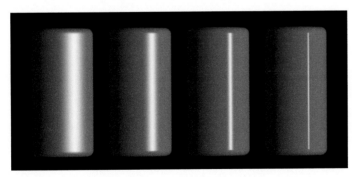

Figure 15.7. Cylinders rendered with specular highlights. All cylinders have $k_a = 0.25$, $k_d = 0.6$, $k_s = 0.2$, and from left to right: $e = 5, 20, 100, 1000$.

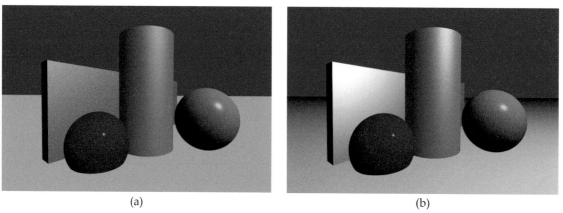

(a)   (b)

Figure 15.8. (a) The scene in Figure 14.7 rendered with specular highlights from a directional light; (b) the scene in Figure 14.10 with specular highlights from a point light. In these images, the left sphere intersects the ground plane.

 ## 15.3 Viewer Dependence

As I discussed in Chapter 14, diffuse shading varies only with the angle between the incoming radiance and the surface normal. We therefore refer to this as *viewer-independent* shading. In contrast, if you look at real objects that have specular highlights, you will notice that the highlights move around as you look at the objects from different directions. This is because a specular highlight is always centered on the direction of mirror-reflection defined by the light, the surface, and the viewer. We therefore refer to specular reflection as *viewer-dependent* shading. For a given point light, a *plane*, and a viewer on the same side of the plane as the light, there is always a single path of mirror-

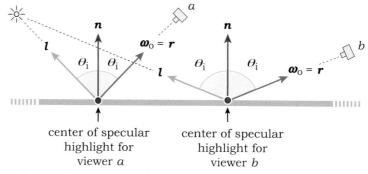

Figure 15.9. The position of the specular highlight changes when the location of the viewer changes. Note that here, $\omega_o = r$.

reflection that connects the light and the viewer. If we keep the surface and light fixed, this path depends on the location of the viewer, as Figure 15.9 illustrates with the dashed lines for two viewers *a* and *b*. For finite flat surfaces and curved surfaces, there may be no paths, multiple paths, or an infinite number of paths (see Exercises 15.1–15.3).

15.4 Colored Highlights

Because the reflected radiance in a specular highlight is a mixture of the ambient, diffuse, and specular reflection, its color is a mixture of the diffuse color of the material and the light color. If the specular highlight is bright enough, that is, the spike in the reflected radiance in Figure 15.6 is long enough, the light color will dominate. In the case of a white light, the highlight will therefore appear white. That's the case for the two spheres in Figure 15.8. On the other hand, if the highlight is dimmer, its color will be just be a brighter version of the diffuse color. That's the case for the cylinder and box in Figure 15.8.

We can make specular highlights a different color from that of the lights by introducing a *specular color* c_s that multiplies the light color in the specular highlight. The modified expression for the reflected radiance is

$$L_o(p, \omega_o) = k_a c_d * (l_s c_l)$$
$$+ \sum_{j=1}^{n} (k_d \, c_d \, / \, \pi) * (l_{s,j} \, c_{l,j}) \, (n \bullet l_j) + \sum_{j=1}^{n} k_s (r_j \bullet \omega_o)^e \, c_s * (l_{s,j} \, c_{l,j}) \, (n \bullet l_j). \quad (15.10)$$

There's nothing new here, as this is in Foley et al. (1995). This modification provides bright specular highlights of any specified color with white lights. I've found, however, that it's most useful with $c_s = c_d$, because this gives us a simple way to render Phong materials with a metallic appearance. The reason is that metals have specular highlights that have the same color as their base color, but metals are not trivial to render accurately. This is therefore just a simple trick. As examples, the left and center cylinders in Figure 15.10 have specular highlights that are the same color as their diffuse colors, and the cylinder on the right has a highlight color that's different from its diffuse color. A lot of colored highlights look good on RGB monitors but don't print well in CMYK. Red is an example. I've therefore included extra examples on the book's website.

Figure 15.10. The specular highlight color is the same as the diffuse color for the left and middle cylinders, but it's a different color for the right cylinder.

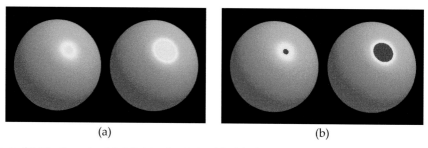

(a)   (b)

Figure 15.11. Specular highlights shaded with (a) the `max_to_one` operator and (b) the `clamp_to_color` operator using red as the overflow color. The right sphere in each image is rendered with a larger value of k_s than the left sphere.

 ## 15.5 Highlights and Overflow

Because specular highlights are the brightest parts of Phong direct illumination, their colors can easily overflow. In Figure 15.11(a), the colors have been clamped with the `max_to_one` tone-mapping operator, and overflow has occurred in both specular highlights. It's particularly noticeable on the right sphere where the highlight has a flat disk-like appearance. That's always a sign that overflow has occurred, at least when $e > 1$. The highlight is also larger than the one on the left, although both materials have the same exponent $e = 10$. In Figure 15.11(b), the overflowed colors are displayed in red.

 ## 15.6 Other Reflection Models

Blinn (1977) made the following simple modification to Phong's specular model:

$$f_{r,s}\,(\mathbf{l},\,\boldsymbol{\omega}_o) = k_s(\mathbf{n} \bullet \mathbf{h})^e,$$

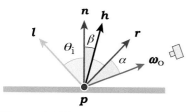

Figure 15.12. The Blinn model for specular reflection uses the halfway vector $\mathbf{h}$.

where $\mathbf{h} = (\mathbf{l} + \boldsymbol{\omega}_o) / \|\mathbf{l} + \boldsymbol{\omega}_o\|$ is the unit vector halfway between $\mathbf{l}$ and $\boldsymbol{\omega}_o$ (see Figure 15.12). The original motivation for this was efficiency, as it doesn't require the reflected vector to be computed, and for a directional light with orthographic viewing, $\mathbf{h}$ is constant.[2] It is, however, still widely used. Note that the angle β between $\mathbf{n}$ and $\mathbf{h}$ is not equal to the angle α between $\mathbf{r}$ and $\boldsymbol{\omega}_o$. A given exponent e will therefore produce a different highlight in each model. Higher values of e are required in the Blinn model to give similar

---

2. Back in the 1970s, when computers were a lot slower than they are today, this was important.

results to the Phong model. Fisher and Woo (1994) and Lewis (1994) provide comparisons between these models. Neither model is based on the physics of specular reflection.

A number of other reflection models have been developed for both diffuse and specular reflection that do model some of the physics of surface reflection. These are *microfacet*-based models, where microfacets are tiny flat reflectors with random sizes and orientations. Depending on how far their average normals differ from the surface normal, they can model smooth to rough surfaces. The facets can also shadow each other by blocking incoming light, mask each other blocking each other's view from the viewing direction, and reflect light using the Fresnel equations, as discussed in Chapter 28.

Oren and Nayar (1994) developed a diffuse reflection model for materials that are not Lambertian. An early specular model was by Cook and Torrance (1981, 1982).

A convenient way to implement different reflection models is to define a material called say, Plastic, with the declaration shown in Listing 15.4. Note that here the BRDFs are pointers to the BRDF base class instead of pointers to

```
class Plastic: public Material {
    public:

        Plastic(void);
        ...

        void
        set_ambient_brdf(BRDF* brdf);

        void
        set_diffuse_brdf(BRDF* brdf);

        void
        set_specular_brdf(BRDF* brdf);

        virtual RGBColor
        shade(ShadeRec& s);

    private:

        BRDF* ambient_brdf;
        BRDF* diffuse_brdf;
        BRDF* specular_brdf;
};
```

Listing 15.4. The class Plastic declaration.

specific derived classes. This allows us to assign any BRDFs to these but prevents Plastic itself from having any user interface for its parameters, as these can be different for each BRDF. Instead, the build functions will have to construct the BRDFs, set their parameters, and assign them to the material using the access functions in Listing 15.4.

 Further Reading

Phong's reflection model (Phong, 1965) was a landmark for computer graphics, and its continued use over the last 40 years is a testament to its simplicity and efficacy, and the fact that it looks right for many materials.

Specular reflection is discussed in many general computer graphics textbooks, such as Foley et al. (1995), Hill and Kelley (2006), and Hearn and Baker (2004). The more specialized books by Glassner (1995), Dutré et al. (2006), and Pharr and Humphreys (2004) discuss specular reflection and microfacet models in terms of BRDFs. Last, but certainly not least, is Hall's wonderful book (Hall, 1988) that discusses the state of the art in shading models in the late 1980s, and provides ray tracing code for just about all the models discussed here.

He et al. (1991) and Ashikhmin et al. (2000) presented sophisticated physically based reflection models. Ashikhmin et al. also presented BRDFs for anisotropic reflection, satin, and velvet. Anisotropic BRDFs are also discussed in Pharr and Humphreys (2003) and Shirley et al. (2005).

 Questions

15.1. In Figure 15.9, suppose a primary ray hits the plane in the center of the specular highlight (the red circles). What is the value of α?

15.2. Figure 15.13 shows two primary rays that hit a flat surface at a and b. Sketch l, n, r, ω_o, and α at these points. Which ray returns the most specular radiance to the camera, and why?

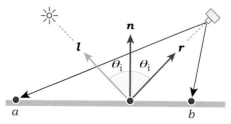

Figure 15.13. Two points on a flat surface that reflect light in a specular manner.

15.3. Consider a box illuminated by a point light as shown in Figure 15.14, with a viewer somewhere in the plane that passes through the light and is parallel to the top face of the box. Is there always a path of mirror-reflection between the light, the top face of the box, and the viewer?

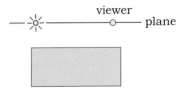

Figure 15.14. A box, a point light, and a viewer.

15.4. For specular reflection, we have $(r \bullet \omega_o)^e = (\cos \alpha)_e > 0$ $\forall\, \alpha \in [0, \pi/2]$ and $\forall\, e > 0$. However, rendered specular reflection only makes a nonzero contribution to an image in the angular range $\alpha \in [0, \alpha_{max}]$, where $\alpha_{max} \to 0$ as $a \to \infty$. In plain English, specular highlights not only look smaller as a increases, but as hit points move away from them, specular reflection actually makes zero contribution to the pixel colors. Why does this happen?

Exercises

15.1. Sketch a curved surface, a point light, and a viewer where there is more than one path of mirror reflection between the light, the surface, and the viewer.

15.2. See if you can think of a configuration where there are an infinite number of paths of mirror reflection between a point light, a surface, and a viewer and sketch them. In this situation, every point on a finite section of the surface (or the whole surface) will be at the center of the specular highlight.

15.3. Repeat Exercise 15.2 for a directional light.

15.4. Derive Equations (15.2) and (15.3) and show that these lead to Equation (15.4) for the reflected vector.

15.5. Prove that the expression (15.6) is reciprocal.

15.6. Implement specular reflection as described in Sections 15.1 and 15.2, and use Figure 15.8 and the figure on the first page of this chapter for testing.

15.7. Figure 15.15 is the figure on the first page of this chapter rendered with $e = 0.25$. Can you explain the shading? Experiment with different values of $e < 1$.

15.8. Implement colored specular highlights as described in Section 15.4.

Figure 15.15. The figure on the first page of this chapter rendered with $e = 0.25$.

15.9. Experiment with colored light sources and specular highlights.

15.10. Implement Blinn's modification discussed in Section 15.6 and compare the results with Phong's original formula.

15.11. Implement the `Plastic` material in Listing 15.4 and use it to experiment with different specular reflection models. See the references cited in the Further Reading section.

16 Shadows

 Objectives

By the end of this chapter, you should:

- understand why shadows are important in ray tracing;
- understand the terminology of shadows;
- understand why it's important to use $t > \varepsilon > 0$ in all ray-object hit functions;
- understand why shadows can be expensive to implement;
- have implemented hard-edged shadows with point and directional lights.

Shadows are everywhere in the real world, both indoors and outdoors. Shadows are also free in the real world, but as you will find out in this chapter, shadows are not free in ray tracing.[1] Here, I'll look at why shadows are important, what they are, why they can be expensive to render, and how to implement hard-edged shadows from point lights.

 16.1 Why Shadows Are Important

Before we look at how shadows are defined, let's look at an image with and without shadows. Figure 16.1(a) shows some simple objects and a ground plane without shadows. Here are some questions about this image:

---

1. This statement is loosely quoted from Mike Murray, circa 1988.

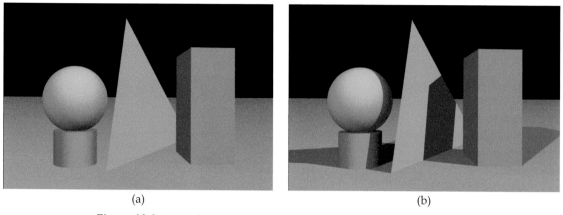

(a)   (b)

Figure 16.1. A simple scene illuminated by a point and a directional light: (a) with no shadows; (b) with shadows.

- How far above the plane are the objects?
- What are the relative distances of the objects from the camera, and by implication, what are their relative sizes?
- How many light sources are there, and from what directions do their illuminations come?
- What type of light sources are present?

It's not possible to answer these questions without shadows, and although shadows can't provide *quantitative* answers to most of these questions, they can provide *qualitative* answers. From Figure 16.1(b), we can see that the cylinder, triangle, and box are either sitting on the plane or penetrate it. The objects are also roughly the same distance from the camera, which allows us to estimate their relative sizes, and there are two directional or point lights. The bottom line here is that shadows provide essential clues for our understanding of images.

Shadows are important for another reason, as well. The ubiquity of shadows in the real world means that their absence in ray-traced images robs the images of an essential element of realism. We expect shadows, and when they are not present, the images often look unnatural.

16.2 Definitions

For directional and point lights, a shadow is part of a scene that doesn't receive any illumination from a given light source because one or more objects in the

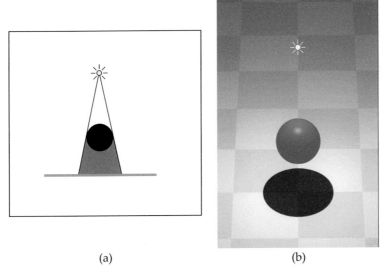

(a)   (b)

Figure 16.2. (a) Schematic diagram of a point light and a sphere with shadow; (b) sphere and plane with shadow, illuminated by a point light.

scene block the illumination. Another way of looking at this is that shadows are the parts of the scene that the light can't see. Shadows are actually three dimensional because the illumination occupies the 3D space between objects, but I'll only render shadows on object surfaces because this is where all of our shading takes place.

The shadows from point and directional lights are hard-edged because surface points either receive full illumination or no illumination from these types of lights (see Figure 16.1(b)). As another example, Figure 16.2(a) is a cross section of a point light's shadow from a sphere that falls on a flat surface. Figure 16.2(b) is a rendered version of this configuration.

Shadows are more complicated for real lights, as these have finite surface area and can be *partially* obscured by objects. The shadows of finite area lights are known as soft shadows and consist of a part where none of the light is visible, called the *umbra*, and a part where some of the light is visible, called the *penumbra*. Figure 16.3 illustrates these for spherical lights illuminating a sphere, where the shadows fall on a flat surface. The graphs along the bottom in Figure 16.3(a)–(c) show the amount of light received as a function of position. This varies from zero in the umbra to a maximum at the edge of the penumbra.[2] As Figure 16.3(d) shows, the umbra can end before it reaches the surface.

---

2. The curves are only sketched and are not based on calculations of the amount of light received.

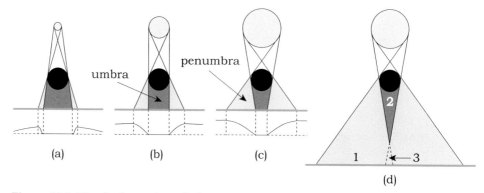

Figure 16.3. The shadows of area lights consist of an umbra and a penumbra. The numbers in (d) refer to Exercise 16.1.

Figure 16.4 shows the configurations in Figure 16.3(a) and (c) rendered with a disk light. Notice that there are no sharp boundaries to the umbra and penumbra. Although the boundaries are precisely defined according to Figure 16.3, we can't tell exactly where they are by looking at the images.

Figure 16.5(a) shows a number of boxes and a plane illuminated by a point light with no distance attenuation. Figure 16.5(b) shows the same scene with the camera at the light location. Notice that no shadows are visible, which demonstrates that the shadows are the part of the scene that the point light can't "see."

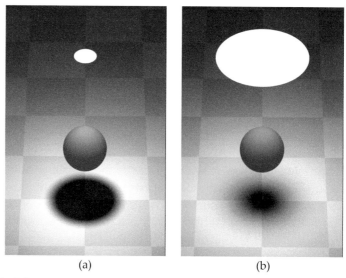

Figure 16.4. Sphere and plane illuminated by a small disk light (a) and by a large disk light (b).

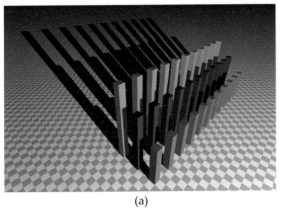
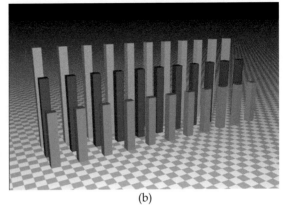

(a)   (b)

Figure 16.5. Boxes and plane illuminated by a point light with shadows visible (a) and with the camera at the light location (b).

 16.3 Implementation

I'll discuss here how to implement shadows for point lights, leaving directional lights for the exercises and area lights for Chapter 18. To compute if a hit point is in shadow from a point light, we have to evaluate the visibility function (13.24) between the hit point and the light's location. The reflected radiance from the light will therefore be

$$L_o(p, \omega_o) = f_r(p, l(p), \omega_o)\, l_s c_l\, V(p, l_p) \cos \theta_l,$$

where l_p is the light's location. Note that we are still using the hemisphere form of the rendering equation, although we have borrowed the visibility function from the area form in Section 13.10.2. The only practical way to evaluate $V(p, l_p)$ is to shoot a ray from the hit point towards the light and see if the ray hits anything between p and the light location. This ray is called a *shadow ray*, as illustrated in Figure 16.6 for a point light.

Here, we shade the hit point a with ambient illumination plus the light's direct illumination because its shadow ray doesn't hit any objects. In contrast, we only shade point b with ambient illumination because its shadow ray does hit an object.

Shadow rays are defined differently from primary rays. A shadow ray's origin is the hit point p being shaded; that is, $o = p$. Its direction is the light's unit direction vector l:

$$d = (l_p - p)/\|p_l - p\|.$$

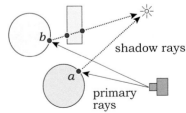

Figure 16.6. Shadow rays for a point light.

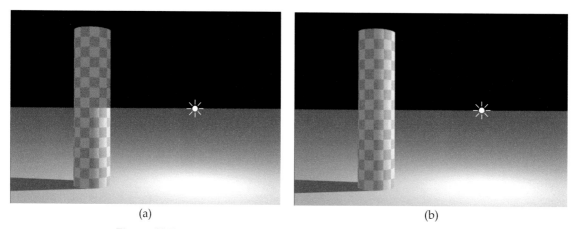

(a)   (b)

Figure 16.7. (a) Incorrect shading of a cylinder from a point light; (b) correct shading.

To find out if a hit point is in shadow, we have to intersect the shadow rays with the objects, but we have to be careful to check that the hit points are between the point being shaded and the light location. Consider Figure 16.7(a), which shows a cylinder illuminated by a point light at the indicated location. The shading is wrong because the cylinder is only shaded with ambient illumination above the height of the light. Figure 16.7(b) shows the correct shading.

Figure 16.8 shows what the problem is in Figure 16.7(a) by using a sample hit point above and below the light. The shadow ray for the hit point below

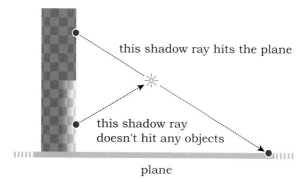

this shadow ray hits the plane

this shadow ray
doesn't hit any objects

plane

Figure 16.8. The top half of the cylinder should not be in shadow because the shadow rays hit the plane after they pass through the light.

the light points up and doesn't hit any objects. This point therefore receives illumination from the light. In contrast, the shadow ray for the hit point above the light points down and hits the plane on the other side of the light. The incorrect shading has occurred because we didn't check that the hit points on the plane are between the light and surface point being shaded.

To implement shadows we need to perform the following tasks:

- incorporate shadow testing into the material shade functions;
- write a function in_shadow for each light type that tests if a hit point can see the light. This evaluates the visibility function $V(p, l_p)$;
- write a function shadow_hit for each object type that intersects a shadow ray with the object.

The following non-physical aspect of lights is also worth implementing. It's a Boolean data member shadows in the Light base class, which you can use to turn shadows on and off in the build functions, individually for each light. There are two reasons for doing this. First, rendering is much quicker when shadows aren't used, a fact that can help when you are adding new features, debugging, or rendering new scenes. Second, it allows you to write the shade functions more efficiently than you can without it. I've included shadows in Figure 14.12 and Listing 14.1.

Listing 16.1 shows the revised Phong::shade function that incorporates shadows.

As an efficiency measure, this function only constructs the shadow ray and tests if the hit point is in shadow when the light casts shadows and the surface is facing "towards" the light, that is, $n \cdot \omega_o > 0$.

Listing 16.2 shows the in_shadow function for a point light. Although this potentially loops over all the objects in the scene, calling each object's shadow_hit function, it checks if the shadow ray hits an object between the hit point being shaded and the light's location and bails out if this happens. It therefore doesn't necessarily have to test the shadow ray for intersection against every object in the scene, but nonetheless, executing this function is still by far the most expensive shading operation.

The shadow_hit functions are also efficiency measures, because we could use the standard hit function for each object. However, these return the normal in the ShadeRec object, which we don't need for shadow testing. The shadow_hit functions therefore don't have a ShadeRec object as a parameter and don't return the normal. This doesn't save much time for simple objects such as spheres and planes, but it can make a difference for objects that are more complicated to intersect. For example, the hit function for axis-aligned boxes described in Chapter 19 has to keep track of the face hit or call a

```
RGBColor
Phong::shade(ShadeRec& sr) {
    Vector3D wo = -sr.ray.d;
    RGBColor L = ambient_brdf->rho(sr, wo) * sr.w.ambient_ptr->L(sr);
    int num_lights  = sr.w.lights.size();

    for (int j = 0; j < num_lights; j++) {
        Vector3D wi = sr.w.lights[j]->get_direction(sr);
        float ndotwi = sr.normal * wi;

        if (ndotwi > 0.0) {
            bool in_shadow = false;

            if (sr.w.lights[j]->casts_shadows()) {
                Ray shadowRay(sr.hitPoint, wi);
                in_shadow = sr.w.lights[j]->in_shadow(shadowRay, sr);
            }

            if (!in_shadow)
                L += (diffuse_brdf->f(sr, wo, wi)
                        + specular_brdf->f(sr, wo, wi)) *
                    sr.w.lights[j]->L(sr) * ndotwi;
        }
    }

    return (L);
}
```

Listing 16.1. The function `Phong::shade`.

```
bool
PointLight::in_shadow(const Ray& ray, const ShadeRec& sr) const {
    float t;
    int num_objects = sr.w.objects.size();
    float d = location.distance(ray.o);

    for (int j = 0; j < num_objects; j++)
        if (sr.w.objects[j]->shadow_hit(ray, t) && t < d)
            return (true);

    return (false);
}
```

Listing 16.2. The function `PointLight::in_shadow`.

```
bool
Plane::shadow_hit(const Ray& ray, float& tmin) const {
    float t = (a - ray.o) * n / (ray.d * n);

    if (t > kEpsilon) {
        tmin = t;
        return (true);
    }
    else
        return (false);
}
```

Listing 16.3. The function `Plane::shadow_hit`.

`find_normal` function. Writing a `shadow_hit` hit function for all objects does increase the code size, but there's not much work involved—essentially, all you have to do is remove code related to shading from the existing hit functions. The `shadow_hit` function for a plane appears in Listing 16.3.

16.4 The Epsilon Factor

In Chapter 3, I used a constant $\varepsilon > 0$ in the plane and sphere hit functions. In fact, I use it for every hit function, and here's why. Figure 16.9 is the same as

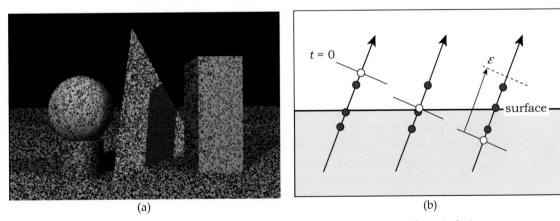

(a)   (b)

Figure 16.9. (a) Salt-and-pepper noise when $\varepsilon = 0$; (b) shadow-ray origins (white circles) and hit points (red circles) can be inside or outside the surface of the object being shaded.

Figure 16.1(b) but rendered with $\varepsilon = 0$. Not pretty, is it? Certainly not an image you'd want to show to your friends. Here's what's happened. Since the shadow rays start at object surfaces, you might think that when they are intersected with the object being shaded, the hit function will return zero for t, but that's not necessarily the case. The finite numerical precision of the intersection calculations means that hit points are rarely exactly on object surfaces. That's not usually a problem for direct illumination without shadows.

It does, however, create a problem for shadow rays for the following reasons. First, shadow-ray origins are primary-ray hit points and can therefore be just inside, or just outside, the surface. For example, the three shadow rays in Figure 16.9(b) have origins indicated by the white circles. Second, because shadow-ray intersection calculations are subject to the same numerical-precision problems as primary rays, their hit points on the object being shaded can also be just inside or just outside the surface, as the red circles in Figure 16.9(b) indicate.

As a result, t can have small positive or negative values, even for a plane, where only a linear equation has to be solved. Here are some values returned by my plane's shadow-ray hit function for the plane in Figure 16.9(a): $t = -1.65296e{-}08$, $2.3816e{-}06$, $4.44553e{-}09$, $-1.14102e{-}6$. Positive and negative values are returned randomly from pixel to pixel. It's the *positive* values that cause the problem because the shadow-ray hit function then returns true, with the result that these surface points are only shaded with ambient illumination. This results in the speckled appearance in Figure 16.9(a), an effect known as *salt-and-pepper noise*. It's a result of the random *self-shadowing* of the surfaces when there shouldn't be any self-shadowing.

In Figure 16.9(b), any hit points above the ray origins have positive t values, and the problem is most acute for the ray on the right, where the origin is inside the surface and can result in larger positive t values. To eliminate self-shadowing, we have to make ε larger than the largest positive t value that's likely to be returned by the shadow_hit function.

We could use a global constant for ε, but not all objects need the same value, and ε would have to be the largest value required for any object. This is about $\varepsilon = 0.001$ for an axis-aligned box and for rendering transparent triangle meshes. However, a value this large can create rendering artifacts for other objects. A better approach is to use a specific static class constant for each geometric object primitive, as this allows you to tailor its value for each object.[3] That's also better design as it doesn't use a global constant. You can declare the constant with the statement

---

3. Primitives are defined on page 354.

```
    static const double kEpsilon;
```

in a primitive's class declaration, but you must initialize it at the start of the primitive's .**cpp** file. For a plane, the code in **Plane.cpp** is

```
    const double Plane::kEpsilon = 0.00001;
```

This approach is still not perfect because it doesn't take into account object sizes. For example, should we use the same value of ε for spheres with radii 0.001 and 1,000,000? Arguably not, but the above approach is practical, and it works.

It's not only shadows that we require $\varepsilon > 0$ for. Reflected and transmitted rays also start on object surfaces, and we need $\varepsilon > 0$ to prevent these rays from recording hits on the objects they start from.

 ## 16.5 Examples

Figure 16.10(a) is a simple example that only involves spheres and a plane. This is based on the scene in Figure 14.21. Figure 16.10(b) shows the scene in Figure 15.8(b) rendered with shadows.

Figure 16.11(a) is a Slinky modeled with a single NURBS[4] surface by Steve Agland. There's a lot of self-shadowing visible on the Slinky. Figure 16.11(b) shows a gray plane and sphere illuminated by red, green, and blue point lights,

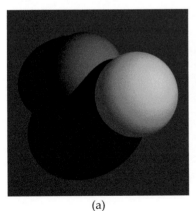 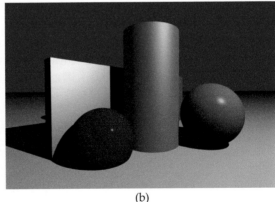

(a)   (b)

Figure 16.10. (a) Plane and two spheres with shadows; (b) the scene in Figure 15.8(b) rendered with shadows.

---

4. NURBS stands for non-uniform rational B-spline (see Rogers (2001)).

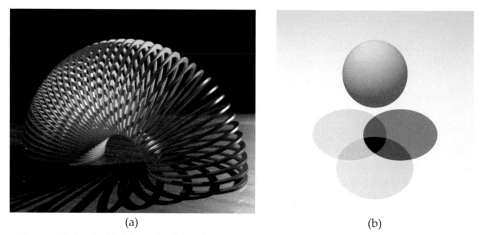

(a)   (b)

Figure 16.11. (a) Rainbow Arch by Steve Agland; (b) colored point lights and shadows.

to illustrate the subtractive primary colors (see Exercise 16.4). You need to look at the RGB version of this image on the book's website to properly appreciate the colors.

 ## 16.6 Costs

Shadows can be more expensive to render than the intersection of primary rays with objects. At each hit point, we need a shadow ray for each directional and point light (see Figure 16.12), and this is where the costs can add up. If there are enough lights in the scene, the costs of intersecting the shadow rays with the objects can exceed that of the primary rays, even when custom functions such as in_shadow are used. The situation is similar for scenes with multiple area lights.

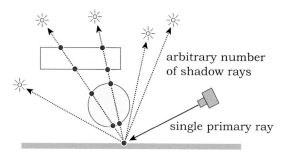

Figure 16.12. A hit point can require an arbitrary number of shadow rays for its shading.

16.7 Shadowing Options

We currently have one shadowing option, where each light can optionally cast shadows. It's also worthwhile implementing two further options, one on the objects and one on the materials.

The objects option is the ability to specify whether an object casts shadows or not. This is essential for performing ambient occlusion with environment lights (see Section 18.10). I've implemented this feature through a Boolean data member shadows in the GeometricObject class because it can then be used for any object and is independent of the material. To implement it, all you have to do is put the statement

```
if (!shadows)
    return (false);
```

at the start of any object's shadow_hit function that you want to use it with and set the object's shadows to false in the build function. The GeometricObject constructor should initialize shadows to true.

The materials option allows us to specify whether a material has shadows cast on it or not. This is sometimes necessary for shading objects inside transparent objects without having to render caustics (see Sections 28.7 and 28.8). I've left this as an exercise.

In summary:

- lights can optionally cast shadows;
- objects can optionally cast shadows;
- materials can optionally have shadows cast on them.

None of these options are physically correct, of course, but they provide great shading flexibility. They are also common in commercial renderers. Bear in mind that commercial computer graphics is more about getting things to look right than being physically correct.

 ## Notes and Discussion

The most spectacular example of a soft shadow is a total solar eclipse, where the umbra is the area of totality and the penumbra is the area of the partial eclipse. Since the Sun is about 378 times larger than the Moon but also, through a remarkable coincidence, about 378 times farther away, they both appear about the same size in the sky. The surface of the Earth is therefore near the end of the

Moon   Earth

Figure 16.13. Scale drawing of the Earth and Moon during a total solar eclipse.

umbra in Figure 16.3(d). As a result, there's no totality in over half the eclipses because the umbra ends before it reaches the surface of the Earth. These are known as *annular* eclipses. Figure 16.13 is a solar eclipse drawn to scale.

 Further Reading

Birn (2006) is a beautiful book that discusses all aspects of digital illumination and shading in a non-technical manner and from an artistic perspective. It has an extensive chapter on shadows. Morrison et al. (1995) discusses solar eclipses, as do most general books on astronomy. Shirley and Morley (2003) discusses an approach to shadows that's similar to the one adopted here, where they have a `hit` and a `shadow_hit` function for each object.

 Questions

16.1. Without the use of shadows, directional lights sometimes give no clues about the size and distance of objects, even with perspective viewing. Figure 16.14 shows the sphere and triangle from Figure 16.1 illuminated with a single directional light and with the camera looking through the center of the sphere. The camera's location is (0.0, 2.4, 20.0) in world coordinates, and the look-at point is (0.0, 2.4, 0.0). In Figure 16.14(a), the sphere has center (0.0, 2.4, 0.0) and radius 1.5, and in Figure 16.14(b), the sphere has center (0, 0, –99,980) and radius 7500, but the images are identical. Why is this?[5]

16.2. Why are no shadows visible in Figure 16.5(b)?

16.3. Is it possible to see some of the shadows in Figure 16.5(b) with the camera at the light location?

16.4. Self-shadowing is where an object casts shadows on itself. What is the condition on the shape of an object that it can be self-shadowing?

5. Although this question isn't on shadows, it's in this chapter because it arose from Figure 16.1.

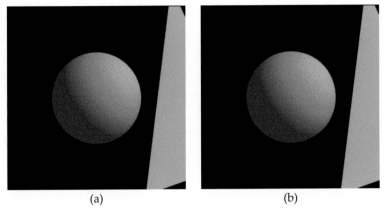

(a)   (b)

Figure 16.14. (a) Small close sphere illuminated with a directional light; (b) large far sphere illuminated with a directional light.

16.5. Why would the `Phong::shade` function in Listing 16.2 take more time to execute if it didn't call the light's `cast_shadows` functions?

 Exercises

16.1. Sketch the outlines of the sphere and the spherical light as they would appear from a location in each of the shadow regions numbered 1 to 3 in Figure 16.3(d).

16.2. Implement shadows for point lights as described here for `Matte` and `Phong` materials. You can use the figure on the first page of this chapter and Figures 16.1 and 16.10 for testing.

16.3. Implement shadows with directional lights, where the reflected radiance for a single light is

$$L_o(p, \omega_o) = f_r(p, l(p), \omega_o)\, l_s c_l\, V(p, l_p) \cos \theta_l.$$

Note that here the visibility function has the hit point p and the light direction l as arguments. The implementation details of `Directional::in_shadow` will be different from `PointLight::in_shadow`.

16.4. By looking at the build function for Figure 16.11(b), try to understand where the colors of the shadows have come from. Render this scene with one, two, and three lights. Change the light colors to cyan, magenta, and yellow. Move the camera farther from the sphere and plane.

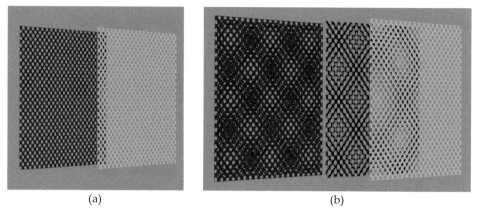

Figure 16.15. (a) Rectangle with a grid of circular holes and its shadow cast on a plane; (b) when two rectangles are used, moiré patterns are created in a number of ways.

16.5.   Figure 16.15(a) shows a yellow rectangle covered with small circular holes and a gray plane. Both are perpendicular to the z-axis and are illuminated with a point light on the z-axis. The holes were created with a *clip map*, for which there is sample code on the book's website. Figure 16.15(b) shows two rectangles (yellow and green) with clip maps and the resulting moiré patterns that are created when the green rectangle is seen through the yellow rectangle, when the yellow rectangle casts shadows on the green rectangle, and when both rectangles cast shadows on the plane. The hole size and spacing are slightly different on each rectangle. Reproduce these images by studying the code and the build functions on the book's website. Experiment with different hole sizes and spacings. In particular, make these the same on each rectangle. Experiment with directional lights parallel to the z-axis and at an angle to it.

16.6.   Render objects that self-shadow, such as the tori in Figure 19.16.

16.7.   Allow materials to optionally have shadows cast on them.

17 Ambient Occlusion

Image courtesy of Mark Howard, Stanford bunny model courtesy of Greg Turk and the Stanford University Graphics Laboratory

 **Objectives**

By the end of this chapter, you should:

- understand how ambient occlusion is computed;
- know how to set up a local orthonormal basis at a hit point;
- have implemented ambient occlusion as a light shader;
- understand some of the limitations of the sampling techniques discussed in Chapter 5.

In Chapter 14, ambient illumination was a constant term throughout a scene. As a result, the surface of any object that only received ambient illumination was rendered with a constant color. Ambient occlusion can significantly increase the realism of the ambient illumination in ray-traced images. The idea is quite simple: the amount of ambient illumination received at a surface point depends on how much of the hemisphere above the point is *not* blocked (occluded) by objects. Figure 17.1 illustrates this in two dimensions for a scene that consists only of a sphere and a box. Because the box isn't visible from point *a* on the sphere, *a* receives ambient light from the whole hemisphere, which is the maximum amount. In contrast, the box is visible from the point *b*

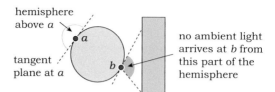

hemisphere
above a

tangent
plane at a

no ambient light
arrives at b from
this part of the
hemisphere

Figure 17.1. Point a on the sphere receives the maximum amount of ambient light because the box isn't visible; point b doesn't receive the maximum amount because the box blocks some of the incoming ambient light.

and blocks some of the incoming ambient illumination, so b does not receive the maximum amount.

Ambient occlusion is still an approximation of diffuse-diffuse light transport. For example, point b can also receive diffuse illumination that's been reflected from the box, but I'll ignore that here. It's computed in Chapter 26.

17.1 Modeling

We can model ambient occlusion by including a visibility term in Equation (14.1) for the incident ambient radiance. The new expression for the incident radiance is

$$L_i(p, \omega_i) = V(p, \omega_i) \, l_s c_l, \tag{17.1}$$

where L_i now depends on p and ω_i. The visibility term is

$$V(p, \omega_i) = \begin{cases} 1 & \text{if the direction } \omega_i \text{ at } p \text{ is not blocked,} \\ 0 & \text{if the direction } \omega_i \text{ at } p \text{ is blocked.} \end{cases} \tag{17.2}$$

As a result, $L_i(p, \omega_i)$ is a binary-valued function: either black or $l_s c_l$, depending on ω_i. The only practical way to estimate the ambient illumination (17.1) is to shoot shadow rays into the hemisphere above p and see how many of them hit objects. We can make the ambient illumination for a given pixel proportional to the number of rays that *don't* hit objects, but how do we distribute the rays? You may think that the best way is a uniform distribution in solid angle. While that would be the best way to estimate the solid angle occluded by the objects, it's not quite what we need. The reason is Lambert's law, as discussed in Section 13.2. This results in the irradiance being proportional to the cosine of the polar angle θ_i at p.

We have to estimate the integral (13.10) for the reflected radiance

$$L_o(p, \omega_o) = \int_{2\pi^+} f_r(p, \omega_i, \omega_o) L_i(p, \omega_i) \cos \theta_i d\omega_i.$$

Using Equation (13.19) for $f_r = f_{r,d} = k_d c_d/\pi$ with k_a instead of k_d, and Equation (17.1) for $L_i(p, \omega_i)$, we have

$$L_o(p, \omega_o) = (k_a c_a/\pi) * (l_s c_l) \int_{2\pi^+} V(p, \omega_i) \cos\theta_i \, d\omega_i. \qquad (17.3)$$

Recall from the discussion of Monte Carlo integration in Section 13.11 that the best estimate for an integral is obtained by using a sample density that matches the integrand. Because of the $\cos\theta_i$ in the integrand, we should therefore shoot the shadow rays with a cosine distribution in the polar angle. As the distribution of objects is unknown, the cosine is the only thing we know about the integrand.

Before we can shoot a shadow ray, we have to set up an orthonormal basis at p, where w is in the direction of the normal at p. Figure 7.4 shows an orthonormal basis set up in this way. Because the orientation of u and v around w doesn't matter, we can use the following construction for (u, v, w):

$$w = n,$$
$$v = w \times up/\|w \times up\|,$$
$$u = v \times w.$$

In practice, it's a good idea to jitter the up vector, in case the surface being shaded is horizontal (see Listing 17.2). Because we only shoot one shadow ray per primary ray, this orthonormal basis will have to be set up for every ray. Provided we have samples on a hemisphere with a cosine distribution, the ray direction for a given sample point $s = (s_x, s_y, s_z)$ is

$$d = s_x\, u + s_y\, v + s_z\, w, \qquad (17.4)$$

which simply projects the 3D sample point onto u, v, and w. By construction, d is a unit vector. Refer to Sections 7.1 and 7.2 to see how the sample points are set up on the hemisphere.

17.2 Implementation

There are two ways we can implement ambient occlusion. One is through a material that's responsible for sampling the hemisphere. Although there's nothing wrong with this approach, we would have to use the material with every object for which we wanted the effect. Since we already have two materials

```
class AmbientOccluder: public Light {
    public:

            AmbientOccluder(void);
            ...

            void
            set_sampler(Sampler* s_ptr);

            virtual Vector3D
            get_direction(ShadeRec& sr);

            virtual bool
            in_shadow(const Ray& ray, const ShadeRec& sr) const;

            virtual RGBColor
            L(ShadeRec& sr);

    private:

            Vector3D u, v, w;
            Sampler* sampler_ptr;
            RGBColor min_amount;
};
```

Listing 17.1. Declaration for the class `AmbientOccluder`.

with an ambient-reflection component, it would be nice to get ambient occlusion working with these without having to change them and without having to add a new material. Fortunately, this is possible by using a light shader. By building ambient occlusion into a new ambient light, it will work for any material that has an ambient-reflection component. All we have to do is use the new light in place of the existing constant ambient light. Listing 17.1 shows the class declaration for the new light, which I've called `AmbientOccluder`.

The member function `set_sampler` appears in Listing 17.2.[1] This function assigns the sampler `sp` (constructed in the build functions) and then maps the samples to the hemisphere with a cosine ($e = 1$) density distribution. Recall from Chapter 5 that when a sampler object is constructed, the samples are only generated in the unit square; it's always the application code's responsibility to distribute them over a hemisphere when required.

---

1. See the Notes and Discussion section for `set_samples`.

```
void
AmbientOccluder::set_sampler(Sampler* s_ptr) {
    if (sampler_ptr) {
        delete sampler_ptr;
        sampler_ptr = NULL;
    }

    sampler_ptr = s_ptr;
    sampler_ptr->map_samples_to_hemisphere(1);
}
```

Listing 17.2. The function `AmbientOccluder::set_sampler`.

```
Vector3D
AmbientOccluder::get_direction(ShadeRec& sr) {
    Point3D sp = sampler_ptr->sample_hemisphere();
    return (sp.x * u + sp.y * v + sp.z * w);
}
```

Listing 17.3. The function `AmbientOccluder::get_direction`.

Listing 17.3 shows the function `get_direction`, which returns the direction of each shadow ray. Notice that this function simply projects the components of the local variable sp onto (u, v, w), as in Equation (17.4).

To test if a shadow ray is blocked by an object, we can use a standard `in_shadow` function. The `in_shadow` function in Listing 17.4 is the same as that for a directional light.

```
bool
AmbientOccluder::in_shadow(const Ray& ray, const ShadeRec& sr) const {
    float t;
    int num_objects = sr.w.objects.size();

    for (int j = 0; j < num_objects; j++)
        if (sr.w.objects[j]->shadow_hit(ray, t))
            return (true);

    return (false);
}
```

Listing 17.4. The function `AmbientOccluder::in_shadow`.

```
RGBColor
AmbientOccluder::L(ShadeRec& sr) {
    w = sr.normal;
    // jitter up vector in case normal is vertical
    v = w ^ Vector3D(0.0072, 1.0, 0.0034);
    v.normalize();
    u = v ^ w;

    Ray shadow_ray;
    shadow_ray.o = sr.hit_point;
    shadow_ray.d = get_direction(sr);

    if (in_shadow(shadow_ray, sr))
        return (min_amount * ls * color);
    else
        return (ls * color);
}
```

Listing 17.5. The function AmbientOccluder::L.

Finally, the function AmbientOccluder::L in Listing 17.5 illustrates how the orthonormal basis is set up and how the functions get_direction and in_shadow are called. Note that L sets up (*u*, *v*, *w*) before it calls get_direction, where these are used.

I use the data member min_amount to return a minimum non-black color when the ray direction is occluded because this results in more natural shading than returning black. It takes into account the fact that all surfaces in real scenes receive some light. The figure on the first page of this chapter and the figures in Section 17.5 demonstrate the benefits of this approach.

All we have to do to get ambient occlusion working is to construct an AmbientOccluder light in a build function and assign it to the world's ambient light.

17.3 A Simple Scene

I'll consider here a simple test scene that consists of a plane and a sphere that just touch. Figure 17.2 illustrates how the ambient illumination varies over the surfaces of both objects. Arrows at the hit points are shadow rays, which either don't hit anything (blue) or hit one of the objects (black). As points on the plane get closer to the sphere, the solid angle it subtends increases, more shadow

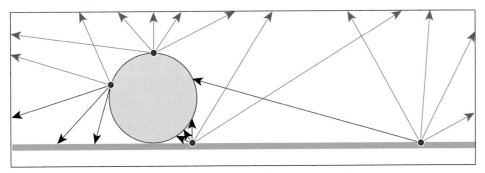

Figure 17.2. Various hit points on the plane and the sphere, with sample shadow rays.

rays hit it, and the ambient illumination that the points receive decreases. A similar situation applies to the sphere. The farther from the top a hit point is, the less ambient illumination it receives.

Listing 17.6 is the build function, which demonstrates how to construct an AmbientOccluder light that uses multi-jittered sampling.

The following images show this scene rendered with various sampling techniques but using only ambient illumination. Figure 17.3(a) was rendered with constant ambient illumination, which provides little information about the scene. Figure 17.3(b) shows the scene as it "should" appear with ambient occlusion. This part was rendered with multi-jittered sampling and 256 rays per pixel. Notice how the ambient occlusion provides a rounded appearance for the sphere and relates it to the plane, like shadows do. Figure 17.3(b) uses min_amount = 0, as do Figures 17.4, 17.6, and 17.7, because this value is best for demonstrating the differences between sampling techniques.

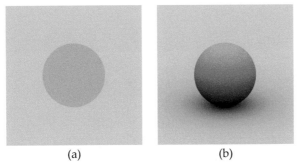

(a)   (b)

Figure 17.3. Sphere and plane scene rendered with constant ambient illumination (a) and ambient occlusion (b).

```
void
World::build(void) {
      int num_samples = 256;

      vp.set_hres(400);
      vp.set_vres(400);
      vp.set_samples(num_samples);

      tracer_ptr = new RayCast(this);

      MultiJittered* sampler_ptr = new MultiJittered(num_samples);

      AmbientOccluder* occluder_ptr = new AmbientOccluder;
      occluder_ptr->scale_radiance(1.0);
      occluder_ptr->set_color(white);
      occluder_ptr->set_min_amount(0.0);
      occluder_ptr->set_sampler(sampler_ptr);
      set_ambient_light(occluder_ptr);

      Pinhole* camera_ptr = new Pinhole;
      camera_ptr->set_eye(25, 20, 45);
      camera_ptr->set_lookat(0, 1, 0);
      camera_ptr->set_view_distance(5000);
      camera_ptr->compute_uvw();
      set_camera(camera_ptr);

      Matte* matte_ptr1 = new Matte;
      matte_ptr1->set_ka(0.75);
      matte_ptr1->set_kd(0);
      matte_ptr1->set_cd(1, 1, 0);  // yellow

      Sphere* sphere_ptr1 = new Sphere (Point3D(0, 1, 0), 1);
      sphere_ptr1->set_material(matte_ptr1);
      add_object(sphere_ptr1);

      Matte* matte_ptr2 = new Matte;
      matte_ptr2->set_ka(0.75);
      matte_ptr2->set_kd(0);
      matte_ptr2->set_cd(1); // white

      Plane* plane_ptr1 = new Plane(Point3D(0), Normal(0, 1, 0));
      plane_ptr1->set_material(matte_ptr2);
      add_object(plane_ptr1);
}
```

Listing 17.6. The build function for Figure 17.3(b). You can also use this build function to render Figures 17.4, 17.6, and 17.7 by using different numbers of samples and assigning a different sampling technique to the ambient occluder's sampler pointer.

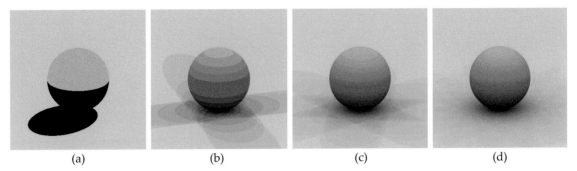

(a) (b) (c) (d)

Figure 17.4. Scene rendered using regular sampling with one sample per pixel (a), 16 samples (b), 64 samples (c), and 256 samples (d).

Ambient occlusion is much better than antialiasing or depth of field for exposing the shortcomings of sampling techniques, as Figure 17.4 illustrates. This figure shows the sphere scene rendered using regular sampling with different numbers of samples per pixel. As you can see, these images are not even approximately correct, although Figure 17.4(d) may appear all right until you look at the image on the book's website. So, what's gone wrong? First, there's only a single set of regular samples to work with (for a given number of samples), so we get correlations. Second, and more importantly, the sample points are mapped onto regular patterns on the hemisphere, as Figure 17.5 illustrates for 256 samples. Even with this large number, there are only 16 $\left(=\sqrt{256}\right)$ evenly spaced azimuth angles used and 16 polar angles. This cre-

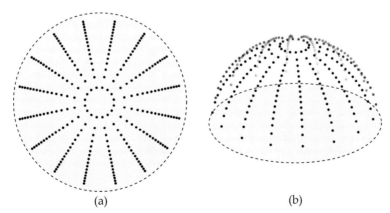

(a) (b)

Figure 17.5. (a) 256 regular samples mapped to a hemisphere with a cosine distribution; (b) 3D view of the samples.

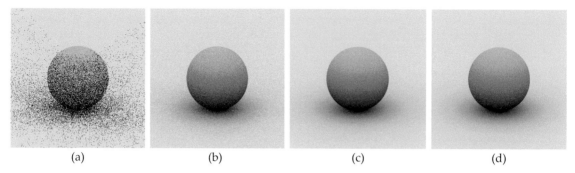

(a)   (b)   (c)   (d)

Figure 17.6. Same as Figure 17.4 but rendered using random sampling.

ates the bands on the sphere and the patterns on the plane (see Question 17.5). Hammersley sampling produces similar results, and for the same reasons. The lesson here is that although uniformly distributed samples are good, *regularly spaced* samples are not good.

Figures 17.6 and 17.7 show, respectively, random and multi-jittered sampling using the same numbers of sample points.

Figures 17.6(a) and 17.6(b) show how noisy the results are with one sample per pixel, but that's understandable because, in general, the wider the angular range of the samples, the more samples you need to reduce noise to acceptable levels. Ambient occlusion is as wide as you can get—the whole hemisphere above each hit point.

The images also illustrate another point: ambient occlusion is black with one ray per pixel. Shades of gray only appear with multiple rays.

Unfortunately, the printed images here can't show you the most important feature: multi-jittered sampling produces results with 64 samples that are as good as random sampling produces with 256 samples. You have to look at

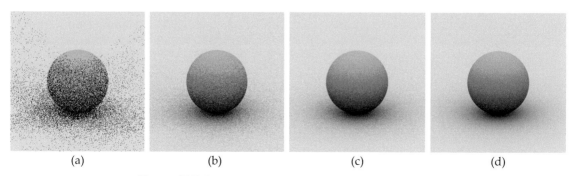

(a)   (b)   (c)   (d)

Figure 17.7. Same as Figure 17.4 but rendered using multi-jittered sampling.

|(a)|(b)|

Figure 17.8. Modified scene rendered with direct illumination from a directional light and constant ambient illumination (a) and with direct illumination and ambient occlusion (b). Multi-jittered sampling was used for the antialiasing and the ambient occlusion, with 100 samples per pixel.

the images on the book's website to see this, where it's obvious. The reason is the superior 1D and 2D distributions of the multi-jittered samples.

Jittered sampling gives better results than random, but not as good as multi-jittered, and *n*-rooks gives results that are similar to random sampling. We can draw the following conclusions from these images:

- Regular sampling is unsuitable for ambient occlusion because of the regular 1D distributions of samples. This results in obvious aliasing artifacts. Hammersley sampling is also unsuitable for the same reasons.

- For this application, multi-jittered sampling is the best of the techniques discussed in Chapter 5 because it allows us to get similar results to random sampling with about one-quarter of the number of samples. That's an important saving in view of the large number of samples that we need in general.

Because we usually render scenes with lights and direct illumination, Figure 17.8 shows the scene illuminated with a directional light. Here, I've decreased the ambient-reflection coefficients for the sphere and plane to stop the direct illumination from washing out the images.

17.4 Two-Sided Objects

In Section 14.6.2, I discussed the issues involved in correctly shading both sides of surfaces with direction illumination. Although these issues don't apply to constant ambient illumination, they do apply to ambient occlusion. The reason is that the shadow rays are shot into the hemisphere around the normal.

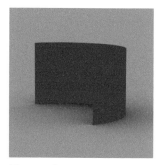

Figure 17.9. A half cylinder rendered with incorrect ambient occlusion.

As an example, Figure 17.9 shows a half cylinder rendered with incorrect ambient illumination, where both sides of the cylinder are the same color.

The problem is the outward-pointing normal to the cylinder, as shown in Figure 17.10(a). If there were no other objects in the scene, both sides of the cylinder would be rendered with full ambient illumination, as illustrated by points a and b, because none of the shadow rays would hit anything. In reality, some shadow rays from points on the inside surface will hit the cylinder, as illustrated by point b in Figure 17.10(b). According to Section 14.6.2, a solution is to use an object whose hit function reverses the normal when a ray hits the inside surface.

Figure 17.11(a) shows the correct ambient-occlusion shading with a two-sided half cylinder; Figure 17.11(b) shows the scene rendered with direct illumination added.

The same situation applies to other open curved objects. Questions 17.6–17.8 are relevant to these shading issues.

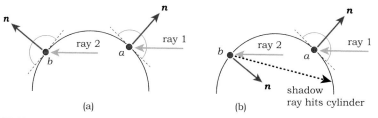

(a)   (b)

Figure 17.10. Ray 1 hits the outside surface of a cylinder at a, and ray 2 hits the inside surface at b. (a) The normal points outwards at both hit points. (b) The normal points inwards at point b, and some of the shadow rays will hit the cylinder.

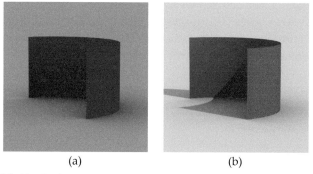

(a)   (b)

Figure 17.11. A half cylinder rendered with correct ambient occlusion (a) and with ambient occlusion and direct illumination (b).

17.5 Other Scenes

Figure 17.12 shows the Stanford bunny rendered with three values of min_amount. In Figure 17.12(a), min_amount = 1.0, and this image is therefore the same as we would get with constant ambient illumination.[2] In Figure 17.2(b), min_amount = 0.25, and in Figure 17.12(c), min_amount = 0.0. Notice that although the images become darker as min_amount decreases, the contrast increases.

Figure 17.13 shows similar effects with the random boxes used in the viewing chapters. Again, notice the difference in contrast in Figure 17.13(a) and (b).

I've found that for most scenes, min_amount = 0.25 provides a good balance between the constant ambient look of min_amount = 1.0 and the equally

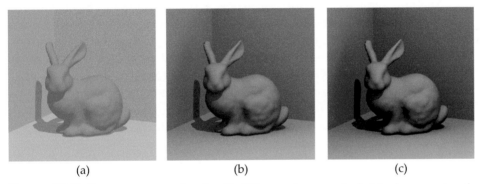

(a)   (b)   (c)

Figure 17.12. Bunny scene rendered with 256 samples per pixel: (a) min_amount = 1; (b) min_amount = 0.25; (c) min_amount = 0.

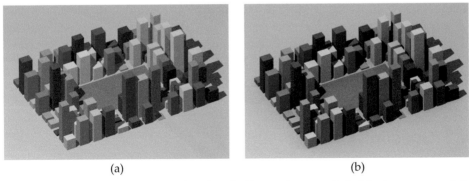

(a)   (b)

Figure 17.13. Random boxes rendered with 64 samples per pixel: (a) min_amount = 1.0; (b) min_amount = 0.25.

---

2. Except for some low-level noise.

unnatural-looking black areas that result from using `min_amount` = 0.0. You should experiment.

 ## Notes and Discussion

Most objects that use samples have a `set_sampler` function and a `set_samples` function. The `set_sampler` function allows a pointer to any type of sampler to be assigned to an object, and it also performs any required mapping of the samples to a disk or a hemisphere. This is the appropriate function to use here because an important function of this chapter is to compare the results of different sampling techniques for ambient occlusion.

The `set_samples` function constructs a default sampler object with the specified number of samples. `AmbientOccluder::set_samples` constructs a multi-jittered sampler object for all (perfect-square) values of `num_samples`. This gives random samples when there is one ray per pixel, in contrast to `ViewPlane::set_samples`, which constructs a uniform sampler when `num_samples` = 1. Performing ambient occlusion with one ray per pixel then results in noisy images such as Figure 17.6(a) instead of images like Figure 17.4(a). You can, of course, decide which you prefer and write the `AmbientOccluder::set_samples` function accordingly.

 ## Further Reading

There hasn't been much written about ambient occlusion. I don't know of any other ray-tracing textbooks that discuss it. It was implemented in RenderMan in about 2002, and I've got most of my information about it from online RenderMan documentation. There's a Wikipedia article at http://www.wikipedia.org/wiki/Ambient_occlusion, which includes links.

 ## Questions

17.1. Consider a scene that consists of a single closed object. Can ambient occlusion be relevant?

17.2. Consider a completely closed environment such as the random boxes scene in Figures 11.11 and 11.12, which includes a sky-dome hemisphere. How can you get ambient occlusion to work in this case?

17.3. Why is *d* a unit vector in Equation (17.4)?

17.4. In Figure 17.2, what fraction of the sphere's surface receives full ambient illumination?

17.5. In Figure 17.4, can you see a relationship between the number of uniform samples used and the number of "spokes" on the plane?

17.6. In Figure 17.11(a), the surface of the cylinder is perpendicular to the plane, and there are no other objects in the scene. Why is the outside surface of the cylinder rendered with a constant color?

17.7. Figure 17.14 shows another view of the cylinder where we can see all of the inside surface. Why does the ambient shading vary from top to bottom, but not horizontally? What fractions of the total ambient illumination do points receive along the top and bottom inside edges of the cylinder?

Figure 17.14. View of the cylinder where all of the inside surface is visible.

17.8. Do the shading issues discussed in Section 17.4 apply to planar objects such as rectangles, disks, and triangles?

17.9. The rectangles in Figure 17.12 meet at a corner behind the bunny with coordinates (-0.13, 0.033, -0.1). Figure 17.15 was rendered with the pinhole camera parameters

```
float delta = 0.01;
camera_ptr->set_eye(-0.13 + delta, 0.033 + delta, -0.1 + delta);
camera_ptr->set_lookat(1.0, 0.5, 1.0);
camera_ptr->set_view_distance(100.0);
```

which is just inside the corner looking out, min_amount = 0.0, and a white background. Can you explain the appearance of the rectangles (which is a question on perspective viewing, not ambient occlusion), and why most of the bunny is black?

17.10. Why are the tops of the boxes the same in both parts of Figure 17.13?

 Exercises

17.1. Implement ambient illumination as a light shader and use the scenes in this chapter to test it. Use ambient occlusion with Matte and Phong materials.

Figure 17.15. A different perspective on the bunny.

17.2. Experiment with different sampling techniques, numbers of samples and sets of samples, values of `min_amount`, objects, and materials.

17.3. The code in Listing 17.5 sets up (u, v, w) as a right-handed system with w parallel to n, and u and v in specific directions in the tangent plane to the surface at the hit point. Investigate how the images are affected when: (a) the directions of u and v are rotated in the tangent plane about w; (b) (u, v, w) form a left-handed system by changing the direction of u or v; (c) u and v are not orthogonal, for example, $u = v$.

17.4. Render Figure 17.12 without the bunny and the directional light. Can you explain the results?

18

Area Lights

Objectives

By the end of this chapter, you should:

- understand how area lights are modeled and rendered;
- have implemented a number of area lights;
- have implemented an environment light.

All real light sources have finite area, and as such, their illumination and soft shadows can add great realism to your images. This is in contrast to the sharp-edged shadows that we get from point and directional lights. The price we have to pay is more sample points per pixel and longer rendering times, but the results are worth it.

I'll discuss here a flexible lighting architecture that will allow you to use a variety of geometric objects as area-light sources. I'll also discuss rectangular and environment lights. There's a lot of work involved in this because it's not just a matter of adding area lights to the existing light classes. We also have to add a new tracer to perform the Monte Carlo integration, add an emissive material, and make changes to the Material, GeometricObject, and Light base classes. If you want to skip this, at least on a first reading, but still want to render soft shadows, look at Exercises 18.1 and 18.2. These cover how to modify point and directional lights to produce good area-light shading effects for a few percent of the work compared to the full implementation.

Because a lot of fiddly programming details are required to implement area lights, most of the classes are on the book's website.

 ## 18.1 Area-Lighting Architecture

One way to implement area lights is to have a separate class for each type of area light. While there's nothing wrong with this approach, you would have to write each class, and a lot of the code would be repeated.

An alternate approach is to have a single area-light class that contains a pointer to a geometric object that provides the illumination through an emissive material. In this approach, the type of object automatically determines the type of light, and the illumination can be computed polymorphically. In principle, this allows any type of geometric object to be a light source, provided we can accurately estimate its incident radiance at a surface point p. I've adopted this approach.

We can use a number of techniques to compute the direct incident radiance. The first is where shadow rays are shot towards sample points on the light surface. Each type of object that's used as an area light source must therefore be able to provide sample points on its surface and the normal at each point. How easy or difficult these tasks are depends on the object. For a planar object such as a rectangle, it's simple to generate uniformly distributed samples on its surface, and the normal is the same at each point. For other objects, such as triangle meshes, the process can be more difficult. This is used with the area form of the rendering equation.

A second technique is where the shadow rays are shot into the solid angle subtended at p by the object and tested for intersection with the light object. This is used with the hemisphere form of the rendering equation, with an added visibility function.

A third technique is where the rays sample the BRDF at p instead of sampling the lights. With this technique, the rays don't have to hit the light surface and don't have to be shadow rays. They can be secondary rays that are traced recursively into the scene to estimate the direct or indirect illumination at p. This technique is used with the hemisphere form of the rendering equation.

Which technique is the most efficient depends on the BRDF at p and on the light source. The BRDF can vary from perfect diffuse reflection to perfect specular reflection, while the solid angle subtended by the light at p can vary

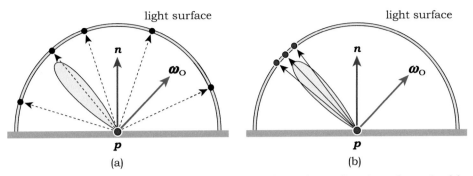

Figure 18.1. Specular BRDF and hemispherical light with ray directions determined by sample points on the light surface (a) and by sampling the BRDF (b).

from very small to the whole hemisphere above p. Figure 18.1 illustrates the case of a specular BRDF and a hemispherical light.

In Figure 18.1(a), the shadow rays are directed to sample points on the light, but most of these are in directions where the BRDF is small. The result will be undersampling of the BRDF and noisy images. In Figure 18.1(b), the rays sample the BRDF, which in this case is more efficient because most of the rays are in directions where the BRDF is not small.

Figure 18.2 illustrates the opposite situation, where the BRDF is Lambertian and the light subtends a small solid angle at p. In this case, sampling the light surface, as illustrated in Figure 18.2(a), is more efficient than sampling the BRDF in Figure 18.2(b) because there, most of the rays miss the light.

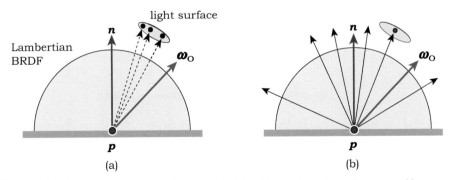

Figure 18.2. Lambertian BRDF and a small light with ray directions determined by sample points on the light surface (a) and by sampling the BRDF (b).

The general technique of choosing the most efficient sampling technique for a given light and BRDF is an example of importance sampling, as discussed in Section 13.11.

In this chapter, I'll use the first technique to estimate the direct illumination from rectangular, disk, and spherical lights, with the area form of the rendering equation.[1] I'll also use the second technique to estimate the direct illumination from environment lights, with the hemisphere form of the rendering equation.

18.2 Direct Rendering

There are two aspects of shading with an area light. The first is rendering the light itself, which can be directly visible, unlike directional and point lights. The second is computing the light's illumination on other objects in the scene. Figure 18.3 illustrates these two aspects, where each ray that hits an area light returns the emitted radiance L_e.

The geometric object that acts as the area light is stored in the `World::objects` array like any other object, so that it can be rendered without special treatment as far as primary and secondary rays are concerned. I attach an `Emissive` material to each such object, which provides the self-emissive term $L_e(p, \omega_o)$ in the rendering equation and its solution (13.29).

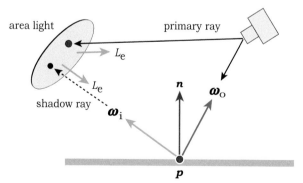

Figure 18.3. An area light can be directly visible as well as providing direct illumination to other objects in the scene.

---

1. Direct lighting is another common name for direct illumination.

18.3 Estimating Direct Illumination

For direct illumination, the exitant radiance $L_o(p', -\omega_i)$ in the area form of the radiance equation (13.25) reduces to the emitted radiance at p'; that is, $L_o(p', -\omega_i) = L_e(p', -\omega_i)$. In addition, L_e is only nonzero on light sources, a fact that allows us to reduce the integration domain from all surfaces in the scene to light-source surfaces only. That's a major simplification. The reflected radiance at a surface point p can then be written as

$$L_r(p, \omega_o) = \int_{A_{\text{lights}}} f_r(p, \omega_i, \omega_o) L_e(p', -\omega_i) V(p, p') G(p, p') dA', \qquad (18.1)$$

where A_{lights} is the set of all light surfaces, and dA' is a differential surface element around p'. As a reminder, ω_i in Equation (18.1) is given by Equation (13.27): $\omega_i = (p' - p)/\|p' - p\|$. If there are n_l area lights in the scene, we can write Equation (18.1) as the following sum over them:

$$L_r(p, \omega_o) = \sum_{k=1}^{n_l} \int_{A_{l,k}} f_r(p, \omega_i, \omega_o) L_e(p', -\omega_i) V(p, p') G(p, p') dA'. \qquad (18.2)$$

Consider a scene that contains a single area light, so that there's a single term in the sum (18.2). The Monte Carlo estimator for the integral is

$$\langle L_r(p, \omega_o) \rangle = \frac{1}{n_s} \sum_{j=1}^{n_s} \frac{f_r(p, \omega_{i,j}, \omega_o) L_e(p'_j, -\omega_{i,j}) V(p, p'_j) G(p, p'_j)}{p(p'_j)}, \qquad (18.3)$$

for n_s sample points p'_j, $j = 1, ..., n_s$. Here, $p(p'_j)$ is the probability density function defined over the surface of the light.

The difficult part is defining the pdf, which can be nontrivial for lights that are not planar. Ideally, we want the pdf to match the contribution of each sample point to the estimator, but that's usually not possible. The simplest choice is to use samples that are uniformly distributed over the light surface, in which case the pdf is just the inverse area of the light: $p(p'_j) = 1/A_l$, for all p'_j. This is particularly suitable for planar lights.

There are two major sources of noise in images generated by (18.3). For points p in the penumbra region of shadows, the visibility function $V(p, p'_j)$ will be zero for some sample points and nonzero for others, and therefore penumbrae are typically noisy, unless we use large numbers of samples. The $1/d^2$ term in the geometric factor $G(p, p'_j)$ can cause large variations in the estimator, and therefore noise, even for points receiving full illumination. This is particularly true for large lights that are close to the surfaces being shaded.

18.4 The Area-Lighting Tracer

Because the Monte Carlo estimator (18.3) involves $G(p, p_j')$ and the pdf, we have to write new material-shade functions to evaluate this estimator and call these from a new tracer. The material functions are called `area_light_shade`, and the tracer is called `AreaLighting`, according to the notation established in Sections 14.5 and 14.7. Listing 18.1 shows the code for the function `AreaLighting::trace_ray`. Note that this only differs from `RayCast::trace_ray` in Listing 14.10 by calling `material_ptr->area_light_shade` instead of `material_ptr->shade`.

 ## 18.5 The Emissive Material

The radiance in the outgoing direction ω_o from a self-emitting material is the emitted radiance L_e. In general, this can depend on location and direction, as indicated by the p and ω_o arguments in $L_e(p, \omega_o)$, but to keep the discussion in this chapter as simple as possible, I'll only consider spatially invariant, isotropic emissive materials, where L_e is independent of p and ω_o.[2] I'll also assume that emissive materials don't reflect or transmit light so that when a primary or secondary ray hits a self-emissive object, no further rays are generated. With these assumptions, the `Emissive` material class is quite simple, as Listing 18.2 shows. In particular, there are no BRDFs involved because it doesn't reflect light.

The emissive material stores a radiance scaling factor l_s and an emitted color c_e, in analogy to light sources. Notice that there is both a `shade` and an `area_light_shade` function. The `shade` function allows us to use the emissive material with other tracers such as `RayCast` and `Whitted` and thereby to render emissive objects in scenes without shading with them. Both functions return the emitted radiance $L_e = l_s c_e$, but only when the incoming ray is on the same side of the object surface as the normal; otherwise, they return black. In other words, an object with an emissive material only emits light on one side of its surface. The constant emitted color and the isotropic emission result in emissive objects being rendered with a constant color.

Listing 18.3 shows the code for `Emissive::area_light_shade`, where the incoming ray is stored in `sr` in the function `AreaLighting::trace_ray`.

---

2. In this context, isotropic means that the emitted radiance is the same in all directions at every point on the light surface.

```
RGBColor
AreaLighting::trace_ray(const Ray ray, const int depth) const {
    ShadeRec sr(world_ptr->hit_objects(ray));

    if (sr.hit_an_object) {
        sr.ray = ray;
        return(sr.material_ptr->area_light_shade(sr));

    else
        return(world_ptr->background_color);
}
```

Listing 18.1. The function AreaLighting::trace_ray.

```
class Emissive: public Material {
    private:

        float ls;                // radiance scaling factor
        RGBColor ce;             // color

    public:

        // constructors, set functions, etc.

        void
        scale_radiance(const float _ls);

        void
        set_ce(const float r, const float g, const float b);

        virtual RGBColor
        get_Le(ShadeRec& sr) const;

        virtual RGBColor
        shade(ShadeRec& sr);

        virtual RGBColor
        area_light_shade(ShadeRec& sr);
};
```

Listing 18.2. Code from the Emissive material class.

I should emphasize that this function is called from AreaLighting::trace_ray
when the nearest hit point of a primary ray or secondary ray is on the surface
of an area light, so that the normal stored in sr is the normal at the hit point. It's

```
RGBColor
Emissive::area_light_shade(ShadeRec& sr) {
        if (-sr.normal * sr.ray.d > 0.0)
                return (ls * ce);
        else
                return (black);
}
```

Listing 18.3. The function `Emissive::area_light_shade`.

therefore part of the *direct rendering* of the area light, not its *direct illumination* on other surfaces, which is handled by the `AreaLight` class.

```
RGBColor
Matte::area_light_shade(ShadeRec& sr) {
    Vector3D wo = -sr.ray.d;
    RGBColor L = ambient_brdf->rho(sr, wo) * sr.w.ambient_ptr->L(sr);
    int num_lights = sr.w.lights.size();

    for (int j = 0; j < num_lights; j++) {
            Vector3D wi = sr.w.lights[j]->get_direction(sr);
            float ndotwi = sr.normal * wi;

        if (ndotwi > 0.0) {
                bool in_shadow = false;

                if (sr.w.lights[j]->casts_shadows()) {
                        Ray shadow_ray(sr.hit_point, wi);
                        in_shadow = sr.w.lights[j]->in_shadow(shadow_ray,
                        sr);
                }

                if (!in_shadow)
                        L += diffuse_brdf->f(sr, wo, wi) * sr.w.lights[j]->L(sr)
                                * sr.w.lights[j]->G(sr) * ndotwi /
                                sr.w.lights[j]->pdf(sr);
        }
    }

    return (L);
}
```

Listing 18.4. The function `Matte::area_light_shade`.

The function `Emissive::get_Le`, which is called from the area light's L function in Listing 18.10, also returns the emitted radiance $l_s c_e$.

 ## 18.6 Other Materials

Since `Emissive::get_Le` is called polymorphically, it has to be added as a virtual function to the base `Material` class. It's not pure virtual there as I've only defined it for the two materials `Emissive` and `SV_Emissive`.[3] We must also add the function `area_light_shade` to the `Material` class, but it has to be defined for every material that we want to render with area-light shading. Listing 18.4 shows the function `Matte::area_light_shade` with shadows. In this context, the area light's `in_shadow` function computes the visibility function $V(p, p'_j)$ in Equation (18.3). You can, of course, turn shadows on or off in the build functions. Notice that the light functions G and pdf are also called polymorphically. As a result, you will have to add these to the `Light` base class as virtual functions, where they can both return 1.0. This will allow you to add point and directional lights to scenes with area lights, as in Figure 18.9.

 ## 18.7 The Geometric Object Classes

A geometric object that's also a light source must provide the following three services to the `AreaLight` class:

- sample points on its surface,
- the pdf at each sample point (which needs the area),
- the normal at each sample point.

To provide the samples, I store a pointer to a sampler object in the geometric object, but to save memory, I only do this with object types that are used for area lights: disks and rectangles, for the time being. We also have to compute the object's inverse area, as the pdf will return this. It's most efficient to compute area once when the object is constructed and to store the inverse area, as this saves a division each time the pdf function is called.

As an example, Listing 18.5 shows the class `Rectangle` with the new data members and member functions in blue. As the functions `sample`, `pdf`, and

---

3. `SV_Emissive` is a spatially varying version of `Emissive` that will allow us to render scenes with textured area lights in Chapter 29.

```
class Rectangle:: public GeometricObject {
    private:

        Point3D p0;
        Vector3D a;
        Vector3D b;
        Normal normal;
        Sampler* sampler_ptr;
        float inv_area;

    public:

        // constructors, access functions, hit functions

        void
        set_sampler(Sampler* sampler);

        virtual Point3D
        sample(void);

        virtual float
        pdf(ShadeRec& sr);

        virtual Normal
        get_normal(const Point3D& p);
};
```

Listing 18.5. The class `Rectangle`.

```
Point3D
Rectangle::sample(void) {
    Point2D sample_point = sampler_ptr->sample_unit_square();
    return (p0 + sample_point.x * a + sample_point.y * b);
}
```

Listing 18.6. The function `Rectangle::sample`.

get_normal will be called polymorphically from AreaLight, they will have to be added as virtual functions to the GeometricObject base class.

The function sample uses the rectangle's corner vertex p_0 and the edge vectors *a* and *b* to generate sample points on the surface. The code is in Listing 18.6.

There is, however, a flaw in this code. Unless the rectangle is a square, the samples will not be uniformly distributed on its surface. The distribution will be stretched in the largest direction, or equivalently, squashed in the smallest direction. Although I'll only use rectangular lights that are square in this chapter, you should test other shapes (see Exercise 18.9). There shouldn't be a major problem unless the light has a skinny shape.

I won't reproduce the functions pdf and get_normal, as these just return the inverse area and the specified normal, respectively.

18.8 The Area Light Class

With code for the other classes out of the way, we can now look at the AreaLight class, the declaration for which is in Listing 18.7.

```
class AreaLight: public Light {
    public:

        // constructors, access functions, etc.

        virtual Vector3D
        get_direction(ShadeRec& sr);

        virtual bool
        in_shadow(const Ray& ray, const ShadeRec& sr) const;

        virtual RGBColor
        L(ShadeRec& sr);

        virtual float
        G(const ShadeRec& sr) const;

        virtual float
        pdf(const ShadeRec& sr) const;

    private:

        GeometricObject* object_ptr;
        Material* material_ptr; // an emissive material
        Point3D sample_point;   // sample point on the surface
        Normal light_normal;    // normal at sample point
        Vector3D wi;      // unit vector from hit point to sample point
};
```

Listing 18.7. The class AreaLight.

```
Vector3D
AreaLight::get_direction(ShadeRec& sr) {
    sample_point = object_ptr->sample();
    light_normal = object_ptr->get_normal(sample_point);
    wi = sample_point - sr.hit_point;
    wi.normalize();

    return (wi);
}
```

Listing 18.8. The function `AreaLight::get_direction`.

The five member functions get_direction, in_shadow, L, G, and pdf are called in this order from Matte::area_light_shade, and so that's the best order to present and discuss them. Because of the area-lighting architecture, where a lot of the work is done in other classes, these functions are all small and simple.

The function get_direction in Listing 18.8 does more than just return the unit direction ω_i from the point being shaded to the sample point; it also stores the sample point, the normal at the sample point, and ω_i in data members. The reason is that these are also required in the functions in_shadow, L, and G. Although it's best for each function to perform a single task, the multitasking in this case is a matter of practical necessity, as a given sample point can only be accessed once.

The geometric object's get_normal function, called from AreaLight:: get_direction, will work for planar objects and objects that are defined by

```
bool
AreaLight::in_shadow(const Ray& ray, const ShadeRec& sr) const {
    float t;
    int num_objects = sr.w.objects.size();
    float ts = (sample_point - ray.o) * ray.d;

    for (int j = 0; j < num_objects ; j++)
        if (sr.w.objects[j]->shadow_hit(ray, t) && t < ts)
            return(true);

    return(false);
}
```

Listing 18.9. The function `AreaLight::in_shadow`.

```
RGBColor
AreaLight::L(ShadeRec& sr) {
    float ndotd = -light_normal * wi;

    if (ndotd > 0.0)
        return (material_ptr->get_Le(sr));
    else
        return (black);
}
```

Listing 18.10. The function `AreaLight::L`.

a single implicit function but will not work for other objects, for example, an axis-aligned box (see the Notes and Discussion section).

The `in_shadow` function in Listing 18.9 tests if the shadow ray hits an object between the hit point and the sample point.

The function `L` in Listing 18.10 checks that the shadow ray hits the light surface on the same side as the normal before returning the material's emitted radiance.

The function `G` in Listing 18.11 computes the cosine term $\cos\theta' = -n'_j \bullet \omega_{i,j}$ divided by d^2. As such, it's not the full geometric factor $G(p, p'_j)$, as the other cosine factor $n \bullet \omega_{i,j}$ is computed separately in `Matte::area_light_shade`.

The function `pdf` in Listing 18.12 simply calls the object's `pdf` function.

```
float
AreaLight::G(const ShadeRec& sr) const {
    float ndotd = -light_normal * wi;
    float d2 = sample_point.d_squared(sr.hit_point);

    return (ndotd / d2);

}
```

Listing 18.11. The function `AreaLight::G`.

```
float
AreaLight::pdf(ShadeRec& sr) {
    return (object_ptr->pdf(sr));
}
```

Listing 18.12. The function `AreaLight::pdf`.

18.9 Example Images

With the above code in place, it's now a simple task to construct area lights. Listing 18.13 shows the relevant code from a build function that constructs a rectangular light. This demonstrates how an area light requires the following three things to be constructed:

- an emissive material;
- a geometric object that's added to the world with the emissive material;
- the area light itself with a pointer to the object.

Notice that the rectangle has shadows set to false. This is necessary to avoid shading artifacts with the function AreaLight::in_shadow in Listing 18.9. The rectangle will be tested for intersection by each shadow ray and would normally return true because each sample point is on its surface. The problem arises because the value of t returned from Rectangle::shadow_hit will be $t_s + \varepsilon$, a fact that can cause random self-shadowing or regular shading artifacts (see Exercise 18.7).

Figure 18.4 shows a scene that consists of four axis aligned-boxes and a ground plane illuminated by a vertical rectangular light. One ray per pixel was used in Figure 18.4(a), which is therefore quite noisy. Figure 18.4(b) was rendered with 100 rays per pixel and has an acceptable amount of noise. Notice that the shadows on the plane are sharp where they leave the boxes. Also notice that there is no illumination on the half of the plane behind the rectangle.

```
Emissive* emissive_ptr = new Emissive;
emissive_ptr->scale_radiance(40.0);
emissive_ptr->set_ce(white);

// define rectangle parameters p0, a, b, normal

Rectangle* rectangle_ptr = new Rectangle(p0, a, b, normal);
rectangle_ptr->set_material(emissive_ptr);
rectangle_ptr->set_sampler(sampler_ptr);
rectangle_ptr->set_shadows(false);
add_object(rectangle_ptr);

AreaLight* area_light_ptr = new AreaLight;
area_light_ptr->set_object(rectangle_ptr);
area_light_ptr->set_shadows(true);
add_light(area_light_ptr);
```

Listing 18.13. Build function code to construct a rectangular light and its associated emissive rectangle.

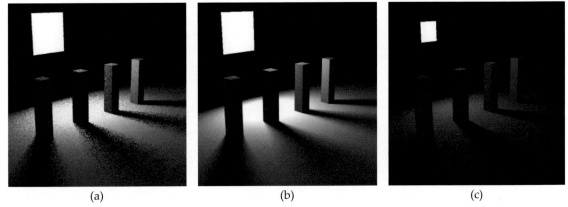

(a)   (b)   (c)

Figure 18.4. (a) A scene with a rectangular light rendered with one ray per pixel; (b) the same scene rendered with 100 rays per pixel; (c) the same scene with a smaller light rendered with 100 rays per pixel.

In Figure 18.4(c), the light area is four times smaller than it is in Figure 18.4(b) and (c), and the illumination is correspondingly smaller, as a result of the pdf. Because we divide by the pdf in the `Matte::area_light_shade` function, the reflected radiance is multiplied by the area of the light. An alternative approach that's more convenient for scene design is to use lights whose total emitted power is specified independently of their surface area (see Exercise 18.10).

Figure 18.5(a) shows the scene rendered with a disk light having the same area as the rectangular light in Figure 18.4(a) and (b). Figure 18.5(b) is the same scene rendered with a spherical light. Notice how similar the shadows are

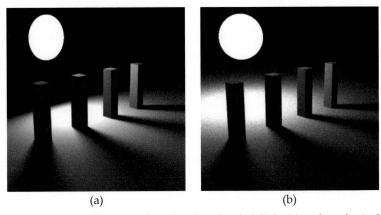

(a)   (b)

Figure 18.5. The scene in Figure 18.4 rendered with a disk light (a) and a spherical light (b). Notice that the spherical light illuminates the whole plane.

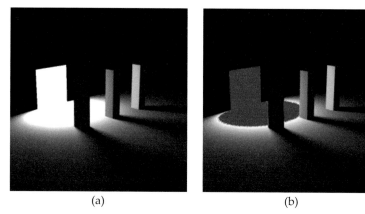

(a)   (b)

Figure 18.6. (a) A scene rendered with a rectangular light that touches the plane; (b) out-of-gamut pixels rendered in red.

for the three light types in Figures 18.4 and 18.5. For lights of similar size and distance from objects, the shadows are relatively insensitive to their shapes. Figure 18.5(a) and (b) were both rendered with 100 rays per pixel, but there is more noise in Figure 18.5(b) because of the simplified spherical-light implementation that I have used (see the Notes and Discussion section).

Figure 18.6 shows a limitation of the direct-illumination model we are using. In Figure 18.6(a), the rectangular light touches the plane, and it appears that the illumination on the plane has overflowed near the light. Indeed, this is the case, as Figure 18.6(b) demonstrates with out-of-gamut pixels shaded red.[4] The geometric reason is the $1/d^2$ factor in $G(p, p'_j)$. As hit points and sample points can be arbitrarily close together, $G(p, p'_j)$ is unbounded. It's also due to the constant pdf and the uniformly distributed sample points. To avoid this overflow, we need to keep area lights at a reasonable distance from object surfaces.

As an example of how this should be done, Shirley and Morley (2003) discusses the direct illumination from a spherical light using the area form of the rendering equation with a pdf that includes the $1/d^2$ term. This cancels the term in $G(p, p'_j)$. It shows a nice image of two spheres that just touch, where one sphere is emissive. There is no overflow in the reflected radiance, and there shouldn't be, of course, because the emitted radiance is always finite.

Another way to avoid the overflow problem is to use the hemisphere form of the rendering equation, which doesn't involve the $1/d^2$ term (see the Further Reading section and Chapter 26).

---

4. The light surface has also overflowed because the scene was rendered with $l_s = 40$, but that's all right: l_s can be as large as we need to provide adequate illumination to the objects in the scene.

18.10 Environment Lights

An *environment light* is an infinitely large sphere that surrounds a scene and provides illumination from all directions. It's often used to simulate the diffuse sky illumination for outdoor scenes. The sphere has an emissive material, which can be a constant color or spatially varying. In the latter case, the colors are often based on a physical sky model, or photographs of the sky. In either case, the results can be beautiful images with soft shading.

A number of figures in Chapters 11 and 12 used a large hemisphere with clouds to add interest to the images, but this wasn't used as an environment light. In those images, rays that didn't hit any objects brought back a cloud-texture color instead of a constant background color. The Uffizi images in Chapter 11 are similar, except that the only object in the scene is a large textured sphere. In this chapter, I'll only consider environment lights with a constant color. Chapter 29 will cover textured environment lights.

I haven't implemented the environment light as an AreaLight because attempting to evaluate the Monte Carlo estimator (18.3) with an infinitely large sphere is problematic. Instead, it's better to use the hemisphere formulation of the rendering equation, where the shadow rays are distributed in solid angle. We still need to use Monte Carlo integration, as the illumination can come from all directions. The shadow rays are shot with a cosine distribution into the hemisphere that's oriented around the normal at each hit point because this is suitable for matte materials. Although this only samples half of the sphere directions, for opaque materials, there's no use sampling the half of the sphere that's below the tangent plane at the hit point, as these points can't contribute to the incident radiance (see the Notes and Discussion section).

The Monte Carlo estimator for the integral in Equation (13.21) is

$$\langle L_r(\boldsymbol{p}, \boldsymbol{\omega}_o) \rangle = \frac{1}{n_s} \sum_{j=1}^{n_s} \frac{f_r(\boldsymbol{p}, \boldsymbol{\omega}_{i,j}, \boldsymbol{\omega}_o) L_i(\boldsymbol{p}, \boldsymbol{\omega}_{i,j}) \cos \theta_{i,j}}{p(\boldsymbol{\omega}_{i,j})}, \tag{18.4}$$

where the pdf $p(\boldsymbol{\omega}_{i,j})$ must now be expressed in terms of a solid-angle measure. In this case, we'll want to make the pdf proportional to $\cos \theta_i = \boldsymbol{n} \cdot \boldsymbol{\omega}_i$, to match the $\cos \theta_i$ term in the integrand, but it must be normalized. Letting $p = c \cos \theta_i$, where c is the normalization constant, we require

$$\int_{2\pi} p(\boldsymbol{\omega}_i) d\boldsymbol{\omega}_i = 1. \tag{18.5}$$

Writing out the integral explicitly gives

$$c \int_0^{2\pi} \int_0^{\pi/2} \cos \theta_i \sin \theta_i d\theta_i d\phi_i = 1 \Rightarrow c = 1/\pi,$$

from Equation (2.12), and hence

$$p = \cos \theta_i /\pi. \tag{18.6}$$

We *should* implement another tracer to evaluate the estimator (18.4), but to save the work of not only implementing a new tracer class but also of writing new shade functions for all of the materials, I've used the AreaLighting tracer. The trick is not to define the G function for the environment light, as this forces the C++ compiler to use the G function defined in the Light base class, which returns 1.0.

Listing 18.14 shows the declaration for the class EnvironmentLight, which doesn't contain a sphere; the code just works as if there is an infinite sphere.

```
class EnvironmentLight: public Light {
    public:
        // constructors etc.

        void
        set_sampler(Sampler* sampler);

        virtual Vector3D
        get_direction(ShadeRec& s);

        virtual RGBColor
        L(ShadeRec& sr);

        bool
        in_shadow(const Ray& ray, const ShadeRec& sr) const;

        virtual float
        pdf(const ShadeRec& sr) const;

    private:

        Sampler* sampler_ptr;
        Material* material_ptr;
        Vector3D u, v, w;
        Vector3D wi;
};
```

Listing 18.14. The class EnvironmentLight.

```
Vector3D
EnvironmentLight::get_direction(ShadeRec& sr) {
    w = sr.normal;
    v = (0.0034, 1, 0.0071) ^ w;
    v.normalize();
    u = v ^ w;
    Point3D sp = sampler_ptr->sample_hemisphere();
    wi = sp.x * u + sp.y * v + sp.z * w;

    return(wi);
}
```

Listing 18.15. The function EnvironmentLight::get_direction.

```
RGBColor
EnvironmentLight::L(ShadeRec& sr) {
    return (material_ptr->get_Le(sr));
}
```

Listing 18.16. The function EnvironmentLight::L.

The classes EnvironmentLight and AmbientOccluder have several features in common. First, their set_sampler functions are the same, where both map the sample points to a hemisphere with a cosine distribution. Second, the mechanism for shooting shadow rays is the same. Both classes have to set up the same *u*, *v*, *w* basis at each hit point, but they do this in different places. Recall from Listing 17.5 that the function AmbientOccluder::L has to set up *u*, *v*, and *w* before it calls the get_direction function. Because the environment light is stored in world::lights, the materials' area_light_shade functions call EnvironmentLight::get_direction before they call EnvironmentLight:: L. We therefore have to set up *u*, *v*, and *w* in get_direction, as shown in Listing 18.15.

The function EnvironmentLight::L is then quite simple, as Listing 18.16 indicates.

Finally, the in_shadow function is the same for both classes, and so I won't reproduce the EnvironmentLight::in_shadow function here.

Listing 18.17 shows how to construct an environment light. Note that the concave sphere for the direct rendering has a finite but very large radius.

Figure 18.7 shows an example scene, where each part illustrates a different illumination component. The scene contains an environment light with

```
Emissive* emissive_ptr = new Emissive;
emissive_ptr->set_ce(1.0, 1.0, 0.5);
emissive_ptr->set_brightness(1.0);

ConcaveSphere* sphere_ptr = new ConcaveSphere;
sphere_ptr->set_radius(1000000.0);
sphere_ptr->set_material(emissive_ptr);
sphere_ptr->set_shadows(false);
add_object(sphere_ptr);

EnvironmentLight* light_ptr = new EnvironmentLight;
light_ptr->set_material(emissive_ptr);
light_ptr->set_sampler(new MultiJittered(num_samples));
light_ptr->set_shadows(true);
add_light(light_ptr);
```

Listing 18.17. A build function fragment that constructs an environment light.

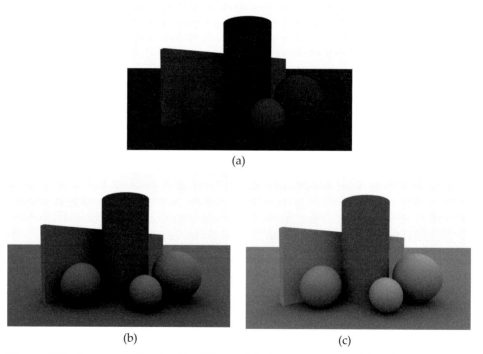

Figure 18.7. A scene rendered with different lighting components: (a) ambient occlusion only; (b) white environment light only; (c) ambient occlusion and environment light. All images were rendered with 100 rays per pixel.

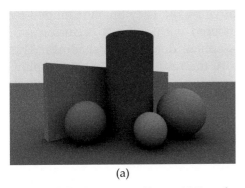
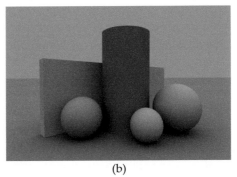

(a)   (b)

Figure 18.8. The scene in Figure 18.7 rendered with ambient occlusion with a yellow environment light (a) and a blue environment light (b).

a white emissive material. Figure 18.7(a) is rendered with ambient occlusion only, where each material has a low ambient reflection coefficient so that the images won't be washed out when we add other illumination components. Figure 18.7(b) is rendered with the environment light but with no ambient illumination. Here, parts of the objects are black where they receive no illumination from the environment light, in the same way that they would be black if they were rendered with ambient occlusion and min_amount = 0. This is no coincidence, as the sampling techniques are the same. Figure 18.7(c) shows the results of using ambient occlusion and the environment light, resulting in a lighter and softer image.

Figure 18.8 shows this scene rendered with a yellow and a blue environment light. As you can see, the color of the light has a dramatic effect on the images.

We can achieve more realistic lighting for outdoor scenes by adding a directional light to simulate direct sunlight. You will be pleased to know that directional and point lights will work without modification with the AreaLighting shader. Figure 18.9 shows the scene in Figure 18.8(a) rendered with an added directional light.

Figure 18.10 shows an environment-light scene without a ground plane, so that the objects are illuminated from all directions. The spheres are from the figure on the first page of Chapter 14 with ran-

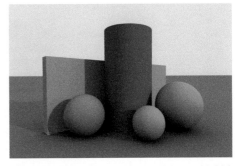

Figure 18.9. The scene in Figure 18.8(a) rendered with ambient occlusion, a yellow environment light, and an orange directional light, to simulate outdoor lighting conditions just after sunrise or before sunset.

dom colors and rendered from the negative z-axis. They are surrounded by a white environment light and also rendered with ambient occlusion (see Question 17.2). The environment light's sphere doesn't cast shadows. This scene provides an opportunity to compare the results of different sampling techniques. Figure 18.10(a) and (b) were rendered with 16 samples per pixel, which is not nearly enough. Multi-jittered sampling was used in Figure 18.10(a) and Hammersley sampling in Figure 18.10(b). The printed images here don't do justice to the ugliness of these images, which are ugly for different reasons: noise in Figure 18.10(a) and texture-like artifacts in Figure 18.10(b). Figure 18.10(c) and (d) use the same sampling techniques with 256 samples per pixel, which is adequate. In this case, both images are good, there being just a faint hint of artifacts in Figure 18.10(d). You need to look at these images on the book's website.

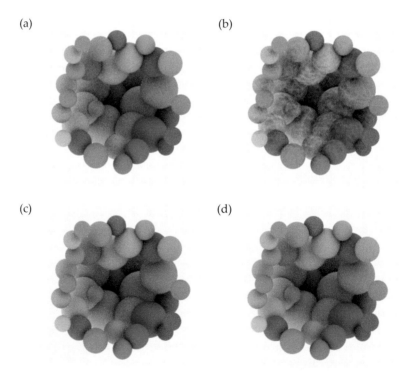

Figure 18.10. Spheres rendered with a white environment light and ambient occlusion: (a) 16 multi-jittered samples for the ambient occlusion and environment light; (c) same as (a) but 256 samples per pixel; (b) 16 Hammersley samples for the ambient occlusion and environment light, (d) same as (a) but 256 samples per pixel.

Notes and Discussion

My spherical light uses a `LightSphere` object, which is a sphere with a sampler object that distributes sample points over its surface with a uniform density. It does this by calling the function `Sampler::map_to_sphere(0)`. The pdf is $p = 1/(4\pi r^2)$, where r is the radius. This implementation results in noisy images because the $\cos\theta'$ term in $G(p, p')$ varies so much. Better implementations are discussed in the references cited in the Further Reading section.

There's a sampling subtlety with the environment light. Recall from Section 18.10 that although the light represents a sphere that surrounds the scene, the shadow rays are distributed in the hemisphere above each hit point p, where the correct pdf measure is $p = \cos\theta_i/\pi$. If we were doing volumetric rendering where p is a point in space, we would have to distribute the shadow rays over the whole sphere that surrounds p. In this case, the correct pdf would be $p = \cos\theta_i/2\pi$ because the integral (18.5) would then be over a sphere. Now, we can also use spherical sampling to render opaque surfaces and still get the correct results, but we would need twice as many samples per pixel to reduce the noise to the same levels as hemisphere sampling produces. The reason is as follows. If we used 100 samples per pixel, only 50 of these would be in the hemisphere above p and therefore able to contribute to the incident radiance, but the reflected radiance L_o from each sample would be multiplied by 2π instead of π. The result would therefore be the same as using the hemisphere sampling except for the increase in noise.

In Chapter 21, I'll discuss how to apply affine transformations to geometric objects, but the technique presented there won't allow us to transform area lights. For example, if we wanted to translate the rectangular light in Figure 18.4, the rectangle object would be translated, but the illumination would stay the same. The reason is that the sample points would not be translated. This isn't a serious problem, as the definitions of disks and rectangles allow us to specify arbitrary locations, sizes, and orientations. Nonetheless, one of the exercises in Chapter 21 will ask you to think about how to apply affine transformations to area lights.

The `AreaLight::get_direction` function in Listing 18.8 calls the geometric object's `get_normal` function, which returns the normal given a sample point on its surface. This will work for planar objects, where the normal is part of the object's definition. It will also work for objects defined by single implicit functions because we can use the gradient operator to compute the normal:

$$n = \nabla(x, y, z)/\nabla\left\|(x, y, z)\right\|.$$

Here, (x, y, z) are the sample-point coordinates. This process will not work for other objects, such as triangle meshes. A solution is to compute and store the normals as the sample points are generated. Geometric information such as the vertex normals can be used for this purpose.

 ## Further Reading

Soft shadows were first rendered with ray tracing by Cook et al. (1984). My area-lighting architecture, where a single area light class contains a pointer to a self-emissive object, is based on the design in Pharr and Humphreys (2004). Some of the implementation details are also based on Dutré et al. (2006). Both of these books contain a comprehensive discussion of ray tracing with area lights.

Shirley and Morley (2003) and Pharr and Humphreys (2004) present techniques for accurately rendering the direct illumination from spherical lights. Shirley's technique is also discussed in Shirley et al. (2005).

Pharr and Humphreys (2004) discusses a sampling pattern called a (0, 2) sequence, which suffers less distortion than other sampling patterns when it's mapped onto long thin rectangles. As such, it may be better than multi-jittered sampling for shading with thin rectangular lights, but, like Hammersley patterns, it's not random. The original literature on this pattern is the book by Niederreiter (1992) and the paper by Kollig and Keller (2002).

Although we can use as many area lights as we like in a given scene, the amount of sampling will be proportional to the number of lights multiplied by the number of samples per pixel. Shirley et al. (1996) developed techniques for efficiently sampling large numbers of area lights. See also Shirley and Morley (2003).

There's a lot more to rendering with area lights than I've presented here, where all the images in the preceding sections were rendered by sampling the light sources and the BRDFs were Lambertian. Pharr and Humphreys (2004) discusses rendering with area lights by sampling the BRDF, which can often work better for specular BRDFs. Of course, scenes can have any combination of BRDFs that range from Lambertian to perfect specular, and area lights that range from small to the whole hemisphere. To handle this situation, a technique called *multiple importance sampling* was developed by Veach and Guibas (1995). See also Veach's PhD thesis (1997). Pharr and Humphreys (2004) has a clear discussion of this for the special case of two BRDFs.

Questions

18.1. Why do the edges of the area lights in Figures 18.4–18.6 appear as if they haven't been antialiased?

18.2. Why doesn't the function `EnvironmentLight::L` in Listing 18.16 have to check that the light is being emitted on the inside surface of the sphere?

18.3. How do directional and area lights work without modification with the `area_light_shade` functions?

18.4. Figure 18.11 shows the scene from Figure 18.7(c) rendered with Phong materials on all objects except the plane. The Phong materials have a red specular color, and the specular exponent varies from 10 to 200. Notice how the specular highlights decrease in brightness as the exponent increases and almost disappear when $e = 200$. Can you explain this? Is there a solution?

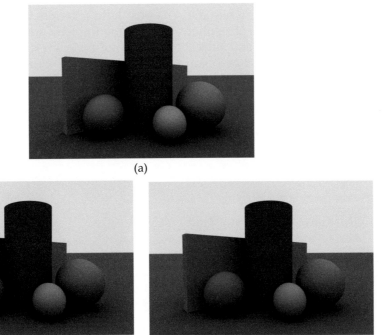

(a)

(b)   (c)

Figure 18.11. Specular highlights from an environment light rendered with $e = 10$ (a), $e = 50$ (b), and $e = 200$ (c).

 **Exercises**

18.1. Here's a simple way to produce soft shadows with a point light. Just jitter the light's location in 3D as in Listing 18.18. I've called this FakeSphericalLight, although the jittered locations are actually in an axis-aligned cube of edge length 2r. That doesn't matter much because of the soft shadows' insensitivity to area-light shapes, as Figures 18.5 and 18.6 demonstrate. The value of r will depend on the light's location and how soft you want the shadows to be.

As far as the direct illumination is concerned, this light is a rudimentary simulation of a cubic *volume light* using multiple point lights, but it will be directly rendered as a self-emissive sphere.

Figure 18.12(a) shows the scene in Figure 18.5(b) rendered with $r = 3.0$ and distance attenuation. The scene contains a sphere with an emissive material centered at the light's location and with radius r, the same as the scene in Figure 18.5(b). Comparing the two figures, which were both rendered with 100 rays per pixel, shows that the shadows are almost identical, but Figure 18.12(a) contains a lot less noise than 18.5(b). There are two reasons for this. First, the fake spherical light's locations are in a 3D volume, while the spherical light's sample points in 18.5(b) are on the surface of a sphere. Second, my implementation of the spherical light is crude and subject to a lot of noise. As a result, Figure 18.12(b) is actually the better looking of the two images. Figure 18.12(b) shows the scene rendered without distance attenuation. There is a large difference in the brightness values between these two images, where $l_s = 250.0$ in Figure 18.12(a) and $l_s = 3.0$ in Figure 18.12(b).

Implement a fake spherical light.

```
Vector3D
FakeSphericalLight::get_direction(ShadeRec& sr) {

    float r = 3.0;
    Point3D new_location;
    new_location.x = location.x + r * (2.0 * rand_float() - 1.0);
    new_location.y = location.y + r * (2.0 * rand_float() - 1.0);
    new_location.z = location.z + r * (2.0 * rand_float() - 1.0);

    return ((new_location - sr.hit_point).hat());
}
```

Listing 18.18. The function FakeSphericalLight::get_direction.

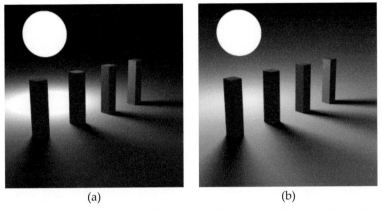

(a)   (b)

Figure 18.12. Illumination from a fake spherical light with distance attenuation (a) and with no distance attenuation (b).

18.2. We can be a bit more "honest" with the fake spherical light by restricting the locations to lie in a sphere instead of a cube. Implement a rejection-sampling technique to enforce this, but make sure that every time `FakeSphericalLight::get_direction` is called, it does return a direction. Compare the results with Figure 18.12.

18.3. Implement a jittered directional light. The figure on the first page of this chapter was rendered with this type of light.

18.4. Implement a rectangular area light as described in this chapter and use the figures in Section 18.7 to test your implementation.

18.5. Implement a disk light and use Figure 18.5(a) to test your implementation. In contrast to the rectangular light, you will need to set up a (u, v, w) basis to compute the sample-point coordinates.

18.6. Experiment with other sampling techniques and numbers of rays per pixel for the figures in Section 18.9.

18.7. The figures in Section 18.9 were rendered with shadows set to false for the rectangle, disk, and sphere. Render the figures with shadows set to true for these objects and compare the results.

18.8. Render some scenes with shadows turned off for the area lights.

18.9. Render the scene in Figure 18.4(a) with a rectangular light of aspect ratio 2 : 1 and two square lights, side-by-side and with the same total area, and compare the results.

18.10. Implement an option on the `AreaLight` class that will allow you to specify the total power of the light as a quantity that's independent of the surface area. This is more convenient for scene design than the current implementation, where the power is proportional to the area.

18.11. Implement an environment light as described in Section 18.10 and use the figures there to test your implementation.

18.12. Implement the function `area_light_shade` for the `Phong` material and reproduce Figure 18.11. Experiment with different values of the Phong exponent e.

18.13. Reproduce the images in Figure 18.10, and experiment with different scene parameters such as the number of samples, the sampling technique, environment-light color, ambient-light conditions, and the material properties of the spheres. You can mix and match different sampling techniques for antialiasing, ambient occlusion, and the environment light.

18.14. Produce some nice images of your own with area and environment lights.

19 Ray-Object Intersections

Image by Mark Langsworth

 ## Objectives

By the end of this chapter, you should:

- understand how bounding boxes can decrease rendering times;
- know how to ray trace a number of object types including triangles and part objects;
- understand why we can only ray trace generic versions of some objects;
- understand the important role that compound objects play in modeling;
- have at your disposal a variety of objects for scene construction.

This chapter allows you to start building a decent collection of object types for modeling and rendering. I'll discuss here how to ray trace axis-aligned bounding boxes as an efficiency measure, as well as triangles, axis-aligned boxes, disks, rectangles, tori, generic objects, and part objects. I'll also discuss the role that compound objects play in modeling and how they can simplify ray-object intersections.

A completely different approach to ray tracing is to only use triangles for modeling. This is certainly possible, because the only object in this book that can't be modeled with triangles is the plane, and you could always substitute a large rectangle or disk for a plane. In addition, all of the curved objects

I discuss have parametric representations that allow them to be tessellated into triangles. This approach is, however, not suitable for us for the following reasons. First, the curved objects are not trivial to tessellate, and second, their accurate representation requires such large numbers of triangles that an acceleration scheme is required to ray trace them with practical ray-tracing times. These processes give you far too much work to do before you can ray trace many of the scenes. Even simple flat objects with curved boundaries such as disks and annuli would need to be tessellated. This approach is also less efficient than using exact mathematical representations of objects with specialized hit functions. Finally, a triangle-only approach doesn't take advantage of ray tracing's unmatched ability to render exact mathematical representations of objects—one of ray tracing's great advantages over other rendering algorithms.

Triangles are still the most important object, as only triangle meshes can accurately represent objects and scenes of arbitrary geometric complexity such as landscapes, plants, buildings, people, characters, and animals (see Chapter 23).

Before we start, here's some notation. A *primitive* is a single geometric object such as a sphere, a triangle, a torus, or an axis-aligned box. In contrast, *compound objects*, to be introduced in Section 19.8, are not primitives, because they consist of other objects—either primitives or other compound objects. In later chapters, I'll discuss grids and triangle meshes—special types of compound objects that can contain millions of other objects. However, the bottom line for ray-object intersections is that although we can write hit functions for compound objects, each ray will ultimately be intersected with the primitives in these objects.

19.1 Bounding Boxes

If an object is expensive to ray trace, we can put a bounding object around it that's inexpensive to ray trace. By definition, a bounding object completely encloses another object, as Figure 19.1 illustrates. If a ray misses the bounding object, it therefore cannot hit the object inside. If the bounding object is significantly quicker to intersect than the object inside, we can usually save time by testing rays with the bounding object first.

The most common bounding objects have the shape of rectangular boxes whose axes are parallel to world coordinate axes. These are known as *axis-aligned bounding boxes*. They are not part of the geometric objects hierarchy because, although we intersect them, we don't render them. This means that their hit function does not have to compute the hit-point coordinates, a fact that simplifies the calculations.

bounding object

expensive object

We can represent a bounding box by its two opposite corners $p_0 = (x_0, y_0, z_0)$ and $p_1 = (x_1, y_1, z_1)$, where $x_0 < x_1$, $y_0 < y_1$, and $z_0 < z_1$. Thanks principally to the work of Kay and Kajiya (1986) and Smits (1998), a ray can be efficiently tested for intersection with a bounding box. The key idea was introduced by Kay and Kajiya, who represented polyhedral bounding volumes as the intersection of infinite slabs. Using this technique, an axis-aligned bounding box is the intersection of the three mutually perpendicular infinite slabs $x \in [x_0, x_1]$, $y \in [y_0, y_1]$, and $z \in [z_0, z_1]$ with the box = $[x_0, x_1] \cap [y_0, y_1] \cap [z_0, z_1]$.

Figure 19.1. The Stanford bunny and a bounding box.

Figure 19.2(a) illustrates the x and y slabs in 2D. Figure 19.2(b) and Figure 19.3 show a few of the many ways that a ray can pass through or miss a 2D axis-aligned box. Let's consider Figure 19.2(b) first, where the ray misses the box. Here, the section of the ray that's inside the x slab, the green interval, does not overlap the red interval where the ray is inside the y slab. The intersection of these two intervals along the ray is therefore empty; that is, $[x_0, x_1] \cap [y_0, y_1] = \varnothing$.

Now look at Figure 19.3(a), where the ray does hit the box and where the x and y intervals along the ray overlap. Figure 19.3(b) shows the ray passing

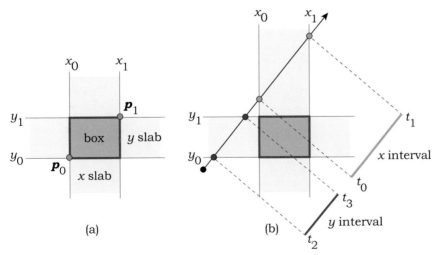

(a)   (b)

Figure 19.2. (a) A 2D axis-aligned box can be defined by the intersection of two infinite slabs; (b) a ray that does not hit the box has x and y intervals that do not overlap.

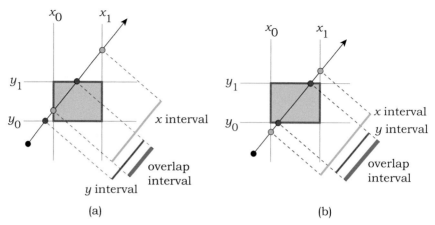

Figure 19.3. Two cases where the ray hits the box: (a) ray passes through adjacent sides; (b) ray passes through opposite sides.

through the box in a different way (entering and exiting on opposite faces), and the y interval is enclosed by the x interval. The condition that the intervals overlap is that the *maximum t-value* for where the ray enters one of the slabs is less than the *minimum t-value* where it leaves one of the slabs.

For ray-tracing purposes, we do, however, have to make a distinction between the ray passing through the box and the ray hitting the box. The above condition is necessary but not sufficient for the ray to hit the box. Figure 19.4(a) shows a ray in the same location as in Figure 19.3(b) but which points away from the box and therefore does not hit it. The bounding-box hit function has to take this into account.

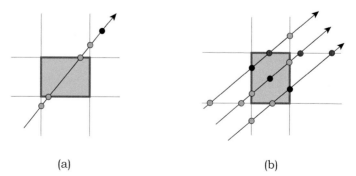

Figure 19.4. (a) This ray passes through the box but doesn't hit it because all of the slab intersections have $t < 0$; (b) various ways that a ray can start on a box face.

There are many other cases where the ray hits or misses the box traveling in the positive or negative x-and y-directions, starts inside one of the slabs, starts inside the box itself or on one of its faces, or is parallel to one of the slabs, either inside the slab, outside the slab, or on one of the slab boundaries. Figure 19.4(b) illustrates three examples. Fortunately, these cases can all be encapsulated in some simple code, and the whole process generalizes easily to 3D.

The bounding-box class is called BBox, where the corner coordinates are stored in six floats: x_0, y_0, z_0, x_1, y_1, z_1, to simplify the application code. They are also public, because they are accessed extensively in the classes Instance (Chapter 21) and Grid (Chapter 22). The code in Listing 19.1 is based on the

```
bool
BBox::hit(const Ray& ray) const {
        double ox = ray.o.x; double oy = ray.o.y; double oz = ray.o.z;
        double dx = ray.d.x; double dy = ray.d.y; double dz = ray.d.z;

        double tx_min, ty_min, tz_min;
        double tx_max, ty_max, tz_max;

        double a = 1.0 / dx;
        if (a >= 0) {
                tx_min = (x0 - ox) * a;
                tx_max = (x1 - ox) * a;
        }
        else {
                tx_min = (x1 - ox) * a;
                tx_max = (x0 - ox) * a;
        }

        double b = 1.0 / dy;
        if (b >= 0) {
                ty_min = (y0 - oy) * b;
                ty_max = (y1 - oy) * b;
        }
        else {
                ty_min = (y1 - oy) * b;
                ty_max = (y0 - oy) * b;
        }

        double c = 1.0 / dz;
```

Listing 19.1. The BBox::hit function.

```
if (c >= 0) {
    tz_min = (z0 - oz) * c;
    tz_max = (z1 - oz) * c;
}
else {
    tz_min = (z1 - oz) * c;
    tz_max = (z0 - oz) * c;
}

double t0, t1;

// find largest entering t value

if (tx_min > ty_min)
    t0 = tx_min;
else
    t0 = ty_min;

if (tz_min > t0)
    t0 = tz_min;

// find smallest exiting t value

if (tx_max < ty_max)
    t1 = tx_max;
else
    t1 = ty_max;

if (tz_max < t1)
    t1 = tz_max;

return (t0 < t1 && t1 > kEpsilon);
}
```

Listing 19.1 (continued). The `BBox::hit` function.

pseudocode in Shirley and Morley (2003) and code in Williams et al. (2005). It relies on properties of IEEE floating-point arithmetic to correctly handle cases where the ray travels exactly in a negative coordinate-axis direction, for example $d = (-1, 0, 0)$.

Two issues we have to address are where to store the bounding boxes and where to call their hit function. One possibility is to store the bounding box in the `GeometricObject` base class, but this would use additional memory (6 floats) for all objects, and not all objects need stored bounding boxes. For

```
bool
Torus::hit(const Ray& ray, double& tmin, ShadeRec& sr) const {
    if(!bbox.hit(ray))
        return(false);

    // remainder of code (see Listing 19.9)
}
```

Listing 19.2. `Torus::hit` code fragment for testing bounding-box intersection.

example, spheres have such simple intersection calculations that bounding boxes are not necessary for their hit functions, axis-aligned boxes are their own bounding boxes, and bounding boxes can't be defined for planes, which are *unbounded* by definition. Because it takes time to intersect the bounding box, using them with simple objects would usually increase their intersection times.

Bounding boxes are most useful for objects with expensive hit functions such as tori, compound objects, beveled objects, and regular grids. These objects need stored bounding boxes, which should be constructed when the object is constructed. The start of the object's `hit` function can then test if the ray hits the bounding box, as illustrated in Listing 19.2 for a torus.

Axis-aligned bounding boxes are also essential for placing geometric objects in acceleration schemes. Consequently, all objects that are included in acceleration schemes must have an access function that returns their bounding box. For objects that store the bounding box, this will just return the box, but for objects such as spheres and triangles, the function will have to compute the bounding box. This won't affect the ray-tracing times, because it's only called while the acceleration scheme is constructed. It will, however, affect the build times, which can be substantial. My `GeometricObject` class therefore has the virtual function

```
virtual BBox
GeometricObject::get_bounding_box(void);
```

which can be overridden for objects to be stored in acceleration schemes.

 ## 19.2 Axis-Aligned Boxes

Axis-aligned boxes are the same shape as axis-aligned bounding boxes but are geometric objects and useful modeling primitives. They are also useful

```
bool
Box::hit(const Ray& ray, double& tmin, ShadeRec& sr) const {

    //same as Listing 19.1 down to the statement float t0, t1;

    int face_in, face_out;

    // find largest entering t value

    if (tx_min > ty_min) {
        t0 = tx_min;
        face_in = (a >= 0.0) ? 0 : 3;
    }
    else {
        t0 = ty_min;
        face_in = (b >= 0.0) ? 1 : 4;
    }

    if (tz_min > t0) {
        t0 = tz_min;
        face_in = (c >= 0.0) ? 2 : 5;
    }

    // find smallest exiting t value

    if (tx_max < ty_max) {
        t1 = tx_max;
        face_out = (a >= 0.0) ? 3 : 0;
    }
    else {
        t1 = ty_max;
        face_out = (b >= 0.0) ? 4 : 1;
    }

    if (tz_max < t1) {
        t1 = tz_max;
        face_out = (c >= 0.0) ? 5 : 2;
    }

    if (t0 < t1 && t1 > kEpsilon) {      // condition for a hit
        if (t0 > kEpsilon) {
            tmin = t0;                    // ray hits outside surface
            sr.normal = get_normal(face_in);
        }
        else {
```

Listing 19.3. The function Box::hit tests if a ray hits an axis-aligned box.

```
                    tmin = t1;                     // ray hits inside surface
                    sr.normal = get_normal(face_out);
            }

            sr.local_hit_point = ray.o + tmin * ray.d;
            return (true);
        }
    else
            return (false);
    }
```

Listing 19.3 (continued). The function Box::hit tests if a ray hits an axis-aligned box.

for teaching ray tracing because the surface is not defined by a single implicit equation. In addition, I'll use them to help illustrate total internal reflection in Chapter 28.

The axis-aligned box class is called Box, and it stores the opposite vertices as six private floats, as they are not used outside the class. Using floats instead of points allows us to make maximum use of the BBox::hit code in Listing 19.1 to intersect the box. The Box hit function has to identify the face that the ray hits and must always return the correct normal. The code also has to handle transparency correctly by taking into account rays that hit an inside surface of the box. The hit-function code is in Listing 19.3. The normal is computed in a separate function shown in Listing 19.4.

```
Normal
Box::get_normal(const int face_hit) const {
    switch (face_hit) {
            case 0:     return (Normal(-1, 0, 0)); // -x face
            case 1:     return (Normal(0, -1, 0)); // -y face
            case 2:     return (Normal(0, 0, -1)); // -z face
            case 3:     return (Normal(1, 0, 0));  // +x face
            case 4:     return (Normal(0, 1, 0));  // +y face
            case 5:     return (Normal(0, 0, 1));  // +z face
    }
}
```

Listing 19.4. The function Box::get_normal.

19.3 Triangles

Most objects in computer graphics are represented by *triangle meshes*—collections of triangles with shared vertices. Commercial rendering and animation packages allow users to model objects with various types of spline-based surfaces such as subdivision surfaces and NURBS and then represent them with triangle meshes for rendering. The reason is that triangles are easily scan-converted in hardware for display purposes, a process that makes the real-time rendering of complex scenes in 3D computer games possible.

Here, I'll explain how to ray trace individual triangles; I'll discuss triangle meshes and acceleration schemes in Chapters 22 and 23. The ray-triangle intersection algorithm involves some mathematics that you may not be familiar with, but I'll explain each step. The presentation here is based on the excellent description in Shirley and Morley (2003).

19.3.1 Definition

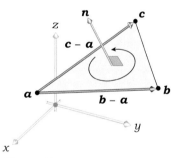

Figure 19.5. Triangle definition.

A triangle is defined by three points in space, *a*, *b*, *c*, which are its vertices (see Figure 19.5). Unless the points are all in a straight line, they define a plane, and therefore a triangle is always flat with a constant normal.[1] A convention is that when we look at a triangle from the side facing the normal, the vertices are ordered *counterclockwise*, as in Figure 19.5. This allows us to compute the unit normal with

$$n = (b-a)\times(c-a)/\|(b-a)\times(c-a)\|. \tag{19.1}$$

The vertices in Equation (19.1) can be cyclically permuted without affecting the result (see Exercise 19.4). For triangle meshes, which are often closed objects, this ensures that the normal for each triangle points outwards.

Listing 19.5 shows a partial declaration of the class `Triangle` and also shows how two `Triangle` constructors can be written.

19.3.2 Intersection

To intersect a ray with a triangle, we first find where it hits the plane and then test if the hit point is in the triangle. The algorithm involves the *barycentric coor-*

---

1. This can be relaxed for rendering triangle meshes with smooth shading (see Chapter 23).

```
class Triangle: public GeometricObject {
    public:

            Point3D     v0, v1, v2;             // vertices
            Normal      normal;

    public:

            Triangle (void);

            Triangle (const Point3D& a, const Point3D& b, const Point3D& c);

            virtual bool
            hit(const Ray& ray, double& tmin, ShadeRec& sr) const;
            ...
};

Triangle::Triangle (void)                       // default constructor
    : GeometricObject(),
      v0(0, 0, 0), v1(0, 0, 1), v2(1, 0, 0),
      normal(0, 1, 0)
{}

Triangle::Triangle (const Point3D& a, const Point3D& b, const Point3D& c)
    : GeometricObject(),
      v0(a), v1(b), v2(c) {
      normal = (v1 - v0) ^ (v2 - v0);           // compute normal
      normal.normalize();
}
```

Listing 19.5. Partial Triangle class declaration and constructor code.

dinates (α, β, γ) for the triangle with vertices (a, b, c), where an arbitrary point p on the plane can be written as

$$p(\alpha, \beta, \gamma) = \alpha a + \beta b + \gamma c, \tag{19.2}$$

with the constraint

$$\alpha + \beta + \gamma = 1. \tag{19.3}$$

Although the coordinates (α, β, γ) are specific to the triangle, they are defined at all points on the plane. For points inside the triangle, they satisfy the inequalities

$$0 < \alpha < 1,$$
$$0 < \beta < 1,$$ (19.4)
$$0 < \gamma < 1$$

(see Figure 19.6). We can use these inequalities to test if the hit point is in the triangle. Although three barycentric coordinates are defined by the triangle, the constraint (19.3) means that only two are independent. This makes sense because we only need two coordinates to specify points on a plane (or any other surface). Equation (19.3) allows us to eliminate one of the coordinates, for example α, by substituting $\alpha = 1 - \beta - \gamma$ into Equation (19.2) to give

$$p(\alpha, \beta, \gamma) = a + \beta(b - a) + \gamma(c - a).$$ (19.5)

In terms of β and γ, the inequalities (19.4) become

$$0 < \beta < 1,$$
$$0 < \gamma < 1,$$ (19.6)
$$0 < \beta + \gamma < 1.$$

When $\beta = 0$ in Equation (19.5), we have

$$p = a + \gamma(c - a),$$ (19.7)

which defines the (infinite) straight line through a and c. This is the γ-axis in Figure 19.6. When the inequality $0 < \gamma < 1$ is taken into account, Equation (19.7) defines the edge $c - a$ of the triangle.

In a similar manner, $\gamma = 0$ and the inequality $0 < \beta < 1$ define the edge $b - a$. Finally, when we substitute $\beta + \gamma = 1$, that is, $\beta = 1 - \gamma$, into Equation (19.5), we get

$$p = b + \gamma(c - b).$$

For $0 < \gamma < 1$, this is the third edge of the triangle $c - b$. Here, β and γ define a *non-orthogonal* coordinate system where the β- and γ-axes are not perpendicular. Non-orthogonal coordinate systems can be complicated to work with, but since the barycentric coordinates are tailor-made for each triangle, they actually simplify the ray-intersection calculations.

To find where the ray hits the plane, we use the ray equation $p = o + t\,d$ for the left-hand side of Equation (19.5):

$$o + t\,d = a + \beta(b - a) + \gamma(c - a).$$ (19.8)

This ray-intersection equation is different from the equations we have to solve for the other objects because there are three unknowns: t, β, and γ, instead of

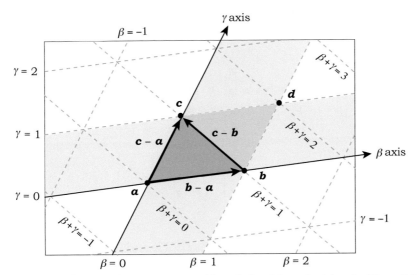

Figure 19.6. The (β, γ) coordinate system and its relationship to the triangle. The solid lines are the (β, γ) coordinate axes, with the origin at a.

just t. Fortunately, Equation (19.8) is linear in the unknowns, and because it's a vector equation, it's equivalent to three scalar equations. We first rearrange the terms so that the unknowns are on the left-hand side:

$$\beta(a - b) + \gamma(a - c) + t\, d = a - o,$$

and then we write out each component:

$$\begin{aligned}
\beta(a_x - b_x) + \gamma(a_x - c_x) + t\, d_x &= a_x - o_x, \\
\beta(a_y - b_y) + \gamma(a_y - c_y) + t\, d_y &= a_y - o_y, \\
\beta(a_z - b_z) + \gamma(a_z - c_z) + t\, d_z &= a_z - o_z.
\end{aligned} \tag{19.9}$$

Equations (19.9) can be rewritten in matrix form as

$$\begin{bmatrix} a & b & c \\ e & f & g \\ i & j & k \end{bmatrix} \begin{bmatrix} \beta \\ \gamma \\ t \end{bmatrix} = \begin{bmatrix} d \\ h \\ l \end{bmatrix}, \tag{19.10}$$

where, to simplify the notation, I've introduced new variables defined as

$$\begin{aligned}
a &= a_x - b_x, & b &= a_x - c_x, & c &= d_x, & d &= a_x - o_x, \\
e &= a_y - b_y, & f &= a_y - c_y, & g &= d_y, & h &= a_y - o_y, \\
i &= a_z - b_z, & j &= a_z - c_z, & k &= d_z, & l &= a_z - o_z.
\end{aligned}$$

We can solve Equations (19.10) with *Cramer's rule*, which expresses the solution in terms of *determinants* (see the Further Reading section). The solution is

$$\beta = \begin{vmatrix} d & b & c \\ h & f & g \\ l & j & k \end{vmatrix} D^{-1}, \ \gamma = \begin{vmatrix} a & d & c \\ e & h & g \\ i & l & k \end{vmatrix} D^{-1}, \ t = \begin{vmatrix} a & b & d \\ e & f & h \\ i & j & l \end{vmatrix} D^{-1}, \qquad (19.11)$$

where

$$D = \begin{vmatrix} a & b & c \\ e & f & g \\ i & j & k \end{vmatrix}. \qquad (19.12)$$

Expanding the determinants in Equations (19.11) and (19.12) allows us to write the expressions for β, γ, and t as

$$\beta = \frac{d(fk - gj) + b(gl - hk) + c(hj - fl)}{a(fk - gj) + b(gi - ek) + c(ej - fi)},$$

$$\gamma = \frac{a(hk - gl) + d(gi - ek) + c(el - hi)}{a(fk - gj) + b(gi - ek) + c(ej - fi)}, \qquad (19.13)$$

$$t = \frac{a(fl - hj) + b(hi - el) + d(ej - fi)}{a(fk - gj) + b(gi - ek) + c(ej - fi)}.$$

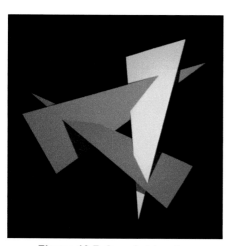

Figure 19.7. Sample triangles.

The above calculations probably seem like a lot of mathematics to go through, and indeed they are, but the end result in Equations (19.13) is simple and easy to convert to code. Listing 19.6 shows the function `Triangle::hit`, which includes early-outs based on the inequalities (19.6). The first early-out rejects points outside the gray strip $\beta \in [0,1]$ in Figure 19.6. The second rejects points outside the grey strip $\gamma \in [0,1]$ and therefore only leaves points in the parallelogram *a*, *b*, *c*, *d*. The third only leaves points in the triangle itself. See Exercise 19.6 for an equivalent set of inequalities.

Figure 19.7 shows three triangles rendered with a matte material and shadows. As this figure demonstrates, ray tracing has no difficulty rendering objects that spatially overlap and interpenetrate.

```
bool
Triangle::hit(const Ray& ray, double& tmin, ShadeRec& sr) const {

    double a = v0.x - v1.x, b = v0.x - v2.x, c = ray.d.x, d = v0.x - ray.o.x;
    double e = v0.y - v1.y, f = v0.y - v2.y, g = ray.d.y, h = v0.y - ray.o.y;
    double i = v0.z - v1.z, j = v0.z - v2.z, k = ray.d.z, l = v0.z - ray.o.z;

    double m = f * k - g * j, n = h * k - g * l, p = f * l - h * j;
    double q = g * i - e * k, s = e * j - f * i;

    double inv_denom  = 1.0 / (a * m + b * q + c * s);

    double e1 = d * m - b * n - c * p;
    double beta = e1 * inv_denom;

    if (beta < 0.0)
        return (false);

    double r = r = e * l - h * i;
    double e2 = a * n + d * q + c * r;
    double gamma = e2 * inv_denom;

    if (gamma < 0.0 )
        return (false);

    if (beta + gamma > 1.0)
        return (false);

    double e3 = a * p - b * r + d * s;
    double t = e3 * inv_denom;

    if (t < kEpsilon)
        return (false);

    tmin = t;
    sr.normal = normal;
    sr.local_hit_point = ray.o + t * ray.d;

    return (true);
}
```

Listing 19.6. Ray-triangle hit function.

19.4 Other Objects

I'll discuss here two more planar objects that are useful for modeling. You can use these individually or combine them with other objects to create more complex objects. They can also be used as area lights.

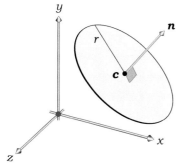

Figure 19.8. Circular disk definition.

19.4.1 Disks

After a plane, a circular disk is the next simplest object to intersect. Figure 19.8 shows an arbitrary disk defined by its center c, radius r, and normal n. Because the center and normal define a plane, the disk's hit function starts with the plane hit-function code from Chapter 3 and then checks if the hit point is within distance r of the center. Listing 19.7 shows the code. Notice that we can avoid computing a square root by using the square of the distance of the hit point from the center.

```
bool
Disk::hit(const Ray& ray, double& tmin, ShadeRec& sr) const {

    float t = (center - ray.o) * normal / (ray.d * normal);

    if (t <= kEpsilon)
        return (false);

    Point3D p = ray.o + t * ray.d;

    if (center.d_squared(p) < r_squared) {
        tmin = t;
        sr.normal = normal;
        sr.local_hit_point = p;
        return (true);
    }
    else
        return (false);
}
```

Listing 19.7. The function `Disk::hit`.

19.4.2 Rectangles

Rectangles have many uses in modeling, for example: open boxes, buildings, parts of beveled boxes in Chapter 21, and as an alternative for a ground plane. Axis-aligned boxes can also be modeled with six rectangles, a technique that's necessary if we want to apply different materials or textures to each face.

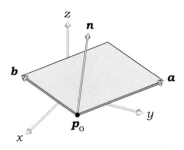

Figure 19.9. A rectangle can be defined by a corner and two perpendicular edges.

The problem with modeling a rectangle is to devise a good user interface, a process that's not as simple as it may seem. The task is to define an arbitrary rectangle without making the user have to think too much when it's constructed. This involves using a sensible definition for the rectangle and its constructors. The definition I'll use is based on a corner p_0 and two adjacent edges defined by vectors a and b (see Figure 19.9).

If a and b define a rectangle, they must be perpendicular. The normal can then be defined as

$$n = a \times b / \|a \times b\|, \qquad (19.14)$$

so that (a, b, n) form a right-handed system. There is, however, a problem with this definition. For an arbitrarily oriented rectangle, how do we specify a and b so that they are perpendicular? As this is not simple to do directly, a better approach is to use a *generic rectangle* (see Section 19.5) and apply affine transformations to it.

It's a lot easier to specify edges that are perpendicular when the rectangle is axis-aligned. In this case, its surface is parallel to one of the coordinate planes, and its edges are parallel to the coordinate axes. Fortunately, these orientations are the most useful for modeling purposes, and we can use a constructor that takes p_0, a, and b as arguments and computes the normal with Equation (19.14). For example, the rectangle with $p_0 = (0, 0, 0)$, $a = (2, 0, 0)$, $b = (0, 0, 3)$ is in the (x, z) plane.

There is, however, still a minor problem with this approach. Suppose, for example, that you want to construct a cube from six squares. For each face, you can use any of the four vertices for p_0, and you will have to make sure that the normal for each face points outwards. My experience is that this requires too much thinking to get the order and directions of a and b correct for the cross product in Equation (19.14). I'll therefore use a constructor that has the normal as an additional parameter. Using this, we only have to make sure the edges are adjacent and of the correct length. Their order and directions don't matter because the normal isn't computed.[2]

---

2. To be on the safe side, the rectangle constructor should still normalize the normal.

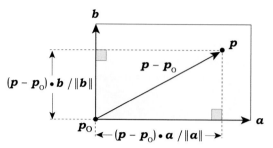

Figure 19.10. The point *p* is in the rectangle when its projections in the *a* and *b* directions cut the edges *a* and *b*.

To test the rectangle for intersection, we first compute the point *p* where the ray hits the rectangle's plane and then subtract p_0 to get the vector $p - p_0$ shown in Figure 19.10. Finally, we project $p - p_0$ onto the two directions *a*

```
bool
Rectangle::hit(const Ray& ray, double& tmin, ShadeRec& sr) const {

        float t = (p0 - ray.o) * normal / (ray.d * normal);

        if (t <= kEpsilon)
                    return (false);

        Point3D p = ray.o + t * ray.d;
        Vector3D d = p - p0;

        float ddota = d * a;

        if (ddota < 0.0 || ddota > a_len_squared)
                    return (false);

        float ddotb = d * b;

        if (ddotb < 0.0 || ddotb > b_len_squared)
                    return (false);

        tmin = t;
        sr.normal = normal;
        sr.local_hit_point = p;

        return (true);
}
```

Listing 19.8. The function `Rectangle::hit`.

and b. Essentially, this process expresses p in the local 2D orthonormal frame defined by p_0, a, and b. The hit point is on the rectangle when the following inequalities are satisfied:

$$0 \le (p - p_0) \bullet a \le \|a\|^2 ,$$
$$0 \le (p - p_0) \bullet b \le \|b\|^2 . \qquad (19.15)$$

See Exercise 19.9.

The rectangle hit function appears in Listing 19.8, where `a_lenSquared` and `b_lenSquared` are data members computed in the constructors. They save up to two multiplications.

 ## 19.5 Generic Objects

19.5.1 Motivation

We can only ray trace objects for which we can do the following two things: derive the ray-intersection equation, and solve it. Arbitrary planes, spheres, triangles, disks, and rectangles present no problems in this regard because we can perform these two tasks regardless of their location, orientation, size, and shape. For a lot of other object types, however, one or both of these tasks is difficult. In the following three examples, deriving the ray-intersection equation is the difficult operation. Consider first the *quadric surfaces*, which are represented by general implicit equations of degree two:

$$ax^2 + by^2 + cz^2 + 2dxy + 2eyz + 2fxz + 2gx + 2hy + 2jz + k = 0. \qquad (19.16)$$

The principal types are ellipsoids, paraboloids, hyperbolic paraboloids, hyperboloids, cones, and cylinders.[3] These can all be ray traced by solving a quadratic equation for the ray parameter, but suppose we want to ray trace an ellipsoid with a specified size, shape, center, and orientation. The difficult part will be to derive the coefficients a–k in Equation (19.16). In this case, it's the arbitrary orientation that creates the difficulty.

The second example is a rectangular box that's been rotated so that it's not axis-aligned. This is an example of a convex polyhedron and can be represented by a series of intersecting planes. Essentially, this is a generalization of the slabs representation of the axis-aligned box. The `Box::hit` algorithm can also be generalized to handle convex polyhedra. The difficult part here is computing the vertices.

---

3. Spheres are a special case of ellipsoids.

The third example is a torus, which is defined by a fourth-degree polynomial that we can only derive easily when the torus is axis-aligned.

Fortunately, there's an elegant procedure that allows us to ray trace the above objects and many other difficult objects. We first define a series of *generic objects* centered on the origin of the world coordinates and axis-aligned. We then apply a sequence of *affine transformations* to these objects to ray trace them in other locations and with arbitrary orientations. This is standard practice in ray tracing, and I'll explain how to do it in detail in Chapter 21. By using this technique, you will only ever have to intersect generic objects. This technique is also essential for ray tracing transformed part objects and compound objects.

19.5.2 Generic Spheres, Disks, and Rectangles

Generic spheres, disks, and rectangles have the following parameter values:

- generic sphere: center = (0, 0, 0), radius = 1.
- generic disk: center = (0, 0, 0), radius = 1, normal = (0, 1, 0).
- generic rectangle: p_0 = (−1, 0, −1), a = (0, 0, 1), b = (1, 0, 0), normal = (0, 1, 0).

In general, I'll only transform the generic versions of these objects, but that's not a hard-and-fast rule. For example, if these objects are parts of a transformed compound object, they may have already been transformed, or be non-generic versions, as required by the compound object's definition.

A rule that is hard-and-fast is as follows. I'll only apply 2D texture mapping to generic objects, to keep the texture-mapping architecture in Chapter 29 as simple as possible.

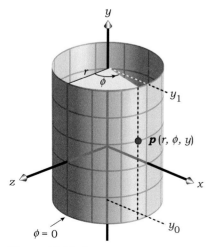

Figure 19.11. Open-cylinder definition.

19.5.3 Generic Open Cylinder

A generic open cylinder is a circular cylinder as defined in Section 2.9.2 and illustrated in Figure 2.12. For convenience, this figure is reproduced in Figure 19.11. Here, the central axis is always the y_w-axis, but the cylinder can have arbitrary values for y_0, y_1, and the radius.

To ray trace an open cylinder we have to intersect a ray with its vertical curved surface, and to do this, we need its equation in implicit form. Fortunately, this is simple to derive. We only have to take the two equations

$$x = r \sin \phi,$$
$$z = r \cos \phi,$$

from Equation (2.2), square both sides, and add them to get

$$x^2 + z^2 - r^2 = 0. \tag{19.17}$$

Note that this doesn't involve y. This is the equation for the infinite cylinder with $y \in (-\infty, \infty)$. The finite cylinder in Figure 19.11 is for $y \in [y_0, y_1]$. Substituting the ray equation into Equation (19.17) gives the quadratic

$$a\,t^2 + b\,t + c = 0,$$

where

$$a = d_x^2 + d_z^2,$$
$$b = 2(o_x d_x + o_z d_z),$$
$$c = o_x o_x + o_z o_z - r^2.$$

The outward-facing unit normal at a hit point p is

$$n = (p_x/r, 0, p_z/r).$$

Because the code for the cylinder hit function is similar to that of the sphere hit function in Listing 3.6, I'll leave its implementation as an exercise. However, see Listing 19.9.

19.5.4 Generic Torus

A torus is a doughnut-shaped object, as illustrated in Figure 19.12.

We can construct a torus as follows. Consider a circle of radius b in the (y, z) plane with center at $z = a$, as shown in Figure 19.13(a). This figure also shows an arbitrary point on the circle at distance z from the y-axis. The equation of the circle is

Figure 19.12. A torus.

$$(z - a)^2 + y^2 - b^2 = 0. \tag{19.18}$$

We generate the torus by rotating this circle through 360° around the y-axis. Figure 19.13(b) is a top-down view of the circle at some stage during the rotation. If we can write down the equation for the rotated circle in terms of x, y, and z, we have the implicit equation of the torus. The key observation is as follows. The red point on the circle in Figure 19.13(a) at distance z along the z-axis maintains the same distance from the y axis as the circle rotates, where it becomes $(x^2 + z^2)^{1/2}$. The equation of the torus is therefore obtained by replacing z in Equation (19.18) with $(x^2 + z^2)^{1/2}$:

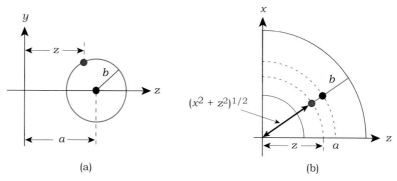

Figure 19.13. Circle used to construct a torus: (a) initial location in the (y, z) plane; (b) rotated location for generating the torus.

$$[(x^2 + z^2)^{1/2} - a]^2 + y^2 - b^2 = 0. \tag{19.19}$$

Squaring Equation (19.19) to get rid of the square root gives

$$f(x, y, z) = (x^2 + y^2 + z^2)^2 - 2(a^2 + b^2)(x^2 + y^2 + z^2) + 4a^2y^2 + (a^2 - b^2)^2 = 0. \tag{19.20}$$

This is the implicit equation of a generic torus whose central axis is the y-axis and that is bisected by the (x, z) plane. Note that this is a *fourth-degree* polynomial in x, y, and z, which is also known as a quartic equation. The two parameters a and b define the shape of the torus; a is called the *swept radius*, and b is called the *tube radius*.[4] These control the size and shape of the torus. Figure 19.14 shows cross sections of tori with different relative values of a and b.

By substituting the ray equation into Equation (19.20), we can derive the equation to solve for the ray parameter t. Unfortunately, there's a fair bit

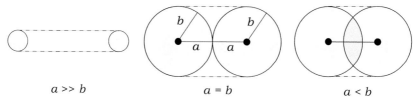

$$a \gg b \qquad\qquad a = b \qquad\qquad a < b$$

Figure 19.14. Tori with different values of a and b. Note that there is no hole in the torus when $a \le b$.

4. The parameter a is also called the *outer radius*, and b is called the *inner radius*.

of algebra involved, but the result is the following fourth-degree polynomial in t:

$$c_4 t^4 + c_3 t^3 + c_2 t^2 + c_1 t + c_0 = 0, \tag{19.21}$$

where the coefficients are

$$c_4 = \left(d_x^2 + d_y^2 + d_z^2\right)^2,$$

$$c_3 = 4\left(d_x^2 + d_y^2 + d_z^2\right)\left(o_x d_x + o_y d_y + o_z d_z\right),$$

$$c_2 = 2\left(d_x^2 + d_y^2 + d_z^2\right)\left[o_x^2 + o_y^2 + o_z^2 - \left(a^2 + b^2\right)\right] + 4\left(o_x d_x + o_y d_y + o_z d_z\right)^2 + 4a^2 d_y^2, \tag{19.22}$$

$$c_1 = 4\left[o_x^2 + o_y^2 + o_z^2 - \left(a^2 + b^2\right)\right]\left(o_x d_x + o_y d_y + o_z d_z\right) + 8a^2 o_y d_y,$$

$$c_0 = 4\left[o_x^2 + o_y^2 + o_z^2 - \left(a^2 + b^2\right)\right]^2 - 4a^2\left(b^2 - o_y^2\right).$$

Since Equation (19.21) is a quartic in t, it can be written in the form

$$(t - t_1)\,(t - t_2)\,(t - t_3)\,(t - t_4) = 0,$$

where t_1–t_4 are the four roots. The fact that there can be from one to four real roots reflects the fact that a ray can hit a torus up to four times. Figure 19.15 illustrates this for four rays in the (x, z) plane. Rays with one or three hits are analogous to rays hitting a sphere once—they involve a tangential intersection with the torus to machine precision. This will rarely happen in practice.

Because we have to solve a quartic to ray trace a torus, these are more difficult to intersect than spheres and planes, but fortunately, help is at hand. Not only can quartics be solved in closed form, but there's public-domain

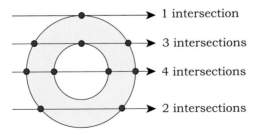

1 intersection

3 intersections

4 intersections

2 intersections

Figure 19.15. Some of the ways that a ray can hit a torus.

```
bool
Torus::hit(const Ray& ray, double& tmin, ShadeRec& sr) const {
        if (!bbox.hit(ray))
                return (false);

        double x1 = ray.o.x; double y1 = ray.o.y; double z1 = ray.o.z;
        double d1 = ray.d.x; double d2 = ray.d.y; double d3 = ray.d.z;

        double coeffs[5];              // coefficient array
        double roots[4];               // solution array

        // define the coefficients

        double sum_d_sqrd = d1 * d1 + d2 * d2 + d3 * d3;
        double e = x1 * x1 + y1 * y1 + z1 * z1 - a * a - b * b;
        double f = x1 * d1 + y1 * d2 + z1 * d3;
        double four_a_sqrd = 4.0 * a * a;

        coeffs[0] = e * e - four_a_sqrd * (b * b - y1 * y1);    // constant term
        coeffs[1] = 4.0 * f * e + 2.0 * four_a_sqrd * y1 * d2;
        coeffs[2] = 2.0 * sum_d_sqrd * e + 4.0 * f * f + four_a_sqrd * d2 * d2;
        coeffs[3] = 4.0 * sum_d_sqrd * f;
        coeffs[4] = sum_d_sqrd * sum_d_sqrd;                     // coefficient of t^4

        // find the roots

        int num_real_roots = SolveQuartic(coeffs, roots);

        bool intersected = false;
        double t = kHugeValue;

        if (num_real_roots == 0)  // ray misses the torus
                return (false);

        // find the smallest root greater than kEpsilon, if any

        for (int j = 0; j < num_real_roots; j++)
                if (roots[j] > kEpsilon) {
                        intersected = true;
                        if (roots[j] < t)
                                t = roots[j];
                }
```

Listing 19.9. The function Torus::hit.

```
        if (!intersected)
                return (false);

        tmin = t;
        sr.local_hit_point = ray.o + t * ray.d;
        sr.normal = computeNormal(sr.local_hit_point);

        return (true);
}
```

Listing 19.9 (continued). The function `Torus::hit`.

C code available for solving them. Schwarze (1990) discusses the solutions of cubic and quartic equations. His code is on the book's website. Herbison-Evans (1995) also discusses the solution of quartic equations.

Listing 19.9 shows the function `Torus::hit`, the first half of which computes the coefficients (19.22) and stores them in a C array. Note that the first coefficient in the array is the constant term c_0, and the last is the coefficient c_4 of t^4. All of the calculations are performed in Schwarze's function `SolveQuartic`, which returns the number of real roots and the roots themselves in the `roots` array. Because the roots in this array are not ordered by increasing t, the following code has to search the array to find the smallest t value.

The normal to the torus is given by the gradient of the function $f(x, y, z)$ in Equation (19.20), evaluated at the hit point:

$$n = \nabla f(x, y, z) = \left(\frac{\partial f}{\partial x}, \frac{\partial f}{\partial y}, \frac{\partial f}{\partial z} \right).$$

See, for example, Thomas and Finney (1996). Performing the partial differentiations gives

$$n_x = 4x \, [x^2 + y^2 + z^2 - (a^2 + b^2)],$$
$$n_y = 4y \, [x^2 + y^2 + z^2 - (a^2 + b^2) + 2a^2],$$
$$n_z = 4z \, [x^2 + y^2 + z^2 - (a^2 + b^2)].$$

As n is not a unit normal, it must be normalized. Figure 19.16 shows three ray-traced tori with the same viewing parameters and $a = 2.0$ but with different values of b.

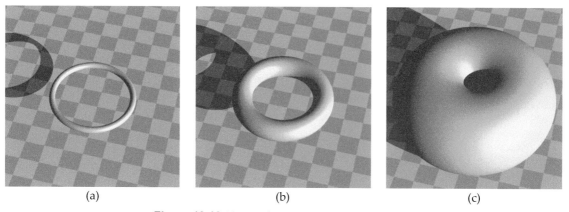

(a)   (b)   (c)

Figure 19.16. Tori with $a = 2.0$ and (a) $b = 0.15$, (b) $b = 0.75$, (c) $b = 2.0$.

19.5.5 Generic Objects and Default Objects

Chapters 29 and 30 cover the texturing of generic objects such as spheres, disks, rectangles, cylinders, tori, and cones (see Exercise 19.12). Generic cylinders, tori, and cones have the following parameter values:

- cylinder: $y_0 = -1$, $y_1 = 1$, radius = 1;
- torus: $a = 2$, $b = 1$;
- cone: height = 2, radius 1.

These are also the *default objects* for each of these object types. For example, if a build function contained the statement `Torus* torus_ptr = new Torus;`, the torus object would have $a = 2$ and $b = 1$. The generic spheres, disks, and rectangles discussed in Section 19.5.2 are also the default objects.

For some of these objects, it may be worthwhile to implement a separate generic version called, for example, `GenericSphere`. The reason is efficiency—a generic sphere, which is a unit sphere at the origin, doesn't need to store the center and radius. The hit function would therefore be simpler than the general version in Listing 3.6, and the rendering of transformed spheres would thus be more efficient (see Exercise 19.19).

 ## 19.6 Shading Issues

It's not possible to discuss intersection completely divorced from shading because these two processes are related. Rays can hit object surfaces on the outside, which is the same side as the normal points, or on the inside, and the shading must always be correct. The shading processes described in Section 14.6.2 rely on the normal being reversed when the ray hits the inside surface. Reversing the normal is the responsibility of the hit functions.

However, if we always reverse the normal in the hit functions, a problem arises with transparent objects, where rays can also hit the inside surfaces. As you'll see in Chapter 27, the transparent-material code reverses the normal in this case, but if the hit function also reverses it, these would cancel, and the transparency code would not work. The solution I have adopted is to use three versions of certain open objects, part objects, and planar objects, as follows:

1. an object whose hit function reverses the normal when a ray hits the inside surface;
2. an object where the normal always points outwards;
3. an object where the normal always points inwards.

For the cylinder, the classes are named as follows: the first version is `OpenCylinder`, the second version is `ConvexCylinder`, and the third version is `ConcaveCylinder`.

 ## 19.7 Part Objects

19.7.1 Theory

All of the finite primitives that I discuss have both implicit and parametric representations. In Chapter 2, I presented the parametric equations of circular cylinders and spheres, but the equations for tori, cones, and other shapes can also be written in parametric form. A *part object* is a parametrically defined primitive where the angles are restricted to subsets of their full ranges. Part objects are valuable modeling tools, as you will see in the following chapters. They are particularly useful for modeling complex transparent objects that are free of interior surfaces. I'll discuss here how to define and render part cylinders, spheres, and tori. There are four steps:

1. specify the desired ranges of the angles in the parametric representation;
2. find the hit point on the complete object;
3. compute the angles at the hit point;
4. only record a hit if the angles are in the specified ranges.

There are some variations in these steps, as cylinders have a single angular parameter, and for spheres we can get by with only calculating one of the angles. Because part objects are open surfaces like the open cylinder, their inside surfaces can be visible. I've therefore defined three versions of part

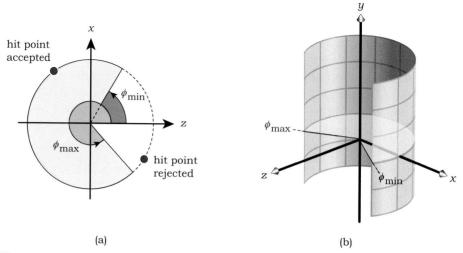

(a)   (b)

Figure 19.17. (a) The azimuth angle is specified between minimum and maximum values; (b) 3D view of a part cylinder.

cylinders, spheres, and tori, as discussed in Section 19.6. The code for the classes `PartCylinder` and `PartSphere` is on the book's website.

19.7.2 Part Cylinders

Part cylinders have arbitrary values for y_0, y_1, and the radius. The angular parameter for a circular cylinder is the azimuth angle ϕ (see Section 2.9.2). To define a part cylinder, we only have to specify the angular range of $\phi \in [\phi_{min}, \phi_{max}]$, where $(\phi_{min}, \phi_{max}) \in [0, 2\pi]$, as illustrated in Figure 19.17(a). 19.17(b) shows a part cylinder in 3D. We only accept hit points when ϕ satisfies $\phi \in [\phi_{min}, \phi_{max}]$.

To compute ϕ at the hit point, we use Equation (2.10) and the code in Listing 2.1.

19.7.3 Part Spheres

Part spheres are centered on the world origin but have arbitrary radii. The polar and azimuth angles in the parametric representation of a sphere belong to the intervals $\theta \in [0, \pi]$ and $\phi \in [0, 2\pi]$ (see Sections 2.5.2 and 2.5.3). To render a part sphere, we need to specify the range for both angles. Fortunately,

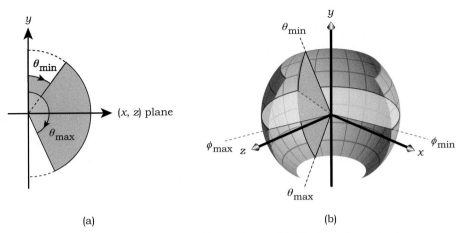

Figure 19.18. (a) Definitions of $\theta_{\min}$ and $\theta_{\max}$; (b) 3D view of a part sphere.

the azimuth angle ϕ is the same as for the cylinder. Figure 19.18(a) illustrates how the minimum and maximum values of θ are defined. Note that because θ is measured from the positive y-axis, a part sphere has $\theta_{\min}$ at the top and $\theta_{\max}$ at the bottom. An example is the lower hemisphere defined by $\theta \in [\pi/2, \pi]$ and $\phi \in [0, 2\pi]$. You can use this to model hemispherical bowls (see Exercise 19.25). Figure 19.18(b) shows a 3D view of a part sphere.

Because $\theta \in [0, \pi]$, we don't need to compute the polar angle itself; instead, we only have to check that the y-coordinate of the hit point satisfies $y \in [r \cos \theta_{\min}, r \cos \theta_{\max}]$. I'll use part spheres to define a fishbowl object in Chapter 28. Listing 19.10 shows the hit function for the `PartSphere` class. This reverses the normal when a ray hits the inside surface of the sphere so that both sides of the surface will be shaded correctly. The part sphere in Figure 19.18(b) was rendered with this code.

19.7.4 Part Tori

The parametric equations for a generic torus are defined with the azimuth and polar angles as shown in Figure 19.19. In Figure 19.19(a), the azimuth angle $\phi \in [0, 2\pi]$ is again the same as it is for cylinders and spheres, but the polar angle in Figure 19.19(b) is defined differently. Here, it's measured counterclockwise from the (x, z) plane and lies in the interval $\theta \in [0, 2\pi]$. We can therefore compute it using the same technique that we use for ϕ.

Figure 19.20 shows a part torus where $\phi \in [\pi/2, 2\pi]$ and $\theta \in [\pi/2, 2\pi]$.

```
bool
ConvexPartSphere::hit(const Ray& ray, double& tmin, ShadeRec& sr) const {
    double t;
    Vector3D  temp    = ray.o - center;
    double a = ray.d * ray.d;
    double b = 2.0 * temp * ray.d;
    double c = temp * temp - r * r;
    double disc = b * b - 4.0 * a * c;

    if (disc < 0.0)
        return(false);
    else {
        double e = sqrt(disc);
        double denom = 2.0 * a;
        t = (-b - e) / denom;               // smaller root

        if (t > kEpsilon) {
            Vector3D hit = ray.o + t * ray.d - center;

            float phi = atan2(hit.x, hit.z);
            if (phi < 0.0)
                phi += TWO_PI;

            if (hit.y <= r * cos_theta_min  && hit.y >= r * cos_theta_max
                    && phi >= phi_min && phi <= phi_max) {
                tmin = t;
                sr.normal = (temp + t * ray.d) / r; // points outwards

                if (-ray.d * sr.normal < 0.0)      // reverse normal
                                                   // when ray hits inside
                        sr.normal = -sr.normal;
                sr.local_hit_point = ray.o + tmin * ray.d;
                return (true);
            }
        }

        t = (-b + e) / denom;               // larger root

        if (t > kEpsilon) {
            Vector3D hit = ray.o + t * ray.d - center;

            float phi = atan2(hit.x, hit.z);
            if (phi < 0.0)
                phi += TWO_PI;

            if (hit.y <= r * cos_theta_min  && hit.y >= r * cos_theta_max
                        && phi >= phi_min && phi <= phi_max) {
                tmin = t;
                sr.normal = (temp + t * ray.d) / r;    // points outwards
```

Listing 19.10. The function PartSphere::hit.

```
                    if (-ray.d * sr.normal < 0.0)      // reverse normal
                                                        // when ray hits inside
                        sr.normal = -sr.normal;

                    sr.local_hit_point = ray.o + tmin * ray.d;
                    return (true);
                }
            }
        }

        return (false);
}
```

Listing 19.10 (continued). The function `PartSphere::hit`.

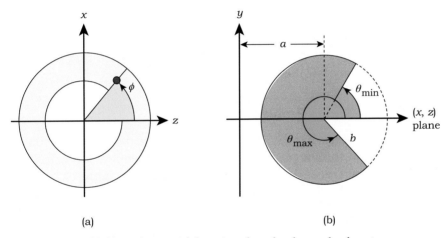

(a)   (b)

Figure 19.19. Definition of the azimuth and polar angles for a torus.

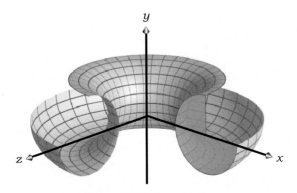

Figure 19.20. A part torus.

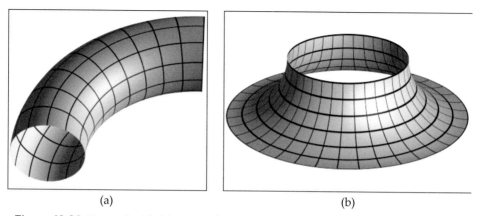

(a)   (b)

Figure 19.21. Part tori with (a) $\phi \in [3\pi/2, 2\pi]$, $\theta \in [0, 2\pi]$; (b) $\phi \in [0, 2\pi]$, $\theta \in [3\pi/2, 2\pi]$.

Part tori are versatile modeling tools, as Figure 19.21 and the exercises demonstrate. Figures 19.20–19.22 were rendered with code that reverses the normal when the ray hits the inside surface.

19.7.5 Angular-Range Problem

Each of the part objects has the zero value of its angle parameters defined at a specific point or in specific planes. A fact of life is that you can't construct a *single* part object that *crosses* the zero values. According to Figure 19.19, the part torus has $\phi = 0$ in the (y, z) plane and $\theta = 0$ in the (x, z) plane. Figure 19.22(a)

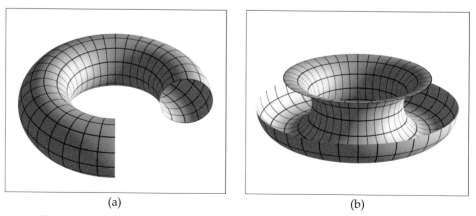

(a)   (b)

Figure 19.22. (a) Part torus that crosses $\phi = 0$, (b) part torus that crosses $\theta = 0$.

shows a part torus defined with $\phi \in [\pi/2, 5\pi/4]$. That's a 2π range, but the section $\phi \in (0, \pi/2)$ is missing. Similarly, the part torus in Figure 19.22(b) is defined with $\theta \in [\pi/2, 5\pi/4]$, and the section $\theta \in (0, \pi/2)$ is missing. If you think the θ range of this looks the same as the torus in Figure 19.20, you're right, except that Figure 19.20 was rendered with $\theta \in [\pi/2, 2\pi]$.

You will need a part torus shape that crosses $\theta = 0$ for the meniscus in the spherical fish bowl that I'll discuss in Chapter 28, and so you will need a solution (see Exercise 19.27). These issues are also relevant to Exercise 21.12, but you can use a completely different solution there.

 ## 19.8 Compound Objects

19.8.1 Benefits

Compound objects are geometric objects that store an array of other geometric objects. I've called the class that implements these Compound. These provide a number of benefits:

- They allow us to treat a collection of objects as a single object, so that we can apply the same set of transformations to them or assign the same material to them.
- They allow us to build objects that consist of more than one part and have a named type in the ray tracer.
- They simplify the implementation of acceleration schemes. For example, the Grid class in Chapter 22 inherits from Compound.
- Most importantly, they allow us to intersect complex objects without having to write any complex hit functions; in fact, objects that inherit from Compound often don't need a hit function of their own.

19.8.2 Implementation

A design principle for compound objects is that they must be able to store geometric objects of any type, including other compound objects. This allows them to be nested. I store the objects in a vector called objects, the same as in the World class. Listing 19.11 shows a partial Compound class declaration.

The internal structure of the compound hit function in Listing 19.12 is similar to the World::hit_objects function in Listing 14.8 because it also has to find the nearest hit point, if any, of the ray with the stored objects. One difference is that the material from the nearest object hit is stored in the GeometricObject base class data member material_ptr. This is neces-

```
class Compound: public GeometricObject {
    public:
        ...
        virtual void
        set_material(const Material* material_ptr);

        void
        add_object(const GeometricObject* object_ptr);

        virtual bool
        hit(const Ray& ray, double& tmin, ShadeRec& sr) const;

        virtual bool
        shadow_hit(const Ray& ray, double& tmin) const;

    protected:

        vector<GeometricObject*> objects;
};
```

Listing 19.11. Declaration of the class Compound.

```
bool
Compound::hit(const Ray& ray, double& tmin, ShadeRec& sr) const {
    float t;
    Normal normal;
    Point3D local_hit_point;
    bool hit = false;
        tmin = kHugeValue;
    int num_objects = objects.size();

    for (int j = 0; j < num_objects; j++)
        if (objects[j]->hit(ray, t, sr) && (t < tmin)) {
            hit = true;
            tmin = t;
            material_ptr = objects[j]->get_material();
            normal = sr.normal;
            local_hit_point = sr.local_hit_point;
        }

    if (hit) {
        sr.t = tmin;
        sr.normal = normal;
        sr.local_hit_point = local_hit_point;
    }

    return (hit);
}
```

Listing 19.12. The function Compound::hit.

```
      void
      Compound::set_material(const Material* material_ptr) {
          int num_objects = objects.size();
          for (int j = 0; j < num_objects; j++)
              objects[j]->set_material(material_ptr);
      }
```

Listing 19.13. The function Compound::set_material.

sary because each object stored in a compound object can have a different material, and the World::hit_objects function needs to store the correct material in its local ShadeRec object. For example, if the ray hits the top annulus of the ring in Figure 19.29(b) and there are no other objects in the scene, World::hit_objects needs to store the yellow material in its ShadeRec object. Note that Compound::hit doesn't store the material in the ShadeRec parameter because the material is always extracted in World::hit_objects, or Compound::hit itself for nested compound objects.

I'll discuss the use of bounding boxes with compound objects in Section 19.8.3.

If you want all of the objects to share the same material, you can arrange this when the individual objects are constructed, or you can use Compound::set_material (see Listing 19.13). This function is the reason that the GeometricObject::set_material function is virtual.

19.8.3 Solid Cylinder

A simple compound object is a solid circular cylinder as shown in Figure 19.23(a). We could model the cylinder as a primitive, but the hit function would be complicated–the cylinder consists of three separate surfaces: the top, the bottom, and the curved side. The fact that rays can hit the curved side in two places, can start anywhere inside, outside, or on one of the surfaces, and can point into or out of the cylinder adds to the complexity.

Fortunately, a compound object that contains two disks and an open cylinder is a much better way to model the cylinder because it eliminates the hit

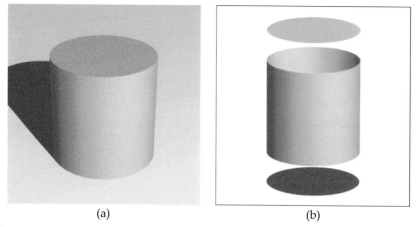

(a)   (b)

Figure 19.23. (a) Rendered solid cylinder, (b) components used in compound object.

function. Figure 19.23(b) shows an exploded view. Since we already have hit functions for these primitives, we just use the hit function in Listing 19.12.

Listing 19.14 shows the class declaration for SolidCylinder class, which inherits from Compound, and the code for one of the constructors. Note that there are no new data members, but see Exercise 19.26. Typically, all the work in implementing a compound object goes into the constructors. A notable exception, however, is the Grid class in Chapter 22.

The idea of constructing complex objects from primitives with simple hit functions is, of course, not new. In fact, it's almost as old as ray tracing itself. Ray tracing triangle meshes, for example, uses the same principle: the triangles are ray traced individually.

The exercises in this chapter cover a number of other compound objects, and in Chapter 21, with affine transformations at our disposal, I'll look at further examples.

For complex compound objects, it's worthwhile storing a bounding box and using it in the hit function. You should compute the bounding box in the constructor and then override the Compound::hit function. Listing 19.15 shows how you could override the hit function for a solid cylinder with a bounding-box test.

An alternate approach is to store a bounding box in the Compound class and test this in the Compound::hit function in Listing 19.12, but this would require every object that you stored in a compound object to be able to return a bounding box.

```
class SolidCylinder: public Compound {
    public:

        SolidCylinder (void);

        SolidCylinder(const float bottom, const float top, const float radius);

        SolidCylinder(const SolidCylinder& cc);
        ...
};

SolidCylinder::SolidCylinder(const float bottom,
            const float top,
            const float radius)
            : Compound() {

    objects.push_back(new Disk(Point3D(0, bottom, 0),              // bottom
                Normal(0, -1, 0),
                radius));

    objects.push_back(new Disk(Point3D(0, top, 0),                // top
                Normal(0, 1, 0),
                radius));

    objects.push_back(new OpenCylinder(bottom, top, radius));    // wall
}
```

Listing 19.14. Class declaration for SolidCylinder, along with a constructor.

```
bool
SolidCylinder::hit(const Ray& ray, double& tmin, ShadeRec& sr) const {
    if (bbox.hit(ray))
        return (Compound::hit(ray, tmin, sr));
    else
        return (false);
}
```

Listing 19.15. The Compound::hit function that tests the bounding box.

Further Reading

A number of ray-object intersection algorithms are described by Haines (1989) and Hanrahan (1989). These are chapters in Glassner (1989). Other books that discuss a variety of intersection algorithms are Hill and Kelley (2006), Akenine-

Möller and Haines (2002), Shirley and Morley (2003), Pharr and Humphreys (2004), and Shirley et al. (2005).

Smits (1998) originally recommended using the properties of IEEE floating-point arithmetic for ray-bounding box intersection. Hill (2001) and Akenine-Möller and Haines (2002) discuss the intersection of a ray with a convex polyhedron. The algorithm is a generalization of the axis-aligned box hit function in Listing 19.3.

The original algorithm for intersecting a ray and a triangle using barycentric coordinates is by Möller and Trumbore (1997). The origin of the code in Listing 19.6 is in Shirley and Morley (2003). Systems of linear equations, Cramer's rule, and determinants are a standard part of linear algebra. See, for example, Anton (2004).

The gradient operator used to compute the normal to a torus in Section 19.5.4 and to a cone in Equation (19.25) is discussed in most calculus textbooks, for example, Thomas and Finney (1996).

 ## Questions

19.1. Can a torus have the shape of a sphere?

19.2. How many times can a ray hit a torus tangentially? Illustrate this with some diagrams.

19.3. Why don't we have to compute the spherical polar angle θ to render a part sphere?

19.4. You can use part objects to render complete objects by specifying the full ranges for the angles, but is there a disadvantage in doing this?

19.5. Since having $\theta = 0$ in the (x, z) plane for a part torus creates modeling problems, would measuring θ from the top of the torus solve the problems?

 ## Exercises

19.1. Implement an axis-aligned bounding box object as described in Section 19.1.

19.2. Write the coordinates of the bounding box corners p_0 and p_1 for an arbitrary sphere. Implement the function BBox Sphere::get_bounding_box. This is in preparation for placing spheres in a grid in Chapter 22.

19.3. Implement an axis-aligned box. You can use the figures in Chapters 8 and 9 for testing purposes. Include a shadow hit function. You should also test the hit function with rays that are parallel to a coordinate axis. An orthographic camera is the best way to do this. Later, you can use the transparent-box images in Chapter 28 to test the hit function with rays that hit the inside surface of the box.

19.4. By cyclically permuting the triangle vertices a, b, and c in Equation (19.1), write two other versions of this equation that give the same normal.

19.5. Implement a triangle as described in Section 19.3 and use Figure 19.7 to test your code. I'll introduce various types of *mesh triangles* in Chapters 23 and 29 that have a different structure, but their hit functions will be basically the same as in Listing 19.6.

19.6. The inequalities (19.6) are equivalent to

$$0 < \beta, \ 0 < \gamma, \ \beta + \gamma < 1 \qquad (19.23)$$

(Shirley and Morley, 2003). You can see this from Figure 19.6. Although the inequalities above are simpler than (19.6), they are not necessarily faster, particularly for rendering triangle meshes where each triangle has a small projected area in the image. The first two inequalities in (19.6) eliminate hit points that are not in finite-width strips on the triangle's plane. In contrast, $0 < \beta$ only eliminates points on half the plane, and $0 < \gamma$ leaves points in a finite fraction of the plane. For example, the point $(\beta, \gamma) = (1.5, 1.5)$ would be eliminated with $0 < \beta < 1$ using (19.6) but survive to $\beta + \gamma < 1$ using the inequalities (19.23). Run timing tests with both sets of inequalities for the triangles in Figure 19.7 and, later, for triangle meshes.

19.7. Implement disks, as described in Section 19.4.1.

19.8. An annulus is a circular ring with specified inner and outer radii and an arbitrary center and normal (see Figure 19.24). Implement an annulus object.

19.9. Convince yourself that the inequalities (19.15) are the correct conditions for a hit point to be on a rectangle.

19.10. Implement rectangles as described in Section 19.4.2.

19.11. Implement a generic open cylinder as described in Section 19.5.3. Make sure that the shading on the inside surface is correct. Render Figure 14.19 with the light at different locations with respect to the camera, in particular, on the opposite side of the cylinder and "inside" the cylinder. Also test this with shadows, as an open cylinder is self-shadowing.

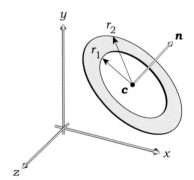

Figure 19.24. An annulus.

19.12. A circular cone is another quadric surface that has many modeling applications. Figure 19.25(a) shows a vertical cross section of a generic cone with height h and radius r in the (x, z) plane. Its bottom edge lies in this plane. The implicit equation for the curved surface is

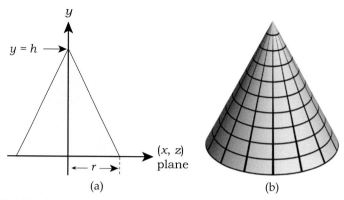

Figure 19.25. (a) Definition of a generic circular cone; (b) rendered cone with $r = 1$ and $h = 2$.

$$(hx/r)^2 - (y - h)^2 + (hz/r)^2 = 0, \tag{19.24}$$

which describes an infinite double cone where the top and bottom pieces meet at $(0, h, 0)$. To render the finite cone, we only record a hit when $y \in [0, h]$.

The normal to the cone is given by the gradient of the implicit function in Equation (19.24). Its components are

$$\mathbf{n} = (2hx/r, -2(y - h), 2hz/r). \tag{19.25}$$

Because you will have to normalize this, you can leave out the 2s. Figure 19.25(b) shows a rendered cone with $r = 1$ and $h = 2$. This cone is open because it has no bottom surface.

Implement a circular cone as described above.

19.13. Prove that Equation (19.20) follows from Equation (19.19).

19.14. Derive the expressions (19.22) for the coefficients c_0–c_4 in Equation (19.21).

19.15. Implement a generic torus and use Figure 19.16 to test your implementation.

19.16. Implement a stored bounding box for a generic torus and compare the rendering times with and without using it in the hit function. You should compute the bounding box in the constructors. You should notice a significant speed-up for rays that don't hit the bounding box.

19.17. Implement part cylinders, part spheres, and part tori as discussed in Section 19.7. To handle all of the modeling situations to be discussed in later chapters, you should implement three versions of each part object (see Section 19.6).

19.18. Implement a part annulus object. You will need this for the beveled wedge object in Section 21.5.

19.19. Implement a GenericSphere object as discussed Section 19.5.5 and use the timing information in the skeleton ray tracer to compare the rendering times of this object and a default sphere.

19.20. Implement the Compound geometric object class from Section 19.8. Include a shadow_hit function.

19.21. How does the compound object hit function work when the compound object is empty? Test an empty object.

19.22. Implement a solid cylinder.

19.23. Implement a solid circular cone (which has a bottom surface).

19.24. A generic thick ring can be defined as shown in Figure 19.26. Implement this as a compound object.

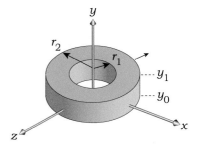

Figure 19.26. A generic thick ring.

19.25. Figure 19.27 shows three hemispherical bowls. Figure 19.27(a) is a thick-walled bowl with a flat rim, Figure 19.27(b) is a thick-walled bowl with a rounded rim, and Figure 19.27(c) appears to be a hemispherical shell with different materials on its inside and outside surfaces, *but it's not*.

Figure 19.28 illustrates how the thick-walled bowls are defined. Model and render these three bowls using the part objects discussed in Section 19.7.

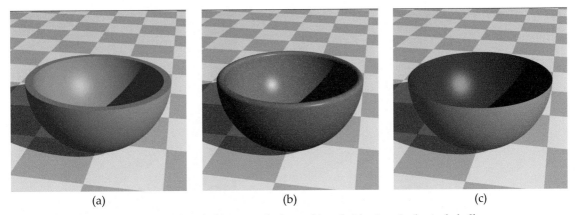

| (a) | (b) | (c) |

Figure 19.27. (a) A flat-rimmed bowl; (b) a round-rimmed bowl; (c) a hemispherical shell that looks like it has different materials on the inside and outside.

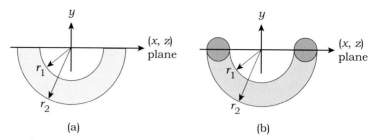

Figure 19.28. Thick-walled hemispherical bowls with a flat rim (a) and a rounded rim (b).

19.26. Figure 19.29 shows a solid cylinder and a thick ring with a different material on each part. For the solid cylinder, you will need access functions to set the color for the bottom, the top, and the wall. With the constructor in Listing 19.14, you would have to use code like the following to set the top material:

```
inline void
OpenCylinder::set_bottom_material(const Material* material_ptr) {
        objects[1]->set_material(material_ptr);
}
```

with similar functions for the other parts. This works, but it's not good code as it's dependent on the order in which the parts are added in the constructor, and it is therefore difficult to maintain. A better approach is to use *named* data members for each part. Implement this for the

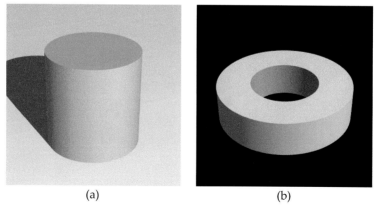

Figure 19.29. Compound objects with a different material on each part: (a) solid cylinder; (b) thick ring.

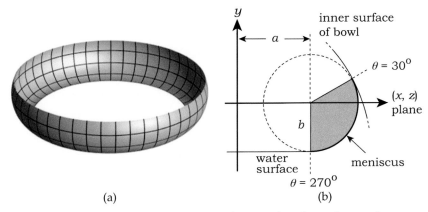

Figure 19.30. (a) A meniscus; (b) cross section of a torus that shows the angular range used in (a).

solid cylinder and thick-walled cylinder. This approach is useful for compound objects with small numbers of components, but it becomes cumbersome for large numbers. For example, the beveled box to be presented in Chapter 21 consists of 26 components, which I have not named. I have also not attempted to render beveled boxes with more than one material.

If you want to construct an object as a "one off," another approach is to construct the parts individually in the build function and then just add them to a compound object. What are its advantages and disadvantages?

19.27. Figure 19.30(a) shows a shape that I'll use in Chapter 28 to model the meniscus for water in a spherical bowl. There, it will add an extra touch of realism to the images. The surface can be constructed with one or more part tori where the range of θ is indicated on the right by the orange sector of the circle. How would you model this surface without changing the definition of the part torus in Section 19.7?

20 Affine Transformations

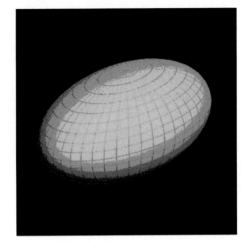

 Objectives

By the end of this chapter, you should:

- understand what affine transformations are;
- understand how to represent transformations with matrices;
- know why we use 4 × 4 matrices for 3D transformations;
- know how to compose a sequence of transformations;
- understand how to define and represent inverse transformations.

Transformations are an essential tool for ray tracing: we use them to alter the size, shape, orientation, and location of geometric objects. Without them, it would not be practical to ray trace objects such as non-axis-aligned rectangular boxes or arbitrary cylinders, cones, and tori. We can also transform cameras, lights, textures, and bump maps. The transformations I'll discuss here are:

- scaling;
- rotation;
- reflection;
- translation;
- shearing.

These are known as *affine transformations* because we can represent them by sets of linear equations and therefore by matrices. As a result, affine transformations preserve straight lines, and a transformed ray is still a ray. This property is important for ray tracing because, in practice, we transform the rays instead of the objects (see Chapter 21).

Although we only need 3D transformations for ray tracing, I'll discuss 2D transformations first because, if you understand these, you'll find it easier to understand the 3D transformations. The discussion here is brief, with no derivations of the primitive transformation matrices, because many general graphics textbooks such as Hearn and Baker (2004) discuss 2D and 3D transformations in detail. In a broader context, the material in this chapter is part of *linear algebra*, as discussed in the Further Reading section.

In matrix notation, we represent points by *column vectors*, for example, $[x \; y]^T$ in 2D and $[x \; y \; z]^T$ in 3D, where T indicates the transpose of the matrix. We multiply these column vectors by transformation matrices on the left. This is how major graphics APIs such as OpenGL represent points. We'll represent vectors and normals in the same way, but as I discussed in Sections 2.6–2.8, vectors, points, and normals transform differently under affine transformations. In Sections 20.1–20.5, I'll only discuss the transformation of points. Section 20.6 involves the transformation of vectors, but the implementation details are in Chapter 21.

This chapter covers background material only and contains no ray tracing. It assumes that you are familiar with matrix notation, definitions, and algebra.

20.1 2D Transformations

Let $p = [x \; y]^T$ be an arbitrary point in the (x, y) plane. An affine transformation applied to p moves it to a new point p related to the original point by the linear equations

$$x' = ax + by,$$
$$y' = cx + dy.$$

These can be written in matrix form as

$$\begin{bmatrix} x' \\ y' \end{bmatrix} = \begin{bmatrix} a & b \\ c & d \end{bmatrix} \begin{bmatrix} x \\ y \end{bmatrix},$$

or

$$p' = Tp, \qquad\qquad (20.1)$$

where

$$T = \begin{bmatrix} a & b \\ c & d \end{bmatrix},$$

is a 2×2 *transformation matrix*. The coefficients a, b, c, and d are floating-point numbers. When these numbers are given specific values, including values returned by function calls, Equation (20.1) can represent most of the specific transformations listed above, in two dimensions. In this section, I'll only consider transformations about the (x, y) coordinate-system origin.

20.1.1 Scaling

We use scaling to change the size and shape of objects. In this case, the transformation matrix M is denoted by $S(a, b)$ and is diagonal:

$$S(a, b) = \begin{bmatrix} a & 0 \\ 0 & b \end{bmatrix}, \tag{20.2}$$

where the *scaling parameters* a and b are numbers. Its effect on the x- and y-components of a point is to transform them to

$$x' = ax,$$
$$y' = by.$$

Figure 20.1 shows some scaling transformations applied to a circular disk. Because the matrix (20.2) scales all points in the (x, y) plane about the origin, a physical analogy is a sheet of rubber nailed to the origin that can be stretched or compressed in various directions. When $a = b$, the scaling is *uniform*, and when $a \neq b$, the scaling is *nonuniform*. With uniform scaling, circles stay circles, but with nonuniform scaling, they are converted to ellipses.

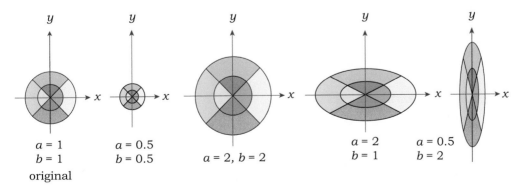

$a = 1$
$b = 1$
original

$a = 0.5$
$b = 0.5$

$a = 2, b = 2$

$a = 2$
$b = 1$

$a = 0.5$
$b = 2$

Figure 20.1. Various 2D scalings applied to the circular disk on the left.

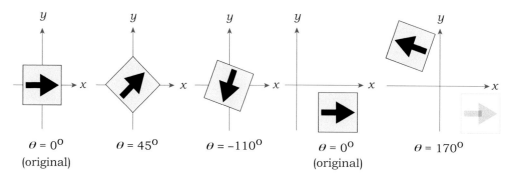

Figure 20.2. Rotating objects about the origin through the indicated angles.

20.1.2 Rotation

The matrix $R(\theta)$ that rotates the (x, y) plane about the origin is

$$R(\theta) = \begin{bmatrix} \cos\theta & -\sin\theta \\ \sin\theta & \cos\theta \end{bmatrix}, \tag{20.3}$$

where θ is the angle of rotation. By convention, a positive rotation is coun-terclockwise. The angle θ in Equation (20.3) is always specified in radians. If you want to specify a rotation angle in degrees, you must convert it to radians before using it in $R(\theta)$ (see Section 2.3.2). The coordinates of a point are trans-formed with $R(\theta)$ according to

$$x' = (\cos\theta)x - (\sin\theta)y,$$
$$y' = -(\sin\theta)x + (\cos\theta)y.$$

Figure 20.2 shows the results of rotating an object through the indicated angles. Normally, we specify $\theta \in [0, \pm 2\pi)$, but θ can be outside these ranges because we can add $2n\pi$, for $n = 0, 1, 2, \dots$ to θ without altering the result. As rotation doesn't change the shape or size of an object, this is an example of a *rigid-body* transformation. These don't deform the objects.

20.1.3 Shearing

In physics, shearing refers to the process of skewing an object by sliding one section against another; this is the process that the shearing transformation simulates. A physical analogy is a deck of cards where you can slide the cards over each other. As shearing is more complex than scaling, I'll discuss shearing along the x-and y-axes separately.

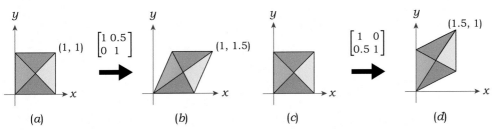

Figure 20.3. (a) and (b) show the effect of shearing a unit square in the x-direction, (c) and (d) illustrate shearing the same square in the y-direction.

The matrix for shearing along the x-axis is

$$M(h_{yx}) = \begin{bmatrix} 1 & h_{yx} \\ 0 & 1 \end{bmatrix}, \tag{20.4}$$

which produces the following transformation equations for the x and y coordinates of a point:

$$x' = x + h_{yx}y,$$
$$y' = y. \tag{20.5}$$

Equations (20.5) show that the new value of x is equal to the original value plus the shearing amount h_{yx} in the x-direction multiplied by the y-coordinate. Here, h_{yx} specifies the amount by which the y-coordinate of the original point determines the x-coordinate of the transformed point. Equations (20.5) also show that the original y-coordinate is unchanged. Figure 20.3(a) and (b) demonstrate the effect of applying the matrix (20.4) with $h_{yx} = 0.5$ to a unit square with one corner at the origin.

Shearing in the y-direction is performed by the matrix

$$M(h_{xy}) = \begin{bmatrix} 1 & 0 \\ h_{xy} & 1 \end{bmatrix}, \tag{20.6}$$

so that $x' = x$, and $y' = y + h_{xy}x$. Figure 20.3(d) shows the results of applying this matrix with $h_{xy} = 0.5$.

The matrices (20.4) and (20.6) can be combined to give

$$M(h_{yx}, h_{xy}) = \begin{bmatrix} 1 & h_{yx} \\ h_{xy} & 1 \end{bmatrix}, \tag{20.7}$$

which shears objects in the (x, y) plane. Figure 20.4 shows the results with $h_{yx} = h_{xy} = 0.5$.

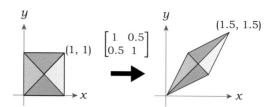

Figure 20.4. Shearing a unit square in the x- and y-directions with shearing factors 0.5.

20.1.4 Reflection

Reflections about the x- and y-coordinate axes are represented by the matrices

$$R_x = \begin{bmatrix} -1 & 0 \\ 0 & 1 \end{bmatrix} \text{ and } R_y = \begin{bmatrix} 1 & 0 \\ 0 & -1 \end{bmatrix},$$

respectively.

20.1.5 Translation

Geometrically, translation is the simplest affine transformation, but paradoxically, it's the one that creates a problem with the above matrix representation. To translate a point, we just add a displacement to the x-and y-coordinates:

$$\begin{aligned} x' &= x + d_x, \\ y' &= y + d_y. \end{aligned} \tag{20.8}$$

So far so good, but the problem becomes apparent when we write these equations in matrix notation:

$$\begin{bmatrix} x' \\ y' \end{bmatrix} = \begin{bmatrix} d_x \\ d_y \end{bmatrix} + \begin{bmatrix} x \\ y \end{bmatrix}. \tag{20.9}$$

Nothing could be simpler than this, but unfortunately, the translated coordinates result from adding a column vector to (x, y) instead of multiplying it by a 2 × 2 matrix. Why is this a problem? It's because we usually have to apply a sequence of transformations to objects, and for reasons of efficiency, programming convenience, and generality, we need to be able to represent all transformations by square-matrix multiplication.[1] Why does this help? The product of any number of square matrices is another square matrix of the same size.

---

1. Another reason is that the matrix representation can be implemented in hardware.

If we apply a sequence of transformation matrices $T_1, T_2, ..., T_n$ to a point, the transformed point will be given by

$$p' = T_n T_{n-1} \cdots T_1 p = Tp,$$

where

$$T = T_n T_{n-1} \cdots T_1. \tag{20.10}$$

is a single matrix. Note that we multiply successive transformation matrices on the left.

A fact of life is that there's simply not enough degrees of freedom in 2×2 matrices to represent translation as a matrix multiplication.

 ## 20.2 3D Homogeneous Coordinates

The solution to the translation problem is to go up a dimension by embedding the (x, y) plane in a 3D space and to use 3×3 matrices to represent *all* 2D transformations. The 3D coordinates are labeled (X, Y, W) and are known as 3D *homogeneous coordinates* (see the Further Reading section). The (x, y) plane is embedded at $W = 1$, has its origin at $(X, Y, W) = (0, 0, 1)$, is parallel to the (X, Y) plane, and has its (x, y) axes parallel to the (X, Y) axes. Figure 20.5 shows the arrangement. A point with coordinates (x, y) is now treated as a 3D point with coordinates $(x, y, 1) = (X, Y, 1)$.

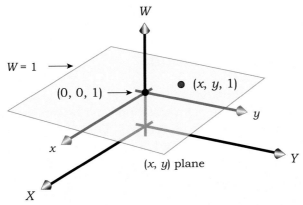

Figure 20.5. The (x, y) plane is embedded at $W = 1$ in the (X, Y, W) coordinate system.

We can now represent translation as the following 3×3 matrix:

$$T(d_x, d_y) = \begin{bmatrix} 1 & 0 & d_x \\ 0 & 1 & d_y \\ 0 & 0 & 1 \end{bmatrix}.$$

Let's apply this to the point $(x, y, 1)$, to make sure it works:

$$p' = \begin{bmatrix} 1 & 0 & d_x \\ 0 & 1 & d_y \\ 0 & 0 & 1 \end{bmatrix} \begin{bmatrix} x \\ y \\ 1 \end{bmatrix} = \begin{bmatrix} x + d_x \\ y + d_y \\ 1 \end{bmatrix},$$

which is exactly what we need according to the Equations (20.8).

We can represent scaling, rotation, and shearing with the following 3×3 matrices, where the original 2×2 matrices are the upper-left 2×2 partitions:

$$S(a, b) = \begin{bmatrix} a & 0 & 0 \\ 0 & b & 0 \\ 0 & 0 & 1 \end{bmatrix},$$

$$R(\theta) = \begin{bmatrix} \cos\theta & -\sin\theta & 0 \\ \sin\theta & \cos\theta & 0 \\ 0 & 0 & 1 \end{bmatrix},$$

$$M(h_{yx}, h_{xy}) = \begin{bmatrix} 1 & h_{yx} & 0 \\ h_{xy} & 1 & 0 \\ 0 & 0 & 1 \end{bmatrix}.$$

Because these transformations leave $W = 1$, they all keep the transformed points in the $(x, y, 1)$ plane.

20.3 3D Transformations

All of the 2D transformations generalize to 3D, but we have to represent them with 4×4 matrices because 3D translation can't be represented by a 3×3 matrix multiplication. Here, we embed the 3D space in a 4D homogeneous coordinate space (X, Y, Z, W), at $W = 1$, and represent points as $(x, y, z, 1)$. All of the 3D affine transformations leave $W = 1$.[2]

---

2. Perspective projection can also be represented by a 4×4 matrix, but it doesn't leave $W = 1$.

20.3.1 Translation

I'll start with translation this time. The translation matrix is

$$T(d_x, d_y, d_z) = \begin{bmatrix} 1 & 0 & 0 & d_x \\ 0 & 1 & 0 & d_y \\ 0 & 0 & 1 & d_z \\ 0 & 0 & 0 & 1 \end{bmatrix},$$

where $T(d_x, d_y, d_z) [x\ y\ z\ 1]^T = [x + d_x\ y + d_y\ z + d_z\ 1]^T$, as required.

20.3.2 Scaling

Scaling about the origin in 3D is a straightforward generalization of 2D scaling, where the 3D scaling matrix is

$$S(a, b, c) = \begin{bmatrix} a & 0 & 0 & 0 \\ 0 & b & 0 & 0 \\ 0 & 0 & c & 0 \\ 0 & 0 & 0 & 1 \end{bmatrix}.$$

Here, a, b, and c are the scaling factors in the (x, y, z) directions, respectively. As expected, applying $S(a, b, c)$ to a 3D point gives $S(a, b, c) [x\ y\ z\ 1]^T = [ax\ by\ cz\ 1]^T$.

As an example, we can transform a sphere into a variety of ellipsoids by scaling it. Figure 20.6(a) shows a unit sphere at the origin, and the other parts of the figure show the results of scaling the sphere with the indicated values of (a, b, c).

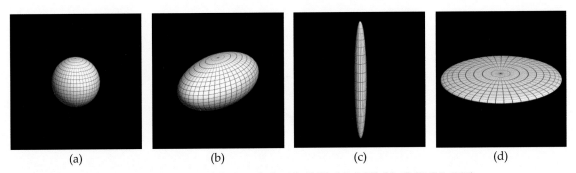

(a)　　　　　(b)　　　　　(c)　　　　　(d)

Figure 20.6. (a) Unit sphere at origin; sphere scaled with (1.25, 1.0, 2.25) (b), (0.25, 2.5, 0.25) (c), and (2.5, 0.25, 2.5) (d). The viewing parameters are the same in each figure.

20.3.3 Rotation

Rotation in 3D is not a straightforward generalization of 2D rotation because there are now three axes about which objects can be rotated. The following sign convention exists for positive rotations about the axes. If we look along the positive part of an axis towards the origin (that is, in the negative axis direction), a positive rotation is counterclockwise. This is consistent with the direction of positive rotations in 2D, which correspond to rotations about the z-axis in 3D. Figure 20.7 shows positive rotations about the x-, y-, and z-axes.

The matrices for these three rotations are

$$R_x(\theta) = \begin{bmatrix} 1 & 0 & 0 & 0 \\ 0 & \cos\theta & -\sin\theta & 0 \\ 0 & \sin\theta & \cos\theta & 0 \\ 0 & 0 & 0 & 1 \end{bmatrix},$$

$$R_y(\theta) = \begin{bmatrix} \cos\theta & 0 & \sin\theta & 0 \\ 0 & 1 & 0 & 0 \\ -\sin\theta & 0 & \cos\theta & 0 \\ 0 & 0 & 0 & 1 \end{bmatrix}, \qquad (20.11)$$

$$R_z(\theta) = \begin{bmatrix} \cos\theta & -\sin\theta & 0 & 0 \\ \sin\theta & \cos\theta & 0 & 0 \\ 0 & 0 & 1 & 0 \\ 0 & 0 & 0 & 1 \end{bmatrix}.$$

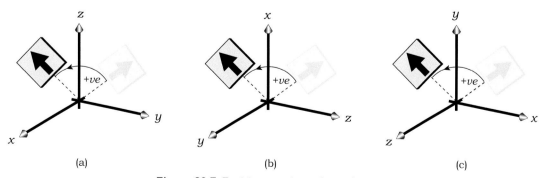

Figure 20.7. Positive rotations about the x-, y-, and z-axes.

20.3.4 Reflection

The primitive reflections in 3D change the sign of a single coordinate and therefore reflect objects across one of the three coordinate planes (y, z), (x, z), and (x, y). They are represented by the following matrices:

$$R_x = \begin{bmatrix} -1 & 0 & 0 & 0 \\ 0 & 1 & 0 & 0 \\ 0 & 0 & 1 & 0 \\ 0 & 0 & 0 & 1 \end{bmatrix}, \quad R_y = \begin{bmatrix} 1 & 0 & 0 & 0 \\ 0 & -1 & 0 & 0 \\ 0 & 0 & 1 & 0 \\ 0 & 0 & 0 & 1 \end{bmatrix}, \quad R_z = \begin{bmatrix} 1 & 0 & 0 & 0 \\ 0 & 1 & 0 & 0 \\ 0 & 0 & -1 & 0 \\ 0 & 0 & 0 & 1 \end{bmatrix}.$$

20.3.5 Shearing

In 3D, objects can be sheared along any of the coordinate axes, in any of the coordinate planes, or combinations of these. The general 3D shearing matrix is

$$M = \begin{bmatrix} 1 & h_{yx} & h_{zx} & 0 \\ h_{xy} & 1 & h_{zy} & 0 \\ h_{xz} & h_{yz} & 1 & 0 \\ 0 & 0 & 0 & 1 \end{bmatrix}, \tag{20.12}$$

which has six shearing parameters. The effect of this matrix on the coordinates of a point is as follows:

$$\begin{bmatrix} x' \\ y' \\ z' \\ 1 \end{bmatrix} = \begin{bmatrix} 1 & h_{yx} & h_{zx} & 0 \\ h_{xy} & 1 & h_{zy} & 0 \\ h_{xz} & h_{yz} & 1 & 0 \\ 0 & 0 & 0 & 1 \end{bmatrix} \begin{bmatrix} x \\ y \\ z \\ 1 \end{bmatrix} = \begin{bmatrix} x + h_{yx}y + h_{zx}z \\ h_{xy}x + y + h_{zy}z \\ h_{xz}x + h_{yz}y + z \\ 1 \end{bmatrix}. \tag{20.13}$$

An example is shearing along the y-axis. With $h_{xy} = 0.75$, the matrix is

$$M = \begin{bmatrix} 1 & 0 & 0 & 0 \\ 0.75 & 1 & 0 & 0 \\ 0 & 0 & 1 & 0 \\ 0 & 0 & 0 & 1 \end{bmatrix},$$

so that $x' = x$, $y' = y + 0.75x$, and $z' = z$, according to Equation (20.13). Fig–ure 20.8 shows the result of applying this shearing transformation to a unit cube centered on the origin.

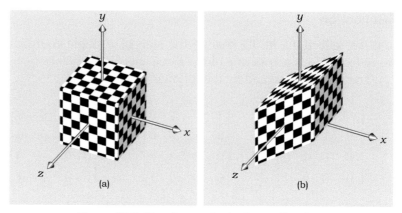

Figure 20.8. Shearing a cube in the y_w-direction.

 20.4 Composition of Transformations

Since we usually need to apply a sequence of transformations to an object, you need to understand how to do this and appreciate that the order of the transformations is important. How it's done is simple in principle—you just specify the transformations in the correct order and build up the composite transformation matrix (20.10) by multiplying each new matrix on the left. It's working out the individual transformations and their order that can be challenging. I'll therefore illustrate this with a few examples.

The first example is the composition of scaling and rotation, which is most easily illustrated in 2D. Figure 20.9(a) shows a square centered on the

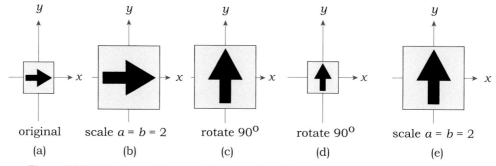

Figure 20.9. This figure illustrates how rotation about the origin commutes with uniform scaling about the origin. (a), (b), and (c) form one sequence of transformations, and (a), (d), and (e) form a second sequence with the same end result.

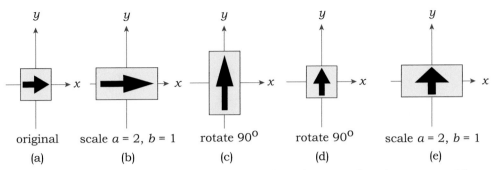

Figure 20.10. This figure illustrates how rotation about the origin doesn't commute with nonuniform scaling about the origin. As in Figure 20.9, there are two sequences. (a), (b), and (c) form one sequence of transformations, and (a), (d), and (e) form a second sequence, this time with a different end result.

origin that is scaled uniformly with $a = b = 2$ in Figure 20.9(b). It's then rotated through 90° to arrive at the orientation in Figure 20.9(c). Figure 20.9(d) and (e) show the result of applying these transformations in reverse order, that is, first rotating by 90° in Figure 20.9(d) and then scaling uniformly in Figure 20.9(e). Notice that the end result is the same. This is always the case for *uniform* scaling and rotation about the same point. In terms of matrices, the rotation and uniform scaling matrices *commute*. This means that their product is independent of the order in which we multiply them:

$$R(\theta)\, S(a, a) = S(a, a)\, R(\theta).$$

The second example is the composition of rotation and nonuniform scaling, as shown in Figure 20.10. Here, we first scale the square with $a = 2$ and $b = 1$ to get the result in Figure 20.10(b) and then rotate it through 90° for Figure 20.10(c). In Figure 20.10(d) and (e), we rotate first and then scale. Notice that the results in Figure 20.10(c) and (e) are different. In this case, the transformation matrices don't commute, and therefore the order of the transformations does matter. We can express this mathematically as

$$R(\theta)\, S(a, b) \neq S(a, b)\, R(\theta)$$

when $a \neq b$ and $R(\theta)$ is any of the rotation matrices (20.11).

The final example is rotation in 3D. We first rotate the box in Figure 20.11(a) through 90° around the x-axis, which leaves it on the z-axis as in Figure 20.11(b). We then rotate it 90° around the y-axis to place it at its final location and orientation on the x-axis in Figure 20.11(c).

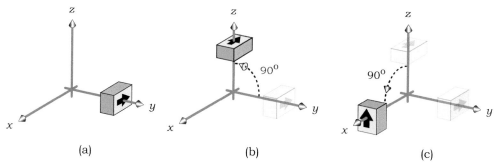

Figure 20.11. (a) Original box on y-axis; (b) box rotated 90° about the x-axis; (c) box then rotated 90° about the y-axis.

If we now perform the rotations in the opposite order, as in Figure 20.12, the end result in Figure 20.12(c) is completely different. The order in which you apply 3D rotations is important, as reflected in the fact that the rotation matrices (20.11) don't commute. In fact, matrices generally don't commute.

Unfortunately, there's no magic formula for the correct sequence of transformations. Often, however, all you have to do is the following. Start with a generic object or some other untransformed object and apply whatever sequence of scaling, shearing, and rotations you need. These will take care of the size, shape, and orientation of the object. Then, translate the object to its desired location. This will avoid problems that can arise from the fact that the transformations I discuss here act around the origin or the coordinate axes. For example, if you translate an object first, and then rotate it, the rotation will still be around a coordinate axis, and this may not give the result you want, as seen

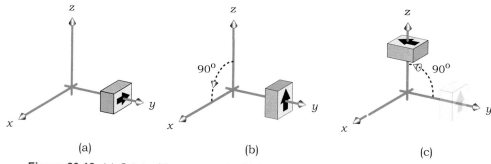

Figure 20.12. (a) Original box on y-axis, (b) box rotated 90° about the y-axis, (c) box then rotated 90° about the x-axis.

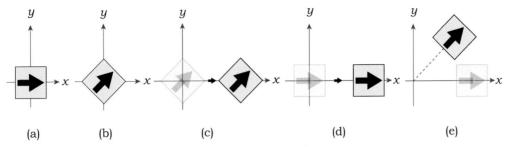

(a)   (b)   (c)   (d)   (e)

Figure 20.13. Rotation and translation don't commute.

Figure 20.13. In Figure 20.13(b) and (c), I've rotated the square 45° about the origin and then translated it in the x-direction. In Figure 20.13(d) and (e), I've translated it first and then rotated it, with a different end result.

We can, of course, rotate objects about lines other than the coordinate axes, a process that I'll explain in Section 20.6. We can also scale objects about arbitrary points and reflect objects through arbitrary planes (see Exercises 20.4 and 20.5).

In the general situation where we apply n transformations, the composite transformation matrix is given by Equation (20.10). If we need to compute this matrix, we can do so by successively multiplying each new transformation matrix on the left. There are, however, only two applications where we need to do this. The first is to perform the roll angle on cameras, which uses a rotation about an arbitrary line. The second and more important application is to compute the bounding box of transformed objects so that they can be placed in a regular-grid acceleration scheme (see Chapter 22).

 20.5 Inverse Transformations

To ray trace transformed objects, we actually need the *inverses* of the above transformations. I'll discuss the reason in Chapter 21.

20.5.1 Individual Inverse Transformations

Inverse transformations have the opposite effects of the "normal," or "forward," transformations discussed above. For example, the inverse of translating an object 20 units in the positive x-direction is translating it 20 units in the negative x-direction, and the inverse of rotating an object 30° about the x-axis is rotating it by −30°. Inverse transformations are represented by the *inverses* of their respective transformation matrices. Fortunately, we can write the inverses by inspection, with the exception of the shearing matrix inverse.

The inverse transformation matrices are as follows:

Translation.

$$T^{-1}(d_x, d_y, d_z) = \begin{bmatrix} 1 & 0 & 0 & -d_x \\ 0 & 1 & 0 & -d_y \\ 0 & 0 & 1 & -d_z \\ 0 & 0 & 0 & 1 \end{bmatrix}.$$

Scaling.

$$S^{-1}(a, b, c) = \begin{bmatrix} 1/a & 0 & 0 & 0 \\ 0 & 1/b & 0 & 0 \\ 0 & 0 & 1/c & 0 \\ 0 & 0 & 0 & 1 \end{bmatrix}.$$

Rotation.

$$R_x^{-1}(\theta) = \begin{bmatrix} 1 & 0 & 0 & 0 \\ 0 & \cos\theta & \sin\theta & 0 \\ 0 & -\sin\theta & \cos\theta & 0 \\ 0 & 0 & 0 & 1 \end{bmatrix},$$

$$R_y^{-1}(\theta) = \begin{bmatrix} \cos\theta & 0 & -\sin\theta & 0 \\ 0 & 1 & 0 & 0 \\ \sin\theta & 0 & \cos\theta & 0 \\ 0 & 0 & 0 & 1 \end{bmatrix},$$

$$R_z^{-1}(\theta) = \begin{bmatrix} \cos\theta & \sin\theta & 0 & 0 \\ -\sin\theta & \cos\theta & 0 & 0 \\ 0 & 0 & 1 & 0 \\ 0 & 0 & 0 & 1 \end{bmatrix}.$$

Shearing. The shearing matrix (20.12) is too complex to write down its inverse by inspection, but that's OK because there's a formula we can use for the inverse of an arbitrary invertible matrix. See, for example, Anton (2004). According to this formula, the inverse of the shearing matrix is

$$M^{-1} = \begin{bmatrix} 1 - h_{yz}h_{zy} & -h_{yx} + h_{yz}h_{zx} & -h_{zx} + h_{yx}h_{zy} & 0 \\ -h_{xy} + h_{xz}h_{zy} & 1 - h_{xz}h_{zx} & -h_{zy} + h_{xy}h_{zx} & 0 \\ -h_{xz} + h_{xy}h_{yz} & -h_{yz} + h_{xz}h_{yx} & 1 - h_{xy}h_{yx} & 0 \\ 0 & 0 & 0 & D \end{bmatrix} D^{-1},$$

where

$$D = 1 - h_{xy}\,h_{yx} - h_{xz}\,h_{zx} - h_{yz}\,h_{zy} + h_{xy}\,h_{yz}\,h_{zx} + h_{xz}\,h_{yx}\,h_{zy}$$

is the determinant of M.

20.5.2 Composite Inverse Transformations

Since we usually have to apply sequences of transformations to objects, the ray tracer will have to compute the composite inverse transformation matrix for a given sequence. Fortunately, the structure of the composite transformation matrix (20.10) makes this a simple procedure. The inverse of a matrix of this form is the product of the individual inverse transformation matrices, but multiplied in the opposite order; that is,

$$T^{-1} = T_1^{-1} T_2^{-1} \cdots T_n^{-1}. \tag{20.14}$$

Notice how the successive inverse matrices are now multiplied on the *right*. Equation (20.14) is an important result because it means that we can build up the inverse matrix as we apply each individual transformation. Some ray-tracing books discuss the numerical inversion of matrices, but numerical inversion is not necessary.

 ## 20.6 Rotation about an Arbitrary Line

This section is heavy-going mathematically and is not essential reading for the following chapters.

Sometimes we need to apply more complicated sequences of transformations than those described in Section 20.4. An example is to rotate an object about an arbitrary line, as shown in Figure 20.14. Here, the line is defined by a point p and a direction d.

Because the process will involve *orthogonal matrices*, here is the definition: an orthogonal matrix is a square matrix for which

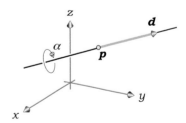

Figure 20.14. An arbitrary line in space as defined by a point p and direction d.

$$M^{-1} = M^{\mathrm{T}}.$$

Simply put, the inverse of an orthogonal matrix is its transpose. Although orthogonal matrices can be of any size, I'll just look at 3×3 matrices and then incorporate them as the upper-left 3×3 partition of 4×4 transformation matrices. Although it may not be obvious at first glance, it follows from the definition of matrix multiplication that the rows and columns of an orthogonal matrix are sets of orthonormal vectors.

As an example, if (u, v, w) is an orthonormal basis, the matrix

$$R = \begin{bmatrix} u_x & u_y & u_z \\ v_x & v_y & v_z \\ w_x & w_y & w_z \end{bmatrix} \tag{20.15}$$

is orthogonal. The transpose is

$$R^T = \begin{bmatrix} u_x & v_x & w_x \\ u_y & v_y & w_y \\ u_z & v_z & w_z \end{bmatrix}, \tag{20.16}$$

and it's not difficult to show that $RR^T = R^TR = I_3$, where I_3 is the 3×3 identity matrix.

The matrix R is useful for ray tracing because it rotates the orthonormal basis vectors (u, v, w) so that they are parallel to the world orthonormal basis vectors (i, j, k), where $i = (1, 0, 0)$, $j = (0, 1, 0)$, and $k = (0, 0, 1)$. Here's how it works for u:

$$R\,u = \begin{bmatrix} u_x & u_y & u_z \\ v_x & v_y & v_z \\ w_x & w_y & w_z \end{bmatrix} \begin{bmatrix} u_x \\ u_y \\ u_z \end{bmatrix} = \begin{bmatrix} u \bullet u \\ v \bullet u \\ w \bullet u \end{bmatrix} = \begin{bmatrix} 1 \\ 0 \\ 0 \end{bmatrix} = i.$$

Similarly,

$$R\,v = \begin{bmatrix} u \bullet v \\ v \bullet v \\ w \bullet v \end{bmatrix} = \begin{bmatrix} 0 \\ 1 \\ 0 \end{bmatrix} = j, \text{ and } R\,w = \begin{bmatrix} u \bullet w \\ v \bullet w \\ w \bullet w \end{bmatrix} = \begin{bmatrix} 0 \\ 0 \\ 1 \end{bmatrix} = k.$$

The above process is an example of a *change of basis* for the orthonormal frame, where R is the *transition matrix*. To see how it helps rotate objects about the line in Figure 20.14, look at Figure 20.15. Figure 20.15(a) shows an orthonormal frame attached to the line with p as the origin and w parallel to the line direction d. In Figure 20.15(b), I've translated the line so that p is at the world origin, and in Figure 20.15(c), I've rotated u, v, and w with R so that they are parallel to the x-, y-, and z-axes. The important thing to notice in Figure 20.15(c) is that the line now lies along the z-axis because it's also been rotated along with u, v, and w. We can show this algebraically as follows. In terms of (u, v, w),

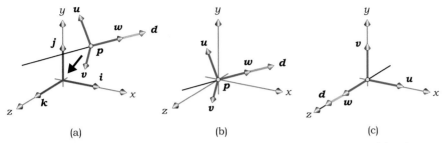

Figure 20.15. (a) A line with attached orthonormal frame, showing the world orthonormal basis vectors; (b) the line translated so that p is at the world origin; (c) the line and its orthonormal frame rotated to place the line along the z-axis.

$$d = dw,$$

where d is the magnitude of d. Applying R to d gives

$$Rd = Rdw = dRw = dk.$$

Now that the line lies along the z-axis, it's simple to rotate objects around it through an angle α by using the z-axis rotation matrix $R_z(\theta)$ in Equation (20.11) with $\theta = -\alpha$. However, that's not the end of the process, because we then have to rotate u, v, w, and the line back to their original orientations in Figure 20.15(b) and then translate p back to its original location in Figure 20.15(a). The complete expression for the composite *inverse* transformation matrix (20.14) for rotating objects about the original line is

$$T^{-1} = T(p_x, p_y, p_z)\, R^T\, R_z(-\alpha)\, R\, T(-p_x, -p_y, -p_z)$$

$$= \begin{bmatrix} 1 & 0 & 0 & p_x \\ 0 & 1 & 0 & p_y \\ 0 & 0 & 1 & p_z \\ 0 & 0 & 0 & 1 \end{bmatrix} \begin{bmatrix} u_x & v_x & w_x & 0 \\ u_y & v_y & w_y & 0 \\ u_z & v_z & w_z & 0 \\ 0 & 0 & 0 & 1 \end{bmatrix} \begin{bmatrix} \cos\alpha & \sin\alpha & 0 & 0 \\ -\sin\alpha & \cos\alpha & 0 & 0 \\ 0 & 0 & 1 & 0 \\ 0 & 0 & 0 & 1 \end{bmatrix} \begin{bmatrix} u_x & u_y & u_z & 0 \\ v_x & v_y & v_z & 0 \\ w_x & w_y & w_z & 0 \\ 0 & 0 & 0 & 1 \end{bmatrix} \begin{bmatrix} 1 & 0 & 0 & -p_x \\ 0 & 1 & 0 & -p_y \\ 0 & 0 & 1 & -p_z \\ 0 & 0 & 0 & 1 \end{bmatrix}.$$

$$(20.17)$$

At the risk of getting you completely confused, the sequence of matrices (20.17) can also be used to rotate the camera around the view direction where we use the forward transformation matrix (20.10). In this case,

$$T = T(e_x - l_x, e_y - l_y, e_z - l_z)\, R^T\, R_z(-\alpha)\, R\, T(-(e_x - l_x), -(e_y - l_y), -(e_z - l_z)). \quad (20.18)$$

Further Reading

There are many good books on linear algebra, but I've found Anton (2004) to be particularly well-written and easy to read. The change of orthonormal basis discussed in Section 20.6 is a standard linear-algebra technique that Anton discusses in Chapter 6. Rotation about an arbitrary line is also discussed in Shirley and Morley (2003). Many general books on computer graphics have an appendix on matrix algebra and discuss homogeneous coordinates. Examples include Foley et al. (1995), Hearn and Baker (2004), and Hill and Kelley (2006).

 Questions

20.1.   What is the unit shearing matrix?
20.2.   What matrix reflects 2D points through the origin?
20.3.   Which of the affine transformations are rigid-body transformations?

 Exercises

20.1.   Prove that the transformation matrices in Section 20.3 perform their respective tasks.
20.2.   Prove that the rotation matrices (20.11) and the uniform scaling matrix $S(a, a, a)$ commute.
20.3.   Prove that the rotation matrices (20.11) don't commute.
20.4.   Derive the composite matrix that scales an object about an arbitrary point.
20.5.   Derive the composite matrix that reflects an object through an arbitrary plane.
20.6.   Prove that the matrices (20.10) and (20.14) are inverses.
20.7.   Prove that the orthogonal matrix (20.15) and its transpose (20.16) are inverses.

21 Transforming Objects

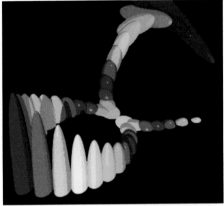

Image courtesy of David Gardner

Objectives

By the end of this chapter, you should:

- understand how to intersect rays with transformed objects;
- understand why instancing is the preferred method;
- be able to transform objects through instancing;
- understand how you can model numerous beveled objects.

In this chapter, I'll put the theory of affine transformations into practice by explaining how to ray trace transformed objects. This will give you a lot of flexibility for modeling purposes.

21.1 Intersecting Transformed Objects

21.1.1 General Theory

How do we intersect rays with transformed objects? The answer is surprising and simple. We don't! Suppose you wanted to ray trace an object with a specified set of affine transforms. Here are the steps:

417

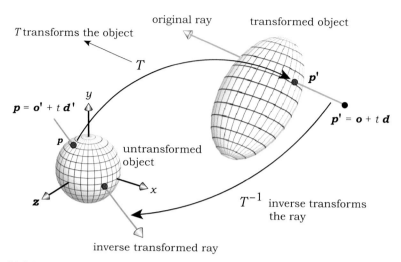

Figure 21.1. Untransformed and transformed objects with the original and inverse transformed rays.

- apply the *inverse* set of transformations to the ray to produce an *inverse transformed* ray;
- intersect the inverse transformed ray with the untransformed object;
- compute the normal to the untransformed object at the hit point;
- use the hit point on the untransformed object to compute where the *original* ray hits the *transformed* object;
- use the normal to the untransformed object to compute the normal to the transformed object.

Figure 21.1 illustrates these procedures, which are standard practice in ray tracing. They are also its neatest trick.

To carry out the above steps, consider a ray with origin o and direction d that hits the transformed object. We need to compute the coordinates of the nearest hit point p' of this original ray and the transformed object. This point will satisfy

$$p' = o + t\,d, \tag{21.1}$$

for some value of t.

There also exists a point p on the untransformed object that's related to p' by Equation (20.1):

$$p' = Tp, \tag{21.2}$$

where T is the composite 4×4 transformation matrix of the form (20.10). If we multiply both sides of Equation (21.2) by the inverse transformation matrix T^{-1}, we get

$$p = T^{-1} p'. \tag{21.3}$$

To inverse transform the ray, we multiply both sides of Equation (21.1) by T^{-1}, which gives

$$T^{-1} p' = T^{-1} o + t T^{-1} d.$$

Using Equation (21.3), we can write this as

$$p = o' + t d', \tag{21.4}$$

where

$$o' = T^{-1} o \tag{21.5}$$

and

$$d' = T^{-1} d \tag{21.6}$$

are the inverse transformed ray origin and direction, respectively. Equation (21.4) is the inverse transformed ray. Figure 21.1 also illustrates this inverse transformation process.

21.1.2 Transforming Points and Vectors

We have to be careful with Equations (21.5) and (21.6) because o is a point and d is a vector, and as we saw in Chapter 20, these transform differently under affine transformations. As a reminder, points are affected by translation, but vectors are not affected.

Let's write the inverse transformation matrix as

$$T^{-1} = \begin{bmatrix} m_{00} & m_{01} & m_{02} & m_{03} \\ m_{10} & m_{11} & m_{12} & m_{13} \\ m_{20} & m_{21} & m_{22} & m_{23} \\ 0 & 0 & 0 & 1 \end{bmatrix},$$

where the rows and columns are numbered from zero instead of one.[1] I'll explain how to compute this matrix in Section 21.1.5.

---

1. This makes the notation in the following equations correspond more closely to the code if you use a 2D array in C to store the matrix elements.

To transform the ray origin, we represent it as a point in 4D homogeneous space $o = [o_x \ o_y \ o_z \ 1]^T$ and multiply it on the left with T^{-1}:

$$o' = \begin{bmatrix} m_{00} & m_{01} & m_{02} & m_{03} \\ m_{10} & m_{11} & m_{12} & m_{13} \\ m_{20} & m_{21} & m_{22} & m_{23} \\ 0 & 0 & 0 & 1 \end{bmatrix} \begin{bmatrix} o_x \\ o_y \\ o_z \\ 1 \end{bmatrix}. \tag{21.7}$$

Writing out the first three components of Equation (21.7) gives

$$\begin{aligned} o'_x &= m_{00}o_x + m_{01}o_y + m_{02}o_z + m_{03}, \\ o'_y &= m_{10}o_x + m_{11}o_y + m_{12}o_z + m_{13}, \\ o'_z &= m_{20}o_x + m_{21}o_y + m_{22}o_z + m_{23}. \end{aligned} \tag{21.8}$$

The transformation of the ray direction does not involve translation, a fact that's handled very naturally in homogeneous coordinates, where directions can be represented by points with $W = 0$ (see the Further Reading section). Accordingly, we represent the ray direction as $d = [d_x \ d_y \ d_z \ 0]^T$ so that

$$d' = \begin{bmatrix} m_{00} & m_{01} & m_{02} & m_{03} \\ m_{10} & m_{11} & m_{12} & m_{13} \\ m_{20} & m_{21} & m_{22} & m_{23} \\ 0 & 0 & 0 & 1 \end{bmatrix} \begin{bmatrix} d_x \\ d_y \\ d_z \\ 0 \end{bmatrix}. \tag{21.9}$$

Writing out the components of Equation (21.9) gives

$$\begin{aligned} d'_x &= m_{00}d_x + m_{01}d_y + m_{02}d_z, \\ d'_y &= m_{10}d_x + m_{11}d_y + m_{12}d_z, \\ d'_z &= m_{20}d_x + m_{21}d_y + m_{22}d_z. \end{aligned} \tag{21.10}$$

21.1.3 Programming Aspects

You will need a `Matrix` class that implements a 4 × 4 matrix. The `Matrix` class in the skeleton ray tracer stores the matrix elements in a public 4 × 4 C array called `m`. To transform 3D points according to Equations (21.8), I've overloaded the * operator in a non-member function defined in the file **Point3D.cpp**. This function appears in Listing 21.1. Note that the second parameter is a `Point3D` reference, not a 4D point; the code simply implements Equations (21.8).

Listing 21.2 shows the code for transforming a vector according to Equations (21.10).

```
Point3D
operator* (const Matrix& mat, const Point3D& p) {
    return (Point3D(mat.m[0][0] * p.x + mat.m[0][1] * p.y + mat.m[0][2] * p.z +
            mat.m[0][3],
            mat.m[1][0] * p.x + mat.m[1][1] * p.y + mat.m[1][2] * p.z +
            mat.m[1][3],
            mat.m[2][0] * p.x + mat.m[2][1] * p.y + mat.m[2][2] * p.z +
            mat.m[2][3]));
}
```

Listing 21.1. The function operator* that transforms a 3D point.


```
Vector3D
operator* (const Matrix& mat, const Vector3D& v) {
    return (Point3D(mat.m[0][0] * v.x + mat.m[0][1] * v.y + mat.m[0][2] * v.z,
            mat.m[1][0] * v.x + mat.m[1][1] * v.y + mat.m[1][2] * v.z,
            mat.m[2][0] * v.x + mat.m[2][1] * v.y + mat.m[2][2] * v.z));
}
```

Listing 21.2. The function operator* that transforms a 3D vector. The function is in the file **Vector3D.cpp**.

21.1.4 Ray Intersection with Transformed Objects

The next step is to intersect the inverse transformed ray (21.4) with the untransformed object. Although this will often be a generic object, it could be any other type of object that's being transformed, for example, a compound object. After we've found the closest hit point p on the untransformed object, we need to find the corresponding hit point p' of the *original ray* with the *transformed object*. To do this, we use the following important property of the transformation process: if the closest hit point p of the inverse transformed ray with the untransformed object occurs at $t = t_0$, the closest hit point p' of the original ray with the transformed object occurs at the same value of t: $t = t_0$.

The proof is as follows. From Equations (21.4)–(21.6),

$$p = o' + t_0 d'$$
$$= T^{-1}o + t_0 T^{-1}d.$$

Multiplying both sides of this equation by T gives

$$Tp = TT^{-1}o + t_0 TT^{-1}d = o + t_0 d = p',$$

as required.

To find the hit point on the transformed object, we simply substitute t_0 into the original ray Equation (21.1).

21.1.5 Inverse of the Transformation Matrix

From the above calculations, it's clear that we need to compute the composite inverse transformation matrix for each transformed object. Fortunately, that's not difficult because of the structure of the inverse matrix as given by Equation (20.14), which is reproduced here:

$$T^{-1} = T_1^{-1} T_2^{-1} \cdots T_n^{-1}. \tag{21.11}$$

The inverse matrices for the individual transformations are all given in Section 20.5. You should compute the matrix (21.11) by multiplying the individual matrices on the right as each transformation is specified in a build function.

21.1.6 Example

The following is a simple example of a generic sphere that's scaled, rotated, and translated. Figure 21.2 illustrates the transformations, starting with the generic sphere on the left and ending with the ellipsoid on the right. Specifically, the sphere is scaled by 2 in the x-direction and 3 in the y-direction, rotated $-45°$ (clockwise) around the x-axis, and then translated 1 unit in the y-direction. Equation (21.12) shows the composite inverse transformation matrix that represents these transformations. Listing 21.7 demonstrates how these transformations can be specified in a build.

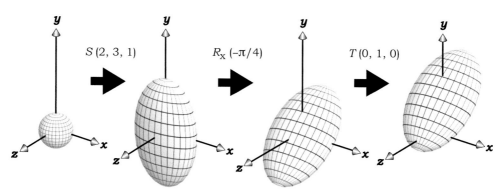

Figure 21.2. Affine transformations applied to a generic sphere.

$$T^{-1} = \begin{bmatrix} 1/2 & 0 & 0 & 0 \\ 0 & 1/3 & 0 & 0 \\ 0 & 0 & 1 & 0 \\ 0 & 0 & 0 & 1 \end{bmatrix} \begin{bmatrix} 1 & 0 & 0 & 0 \\ 0 & 1/\sqrt{2} & -1/\sqrt{2} & 0 \\ 0 & 1/\sqrt{2} & 1/\sqrt{2} & 0 \\ 0 & 0 & 0 & 1 \end{bmatrix} \begin{bmatrix} 1 & 0 & 0 & 0 \\ 0 & 1 & 0 & -1 \\ 0 & 0 & 1 & 0 \\ 0 & 0 & 0 & 1 \end{bmatrix}. \quad (21.12)$$

$$\underbrace{}_{\text{inverse scale}} \qquad \underbrace{}_{\text{inverse rotate}} \qquad \underbrace{}_{\text{inverse translate}}$$

21.2 Transforming Normals

21.2.1 Theory

For shading purposes, we need the normal at the hit point on the transformed object. Fortunately, there's a simple relationship between this normal and the normal at the hit point on the untransformed object. Although I'll just quote the result here, you can find the derivation in Foley et al. (1995), p. 217, and Shirley et al. (2005), Chapter 6.

Let n be the normal to the untransformed object at the intersection with the inverse transformed ray, as illustrated in Figure 21.3. The normal n' to the transformed object is given by

$$n' = T^{-T} n', \quad (21.13)$$

where $T^{-T} = (T^{-1})^{T}$ is the *transpose* of the inverse transformation matrix. The normal transforms in this way because it has to remain perpendicular to the object surface (see Figure 2.8).

Do we have to store the transpose of T^{-1} in addition to T^{-1}? No, because T^{-1} and T^{-T} store the same information; the transpose of T^{-1} is simply obtained

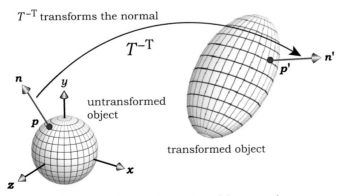

Figure 21.3. Transformation of the normal.

```
Normal
operator* (const Matrix& mat, const Normal& n) {
      return (Normal(   mat.m[0][0] * n.x + mat.m[1][0] * n.y + mat.m[2][0] * n.z,
             mat.m[0][1] * n.x + mat.m[1][1] * n.y + mat.m[2][1] * n.z,
             mat.m[0][2] * n.x + mat.m[1][2] * n.y + mat.m[2][2] * n.z));
}
```

Listing 21.3. The function `operator*` that transforms a normal. The function is in the file **Normal.cpp**.

by swapping the rows and columns. Since normals are directions, we can represent these in homogeneous coordinates with $W = 0$, in the same way that we represent vectors. Normals are also not affected by translation. For a given inverse transformation matrix T^{-1} and normal $n' = [\, n'_x \;\; n'_y \;\; n'_z \;\; 0\,]$ on the untransformed object, we can define the operation in Equation (21.13) by writing it in matrix form

$$
n = \begin{bmatrix} m_{00} & m_{01} & m_{02} & m_{03} \\ m_{10} & m_{11} & m_{12} & m_{13} \\ m_{20} & m_{21} & m_{22} & m_{23} \\ 0 & 0 & 0 & 1 \end{bmatrix}^{\mathrm{T}} \begin{bmatrix} n_x \\ n_y \\ n_z \\ 0 \end{bmatrix} = \begin{bmatrix} m_{00} & m_{10} & m_{20} & 0 \\ m_{01} & m_{11} & m_{21} & 0 \\ m_{02} & m_{12} & m_{22} & 0 \\ m_{03} & m_{13} & m_{23} & 1 \end{bmatrix} \begin{bmatrix} n_x \\ n_y \\ n_z \\ 0 \end{bmatrix}. \tag{21.14}
$$

Writing out the first three components of Equation (21.14) gives

$$
\begin{aligned}
n'_x &= m_{00}n_x + m_{10}n_y + m_{20}n_z, \\
n'_y &= m_{01}n_x + m_{11}n_y + m_{21}n_z, \\
n'_z &= m_{02}n_x + m_{12}n_y + m_{22}n_z.
\end{aligned} \tag{21.15}
$$

21.2.2 Programming Aspects

The function that implements the transformation equations (21.15) appears in Listing 21.3. Because the resulting normal will not be of unit length, you will have to normalize it. Listing 21.6 illustrates where you should do this.

21.3 Directly Transforming Objects

There are two ways to implement transformations. One is directly in the objects, where we store the inverse transformation matrix in the `GeometricObject` class and provide a set of transformation functions to construct the matrix. We also have to store a Boolean variable that's set to true when an object has been transformed.

This approach has a number of associated costs. The first is memory, as all objects then have to store the matrix whether they are transformed or not, and this requires 16 floats.[2] This can significantly increase the memory footprint for large scenes, with an attendant increase in render times if it slows memory access.

The second cost is in the object hit functions. Listing 21.4 shows the plane hit function from Listing 3.5, amended to handle transformations. Here, we have to test if the object has been transformed and, if it has, compute the inverse transformed ray. This test is also required before the normal is computed. These tests take time.

```
bool
Plane::hit(const Ray& ray, double& tmin, ShadeRec& sr) const {
    if (transformed) {
        ray.o = inv_matrix * ray.o;
        ray.d = inv_matrix * ray.d;
    }

    float t = (a - ray.o) * normal  / (ray.d * normal );

    if (t > kEpsilon) {
        tmin = t;

        if (transformed) {
            sr.normal = inv_matrix * normal ;
            sr.normal.normalize();
        }
        else
            sr.normal = normal ;

        sr.local_hit_point = ray.o + t * ray.d;

        return (true);
    }

    return (false);
}
```

Listing 21.4. Ray-plane hit function with affine transformations.

---

2. You could get by with 12 floats if you don't store the last row.

The third cost is programming effort because these tests and transformations have to be in the `hit` function and `shadow_hit` function of every object type.

 ## 21.4 Instancing

The second way to implement transformations is called *instancing*, and it avoids all of the above problems. To see what instancing is, consider an object that takes up a lot of memory, say a large triangle mesh with millions of triangles. Suppose we can only fit a few of these objects in memory, but we want to render a scene that contains a large number of them with different materials, locations, sizes, etc. We can do this by storing a single version of the object and constructing a number of *instance objects* that contain a pointer to the object, an inverse transformation matrix, and a material. We need a separate instance for each version of the object. Figure 21.4 shows an example where I've stored a single Stanford bunny but rendered it 64 times with different materials. I'll explain after Listing 21.6 how each bunny was rendered with a different material.

The above example demonstrates how instances can save memory for large objects, but the memory savings are broader than that because we don't have to store the matrix in the `GeometricObject` class. I've implemented

Figure 21.4. Sixty-four Stanford bunnies created by storing a single bunny and using instances.

instances in an `Instance` class that inherits from `GeometricObject` and can therefore have its own hit function where all of the transformation-specific code resides. This only has to be written once, and we don't have to change the hit functions of any other objects to implement instancing.

Listing 21.5 shows part of the declaration for the class `Instance`. The `transform_the_texture` data member is used to attach textures to transformed objects, as I'll explain in Chapter 29.

Listing 21.6 shows the `Instance` hit function. Although this is a short function, it performs a number of operations, some in subtle ways. You will need to study this function in conjunction with the functions `World::hit_objects` and `Compound::hit` because it can be called from these. In fact, this is the most connected function in the ray tracer. A couple of obvious facts are that it transforms a local copy of the ray, and it doesn't test that the object is transformed. It can't transform the ray parameter because that's `const`, and for good reason. If any hit function changed the ray, the functions `World::hit_objects`

```
class Instance: public GeometricObject {
    public:

        Instance(void);
        Instance(const Object* obj_ptr);
        ...


        virtual bool
        shadow_hit(const Ray& ray, double& tmin) const;

        virtual bool
        hit(const Ray& ray, double& tmin, ShadeRec& sr) const;

        void
        translate(const float dx, const float dy, const float dz);

        // other transformation functions

    private:

        GeometricObject* object_ptr;       // object to be transformed
        Matrix inv_matrix;                 // inverse transformation matrix
        bool transform_the_texture;        // do we transform the texture
};
```

Listing 21.5. Partial declaration of the class `Instance`.

```
bool
Instance::hit(const Ray& ray, float& t, ShadeRec& sr) const {

    Ray inv_ray(ray);
    inv_ray.o = inv_matrix * inv_ray.o;
    inv_ray.d = inv_matrix * inv_ray.d;

    if (object_ptr->hit(inv_ray, t, sr)) {
        sr.normal = inv_matrix * sr.normal;
        sr.normal.normalize();

        if (object_ptr->get_material())
            material_ptr = object_ptr->get_material();

        if (!transform_the_texture)
            sr.local_hit_point = ray.o + t * ray.d;

        return (true);
    }

    return (false);
}
```

Listing 21.6. The function `Instance::hit`.

and `Compound::hit` would not work; the same ray has to be tested against all objects. Something that may not be obvious is that operator * is overloaded in four ways. The first three are for transforming points, directions, and normals, as in Listings 21.1–21.3, respectively, and the fourth is for multiplying a vector by a `double` on the left.

What is not obvious is that the hit function is designed to work for arbitrarily nested instances, meaning that the stored object may be another instance. This is critical for modeling flexibility. When this happens, `Instance::hit` is called recursively until the object is untransformed.[3] The ray is progressively inverse transformed before each recursive call so that the most transformed ray is ultimately intersected with an untransformed object.

---

3. An untransformed compound object could still have transformed components, as the beveled cylinder discussed in Section 21.5 demonstrates. Any transformed components would trigger further recursive calls.

Instance::hit also has to return the unit normal on the *transformed* object through its ShadeRec parameter. The object_ptr->hit function returns the unit normal *n* on the untransformed object, and the normal (21.13) on the transformed object is then progressively built up with the statement sr.normal = inv_matrix * sr.normal as the recursion stack unwinds. I've normalized the normal at each level because the code doesn't keep track of the recursion depth and therefore has no way of knowing when it's at the top level.

The code

```
if (object_ptr->get_material())
    material_ptr = object_ptr->get_material();
```

may look strange, but it performs a critical task. Each instance object has access to at least two materials. In the simplest case, the object being transformed will store a single material. This could be a primitive or something much more complex, such as one of the bunnies in Figure 21.4. The instance object also inherits a material pointer from GeometricObject, which has to be assigned a material somewhere before the hit function returns. If this isn't done, the pointer will remain null, and the ray tracer could crash if it attempts to shade the transformed object. A simple guideline is as follows: If the build function assigns a material to the object being transformed, the instance hit function assigns this material to the instance material pointer. If the build function doesn't assign a material to the object, it must assign a material to the instance. In this case, each instance of an object can have a different material (see Exercise 21.4).

The instance hit function checks if the object's material pointer is not null before assigning it to its own material. It also correctly handles the case where the object being transformed is a compound object containing multiple materials. In this case, the Compound::hit function will return the correct material for the nearest primitive that the ray ultimately hits. A simple example is the multicolored ring in Figure 21.14, where each primitive component has its own material. A more complicated example is the bunnies in Figure 21.4, where the material for each triangle is not stored with the triangle but instead is stored in the grid.

In common with all hit functions, Instance::hit returns the minimum *t* value at the hit point when the ray hits the object. This is passed up the recursion stack without change.

I'll discuss how the texture statement works in Chapter 30, because that's most easily explained in a texturing context.

Listing 21.7 shows the build function for the ellipsoid on the right in Figure 21.2. Note the syntax used to construct the instance:

```
Instance* ellipsoid_ptr = new Instance(new Sphere);
```

This is the only statement that refers to the `Instance` class. The rendered result appears in Figure 21.5. Alternatively, you could construct a default instance object and set the object with an `Instance::set_object` function.

```
void
world::build(void) {
        vp.set_hres(400);
        vp.set_vres(400);
        vp.set_samples(16);

        tracer_ptr = new RayCast(this);

        Pinhole* camera_ptr = new Pinhole;
        camera_ptr->set_eye(100, 0, 100);
        camera_ptr->set_lookat(0, 1, 0);
        camera_ptr->set_vpd(8000);
        camera_ptr->compute_uvw();
        set_camera(camera_ptr);

        PointLight* light_ptr = new PointLight();
        light_ptr->set_location(50, 50, 1);
        light_ptr->scale_radiance(3.0);
        add_light(light_ptr);

        Phong* phong_ptr = new Phong;
        phong_ptr->set_cd(0.75);
        phong_ptr->set_ka(0.25);
        phong_ptr->set_kd(0.8);
        phong_ptr->set_ks(0.15);
        phong_ptr->set_exp(50);

        Instance* ellipsoid_ptr = new Instance(new Sphere);
        ellipsoid_ptr->set_material(phong_ptr);
        ellipsoid_ptr->scale(2, 3, 1);
        ellipsoid_ptr->rotate_x(-45);
        ellipsoid_ptr->translate(0, 1, 0);
        add_object(ellipsoid_ptr);
}
```

Listing 21.7. The build function for the ellipsoid in Figure 21.2.

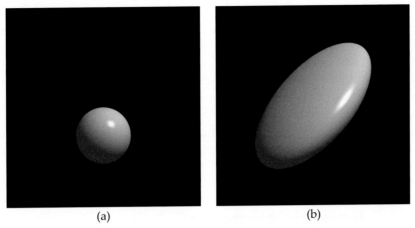

(a)   (b)

Figure 21.5. (a) Generic sphere; (b) ellipsoid constructed with the build function in Listing 21.7.

If an object constructor takes arguments, it can still be called with the instance constructor. For example:

```
Instance* box_ptr = new Instance (new Box(Point3D(-1, -1, -5), Point3D(1, 1, -3)));
```

As an example of the code that builds the inverse transformation matrix, Listing 21.8 shows the `Instance::translate` function. The other transformation functions are similar. The code in Listing 21.8 relies on the fact that the `Matrix` default constructor initializes a matrix to a unit matrix.

```
void
Instance::translate(const float dx, const float dy, const float dz) {

    Matrix inv_translation_matrix;        // temporary matrix

    inv_translation_matrix.m[0][3] = -dx;
    inv_translation_matrix.m[1][3] = -dy;
    inv_translation_matrix.m[2][3] = -dz;

    // post-multiply for inverse translation
    inv_matrix = inv_matrix * inv_translation_matrix;
}
```

Listing 21.8. The function `Instance::translate`.

To summarize: The benefits of using instances to transform objects are that object hit functions are simpler and run marginally faster and the transformation code only has to be written once. Objects are also smaller because the matrix is only stored in the instances. The disadvantages are that the transformed object hit functions are accessed through an additional indirection and the build-function syntax is slightly more complex.

At this stage, the `Instance` class is not complete, as we still have to deal with the issue of computing and storing the (forward) transformation matrix. I'll cover that in Chapter 22. The `Instance::hit` function is, however, in its final form.

21.5 Beveled Objects

Figure 21.6 shows three compound objects that we can model using the objects from Chapter 19 and transformations. Here, each object has been transformed.

Figure 21.7 shows *beveled* versions of these objects, where the sharp edges are now rounded. This is a more accurate way of modeling many common

Figure 21.6. Transformed compound objects.

Figure 21.7. Compound objects with beveling.

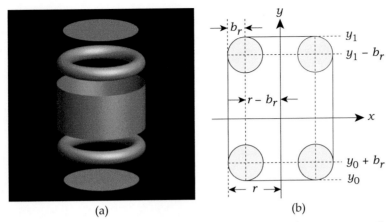

Figure 21.8. (a) Exploded view of a beveled cylinder, (b) how the components fit together.

objects, which often have rounded edges. The beveling also creates more interesting images because the bevels can show specular highlights.

Beveling is common in commercial modeling and rendering packages, where it's usually implemented using triangle meshes. In contrast, we have enough primitives at our disposal to model a number of parameterized beveled objects, such as those shown in Figure 21.7, without using triangles. Why discuss beveling here, and not in Chapter 19? The reason is that the *untransformed* versions of these beveled objects all contain *transformed* components.

The beveled cylinder is particularly simple to model, as the exploded view in Figure 21.8(a) indicates. We just add two tori to the solid cylinder from Chapter 19 and parameterize it with the minimum and maximum y values, the cylinder radius, and the bevel radius. Figure 21.8(b) shows how the parts fit together. Note that only a quarter of each torus is visible. The catch is that the tori have to be translated in the y direction.

Listing 21.9 shows a constructor for the `BeveledCylinder` class that illustrates how to construct the bevels. You should compare this with Listing 19.14 for the solid cylinder.

The beveled box is by far the most complex object in Figure 21.7, with 26 components: eight spheres, six rectangles, and 12 open cylinders. The use of a bounding box considerably speeds the rendering of this object. See Listing 19.15 for an example of how to do this.

Finally, Figure 21.9(a) shows three examples of a beveled wedge object. This is the most complex beveled object in the collection, with 30 primitives: eight spheres, eight open cylinders, two part cylinders, four part tori, two rect-

```
BeveledCylinder::BeveledCylinder(const float bottom,
        const float    top,
        const float    radius,
        const float    bevel_radius)
        : Compound() {
    objects.push_back(new Disk(Point3D(0, bottom, 0),           // bottom
            Normal(0, -1, 0),
            radius - bevel_radius));

    objects.push_back(new Disk(Point3D(0, top, 0),              // top
            Normal(0, 1, 0),
            radius - bevel_radius));

    objects.push_back(new OpenCylinder(bottom + bevel_radius,   // vertical wall
            top - bevel_radius,
            radius));

    Instance* bottom_bevel_ptr = new Instance(new Torus(radius - bevel_radius,
                                        bevel_radius));
    bottom_bevel_ptr->translate(0, bottom + bevel_radius, 0);
    objects.push_back(bottom_bevel_ptr);

    Instance* top_bevel_ptr = new Instance(new Torus(radius - bevel_radius,
                                        bevel_radius));
    top_bevel_ptr->translate(0, top - bevel_radius, 0);
    objects.push_back(top_bevel_ptr);
}
```

Listing 21.9. A parameterized constructor for the BeveledCylinder class.

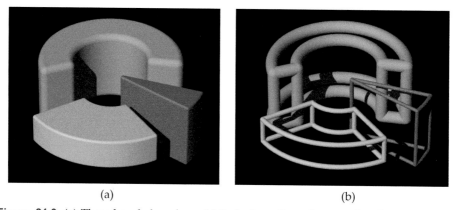

(a)   (b)

Figure 21.9. (a) Three beveled wedges; (b) "wireframe" versions rendered using only the spheres, open cylinders, and tori.

angles, and six part annuli. Figure 21.9(b) shows the same objects as in Figure 21.9(a) with part of their outer surfaces removed.

Figure 21.10 shows a top-down view of a beveled wedge. The parameters are the y extents y_0, y_1, the inner and outer radii r_0, r_1, the minimum and maximum azimuth angles ϕ_0, ϕ_1, and the bevel radius b_r. The bevel radius is the common radius of the spheres, open cylinders, and part tori. The beveled wedge class is on the book's website.

There are a number of restrictions on the parameters: we must have $r_1 > r_0 > 0$ with minimum separations between 0, r_0, and r_1 that depend on the other parameters, particularly b_r; similarly, we must have $y_1 > y_0$ and $0° < \phi_0 < \phi_1 < 360°$ with minimum separations. Setting $\phi_0 = 0°$ and $\phi_1 = 360°$ will not result in a beveled thick ring like the one illustrated in Figure 21.7 (see Figure 21.17).

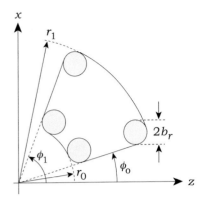

Figure 21.10. Beveled-wedge parameters in the (x, z) plane.

In spite of these limitations, the beveled wedge is a most useful modeling object, particularly for architecture. Figure 21.11 shows two examples using noise-based textures from Chapter 31. Figure 21.11(a) is a rosette rendered with marble; Figure 21.11(b) is a wall with an archway rendered with marble and sandstone. The beveled wedges in these figures were stored in grids to improve the rendering times. Because of their complexity, a tight bounding box is critical for reasonable rendering times, particularly when large numbers of the wedges are stored in a grid. A trivial bounding box is $p_0 = (-r_1, y_0, -r_1)$, $p_1 = (r_1, y_1, r_1)$, and it's also possible to compute a reasonably tight bounding box

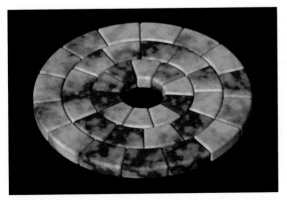

Figure 21.11. (a) A rosette modeled with beveled wedges; (b) a wall with an archway modeled with beveled wedges and beveled boxes.

when $r_1 - r_0 \ll r_1$ and $\phi_1 - \phi_0 \ll 360°$. The complete BeveledWedge class is on the book's website.

 # Further Reading

Hill (1990) was the first general graphics textbook to discuss transformations in ray tracing but used 3×3 matrices to represent scaling, rotation, reflection, and shearing and a vector to represent translation. The most recent edition of Hill and Kelley (2006) uses 4×4 matrices. Wilt (1994) has transformations in the code as 4×4 matrices but doesn't appear to discuss them in the text. Shirley and Morley (2003) discusses transformations the way I've implemented them using instancing. The main difference between the two implementations is that they use a single class for vectors, points, and normals. The first edition of this book, Shirley (2000), was the inspiration for my use of instances.

 # Notes and Discussion

The Instance Hit Function

I wish I could say that I wrote the Instance::hit function in one go, but I didn't. This function evolved over several years as I added features to the ray tracer that it couldn't handle. The part that gave me the most trouble was the if statement for transforming the texture. I'll discuss this in Chapter 30.

Transformation Code

You will need to perform transformations on textures as well as geometric objects, and you may also want to transform the camera. With the current architecture, you will end up with repeated transformation code. A possible way to avoid this is to provide a *transforms* class whose objects can provide transformation services to other objects. This could encapsulate all of the transformations code in one place, but before you try this, you need to read Chapter 22. As it turns out, not all objects require the same transformation code. Instances need extra code in their transformation functions so that we can place transformed objects in grids. Textures and bump maps don't need this extra code. There's also the issue of transforming area lights with their sample points (see Exercise 21.15).

Important Point

Transforming the direction with Equations (21.10) can result in a ray direction that is not a unit vector when the inverse transformed ray is intersected with the object in the function `Instance::hit`. This is why you should not assume that the ray direction is a unit vector in any hit function.

Questions

21.1. Which transformations can change the length of the ray direction?

21.2. Which transformations can change the length of the normal?

21.3. The last statement in Listing 21.8 is `inv_matrix = inv_matrix * inv_translation_matrix;`. Suppose this were the *first* transformation that you applied to an object. What should the matrix `inv_matrix` be on the right-hand side of the assignment? How can you make sure it will always be this matrix in this situation? Is this question relevant to the other transformations?

21.4. The middle beveled cylinder in Figure 21.12 was constructed to be twice the height of the left cylinder. The right cylinder was constructed to be the same height as the left cylinder and was then scaled by a factor of two in the y-direction. Why is this different from the middle cylinder? The bevel radius is the same for all cylinders.

21.5. Figure 21.13 shows a nice speckled sphere with holes, except that it's not really a sphere. It's a beveled cylinder with $y_0 = -1$, $y_1 = 1$, radius = 1, and bevel radius = 1. Can you explain what has happened?

Figure 21.12. Three beveled cylinders.

Figure 21.13. A speckled sphere. Notice the shadow visible through the sphere and the speckles of light in the shadow.

 Exercises

21.1. Implement instances and test your code with the ellipsoid in Figure 21.5.

21.2. Figure 21.14 shows a multicolored thick ring that has been rotated and translated, using a nested instance object. See the build-function code fragment in Listing 21.10. Use this as a further test of your `Instance` class. The complete build function is on the book's website.

Figure 21.14. Transformed multicolored ring with shadows.

```
Instance* rotated_ring_ptr = new Instance(ring_ptr);
rotated_ring_ptr->rotate_z(-45);

Instance* translated_ring_ptr = new Instance(rotated_ring_ptr);
translated_ring_ptr->translate(1, 0, 0);
add_object(translated_ring_ptr);
```

Listing 21.10. Code fragment from the build function for Figure 21.14.

21.3. Write the function `Instance::shadow_hit` and test that shadows work correctly with instances. You can use Figure 21.14 for testing purposes because the ring: casts a shadow on the plane, self-shadows, and has a shadow cast on it by the sphere.

21.4. Figure 21.15 shows 25 randomly colored ellipsoids constructed from a single generic sphere. Use this image to test the ability of the `Instance` class to create multiple transformed objects with different materials. Although I have seeded `rand` to generate these ellipsoids, you may get different colors and shapes.

21.5. Apply further transformations to the ellipsoid in Figure 21.5 but, as always, be careful with their order.

21.6. Figures 19.27(b) and 19.28(b) show a generic hemispherical bowl with a rounded rim. If you have implemented this, the simplest way to render this type of bowl in arbitrary locations, etc., is to use instances to transform it. Experiment with this.

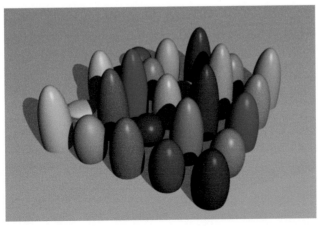

Figure 21.15. Ellipsoids generated from a single generic sphere, which is not rendered.

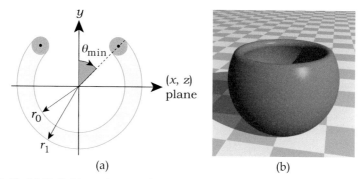

(a)   (b)

Figure 21.16. (a) Definition of a round-rimmed bowl; (b) rendered bowl with an opening angle of 120°.

21.7. Figure 21.16(a) shows the definition of a slightly more general round-rimmed bowl that has an arbitrary opening angle at the top. It consists of a translated torus for the rim and two part spheres centered on the origin. The simplest way to specify the opening angle is to use θ_{min}, as indicated in Figure 21.16(a), because then θ_{min} is also the minimum polar angle for the part spheres, as illustrated in Figure 19.18(a). The actual opening angle will be smaller than this because half of the torus is inside the cone defined by the y-axis and θ_{min}, but that's not as easy to work with.

To model the rim, we start with a generic torus with parameters

$$a = [(r_1 + r_2)/2] \sin \theta_{min},$$
$$b = (r_2 - r_1)/2$$

and translate it by $[(r_1 + r_2)/2] \cos \theta_{min}$ in the y-direction.

Part of the rim and the outer part sphere will be components of a spherical fishbowl, to be discussed in Chapter 28. Implement this bowl and use Figure 21.16(b) to test it. Note the apparent anomalous specular highlight shading when the highlight on the sphere hits the torus. This is correct, but try to work out why it happens. Here are some hints. The curvature of the torus is quite different from the curvature of the sphere, and the specular highlights are a different shape. You can see this from the specular highlight on the back of the rim. Render the bowl without the outer sphere. Also, render the bowl with its center, the eye point, and the (point) light location in a straight line and note how the anomalous shading disappears.

21.8. Implement the objects in Figure 21.6 and render this scene.

21.9. Implement the beveled objects in Figure 21.7 and render this scene. Experiment with different parameters, for example, the bevel radii.

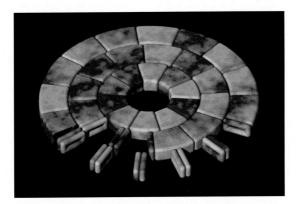

Figure 21.17. The result of adding offsets to the ϕ_0 angles in the outer two rings.

Implement bounding boxes for these beveled objects and compare the rendering speeds.

21.10. Get the beveled wedge object running in your ray tracer and test it with Figure 21.9(a).

21.11. Reproduce the rosette and archway images in Figure 21.11.

21.12. If you look closely at the rosette in Figure 21.11(a), you'll notice that the radial edges of several wedges line up. The reasons are as follows. Three edges line up on the left because the first wedge in each ring starts with $\phi_0 = 0$. Other edges line up because the number of wedges in each ring must divide 360 a whole number of times, and there's not a huge choice of numbers to pick from. From the inner to the outer ring, I've used 10, 12, and 15 wedges. You may think that a simple way to prevent this alignment would be to add an offset to ϕ_0 in each ring, which rotates the wedges around the y-axis, but this will not work. Figure 21.17 shows the results of using offsets of zero for the inner ring, 63° for the middle ring, and 126° for the outer ring. What has happened here? Why are some parts of the wedges rendered and not others? Can you think of a solution?

21.13. Put mortar between the wedges and blocks in the rosette, the archway, and the wall in Figure 21.11.

21.14. Use beveled wedges and beveled boxes to produce some nice images of your own. A medieval castle would look good.

21.15. Implement a technique that will allow you to transform area lights. The instance mechanism described here will allow you to transform the area light objects but not the sample points on them.

22 Regular Grids

22.1 Description
22.2 Construction
22.3 Traversal
22.4 Testing
22.5 Grids and Transformed Objects
22.6 Comparison with BVHs

 Objectives

By the end of this chapter, you should:

- understand how regular-grid acceleration schemes work;
- appreciate the speed-up factors they can achieve;
- know how to place transformed objects in grids;
- have implemented a regular grid.

In previous chapters, I emphasized the importance of writing simple, efficient code, particularly in the hit functions. In Chapter 19, I discussed bounding boxes as a technique for accelerating the intersection of objects with complex hit functions. Despite this, the current ray tracer is still hopelessly inefficient for ray tracing large numbers of objects, the reason being that each ray is intersected with each object. This is known as *exhaustive ray tracing* where the rendering time is proportional to the number of objects in the scene.

A number of acceleration techniques have been developed that can dramatically reduce the rendering times for large numbers of objects by dramatically reducing the number of objects that each ray has to intersect. Common techniques use bounding volume hierarchies (BVHs), octrees, binary space partition (BSP) trees, kd-trees, and regular grids (see the Further Reading section).

Without using one of these techniques, it's not feasible to ray trace large numbers of objects. All commercial ray tracers incorporate an acceleration scheme, otherwise they would not be useful in a commercial context, where complex scenes, often containing millions of objects, are the norm.

I'll discuss regular grids here because of their conceptual simplicity, excellent performance, robustness, and their ability to handle rays that start inside them with little extra programming effort.

22.1 Description

The following is a short description of what a regular grid is and how it works. A regular grid has the shape of an axis-aligned box that contains a group of objects. Figure 22.1(a) illustrates the idea in 2D. The box is subdivided into a number of *cells* that also have the shape of an axis-aligned box and are all the same size. Essentially, a regular grid is a spatial subdivision scheme that divides part of world space into a regular 3D cellular structure, hence the name. Roughly speaking, each cell stores a list of the objects that are in it, or partly in it, or may be in it.

A ray that hits the grid only passes through certain cells, (shown shaded in Figure 22.1(b)), and is only intersected with the objects in these cells. This can save a lot of time, particularly when there are a large number of objects in the grid, as the ray will only be intersected with a small fraction of the objects.

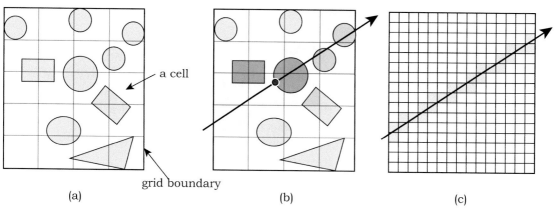

(a)   (b)   (c)

Figure 22.1. (a) 2D grid with objects, boundary, and cells; (b) a ray that passes through the grid hits the large dark sphere, as indicated by the red dot; (c) with a finer grid structure, the savings are more evident.

The situation is, however, better than that. The cells are tested strictly in the order that the ray traverses them as t increases. This means, roughly speaking again, that the first object that the ray hits is the nearest one, and the process then stops for that ray. This is the large sphere in Figure 22.1(b). The savings are better illustrated when there are more cells, as in Figure 22.1(c), and, of course, the savings are even higher in 3D.

For a scene with a large number n of objects, a grid will have $O(\sqrt[3]{n})$ cells in each direction, and rays will therefore be intersected with $O(\sqrt[3]{n})$ objects. That's the worst-case scenario, however, where the rays traverse the whole grid. For densely packed objects such as the spheres in Section 22.4.3, where the rays don't penetrate far into the grid, the number of objects intersected can be closer to $O(\log n)$ (see Table 22.2). The same situation applies to the hierarchical grids in Section 23.5. These types of asymptotic time complexities are a unique advantage that ray tracing has over algorithms whose render times are always proportional to n.

 ## 22.2 Construction

To construct a grid, we have to perform the following three tasks:

1. add the objects;
2. compute the bounding box;
3. set up the cells.

Grids are geometric objects so that they can be intersected like any other object; they can also be nested—an important modeling characteristic. They also inherit from Compound, for two reasons. First, grids *are* compound objects because they consist of more than one component. Second, when we add objects to a grid, we need a temporary place to store them before we set up the cells; the Compound::objects data structure is convenient for this and simplifies the grid implementation. For example, it has code for assigning the same material to each object in the grid. Listing 22.1 shows a simplified declaration of the class.[1]

Adding an object to a grid is simple, as the following example shows. If we have the statement

```
Grid* grid_ptr = new Grid;
```

---

1. I'll add other data members and member functions in Chapter 23 to handle triangle meshes.

```
class Grid: public Compound {
    public:

        Grid(void);

        // other constructors, etc.

        virtual BBox
        get_bounding_box(void);

        void
        setup_cells(void);

        virtual bool
        hit(Ray& ray, float& tmin, Shading& s);

        virtual bool
        shadow_hit(Ray& ray, float& tmin);

    private:

        vector<GeometricObject*> cells;   // cells are stored in a 1D array
        BBox bbox;              // bounding box
        int nx, ny, nz;         // number of cells in the x-, y-, and z-directions

        Point3D               // compute minimum grid coordinates
        min_coordinates(void);

        Point3D               // compute maximum grid coordinates
        max_coordinates(void);
};
```

Listing 22.1. Declaration of the class `Grid`.

in a build function and have constructed a sphere called `sphere_ptr`, we use
the statement

```
grid_ptr->add_object(sphere_ptr);
```

Here, `add_object` is inherited from `Compound` and adds the sphere pointer to
the `Compound::objects` array.

To help illustrate how we compute the grid's bounding box, Figure 22.2(a)
shows the objects from Figure 22.1 with their bounding boxes. The grid's bounding box is the union of the bounding boxes of the objects, as Figure 22.2(b)

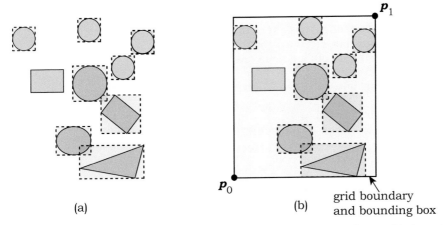

Figure 22.2. (a) Objects to be placed in a grid with their bounding boxes; (b) the grid's bounding box.

illustrates. This also defines the grid's dimensions in the x-, y-, and z-directions because of its axis-aligned box shape.

The code for computing p_0 and p_1 is simple and is in the functions `min_coordinates` and `max_coordinates`, which are called from the `setup_cells` function. These points do not have to be stored in the grid. Listing 22.2 shows the code for `get_min_coordinates`, where `kEpsilon` is subtracted from the coordinates to make the grid slightly larger than the union of the objects' bounding boxes. The function `get_max_coordinates` is analogous (see Question 22.6).

The next step is to divide the grid into the cells, which should be as cubical in shape as possible for intersection efficiency. We also have to consider how many cells to use. Although the cells are critical to the operation of the grid, they don't need to be constructed or stored as separate objects. Instead, I'll simulate them by indexing the 1D array of object pointers called `cells` in Listing 22.1.

Let n_x, n_y, and n_z be the number of cells in the x_w-, y_w-, and z_w-directions, respectively, let w_x, w_y, and w_z be the dimensions of the grid, and let n be the number of objects to be placed in the grid. The following expressions, which are similar to those in Shirley (2000), can be used to calculate n_x, n_y, and n_z so that the cells are roughly cubical:

$$s = (w_x w_y w_z / n)^{1/3},$$
$$n_x = \text{trunc}\,(m w_x / s) + 1,$$
$$n_y = \text{trunc}\,(m w_y / s) + 1,$$
$$n_z = \text{trunc}\,(m w_z / s) + 1.$$

$$(22.1)$$

```
Point3D
Grid::min_coordinates(void) {
    BBox bbox;
    Point3D p0(kHugeValue);

    int num_objects = objects.size();

    for (int j = 0; j < num_objects; j++) {
        bbox = objects[j]->get_bounding_box();

        if (bbox.x0 < p0.x)
            p0.x = bbox.x0;
        if (bbox.y0 < p0.y)
            p0.y = bbox.y0;
        if (bbox.z0 < p0.z)
            p0.z = bbox.z0;
    }

    p0.x -= kEpsilon; p0.y -= kEpsilon;, p0.z -= kEpsilon;

    return (p0);
}
```

Listing 22.2. The function `Grid::min_coordinates`.

Here, m is a multiplying factor that allows us to vary the number of cells. The + 1 in the formulae guarantees that the number of cells in any direction is never zero. From Equations (22.1), the total number of cells $n_x n_y n_z$ is approximately $m^3 n$, provided $n_x \gg 1$, $n_y \gg 1$, and $n_z \gg 1$, which is usually the case. When $m = 1$, the number of cells is approximately equal to the number of objects, but that's usually not the best value to use. If we have too many cells, the ray tracer wastes time testing for object intersections in empty cells, but if there are too few cells, it intersects too many objects. In the limit of a single cell ($n_x = n_y = n_z = 1$), we essentially don't have a grid, and there is no speed-up. Grids seem to have a sweet spot when there are about 8–10 times more cells than objects, because that's when they are most efficient. By default, I use a factor of 8, which corresponds to $m = 2$. You should experiment with different values of m and compare the render speeds (see Exercises 22.5 and 22.6). The expressions (22.1) are easily translated into code, as Listing 22.4 shows.

Now to the indexing. According to Listing 22.1, the cells are represented by

$$\text{vector<GeometricObject*>} \quad \text{cells;} \tag{22.2}$$

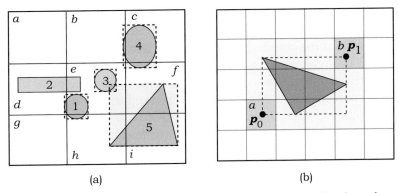

Figure 22.3. (a) Cells and objects; (b) cells overlapped by the bounding box of an object.

which is a 1D array of length $n_x n_y n_z$. The index of the (i_x, i_y, i_z) cell is

$$\text{index} = i_x + n_x i_y + n_x n_y i_z, \tag{22.3}$$

which is the standard way that C and C++ programs store "3D" data structures in 1D arrays.

I place the objects into the cells by storing, for each cell, a "list" of all objects whose bounding boxes overlap the cell. The list will be empty if no bounding boxes overlap a cell, but the fact that the bounding box of an object overlaps a cell doesn't mean that any part of the object is inside the cell. Figure 22.3(a) illustrates some of the possibilities for five objects and nine cells.

Table 22.1 lists the cells and their contents. Notice how objects 1, 2, 4, and 5 are in more than one cell.

Cell	Objects
a	empty
b	4
c	4
d	1 and 2
e	1, 2, 3, 4, 5, but only 1, 2, and 3 are actually in the cell
f	4 and 5
g	1, but object 1 is not in the cell
h	1 and 5
i	5

Table 22.1. The cells in Figure 22.3(a) and their contents.

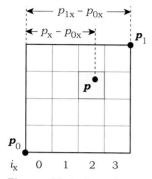

Figure 22.4. A grid with four cells in the x-direction and a point p for which we wish to calculate the x cell index.

To discover which cells an object must be added to, we first compute the cells that contain the minimum and maximum corners of the object's bounding box. Figure 22.3(b) illustrates this for a triangle, where p_0 and p_1 are in the cells labeled a and b, respectively. We need to compute which grid cell a given point p in world coordinates lies in. The cells are indexed with integers in the ranges $(i_x, i_y, i_z) \in [0, n_x - 1] \times [0, n_y - 1] \times [0, n_z - 1]$. Figure 22.4 shows a grid with four cells in the x-direction indexed with $i_x \in [0, 3]$, where p_0 and p_1 are the opposite corners of the grid. This figure also shows the distance $p_x - p_{0x}$ between p and p_0 in the x-direction and the grid extent $p_{1x} - p_{0x}$ in the x-direction.

If we compute the ratio of these distances, multiply it by n_x, and truncate the result to an integer, we almost have what we need:

$$f(p_x) = (p_x - p_{0x})/(p_{1x} - p_{0x}) \in [0.0, 1.0], \qquad (22.4)$$
$$i_x = \left\lfloor n_x f(p_x) \right\rfloor \in [0, n_x].$$

For $n_x = 4$, this produces the integer-valued step function in Figure 22.5(a).

The problem is that the point p can, and will, be located on any face of the grid's bounding box. The negative face, where $p_x = p_{0x}$, isn't a problem because small negative values of the right-hand side resulting from round-off errors are truncated to zero. The problem lies with the positive face where $p_x = p_{1x}$. Here, values of the right-hand side that are ≥ 1.0 return n_x, which is out of range. We could fix this by adding an if statement

$$\text{if } (i_x = n_x)$$
$$i_x = n_x - 1,$$

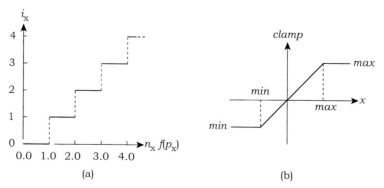

Figure 22.5. (a) The graph of i_x from Equation (22.4) for $n_x = 4$; (b) the graph of the clamp function from Listing 22.3.

```
inline float
clamp(float x, float min, float max) {
    return (x < min ? min : (x > max ? max : x));
}
```

Listing 22.3. The clamp function.

but it can be fixed more generally by using the clamp function in Listing 22.3. This clamps the first parameter between the last two parameters, using linear interpolation to join the minimum and maximum values. Its graph is in Figure 22.5(b). As this is a utility function, it is in the file **Maths.h**.

I call clamp six times with max = $n_x - 1$ to insert each object in the grid, truncating its output to an integer (see Listing 22.4).

The final construction step is to add each object to the cells that its bounding box overlaps. Figure 22.3(b) illustrates this in 2D for a triangle, where the bounding rectangle overlaps the light gray cells. The representation (22.2) of storing an object pointer in each cell is not the only representation that we can use. Exercise 22.7 covers two alternatives. I use (22.2) because it has a small memory footprint and runs the fastest on my computer. It does, however, have the most complicated code for inserting the objects into the cells because each cell will need to have one of the following types of information stored in it:

- the null pointer if there are no objects;
- an object pointer if there is one object;
- a compound-object pointer if there is more than one object.

As a result, the code needs to keep track of how many objects are in each cell, for which I use a temporary array. Listing 22.4 shows the function Grid:: setup_cells. This function is called from each build function that constructs a grid but only after all of the objects have been added to the grid. Listing 22.8 is an example of a build function that does this.

```
void
Grid::setup_cells(void) {
    // find the minimum and maximum coordinates of the grid

    Point3D p0 = min_coordinates();
    Point3D p1 = max_coordinates();
```

Listing 22.4. Code for storing objects in cells.

```
// store them in the bounding box

bbox.x0 = p0.x; bbox.y0 = p0.y; bbox.z0 = p0.z;
bbox.x1 = p1.x; bbox.y1 = p1.y; bbox.z1 = p1.z;

// compute the number of cells in the x-, y-, and z-directions

int num_objects = objects.size();
float wx = p1.x - p0.x;           // grid extent in x-direction
float wy = p1.y - p0.y;           // grid extent in y-direction
float wz = p1.z - p0.z;           // grid extent in z-direction
float multiplier = 2.0;           // about 8 times more cells than objects
float s = pow(wx * wy * wz / num_objects, 0.3333333);
nx = multiplier * wx / s + 1;
ny = multiplier * wy / s + 1;
nz = multiplier * wz / s + 1;

// set up the array of cells with null pointers

int num_cells = nx * ny * nz;
cells.reserve(num_objects);

for (int j = 0; j < num_cells; j++)
    cells.push_back(NULL);

// set up a temporary array to hold the number of objects stored in each cell

vector<int> counts;
counts.reserve(num_cells);

for (int j = 0; j < num_cells; j++)
    counts.push_back(0);

// put objects into the cells

BBox obj_bbox;      // object's bounding box
int index;          // cells array index

for (int j = 0; j < num_objects; j++) {
    obj_bbox =  objects[j]->get_bounding_box();

    // compute the cell indices for the corners of the bounding box of the
    // object

    int ixmin = clamp((obj_bbox.x0 - p0.x) * nx / (p1.x - p0.x), 0, nx - 1);
```

Listing 22.4 (continued). Code for storing objects in cells.

```
int iymin = clamp((obj_bbox.y0 - p0.y) * ny / (p1.y - p0.y), 0, ny - 1);
int izmin = clamp((obj_bbox.z0 - p0.z) * nz / (p1.z - p0.z), 0, nz - 1);
int ixmax = clamp((obj_bbox.x1 - p0.x) * nx / (p1.x - p0.x), 0, nx - 1);
int iymax = clamp((obj_bbox.y1 - p0.y) * ny / (p1.y - p0.y), 0, ny - 1);
int izmax = clamp((obj_bbox.z1 - p0.z) * nz / (p1.z - p0.z), 0, nz - 1);

// add the object to the cells

for (int iz = izmin; iz <= izmax; iz++            // cells in z direction
    for (int iy = iymin; iy <= iymax; iy++)    // cells in y direction
        for (int ix = ixmin; ix <= ixmax; ix++) {    // cells in x
                                                     // direction
            index = ix + nx * iy + nx * ny * iz;

            if (counts[index] == 0) {
                cells[index] = objects[j];
                counts[index] += 1;        index = 1
            }
            else {
                if (counts[index] == 1) {
                    // construct a compound object
                    Compound* compound_ptr = new Compound;
                    // add the object already in cell
                    compound_ptr->add_object(cells[index]);
                    // add the new object
                    compound_ptr->add_object(objects[j]);

                    // store compound in current cell
                    cells[index] = compound_ptr;
                    // index = 2
                    counts[index] += 1;
                }
                else {                // counts[index] > 1
                    // just add current object
                    cells[index]->add_object(objects[j]);

                    // for statistics only
                    counts[index] += 1;
                }
            }
        }
    }
}
```

Listing 22.4 (continued). Code for storing objects in cells.

```
// erase Compound::Objects, but don't delete the objects

objects.erase (objects.begin(), objects.end());

// code for statistics on cell objects counts can go in here

// erase the temporary counts vector

counts.erase (counts.begin(), counts.end());
}
```

Listing 22.4 (continued). Code for storing objects in cells.

 ## 22.3 Traversal

As the grid has a long hit function, it's worthwhile looking at this in stages. The following is top-level pseudocode.

```
if the ray misses the grid's bounding box
    return false

if the ray starts inside the grid
    find the cell that contains the ray origin
else
    find the cell where the ray hits the grid from the
        outside

traverse the grid
```

Testing the ray for intersection with the bounding box at the start of the hit function isn't just an efficiency measure. The minimum and maximum t values in the x-, y-, and z-directions that are computed in the process are used in the subsequent traversal code. This prevents us from just calling the bounding-box hit function in Listing 19.1, as it doesn't return these values.

The hit function must be able to handle rays that start inside or outside the grid. Even with ray casting, we can put the camera inside the grid, and all the primary rays will then start inside. Shadow rays with any type of ray tracing also start inside the grid when we shade the objects in the grid. Finding the cell from which to start the traversal process is a simple application of the clamp function, as the code in Listing 22.5 shows. This is taken from the hit function, where ox, oy, and oz are the ray-origin coordinates, x0, y0 ... z1 are

```
int ix, iy, iz;

if (bbox.inside(ray.o)) {
        ix = clamp((ox - x0) * nx / (x1 - x0), 0, nx - 1);
        iy = clamp((oy - y0) * ny / (y1 - y0), 0, ny - 1);
        iz = clamp((oz - z0) * nz / (z1 - z0), 0, nz - 1);
}
else {
        Point3D p = ray.o + t0 * ray.d;
        ix = clamp((p.x - x0) * nx / (x1 - x0), 0, nx - 1);
        iy = clamp((p.y - y0) * ny / (y1 - y0), 0, ny - 1);
        iz = clamp((p.z - z0) * nz / (z1 - z0), 0, nz - 1);
}
```

Listing 22.5. Code fragment from `Grid::hit`.

the grid's bounding-box vertices, and `t0` is the t value where the ray hits the bounding box.

The following is an example of how the ray can traverse the grid after hitting it from the outside. Figure 22.6(a) shows a ray that hits the cell labeled a. We test if the ray hits any objects in this cell, but since it's empty, we proceed to test the other cells that the ray passes through, in the order of increasing t. The next two are the cells b and c. This process of stepping the ray through the grid is analogous to Bresenham's classic algorithm for scan-converting lines (Bresenham, 1965, see also Foley et al., 1995). In this context, the technique is known as a 3D digital differential analyzer (3DDDA) and was developed by Fujimoto et al. (1986). In Figure 22.6(a), the ray is tested for intersection with

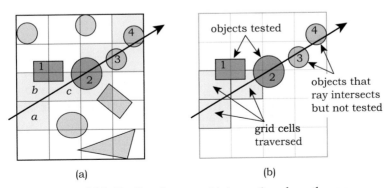

Figure 22.6. Finding the nearest intersection along the ray.

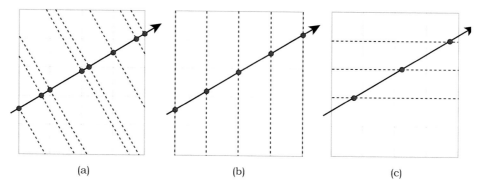

(a)   (b)   (c)

Figure 22.7. Intersections with the cell boundaries are equally spaced in the x-, y-, and z-directions.

the box 1 in cell b, which it misses, and then again in cell c, which it misses again. The ray is also tested with the sphere 2 in cell c, which it hits.

That is the end of the process as far as this ray is concerned; *by construction*, the hit point on object 2 is the closest hit point of all objects along the ray.

Although the ray passes through objects 3 and 4, these are not tested for intersection because of the intersection with the sphere 2. The other objects in the grid are also not tested (see Figure 22.6(b)).

To step a ray through the grid, we use the following astute observation by Amanatides and Woo (1987). Even though the intersections of the ray with the cell faces are unequally spaced along the ray, as indicated in Figure 22.7(a), the intersections in the x-, y-, and z-directions are equally spaced, as Figure 22.7(b) and (c) demonstrate. This simplifies the code, because it allows us to compute the ray parameter increments across the cells in the x-, y-, and z-directions. For a single cell, these are

$$dt_x = (t_{xmax} - t_{xmin})/n_x,$$
$$dt_y = (t_{ymax} - t_{ymin})/n_y,$$
$$dt_z = (t_{zmax} - t_{zmin})/n_z.$$

To simplify the following discussion, I'll consider a ray traveling in the positive x- and y-directions in a 2D grid. For each cell, we have to work out if the next cell that the ray passes through is one across in the x-direction or one up in the y-direction. Figure 22.8 illustrates two configurations where the current cell is dark-shaded and the ray has entered it on an x (vertical) face. It could alternatively enter on a y face and have any positive gradient.

If t_0 is the ray parameter where the ray enters the current cell, we compute t_{xnext}, the t value where it hits the next x face, and t_{ynext}, where it hits the

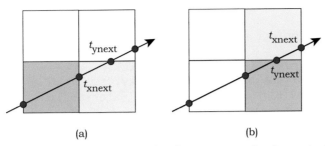

(a)   (b)

Figure 22.8. At each cell, we have to decide to go across for the next cell, or up.

next y face. If $t_{xnext} < t_{ynext}$, we go across, as in Figure 22.8(a); otherwise, we go up, as in Figure 22.8(b). To incorporate this into a working algorithm, we have to do the following:

1. compute t_{xnext} and t_{ynext} for the initial cell;
2. specify a condition to terminate the algorithm;
3. step the ray though the grid.

Listing 22.6 is the code for Steps 1 and 2 (in 3D), where the initial cell coordinates ix, iy and iz have been computed by the code in Listing 22.5. The

```
float dtx = (tx_max - tx_min) / nx;
float dty = (ty_max - ty_min) / ny;
float dtz = (tz_max - tz_min) / nz;

float tx_next, ty_next, tz_next;
int ix_step, iy_step, iz_step;
int ix_stop, iy_stop, iz_stop;

tx_next = tx_min + (ix + 1) * dtx;
ix_step = +1;
ix_stop = nx;

ty_next = ty_min + (iy + 1) * dty;
iy_step = +1;
iy_stop = ny;

tz_next = tz_min + (iz + 1) * dtz;
iz_step = +1;
iz_stop = nz;
```

Listing 22.6. Set-up code for grid traversal.

```
while (true) {
    GeometricObject* object_ptr = cells[ix + nx * iy + nx * ny * iz];

    if (tx_next < ty_next && tx_next < tz_next) {
        if (object_ptr && object_ptr->hit(ray, t, sr) && t < tx_next) {
            material_ptr = object_ptr->get_material();
            return (true);
        }

        tx_next += dtx;
        ix += ix_step;

        if (ix == ix_stop)
            return (false);
    }
    else {
        if (ty_next < tz_next) {
            if (object_ptr && object_ptr->hit(ray, t, sr) && t <
                ty_next) {
                material_ptr = object_ptr->get_material();
                return (true);
            }

            ty_next += dty;
            iy += iy_step;

            if (iy == iy_stop)
                return (false);
        }
        else {
            if (object_ptr && object_ptr->hit(ray, t, sr) && t < tz_
            next) {
                material_ptr = object_ptr->get_material();
                return (true);
            }

            tz_next += dtz;
            iz += iz_step;

            if (iz == iz_stop)
                return (false);
        }
    }
}
```

Listing 22.7. Grid traversal in 3D.

variables ix_stop, iy_stop, and iz_stop will tell the algorithm when the ray is about to exit the grid.

Listing 22.7 shows how the grid is traversed in 3D. If the cell is empty, the object pointer will be null, which has to be checked before the hit function is called. Because of the lazy evaluation of the && operator in C++, the hit function will only be called when there is an object present. Note that a hit is only recorded when a hit occurs for $t < t_{xnext}$ or $t < t_{ynext}$, to confine any hits to the current cell.

The full hit function is on the book's website as part of the Grid class.

 ## 22.4 Testing

Grids are complex objects that you need to test thoroughly. This section contains some tips for doing this and some test scenes.

22.4.1 Testing Tips

Turn the grid off. Unless you are rendering huge numbers of objects, you can always render test scenes with and without using the grid and compare the results. If the grid is working correctly, the results must be identical. This technique is applicable to all rendering situations. It's usually not much work to change the build functions. To use the grid, you add objects to the grid as they are constructed and then add the grid to the world. To turn the grid off, you add the objects to the world but don't add the grid to the world.

Use all types of rays. Test the grid with primary, secondary, and shadow rays that start inside and outside the grid. This will involve you placing the camera inside the grid and, in later chapters, using reflective and transparent materials.[2]

Use special configurations. Grids will sometimes work correctly when rays travel at arbitrary angles to the coordinate axes but fail when they are parallel to the axes or the coordinate planes. The reason is that in this case, the grid hit function divides by zero. Use tests where rays have these orientations. You should also test a grid that's centered on the world axis and has axis-aligned objects.

---

2. The random box city figures in Chapter 11 were also rendered using a grid, and in Figure 11.12, the camera is inside the grid.

Use a single object. Test the grid with a single object, for example, a sphere centered on the origin, an axis-aligned cube centered on the origin, and an axis-aligned cube with one vertex at the origin. The cube in this last example has three of its faces in coordinate planes. Place the camera inside the cube. Use a single cell and multiple cells. Also, test the grid by looking along the world coordinate axes.

22.4.2 Eight Boxes

Figure 22.9(a) shows a grid with eight axis-aligned boxes. Although this is a simple scene, it's a tough test because of the symmetries involved and the axis alignment of the objects and the lights. Figure 22.9(b) shows a vertical cross section through the four "front" boxes in Figure 22.9(a).

The boxes are arranged so that the grid's bounding box is a cube centered on the origin with one box at each corner. Each box therefore has three faces in the bounding-box faces. There are four cells in each direction, as indicated by the dashed lines in Figure 22.9(b), and the size of the bottom four boxes is such that their three faces inside the grid lie on cell faces. The scene is illuminated by six directional lights in the $\pm x$-, $\pm y$-, and $\pm z$-directions, so that the shadow rays, which all start inside the grid or on its boundary, travel parallel to the coordinate axes in both directions.

The only way to get all of the primary rays parallel to a coordinate axis is to use an orthographic camera. Figure 22.10(a) is an orthographic view look-

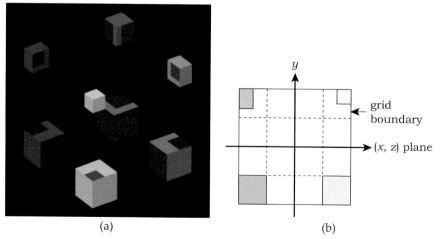

(a)   (b)

Figure 22.9. (a) Orthographic view of eight boxes in a grid; (b) vertical cross section of the grid, showing its bounding box and cells.

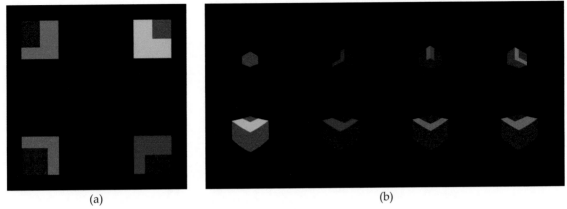

Figure 22.10. (a) Orthographic view of the cubes looking down the y-axis; (b) spherical panoramic view from the center of the grid.

ing down the y-axis where the eye point is at the origin. This places all of the ray origins in the (x, z) plane and on cell faces. Only the bottom four boxes are visible, but the shadow rays still intersect the other boxes.

Figure 22.10(b) shows a $360° \times 180°$ spherical panoramic view from inside the grid where the eye point is at the origin. As such, it's at a corner of 8 cells. The view direction is along the negative x-axis. This demonstrates that shadows are working for the three lights coming from the negative coordinate axis directions (see Question 22.4).

22.4.3 Random Spheres

If your grid can correctly render the boxes in Section 22.4.2, it's probably in good shape, but that scene doesn't have enough objects to demonstrate the speed advantages of grids. Random spheres in a cube are a simple way to do this, as indicated in Listing 22.8. Here, the spheres are randomly placed in a cube that's centered on the origin, their radii are scaled according to the number of spheres, and their colors are random.[3]

Some results are shown in Figure 22.11, where Figure 22.11(a)–(d) were rendered with a pinhole camera on the z-axis with one ray per pixel, a single directional light, and no shadows. The million-spheres grid used about 250 MB of RAM on my computer, but you could save memory by letting the spheres

---

3. The code for generating the spheres in Listing 22.8 is by Peter Shirley.

```
void
World::build(void) {
    // construct viewplane, integrator, camera, and lights

    int num_spheres = 100000;
    float volume = 0.1 /  num_spheres;
    float radius = pow(0.75 * volume / 3.14159, 0.333333);

    Grid* grid_ptr = new Grid;
    set_rand_seed(15);

    for (int j = 0; j <  num_spheres; j++) {
        Matte* matte_ptr = new Matte;
        matte_ptr->set_ka(0.25);
        matte_ptr->set_kd(0.75);
        matte_ptr->set_cd(randf(), randf(), randf());

        Sphere* sphere_ptr = new Sphere;
        sphere_ptr->set_radius(radius);
        sphere_ptr->set_center( 1.0 - 2.0 * rand_float(),
                1.0 - 2.0 * rand_float(),
                1.0 - 2.0 * rand_float());
        sphere_ptr->set_material(matte_ptr);
        grid_ptr->add_object(sphere_ptr);
    }

    grid_ptr->setup_cells(); // must be called after all the
                             // spheres have been added
    add_object(grid_ptr);
}
```

Listing 22.8. Partial build function for a grid of random spheres.

share a common material. Figure 22.11(e) is a three-faced view of 100,000 spheres with shadows.

Table 22.2 compares the render times for the face-on views using the grid and using exhaustive ray tracing. All images were rendered at a resolution of 400×400 pixels on a 450 MHz G3 Macintosh with 512 MB RAM. The table also shows the speed-up factors, which increase as the number of spheres increases. The speed-up for one million spheres is estimated using linear extrapolation. A value of $m = 2$ in Equation (22.1) was used, which results in eight times more cells than objects.

The figure on the first page of this chapter is a perspective view of 1000 spheres with the camera inside the grid. Note the extreme perspective distortion.

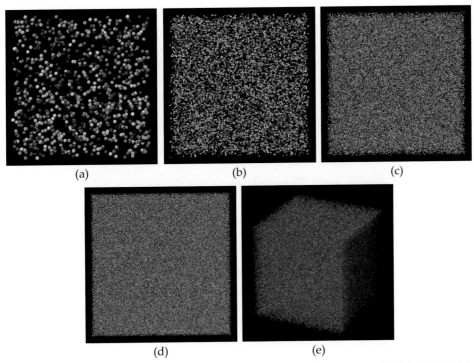

Figure 22.11. Face-on views of a cube of random spheres with 1000 (a), 10,000 (b), 100,000 (c), and one million (d) spheres; (e) three-faced view of 100,000 spheres with shadows.

Number of	Render Times in Seconds		Grid Speed-Up
Spheres	With Grid	Exhaustive	Factors
10	1.5	2.5	1.6
100	2.0	16	8
1000	2.7	164	61
10,000	3.8	2041	537
100,000	4.7	22169 (6 hours)	4717
1,000,000	5.2	forget it!	≈ 46,307

Table 22.2. Render times for random spheres in a cube.

22.4.4 Some Issues

A random cube of spheres is ideal for the grid structure, particularly when there are large numbers of spheres uniformly distributed in the cube. The fact that the rays don't penetrate the grid very far before they hit a sphere also contributes to the low rendering times. This is demonstrated by the fact that render times for 100,000 and one million spheres are not much different. The triangle meshes in Chapter 23 provide more realistic tests for the grid.

As discussed in Chapter 1, I use doubles for the Sphere, Vector3D, and Point3D data members and for the object-intersection calculations. I couldn't render more than about 10,000 of these spheres with floats, due to numerical-precision problems; the spheres were just too small. My students who use PCs don't have this problem.

 ## 22.5 Grids and Transformed Objects

For modeling and rendering flexibility, we must be able to include transformed objects in grids. To do this, we need the axis-aligned bounding boxes of the transformed objects, as Figure 22.12 illustrates for a transformed sphere.

Unfortunately, it's difficult to compute the axis-aligned bounding box of an arbitrary object that has been subject to an arbitrary sequence of transformations. It's even difficult for the transformed object in Figure 22.12, which is just a rotated ellipsoid.

In practice, we have to settle for second best, which is the *axis-aligned bounding box of the original object's transformed bounding box*. Did you get that? Don't worry; Figure 22.13 illustrates what I'm talking about. For example, let's scale the sphere on the left to produce an ellipsoid and its bounding box defined by p'_0 and p'_1. Now rotate this and the bounding box to produce the rotated

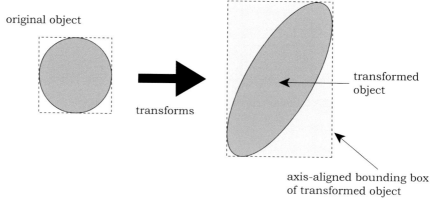

Figure 22.12. This figure illustrates the axis-aligned bounding box of a transformed object.

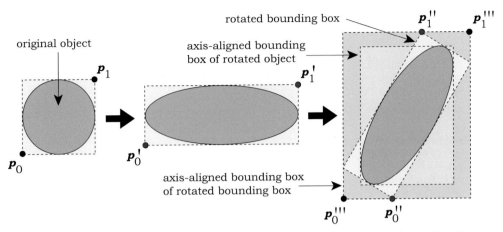

Figure 22.13. The axis-aligned bounding box of the rotated bounding box is larger than the axis-aligned bounding box of the rotated object.

ellipsoid and rotated bounding box p_0'' and p_1'' on the right. This bounding box is the tightest fit to the ellipsoid, but because it's no longer axis-aligned, we can't use it. We also can't easily compute the axis-aligned bounding box of the rotated ellipsoid, indicated by the green rectangle. So, what can we do? We can compute the axis-aligned bounding box of the rotated bounding box, as defined by p_0''' and p_1''' and as indicated by the gray rectangle. As you can see, it's larger than the axis-aligned bounding box of the rotated object, with the result that the transformed object will be placed in more grid cells than necessary. But this just affects the efficiency of the grid; the results will still be correct, of course. Axis-aligned boxes computed this way are often loose fits to the objects, particularly when scaling or shearing is combined with rotation, but it's the best we can do.

Because the rotated vertices p_0'' and p_1'' in Figure 22.13 don't define the extremities of the axis-aligned box of the rotated bounding box, we need to transform all eight vertices of the original object's bounding box and use these transformed vertices to work out the minimum and maximum vertices p_0''' and p_1'''. The catch is that we need to use the *forward* transformations, not their inverses. The instance objects thus need access to the transformation matrix as well as its inverse. Fortunately, we only need the bounding boxes during grid construction; they are not used to ray trace the transformed objects. The transformation matrix, which I've called `forward_matrix`, can therefore be static in the `Instance` class. We must, however, store the bounding box with each instance because it has to be accessed three times during the grid construc-

```
class Instance: public GeometricObject {
     public:

          // constructors, etc.

          void
          compute_bounding_box(void);

          virtual BBox
          get_bounding_box (void);

          virtual bool
          shadow_hitt(const Ray& ray, float& tmin) const;

          virtual bool
          hit(const Ray& ray, float& tmin, ShadeRec& sr) const;

          void
          translate(const float dx, const float dy, const float dz);

          // other transformation functions

     private:

          GeometricObject* object_ptr;    // object to be transformed
          Matrix inv_matrix;              // inverse transformation matrix
          bool transform_texture;         // do we transform textures?

          static Matrix forward_matrix;   // transformation matrix
          BBox bbox;                      // bounding box
};
```

Listing 22.9. New declaration of the class Instance.

tion. It's used twice to compute the grid's dimensions and once to place the transformed objects in the grid.[4] The revised declaration of the Instance class appears in Listing 22.9, where the new member functions and data members are in blue.

The forward_matrix data member needs to be initialized to the unit matrix at the start of the **Instance.cpp** file with the code

---

4. You would only need to use the bounding box twice if you combined the min_coordinates and max_coordinates functions.

```
Matrix
Instance::forward_matrix;          // invoke default Matrix
                                   // constructor
```

The transformation matrix must be built up at the same time as the inverse matrix is built up. Listing 22.10 illustrates how to do this with the `Instance::translate` function, where I've added the `forward_matrix` code to the function in Listing 21.8. Note that the translation matrix is pre-multiplied in accordance with Equation (20.10). The other transformation functions will need similar code added.

The last thing to do when constructing an instance is to call the function `Instance::compute_bounding_box`. If you want to store a transformed object in a grid, you must call this function in the build function. I haven't reproduced the code for this function here because it's lengthy and not particularly interesting, except for one point. After it has finished with the transformation matrix, it must set it back to the identity matrix, ready for the next instance. Remember: there is only one copy of a `static` variable.

Figure 22.14 shows a spherical panoramic view of a grid that contains 25 random spheres that were constructed by scaling and translating generic spheres.

```
void
Instance::translate(const float dx, const float dy, const float dz) {

    Matrix inv_translation_matrix;  // temporary inverse translation matrix
    Matrix translation_matrix;      // temporary translation matrix

    inv_translation_matrix.m[0][3] = -dx;
    inv_translation_matrix.m[1][3] = -dy;
    inv_translation_matrix.m[2][3] = -dz;

    inv_matrix = inv_matrix * inv_translation_matrix;     // post-multiply

    translation_matrix.m[0][3] = dx;
    translation_matrix.m[1][3] = dy;
    translation_matrix.m[2][3] = dz;

    forward_matrix = translation_matrix * forward_matrix; // pre-multiply

}
```

Listing 22.10. The function `Instance::translate` with the `forward_matrix` code included.

Figure 22.14. Twenty-five random spheres in a grid.

The lines on their surfaces, which are textures, help to illustrate the distortions produced by the panoramic camera. All of the spheres are the same size.

The bunnies in Figure 21.4 are stored in a grid after being translated. Because each bunny is also a grid, this figure illustrates nested grids. You should be able to reproduce this after you have finished Chapter 23.

22.6 Comparison with BVHs

Bounding volume hierarchies are more adaptive to the scene geometry than grids because the cell sizes and locations are determined by the objects. They can therefore be more efficient for scenes where the objects are unevenly distributed in space, such as triangle meshes. They have a much simpler, recursively defined hit function than the grid. Their construction is not as straightforward as the grid's because they require a *cost-function* heuristic for optimal performance. The analogous cost function for grids is the number of cells per object. Compared to a grid, it's more trouble to handle rays that start inside a BVH, because these rays can start arbitrarily deep in the hierarchy.

Further Reading

Most of the fundamental breakthroughs in ray-tracing acceleration occurred during the 1980s. The reason is that ray tracing was so slow on the machines of the time that people started to think about how to make it run faster, right from the start. The following are some of the significant contributions.

The earliest papers on acceleration, by Rubin and Whitted (1980) and Weghorst et al. (1984), used bounding volume hierarchies. The first spatial subdivision algorithms were by Glassner (1984), who used octrees, and Kaplan (1985), who used kd-trees. The regular grid and its 3DDDA traversal algorithm originated with Fujimoto et al. (1986). Goldsmith and Salmon (1987) described an algorithm for automatically generating bounding volume hierarchies because the hierarchies of the time were either built by hand or were just based on the scene data structure. They were therefore less than optimal in terms of performance. Kirk and Arvo (1988) provide an excellent survey of acceleration techniques as they existed in 1988. Samet (1990a, 1990b) and Langetepe and Zachmann (2006) are books on spatial data structures.

My discussion of regular grids is based on Shirley (2000), who recommended that each cell store an object pointer and presented pseudocode for the hit function. Some aspects of the regular grid are also presented in Shirley et al. (2005).

Shirley and Morley (2003) has the complete code for a bounding volume hierarchy. Pharr and Humphreys (2004) discusses regular grids and kd-trees.

Questions

22.1. Figure 22.15 is similar to Figure 22.6, but here, the ray hits the box behind the sphere. Would this situation cause problems for the grid hit function? Consider the cells that the ray traverses before it gets to the sphere. In each of these cells the ray will be tested against the box, whose hit function will return true.

22.2. One of the geometric objects can't be stored in a grid. Which one is it, and what is the reason?

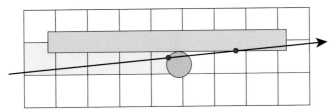

Figure 22.15. The ray hits the box behind the sphere.

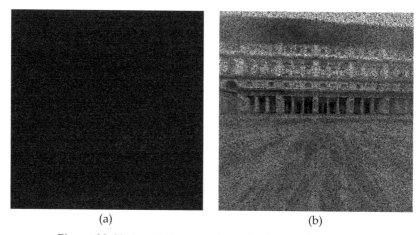

(a)   (b)

Figure 22.16. A grid that contains a single axis-aligned box.

22.3. There are certain shadows visible in Figure 22.10(a). In which directions do the shadow rays travel that created these?

22.4. How can you tell from Figure 22.10(b) that shadows are working correctly for the directional lights in the negative x-, y-, and z-directions?

22.5. Which transformations leave the transformed bounding box axis-aligned?

22.6. Consider a scene that consists of a grid that contains a single axis-aligned box with a brown matte material, a pinhole camera and a point light inside the box, and the Uffizi image on a large surrounding sphere. The scene will be rendered with ray casting. Figure 22.16(a) shows the inside of the box illuminated by the point light. Definitely not an interesting image. Figure 22.16(b) is the same scene rendered *without* the grid's bounding box being expanded with kEpsilon in the functions get_min_coordinates and get_max_coordinates. In this case, the grid is exactly the same size as the axis-aligned box's bounding box. Can you explain this noisy image of the Uffizi buildings?

 Exercises

22.1. Implement the Grid class on the book's website and use the scenes in Section 22.4 to test it.

22.2. Section 22.4 only covered a few of the many tests that you should perform on the boxes grid. Here are a few more suggestions. Use the orthographic camera to look at the cubes from the positive and negative x-,

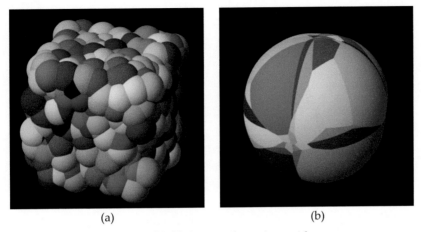

(a) (b)

Figure 22.17. Large spheres in a grid.

y-, and z-directions. Also use it to look parallel to the coordinate planes where the primary rays aren't parallel to a coordinate axis. Use the perspective camera with the eye point at various locations outside the grid, on the grid faces, and inside the grid.

22.3. Make the random spheres in Section 22.4.3 larger and see how this affects the build times, memory footprints, and rendering times. As an example, Figure 22.17(a) shows 1000 spheres that are 10 times larger than those in Figure 22.11(a), and in Figure 22.17(b), the spheres are 250 times larger.

22.4. In Figures 22.9 and 22.10, I hard-wired $n_x = n_y = n_z = 4$ into the `Grid::setup_cells` function. Give the user the option to set a common value for these in the build functions.

22.5. My grid implementation hard-wires in the value $m = 2$. Give the user the option to set this in the build functions.

22.6. Experiment with various values of m in Equations (22.1) and compare the speeds.

22.7. Below are two alternative ways to represent the cells. Compare the build times, memory footprints, and rendering times with the representation (22.2).

```
vector<Compound*> cells;
vector<vector<GeometricObject*> > cells;
```

These will affect the function `Grid::setup_cells`, which will be simpler than the version in Listing 22.4, and will also affect the hit functions. In

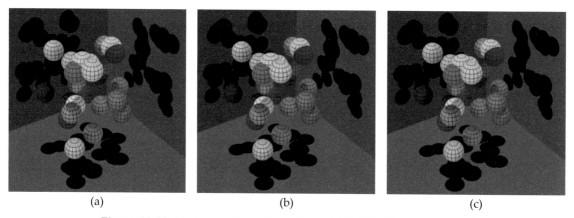

(a)   (b)   (c)

Figure 22.18. (a) Twenty-five spheres in a grid; (b) 25 ellipsoids in a grid; (c) 25 spheres in a scaled grid.

the Compound object representation, some of the objects will be empy (see Exercise 19.21).

22.8. Get a grid to cast shadows on another object. A good test would be either the boxes grid or the random spheres and some planes. Figure 22.18(a) is an example of the latter. Include a case where the plane cuts through the grid, as this would be another test for the grid's regular hit function.

22.9. Figure 22.18(a) shows 25 random spheres in a grid, with three planes and shadows. In Figure 22.18(b), the spheres have been individually scaled by $(a, b, c) = (1.0, 0.25, 1.0)$ before they have been added to the grid. In Figure 22.18(c), the grid has been scaled by the same amounts instead of the spheres. Although the spheres are the same shape in both images, the results are different. Can you explain this? It might help to render the images with the camera on the positive x- or z-axis. Reproduce these figures.

22.10. Check that nested instances work when you store them in a grid.

22.11. Implement a bounding volume hierarchy (BVH) acceleration scheme and compare its performance with the regular grid for a variety of scenes, including triangle meshes.

23 Triangle Meshes

Image courtesy of Tania Humphreys, Isis and
Ganesh models courtesy of Cyberware

 Objectives

By the end of this chapter, you should:

- understand the importance of triangle meshes for modeling complex objects;
- be able to render triangle meshes using a regular grid;
- be able to read triangle-mesh data from PLY files.

Commercial modeling, rendering, and animation packages allow users to model objects using a variety of techniques. For example, complex surfaces can be modeled using NURBS or subdivision surfaces, constructive solid geometry can be used to build complex objects from simple components, and some packages also employ a variety of primitives as we do. Regardless of the techniques used for modeling, the objects are displayed in the modelers using triangles or wireframes. There are good reasons for this:

- the underlying mathematical surfaces are difficult to render directly, particularly in real time;
- the surfaces can be polygonized with user control on the number of triangles;
- triangle and wireframe meshes can be rendered in the hardware of graphics cards.

Not all triangle meshes are based on mathematical models. Objects such as the Stanford bunny have been laser scanned and the resulting data converted to triangles (Turk and Levoy, 1994).

Because it's also difficult to ray trace NURBS and subdivision surfaces, it's essential for commercial ray tracers to be able to render triangle meshes. It's also essential to use an acceleration technique because most meshes contain large numbers of triangles. I'll use the regular grid from Chapter 22 with a number of triangle-mesh member functions added. Because some of these functions are long or have complex syntax, I'll only describe them briefly here or present them in pseudocode.

23.1 Tessellating a Sphere

23.1.1 Flat Shading

We can start by tessellating[1] a generic sphere because this illustrates the procedure of approximating curved surfaces by triangles. The code for generating the triangles is based on the parametric representation of a sphere in Equations (2.3) with $r = 1$ and is on the book's website in the function `Grid::tessellate_flat_sphere`.

The tessellation parameters are the numbers of triangles in the azimuth and polar directions, which I'll refer to as m and n, respectively. Figure 23.1 shows the sphere approximated with different numbers of triangles and rendered with Phong shading. As m and n increase, the triangles become an increasingly accurate representation of the sphere. I've used the `Triangle` class from Chapter 19 and a directional light so that each triangle will be rendered with constant ambient, diffuse, and specular shading.[2] The flat shading affects specular reflection more than it does diffuse because specular reflection varies more rapidly across surfaces than diffuse. As a result, the specular highlight is missing in Figure 23.1(a), covers a single triangle in Figure 23.1(b) and (c), and makes the triangulation more apparent than the diffuse reflection does in Figure 23.1(d). In general, we require large numbers of flat-shaded triangles to correctly render specular highlights. Notice that in Figure 23.1(c) and (d), the

---

1. Tessellation means to arrange objects so that there are no gaps or overlaps. The sphere triangles have these properties. Mosaics and floorboards are real-world examples of tessellation. The 2D checker textures in Chapter 30 are further computer examples.

2. The specular reflection does vary with position, but in this figure, the triangles are too small for this to be noticeable.

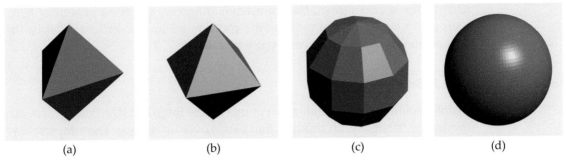

(a) (b) (c) (d)

Figure 23.1. Sphere tessellated with: (a) $m = 3$, $n = 2$; (b) $m = 4$, $n = 2$; (c) $m = 10$, $n = 5$; (d) $m = 100$, $n = 50$.

```
BBox
Triangle::get_bounding_box(void) {
      double delta = 0.000001;

      return(BBox(min(min(v0.x, v1.x), v2.x) - delta,
                  max(max(v0.x, v1.x), v2.x) + delta,
                  min(min(v0.y, v1.y), v2.y) - delta,
                  max(max(v0.y, v1.y), v2.y) + delta,
                  min(min(v0.z, v1.z), v2.z) - delta,
                  max(max(v0.z, v1.z), v2.z) + delta));
}
```

Listing 23.1. The function `Triangle::get_bounding_box`.

sphere seems to be mainly composed of quadrilaterals instead of triangles (see Question 23.2).

To place triangles in a grid, we must be able to compute their bounding boxes. This is a relatively simple task, as the code in Listing 23.1 indicates, but triangles can have degenerate bounding boxes whose extent in one of the coordinate-axis directions is zero (see Question 23.3). The variable `delta` avoids this by displacing the corners of the box by a small amount. Here, `min` and `max` are utility functions defined in **Maths.h**.

Another way of rendering triangles is to vary the shading across each triangle based on the orientation of the surface they represent. By doing this, the surface will appear to be curved instead of consisting of flat facets. Again, a sphere is a good way to introduce this process. Figure 23.2 shows a triangle whose vertices are on the surface of a sphere. The sphere's normal at

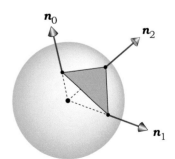

Figure 23.2. The normal at every point on the surface of a sphere points radially out from the sphere center.

each vertex is also shown. Each normal is different, and for a generic sphere, their components are the same as the coordinates of the vertices. That is, the unit normal at vertex i is given by $n_i = v_i$, for $i = 0, 1, 2$.

23.1.2 Smooth Shading

By interpolating the normals at hit points on the interior of the triangle, we can render the triangle with shading that varies over its surface. The simplest way to interpolate the normals is to use a bilinear combination. The most convenient expression involves the barycentric coordinates at the hit points, which we have already computed in the triangle hit function:

$$n = (1 - \beta - \gamma)n_0 + \beta n_1 + \gamma n_2. \tag{23.1}$$

The expression (23.1) reduces to the vertex normals at each vertex, but just as importantly, it's continuous across the triangle boundaries (see Exercise 23.3). If we render the triangles this way, the continuous shading across the triangle edges will make them invisible, and the sphere's surface will appear smooth, but we can't use the Triangle class. I've therefore implemented a class called SmoothTriangle that stores the three normals as well as the vertices and uses the expression (23.1) to compute the normal. As such, it's a memory hog, but that's OK for demonstration purposes. The grid function Grid::tessellate_smooth_sphere constructs the smooth triangles. The results in Figure 23.3 use the same numbers of polygons as in Figure 23.1.

Notice how the specular highlight is now more accurately rendered, even when it's on a single triangle, as in Figure 23.3(a) and (b); however, see Question 23.4. Also, notice the incongruous appearance of the objects in

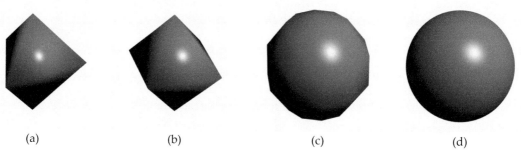

(a)   (b)   (c)   (d)

Figure 23.3. Sphere tessellated with: (a) $m = 3$, $n = 2$, (b) $m = 4$, $n = 2$, (c) $m = 10$, $n = 5$, (d) $m = 100$, $n = 50$. Rendered with smooth shading.

Figure 23.3(a)–(c) where the polygonal silhouette is at odds with the smoothly shaded surface.

Provided we can compute the vertex normals, we can always render a polygon mesh with smooth shading. However, if you want to use triangles to represent an object with sharp edges, such as a polyhedron, you should of course use flat shading.

23.2 A Mesh Data Structure

It wastes memory to store the vertices and normals with each triangle because each vertex is shared by a number of triangles. In fact, for an arbitrary closed triangle mesh with a large number of triangles, each vertex is shared by an average of six triangles. This can be proved using the *Euler characteristic* of a surface, a deep and beautiful result from topology[3] (see Haines (2001)). As an illustration, Figure 23.4 is a sphere with the triangle edges rendered. In this figure, 16 polygons share the top and bottom vertices, four share the top and bottom row of vertices, but six share the other vertices, which are in the majority.

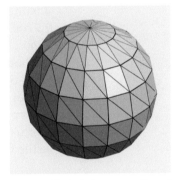

Figure 23.4. Sphere tessellated with $m = 8$, $n = 16$.

We can save memory by only storing the coordinates and normal once for each vertex in an auxiliary data structure and giving the triangles access to the vertex information. I'll still store a single normal in each triangle to save time during scene construction. This type of data structure is called a *triangle mesh* and is commonly used in commercial graphics software. For example, OpenGL and Direct3D both support polygon meshes, and graphics cards support them as well, because it's more efficient to only have to transform vertex information once (see Akenine-Möller and Haines (2002)).

I've implemented triangle meshes with a Mesh data structure that holds the vertex information and with a series of *mesh triangles* that work with it. The declaration of the Mesh class is in Listing 23.2, where all data members are public for ease of access. Note that this is not a geometric object.

Figure 23.5 shows the mesh triangle inheritance chart where the base class MeshTriangle inherits directly from GeometricObject. This triangle class gains access to the mesh data structure by storing a pointer to the mesh and three indices into the vertices and normals arrays in the mesh.

---

3. Leonhard Euler was a Swiss mathematician who lived from 1707 to 1783.

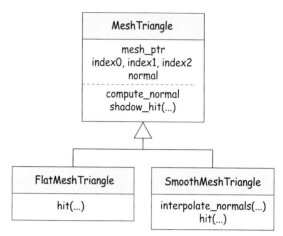

Figure 23.5. Mesh triangle classes.

Listing 23.3 shows the hit function for the `FlatMeshTriangle` class. Note that the code inside the function is the same as in Listing 19.6 except for the first three lines, which illustrate how the vertices are extracted from the mesh.

Although it's possible to rewrite the `Grid` functions for tessellating spheres and other objects so that they create triangle meshes, it's not a trivial process. It's also not worth the effort because data files that have been created by other programs provide a far more varied source of mesh triangle data. I'll therefore only discuss triangle meshes that are read from files, after first discussing a simple file format.

```
class Mesh {
     public:

               vector<Point3D> vertices;          // vertices
               vector<int> indices;               // vertex indices
               vector<Normal> normals;            // average normal at each vertex
               vector<vector<int>> vertex_faces;  // the faces shared by each vertex
               vector<float> u;          // u texture coordinate at each vertex
               vector<float> v;          // v texture coordinate at each vertex
               int num_vertices;         // number of vertices
               int num_triangles;        // number of triangles

               // constructors, etc.
};
```

Listing 23.2. Declaration of the class `Mesh`. The data members u and v are used in Chapter 29.

```
bool
FlatMeshTriangle::hit(const Ray& ray, float& tmin, ShadeRec& sr) const {

    Point3D v0(mesh_ptr->vertices[index0]);
    Point3D v1(mesh_ptr->vertices[index1]);
    Point3D v2(mesh_ptr->vertices[index2]);

    double a = v0.x - v1.x, b = v0.x - v2.x, c = ray.d.x, d = v0.x - ray.o.x;
    double e = v0.y - v1.y, f = v0.y - v2.y, g = ray.d.y, h = v0.y - ray.o.y;
    double i = v0.z - v1.z, j = v0.z - v2.z, k = ray.d.z, l = v0.z - ray.o.z;

    double m = f * k - g * j, n = h * k - g * l, p = f * l - h * j;
    double q = g * i - e * k, r = e * l - h * i, s = e * j - f * i;

    double inv_denom = 1.0 / (a * m + b * q + c * s);

    double e1 = d * m - b * n - c * p;
    double beta = e1 * inv_denom;

    if (beta < 0.0 || beta > 1.0)
        return (false);

    double e2 = a * n + d * q + c * r;
    double gamma      = e2 * inv_denom;

    if (gamma < 0.0 || gamma > 1.0)
        return (false);

    if (beta + gamma > 1.0)
        return (false);

    double e3 = a * p - b * r + d * s;
    double t = e3 * inv_denom;

    if (t < kEpsilon)
        return (false);

    tmin = t;
    sr.normal = normal;                          // for flat shading
    sr.local_hit_point = ray.o + t * ray.d;      // for texture mapping

    return(true);
}
```

Listing 23.3. The function `FlatMeshTriangle::hit`.

23.3 PLY Files

PLY files were developed by Greg Turk in the mid 1990s for storing single poly-gon meshes (Turk and Levoy, 1994). They can be ASCII or binary. The website is http://www-static.cc.gatech.edu/projects/large_models/ply.html. The only type of PLY file that I'll discuss in this chapter contains a list of triangle vertex coordinates as (x, y, z) triples and a list of triangular faces that consist of indices into the vertex list. The structure of a PLY file of this type consists of a header, a vertex list, and a face list.

As a simple example, the PLY file in Listing 23.4 describes the two tri-angles that are illustrated in Figure 23.7.

The header in an ASCII PLY file consists of a number of carriage-return terminated ASCII strings, the first of which is the single word `ply`, and the sec-ond of which specifies the file type and version number. Comments are lines that start with the keyword `comment`, and they can only appear in the header. The header is terminated by the keyword `end_header`.

A PLY file can describe an arbitrary number of user-defined *element types*, each of which can have an arbitrary number of user-defined *properties*. The names of all elements and properties are also user-defined. The header speci-fies the name and number of each element with the keyword `element` and

```
ply
format ascii 1.0
comment author: Kevin Suffern
comment this file contains two triangles
element vertex 4
property float x
property float y
property float z
element face 2
property list int int vertex_indices
end_header
-1.0 0.0 -1.0
-1.0 -1.0 1.0
1.0 0.0 1.0
1.0 -1,0 -1.0
3 0 1 2
3 0 2 3
```

Listing 23.4. A simple PLY file.

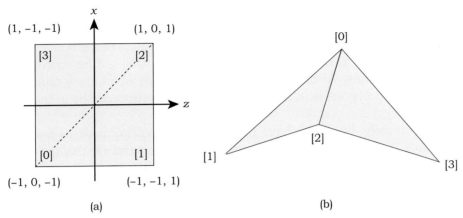

Figure 23.6. (a) Top-down view of the triangles defined in Listing 23.4; (b) 3D view of the triangles.

the name and type of each property with the keyword `property`. The general syntax is

```
element <name> <number>
property <type> <name>
property <type> <name>
property <type> <name>
...
```

All of the PLY files I'll use have two element types called `vertex` and `face`, as these are common names that most PLY files have. Each vertex has three properties of type `float` called x, y, and z, as in Listing 23.4. The data for the vertices follow the header, one vertex per line. Figure 23.6(a) shows a top-down view of the four vertices in this example, numbered 0–3 because they will be stored in a `vector` according to Listing 23.2.[4]

PLY file faces always have a single property, which is a list whose first element is the number of vertices per face and whose remaining elements are the vertex indices into the vertices array. The `face` property syntax specifies this with `list int int`, where the two ints specify that the number of indices and the indices themselves are integers. The PLY file in Listing 23.4 defines two triangle faces in the last two lines. Figure 23.6(b) shows a 3D view of the triangles, where the first triangle is defined by the vertices 0, 1, and 2 and the

---

4. The vertex numbers are not stored in the PLY files.

second by the vertices 0, 2, and 3. Note that the vertices are ordered counterclockwise when viewed from the top.

PLY files are actually a lot more flexible than this. They can store additional information at the vertices, for example, normals, texture coordinates, or RGB color values. Also, faces can be polygons with an arbitrary number of vertices, and polygons with different numbers of vertices can be in the same PLY file.

Fortunately, you don't have to worry about writing code to read PLY files; Greg Turk has written an extensive PLY software package that includes a parser. I've incorporated some of this into the `Grid` class. You will need to add the file **PLY.c** to your project and `#include` the file **PLY.h** in **Grid.h** or **Grid.cpp**. These files are straight from the PLY package with no modifications; they provide the PLY file definitions and basic functions for reading (and writing) PLY files. They are written in C, not C++.

I've added grid member functions called `read_flat_triangles` and `read_smooth_triangles` that call the function `read_ply_file`. This last function does the actual reading with the specified triangle type, flat or smooth, supplied as an argument. It's also part of the PLY package, but I've modified it to add the vertices to the mesh, construct the mesh triangles, and add them to the grid. Because it's a long function, allowing it to construct either type of triangle saves a lot of repeated code. You should study this function carefully.

If you ray trace PLY files that you download from the web or get from other sources, there may be additional properties on the vertex lines. The code in **PLY.c** and `read_ply_file` will still parse these files correctly provided the vertex coordinates are the first three numbers on each line.

You can find a number of PLY files, including the Stanford bunny, a horse, a dragon, and a Buddha, at the Georgia Institute of Technology Large Geometric Objects Archive at http://www-static.cc.gatech.edu/projects/large_models/. This site also has the skeleton-hand model that was rendered by Jimmy Nguyen in the figure on the first page of Chapter 1.

 ## 23.4 Examples

23.4.1 Two Triangles

I'll start with the two triangles defined in Listing 23.4, which are rendered as flat triangles in Figure 23.7(a).

Listing 23.5 shows the section of the build function for Figure 23.7(a) that constructs the grid with a mesh object and reads the PLY file. The PLY file must be in the same directory as the ray tracer.

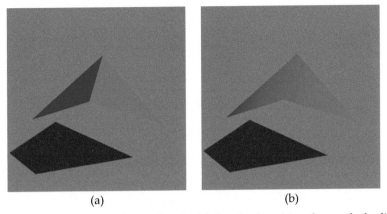

(a)   (b)

Figure 23.7. Two mesh triangles rendered with flat shading (a) and smooth shading (b).

```
void
World::build(void) {

    // construct view plane, tracer, camera, and light

    Matt* matt_ptr1 = new Matt;
    matt_ptr1->set_ka(0.1);
    matt_ptr1->set_kd(0.75);
    matt_ptr1->set_cd(0.1, 0.5, 1.0);

    const char* file_name = "TwoTriangles.ply";
    Grid* grid_ptr = new Grid(new Mesh);
    grid_ptr->read_flat_triangles(file_name);        // read ply file
    grid_ptr->set_material(matt_ptr1);
    grid_ptr->setup_cells();
    add_object(grid_ptr);

    // construct ground plane
}
```

Listing 23.5. Build function for Figure 23.7(a).

Figure 23.7(b) shows the triangles rendered with smooth shading. This results from calling `Grid::read_smooth_triangles` in the build function, the code for which is in Listing 23.6.

```
void
Grid::read_smooth_triangles(char* file_name) {
        read_ply_file(file_name, smooth);
        compute_mesh_normals();
}
```

Listing 23.6. The function `Grid::read_smooth_triangles`.

23.4.2 Computing the Normals

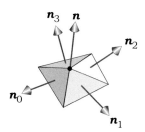

Figure 23.8. Each triangle that shares a vertex has its own normal.

The problem with rendering arbitrary triangle meshes with smooth shading is that, unlike the sphere discussed above, there is no convenient formula for the normal at each vertex. Although some PLY files contain the normals, the files I discuss here don't, and we therefore have to compute them. Figure 23.8 shows a vertex where four triangles meet, each of which has its own normal. We compute the normal n at the common vertex as the normalized sum of these normals. In other words, the normal is the average of the triangle normals that share the vertex, normalized to unit length.

The pseudocode in Listing 23.7 is an algorithm that computes the vertex normals by using the fact that each triangle stores the three vertex indices.

Although this is simple and correct, it has the following serious problem. It runs in $O(num\_vertices \times num\_triangles)$ time and is therefore only practical for small meshes. Consider the largest Stanford bunny PLY file with $num\_vertices = 35,947$ and $num\_triangles = 67,541$, which is not a huge file. This algorithm would require 10^9 operations. For the dragon PLY file, it would require about 10^{11} operations.

```
for each vertex {
        normal = zero normal
        for each triangle {
                if the triangle has the vertex's index
                        add the triangle normal to normal
        }
        normalize the normal
}

add the normal to the mesh
```

Listing 23.7. An algorithm to compute the normal at each vertex.

```
for each vertex {
        normal = zero normal
        for each triangle that shares the vertex
                add the triangle normal to normal
        normalize the normal
}

add the normal to the mesh
```

Listing 23.8. An algorithm that computes the normal at each vertex in $O(num\_vertices)$ time.

To make this process practical, we need an algorithm that runs in $O(num\_vertices)$ time. The pseudocode in Listing 23.8 shows such an algorithm. The crucial difference is that this algorithm only considers triangles that share each vertex. The catch is: how do we find them? The required information has to be stored while the file is being read, and this is where the Mesh data member vertex_faces is used. Note that this is an array of arrays, and it allows us to store a list of all of the triangles that share each vertex, no matter how many there are. The code for doing this is in Grid::read_ply_file and is executed each time a smooth mesh triangle is constructed. The triangle number, starting at zero for the first triangle read, is added to the three vertices that belong to the triangle.

The code for the algorithm in Listing 23.8 is in the function Grid::compute_mesh_normals, which I won't reproduce here because the syntax is somewhat complex. This calls the get_normal function for each smooth mesh triangle on average six times. To avoid computing the normal each time, I compute the normal (once) and store it in each triangle (flat and smooth) when the triangle is constructed. This is a classic space-time trade-off but for scene-construction time in this case instead of rendering time. Listing 23.6 shows where the compute_mesh_normals function is called.

Listing 23.9 shows the code for the function SmoothMeshTriangle::interpolate_normal, which uses the formula (23.1). This is called from the function SmoothMeshTriangle::hit, whose code I won't reproduce here because there's only one statement that's different from the flat mesh triangle hit function in Listing 23.3: sr.normal = normal is replaced with sr.normal = interpolate_normal(beta, gamma).

Figure 23.9 shows the horse and the dragon models rendered with smooth shading.

The memory savings I get from using meshes with PLY files are rather modest, about 20% for flat triangles and about 25% for smooth triangles,

```
Normal
SmoothMeshTriangle::interpolate_normal(const float beta, const float gamma)
const {

    Normal normal((1 - beta - gamma) * mesh_ptr->normals[index1]
            + beta * mesh_ptr->normals[index2]
            + gamma * mesh_ptr->normals[index3] );
    normal.normalize();

    return (normal);
}
```

Listing 23.9. The function SmoothMeshTriangle::interpolate_normal.

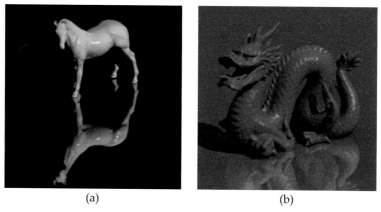

(a)   (b)

Figure 23.9. (a) Horse PLY model courtesy of Cyberware (image courtesy of Daniel Kaestli); (b) dragon PLY model courtesy of the Stanford University Computer Graphics Laboratory.

compared with using non-mesh triangles. However, the savings increase as more information is stored at the vertices, for example, texture coordinates in Chapter 29.

23.4.3 Multiple-Mesh Objects

Because PLY files can only contain a single polygon mesh, a single PLY file can't describe complex models that consist of multiple meshes, and which are the norm in commercial graphics. That's not a problem for us, however, because we can nest grids. The penguin in Figure 23.10 is an example that consists of 11 parts described by 11 PLY files. I've stored these in a separate grid, and rendered them with different colors to highlight the different parts. As such, the

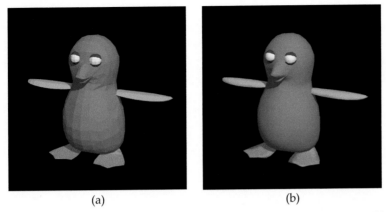

Figure 23.10. Penguin model courtesy of Naomi Hatchman. (a) Flat shading; (b) smooth shading.

penguin is a two-level grid object. All of the resources you need to reproduce these images are on the book's website.

 ## 23.5 Hierarchical Instance Grids

This section is purely for fun, meaning that it's not necessary for the following chapters. The technique I'll describe here will allow you to render scenes with an astronomical numbers of objects, provided they are all instances of the same object.

The basic idea is quite simple, as Figure 23.11 demonstrates. On the left we have a single geometric object, from which we create nine instances in a

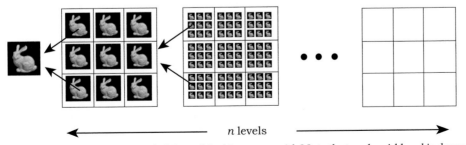

n levels

Figure 23.11. Construction of a hierarchical instance grid. Note that each grid level is *drawn* successively smaller here so that they will fit in the figure. There's no scaling required in the construction.

regular 3×3 arrangement by translating the object in the x- and z-directions. We store these in a grid. As the resulting grid is also a geometric object, we next create nine instances of it by translation and store these in another grid. This produces $(3 \times 3)^2 = 27$ instances. We then repeat this process for n levels, after which the total number of instances is $(3 \times 3)^n$.

```
const char* file_name = "Bunny69K.ply";
Grid* bunny_ptr = new Grid(new Mesh);
bunny_ptr->read_smooth_triangles(file_name);
bunny_ptr->set_material(phong_ptr);
bunny_ptr->setup_cells();

int num_levels = 8;           // number of levels
int instances_grid_res = 10;  // initial number of bunnies in x- and z-directions
double gap = 0.05;            // initial distance between instances
double size = 0.1;           // bunny size

Grid* current_grid_ptr = bunny_ptr;   // initially, just the bunny

for (int level = 0; level < num_levels; level++) {
    Grid* instance_grid_ptr = new Grid;           // temporary grid

    for (int i = 0; i < instances_grid_res; i++) {      // xw direction
        for (int k = 0; k < instances_grid_res; k++) {  // zw direction
            Instance* instance_ptr = new Instance;
            // add whole grid up to this level
            instance_ptr->set_object(current_grid_ptr);
            instance_ptr->set_material(phong_ptr);
            instance_ptr->translate(i * (size + gap), 0.0, k * (size + gap));
            instance_ptr->compute_bounding_box();
            instance_grid_ptr->add_object(instance_ptr);
        }
    }

    size = instances_grid_res * size + (instances_grid_res - 1) * gap;
    gap = 0.05 * size;
    instance_grid_ptr->setup_cells();
    current_grid_ptr = current_grid_ptr;
}

add_object(current_grid_ptr);
...
```

Listing 23.10. Part of a build function for a hierarchical instance grid.

In general, if we use an $m \times m$ arrangement of instances with n levels of grids, the number of instances is $(m \times m)^n = m^{2n}$. I call this a *hierarchical instance grid*. For example, if $m = 10$ and $n = 8$, we have $(100)^8 = 10^{16}$ instances. The recursive hierarchical structure of the grid saves a lot of memory compared with trying to store all of the instances in a single grid.

Listing 23.10 is part of a build function that demonstrates how to build a hierarchical instance grid.

Figure 23.12 shows perspective views of a grid with $m = 10$ and $n = 8$ that contains 10^{16} high-resolution bunnies and 6.9541×10^{20} triangles. The whole grid appears in Figure 23.12(a), while Figure 23.12(b)–(d) are rendered with zoom factors of 10^3, 10^6, and 10^8, respectively. There is a lot of aliasing in Figure 23.12(a), (b), and (c). Slightly less than half of the triangles per bunny are visible in the images.

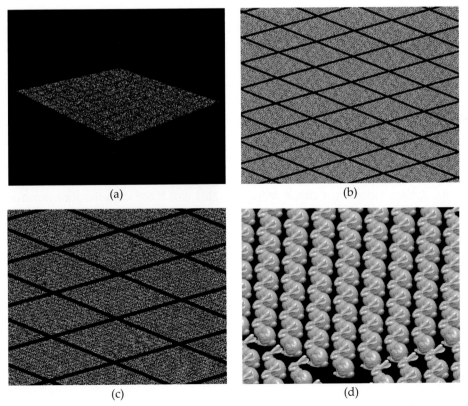

(a)

(b)

(c)

(d)

Figure 23.12. A hierarchical instance grid rendered with successive zoom factors.

Further Reading

Akenine-Möller and Haines (2002) contains good discussions on the use of triangles and other polygons in computer graphics. The Stanford bunny, skeleton, and other PLY models can be found at the Geogia Institute of Technology Large Geometry Models Archive at http://www.cc.gatech.edu/projects/large_models/index.html. Cyberware's website at http://www.cyberware.com has the Ganesh, horse, Isis, and other PLY models. The Stanford University Computer Graphics Laboratory has the dragon, Stanford bunny, and other PLY models at http://graphics.stanford.edu. The dragon model was first discussed by Curless and Levoy (1996). There are many other sources of polygon models on the web. Greg Turk's home page at http://www-static.cc.gatech.edu/~turk/ has a list of sites.

 Questions

23.1. Consider an arbitrary point on the surface of a generic sphere. Why are the components of the unit normal the same as the coordinates of the point?

23.2. Why do the sphere models in Figure 23.1(c) and (d) seem to consist of quadrilaterals, except for the triangles that meet at the top and bottom?

23.3. How can triangles have degenerate bounding boxes?

23.4. Is the specular highlight in Figure 23.3 really accurate? Notice how it grows in size as the number of triangles increases. Why does this happen?

23.5. Which primitives other than triangles can have degenerate bounding boxes?

23.6. Can you explain why the algorithm in Listing 23.8 operates in $O(num\_vertices)$ time?

23.7. How can you tell that the penguin in Figure 23.10(b) consists of polygons?

 Exercises

23.1. Reproduce Figures 23.1 and 23.3 and experiment with different values of m and n.

23.2. In the build function for Figure 23.3(d), replace the grid with a generic sphere and compare the results.

23.3. Derive the formula (23.1) for the interpolated normal. Hint: the expression is of the form

$$\boldsymbol{n} = a\boldsymbol{n}_1 + b\boldsymbol{n}_2 + c\boldsymbol{n}_3.$$

where a, b, and c are constants. Use the boundary conditions to find these.

23.4. There are low, medium, and high polygon resolution bunny PLY files on the book's website, with test images. Render these with flat and smooth shading.

23.5. Figure 23.13 shows a goldfish model that I'll use in Section 28.8. Render this using the low- and high-resolution PLY files on the book's website.

23.6. Download other PLY files from the web, for example, the dragon, Buddha, and horse models, and render these.

23.7. Implement the penguin from Section 23.4.3. There are low- and high-resolution versions on the book's website.

Figure 23.13. High-resolution goldfish model courtesy of James McNess.

Figure 23.14. A 3D hierarchical instance grid of spheres. Image courtesy of Simon Biber.

23.8. Implement a 2D hierarchical instance grid and experiment with different values of the parameters. See how many spheres and triangles you can render.

23.9. A 3D hierarchical instance grid is much more efficient for storing instances than the 2D structure in Listing 23.10. Write a 3D version of this algorithm and see how many triangles, or other objects, you can store and render. As an example, Figure 23.14 shows 4.3×10^{36} spheres in a 3D grid.

24   Mirror Reflection

Reflective spheres by Burt Flugleman, Rundle Street Mall, Adelaide. Photograph by Kevin Suffern.

Objectives

By the end of this chapter, you should:

- understand how mirror reflections are modeled in ray tracing;
- have seen some interesting examples of reflections;
- have implemented a reflective material.

    I'll discuss here how ray tracing simulates part of the indirect illumination in a scene. This ray-tracing technique was first developed by Whitted (1980) and is often referred to as Whitted-style ray tracing. Up until now, we have only ray traced the primary rays, but here we will trace the reflected rays as they bounce between reflective objects in the scene. The part of the indirect illumination that this models is the specular-to-specular light transport with perfect specular reflection.

When a ray hits an object whose material is reflective, we calculate a *reflected ray* at the hit point, in the direction of mirror reflection. This was illustrated in Figures 15.1 and 15.2, as specular highlights require the same direction. The reflected rays are examples of secondary rays and can themselves hit objects and give rise to further reflected rays. The ability to trace reflected rays allows reflections to be rendered. As a result, objects can appear more than once in an image, and parts of the scene that are hidden from the camera in ray casting can be visible.

 ## 24.1 The Illumination Model

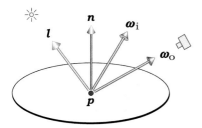

Figure 24.1. With indirect illumination, incident radiance at a surface point can arrive from any direction ω_i.

When indirect illumination is taken into account, incident radiance can arrive at a surface point from any direction ω_i in the hemisphere, not just from the light sources.[1] See Figure 24.1, where ω_i is an arbitrary direction and the reflected radiance in the direction ω_o is the sum of a direct and an indirect term, as discussed in Section 14.1.

For a point p on the surface of a non-emissive object, we can write the rendering equation (13.21) as

$$L_r(p, \omega_o) = L_{\text{direct}}(p, \omega_o) + L_{\text{indirect}}(p, \omega_o),$$

where $L_{\text{direct}}(p, \omega_o)$ is given by Equation (18.1) and $L_{\text{indirect}}(p, \omega_o)$ is

$$L_{\text{indirect}}(p, \omega_O) = \int_{2\pi^+} f_r(p, \omega_i, \omega_O) L_i(r_c(p, \omega_i), -\omega_i) \cos\theta_i d\omega_i. \qquad (24.1)$$

Here, $L_i(r_c(p, \omega_i), -\omega_i)$ is the incident radiance in the direction ω_i obtained by shooting a reflected ray into the hemisphere above p. In general, the integral in Equation (24.1) can be difficult to evaluate, but it's simple in this chapter as we are only going to consider the special case of perfect mirror reflection at p. This is illustrated in Figure 24.2(a) where a primary ray r_0 intersects an object at p and is reflected in the direction of perfect mirror reflection. We implement this by constructing a reflected ray r and tracing it into the scene. Figure 24.2(b) shows the directions in 3D, where we need to compute the reflected radiance

---

1. Of course, incident radiance can also arrive from any direction from an environment light, but that's direct illumination computed with Monte Carlo integration.

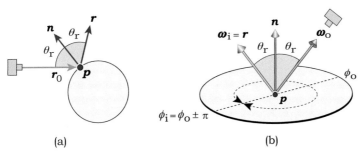

(a)   (b)

Figure 24.2. (a) Perfect mirror reflection at a surface point p; (b) 3D directions and angles at p for perfect mirror reflection.

in the direction $\omega_o = r_0$ from the incident radiance in the direction $\omega_i = r$. For perfect mirror reflection, $\theta_i = \theta_o = \theta_r$, and $\phi_i = \phi_o \pm \pi$. From Equation (15.4), r is given by

$$r = -\omega_o + 2(n \bullet \omega_o)\, n. \qquad (24.2)$$

Because the incident radiance comes from a single direction, the expression for the reflected radiance in the direction ω_o is

$$L_{\text{indirect}}(p, \omega_o) = f_{r,s}(p, \omega_i, \omega_o) L_i(p, \omega_i), \qquad (24.3)$$

where $f_{r,s}$ is the perfect specular BRDF (see Nicodemus et al. (1977)). Note that there is no $\cos\theta_i$ term in this expression. The reason is shown in Figure 24.3, where Figure 24.3(a) shows a beam of light with a small incidence angle that's

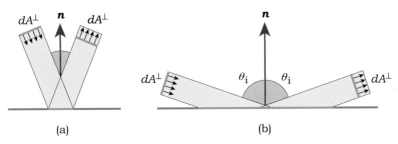

(a)   (b)

Figure 24.3. When a beam of light is reflected from a perfect mirror, its cross section area is unchanged after reflection and is therefore independent of the angle of incidence θ_i.

reflected from a perfect mirror. Because there's no scattering, its cross section area is the same before and after the reflection. This applies for all incidence angles, so that for the larger incidence angle in Figure 24.3(b), where the beam hits the mirror over a larger area because of the $\cos \theta_i$ term, the cross sections before and after reflection are still the same. The cross section of the reflected beam is therefore independent of θ_i, and so is the reflected radiance, as it's specified perpendicular to the beam's direction.

There are a number of ways that we can model specular reflection in the BRDF. A physically correct model for smooth materials uses the Fresnel equations $f_{r,s} = F(p, \omega_o)$, where F depends on the angle of incidence θ_i, but I'll discuss these in Chapter 28. In this chapter, I'll discuss a simpler reflection model where $f_{r,s}$ is a constant. The expression is $f_{r,s} = \rho_s = k_r c_r$, where $k_r \in [0, 1]$ is the *reflection coefficient* and c_r is the *reflection color*. In this case, Equation (24.3) becomes

$$L_{\text{indirect}}(p, \omega_o) = k_r c_r L_i(p, \omega_i). \tag{24.4}$$

We can design a BRDF so that the integral (24.1) reduces to the expression (24.4). The BRDF must be zero for all values of $\theta_i \neq \theta_r$ and $\phi_i \neq \phi_o \pm \pi$. When $\theta_i = \theta_r$ and $\phi_i = \phi_o \pm \pi$, it must have a singularity and must therefore involve delta functions. The expression is

$$f_{r,s}(p, \omega_i, \omega_o) = 2 k_r c_r \delta(\sin^2\theta_r - \sin^2\theta_i)\, \delta(\phi_o \pm \pi - \phi_i), \tag{24.5}$$

(Nicodemus et al., 1977). See Exercise 24.1. The BRDF (24.5) is not quite what we want, however. The rendering equation integrals always have the $\cos \theta_i$ term present, and if we used (24.5), the resulting expression for $L_r(p, \omega_o)$ would be

$$L_{\text{indirect}}(p, \omega_o) = k_r c_r L_i(p, \omega_i) \cos \theta_i.$$

Fortunately, this is simple to fix by dividing (24.5) by $\cos \theta_i$:

$$f_{r,s}(p, \omega_i, \omega_o) = 2 k_r c_r \delta(\sin^2\theta_r - \sin^2\theta_i)\, \delta(\phi_o \pm \pi - \phi_i)/\cos \theta_i, \tag{24.6}$$

as this cancels the $\cos \theta_i$ term in the rendering equation.

Again, if the delta functions and integrals bother you, don't worry. The implementation in the Section 24.2 is quite simple. The above analysis boils down to the function `PerfectSpecular::sample_f` in Listing 24.2, which contains just three simple lines of code.

There is, however, a lot more to reflections than discussed above; in scenes with more than one reflective object, rays can bounce between them. See Figure 24.4, where the single primary ray r_0 gives rise to the reflected rays r_1, r_2, and r_3. Notice how the reflected rays all start on object surfaces.

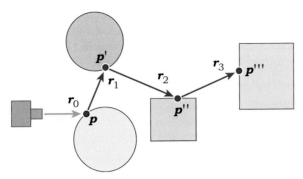

Figure 24.4. Reflected rays generated from a single primary ray r_0.

Each successive reflection corresponds to a recursive application of the ray-casting operator $r_c(p, \omega_i) = r(p, \omega_i)$, as shown in Figure 24.5 for two reflections.

The expressions $L_i(r(p, \omega_i), -\omega_i)$ can be successively substituted into Equation (24.1) to get a theoretical solution to the rendering equation that's analogous to Equation (13.29), but for practical ray-tracing purposes, we can proceed as follows. We trace the reflected ray r_1, which will result in one of the following outcomes:

1. It doesn't hit any objects, in which case it returns the background color to p.
2. It hits a light source, in which case it returns L_e to p.
3. Its nearest hit point p' is on a non-reflective object, in which case the direct illumination is computed at p' and returned to p.

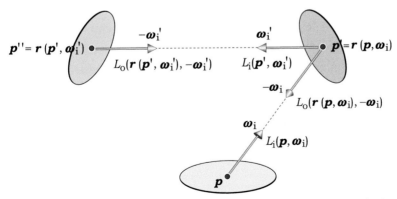

Figure 24.5. Incident radiance returned along reflected rays at p and p', where both reflected rays hit an object.

4. Its nearest hit point p' is on another reflective object, in which case the direct illumination is computed at p', and the reflected ray r_2 is traced. The radiance returned to p' by r_2 is then added to the direct illumination, and the combined radiance is returned to p.

In Case 4, we trace the reflected rays recursively until either one of Cases 1, 2, or 3 occurs, or some specified maximum number of bounces has been reached. This is the process that simulates the specular-to-specular light transport in a scene. The radiance returned to the camera by the ray r_0 is determined by the material properties of all of the objects that the reflected rays have hit. Of course, Cases 1–4 can also apply to the primary ray r_0. If the scene contains area lights, we need to use Monte Carlo integration to evaluate the direct illumination at each hit point, but we don't have to do this for the indirect illumination, as there are no integrals to evaluate.

 ## 24.2 Implementation

24.2.1 Things to Do

To implement reflections, we need to perform the following tasks:

1. Add a data member `max_depth` to the view plane to specify the maximum number of bounces.[2]
2. Allow the ray tracer to keep track of how many bounces a ray has had by adding a data member `depth` to the `ShadeRec` class.
3. Implement a new tracer class called `Whitted` whose `trace_ray` function uses its `depth` parameter to store the depth of each ray in the `ShadeRec` object.
4. Implement a `PerfectSpecular` BRDF.
5. Implement at least one reflective material that constructs the reflected rays and ray traces them.

Fortunately, we don't have to do either of the following tasks:

1. Alter any of the cameras' `render_scene` functions. Because the variable `depth` specifies how many bounces a ray has had, its value for primary rays is zero. The `render_scene` functions already set `depth` to zero for each primary ray and pass this value into the tracer's `trace_ray` function.

---

2. The name `max_bounces` may be more appropriate, but as reflections are implemented through recursive function calls, `max_depth` is also appropriate and ties in better with the fact that each ray is at a particular recursion depth.

2. Write new shade functions for existing materials. We could write functions called whitted_shade for all materials, but for the Matte and Phong materials, the code inside would be the same as in their existing shade functions. The approach I've adopted is to write shade functions for the reflective materials that construct and handle the reflected rays. This way, we can ray trace scenes with Matte, Phong, and reflective materials, and illuminated with directional and point lights, without altering the existing materials.

A great benefit of using tracers is that they allow us to implement reflections with minimal changes to existing classes.

If you want to ray trace scenes with reflective materials and area lights, you will have to write an area_light_shade function for the reflective materials and use the AreaLighting tracer. I've left this as an exercise.

24.2.2 The Whitted Tracer

Listing 24.1 shows the function whitted::trace_ray, which returns black when the depth parameter is greater than max_depth and stores depth in the ShadeRec object. This function will be called recursively from a reflective material's shade function, which you will also need to look at to fully understand how trace_ray works (see Section 24.2.4).

```
RGBColor
whitted::trace_ray(const Ray ray, const int depth) const {
    if (depth > world_ptr->vp.max_depth)
        return (black);
    else {
        ShadeRec sr(world_ptr->hit_objects(ray));

        if (sr.hit_an_object) {
            sr.depth = depth;
            sr.ray = ray;

            return (sr.material_ptr->shade(sr));
        }
        else
            return (world_ptr->background_color);
    }
}
```

Listing 24.1. The function whitted::traceRay.

```
RGBColor
PerfectSpecular::sample_f(const ShadeRec& sr, const Vector3D& wo,
Vector3D& wi) const {
    float ndotwo = sr.normal * wo;
    wi = -wo + 2.0 * sr.normal * ndotwo;

    return (kr * cr / (sr.normal * wi));
}
```

Listing 24.2. The function `PerfectSpecular::sample_f`.

24.2.3 The Perfect Specular BRDF

Perfect mirror reflection is implemented in the `PerfectSpecular` BRDF, which stores k_r and c_r. To implement reflections, we use the BRDF function `sample_f` to compute the direction of the reflected ray, as well as computing the reflected radiance (see Section 13.9.1 and, in particular, Table 13.1). Because the reflected ray is always in the direction of mirror reflection, there is no random sampling of the BRDF. As a result, the function `PerfectSpecular::sample_f` in Listing 24.2 is simple. Here, I've used $\omega_i = -\omega_o + 2(n \bullet \omega_o) n$, which follows from Equation (24.2).

Since we don't use the functions `PerfectSpecular::rho` and `PerfectSpecular::f`, these don't have to be defined. The inherited versions from the base class BRDF just return black.

24.2.4 A Reflective Material

I've implemented a material called `Reflective` that inherits from `Phong` so that it can use the function `Phong::shade` for the direct illumination. This is a traditional reflective material that allows surfaces to be rendered with ambient, diffuse, and specular direct illumination, as well as reflections. The only data member that `Reflective` has to store directly is the perfect specular BRDF, as indicated in Listing 24.3

The shade function for the `Reflective` class is in Listing 24.4. Notice that this function makes a recursive call to `trace_ray`, an action that results in the shade function also being recalled recursively from `whitted::trace_ray` in Listing 24.1. This is "recursion by stealth" because neither function calls itself directly. Because `trace_ray` is called recursively, its ray parameter

```
class Reflective: public Phong {
    public:

    // constructors, access functions, etc.

    virtual RGBColor
    shade(ShadeRec& sr);

    private:

        PerfectSpecular* reflective_brdf;
}
```

Listing 24.3. The class `Reflective`.

```
RGBColor
Reflective::shade(ShadeRec& sr) {
    RGBColor L(Phong::shade(sr));          // direct illumination

    Vector3D wo = -sr.ray.d;
    Vector3D wi;
    RGBColor fr = reflective_brdf->sample_f(sr, wo, wi);
    Ray reflected_ray(sr.hit_point, wi);

    L += fr * sr.w.tracer_ptr->trace_ray(reflected_ray, sr.depth + 1) *
    (sr.normal * wi);

    return (L);
}
```

Listing 24.4. `Reflective` material code.

must be const Ray ray instead of the more efficient ray reference const Ray& ray. Pass by value is necessary here because each stack frame of trace_ray requires its own copy of the ray. At any time, there can be up to max_depth distinct rays in the recursion stack. A reference would only work for ray casting (see Question 24.1).

How do we break out of this sequence of mutually recursive function calls? It's the + 1 in the sr.depth + 1 argument of trace_ray. This is a critical part of the code, as it provides the escape mechanism that you always need with recursive programming (see Question 24.2).

```
...
int num_samples = 1;

vp.set_hres(600);
vp.set_vres(400);
vp.set_samples(num_samples);
vp.set_max_depth(10);

tracer_ptr = new Whitted(this);

Reflective* reflective_ptr1 = new Reflective;
reflective_ptr1->set_ka(0.25);
reflective_ptr1->set_kd(0.5);
reflective_ptr1->set_cd(0.75, 0.75, 0);
reflective_ptr1->set_ks(0.15);
reflective_ptr1->set_exp(100);
reflective_ptr1->set_kr(0.75);
reflective_ptr1->set_cr(white);
...
```

Listing 24.5. Build function fragment for a scene with reflective materials. Only the set functions set_kr and set_cr are data members of the Reflective class; the others are inherited from the Phong class.

 ## 24.3 Reflective Objects

We can now look at images of a scene that contains reflective objects. The reflective materials in these images have c_r = white, so that no color is added through the reflections. Listing 24.5 is a fragment from the build function for this scene that demonstrates how to construct the view plane, the Whitted tracer, and one of the reflective materials.

Figure 24.6(a) shows the scene rendered with max_depth = 0, which is the same as ray casting. I've put grid lines on the plane, as these help to visualize the reflections, but you can easily render these images with a matte material on the plane.[3]

Figure 24.6(b) displays the results of using max_depth = 1, for a single bounce. As you can see, the reflections dramatically alter the appearance of the three reflective objects (see Questions 24.3 and 24.4).

---

3. The build function defines a matte material for this purpose.

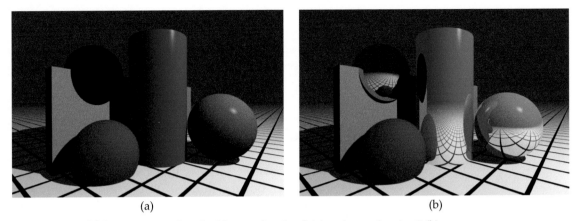

(a)   (b)

Figure 24.6. A scene rendered with `max_depth` = 0 (a) and `max_depth` = 1 (b).

The black sphere in Figure 24.6(a) demonstrates how we can model an uncolored mirror with the `Reflective` material: just set all components of the direct illumination to zero. With no direct illumination, the only reflected radiance comes from the reflected rays.

Figure 24.7(a) shows the results of rendering the scene with `max_depth` = 10. The only differences between this image and Figure 26.6(b) are in the inter-reflections between the reflective spheres and the cylinder. Most reflected rays hit a non-reflective object or leave the scene without hitting

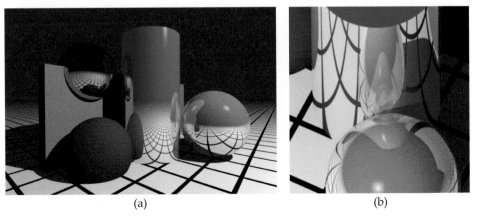

(a)   (b)

Figure 24.7. (a) The scene from Figure 24.6 rendered with `max_depth` = 10; (b) close-up view of the yellow-green sphere and the cylinder from a different viewpoint than in (a).

another reflective object, with the result that the inter-reflections are the only places where multiple reflections can build up. Figure 24.7(b) shows a close-up view of the yellow-green sphere and reflections on the cylinder from a different camera location. There are further examples of inter-reflections in the following sections.

24.4 Inconsistencies

An inconsistency in the `Reflective` material is that the direct illumination models glossy specular reflection, but the indirect illumination models perfect specular reflection. This puts the mirror-sharp reflections at odds with the specular highlights, a factor that has contributed to the ray-traced appearance of traditional ray-traced images. To be consistent, if we render a reflective object with specular highlights, we should use the same amount of glossiness for the reflections. As an example, the center sphere in Figure 24.8(a) is rendered with the `Reflective` material, and in Figure 24.8(b), it is rendered with glossy reflections. I'll discuss how to implement these in Chapter 25.

Another inconsistency occurs if we don't enforce $k_r = k_s$. These should be the same, as they both specify specular reflection, but for shading flexibility, I won't enforce this.

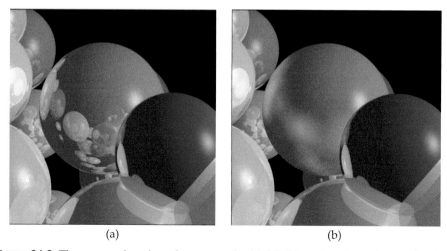

(a)   (b)

Figure 24.8. The green sphere has glossy specular highlights and perfect mirror reflections (a) and glossy reflections (b).

Figure 24.9. Colored reflective balls. Photograph by Kevin Suffern.

 ## 24.5 Colored Reflectors

Highly polished materials often don't have any diffuse reflection component or Phong specular highlights. Such materials can also be brightly colored, such as the balls in Figure 24.9.

We can simulate this type of material with the Reflective class by setting $k_a = k_d = k_s = 0.0$ and using a reflective color c_r that's not white. Figure 24.10 shows several colored spheres rendered this way. Notice the complex pattern of inter-reflections and the color mixing in them. There are no light sources, and the scene was rendered with max_depth = 10. Because it can be a lot of work to set $k_a = k_d = k_s = 0.0$ in the build functions for every reflective material that you want to render with no direct illumination, it's a good idea to implement another reflective material that doesn't have a Phong component (see Exercise 24.7).

Figure 24.10. Colored reflective spheres.

Figure 24.11 shows Figure 11.12(a) rendered with random colored reflective materials on the buildings.

Figure 24.11. City scene rendered with reflective buildings.

 ## 24.6 Real and Virtual Images

You will be able to better understand ray-traced images that contain reflections if you know where the reflections are in 3D space. I'll therefore describe here some of the optics of mirrors, but unfortunately, in the optics literature, reflections of objects in mirrors are referred to as "images." You may find this a bit confusing, as this whole book is about rendering ray-traced images of 3D scenes. Because I'll have to use the correct optics terminology, in the following discussion, the word "image" will refer to a 3D reflection in the real world. Also note that the discussion below is quite brief. After all, this isn't an optics textbook. The references cited in the Further Reading section discuss the formation of images from mirrors in much more detail.

Optics images are basically of two types: *real* and *virtual*. With a real mirror, a virtual image is one that's formed with no light actually coming from the image. As a simple example, a plane mirror only forms virtual images. These are the same distances behind the mirror plane that the real objects are in front of it. Figure 24.12 illustrates this for a single point p on an object and its image p'. This is a vir-

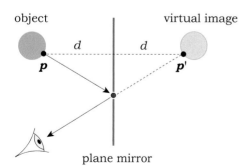

Figure 24.12. A point p and its virtual image p' are on opposite sides of a plane mirror and the same distance from it.

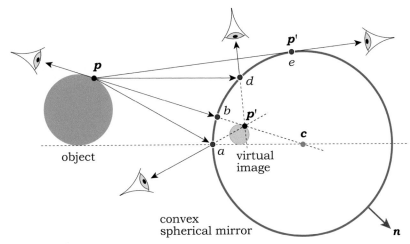

Figure 24.13. When viewed from the outside, a reflective sphere forms a virtual image inside the sphere. Here, *c* is the center of the sphere.

tual image because the light ray that forms the image is reflected from the mirror and doesn't pass through p'. The light only appears to come from p'.

A convex mirror only forms virtual images, which, again, are behind the mirror. Figure 24.13 illustrates the formation of a virtual image for a single point p and a convex spherical mirror. For a mirrored sphere, the images are inside the sphere. This figure shows how the reflected rays at *a*, *b*, and *d*, when we extend their directions back into the sphere, all pass through the image point p'.[4] By construction, this is the same point for all viewing angles between *a* and *d*. If you look at the reflection of a light source on a reflective sphere, you will see that, as you move your head, the reflection seems to stay in the same 3D location inside the sphere. But this doesn't apply to all viewing angles. For reflection points outside the arc *a–d*, the reflected rays' extensions can't pass through the same point p' without violating the law of reflection. For example, p' would appear at *e* for the grazing ray that touches the sphere at this point.

In contrast, a concave mirror can form real and virtual images depending on where the object is in relationship to the mirror and, thus, can form more types of images than convex mirrors. Figure 24.14 shows one example of the formation of a real image inside a spherical mirror for a single point p. In this

---

4. The letters *a*, *b*, *d*, and *e* are just labels for the points and are therefore not bold.

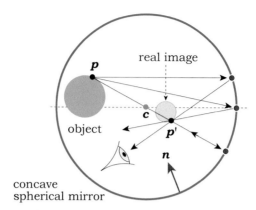

Figure 24.14. Formation of a real image inside a hollow sphere with an image on its inside surface.

case, the image is real because the rays reflected off the inside surface of the sphere pass through the image point p'.

In Section 24.7, I'll show ray-traced examples of the types of images in Figures 24.12–24.14.

24.7 Examples

We can use reflections to create many beautiful and interesting images. I hope that after you have looked at the following examples, you'll want to create your own images.

24.7.1 Sphere Reflections

It's not always obvious that reflections on a sphere are inside the sphere. For example, Figure 24.15(a) shows a small reflective sphere, a rectangle, and a large self-luminous sphere with grid lines. Figure 24.15(b) shows a close-up view of the reflections of the rectangle and large sphere on the small sphere. There are also specular highlights from point and directional lights visible. Here, it's hard to see that the reflections are inside the sphere because its surface isn't visible. Placing grid lines on the surface helps, as in Figure 24.15(c), particularly when they are rendered over the reflections.

However, stereo pairs are the most effective way to demonstrate where the reflections are (see Figure 24.16). This shows that the specular highlights are also underneath the surface, as a result of these being the reflections of the point and directional lights.

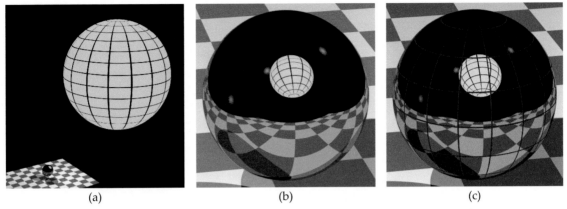

(a)   (b)   (c)

Figure 24.15. (a) Scene with two spheres and a checkered rectangle; (b) close-up view of reflections on the small sphere; (c) same as (b) but with grid lines added to the reflective sphere.

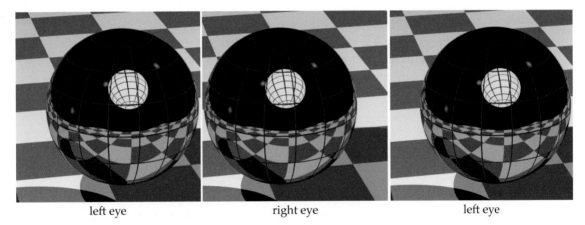

left eye   right eye   left eye

Figure 24.16. Stereo pair of Figure 24.15(c). If you can't view these naturally, you will have to use a stereoscope.

24.7.2 Hall of Mirrors

One of the best ways to illustrate reflections is to simulate a hall of mirrors. This is a configuration where there are two parallel mirrors, often on opposite sides of a room, where you can see multiple reflections. The scene in Figures 24.17 and 24.18 consists of six planes that intersect to form a cube with parallel mirrors near two opposite walls, a mirror near a third wall, a mirror near the floor, and a reflective sphere in the middle. The sphere is the only reflective object

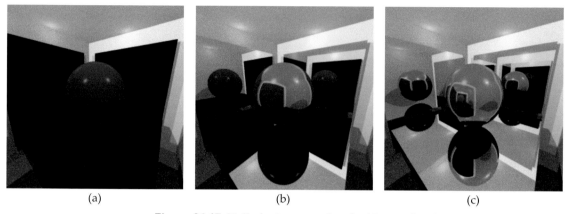

(a)   (b)   (c)

Figure 24.17. Hall of mirrors rendered with `max_depth` = 0, 1, and 2.

with a direct-illumination component. The wall mirrors have $k_r = 0.9$. The scene is illuminated with four point lights near the ceiling.

Figure 24.17(a) was rendered with `max_depth` = 0, so there are no reflections. This is not a pretty sight. Figure 24.17(b) was rendered with `max_depth` = 1 and doesn't look much better, but it does show that the sphere is reflective and shows the first reflection off the mirrors. Figure 24.27(c) was rendered with `max_depth` = 2.

Figure 24.18(a) was rendered with `max_depth` = 19, where the result finally looks like a hall of mirrors. The wall mirrors have a faint green reflection color

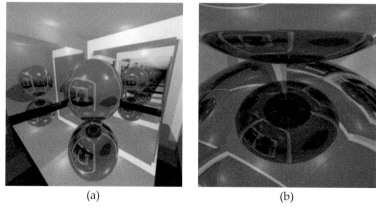

(a)   (b)

Figure 24.18. (a) Hall of mirrors with `max_depth` = 19; (b) close-up view of the multiple reflections between the floor mirror and the sphere.

to simulate the green color that multiple reflections from real mirrors pick up as they travel through the panes of glass. Figure 24.18(b) is a close-up view of the floor mirror rendered with max_depth = 19.

24.7.3 Self-Reflection

Non-convex objects can exhibit *self-reflection*, where the objects can appear reflected on their own surfaces. Tori exhibit this, as you can see from the beautiful image of two reflective tori in Figure 24.19. What is the small pink reflection on the lower right part of the blue torus?

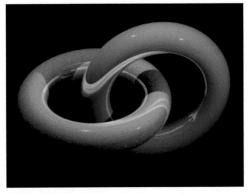

Figure 24.19. Two reflective tori. Image courtesy of Daniel Kaestli.

24.7.4 Four Spheres

Figure 24.20(a) shows four reflective spheres arranged so that their centers are at the vertices of a regular tetrahedron and their radii are such that they just touch. If you think these spheres look strange, they are. Their reflection parameters are $k_a = 1.0$ and $k_r = 1.0$. I've chosen these values to emphasize the inter-reflections of the spheres, which consequently are quite bright. If we place the camera in the space between the spheres, we find that something wonderful happens: the reflected rays line up in the form of a classic early twentieth-century fractal called the Sierpinski gasket (Sierpinski, 1915, Mandelbrot, 1972,

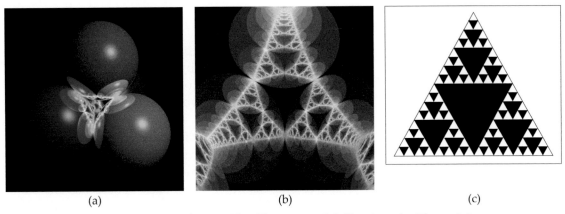

(a)   (b)   (c)

Figure 24.20. (a) Four reflective spheres with a Phong material, illuminated with a point light; (b) the same spheres rendered with the camera in the space between them, but using ambient illumination only; (c) illustration of the Sierpinski gasket fractal.

Suffern 1994, Suffern 2000). An example image rendered with ambient illumination only and `max_depth` = 12 is in Figure 24.20(b). Figure 24.20(c) is a version of the Sierpinski gasket to demonstrate that the pattern of reflections in Figure 24.20(b) has the same recursive structure, although it's somewhat distorted. Fractals have an infinite amount of detail and, as such, are only mathematical abstractions. The real fractal from Figure 24.20(c) is obtained by repeating the recursive subdivision of the triangle an infinite number of times, instead of just four times as shown. This figure is called a *band-limited* fractal because it contains a finite amount of detail.

In the same way, Figure 24.20(b) is also a band-limited fractal because of the finite recursion depth and the finite number of pixels. If you zoomed into any part of the white lines, you would find that they are composed of disks. These are just the reflections of the spheres, visible in larger versions at lower recursion depths in the same figure. If you then increased the recursion depth, you would get back an image similar to Figure 24.20(b) because the Sierpinksi gasket, like most fractals, is *self-similar*. This means that any part, examined at any level of detail, looks similar to any other part. You can keep increasing the recursion depth until you run out of numerical precision or stack space, but you will always have a finite amount of detail.

The fractal image appears bright because $k_a = k_r = 1.0$. As k_r decreases, it rapidly fades, and for real reflective materials, where k_r is about 0.04 at normal incidence, it doesn't appear at all. The reason is that as the recursion depth increases, the rays are reflected at closer to normal incidence before turning around and escaping from the system. This is illustrated in Figure 24.21. However, the value of k_r doesn't affect the angle of reflection, and so the rays still line up in the Sierpinski gasket pattern. In fact, if we rendered Figure 24.20(b) with the pixels colored with the number of bounces before the ray escapes (the escape time), the same pattern would appear (see Sweet et al. (2001)).

The rich reflective environment between the spheres provides many possibilities for creating different optical effects. Figure 24.22, *Anemones* (Suffern, 1996, Suffern, 2000), is one example. Here, each sphere has the same material, but the color depends on the recursion depth of the ray. If you are after artistic expression instead of physical simulation, ray tracing allows you to do anything you want.

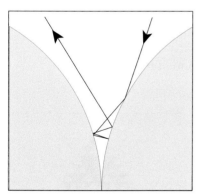

Figure 24.21. This figure shows the path of a typical ray that bounces between the spheres. The reflected directions become almost normal to the spheres before the ray turns around and escapes.

Figure 24.22. *Anemones*, Kevin Suffern, 1996.

24.7.5 Reflections in a Hollow Sphere

In the early 1990s, I wondered what it would be like if I stood inside a hollow sphere with a mirror on its inside surface. Although I've never seen what my reflections would look like, this started a project of ray tracing spheres inside a hollow sphere. An early result was *Blue Glass* (Suffern, 1993, Suffern et al., 1993), as shown in Figure 24.23(a). This was produced by placing a blue and

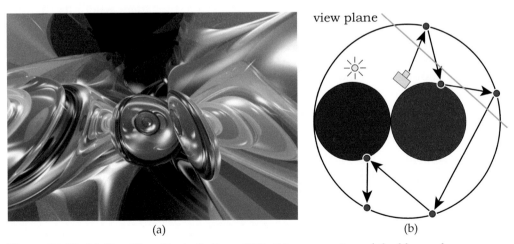

(a)   (b)

Figure 24.23. (a) *Blue Glass*, Kevin Suffern, 1993; (b) cross section of the blue and gray spheres inside the hollow sphere.

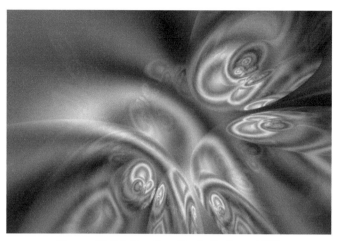

Figure 24.24. *Creation*, Kevin Suffern, 1997.

a gray sphere inside the hollow sphere and ray tracing their reflections on the inside surface of the hollow sphere with max_depth = 13. Figure 24.23(b) shows the arrangement of the spheres, point light, and camera inside the hollow sphere. The spheres inside have the dark diffuse colors as shown in Figure 24.23(b) and are rendered with a Phong material. The dark colors are necessary to prevent the image from becoming washed out at high recursion depths.[5] The hollow sphere has $k_r = 1.0$.

Figure 24.24 shows another example, called *Creation*, where the hollow sphere has a gray diffuse color and there are four black reflective spheres inside. A fifth sphere at the center of the hollow sphere has a material that simulates an interference film to create rainbow colors. The maximum recursion depth is 8. As the resulting image doesn't reproduce particularly well in CMYK, I've included an RGB version on the book's website.

24.7.6 Making Mirages

An optical device called the Mirage 2000, manufactured by Opti-Gone Associates, creates real images of objects using two concave paraboloidal mirrors. A paraboloidal surface is defined by the equation

$$y = a(x^2 + z^2),$$
(24.7)

---

5. Figure 24.23(a) has been contrast enhanced in Photoshop for artistic purposes.

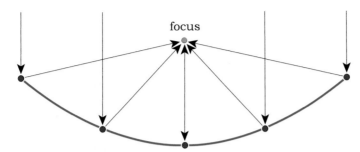

Figure 24.25. A paraboloidal surface focuses all light that hits it parallel to its central axis onto its focus point.

where a is a constant. Paraboloids have the useful property that they focus all light that travels parallel to their central axis onto a single point called the *focus*, with coordinates $f = (0, 1/(4a), 0)$ (see Figure 24.25). This is why they are sometimes used as telescope mirrors.

The Mirage 2000 device consists of two paraboloids, as shown in Figure 24.26, with a circular hole in the top paraboloid. This creates a real image of an object placed in the center of the bottom paraboloid from light that hits both paraboloids. The image floats in space above the opening.

We can simulate this device by ray tracing the paraboloids with a maximum depth of at least 2; Figure 24.26 shows the path of a typical ray. Figure 24.27(a) shows a view of the device with a yellow reflective sphere inside that has grid lines on its surface. The sphere itself is not visible in this image, but its real image is. In Figure 24.27(b), the top has been removed to show the sphere sitting on the bottom paraboloid, along with its reflections.

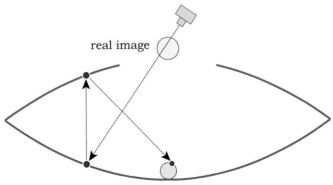

Figure 24.26. When we ray trace a model of the Mirage 2000 device, the real image of an object at the bottom is produced by rays that reflect off of both paraboloids.

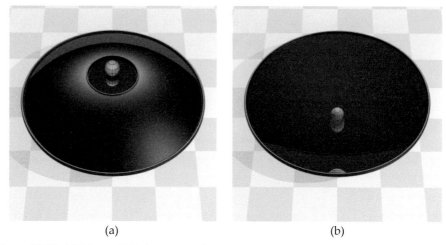

(a)   (b)

Figure 24.27. (a) Mirage 2000 device simulation; (b) image with the top removed showing the sphere and its reflection on the bottom paraboloid. Images courtesy of Tania Humphreys.

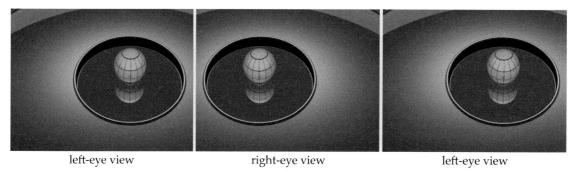

left-eye view   right-eye view   left-eye view

Figure 24.28. Stereo pair of the Mirage 2000 device. Images courtesy of Tania Humphreys.

The best way to visualize the real image is with stereo pairs, as these allow you to view the image in 3D (see Figure 24.28). The image floats above the opening, as demonstrated in Figure 24.26.

24.7.7 Beveled Objects

The compound objects discussed in Chapters 19 and 21 look good when they are rendered with reflective materials, provided they have sharp edges. Figure 24.29(a) and (b) display a thick ring and a cube, respectively. In these images, there are sharp transitions between the reflections on adjacent surfaces

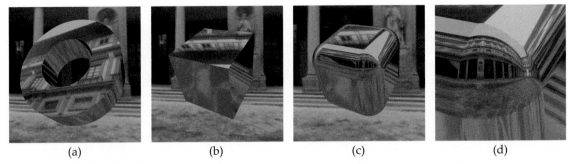

(a)	(b)	(c)	(d)

Figure 24.29. Reflective objects with the Uffizi Gallery background: (a) thick ring; (b) cube; (c) beveled cube; (d) close-up view of a corner of the beveled cube where each component now has a different color to show the boundaries.

because of the discontinuities in the normals, but we expect that. In contrast, the beveled box in Figure 24.29(c) is not as successful because there seem to be discontinuities in the reflections across the boundaries of the various components. Although the normals are continous across the boundaries, there are discontinuities in the curvatures, which cause rapid changes in the normals. Figure 24.29(d) shows a close up of one of the corners of the beveled box where each component has a different color. Our beveled objects are more successful when they are rendered with matte materials. Modeling beveled objects with polygonized NURBS surfaces or subdivision surfaces may help to solve this problem (see the Further Reading section).

The images in Figure 24.29 are a good test that reflections work correctly with transformed objects. The ring and cube are rotated, and the ring and beveled box also have transformed components.

24.7.8 Triangle Meshes

Figures 23.1 and 23.3 demonstrated the differences in shading that occur when we render triangle meshes with flat and smooth shading. There, the differences were particularly striking for the specular highlights. The differences can be just as striking for reflective materials, and for the same reason: the sensitivity of the reflected ray directions to the surface normals.

Let's start with the sphere again. Figure 24.30(a) shows a 10,000-triangle sphere mesh rendered with flat shading, where the facets are obvious. In contrast, Figure 24.30(b) shows the same mesh rendered with smooth shading. This looks like a ray-traced sphere, a fact that's confirmed in Figure 24.30(c), which is a ray-traced sphere. The book's website contains the difference image between Figure 24.30(b) and (c), which is almost black.

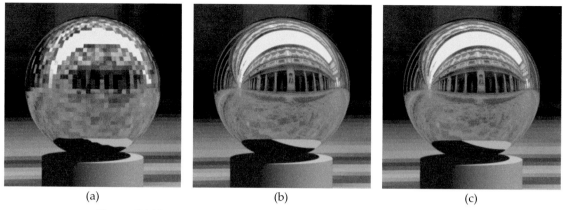

(a)   (b)   (c)

Figure 24.30. (a) Sphere triangle mesh with flat shading. There are some aliasing artifacts near the center of the sphere on some facets. (b) The same mesh with smooth shading. (c) Ray-traced sphere.

The Stanford bunny highlights some issues with reflective triangle meshes that are not apparent with the sphere. For example, smooth shading is not always the best technique; it all depends on the resolution of the triangle mesh and on the effects you want to achieve. Figure 24.31(a) shows a low-resolution (3K) Stanford bunny rendered with a reflective material and flat shading. In this case, the low number of triangles and the flat shading results in an appearance like cut glass, even though the material isn't transparent. Figure 24.31(b) shows the same mesh rendered with smooth shading, where there is a large difference in appearance. Figure 24.31(c) shows the high-resolution (69K) model rendered with flat shading. This image looks messy. Figure 24.31(d) shows the 69K model rendered with smooth shading. The additional detail in this model results in confusing-looking reflections.

(a)   (b)   (c)   (d)

Figure 24.31. Reflective Stanford bunny models rendered with flat and smooth shading.

Figure 24.31 indicates that the Stanford bunny is not particularly effective as a purely reflective object, although I personally like Figure 24.31(a). The low-resolution model is inaccurate, while the high-resolution model is too lumpy, as the figure on the first page of Chapter 17 demonstrates. The high-resolution model works much better as a non-reflective object.

The images in Figure 24.31 were rendered with max_depth = 3 because the bunny models are self-reflective. Figure 24.32 shows the 69K model rendered with max_depth = 1, which can't render self-reflections (see Question 24.6). The number of bounces required to correctly render self-reflections depends on the triangle mesh and the viewing parameters. There's no general upper limit.

Figure 24.32. The 69K Stanford bunny model rendered with max_depth = 1.

The images in this section are a good test that reflections work with uniform grids, where the reflected rays start, and sometimes end, inside the grids. See also Exercise 24.23.

Further Reading

The original formulation of recursive ray tracing for rendering perfect specular reflection is in Whitted's landmark paper Whitted (1980), where he also modeled perfect transmission. This is why the tracer is called whitted. This topic is discussed in many books, such as Glassner (1989), Hall (1988), Foley et al. (1995), Wilt (1994), Watt (2000), Hill and Kelley (2006), Shirley and Morley (2003), Hearn and Baker (2004), Pharr and Humphreys (2004), and Shirley et al. (2005).

The inconsistency in Section 24.4 between glossy and perfect specular reflection was discussed by Watt (2000).

There is a lot of information available on real and virtual images on the Web and in optics textbooks. Hecht (1997) has an extensive discussion on this topic.

Suffern (2000) discusses how Figure 24.20(b) was generated and presents a similar image using six spheres at the vertices of a regular octahedron. Korsh and Wagner (1991) demonstrate that the reflections between spheres are chaotic and result in fractal images. Sweet et al. (1999) and Sweet et al. (2001) discuss experiments with real reflective spheres and a digital camera. Suffern et al. (1993) discusses how Figure 24.23(a) was created. Musgrave (2003a) is an excellent introduction to fractals.

The Opti-Gone Associates website at http://www.optigone.com has specifications for the nine-inch Mirage 2000 model that Figures 24.26–24.28 are based on. This site also has many useful links.

Rogers (2001) is an excellent book on NURBS. A recent book on subdivision surfaces is Warren and Weimer (2002). Subdivision surfaces are also discussed in Pharr and Humphreys (2004).

Questions

24.1. Recall that the ray parameter in `Whitted::trace_ray` in Listing 24.1 can't be a reference because of the recursion. Although the function `Reflective::shade` in Listing 24.4 is also called recursively, we can still use a reference for its `ShadeRec` parameter. Why does this work?

24.2. How does the + 1 in the `sr.depth + 1` argument passed to `Whitted::trace_ray` in Listing 24.4 stop the recursion?

24.3. In Figure 24.6(b), the parts of the cylinder and green sphere that don't have reflections of other objects are lighter than they are in Figure 24.6(a). Can you explain this?

24.4. The reflections of the plane on the cylinder in Figure 24.6(b) have a blue color. Where does this color come from?

24.5. Figure 24.33(a) is a close-up view of the sphere on top of the box in Figure 24.6. This sphere is rendered with $k_r = 0.75$. In Figure 24.33(b), the

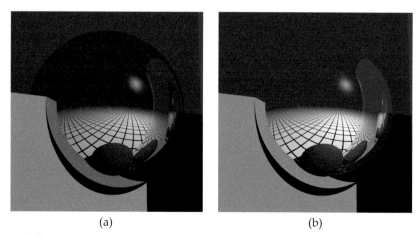

(a)   (b)

Figure 24.33. Close-up views of the sphere on top of the box in Figure 24.6 rendered with $k_r = 0.75$ (a) and $k_r = 1.0$ (b).

sphere has been rendered with $k_r = 1.0$. Why is the top part of the sphere the same color as the background color?

24.6. Figure 24.34 shows the scene in Figure 24.10 rendered with `max_depth` = 1. Can you explain this image? Exercise 24.3 is also relevant to this question.

24.7. How do the flat mirrors in the hall of mirrors images differ from household mirrors?

24.8. There's a lot of perspective distortion in the hall of mirrors images in Figures 24.17 and 24.18, caused by the fact that the camera has to be inside the box. You can see the distortion in the sphere reflections, particularly the reflection on the bottom mirror. However, the direct image of the sphere has a circular outline. Why is this? Does this sphere appear distorted?

Figure 24.34. The Uffizi spheres rendered with `max_depth` = 1.

24.9. In Figure 24.17(c), look at the reflection of the sphere in the mirror on the left wall. Why are there reflections on the top part but not on the bottom part?

24.10. Figure 24.35 shows another hall of mirrors image, this one inspired by the work of Roy Hall, who rendered a similar scene in the 1980s. His hall of mirrors appears on the cover of his book (Hall, 1988). Here, there are three spheres inside the box whose direct images show perspective distortion, again because they are close to the camera. Notice that in this case, their reflections don't appear distorted. Why is this?

Figure 24.35. Hall of mirrors image rendered with `max_depth` = 20.

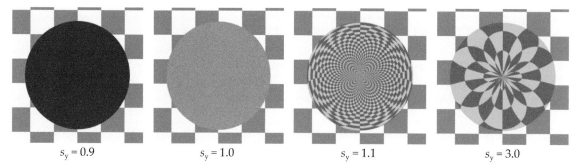

$s_y = 0.9$ $s_y = 1.0$ $s_y = 1.1$ $s_y = 3.0$

Figure 24.36. A cone scaled by the indicated amounts in the y-direction.

24.11. Figure 24.36 shows a reflective generic circular cone that has been scaled in the y-direction by various amounts. The cone is sitting on a horizontal checker plane, and these are orthographic views with the camera looking directly down the central axis of the cone (the y-axis). The background color is dark green, and the images are rendered with max_depth = 1. The scaling factors are indicated under each image. Can you explain these images? As a reminder from Chapter 19, a generic circular cone has height 2 and radius 1 so that its curved surface makes an angle of 45° to the horizontal.

24.12. Figure 24.37 shows an orthographic view of two orange spherical mirrors with vertical central axes. The rims of the mirrors are in the (x, z) plane and just fill the hole in a light-green horizontal annulus. The view direction is vertically down. Above the camera is a horizontal plane with a black-and-white checker. One of these mirrors is convex, and the other is concave, as the vertical cross sections in Figure 24.38 illustrate. Which is which in Figure 24.37?

24.13. Figure 24.39 is a open cylinder with a colored reflective material that has no direct-illumination component. There are no light sources in the scene. The only other object in the scene is the large yellow environment-light sphere used in Section 18.10. The camera is at the center of the cylinder and is looking horizontally at its inside surface. The scene was rendered with max_depth = 10. What are the color bands, and what is the dark region across the middle of the image?

24.14. Figure 24.40(a) shows three reflective spheres that just touch, rendered with $k_r = 1$ and no light sources. The reflection colors are the CMY primaries yellow (1, 1, 0), cyan (0, 1, 1), and magenta (1, 0, 1). This image was rendered with max_depth = 15. In Figure24.40(b), the colors are the RGB primaries red (1, 0, 0), green (0, 1, 0), and blue (0, 0, 1). This was rendered with max_depth = 1 because increasing max_depth makes no difference to this image. It's best to look at these images on the book's website.

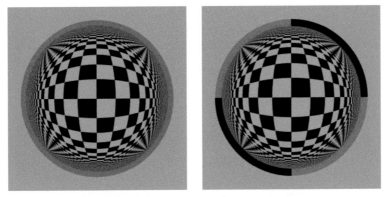

Figure 24.37. A concave and a convex mirror.

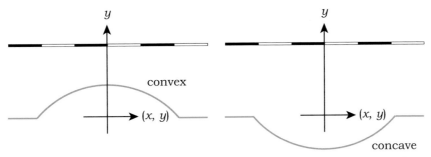

Figure 24.38. Vertical cross section views of the mirrors in Figure 24.37. In this figure, the checkers are not drawn to scale, and the checker plane is not drawn at its true height above the (x, z) plane.

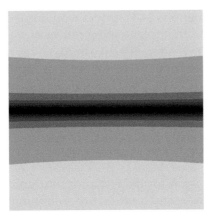

Figure 24.39. A reflective open cylinder surrounded by a large yellow sphere that's directly visible at the top and bottom of the image.

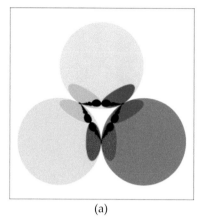

(a)   (b)

Figure 24.40. (a) CMY colored reflective spheres; (b) RGB colored reflective spheres.

Can you explain the reflections? Why does increasing `max_depth` make a difference in Figure 24.40(a) but not in Figure 24.40(b)?

 # Exercises

There are enough exercises here to keep you busy for a lifetime. I've been experimenting with reflections for art and science since the early 1990s and have barely scratched the surface.

24.1. Show that when you substitute Equation (24.5) into the integral (24.1), the result is Equation (24.4). If you would rather skip this exercise and get straight on with implementing reflections, I wouldn't blame you.

24.2. Add the ability to render reflective materials as discussed in Section 24.2. Use the images in Section 24.3 to test your implementation.

24.3. In Figure 24.4, show that the radiance returned by the primary ray r_0 is given by

$$L = L_{\text{direct}}(p) + k_r(p)\, L_{\text{direct}}(p') + k_r(p)\, k_r(p'')\, L_{\text{direct}}(p'')$$
$$+ k_r(p)\, k_r(p')\, k_r(p'')\, L_{\text{direct}}(p''').$$

24.4. Write the expression for the radiance returned by a primary ray when there are n bounces and there is direct illumination at each hit point.

24.5. What is the analogous expression for n bounces when there is no direct illumination at the hit points? How can this be nonzero?

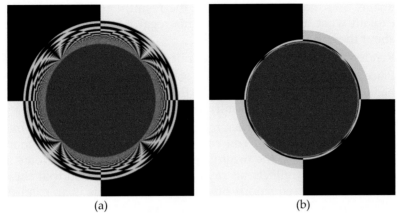

(a)   (b)

Figure 24.41. Orthographic view of a reflective sphere above a checker plane: (a) sphere completely above the plane; (b) most of the sphere below the plane.

24.6. This exercise requires some simple trigonometry. Figure 24.41(a) shows a yellow reflective *unit* sphere above a horizontal checker plane. The background color is dark green, and the scene is rendered with an orthographic camera looking vertically down on the sphere and plane. The plane is reflected on the sphere. Here are some questions:

(a) Where is the horizon in this image?

(b) What is the radius of the green disk?

(c) Does the radius depend on the sphere's height above the plane?

In Figure 24.41(b), most of the sphere is underneath the plane, and the reflection of the plane has changed. When the center of the sphere is a certain distance below the plane, the plane's reflection will disappear.

(d) At what distance below the plane does this happen?

(e) Is there a relationship between the answers to (b) and (d)?

24.7. Implement a reflective material that doesn't have a direct-illumination component.

24.8. Implement the hall of mirrors from Section 24.7.2. If you have done Exercise 24.7, you can use the new reflective material for the mirrors and use these images for testing.

28.9. Add a mirror on the fourth wall of the hall of mirrors scene.

28.10. Experiment with mirrors of different colors in the hall of mirrors scene.

24.11. In the hall of mirrors build function, reverse the normal on all of the mirrors so that they point out of the box and re-render the max_depth = 19 image. You may be surprised by the result; I certainly was. Can you explain what has happened? In this regard, is there anything unique about the hall of mirrors?

24.12. Render a stereo pair of the hall of mirrors scene with max_depth = 19.

24.13. Place some objects, a camera, and some light sources inside a cube that has a mirror material and ray trace the scene with high recursion depths. This is the ultimate hall of mirrors.

24.14. Model and render a *corner reflector*. This consists of three mutually perpendicular mirrors. You can use three triangles in the coordinate planes that meet at the origin and touch along the coordinate axes. A corner reflector reflects all rays back in the direction that they came from, after two reflections off of the mirrors. This is an example of a *retro-reflector*. An array of corner reflectors was placed on the moon by the Apollo 11 astronauts in 1969 so that the distance between the Earth and the moon could be measured by bouncing a laser beam off of the mirrors.

24.15. Implement the four-spheres scene in Figure 24.20 and experiment. Here are some of the many things you can do. Use different values of k_r to see what effect these have on the images. Zoom into part of the fractal and, to see what it looks like, then increase the recursion depth. Use a fisheye camera, as this will allow you to see the reflections from all directions in the one image. Figure 24.42 is an example.

24.16. A tetrahedron is the simplest Platonic solid, of which there are four others: the hexahedron, the octahedron, the icosahedron, and the dodecahedron. Use spheres at the vertices of the other Platonic solids and see what type of fractals result. Their vertex coordinates are on the book's website.

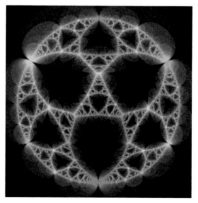

Figure 24.42. Fisheye camera view of the four-spheres scene in Figure 24.20(b).

24.17. Use spheres of different sizes that just touch and see what sort of images you can produce.

24.18. Place some objects, a camera, and some lights inside a hollow mirrored sphere and see what type of images you can render. Experiment with a fisheye camera and with a stereoscopic fisheye camera. Also experiment with the camera inside a hollow ellipsoid.

24.19. Implement a reflective paraboloid, place the camera on the central axis, and place an object such as a sphere or a solid cylinder on the axis between the camera and the surface. Experiment with different locations for the object and camera on the concave side of the paraboloid. Move the camera and the object off the central axis. You should also look at an optics textbook that discusses the types of real and virtual images that can be generated by a concave paraboloid. A paraboloid class is on the book's website.

24.20. Implement a model of the Mirage device and reproduce the images in Section 24.7.6. Experiment with different objects, camera locations, etc. You will have to implement a part paraboloid for the top surface.

24.21. Render some reflective tori.

24.22. Write a version of the function area_light_shade for the Reflective material that's able to handle recursive calls. You can use the function Whitted::traceRay in Listing 24.1 as a model. Experiment with environment lights and area lights. Figure 24.43 is a test image.

Figure 24.43. A scene rendered with reflective objects, an environment light, and ambient occlusion.

24.23. Reproduce Figure 24.30 and experiment with different tessellation resolutions for the sphere, starting with $m = 3$, $n = 2$, as shown in Figure 23.1(a).

24.24. Reproduce some of the images in Figure 24.31.

24.25. See if you can purchase some reflective spheres, a convex spherical mirror, a concave spherical mirror, and a concave paraboloidal mirror. Although ray tracing reflections is a lot of fun, nothing beats real-time ray tracing with real mirrors, particularly big ones! If you can't buy any, try reflective metal food bowls. Even a spoon will give you some images.

25 Glossy Reflection

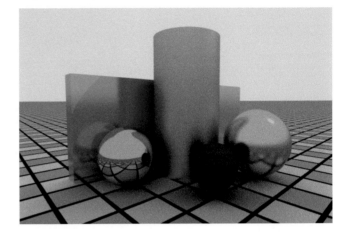

 Objectives

By the end of this chapter, you should:

- understand what glossy reflection is;
- understand how it can be modeled in ray tracing;
- have implemented glossy reflection in your ray tracer;
- have more tools to produce nice images.

In this chapter, you will learn how to render glossy reflections. Many real materials are imperfect reflectors, where the reflections are blurred to various degrees due to surface roughness that scatters the incident radiance. The use of glossy reflections will allow us to remove the main inconsistency discussed in Section 24.4 by treating specular highlights and reflections in a consistent manner. Figure 25.1 is a photograph of three glossy spheres.

25.1 Modeling

Consider a ray that hits a surface from the direction ω_o and its associated direction of mirror reflection r, as illustrated in Figure 25.2. We can simulate glossy reflection by choosing a random direction for the reflected ray instead of using

Figure 25.1. Glossy spheres. Photograph by Kevin Suffern.

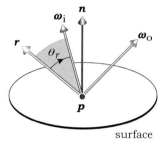

Figure 25.2. The reflected ray direction $\boldsymbol{\omega}_i$ makes an angle θ_r with the direction of mirror reflection r.

surface

the direction of mirror reflection, but how do we choose the direction? To make the simulation consistent with the specular-highlights model in Chapter 15, we should use the same cosine power formula. The density d in solid angle of the reflected rays around the mirror reflection direction r is then given by

$$d = (\cos \theta_r)^e, \tag{25.1}$$

where θ_r is the angle between r and $\boldsymbol{\omega}_i$ and e is the specular exponent.

A suitable BRDF for this purpose is

$$f_{r,s}(\boldsymbol{p}, \boldsymbol{\omega}_i, \boldsymbol{\omega}_o) = c\,k_r c_r \cos(\theta_r)^e = c\,k_r c_r (r \bullet \boldsymbol{\omega}_i)^e, \tag{25.2}$$

where c is a normalization constant. This constant is proportional to $e + 1$, so that $c \to \infty$ as $e \to \infty$. It expresses the fact that as e increases, the BRDF (25.2) becomes more concentrated around the direction of mirror reflection. In the limit $e = \infty$, the BRDF becomes a delta function.

Substituting Equation (25.2) into (24.1) gives the following expression for the reflected radiance in the $\boldsymbol{\omega}_o$ direction:

$$L_{\text{indirect}}(\boldsymbol{p}, \boldsymbol{\omega}_O) = c\,k_r c_r \int\limits_{2\pi^+} (\boldsymbol{\omega}_i \bullet r)^e \, L_o(r_c(\boldsymbol{p}, \boldsymbol{\omega}_i), -\boldsymbol{\omega}_i) \cos\theta_i d\omega_i. \tag{25.3}$$

Because there are no delta functions in this integrand, we have to estimate its value using Monte Carlo integration. The estimator is

$$\langle L_r(\boldsymbol{p}, \boldsymbol{\omega}_o) \rangle = \frac{c\,k_r c_r}{n_s} \sum_{j=1}^{n_s} \frac{(\boldsymbol{\omega}_{i,j} \bullet r)^e \, L_o(r_c(\boldsymbol{p}, \boldsymbol{\omega}_{i,j}), -\boldsymbol{\omega}_{i,j}) \cos\theta_{i,j}}{p(\boldsymbol{\omega}_{i,j})}. \tag{25.4}$$

In this expression, the measure of the pdf is solid angle in the hemisphere at p. Because the choice of pdf determines the directions of the rays shot into the hemisphere, to use the distribution (25.1), the pdf should be proportional to the BRDF; that is,

$$p(\boldsymbol{\omega}_{i,j}) \propto (\boldsymbol{r} \bullet \boldsymbol{\omega}_i)^e. \tag{25.5}$$

A problem with this approach is that it ignores the $\cos\theta_i$ term in Equation (25.3). If we want the glossy reflection to be consistent with perfect specular reflection in the limit $e \to \infty$, we need to get rid of this term. One way would be to make $p(\boldsymbol{\omega}_{i,j})$ proportional to the product of the BRDF and $\cos\theta_i = \boldsymbol{n} \bullet \boldsymbol{\omega}_i$:

$$p(\boldsymbol{\omega}_{i,j}) \propto (\boldsymbol{r} \bullet \boldsymbol{\omega}_i)^e(\boldsymbol{n} \bullet \boldsymbol{\omega}_i),$$

but then the ray directions should also be derived from this product. Unfortunately, that's difficult to do. In spite of not being able to sample this correctly, I'll still use it with

$$p(\boldsymbol{\omega}_{i,j}) \propto c(\boldsymbol{r} \bullet \boldsymbol{\omega}_i)^e(\boldsymbol{n} \bullet \boldsymbol{\omega}_i), \tag{25.6}$$

but I'll keep the distribution (25.1) for the ray directions. With this pdf, the BRDF normalization constant c cancels. The inconsistency in the pdf (25.6) and the ray direction distribution approaches zero as $e \to \infty$.

With this choice of pdf, the estimator (25.4) simplifies to

$$\langle L_r(\boldsymbol{p}, \boldsymbol{\omega}_o) \rangle = \frac{k_r c_r}{n_s} \sum_{j=1}^{n_s} L_o(r_c(\boldsymbol{p}, \boldsymbol{\omega}_{i,j}), -\boldsymbol{\omega}_{i,j}), \tag{25.7}$$

where each randomly reflected ray is treated in the same way as perfect mirror reflection was treated in Chapter 24. The only source of noise in Equation (25.7) is variations in the radiance returned by the reflected rays. This model has k_s, c_s, and e as parameters and, as you will see, produces nice blurred reflections that approach perfect mirrors as $e \to \infty$. Physically based models of glossy reflection are much more complex (see the Further Reading section).

Figure 25.3 shows the plane through the hit point that's perpendicular to $\boldsymbol{r}$. I'll call this the *normal plane*. It's relevant to the modeling because the hemisphere over which the ray directions are distributed is oriented around $\boldsymbol{r}$, instead of $\boldsymbol{n}$ as in previous chapters. The black dots sketched on the hemisphere

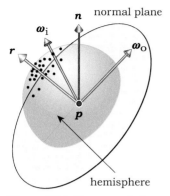

Figure 25.3. The normal plane at a hit point is perpendicular to the direction of mirror reflection.

show where reflected rays may penetrate the hemisphere. The ray directions will all be on the "*r*" side of the normal plane.

In this context, Figure 15.4 shows how the exponent *e* controls the distribution of the samples over the hemisphere and concentrates them around *r* as *e* increases. We can therefore use *e* to control the amount of glossiness. Because materials become more glossy as the samples spread out over the hemisphere, the smaller *e* is, the more glossy the material will be. This continues down to *e* = 1, which is Lambertian reflection but oriented around *r*, not *n*.

We can express the reflected ray direction ω_i in terms of an orthonormal basis (*u*, *v*, *w*), where *w* is parallel to *r*, and *u* and *v* are in the normal plane. The orientation of *u* and *v* around *r* doesn't matter because the distribution of samples on the hemisphere is rotationally symmetric about *r*. Provided we have samples on a hemisphere with a cosine power distribution, the ray direction is given by the same expression as Equation (17.4):

$$\omega_i = s_x\, \boldsymbol{u} + s_y\, \boldsymbol{v} + s_z\, \boldsymbol{w} \qquad (25.8)$$

Finally, we have to deal with the fact that Equation (25.8) can generate rays that lie below the object's surface at the hit point. To see how this happens, consider an incoming ray that hits a surface with different incident angles, as in Figure 25.4. In Figure 25.4(a), the incoming ray direction ω_o is normal to the surface and therefore coincident with *r* and *n*. This is the only case where the hemisphere that's centered on *r* lies entirely above the surface. In

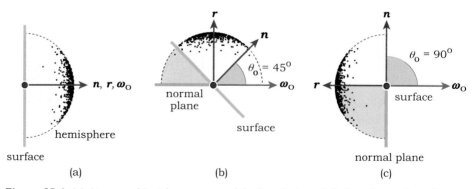

Figure 25.4. (a) At normal incidence, none of the hemisphere is below the surface; (b) part of the hemisphere is below the surface; (c) at grazing incidence, half of the hemisphere is below the surface.

Figure 25.4(b), the incident angle is 45°, and the cyan section of the hemisphere is below the surface[1]. In Figure 25.4(c), the incoming ray is tangent to the surface, and half the hemisphere is below the surface, a situation that occurs at object silhouettes as seen from the camera or ray origin. The *fraction* of reflected rays that lie below the surface depends on the angle of incidence and the value of e but is roughly 50% at grazing incidence for all values of e.

Figure 25.5. Incorrect rendering of a glossy sphere.

Figure 24.5(a) is a test scene that consists of a glossy sphere and a blue background color. This image was rendered with the estimator (25.7), $e = 1$, $k_r = 0.8$, $c_r = $ white, 100 rays per pixel, and all reflected rays traced. The color of the sphere should be constant, but as you can see, it's not. The problem is that the rays under the surface hit the inside of the sphere, and since the sphere's material has no direct shading component, they return zero radiance. As a result, the sphere is only half as bright at the silhouette as it is in the center.

Fortunately, there's a simple solution. We just reflect any rays that are below the surface through r, a process that puts them above the surface. Figure 25.6 illustrates how this works, where rays below the surface (the gray dots) are reflected to become the red dots. This introduces some bias in the distribution, where there are more rays than normal towards the periphery of the distribution, as in Figure 25.6(a). However, the bias decreases as the fraction of reflected rays increases, and it disappears at the silhouette, as in Figure 25.6(b).

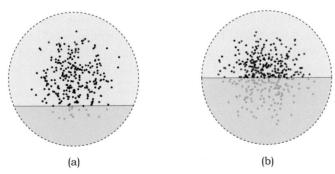

(a)   (b)

Figure 25.6. Rays below the surface (cyan segments of the hemisphere) are reflected through r (at the center of the disks) to the red dots, above the surface.

---

1. For $\theta_1 = 45°$, ω_o is in the normal plane.

The test for the initial ray being below the tangent plane is $\mathbf{n} \bullet \boldsymbol{\omega}_i < 0$, and the expression for the reflected ray direction is

$$\boldsymbol{\omega}_i = -s_x \, \mathbf{u} - s_y \, \boldsymbol{v} + s_z \, \boldsymbol{w}.$$

Figure 25.7. Correct rendering of a glossy sphere.

A bad feature of this technique is that as the fraction of the hemisphere below the surface increases, any stratification of the samples is progressively destroyed. Recall from Chapter 5 that one of the benefits of stratification is that samples generated with widely different random number pairs, for example, (0.001, 0.05) and (0.95, 0.99), are expected to be far apart on the unit square and therefore far apart on the hemisphere. By reflecting the rays through r, these two samples can end up arbitrarily close to each other. We'll just have to live with this, because the alternative of just sampling the part of the hemisphere above the surface is difficult. Fortunately, the results are still good. Figure 25.7 shows the results of using this technique for the test sphere, which is now correctly rendered, although arguably not as interesting to look at.

 ## 25.2 Implementation

There's not much work required to implement glossy reflection, as we already have a glossy specular BRDF that was used in Chapter 15 for modeling specular highlights. The existing data members ks and cs can be used for k_r and c_r, respectively, and exp can still be used for e. We have to add a sampler object and write the sample_f function. Listing 25.1 shows the function Glossyspecular:: set_samples, which sets up multi-jittered samples. This function will be called by the material that implements glossy reflection (see Listing 25.3). You should

```
void
GlossySpecular::set_samples(const int num_samples, const float exp) {
    sampler_ptr = new MultiJittered(num_samples);
    sampler_ptr->map_samples_to_hemisphere(exp);
}
```

Listing 25.1. The function Glossyspecular::set_samples. Notice that this maps the samples to a hemisphere with the specified cosine power distribution.

```
RGBColor
GlossySpecular::sample_f(const ShadeRec& sr,
        const Vector3D& wo,
        Vector3D& wi,
        float& pdf) const {

    float ndotwo = sr.normal * wo;
    Vector3D r = -wo + 2.0 * sr.normal * ndotwo;   // direction of mirror
                                                   // reflection

    Vector3D w = r;
    Vector3D u = Vector3D(0.00424, 1, 0.00764) ^ w;
    u.normalize();
    Vector3D v = u ^ w;

    Point3D sp = sampler_ptr->sample_hemisphere();
    wi = sp.x * u + sp.y * v + sp.z * w;        // reflected ray direction

    if (sr.normal * wi < 0.0)              // reflected ray is below surface
        wi = -sp.x * u - sp.y * v + sp.z * w;

    float phong_lobe = pow(r * wi, exp);
    pdf = phong_lobe * (sr.normal * wi);

    return (ks * cs * phong_lobe);
}
```

Listing 25.2. The function `Glossyspecular::sample_f`.

also have a `set_sampler` function that sets a user-specified sampler, as this will allow you to experiment with different sampling techniques.

The function `Glossyspecular::sample_f` in Listing 25.2 is the version that has the pdf as a parameter because it has to return this. It also computes the direction ω_i of the reflected ray according to Equation (25.8), computes the pdf according to Equation (25.6) but without the c, and returns the BRDF in Equation (25.2), again without the c.

I'll use the `AreaLight` tracer for glossy reflection because, again, it saves us writing a new tracer and allows us to render glossy reflections with all of the light sources.

We also need a `GlossyReflector` material that inherits from `Phong` and has its own `GlossySpecular` BRDF. This allows us to include direct illumination and to set the direct and indirect glossy reflection components independently, including having no direct specular reflection. Listing 25.3 shows

```
class GlossyReflector: public Phong {
    public:

        // constructors etc.

        void
        set_samples(const int num_samples, const float exp);

        void
        set_kr(const float k);

        void
        set_exponent(const float exp);

        virtual RGBColor
        area_light_shade(ShadeRec& sr);

    private:

        GlossySpecular* glossy_specular_brdf;
};

inline void
GlossyReflector::set_samples(const int num_samples, const float exp) {
    glossy_specular_brdf->set_samples(num_samples, exp);
}

inline void
GlossyReflector::set_kr(const float k) {
    glossy_specular_brdf->set_ks(k);
}

inline void
GlossyReflector::set_exponent(const float exp) {
    glossy_specular_brdf->set_exp(exp);
}
```

Listing 25.3. Sample code from the GlossyReflector class.

part of the class declaration for GlossyReflector, along with three access functions. Note that set_samples just calls the function glossy_specular_brdf->set_samples from Listing 25.1, and set_kr sets glossy_specular_brdf::ks. The set functions for c_r (not shown) similarly set glossy_specular_brdf::cs. The set_exponent function sets e in glossy_specular_brdf and is required

```
RGBColor
GlossyReflector::area_light_shade(ShadeRec& sr) {
    RGBColor L(Phong::area_light_shade(sr));      // direct illumination
    Vector3D wo(-sr.ray.d);
    Vector3D wi;
    float    pdf;
    RGBColor fr(glossy_specular_brdf->sample_f(sr, wo, wi, pdf));
    Ray reflected_ray(sr.hit_point, wi);

    L += fr * sr.w.tracer_ptr->trace_ray(reflected_ray, sr.depth + 1) *
    (sr.normal * wi) / pdf;

    return (L);
}
```

Listing 25.4. The function GlossyReflector::area_light_shade.

as a separate function from the inherited function set_exp, which sets e in
Phong:specular_brdf.

Listing 25.4 shows the function GlossyReflector::area_light_shade,
where the radiance is divided by the pdf.

25.3 Results

A good place to start is the scene in Figure 24.30(c) with a glossy reflector
material on the sphere, as this will allow us to compare the results with mirror reflection. Listing 25.5 is a fragment from the build function that illustrates
how to set up the glossy reflector material, which, in this case, has no direct-
illumination component.

Figure 25.8 shows the results for six values of e that range from $e = 1.0$
in Figure 25.8(a) to $e = 100000.0$ in Figure 25.8(f). Figure 25.8(a), which is
Lambertian reflection, shows no reflected image. There is some image visible in Figure 25.8(b) with $e = 10.0$. The images become progressively sharper
in Figure 25.8(c)–(e). Figure 25.8(f) is visually identical to Figure 24.30(c).
The more glossy the material, the more rays per pixel we need to reduce the
noise to acceptable amounts. These images were rendered with multi-jittered
sampling and 256 samples per pixel in Figure 25.8(a) and (b), 100 samples in
Figure 25.8(c) and (d), and 25 samples in Figure 25.8(e) and (f). See Figure 25.13
for the consequences of using fewer samples per pixel and of using non-
random sampling patterns.

```
int nun_samples = 100;
...

float exp = 100.0;
GlossyReflector* glossy_ptr = new GlossyReflector;
glossy_ptr->set_samples(num_samples, exp);
glossy_ptr->set_ka(0.0);
glossy_ptr->set_kd(0.0);
glossy_ptr->set_ks(0.0);
glossy_ptr->set_exp(exp);
glossy_ptr->set_cd(1.0, 1.0, 0.3);
glossy_ptr->set_kr(0.9);
glossy_ptr->set_exponent(exp);
glossy_ptr->set_cr(1.0, 1.0, 0.3); // lemon
```

Listing 25.4. Code fragment from the build function for Figure 25.8.

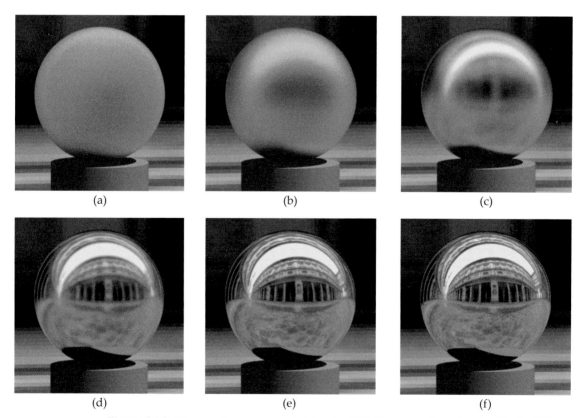

Figure 25.8. Glossy sphere surrounded by the Uffizi image and rendered with the following values of e: (a) 1.0; (b) 10.0; (c) 100.0; (d) 1000.0; (e) 10000.0; (f) 100000.0.

Figure 25.9. Thin blocks with glossy reflection and direct illumination. From left to right, $e = 100000.0, 10000.0, 1000.0, 100.0$. This was inspired by a grayscale figure in Westlund and Meyer (2001).

The glossy blocks in Figure 25.9 include ambient and diffuse shading. Notice how the reflections on all of the blocks are sharp where they touch the plane (on which they are sitting). This image was rendered with multi-jittered sampling and 256 samples per pixel because of the block on the right.

Figure 25.10(a) shows the hall of mirrors from Section 24.7.2 with the camera looking at the mirror on the back wall. This was rendered with `max_depth = 19`. Figure 25.10(b) shows the scene where the two mirrors on the front and back walls have a glossy reflector material with $e = 25000.0$. Notice how

(a)   (b)

Figure 25.10. Hall of mirrors rendered with perfect specular reflection (a) and with glossy reflection with e = 25000.0 (b).

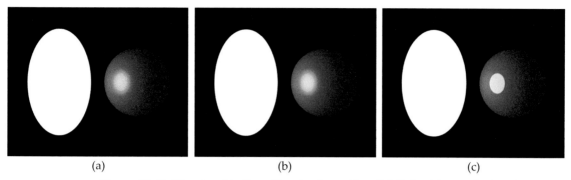

(a)   (b)   (c)

Figure 25.11. Direct and indirect illumination with a disk light: (a) specular highlight with $e = 25$; (b) glossy reflection with $e = 25$; (c) simulation of mirror reflection with $e = 100000$. Images rendered with 100 multi-jittered samples per pixel.

the reflections become more blurred with each bounce, in spite of the high value of e.

Figure 25.11 shows how we can use the `GlossyReflector` material to simulate different optical effects. This figure shows a glossy sphere illuminated by a disk light. In Figure 25.11(a), the sphere is only shaded with direct illumination, where $k_s = 0.65$ and $e = 25$, and so the bright area is the specular highlight. In Figure 25.11(b), there's no direct specular reflection, but there is glossy reflection with $k_r = 0.65$ and $e = 25$ again. The bright area is now the reflection of the light. Notice that there's little visible difference between these two images, demonstrating that specular highlights are the smeared-out reflections of the lights. Finally, Figure 25.11(c) is the same as Figure 25.11(b) but rendered with $e = 100000.0$ to simulate a perfect mirror. We could, of course, get this same effect with a `Reflective` material on the sphere.

Further Reading

Hunter (1937) provided the original definitions and measurement of gloss. The technical definition of gloss involves a parameter $\lambda \in [0, 100]$, but there's no simple relation between λ and e. Wallace et al. (1987) first presented images of glossy reflection using a combination of radiosity and ray tracing. Westlund and Meyer (2001) discusses the technical definition of gloss and presents some nice ray-traced images of glossy materials. Ashikhmin and Shirley (2001, 2002) discuss Monte Carlo techniques for ray tracing anisotropic glossy reflections. Shirley and Morley (2003) discusses glossy reflection with the pdf (25.6).

Dutré et al. (2003) discusses a model for glossy reflection that is similar to the model used in this chapter and discuss various pdfs that could be used, along with their advantages and disadvantages. Pharr and Humphreys (2004) discusses Monte Carlo techniques for ray tracing glossy reflection based on the Blinn (1967) microfacet distribution and on Ashikhmin and Shirley's anisotropic model. These models are considerably more complex than the model presented here.

 ## Questions

25.1. Figure 25.12 shows a glossy sphere with $e = 100$ and a checker plane. Can you explain the crescent-shaped reflections of the plane and background color on the sphere? These are visible near where the sphere cuts the horizon.

25.2. Figure 25.13(a) is the sphere in Figure 25.8(a) with $e = 1$ but rendered with one random sample per pixel. As expected, the sphere surface is completely covered with noise. Figure 25.13(b) is rendered with one regular sample per pixel, and Figure 25.13(c) is rendered with one Hammersley sample per pixel. Can you explain the mirrored appearance of this Lambertian sphere in Figure 25.13(b) and (c)? What do these images tell you about the suitability of uniform and Hammersley sampling for simulating glossy reflection? See also Exercise 25.4.

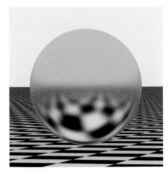

Figure 25.12. Glossy sphere and checker plane.

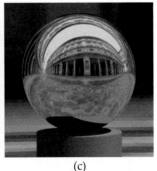

(a)　　　　　　　　　(b)　　　　　　　　　(c)

Figure 25.13. The Lambertian sphere in Figure 25.8(a) rendered with one sample per pixel and the following sampling patterns: (a) random; (b) regular; (c) Hammersley.

Exercises

25.1. Implement glossy reflection as described in this chapter, and use the scene in Figure 25.8 to test your implementation.

25.2. As the scene in Figure 25.8 has a point light, add a specular highlight to the sphere with the same specular parameters as used for the glossy reflection.

25.3. Add ambient and diffuse illumination to the sphere in Figure 25.8.

25.4. Experiment with different sampling patterns in Figures 25.8 and 25.9 and different numbers of samples per pixel, starting with one sample.

25.5. Render the hall of mirrors in Figure 25.10 with different values of e, max_depth, numbers of samples, and sampling patterns.

25.6. Render the sphere and checker plane in Figure 25.12 with different values of e and numbers of samples.

25.7. Render some glossy objects illuminated with area lights. An example is the figure on the first page of this chapter, where the plane, large sphere, cylinder, and box are glossy and where the scene is illuminated by a point light and an environment light. Notice the color bleeding onto the plane, which has $e = 1.0$. You can render this scene without the texture on the plane.

25.8. In the figure on the first page of this chapter, the glossy objects have two specular highlights, one from the point light and the other from the environment light. Re-render this image with the specular highlight color set to red and compare the results with the existing image. Start with one sample per pixel.

25.9. Render some nice glossy-reflection images of your own.

26 Global Illumination

Image courtesy of Steven Parker

Objectives

By the end of this chapter, you should:

- understand how path tracing works;
- know how to combine direct and indirect illumination in a path tracer;
- appreciate path tracing's abilities and limitations.

 26.1 Light Transport

In previous chapters, we looked at direct illumination from a variety of light sources and at indirect illumination with perfect specular and glossy specular reflection. There are, however, many other ways that light can be transported in a scene. The general situation is reflection between surfaces with arbitrary BRDFs. An example is reflection between Lambertian surfaces, which we have approximated with the ambient term.

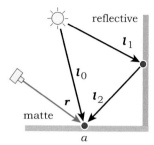

Figure 26.1. A simple situation that can't be handled by Whitted ray tracing. The point a receives light directly along the path l_0 and indirectly along the path l_1 and l_2. Whitted ray tracing can simulate the direct illumination at a but not the indirect illumination.

Another example is light that's reflected from a specular surface onto a matte surface, as illustrated in Figure 26.1. Here, the point a receives incident radiance from the light source in two ways. The first is direct illumination from the ray l_0; the second is indirect illumination reflected via rays l_1 and l_2. Suppose that a primary ray r hits the matte surface at a and that we are attempting to shade this point. Chapters 14–18 have thoroughly covered how to compute the direct illumination, but there's a problem with the indirect illumination. The ray tracer can't "discover" the path l_1 and l_2 from the light to a. The additional reflected radiance along r, which is known as a *caustic*, is therefore not rendered. A simple example is a plane mirror that reflects light onto a matte surface.

Global illumination algorithms try to simulate all light-transport mechanisms that contribute to an image. In Section 26.2, I'll present an algorithm that will do this in theory, given enough samples per pixel and sufficient rendering time.

 ## 26.2 Path Tracing

26.2.1 Description

Path tracing is a conceptually simple, brute-force technique for computing the direct and indirect illumination in scenes with area light sources. Figure 26.2 illustrates how this works. Each ray is followed through the scene until it hits a light surface, the maximum recursion depth is reached, or the ray leaves the

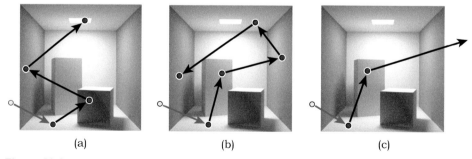

(a)   (b)   (c)

Figure 26.2. In a path-tracing environment, three things can happen along a ray path: (a) a ray hits a light source; (b) the maximum recursion depth (four, in this case) is reached; (c) a ray leaves the scene (provided it's not a closed environment). The grayscale image used in this scene is courtesy of Steven Parker.

scene. At each hit point, a pdf is sampled by calling the `sample_f` function of a BRDF. This determines the ray direction. There are no restrictions on the BRDFs, which can range from Lambertian to perfectly specular, or transparent. This allows a path tracer to simulate all types of light transport between surfaces by treating all materials as reflective in the sense that reflected rays are generated and traced at hit points. The exception is emissive materials, which are not reflective in this sense. A single primary ray and its reflected rays is called a *ray path*, or just a *path*.

When the background color is black, the only way that a path tracer can return a nonzero radiance value is for the path to eventually hit a light source. This means that pure path tracing can't be used with point and directional lights, as there are no light surfaces for the rays to hit. .

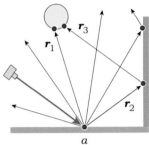

Figure 26.3. Sample path-traced rays for a Lambertian and a perfect mirror surface. Ray r_1 simulates direct illumination at a. Rays r_2 and r_3 simulate perfect-specular-to-diffuse light transport.

Figure 26.3 shows the configuration in Figure 26.1, where the bottom surface is Lambertian and the reflective surface is perfectly specular. To avoid clutter, the cyan primary ray represents a number of primary rays for a single pixel, which of course will all be slightly different. For a Lambertian surface, the reflected ray directions are distributed in a hemispherical cosine distribution around the normal. If any of these rays hit the mirror, they are reflected in the direction of perfect mirror reflection. Now, if we use enough samples, and if the light source is large enough, some rays reflected from the matte surface will hit the light. An example is ray r_1. These rays simulate direct illumination on the matte surface. Other rays, such as ray r_3, will hit the light after bouncing off of the mirror, in essence discovering paths like l_1 and l_2 in Figure 26.1 and allowing us to render caustics on the matte surface.

Figure 26.4(a) shows sample rays when both surfaces are Lambertian, so that all secondary rays are randomly oriented. Again, some rays will hit the light after being reflected from the vertical surface. These rays simulate diffuse-to-diffuse light transport. When there's color transfer between the surfaces, as there always will be when the surfaces are colored, the effect is known as *color bleeding* (Birn, 2006). From all of the rays shown in Figure 26.4(a), the radiance flow diagram in Figure 26.4(b) shows that only two paths return radiance to the pixel.

Another point about path tracing is that there are no actual lights stored in the world. A light source is simply an object with an emissive material. As a result, any objects can act as a light, including complex triangle meshes. There is also no need to generate sample points on light surfaces.

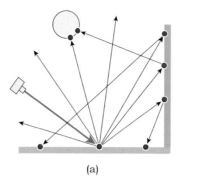 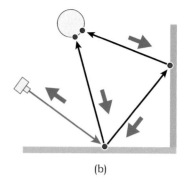

(a)   (b)

Figure 26.4. (a) Rays scattered from two Lambertian surfaces; (b) only two paths in (a) return radiance to the pixel, because only two rays hit the light surface.

To evaluate the radiance value of each pixel, we use the hemisphere formulation of the rendering equation (13.21) with the Monte Carlo estimator

$$\langle L_\mathrm{r}(\boldsymbol{p},\boldsymbol{\omega}_\mathrm{o})\rangle = \frac{1}{n_\mathrm{s}}\sum_{j=1}^{n_\mathrm{s}} \frac{f_\mathrm{r}(\boldsymbol{p},\boldsymbol{\omega}_{\mathrm{i},j},\boldsymbol{\omega}_\mathrm{o})L_\mathrm{i}(\boldsymbol{p},\boldsymbol{\omega}_{\mathrm{i},j})\cos\theta_{\mathrm{i},j}}{p(\boldsymbol{\omega}_{\mathrm{i},j})}. \tag{26.1}$$

As path tracing is recursive, $L_\mathrm{i}(\boldsymbol{p},\boldsymbol{\omega}_\mathrm{i})$ is evaluated with the ray-casting operator (Equation (13.22)). The recursive evaluation of the interval with an infinite maximum recursion depth results in the series solution (13.29) of the rendering equation. In terms of image display, path tracing can produce exact solutions of the rendering equation when we use enough samples and a high enough value of `max_depth`. The path tracer discussed here won't produce a solution of the full rendering equation because of the non-reflective emissive materials. Ray paths that hit a light source terminate at the light, as in Figure 26.2(a).

Is there a catch? Unfortunately, there is. With the exception of environment lights, light sources are usually small compared to other objects in a scene, or they subtend small solid angles at most surface points. In this situation, path tracing is particularly inefficient because the fraction of ray paths through a scene that actually hit a light surface will be small. With small numbers of samples, many pixels will be black because none of their ray paths hit a light surface. The result is generally very noisy images unless we use large numbers of samples per pixel. Some scenes can require thousands of samples to reduce noise to acceptable amounts, resulting in long rendering times.

26.2.2 Implementation

I'll implement path tracing with the following:

- a PathTrace tracer;
- a sample_f function that returns a pdf, for all BRDFs that are used with path tracing;
- a path_shade function for all materials that are used with path tracing;
- a sampler object in the BRDF base class.

Listing 26.1 shows the function PathTrace::trace_ray. Note that the only difference between this and the function Whitted::trace_ray in Listing 24.1 is the function call material_ptr->path_shade instead of material_ptr->shade.

I'll only discuss path tracing with Lambertian and perfectly specular materials. Path tracing with glossy reflection is left as an exercise.

The function Lambertian::sample_f in Listing 26.2 sets up an orthonormal basis with $w = n$ and then samples the hemisphere centered on the normal with a cosine distribution. This requires an (inherited) sampler object in the Lambertian BRDF Matte::diffuse_brdf, with a cosine distribution of sample points. Finally, Lambertian::sample_f computes the pdf = $\cos \theta_i/\pi$ from Equation (18.6) and returns $k_d c_d/\pi$.

I'll also implement a new sample_f function in Listing 26.3 for the perfectly specular BRDF that returns a pdf to make the code consistent with

```
RGBColor
PathTrace::trace_ray(const Ray ray, const int depth) const {
    if (depth > world_ptr->vp.max_depth)
        return(black);
    else {
        ShadeRec sr(world_ptr->hit_objects(ray));

        if (sr.hit_an_object) {
            sr.depth = depth;
            sr.ray = ray;

            return(sr.material_ptr->path_shade(sr));
        }
        else
            return(world_ptr->background_color);
    }
}
```

Listing 26.1. The function PathTrace::trace_ray.

```
RGBColor
Lambertian::sample_f(const ShadeRec& sr,
         const Vector3D& wo,
         Vector3D& wi,
         float& pdf) const {

    Vector3D w = sr.normal;
    Vector3D v = (0.0034, 1.0, 0.0071) ^ w;
    v.normalize();
    Vector3D u = v ^ w;

    Point3D sp = sampler_ptr->sample_hemisphere();
    wi = sp.x * u + sp.y * v + sp.z * w;
    wi.normalize();
    pdf = sr.normal * wi * invPI;

    return (kd * cd * invPI);
}
```

Listing 26.2. The function `Lambertian::sample_f`.

```
RGBColor
PerfectSpecular::sample_f(const ShadeRec& sr,
         const Vector3D& wo,
         Vector3D& wi,
         float& pdf) const {
    float ndotwo = sr.normal * wo;
    wi = -wo + 2.0 * sr.normal * ndotwo;
    pdf = sr.normal * wi;

    return (kr * cr);
}
```

Listing 26.3. The function `PerfectSpecular::sample_f`.

the other new `sample_f` functions. The pdf is just $\cos \theta_i$ to cancel the $\cos \theta_i$ term in the Monte Carlo estimator (26.1). You should compare this with the `PerfectSpecular::sample_f` function in Listing 24.2 that's used for Whitted ray tracing and returns $k_r c_r / \cos \theta_i$.

Listing 26.4 shows the function `Matte:path_shade`. Note that this doesn't explicitly compute the direct illumination.

As a final code example, the `path_trace` function for the `Reflective` material appears in Listing 26.5. By comparing this with the `Reflective::`

```
RGBColor
Matte::path_shade(ShadeRec& sr) {
    Vector3D wi;
    Vector3D wo = -sr.ray.d;
    float pdf;
    RGBColor f = diffuse_brdf->sample_f(sr, wo, wi, pdf);
    float ndotwi = sr.normal * wi;
    Ray reflected_ray(sr.hit_point, wi);

    return (f * sr.w.tracer_ptr->trace_ray(reflected_ray, sr.depth + 1)
            * ndotwi / pdf);
}
```

Listing 26.4. The function `Matte:path_shade`.

```
RGBColor
Reflective::path_shade(ShadeRec& sr) {
    Vector3D wo = -sr.ray.d;
    Vector3D wi;
    float pdf;
    RGBColor fr = reflective_brdf->sample_f(sr, wo, wi, pdf);
    Ray reflected_ray(sr.hit_point, wi);

    return (fr * sr.w.tracer_ptr->trace_ray(reflected_ray, sr.depth + 1)
            * (sr.normal * wi) / pdf);
}
```

Listing 26.5. The function `Reflective::path_shade`.

shade function in Listing 24.4, you will see that both functions return the same expression for the reflected radiance: $k_r c_r L_i(p, \omega_i)$, ignoring the direct-illumination component in Listing 24.4. They just do it in slightly different ways. In both cases, the $\cos \theta_i$ term is cancelled.

 ## 26.3 Results

26.3.1 Environment Light

The easiest type of scene to render with path tracing has an environment light as the only source of illumination. Because an environment light has the largest possible angular extent, it doesn't need any more samples to path trace than

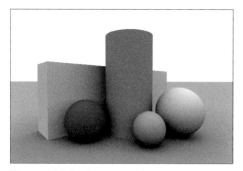

Figure 26.5. Scene rendered with direct illumination from an environment light, zero ambient illumination, and 100 samples per pixel.

its direct illumination required in Section 18.10. For a comparison with path tracing, Figure 26.5 shows a scene rendered with direct illumination from sampling a white environment light but with zero ambient illumination.

Figure 26.6 shows the same scene rendered with path tracing. Figure 26.6(a) has zero bounces (max_depth = 0) so that the objects are black. At least one bounce is required to bring back radiance, unless a primary ray hits an emissive object. Figure 26.6(b) was rendered with one bounce, and the resulting image is identical to Figure 26.5 except for the noise details (see Question 26.2). Path tracing with max_depth = 1 results in direct illumination.

Figure 26.6(c) was rendered with max_depth = 5 and illustrates diffuse-diffuse light transport, the effects of which are obvious by comparing the

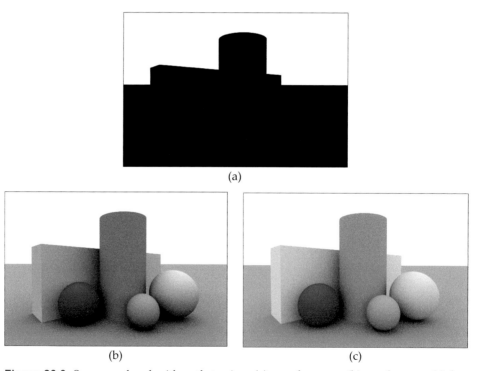

Figure 26.6. Scene rendered with path tracing: (a) zero bounces; (b) one bounce; (c) five bounces.

objects in Figure 26.6(b) and (c). Color bleeding from the green plane and the orange sphere onto the other objects is, however, subtle.

26.3.2 The Cornell Box

The Cornell box is a real cubic box with five faces, built in the Program of Computer Graphics at Cornell University, initially to test radiosity algorithms (Goral et al., 1984). Various versions have been used ever since for testing a variety of graphics algorithms, including ray tracing. Figure 26.7 shows path-traced images of an early version with a rectangular light in the ceiling and two white boxes on the floor. These images were rendered with matte surfaces and `max_depth` = 10. The only difference between them is the number of samples per pixel. Figure 26.7(a) was rendered with one sample, with the result that most of the pixels are black; a single path has only a small probability of hitting the light, even after a maximum of 10 bounces. Many rays will leave the box with fewer bounces than this. Figure 26.7(b) used 100 samples per pixel, which produces a meaningful image but with a large amount of noise. Noisy images such as this are a common characteristic of path tracing due to the inefficient sampling of the lights. The sampling is like that depicted in Figure 18.2(b). The smaller the lights are, the more samples we need to reduce noise to acceptable levels, and the brighter the lights have to be to achieve reasonable lighting levels. In Figure 26.7, the light color is (1.0, 0.73, 0.4), but the radiance is scaled by 100.0.

Figure 26.7(c) and (d) were rendered with 1024 and 10,000 samples, respectively. As you can see, there's noise present in both images. Notice the strong color bleeding onto the walls of the boxes that face the colored walls. Color bleeding is also present on the floor, ceiling, and back wall.

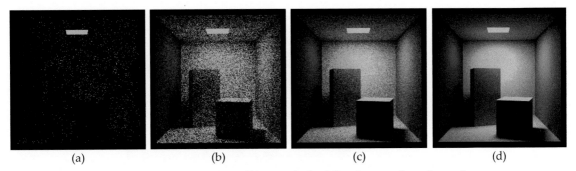

(a)   (b)   (c)   (d)

Figure 26.7. Path-traced images of the Cornell box with the following number of samples per pixel: (a) 1; (b) 100; (c) 1024; (d) 10,000.

In contrast to Figure 26.7, the beautiful figure on the first page of this chapter, by Steven Parker at the University of Utah, is free of noise but was rendered with over 100,000 rays per pixel (see the Notes and Discussion section).

26.3.3 Reflective Surfaces and Caustics

To demonstrate caustics, Figure 26.8 shows a Lambertian plane and a vertical reflective rectangle illuminated by a sphere with an emissive material. The sphere is light green, the rectangle is a perfect mirror with an orange color, and the plane is white. You can see the reflection, with its faint orange tint, on the plane in front of the mirror.

Much more interesting caustics are created from curved reflectors, which can concentrate the reflected light. Figure 26.9(a) shows the scene from Figure 26.8 with the flat mirror replaced by a concave half cylinder. The result is a beautiful cardioid caustic that's characteristic of the caustics formed by concave cylindrical reflectors. As this image was rendered with max_depth = 2, a lot of reflections and caustics are therefore not rendered. For example, notice that the caustic is not reflected in the mirror. Fortunately, this is simple to remedy by increasing max_depth. Figure 26.9(b) shows the result of using max_depth = 5. This image shows other caustics on the plane due to multiple reflections, shows the reflections of the caustics, and shows self-reflections of the cylinder (see Question 26.3). Figure 26.9(c) is a top-down view of the scene that provides a different view of the caustics and demonstrates that the sphere is not aligned with the cylinder.

You can see this type of caustic in coffee mugs and other cylindrical containers. Just have a strong light shining in it. Because the light in Figure 26.9 is

Figure 26.8. In this figure, the path tracer has rendered the light reflected from a mirror onto a matte surface by simulating light paths like l_1 and l_2 in Figure 26.1.

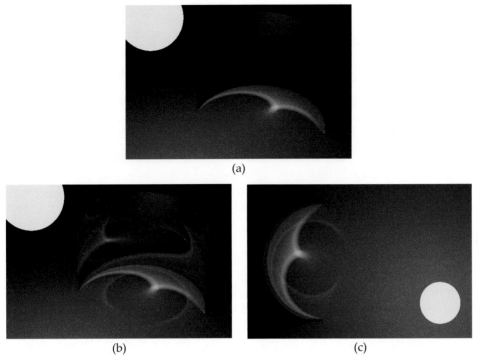

(a)

(b)   (c)

Figure 26.9. Caustics formed by a spherical light and a cylindrical reflector: (a) `max_depth` = 2; (b) `max_depth` = 5; (c) top-down view with `max_depth` = 5. These images were rendered with 71 × 71 = 5041 samples per pixel.

reasonably large, the caustics are broad with soft boundaries. These caustics become thinner and sharper as the light source becomes smaller or farther away. Caustics from point and directional lights are the thinnest and sharpest, and although we can't render these with path tracing, photon mapping can be used for this purpose (see the Further Reading section).

26.4 Sampling the Lights

Because the sampling of small light sources is so inefficient in path tracing, it's worthwhile considering a hybrid approach, where the direct illumination is computed by sampling the lights, and path tracing is only used for the indirect illumination. Part of the rationale is that the direct illumination varies rapidly, particularly in shadows, while the indirect illumination usually varies more

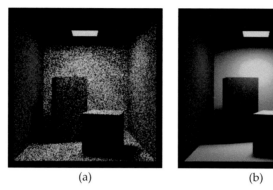

(a)   (b)

Figure 26.10. Cornell box rendered with 100 samples per pixel and the following techniques: (a) path tracing with `max_depth` = 1 to simulate the direct illumination; (b) direct illumination by sampling the light.

slowly. A light-sampling approach for the direct illumination, as presented in Chapter 18, will therefore result in less noise.

Figure 26.10(a) displays the direct illumination for the Cornell box scene using path tracing with 100 samples per pixel. Notice that the ceiling and the shadow umbrae are black. For comparison, Figure 26.10(b) shows the direct illumination that results from sampling the light with 100 samples per pixel. As you can see, this has much less noise than Figure 26.10(a).

If we use this approach with path tracing, we have to be careful not to render the direct illumination twice. Fortunately, that's simple to arrange by making minor modifications to the existing path-tracing code or, preferably, writing a new tracer. An example configuration appears in Figure 26.11, which shows the radiance flow along various rays that hit a light source. There are three primary rays: one hits the light, and two hit a surface. The light returns the emitted radiance along all rays that hit it except those at `depth` = 1. At the hit point a, the shadow ray returns the emitted radiance L_e, but the secondary path-traced ray at `depth` = 1, which hits the light, returns zero radiance. At point c, the path-traced ray that hits the light is at `depth` = 2 and returns L_e, as in normal path tracing.

This can be implemented with another tracer, called, say, `GlobalTrace`, and corresponding material `global_shade` functions. I won't reproduce the function `GlobalTrace::trace_ray` here because it only differs from `PathTrace::trace_ray` in Listing 26.1 by calling `material_ptr-global_shade` instead of `material_ptr->path_shade`. The `Emissive::global_shade` function in Listing 26.6 returns black when the ray depth is one.

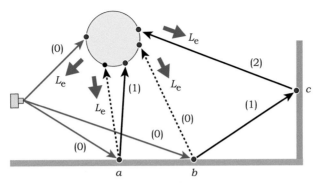

Figure 26.11. This figure illustrates which rays return the emitted radiance after hitting a light source. The thin cyan arrows are primary path-traced rays, the dashed arrows are shadow rays, and the black arrows are secondary path-traced rays. The numbers in parentheses are the recursion depths of the rays. A shadow ray has the same recursion depth as the incoming ray.

The `Matte:global_shade` function in Listing 26.7 computes the direct illumination when the depth is zero.

This simple approach handles purely diffuse environments such as the Cornell box and will also render the caustics and their reflections in Figure 26.9 because these are all rendered with depth > 1. What it will not render, however, are reflections of lights on objects that are directly visible from the camera. The reflection of the spherical light on the rectangle in Figure 26.8 is an example. This won't appear because the reflected ray that hits the light in this case has depth = 1. The problem can be fixed with the grubby piece of programming in

```
RGBColor
Emissive::global_shade(ShadeRec& sr) {

    if (sr.depth == 1)
        return (black);

    if (-sr.normal * sr.ray.d > 0.0)
        return (ls * ce);
    else
        return (black);
}
```

Listing 26.6. The function `Emissive::global_shade`.

```
RGBColor
Matte::global_shade(ShadeRec& sr) {
    RGBColor L;

    if (sr.depth == 0)
        L = area_light_shade(sr);

    Vector3D wi;
    Vector3D wo = -sr.ray.d;
    float pdf;
    RGBColor f = diffuse_brdf->sample_f(sr, wo, wi, pdf);
    float ndotwi = sr.normal * wi;
    Ray reflected_ray(sr.hit_point, wi);
    L += f * sr.w.tracer_ptr->trace_ray(reflected_ray, return_le,
        sr.depth + 1) * ndotwi / pdf;

    return (L);
}
```

Listing 26.7. The function `Matte::global_shade`.

Listing 26.8, which assigns `depth` = 2 to these rays. The reason for using this hack is that our shading architecture doesn't provide a simple way of telling the `Emissive` material that some rays with `depth` = 1 should return L_e. That's not a huge problem, as I'm not going to pursue this type of rendering very far, due to a much bigger problem.

```
RGBColor
Reflective::global_shade(ShadeRec& sr) {
    Vector3D wo = -sr.ray.d;
    Vector3D wi;
    float pdf;
    RGBColor fr = reflective_brdf->sample_f(sr, wo, wi, pdf);
    Ray reflected_ray(sr.hit_point, wi);

    if (sr.depth == 0)
        return (fr * sr.w.tracer_ptr->trace_ray(reflected_ray, sr.depth
                + 2) * (sr.normal * wi) / pdf);
    else
        return (fr * sr.w.tracer_ptr->trace_ray(reflected_ray, sr.depth
                + 1) * (sr.normal * wi) / pdf);
}
```

Listing 26.8. The function `Reflective::global_shade`.

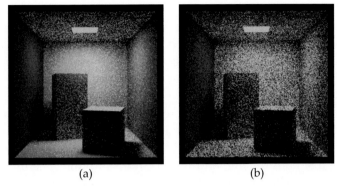

(a)   (b)

Figure 26.12. (a) The Cornell box rendered with direct illumination by sampling the light and path tracing with `max_depth` = 10 to simulate the indirect illumination; (b) the Cornell box rendered with pure path tracing with `max_depth` = 10.

Figure 26.12(a) shows the Cornell box rendered using the global tracer with 100 samples per pixel. To allow a side-by-side comparison, Figure 26.12(b) repeats Figure 26.7(b), where path tracing has been used for the direct and indirect illumination. Figure 26.12(a) is arguably the better image because at least the direct illumination is relatively noise free. The noisy indirect illumination is, however, visually incongruous with the smooth direct illumination.

The real problem here is that when the light sources are small, the simple path tracer we are using for the indirect illumination still needs huge numbers of samples to reduce noise to acceptable levels. To achieve results for the indirect illumination that are as noise-free as the direct illumination, while using no more samples, we require a more sophisticated approach. Several techniques based on *bidirectional path tracing* are quite effective. In bidirectional path tracing, rays are traced from the light sources as well as from the camera. I can't discuss these here due to time and length considerations, but references are listed in the Further Reading section.

Notes and Discussion

My sampling architecture has problems with Figure 26.7(d) because of the large number of samples. With 10,000 samples per pixel, 83 sets of samples, and a different multi-jittered sampler object for the view plane and each material, the total storage is over 450 MB. The other problem was at my first rendering attempt, the ray tracer crashed after about 90% was rendered. The cause was the variable `sampler::count`, which was declared as a `long` and overflowed when it exceeded $2^{31} - 1 = 2{,}147{,}483{,}647$. On my system, a `long` is 4 bytes. Declaring `count` as an `unsigned long`, which allows twice as many samples to be accessed, allowed the image to be rendered. I tried using fewer sets and using a single shared sampler object, but the result was bad aliasing artifacts. Admittedly, I didn't design the sampler architecture with this type of application in mind.

The Cornell box materials are presented as measured reflectances at 4 nm intervals from 400 nm to 700 nm and are assumed to be Lambertian. Steven Parker's figure on the first page of this chapter is a spectral rendering using six wavelengths, path tracing, and importance sampling. The image was initially rendered at 4048 × 4048 pixels, and took 17,000 hours to render on a 175 MHz RS10000 chip. In contrast, my images used approximate RGB colors for the materials and the `max_to_one` tone-mapping operator discussed in Section 14.9. As a result of the tone mapping, the light surface is rendered with its true color regardless of how bright it is, instead of white. My shadows are also darker.

 Further Reading

Path tracing was invented by Kajiya (1986) as a solution to the rendering equation. Its origins go back to the distribution ray tracing introduced by Cooke et al. (1984). Today, there are a number of books that discuss path tracing. These include Dutré et al. (2003), Jensen (2001), Pharr and Humphreys (2004), Shirley and Morley (2003), and Shirley et al. (2005).

The Cornell box website is at http://www.graphics.cornell.edu/online/box, from where you can download the data, photographs, and rendered images.

Bidirectional path tracing was developed independently by Lafortune and Willems (1993, 1994) and Veach and Guibas (1994, 1995). This can result in a dramatic reduction in the noise compared with simple path tracing.

Metropolis light transport was developed by Veach and Guibas (1997). This technique works well for scenes that involve light paths that other techniques have difficulty sampling. It is based on a sampling technique developed by Metropolis et al. (1953) for computational physics.

Photon mapping is a bidirectional path tracing algorithm developed by Jensen (1995, 1996a, 1996b). It's also discussed in the book Jensen (2001). There are separate photon maps for rendering caustics and simulating indirect illumination.

Although I've used a constant value of `max_depth` to control the number of bounces in path tracing, the standard technique for doing this is called

Russian roulette. Here, a probability, based on the reflectance at a hit point, is used to determine if a path is terminated or continued. The results are the same as using an infinite value of max_depth, but at the cost of increased noise. Russian roulette has been used since the 1940s (Hammersley and Hanscomb, 1964) and was first used for image synthesis by Kirk and Arvo (1988). Most of the books cited above discuss this technique.

 Questions

26.1. Why is there no explicit computation of the direct illumination in the Matte:path_shade function in Listing 26.4?

26.2. In Figure 26.5, the environment light has sample points on the hemisphere with a cosine distribution centered on the y-axis. These points determine the directions of all shadow rays from object surfaces. In Figure 26.6(b), secondary ray directions are in a cosine distribution centered on the surface normal at each hit point. Since the ray directions ω_i are different in each image and the reflected radiance is always proportional to $n \bullet \omega_i$, why are these images the same?

26.3. How many different caustics can you see on the plane in Figure 26.9(b)?

26.4. Why are the caustics in Figure 26.9(b) different colors?

26.5. Why can't we see the reflection of the caustic in Figure 26.9(a)?

 Exercises

26.1. Implement path tracing as described in Section 26.2 and use the images in Section 26.3 for testing your implementation.

26.2. Render the Cornell box scene in Figure 26.7 with different values of max_depth.

26.3. With the Cornell box scene, try to reduce the number of samples stored for a given value of num_samples. There are several ways you can do this: have the view plane and the materials share the same sampler object, reduce the number of sets of sample patterns, or use some combination of these.

26.4. By drawing some diagrams analogous to Figure 26.3, try to understand how all of the caustics in Figure 26.9 are formed.

26.5. By drawing some diagrams analogous to Figure 26.3, try to understand how the reflections of the caustics in Figure 26.9(b) are formed. Start with the cardioid caustic. This should tell you why there is no reflection of this in Figure 26.9(a).

26.6.   For the scene in Figure 26.8, experiment with concave part cylinders with different angular ranges and light locations. Include a full cylinder with the light inside.

26.7.   Path trace some scenes that contain the Stanford bunny. Experiment with different types of lights, including an environment light, and with different materials on the bunny, such as `Matte`, `Reflective`, and `GlossyReflector`.

26.8.   Use the Stanford bunny as a light source.

26.9.   Render the scene in Figure 26.9 with a `GlossyReflector` material on the cylinder.

26.10. Find out how Russian roulette works and implement it with your path tracer. Compare the results with using `max_depth`. In particular, render the scene in Figure 26.9, where you can see inter-reflections of the cylinder.

26.11. Render Figure 18.6 with path tracing and compare the results.

27 Simple Transparency

Photograph courtesy of Steve Agland

 Objectives

By the end of this chapter, you should:

- understand the concepts and physical processes of transparency;
- understand the practical issues involved in correctly ray tracing transparent objects;
- understand how a simplified model of transparency is implemented in ray tracing;
- have added the ability to ray trace transparent objects to your ray tracer;
- have ray traced a variety of transparent objects.

Transparency is my favorite ray-tracing topic. Ray tracing can accurately simulate the natural beauty of transparent objects, such as the sphere in the photograph on the first page of this chapter, or the sparkle of a diamond. Figure 27.1(a)–(c) are by my students, and there are many other nice images in this chapter.

Getting transparency correct is not trivial, but in this chapter and Chapter 28, I'll guide you through the physical processes you need to simulate in order

(a)

(b)

(c)

Figure 27.1. (a) Opaque and transparent spheres. Image courtesy of Vinh Wong. (b) Reflective sphere inside a transparent cube. Image courtesy of Adeel Khan. Notice the fractal pattern on the surface of the sphere. (c) Transparent blocks. Image courtesy of Nathan Andrews.

to render transparent objects, as well as how to implement them. Transparent materials, or *media*, as they are called, allow light to pass through them. Common examples include glasses, clear plastics, and gases such as air. In physics, these are called *dielectrics*.

In this chapter, I'll discuss what happens when a ray hits the boundary between two dielectrics: refraction, the transmitted ray, and total internal reflection. I'll use a simplified model for transparency with constant reflection and transmission coefficients and no color. This will allow you to concentrate on the core issues but still get nice results. A restriction is that the techniques used here will not allow you to ray trace nested transparent objects, but by getting the foundations correct first, you'll find it easier to implement a more physically accurate and flexible model of transparency in Chapter 28.

Before we start, here are a couple of handy hints. Use a background color other than black when you ray trace transparent objects, at least initially. Unless your objects are in a completely enclosed environment, you'll probably see the background color refracted through them, and if it's black, parts of your objects will also look black. This can be confusing, as some objects can trap rays, and parts of them will appear black because of that. The thin black strips on the ellipsoid and torus in Figures 27.24(a) and 27.29 are examples. You should avoid dark shadows for the same reason.

 ## 27.1 Index of Refraction

Let's briefly discuss some physics. You may have heard from relativity theory that the speed of light is a constant c, with value $c = 2.99 \times 10^7$ m per second. In fact, light only travels at this speed in a *perfect vacuum*. Whenever light travels through a transparent medium, including the earth's atmosphere, it interacts with the medium's molecules and, as a result, travels at a lower speed. We define the *absolute index of refraction η* of a medium to be the ratio of the speed of light in a vacuum c to its speed v in the medium:

$$\eta = c/v.$$

This is discussed in most optics textbooks, for example, Hecht (1997). Since $v < c$ for all media, we always have $\eta > 1$. From now on, I'll refer to η as the *index of refraction*, or *ior* for short. This is one of the most important properties of transparent media in optics and ray tracing. Table 27.1 lists the indices of refraction for some well-known media.

Medium	Index of Refraction
perfect vacuum	1.0
air (1 atm, 20° C)	1.0003
ice	1.31
water	1.33
ethyl alcohol	1.36
fused quartz	1.46
acrylic (Plexiglas, Perspex)	1.49
crown glass	1.52
polyester resin	1.56
dense flint glass	1.66
diamond	2.42

Table 27.1. Indices of refraction for common media.

27.2 Surface Physics and Refraction

Consider a ray from the direction ω_o that hits the boundary between two transparent media, as shown in Figure 27.2. A reflected ray r in the direction of mirror reflection is generated at the hit point, as in perfect specular reflection, but now a transmitted ray in the direction t *may* also be generated. If the boundary is optically smooth, the incident, reflected, and transmitted rays will all be in the plane of incidence, with ω_o and t on opposite sides of the boundary, and the transmission will be perfectly specular.[1] The two indices of refraction are η_{out} and η_{in}, and if one of the media is air, we can take its ior to be 1.0 with little error, according to Table 27.1.

The relevant quantity for ray tracing is the ratio η of the two indices of refraction:

$$\eta = \eta_{in}/\eta_{out}. \tag{27.1}$$

We call η the *relative index of refraction*. Note that it's *not* defined as $\eta = \eta_{out}/\eta_{in}$. Also note that I'm using the same symbol η for absolute and relative indices of refraction.

To trace rays through transparent objects, we need an expression for the transmitted ray direction t. Notice from Figure 27.2 that t doesn't point in the

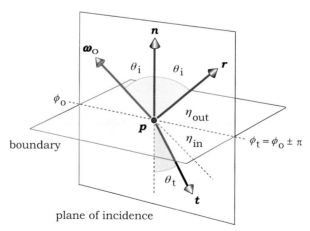

Figure 27.2. Reflected and transmitted rays at the boundary between two transparent media.

---

1. A surface is optically smooth if any roughness features are much smaller than the wavelengths of light. Panes of glass, sheets of acrylic, camera lenses, and telescope mirrors are examples.

same direction as the incident ray. This is because the direction of light changes as it crosses the boundary between media with different indices of refraction, a phenomenon known as *refraction*. It's a result of the different speeds of light in the two media.

In Figure 27.2, θ_i is the angle of incidence as discussed in Section 15.1, and θ_t is the *angle of refraction*. This is the polar angle between the normal direction on the transmitted ray's side of the boundary and the transmitted ray. The relationship between these two angles was worked out by Willebrord Snell in 1621 and is known as *Snell's law* or the *law of refraction*:

$$\frac{\sin\theta_i}{\sin\theta_t} = \frac{\eta_{in}}{\eta_{out}} = \eta. \tag{27.2}$$

Armed with the law of reflection from Chapter 15 and Snell's law, we can derive an expression for the transmitted direction t, but I'll just quote the result here. You can find the derivation in Glassner (1989) and Shirley and Morley (2003). The expression for t is

$$t = \frac{1}{\eta}\omega_o - \left(\cos\theta_t - \frac{1}{\eta}\cos\theta_i\right)n, \tag{27.3}$$

where

$$\cos\theta_i = n \bullet \omega_o$$

and

$$\cos\theta_t = \left[1 - \frac{1}{\eta^2}(1 - \cos^2\theta_i)\right]^{1/2}. \tag{27.4}$$

By construction, t is a unit vector. Notice from Equations (27.2)–(27.4) that t depends only on θ_i and η.

Now, here's an important question. Since the direction of the light changes as it crosses the boundary, the transmitted ray is bent away from the direction ω_o of the incoming ray. In which direction is it bent? The answer is simple:

- When light passes from a medium with a smaller ior to a medium with a larger ior, t is bent towards the normal direction at the hit point (see Figure 27.3).

- When light passes from a medium with a larger ior to a medium with a smaller ior, t is bent away from the normal direction at the point of intersection (see Figure 27.4).

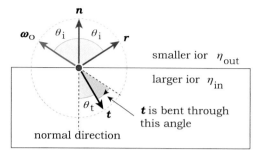

Figure 27.3. Direction change of t when $\eta > 1$.

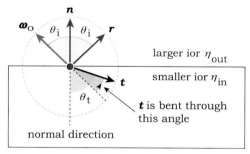

Figure 27.4. Direction change of t when $\eta < 1$.

27.3 Total Internal Reflection

The fact that the transmitted ray is bent *away* from the normal direction when $\eta < 1$ leads to the optical phenomenon called *total internal reflection*. To illustrate this, Figure 27.5 shows a sequence of rays that hit a surface point with increasing incident angles. I've drawn these rays hitting the inside surface of the object because $\eta_{in} > \eta_{out}$. This gives $\eta < 1$ for rays passing out of the object, since the relative index of refraction is now $\eta = \eta_{out}/\eta_{in}$, that is, its value is the inverse of when the ray hits the outside of the object. Note that I've drawn the normal on the *same* side of the boundary as the incident ray because, in this situation, the shading code will reverse it before it computes t. You can see total internal reflection in action if you are underwater and looking up (see Exercise 27.3).

As θ_i increases in Figure 27.5, notice how the transmitted ray bends towards the boundary, until θ_i reaches the *critical angle* θ_c in Figure 27.5(c). At this point, the transmitted ray is parallel to the boundary, and the angle of refraction is $\theta_t = \pi/2$.

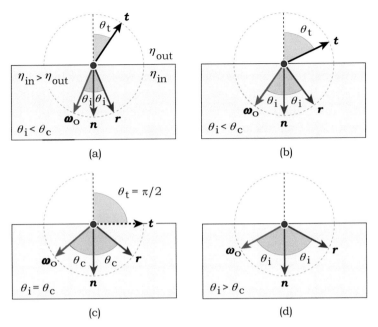

Figure 27.5. Total internal reflection: (a) and (b) $\theta_i < \theta_c$; (c) $\theta_i = \theta_c$; (d) $\theta_i > \theta_c$.

What happens to the transmitted ray when $\theta_t > \theta_c$? The answer is that it doesn't exist. In Figure 27.5(a) and (b), the energy in the incident ray is split between t and r, but as the direction of t approaches the boundary, the energy it carries decreases, while the energy carried in the reflected ray r increases. By the time t is parallel to the boundary, there is, in fact, no energy in it. That's why it's drawn as a dashed line in Figure 27.5(c). When total internal reflection occurs, *all* of the energy from the incident ray goes into the reflected ray. The Fresnel equations that I'll discuss in the following chapter specify the exact energy split between t and r as a function of θ_i and η.

To produce correct images, total internal reflection must be taken into account when we ray trace transparent objects. We must test for this condition at each ray–transparent-object hit point and, if it occurs, take the appropriate action. Since the condition is $\theta_i > \theta_c$, you may think that we have to compute θ_c, but this isn't necessary—there's a simpler but equivalent test. Notice that the expression for θ_t in Equation (27.4) involves a square root. If the expression inside the square root is negative, θ_t is imaginary, and t is therefore complex. This is another way of saying that t doesn't exist as a real ray. Since the expression inside the square root becomes zero when $\theta_i = \theta_c$, we can use the inequality

$$1 - \frac{1}{\eta^2}(1 - \cos^2\theta_i) < 0 \qquad (27.5)$$

as the condition for total internal reflection.

Total internal reflection doesn't only occur when a ray hits the inside surface of an object. If we ray trace an object whose ior is less than the surrounding medium, total internal reflection can occur when a ray hits it from the outside. Figure 27.15 shows an example.

27.4 The Illumination Model

The shading model for transparency is an extension of the model for reflective materials in Chapter 24. The exitant radiance at a point p is

$$L_r(p, \omega_o) = L_{direct}(p, \omega_o) + L_{indirect}(p, \omega_o),$$

where the indirect radiance now has a reflected and a transmitted component:

$$L_{indirect}(p, \omega_o) = L_r(p, \omega_o) + L_t(p, \omega_o). \qquad (27.6)$$

$L_r(p, \omega_o)$ is given by Equation (24.1), and the transmitted term is

$$L_t(p, \omega_o) = \int_{2\pi^-} f_{t,s}(p, \omega_i, \omega_o) L_o(r_c(p, \omega_i), -\omega_i)|\cos\theta_i|d\omega_i, \qquad (27.7)$$

where $f_{r,s}(p, \omega_i, \omega_o)$ is the *bidirectional transmission distribution function* (BTDF) for perfect specular transmission.

For ray tracing an isolated closed transparent object from the outside, we must trace the reflected and transmitted rays to a maximum recursion depth (max_depth) of at least two because it takes at least two bounces for the transmitted rays to come out of the object. Figure 27.6 shows a sequence of rays through various transparent objects drawn to a maximum depth of four.

As each ray-object intersection can generate two new rays, we can represent these with a binary tree, as in Figure 27.7. This is known as a *ray tree*, and if the reflected rays are followed before the transmitted rays, the tree will be traversed in a depth-first, left-to-right order. The numbering of the rays in Figures 27.6 and 27.7 reflect this order.

Not every ray-object intersection results in two new rays—sometimes only one ray is generated, and sometimes no rays. For example, no new rays are generated at point a in Figure 27.6 because the object is opaque and non-reflective. No transmitted ray is generated when there's total internal reflec-

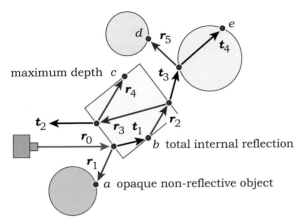

Figure 27.6. Transparent objects with reflected and transmitted rays.

tion, as at point b, and no new rays are generated if the maximum recursion depth has been reached, which it has at points c, d, and e. Unless max_depth is reached, a reflected ray is always generated, as the transparent materials we will model are also reflective.

If all rays in the ray tree are traced, the ray r_0 will end up generating a total of $2^{\text{max\_depth} + 1}$ secondary rays down to max_depth. This can result in long rendering times and make it impossible to ray trace some transparent objects (see Section 27.8).

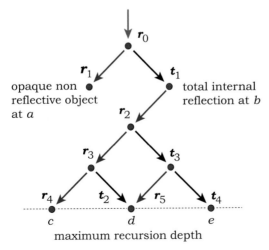

Figure 27.7. The ray tree that corresponds to Figure 27.6.

The BTDF in Equation (27.7) will only be nonzero for the direction t and will therefore involve a delta function. But before we can write a formula for it, we need to take into account the fact that refraction causes the radiance along a ray to change as it crosses the boundary between two dielectrics. Figure 27.8 shows a differential cone of incident radiance crossing a boundary. When the radiance passes from a medium of smaller η to one of larger η, the angle of the cone decreases, thus increasing the radiance; conversely, when it passes from a medium of larger η to one of smaller η, the angle decreases, and so does the radiance.

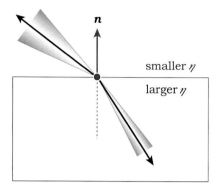

Figure 27.8. The angle of a differential cone of incident radiance changes as it crosses the boundary between two dielectrics.

By considering the amount of differential flux that crosses the boundary, and using Snell's law and the angle relation $\phi_t = \phi_o \pm \pi$ (Figure 27.2), we can derive the following relation between the incident radiance L_i and the transmitted radiance L_t:

$$L_t = k_t \left(\frac{\eta_t^2}{\eta_i^2} \right) L_i \tag{27.8}$$

(see Pharr and Humphreys (2004)). In Equation (27.8), η_i is the ior on the incident radiance side of the boundary, and η_t is the ior on the exitant radiance side. The quantity $k_t \in [0, 1]$ is the *transmission coefficient*. This specifies the fraction of flux that's transmitted across the boundary in the same way that k_r specifies the fraction of flux that's reflected. By conservation of energy, we have $k_r + k_t = 1$.

We can write the BTDF as

$$f_{t,s}(p, \omega_i, \omega_o) = k_t \left(\frac{\eta_t^2}{\eta_i^2} \right) \frac{\delta(\omega_i - t(n, \omega_o))}{|\cos\theta_i|}, \tag{27.9}$$

where $t(n, \omega_o)$ is given by Equation (27.3) and $|\cos\theta_i|$ is in the denominator to cancel this term in Equation (27.7). There's no $\cos\theta_i$ term in the expression for the transmitted radiance because it's perfect specular transmission. From Equations (27.7) and (27.8), the transmitted radiance is

$$L_t(p, \omega_o) = k_t \left(\frac{\eta_t^2}{\eta_i^2} \right) L_i(p, \omega_i), \tag{27.10}$$

where $L_i(p, \omega_i) = L_o(r_c(p, \omega_i), -\omega_i)$ is the radiance incident along the transmitted ray t.

Although the expression (27.10) is simple, we have to be careful when we apply it. Why? It's easy to get the η_t^2 / η_i^2 term upside down. To illustrate the correct quantities to use, Figure 27.9 shows some sample transmitted rays. The thick arrows show the direction of radiance transfer, which, as always, is opposite of the ray directions.

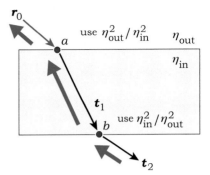

Figure 27.9. Ray and radiance-transfer directions through a transparent object.

Here are the expressions to use:

- At point a, the incident ray r_0 hits the outside of the object, the transmitted ray t_1 is inside the object, but the radiance transfer is from inside to outside, so $\eta_i = \eta_{in}$, $\eta_t = \eta_{out}$, and we use $\eta_{out}^2 / \eta_{in}^2$ in Equation (27.10).

- At point b, the incident ray t_1 hits the inside of the object, the transmitted ray t_2 is outside the object, but the radiance transfer is from outside to inside, so $\eta_i = \eta_{out}$, $\eta_t = \eta_{in}$, and we use $\eta_{in}^2 / \eta_{out}^2$ in Equation (27.10).

27.5 Practical Aspects

Here are a number of important points about ray tracing transparent objects. Although we've discussed most of these above, it's useful to have them all in one place as a check list.

- If we are not at `max_depth`, a reflected ray is always created at a ray-object hit point because the transparent material we model in this chapter is reflective.
- If we are not at `max_depth`, a transmitted ray is created at a ray-boundary intersection unless there is total internal reflection.
- Transmitted rays can be inside or outside transparent objects.
- Reflected rays can be inside or outside transparent objects.
- What happens at a ray-boundary intersection depends only on the incidence angle θ_i, and the relative index of refraction η.
- When a ray hits a transparent object from the inside, we must do the following three things before we compute the transmitted ray:
  1. change the sign of $\cos \theta_i$;
  2. reverse the direction of the normal;
  3. *invert* the value of η (that is, replace η with $1/\eta$).

  As these changes will be handled by local variables in the BTDF `sample_f` function, they only apply to the computation of t.

- Depending on the value of η, total internal reflection can occur when a ray strikes a transparent object from the inside or the outside. We must therefore test for total internal reflection at every ray-object hit point.
- When total internal reflection occurs, we set the reflection coefficient to 1 because this models the way real transparent materials behave.
- Other than the inversion of η, all optical properties of a transparent material are the same on its inside and outside surfaces.

The condition that a ray hits the inside surface of an object is

$$\cos \theta_i = \boldsymbol{n} \bullet \boldsymbol{\omega}_o < 0,$$

from Section 14.6.2. A ray that hits the inside surface of an object can be a transmitted ray, a reflected ray, or, if the camera is inside the object, a primary ray.

Because we only reverse the normal to compute $\boldsymbol{t}$, we compute reflected rays off of the inside surface with the normal pointing *outwards*. An interesting point is that the code in Listing 24.2 still correctly computes the reflected ray direction (see Question 27.1).

 ## 27.6 Implementation

The simple transparent material I'll discuss here uses a single index of refraction $\eta = \eta_{in}$. This is all we need to render isolated transparent objects in air where $\eta_{out} = 1$, but it will also allow us to render other transparent objects such as air bubbles in water by using the appropriate value of η.

The BTDF classes define a function `tir` to check for total internal reflection and a function `fresnel` to compute the Fresnel equations. These are in addition to the functions `f`, `sample_f`, and `rho`. The classes are arranged in an inheritance structure, as indicated in Figure 27.10. I'll use the `PerfectTransmitter` BTDF in this chapter and the `FresnelTransmitter` BTDF in Chapter 28.

The `PerfectTransmitter` BTDF stores k_t and η. Listing 27.1 shows the function `PerfectTransmitter::tir`.

Listing 27.2 shows the function `PerfectTransmitter::sample_f`, which computes the transmitted ray direction and returns it in the parameter `wt`, but this will only be called when there is no total internal reflection. As there's no color involved with transmission in this chapter, the return value is multiplied by white so that it will return an `RGBColor`.

The material `Transparent` inherits from `Phong` so that we can render transparent objects with specular highlights. These help the visualization of trans-

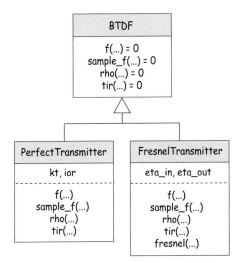

Figure 27.10. The BTDF inheritance chart.

```
bool
PerfectTransmitter::tir(const ShadeRec& sr) const {
    Vector3D wo(-sr.ray.d);
    float cos_thetai = sr.normal * wo;
    float eta = ior;

    if (cos_thetai < 0.0)
        eta = 1.0 / eta;

    return (1.0 - (1.0 - cos_thetai * cos_thetai) / (eta * eta) < 0.0);
}
```

Listing 27.1. The function `PerfectTransmitter::tir`.

parent objects when they are illuminated with point and directional lights, although they do create the same inconsistency that we had with the reflective materials in Chapter 24. Listing 27.3 shows the class declaration for the material `Transparent`. This contains a BRDF to handle reflections, a BTDF to handle the transparency, and three BRDFs inherited from the `Phong` material.

The function `Transparent::shade` appears in Listing 27.4. Note that when there is total internal reflection, the radiance is just incremented by the amount returned by the reflected ray, without multiplying it by the BRDF and $\cos \theta_i$. This is a fix to save us the trouble of getting the BRDF to use $k_r = 1$ in this case and the regular value of k_r when there's no total internal reflection.

```
RGBColor
PerfectTransmitter::sample_f(const ShadeRec& sr,
        const Vector3D& wo,
        Vector3D& wt) const {
    Normal n(sr.normal);
    float cos_thetai = n * wo;
    float eta = ior;

    if (cos_theta_i < 0.0) {
        cos_theta_i = -cos_theta_i;
        n = -n;
        eta = 1.0 / eta;
    }

    float temp = 1.0 - (1.0 - cos_theta_i * cos_theta_i) / (eta * eta);
    float cos_theta2 = sqrt(temp);
    wt = -wo / eta - (cos_theta2 - cos_theta_i / eta) * n;

    return (kt / (eta * eta) * white / fabs(sr.normal * wt));
}
```

Listing 27.2. The function `PerfectTransmitter::sample_f`.

```
class Transparent: public Phong {
    public:

        // constructors, etc.

        virtual RGBColor
        shade(ShadeRec& sr);

    private:

        PerfectSpecular*  reflective_brdf;
        PerfectTransmitter* specular_btdf;
};
```

Listing 27.3. The `Transparent` class declaration.

Because the `Transparent` material implements perfect specular reflection and transmission, and because the following sections will only use point and directional lights, we can use the `Whitted` tracer. That's also appropriate, as this is part of Whitted ray tracing.

```
RGBColor
Transparent::shade(ShadeRec& sr) {
    RGBColor L(Phong::shade(sr));

    Vector3D wo = -sr.ray.d;
    Vector3D wi;
    RGBColor fr = reflective_brdf->sample_f(sr, wo, wi);      // computes wi
    Ray reflected_ray(sr.hit_point, wi);

    if(specular_btdf->tir(sr))
        L += sr.w.tracer_ptr->trace_ray(reflected_ray, sr.depth + 1);
        // kr = 1.0
    else {
        Vector3D wt;
        RGBColor ft = specular_btdf->sample_f(sr, wo, wt);    // computes wt
        Ray transmitted_ray(sr.hit_point, wt);

        L += fr * sr.w.tracer_ptr->trace_ray(reflected_ray, sr.depth + 1)
            * fabs(sr.normal * wi);
        L += ft * sr.w.tracer_ptr->trace_ray(transmitted_ray, sr.depth + 1)
            * fabs(sr.normal * wt);
    }

    return (L);
}
```

Listing 27.4. The function `Transparent::shade`.

 ## 27.7 Transparent Spheres

27.7.1 General Analysis

Transparent spheres are great for testing your transparency code because their simple shape allows us to calculate exactly what happens to rays that are transmitted through them. But as you'll see, they can't demonstrate total internal reflection off of their inside surfaces when we ray trace them from the outside.

I'll analyze here what happens when we ray trace a transparent sphere from the outside and the whole sphere is visible in the image. To do this, we only have to examine rays that hit a unit sphere centered at the origin, although we will have to look at the cases $\eta \geq 1$ and $\eta < 1$ separately. There is also some mathematics involved, but it's elementary, and the analysis will all be 2D in the (x, y) plane.

Here's a question to start with. Do all rays that hit the sphere generate a transmitted ray inside the sphere? To answer this, consider Figure 27.11, which shows the cross section in the (x, y) plane of a unit sphere and an incoming ray r_0. This ray is parallel to the x-axis and distance $b \in [0, 1]$ from it, where b is called the *impact parameter*.[2] Because of symmetry, b is the only parameter we have to consider (see Question 27.2).

Since the x- and y-coordinates of the hit point a satisfy

$$x^2 + y^2 = 1,\tag{27.11}$$

it's simple to show that the coordinates of a are

$$x = (1 - b^2)^{1/2},\tag{27.12}$$
$$y = b$$

(see Exercise 27.1). The unit normal at the hit point is then

$$n = (x, y) = [(1 - b^2)^{1/2}, b].$$

Since $r_0 = (-1, 0)$, $\cos \theta_i$ is given by

$$\cos \theta_i = -r_0 \bullet n = -(-1, 0) \bullet [(1 - b^2)^{1/2}, b]$$
$$= (1 - b^2)^{1/2}.\tag{27.13}$$

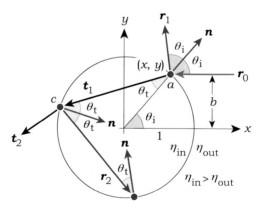

Figure 27.11. Reflected and transmitted rays generated by a ray r_0 that hits a unit sphere with impact parameter b. The lengths of the (unit) normals and the sphere are not drawn on the same scale.

2. "Impact parameter" is a physics term.

Equations (27.4) and (27.13) then give

$$\cos \theta_i = (1 - b^2/\eta^2)^{1/2}. \tag{27.14}$$

From Equation (27.14), total internal reflection will occur at a when

$$1 - b^2/\eta^2 < 0$$

or

$$b > \eta, \tag{27.15}$$

a beautifully simple result.

27.2.2 The Case $\eta \geq 1$

When $\eta \geq 1$, Equation (27.15) can't be satisfied, because $b \in [0, 1]$. Therefore, when we ray trace a sphere whose index of refraction is *larger* than that of the surrounding medium, total internal reflection can't occur when the rays hit the sphere from the outside.[3] That is, all rays generate a transmitted ray inside. In the special case $\eta = 1$, rays that are tangent to the sphere, that is, have $b = 1 = \eta$, are at the critical angle. In this case, no transmitted rays are generated, but this has no effect on the images. Do you know why?

We can now look at some images. The scene I'll use contains a reflective and a transparent sphere with a checkerboard rectangle, two point lights, and a directional light. Figure 27.12 is a view of the spheres looking vertically down to show their relative locations.

Listing 27.5 shows how to construct the transparent sphere.

A problem with transparency is that we often don't have an intuitive idea of what the images should look like. Therefore, when you ray trace a new transparent object type, how can you tell if the images are correct? It's always a good idea to start with $\eta = 1$. Although that's not physically correct, the lack of refraction will immediately tell you if the rays are going through the object correctly. If that's not happening, you can fix any problems at this

Figure 27.12. A reflective and a transparent sphere.

---

3. Rays that start inside the sphere *can* be totally internally reflected. These include camera rays if the camera is inside the sphere and rays reflected from objects inside the sphere. This is discussed in Chapter 28.

```
void
World::build(void) {
    ...
    // transparent sphere

    Transparent* glass_ptr = new Transparent;
    glass_ptr->set_ks(0.5);
    glass_ptr->set_exp(2000.0);
    glass_ptr->set_ior(1.5);
    glass_ptr->set_kr(0.1);
    glass_ptr->set_kt(0.9);
    Sphere* sphere_ptr1 = Sphere(Point3D(0.0, 4.5, 0.0), 3.0);
    sphere_ptr1->set_material(glass_ptr);
    add_object(sphere_ptr1);
    ...
}
```

Listing 27.5. Part of the build function for Figures 27.12–27.14 that demonstrates how to construct the transparent sphere.

stage. That's one reason I've included a number of images here with $\eta = 1$. Another reason is that $\eta = 1$ allows us to see some (often subtle) optical effects that are masked by refraction.

Figure 27.13 shows three views of the scene with $\eta = 1$ and different values of max_depth. The transparent sphere is visible in each image through its specular highlights and faint color changes and reflections. Here are

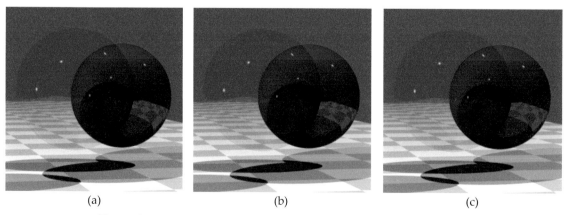

(a)   (b)   (c)

Figure 27.13. A reflective and a transparent sphere rendered with $\eta = 1$: (a) max_depth = 2; (b) max_depth = 4; (c) max_depth = 5.

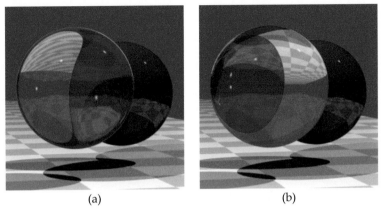

(a)   (b)

Figure 27.14. The spheres with `max_depth` = 5: (a) η = 1.1; (b) η = 1.5.

some questions to think about before reading further. In Figure 27.13(a), with `max_depth` = 2, why does the scene appear slightly darker when seen through the transparent sphere? (Figure 27.32(a) shows the same effect). In Figure 7.13(b), with `max_depth` = 4, what is the dark disk near the middle of the red sphere? What has happened to it in Figure 27.13(c), where `max_depth` = 5? In Figure 27.13(b) and (c), a faint image of the checkers is visible in the top part of the transparent sphere, and a faint image of the red sphere is also visible. How are these formed? These optical effects are easier to see in the images on the book's website.

Figure 27.14 shows the effects of changing the index of refraction. In Figure 27.14(a), η = 1.1, and in Figure 27.14(b), η = 1.5, which corresponds to a glass sphere in air. Before you read Section 27.7.4, see if you can work out how the image seen through the sphere changes as η increases.

27.7.3 The Case $\eta < 1$

When $\eta < 1$, Equation (27.15) is satisfied for $b > \eta$. Consequently, when we ray trace a sphere from the outside whose index of refraction is *smaller* than that of the surrounding medium, total internal reflection will occur, provided the whole sphere is visible. Such rays are totally internally reflected *off* of the sphere, and no internal transmitted rays are created.

If we change the index of refraction of the sphere to η = 0.75, which corresponds to an air bubble in water, Figure 27.15(a) can be the result if we are not careful. Here, the most striking feature is the large dark ring caused by total internal reflection when $b > 0.75$. This is not correct, however, because I've

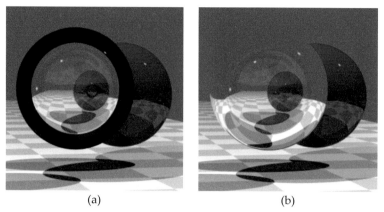

(a)   (b)

Figure 27.15. Ray traced air bubble in water: (a) $k_r = 0.1$ when there is total internal reflection; (b) $k_r = 1.0$ when there is total internal reflection.

deliberately left $k_r = 0.1$ in this region. In Figure 27.15(b), I've used the correct value $k_r = 1$, and the ring becomes a perfect mirror. Notice that the boundary between the top part of the sphere and background isn't visible.

27.7.4 What Happens to Rays that Enter the Sphere?

We can't completely understand the previous images unless we analyze what happens to the rays that enter the sphere. In particular, we need to find out if total internal reflection can occur when rays hit the sphere from the inside. Again, I'll only consider ray tracing a transparent sphere from the outside and assume that the whole sphere is visible in the image. In Figure 27.11, the internally transmitted ray t_1 hits the sphere from the inside at point c. Although I've drawn Figure 27.11 for $\eta > 1$, this will not affect the calculations below.

Because of symmetry, the angle that t_1 makes with the inward-pointing normal at c is the same as the angle of refraction θ_t at a. For calculations at c, this angle is the angle of incidence θ_i, and it follows from Equation (27.14) that

$$\cos\theta_i = (1 - b^2/\eta^2)^{1/2}. \tag{27.16}$$

The cosine of the angle of refraction θ_t for the external transmitted ray t_2 at c is given by Equation (27.4) again, where we have to use the reciprocal of η on the right-hand side. Consequently,

$$\cos\theta_t = [1 - \eta^2(1 - \cos^2\theta_i)]^{1/2}. \tag{27.17}$$

Substituting (27.16) into (27.17) gives the simple result

$$\cos \theta_t = (1 - b^2)^{1/2}. \tag{27.18}$$

Note that this expression is independent of η.

Since $1 - b^2$ can't be negative, Equation (27.17) tells us that regardless of the value of η, no rays transmitted through the sphere are totally internally reflected when they hit the sphere from the inside.

There is, however, one final question to answer. What happens to the internally reflected ray r_2 at c? Can this ray be totally internally reflected? No—symmetry guarantees that this ray hits the inside of the sphere at the same angle as the transmitted ray t_1 does at c. The same fact holds for any further internally reflected rays that are created from r_2. We therefore have the following result: no total internal reflection occurs from inside a sphere when the sphere is ray traced from the outside.

This means that all rays that enter the sphere bring back some radiance from the scene through their external transmitted rays, even if it's just the background color. I'll discuss in Chapter 28 how many of these transmitted rays make a significant contribution to the image.

In Figure 27.11, notice that although the incoming ray r_0 is horizontal, the external transmitted ray t_2 points towards the x-axis. Since r_0 is arbitrary, this applies to all externally transmitted rays, and as a result, the part of the scene that's visible through a transparent sphere *may* be inverted through the x-axis. In a 3D scene, the x-axis here corresponds to a line from the camera location through the center of the sphere. In a ray-traced image, the inversion is through the projected center of the sphere. Figure 27.16 attempts to illustrate this schematically, but to really appreciate the effect, you need to watch the animation **ChangingEta. mov** on the book's website, where η changes from frame to frame. Images for specific values of η, such as Figure 27.12, don't convey enough information for you to see this.

It's important to realize, however, that this is not the whole story. The inversion of all of the scene that's seen through the sphere only happens when the camera and objects are not close to the sphere. When objects, the camera, or both are close to the sphere, the situation is more complex (see Questions 27.9 and 27.10).

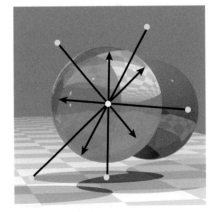

Figure 27.16. Inversion of the scene through a transparent sphere. Arrows indicate points in the scene (yellow dots) and where they are seen through the sphere.

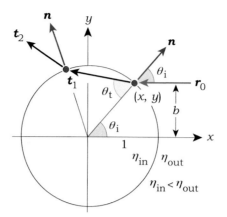

Figure 27.17. Reflected and transmitted rays generated by a ray r_0 that hits a unit sphere with impact parameter b, where the sphere has $\eta < 1$.

Figure 27.17 shows that when $\eta < 1$, the externally transmitted ray t_2 points away from the x-axis. As a result, the part of the scene that's visible through the sphere is not inverted and appears reduced in size. Figure 27.15 is an example.

27.8 Transparent Compound Objects

In Chapter 19, I discussed how to construct compound objects such as cylinders and bowls from disks, open cylinders, and part spheres; in Chapter 21, I discussed beveled objects. To ray trace these objects with transparent materials, we must be careful with the normals, as these must always point out of the object. Figure 27.18 shows three examples. The simplest is a solid cylinder where the curved surface must be modeled with a *convex* open cylinder. In particular, we can't use an object that reverses the normal when a ray hits its inside surface, as discussed in Section 19.5.3. The next example is a thick ring that's modeled with a convex open cylinder for the outer curved surface and a *concave* open cylinder for the inner surface. The last example is a flat-rimmed hemispherical bowl where I've used a convex hemisphere for the outer curved surface and a concave hemisphere for the inner surface.

Figure 27.19 shows ray-traced images of the objects in Figure 27.18, which all exhibit total internal reflection off of their inside surfaces.

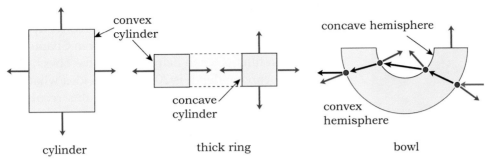

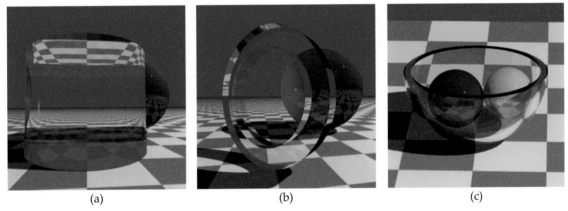

Figure 27.18. Vertical cross sections of a transparent cylinder, a thick ring, and a hemispherical bowl, showing the directions of the normals. The bowl part also shows sample transmitted rays.

Figure 27.19. Rendered transparent cylinder, thick ring, and bowl.

As we saw in Figure 24.29, beveled objects don't work particularly well with reflective materials. It's no surprise then, that they also don't work well with transparent materials, and for the same reason. In fact, transparency makes the problem worse because each ray uses at least two normals to traverse a transparent object. There's also another problem in that there can't be any interior surfaces. As a result, we can't use the beveled box from Chapter 21. Instead, we have to use a *beveled box shell* object constructed from part spheres and cylinders, in contrast to the beveled box, which used whole spheres and open cylinders. This considerably complicates the modeling because we have to specify the angular range for each of the eight part spheres and 12 part cylinders. In addition, these have to be convex, but there's more. We also need versions of the rectangles where the normals point outwards.

Figure 27.20. A beveled box shell rendered with `max_depth` = 20.

After all this modeling, the result in Figure 27.20 is not an attractive-looking object, although it is correctly rendered. I've used the transparent material from Chapter 28 with a lemon filter color to help visualize the object. The maximum recursion depth is 20. I have no idea what the beveled box would look like because, at this recursion depth, I can't even render a single pixel; the interior surfaces of the spheres and cylinders result in a combinatorial explosion of secondary rays—up to 2^{21} for each primary ray. Adaptive ray culling may help, but I don't have that implemented. In conclusion, the beveled box shell wasn't worth the modeling effort, but the code is on the book's website in case you want to experiment with it.

In spite of these problems, some transparent objects with beveled surfaces can be successful. See the glass of water and fishbowls in Chapter 28, where the water meniscus and the round edges have small radii compared with the overall dimensions of the objects.

27.9 Leaving Out the Etas

What difference do you think would it make to the appearance of transparent objects if the factor η_t^2 / η_i^2 were left out of the expression (27.10) for the transmitted radiance? For the objects rendered up to this point in this chapter, the answer is absolutely nothing. The reason is symmetry. When we ray trace an isolated transparent object with a closed boundary, no matter how complex its shape, the transmitted rays will enter and leave it the same (even) number of times. Because the η factors are inverses for rays entering and leaving the object, they cancel in the expression for the transmitted radiance (see Exercise 27.13).

It makes a difference for "open" transparent objects such as planar and part objects. For example, we can put water in the bowls from Chapters 19 and 21 by adding a transparent disk for the water surface. It also makes a difference when the camera is inside a transparent object.

The scene in Figure 27.21(a) contains two vertical transparent disks. The disk nearer the camera has the normal (0, 0, 1) pointing towards the camera; the disk further from the camera is smaller, and has the normal (0, 0, −1) pointing away from the camera. The disks are rendered with $\eta = 1.5$. Rays that pass through both disks are like rays that pass through any other transparent objects, and the radiance they return to the camera is unaffected by the factor

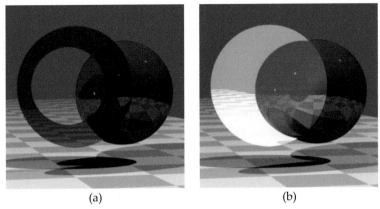

(a)   (b)

Figure 27.21. (a) A scene that contains two parallel transparent disks whose normals point in opposite directions; (b) a single disk whose normal points away from the camera.

η_t^2 / η_i^2. In contrast, rays that only pass through the front disk have their radiance reduced by a factor of $\eta_t^2 / \eta_i^2 = 1.5^2 = 2.25$.

The scene in Figure 27.21(b) contains a single transparent disk, where its normal $(0, 0, -1)$ points away from the camera. Primary rays that pass through the disk have their radiance increased by 2.25, resulting in the washed-out appearance of the scene as viewed through the disk. As this is what can happen to the whole scene when you place the camera inside a transparent object, it's quite relevant to the rendering of transparent objects. I'll discuss how to handle this situation in Section 28.6.3.

 Further Reading

As with perfect specular reflection, Whitted was the first person to implement perfect specular transmission with illumination by point lights. See Whitted (1980). Many of the references cited in Chapter 24 also discuss perfect specular transmission: Glassner (1989), Hall (1988), Foley et al. (1995), Wilt (1994), Watt (2000), Hill and Kelley (2006), Shirley and Morley (2003), Hearn and Baker (2004), Pharr and Humphreys (2004), and Shirley et al. (2005).

You can find the theory presented in Sections 27.1–27.3 in most optics textbooks, for example, Hecht (1997).

Although the theory of ray tracing transparent spheres presented in Section 27.7 is probably not new, I haven't seen it written up anywhere.

Questions

27.1. Why don't we have to write a new version of the BRDF function `PerfectSpecular::sample_f` in Listing 24.2, for the material `Transparent`? Specifically, why does this function correctly compute the reflected ray direction when a ray hits the inside surface of a transparent object and the normal points outwards? Hint: see Exercise 24.11.

27.2. Why is the configuration in Figure 27.11 the most specifc that we need to analyze a sphere? In particular, why doesn't the analysis depend on how close the camera is to the sphere?

27.3. What do you think the transparent sphere in Section 27.7 would look like if you ray traced it with `max_depth` = 0 or 1?

27.4. What is the minimum depth we need to see through a transparent sphere?

27.5. The function `Transparent::shade` in Listing 27.4 traces reflected rays before transmitted rays. Would it make any difference to the images if this order were reversed?

27.6. The sphere in Figure 27.15 has $\eta = 0.75$ to simulate an air bubble in water. Where does this value of η come from? What is the corresponding value for an air bubble in acrylic?

27.7. Why is the top of the sphere in Figure 27.15(b) exactly the same color as the background?

27.8. Why are air bubbles in water and clear plastic so shiny?

27.9. The inversion shown in Figure 27.16 doesn't always happen over the whole sphere. Figure 27.22 shows the text "Ray Tracing from the Ground Up" on a flat surface just behind a colored transparent sphere. Note that most of the text seen through the sphere is not inverted and that there are two images of the "o" and the "t". Can you explain this? Here, the

Figure 27.22. Transparent sphere in front of text.

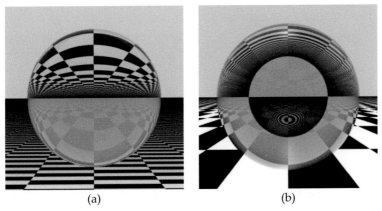
(a)   (b)

Figure 27.23. A transparent sphere with the camera far from the sphere (a) and close to the sphere (b).

text surface just touches the sphere, which has an index of refraction of 1.5 and a radius of 0.76. The camera is 8 units from the sphere center.

27.10. On the same theme as Question 27.9, Figure 27.23(a) shows a sphere of radius one at the origin with the camera on the z-axis at $z = 20.0$. Here, the whole sphere inverts the scene. In Figure 27.23(b) the camera is at $z = 1.25$. Notice the central region of the sphere, where there is no inversion. Can you explain this? If you look through a real transparent sphere with your eye on the surface, you will see the world the right way up, as in the central region here, but the view will be so blurred that you will hardly be able to tell what you are looking at.

27.11. Things look blurred when you look through a sphere close up because spheres don't perfectly focus light that passes through them. For example, a parallel beam of light will not be focused to a single point. How, then, can the ray tracer create perfectly sharp images of the scene, even when the camera is close to the sphere as in Figure 27.23(b)?

27.12. Figure 27.24(a) shows a transparent ellipsoid that has a thin black strip around its silhouette. As this is only a few pixels wide, it's easier to see it in the image on the book's website. The strip results from the total internal reflection of rays off of the inside surface of the ellipsoid. For the pixel in the strip pointed to by the arrow in Figure 27.24(a), Figure 27.24(b) shows the totally internally reflected rays inside the ellipsoid to max_depth = 8. The ray at the lower left is the primary ray, and this image also shows the externally reflected ray where the primary ray hits the ellipsoid.

As the ellipsoid is rendered with instancing, as described in Chapter 21, the inverse transformed rays are actually intersected with a generic sphere. However, as we proved in Section 27.7.3, no rays are

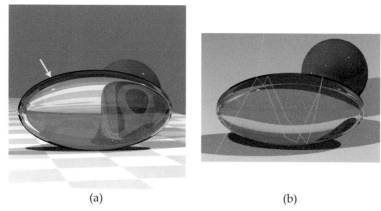

(a)   (b)

Figure 27.24. (a) A transparent ellipsoid with $\eta = 1.5$; (b) the ellipsoid in (a) rendered with ray-visualization software that shows some of the rays generated from the primary ray that hits the ellipsoid at the point indicated by the arrow. Image and software courtesy of Alister McKinley. This image was rendered from a higher camera location to show the primary ray, but all of the visualized rays apply to (a). A matte plane was used instead of the rectangle (a), but that doesn't affect the rays.

totally internally reflected off of the inside surface of a sphere when the sphere is ray traced from the outside. How, then, is the ray tracer able to simulate total internal reflection for the ellipsoid?

27.13. This question is analogous to Question 24.12. Figure 27.25 shows an orthographic view looking down the positive z-axis on a horizontal plane at $z = -50.0$ with black and orange checkers (and one cyan checker). In the (x, z) plane, there is a large transparent annulus with

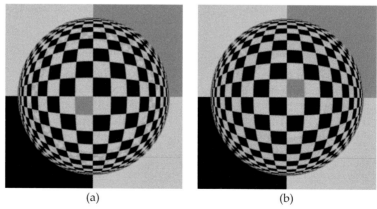

(a)   (b)

Figure 27.25. Transparent hemispheres and a checker plane. These are open transparent objects like the disks in Figure 27.21.

a small hole centered on the z-axis. Just filling the hole is a transparent hemisphere whose rim is in the (x, z) plane. The index of refraction is 1.5 for both objects. In one image, the hemisphere is above the (x, z) plane and is therefore convex towards the camera; in the other image, the hemisphere is below the (x, z) plane and is therefore concave towards the camera. Which is which?

Figure 27.26. A scene that contains two parallel transparent disks whose normals point in the same direction.

Here are some related questions. The horizon of the checker plane is not visible through the hemisphere in either image. Why is this? Would moving the plane farther down the z-axis change the situation?

27.14. What is the minimum depth we need to see through a transparent torus?

27.15. What is the minimum depth we need to see through a transparent thick ring, like the ring in Figure 27.19?

27.16. The disks in Figure 27.26 have their normals pointing in the same direction: $(0, 0, 1)$. Can you explain this image?

Exercises

27.1. Derive expressions (27.12) for the hit-point coordinates in Figure 27.11.

27.2. Derive expression (27.14) for $\cos \theta_t$.

27.3. Figure 27.27 shows what happens if you were underwater looking up. Because of total internal reflection, the only part of the world above the

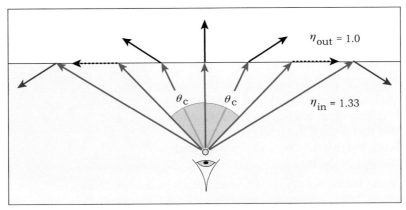

Figure 27.27. Looking up underwater.

Figure 27.28. Transparent ellipsoid with $\eta = 0.75$.

water that you can see is from light that comes in from a cone with half angle θ_c. Compute θ_c in degrees.

27.4. Prove that for a full ray tree, the number of secondary rays generated is $2^{\text{max\_depth}+1}$. Hint: you can express the answer as the partial sum of a geometric series (see Chapter 2). How many individual rays are there at max_depth?

27.5. Implement transparency with the Transparent material described in Section 27.6. Reproduce the Figures in Section 27.7 and include max_depth = 0 and 1.

27.6. According to Table 27.1, when ice is viewed from underwater, the relative index of refraction is $\eta = 0.98$. Render the transparent sphere in Section 27.7 with this value of η.

27.7. Your transparency code must work correctly with transformed objects. Test your implementation with the transparent ellipsoids in Figures 27.24(a) and 27.28. Notice how the specular highlights on the ellipsoids are elongated.

27.8. Figure 27.29 shows a transparent torus that has been rotated and translated. Implement a transparent torus and use this image to check your results. Note the black strips at the top and bottom of the torus.

27.9. Your transparency code must also work with triangle meshes. Figure 27.30 shows a transparent 16K

Figure 27.29. A transparent torus with $\eta = 1.5$.

Figure 27.30. Transparent Stanford bunny.

bunny rendered with smooth triangles, $\eta = 1.5$, and `max_depth` = 10, which you can use for testing. This image took a long time to render because of the binary tree of rays generated by the mesh. I'll cover transparent triangle meshes in more detail in Chapter 28.

27.10. The scene in Figure 27.31(a) contains a magnifying glass, which is a convex lens with a cross section like that shown in Figure 27.31(b). Model a magnifying glass using the objects discussed in Chapter 19, and render some images with it. Also model a concave lens and render some images with it. A representative cross section of a concave lens is also shown in Figure 27.31(b).

27.11. Render the scenes in Figure 27.19.

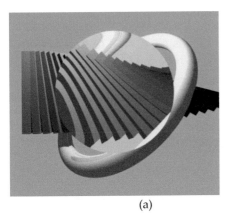

(a)

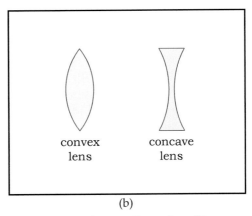

(b)

Figure 27.31. (a) A magnifying glass modeled and rendered by Peter Brownlow; (b) convex and concave lens cross sections.

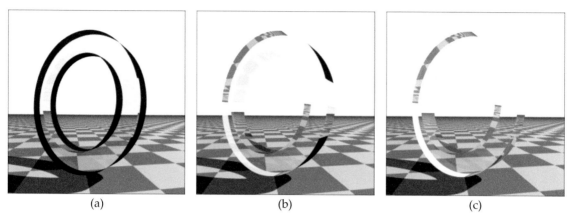

(a)   (b)   (c)

Figure 27.32. Thick ring rendered with `max_depth` = 2 (a), `max_depth` = 3 (b), and a higher value of `max_depth` (c).

27.12. Figure 27.32 shows the thick ring from Figure 27.19 rendered on a white background using different values of `max_depth`. All images were rendered with $k_r = 0.1$ and $k_r = 0.9$. In Figure 27.32(a), the dark areas on the curved surfaces are due to total internal reflection of the rays off of the inside surfaces of the cylinder. When this occurs, rays need more than two bounces to get through the ring. Notice how the background as seen through the two flat faces is not white. By sketching the secondary rays, prove that the radiance returned by the primary rays in this area is (0.91, 0.91, 0.91). In Figure 27.32(b), `max_depth` = 3, resulting in more rays getting through and the background color appearing to be white. Prove that the primary-ray radiance in this case is (0.991, 0.991, 0.991). In Figure 27.32(c), rendered with a higher value of `max_depth`, part of the cylinder is now almost invisible against the background. Render this scene with values of `max_depth` increasing from 2 to find out how high `max_depth` is in Figure 27.32(c). Also, find out how high `max_depth` must be before the image stops changing.

27.13. Prove that the radiance transmitted through a transparent object with a single boundary is independent of the term η_t^2 / η_i^2 in Equation (27.10). You can do this by writing the expression for the transmitted radiance for a single entry and exit. Why is this sufficient?

28 Realistic Transparency

Image courtesy of John Avery

 Objectives

By the end of this chapter, you should:

- understand how real materials reflect and transmit light;
- understand how color filtering is modeled.
- have implemented a physically correct transparent material;
- know how nested transparent objects are modeled.

I'll present here a physically correct model for reflection and transmission at the boundary of two dielectrics. I'll also discuss color filtering, as this will allow you to render colored transparent objects and more realistic-looking transparent objects than you could in Chapter 27. The new material will be used to demonstrate how transparency works with rectangular boxes and spheres; this time placing the camera inside a transparent sphere.

Another advantage of the new material is that it can be used to render nested transparent objects, thereby greatly increasing its modeling capabilities. As examples, I'll demonstrate how to model and render glasses of water and fishbowls.

Finally, I'll use path tracing to render caustics from transparent objects.

28.1 The Fresnel Equations

The Transparent material in Chapter 27 is unrealistic because it has constant values for k_r and k_t. In contrast, the values of k_r and k_t for real dielectrics vary strongly with the incident angle θ_i. How these quantities vary is described by the *Fresnel equations*, derived by the French physicist and mathematician Augustin-Jean Fresnel (1788-1827). These equations specify how light is reflected and transmitted at the boundary of two dielectrics with optically smooth surfaces, and as such, they describe perfect specular reflection and transmission.

As Fresnel's research was based on the wave theory of light, he derived separate equations for light polarized parallel and perpendicular to the boundary. Equations (28.1) and (28.2) are accurate approximations of his reflectance formulae for dielectrics:

$$r_\parallel = \frac{\eta \cos\theta_i - \cos\theta_t}{\eta \cos\theta_i + \cos\theta_t}, \tag{28.1}$$

$$r_\perp = \frac{\cos\theta_i - \eta \cos\theta_t}{\cos\theta_i + \eta \cos\theta_t}, \tag{28.2}$$

where $\eta = \eta_{in}/\eta_{out}$, and $r_\parallel$ and $r_\perp$ are the reflected amplitudes of light waves polarized parallel and perpendicular to the boundary, respectively. See Hecht (1997) for a discussion of polarization, an explanation of reflected amplitude, and the derivation of these equations. Note that Equations (28.1) and (28.2) only depend on θ_i and η because θ_t is given in terms of θ_i and η by Equation (27.4).

For unpolarized light, the *Fresnel reflectance* k_r is given by

$$k_r = \frac{1}{2}(r_\parallel^2 + r_\perp^2). \tag{28.3}$$

Equation (28.3) involves the squares of $r_\parallel$ and $r_\perp$ because k_r specifies the fraction of incident power reflected from a surface, and the power of a light wave is proportional to the square of its amplitude.

By conservation of energy, the *Fresnel transmittance* k_t is

$$k_t = 1 - k_r. \tag{28.4}$$

A simple analysis of Equations (28.1)–(28.4) can tell us how dielectrics behave at normal and grazing incidence.

28.1.1 Normal Incidence

At normal incidence, $\theta_i = \theta_t = 0$, and Equations (28.1) and (28.2) reduce to

$$r_\| = \frac{\eta - 1}{\eta + 1}, \quad r_\perp = -\frac{\eta - 1}{\eta + 1} = -r_\|$$

Consequently,

$$k_r = \frac{(\eta - 1)^2}{(\eta + 1)^2}, \quad k_t = \frac{4\eta}{(\eta + 1)^2}. \tag{28.5}$$

An interesting fact is that the expressions (28.5) satisfy

$$k_r(\eta) = k_r(1/\eta), \; k_t(\eta) = k_t(1/\eta) \tag{28.6}$$

so that k_r and k_t have the same values when light enters and exits a dielectric medium at normal incidence.

At the boundary between air and glass, where $\eta = 1.5$ when the light is entering the glass, Equation (28.5) gives $k_r = 0.04$. This means that glass at normal incidence reflects only 4% of the light that hits it and, by Equation (28.4), transmits 96% of the light. Does this mean that a perfectly clear pane of glass transmits 96% of the light that hits it at normal incidence? No (see Section 28.5).

28.1.2 Grazing Incidence

At grazing incidence, $\theta_i = \pi / 2$ so that $\cos \theta_i = 0$, and from Equations (28.1) and (28.2), $r_\| = r_\perp = -1$. Don't worry about the minus sign, which has to do with the polarization of light. The relevant fact for us is that Equations (28.3) and (28.4) reduce to

$$k_r = 1 \text{ and } k_t = 0, \tag{28.7}$$

respectively. Since equations (28.1) and (28.2) apply to all dielectric media, Equation (28.7) provides the following important result: All optically smooth dielectrics become perfect mirrors at grazing incidence.

You can see an example of this by looking at a pane of glass and turning it so that you are looking almost parallel to it. At near grazing incidence, you can no longer see through it, and it becomes a mirror. Even the cover of this book will behave in a similar manner.

Figure 28.1 displays graphs of k_r and k_t for $\eta = 1.5$ (glass in air) over the whole range of incidence angles $\theta_i \in [0, \pi/2]$. Notice how glass has almost constant Fresnel reflectance of 4%–5% up to $\theta_i \approx 50°$ and then approaches a perfect mirror steeply as $\theta_i \to \pi/2$. These curves also demonstrate how the arbitrary

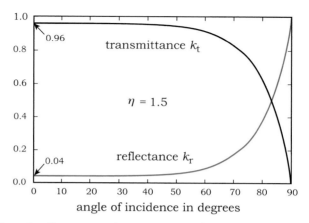

Figure 28.1. Fresnel reflectance and transmittance for glass as a function of incidence angle.

constant values $k_r = 0.1$ and $k_t = 0.9$ used in Chapter 27 are not even approximately correct.

28.1.3 Total Internal Reflection

We need to be careful when using equations (28.1)–(28.3), as they are not valid when there's total internal reflection. When this occurs, $k_r = 1$ and $k_t = 0$, as in Chapter 27. Figure 28.2 shows graphs of k_r and k_t as functions of incidence

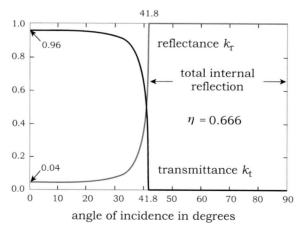

Figure 28.2. Graphs of k_r and k_t for $\eta \approx 0.666$ as functions of θ_i. The gradients of k_r and k_t become infinite as $\theta_i \to \theta_c$ from the left.

angle at a glass-air boundary where $\eta = 1/1.5 \approx 0.666$. For this value of η, the critical angle is $\theta_c \approx 41.8°$.

It's worth emphasizing that the Fresnel equations don't alter the reflection and refraction angles; they only specify k_r and k_t and therefore help to determine the radiance distribution between the reflected and transmitted rays.[1] Snell's law still applies.

28.2 Color Filtering

Dielectrics attenuate light that passes through them because the light interacts with their molecules. As a result, some of the light is scattered, with the amount increasing with the distance traveled. If the amount of scattering depends on the wavelength of the light, the dielectric will be colored. Dielectrics are examples of *participating media*.

We can model this as follows. Consider a ray that travels a differential distance dx through an attenuating medium. The fraction of the radiance attenuated is given by

$$dL/L = -\sigma dx, \tag{28.8}$$

where σ is the *attenuation coefficient*. Equation (28.8) is a *differential equation* whose solution is

$$L(d) = L_0 e^{-\sigma d}, \tag{28.9}$$

where d is the distance traveled in the medium and L_0 is the value of L when $d = 0$. The references in the Further Reading section derive this solution. Equation (28.9) is known as the *Beer-Lambert law*. Its most important property is that the radiance decreases exponentially with distance traveled.

Since L is an RGB color in our ray tracer, we need three versions of Equation (28.9), one each for the red, green, and blue color components. We could use an RGB color for the attenuation coefficient, $\sigma = (\sigma_r, \sigma_g, \sigma_b)$, but it's more convenient to re-write these equations in terms of a *filter color* c_f:

$$L(d) = c_f^d L_0, \tag{28.10}$$

where $c_f = e^{-\sigma}$. If there's no color filtering, $c_f = (1, 1, 1) =$ white.

---

1. The Fresnel equations don't *completely* determine the radiance distribution because of the η^2 factor for the transmitted rays.

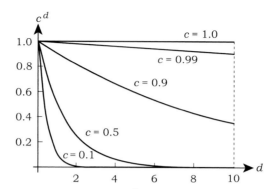

Figure 28.3. Plots of c^d for various values of c.

To demonstrate how quickly exponential attenuation can decrease the transmitted radiance, Figure 28.3 shows graphs of c^d, where $c \in [0, 1]$ can be a component of c_f. Notice how quickly the curves with $c = 0.5$ and $c = 0.1$ approach zero as d increases.

Figure 28.4 illustrates radiance transfer through a dielectric medium with color filtering. If the radiance that leaves b is L_b, the radiance L_a that arrives at a is

$$L_a = c_f^d L_b = (c_{f,r}^d, c_{f,g}^d, c_{f,b}^d) * (L_{b,r}, L_{b,g}, L_{b,b})$$
$$= (c_{f,r}^d L_{b,r}, c_{f,g}^d L_{b,g}, c_{f,b}^d L_{b,b}),$$

(28.11)

where d is the distance between the hit points a and b.

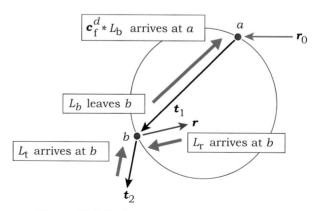

Figure 28.4. Radiance attenuation in a dielectric.

To evaluate the expression (28.11), we need to know the length of the t_1 ray's path through the medium, but fortunately, this is the ray parameter t where it hits the object at b. Provided the ray's direction is a unit vector, t specifies distance along the ray. Color filtering will not work correctly if your ray directions aren't normalized. We have to apply color filtering to all rays, reflected and transmitted, that travel through transparent media. Color filtering also has to work correctly with objects that have been scaled (see Figure 28.49).

 ## 28.3 Implementation

To implement the Fresnel equations, color filtering, and dielectrics that can be nested, we need a BRDF to handle the reflection, a BRDF to handle the transmission, and a new transparent material. I've called these `FresnelReflector`, `FresnelTransmitter`, and `Dielectric`, respectively. The BRDF will need to store η_{in} and η_{out} so that it can compute the Fresnel reflectance; the BRDF will also need to store these to compute the Fresnel transmittance.

Listing 28.1 shows the function `FresnelReflector::fresnel`, which computes the reflectance. After checking if the ray hits the inside surface, the complex-looking code that follows is just a straightforward implementation of Equations (28.1)–(28.3). The BTDF has the same function, to compute the transmission with Equation (28.4) (see Exercise 28.43). This function will not be called when there is total internal reflection.

The dielectric material's `shade` function calls the `FresnelReflector::sample_f`, `FresnelTransmitter::tir`, and `FresnelTransmitter::sample_f` functions, but because these are almost the same as the functions `PerfectSpecular::sample_f` in Listing 24.2, `PerfectTransmitter::tir` in Listing 27.1, and `PerfectTransmitter::sample_f` in Listing 27.2, I won't reproduce them here.

Listing 28.2 shows part of the `Dielectric` class declaration. This inherits from `Phong` so that we can render specular highlights. We should use the Fresnel equations for k_s, but this makes the highlights too dim. As they are artificial anyway, we can set k_s independently. The `Dielectric` material stores the interior and exterior filter colors because color filtering only occurs as rays traverse the medium. The filter colors are therefore not relevant to the BRDF and BTDF.

The function `Dielectric::shade` in Listing 28.3 may appear complex at first sight, but its structure is actually quite simple. If there's total internal reflection, it traces a reflected ray that can be inside or outside the

```
float
FresnelReflector::fresnel(const ShadeRec& sr) const {
    Normal normal(sr.normal);
    float ndotd = -normal * sr.ray.d;
    float eta;

    if (ndotd < 0.0) {                      // ray hits inside surface
        normal = -normal;
        eta = eta_out / eta_in;
    }
    else
        eta = eta_in / eta_out;

    float cos_theta_i = -normal * sr.ray.d;
    float temp = 1.0 - (1.0 - cos_theta_i * cos_theta_i) / (eta * eta);
    float cos_theta_t = sqrt (1.0 - (1.0 - cos_theta_i * cos_theta_i) /
            (eta * eta));
    float r_parallel = (eta * cos_theta_i - cos_theta_t) /
            (eta * cos_theta_i + cos_theta_t);
    float r_perpendicular = (cos_theta_i - eta * cos_theta_t) /
            (cos_theta_i + eta * cos_theta_t);
    float kr = 0.5 * (r_parallel * r_parallel + r_perpendicular
            * r_perpendicular);

    return (kr);
}
```

Listing 28.1. The function `FresnelReflector::fresnel`.

```
class Dielectric: public Phong {
    public:
        ...

        virtual RGBColor
        shade(ShadeRec& s);

    private:

        RGBColor cf_in;          // interior filter color
        RGBColor cf_out;         // exterior filter color

        FresnelReflector* fresnel_brdf;
        FresnelTransmitter* fresnel_btdf;
};
```

Listing 28.2. Partial declaration of the `Dielectric` class.

```
RGBColor
Dielectric::shade(ShadeRec& sr) {
    RGBColor L(Phong::shade(sr));

    Vector3D wi;
    Vector3D wo(-sr.ray.d);
    RGBColor fr = fresnel_brdf->sample_f(sr, wo, wi);          // computes wi
    Ray reflected_ray(sr.hit_point, wi);
    float t;
    RGBColor Lr, Lt;
    float ndotwi = sr.normal * wi;

    if(fresnel_btdf->tir(sr)) {                     // total internal reflection
        if (ndotwi < 0.0) {
            // reflected ray is inside

            Lr = sr.w.tracer_ptr->trace_ray(reflected_ray, t, sr.depth + 1);
            L += cf_in.powc(t) * Lr;           // inside filter color
        }
        else {
            // reflected ray is outside

            Lr = sr.w.tracer_ptr->trace_ray(reflected_ray, t, sr.depth + 1);
            // kr = 1
            L += cf_out.powc(t) * Lr;          // outside filter color
        }
    }
    else {             // no total internal reflection
        Vector3D wt;
        RGBColor ft = fresnel_btdf->sample_f(sr, wo, wt);      // computes wt
        Ray transmitted_ray(sr.hit_point, wt);
        float ndotwt = sr.normal * wt;

        if (ndotwi < 0.0) {
            // reflected ray is inside

            Lr = fr * sr.w.tracer_ptr->trace_ray(reflected_ray, t,
                sr.depth + 1) * fabs(ndotwi);
            L += cf_in.powc(t) * Lr;           // inside filter color

            // transmitted ray is outside

            Lt = ft * sr.w.tracer_ptr->trace_ray(transmitted_ray, t,
                sr.depth + 1) * fabs(ndotwt);
            L += cf_out.powc(t) * Lt;          // outside filter color
        }
```

Listing 28.3. The function Dielectric::shade.

```
      else {
            // reflected ray is outside

            Lr = fr * sr.w.tracer_ptr->trace_ray(reflected_ray, t,
                  sr.depth + 1) * fabs(ndotwi);
            L += cf_out.powc(t) * Lr;              // outside filter color

            // transmitted ray is inside

            Lt = ft * sr.w.tracer_ptr->trace_ray(transmitted_ray, t,
                  sr.depth + 1) * fabs(ndotwt);
            L += cf_in.powc(t)) * Lt;              // inside filter color
      }
  }

  return (L);
}
```

Listing 28.3 (continued). The function `Dielectric::shade`.

medium. If there's no total internal reflection, it traces a reflected and a transmitted ray, one of which will be inside and the other outside. At this level, the algorithm is the same as `Transparent::shade` in Listing 27.4. The complication in this case is the color filtering. Before any ray is traced, we have to find out if it's inside or outside, as this determines which filter color must be used.

This function calls a special version of `trace_ray` that returns the ray parameter at the nearest hit point, for use in the color filtering. The `Whitted` tracer version of this function is in Listing 28.4. The difference between this function and the regular version of `Whitted::trace_ray` in Listing 24.1 is that this assigns `sr.t` to `tmin` when the ray hits an object and assigns `kHugeValue` to `tmin` when no object is hit. The latter assignment ensures that the color filtering works correctly for rays that are outside transparent objects and for one-sided objects.

Instead of using a special version of `trace_ray`, why don't we do the following? Change the function `World::hit_objects` in Listing 14.8 to store `kHugeValue` in `sr.t` when no object is hit (one line of code), use the regular version of `trace_ray` in `Dielectric::shade`, and use `sr.t` in instead of `t` to compute the color filtering. That's a lot simpler, but unfortunately, it won't work. The reason is that the `ShadeRec` object in `trace_ray` is not the same `ShadeRec` object that's passed in as the parameter to `Dielectric::shade`.

```
RGBColor
whitted::trace_ray(const Ray ray, float& tmin, const int depth) const {
    if (depth > world_ptr->vp.get_max_depth())
        return(black);
    else {
        ShadeRec sr(world_ptr->hit_objects(ray));

        if (sr.hit_an_object) {
            sr.depth = depth;
            sr.ray = ray;
            tmin = sr.t;
            return (sr.material_ptr->shade(sr));
        }
        else {
            tmin = kHugeValue;
            return (world_ptr->background_color);
        }
    }
}
```

Listing 28.4. The function whitted::trace_ray.

28.4 Images

28.4.1 Fresnel Effects

For curved objects, the effects of using the Fresnel equations are often subtle.
The transparent sphere from Section 27.7 is an example, but before we look at
that, Listing 28.5 demonstrates how to set up a Dielectric material with an
ior of 1.5, the same specular highlights as used in Section 27.7, and no color
filtering.

```
Dielectric* dielectric_ptr = new Dielectric;
dielectric_ptr->set_ks(0.2);
dielectric_ptr->set_exp(2000);
dielectric_ptr->set_eta_in(1.5);
dielectric_ptr->set_eta_out(1.0);
dielectric_ptr->set_cf_in(1.0);
dielectric_ptr->set_cf_out(1.0);
```

Listing 28.5. Sample code for specifying a Dielectric material.

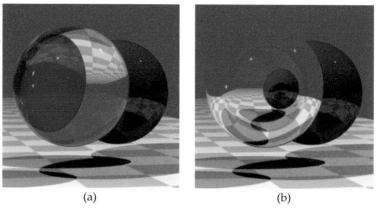

(a)   (b)

Figure 28.5. (a) Figure 27.14(b) rendered with a Dielectric material for the sphere; (b) Figure 27.15(b) rendered with a Dielectric material.

Figure 28.5(a) displays the sphere in Figure 27.14(b) rendered with the Dielectric material. The main differences are near the silhouette, where the Fresnel reflectance approaches one, increasing the brightness of the reflections. This is particularly noticeable on the lower part of the sphere, where the rectangle is reflected. The opposite effect happens away from the silhouette, where the reflectance is less than the constant value $k_r = 0.1$ used in Figure 27.14(b), resulting in the reflection of the rectangle being fainter.

In Figure 28.5(b), where the sphere is an air bubble in water, the differences are in the part of the sphere where the rays get through. Again, the reflection of the rectangle is fainter, but the reason this time is that the Fresnel reflectance from the inside surface, where $\eta = 1.33$, is less than $k_r = 0.1$. Although I don't have a graph of k_r for $\eta = 1.33$, it would be similar to the $\eta = 1.5$ curve; its value at normal incidence is 0.02.

It's instructive to render a completely transparent sphere with no other objects, no lights, and a white background, because this will illustrate the general behavior of smooth transparent objects. Figure 28.6(a) shows a sphere with $\eta = 1.5$ rendered with max_depth = 1, so that the transmitted rays don't get out. The color at the sphere's center is (0.04, 0.04, 0.04), as expected (why?), and it gets lighter near the silhouette, as $f_r \to 1.0$. Right at the silhouette, you might expect (as I did) that the color would approach white due to the perfect mirror reflection, but that doesn't happen. The sphere has a sharp non-white silhouette caused by difficulties in sampling the k_r curve in Figure 28.1. Although the slope of f_r is finite at $\theta_i = \pi/2$, it is large. As a result, a value of θ_i that's less than $\pi/2$, by even a small amount, can result in a value of $f_r = 0.85$

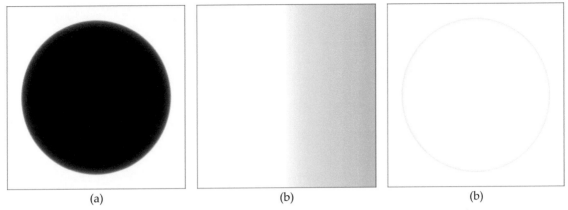

(a)   (b)   (b)

Figure 28.6. A transparent sphere with $\eta = 1.5$: (a) rendered with max_depth = 1; (b) zoomed-in view of the sphere boundary; (c) max_depth = 3.

to 0.95. Figure 28.6(b) shows part of the silhouette zoomed by a factor of 10^4, where it's lighter but still not white. Therefore, any smooth transparent object with $\eta > 1.0$ will have brighter reflections near its silhouette, but a perfect mirror will generally not be visible.

Figure 28.6(c) shows the sphere rendered with max_depth = 3, where it's white in the center, but why is it dark near the silhouette? This is again caused by sampling the Fresnel reflectance and transmission curves in Figures 28.1 and 28.2, but also by not using a high enough maximum recursion depth. Sampling the Fresnel equations when a ray hits the inside surface is even more problematic than when it hits the outside, because it's the curves in Figure 28.2 that are applicable. Although there's no total internal reflection, we do have $\theta_i = \theta_c$ at the silhouette, where the slopes are infinite. We have to ray trace this sphere with max_depth = 7 before it disappears, but why should it disappear? The short answer is conservation of energy (see Section 28.5). In this sphere, up to the first six external transmitted rays can theoretically return some radiance to the pixel when $\eta > 1.5$. The number will vary with η.

Flat surfaces are better than curved surfaces for demonstrating the effects of the Fresnel equations. Figure 28.7 shows an example rendered with a rectangular fisheye camera view. The scene consists of a horizontal checker plane with black and orange checkers and a thin transparent ($\eta = 1.5$) solid cylinder of radius 250 above the plane, whose lower surface is 10 units from the plane. The checkers have the same color as they do in Figure 27.25. The camera is just above the plane and looking at the cylinder. Figure 28.7(a) was rendered with $k_r = 0.1$, and so the color of the cylinder is the transmitted background color,

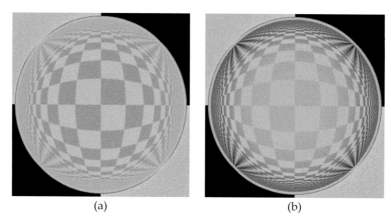

(a)   (b)

Figure 28.7. Fisheye views of a transparent cylinder and a checker plane: (a) $k_r = 0.1$, $k_t = 0.9$; (b) Fresnel reflectance and transmission.

plus faint reflections of the checkers. In Figure 28.7(b), which was rendered with the `Dielectric` material, the checker reflections are fainter in the center of the cylinder, where $k_r = 0.04$, but become much brighter towards the edge, where k_r is larger. But even here, the sampled values of k_r are no larger than about 0.79.

28.4.2 Color Filtering

Color filtering is a subtractive process because it removes radiance from rays. A good example to start with uses the CMY subtractive primaries

$$yellow = (1, 1, 0),$$
$$cyan = (0, 1, 1),$$
$$magenta = (1, 0, 1)$$

for the filter colors. A filter color component that's zero blocks all light, regardless of how small the ray path length is. In contrast, a component that's equal to one let's all light through, regardless of how long the path length is. For example, yellow lets all the red and green through and blocks the blue.

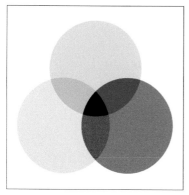

Figure 28.8. Solid cylinders with pure yellow, cyan, and magenta filter colors.

Figure 28.8 illustrates these colors using three solid cylinders that overlap in the line of sight, with a white background. This figure illustrates the following properties of the CMY primary colors:

white – yellow – cyan = green,
white – cyan – magenta = blue,
white – yellow – magenta = red,
white – yellow – cyan – magenta = black.

The following examples demonstrate how the yellow and green colors arise. White light filtered through a yellow medium:

$$= (1^d, 1^d, 0) * (1, 1, 1)$$
$$= (1, 1, 0) * (1, 1, 1) = (1, 1, 0)$$
$$= \text{yellow}.$$

White light filtered through cyan and yellow media:

$$= (1, 1, 0) * (0, 1, 1) * (1, 1, 1)$$
$$= (0, 1, 0)$$
$$= \text{green}.$$

No real media behave exactly like these filters because all real media transmit light over finite ranges of wavelength. You should compare Figures 28.8 and 24.40(a), as these illustrate the same processes using different techniques. We can also use the RGB primaries as filter colors, but see Question 28.1.

The real beauty of colored transparency comes out when we use filter colors where some of the components are less than one. This not only gives us an almost unlimited number of colors to use but provides attenuation that does depend on path length. Many objects can be used to demonstrate this—examples include triangle meshes, solid cylinders, and axis-aligned boxes, particularly when the boxes are long and thin or flat and wide. A certain physical process, however, has the effect of preventing short path lengths from occurring in many curved objects. Consider the spheres in Figure 28.9, where the filter

Figure 28.9. Colored transparent spheres rendered with a white background.

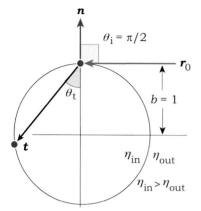

Figure 28.10. Tangential intersection of a ray with a unit sphere.

color is $c_f = (0.65, 0.45, 0.0)$. As the spheres get smaller, the color gets brighter, because the path lengths are smaller, but notice how the color doesn't vary much across each sphere.

The reason is illustrated in Figure 28.10, where a ray hits a unit sphere tangentially.

In this situation, the transmitted angle is

$$\theta_t = \cos^{-1}((\eta^2 - 1)^{1/2}/\eta), \tag{28.12}$$

from Equation (27.14). This is also the critical angle θ_c. A simple calculation shows that for a sphere of radius r, the path length of the transmitted ray through the sphere is

$$d = \frac{r}{\eta}(\eta^2 - 1)^{1/2}. \tag{28.13}$$

For $\eta = 1.5$, which is the value used in Figure 28.10, $d = 1.49$. This is also the minimum path length through a unit sphere. This process doesn't just happen for spheres, of course; it happens along the silhouette of any smooth object when $\eta > 1$. However, if it only applied at the silhouettes, it wouldn't have any effect on the images. The refraction angle increases towards θ_c in a continuous manner as rays approach the silhouette. Figure 28.27 shows other rays going through a sphere.

A good object for creating different path lengths is a concave lens, as shown in Figure 28.11. This consists of two concave part spheres and a concave

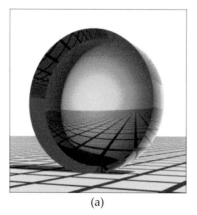
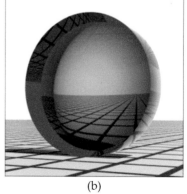

(a)   (b)

Figure 28.11. Concave lenses rendered with $c_f = (0.65, 0.45, 0)$ (a) and $c_f = (0.0, 0.5, 0.5)$ (b).

open cylinder. It's parameterized so that we can specify the radius, the rim thickness, and the minimum distance between the part spheres in the middle. In Figure 28.11, the radius is 4, the rim thickness is 2, but the minimum distance is only 0.1 in Figure 28.11(a) and 0.35 in Figure 28.11(b). The book's website has images using other filter colors.

28.4.3 Triangle Meshes

Figure 28.12 shows the Stanford bunny and horse rendered with color filtering. Again, a white background with no other objects is best for showing the effects of color filtering. Figure 28.12(a) is the bunny rendered with max_depth = 2 to demonstrate that most rays get straight through. The dark areas are caused by total internal reflection. You can see the Fresnel equations working near the silhouette, and on one of the ears. Figure 28.12(b) is rendered with max_depth = 10, and here the sharp changes in color are due to rays being totally internally reflected different numbers of times before getting out. The ears are light-colored because they are thin. The horse in Figure 28.12(c) shows even more variation in path length.

Of course, you are more likely to want to render transparent triangle meshes in scenes with other objects, where the refracted image of the scene may be important. Figure 28.13 shows three Stanford bunny models rendered with a grid of lines behind it. The smooth-shaded models are the 3K model in Figure 28.13(a) and the 69K model in Figure 28.13(c). Figure 28.13(b) is the 16K model with flat shading, probably not a good idea unless you are after special

(a)   (b)   (c)

Figure 28.12. (a) Stanford bunny rendered with c_f = (0.65, 0.45, 0) and max_depth = 2; (b) max_depth = 10; (c) horse model rendered with c_f = (0.65, 0.65, 0.1) and max_depth = 10.

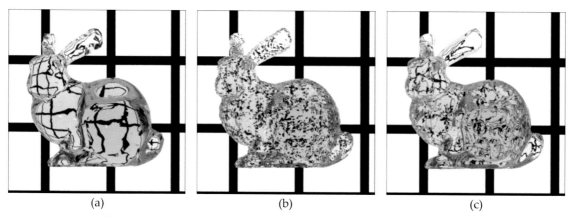

Figure 28.13. Transparent Stanford bunny models and grid lines: (a) 3K model with smooth shading; (b) 16K model with flat shading; (c) 69K model with smooth shading.

Figure 28.14. 97K horse model rendered with smooth shading.

effects. Note how messy the grids appear with the 69K model. The reason is that this model is quite lumpy, as the figure on the first page of Chapter 17 demonstrates. The 3K model shows a clearer image because the lumps are smoothed out.

In contrast, the horse model in Figure 28.14 forms clear images from nearly all parts of its body, including the legs, because it's a smoother model.

28.4.4 Nested Spheres

Figure 28.15(a) and (b) show three nested concentric transparent spheres with color filtering, to demonstrate how the Dielectric material can be used to model nested transparent objects. The outer sphere is blue-colored glass, the middle sphere is lemon-colored diamond, and the inner sphere is mauve-colored water. The appropriate values of eta_in and eta_out have to be specified for the glass-air boundary, the diamond-glass boundary, and the water-diamond boundary. If you do this correctly for the three spheres and use a high enough value of max_depth, the transparency code should run automatically. See if you can work out the value of max_depth to get the rays through before you look at the build function. Figure 28.15(c) shows the diamond sphere by itself. A general rule for build functions is that to remove

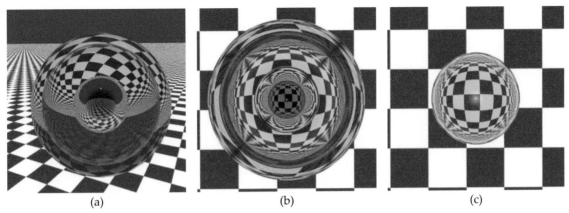

(a)   (b)   (c)

Figure 28.15. (a) Three concentric spheres viewed from an angle; (b) top-down view; (c) the diamond sphere by itself.

objects, all you have to do is comment out the appropriate `add_object` functions, but this won't always work for nested transparent objects. You can remove the water sphere, because it's inside the other two spheres, but just removing the glass sphere won't leave a diamond sphere; the resulting relative index of refraction will be η = 1.61 instead of 2.42. You will also have to change `eta_out` from 1.5 to 1.0.

Figure 28.16. Low-resolution bunny model and area light.

28.4.5 Area Lights

Figure 28.16 shows a low-resolution bunny model illuminated by a large rectangular light that's not directly visible in the image. The white areas on the bunny are the reflections of the light off of the outside surface, while the orange areas are the reflections of the light off of the inside surface.

 ## 28.5 Transparent Boxes

Because rectangular boxes consist of planar faces, we can use them to demonstrate total internal reflection as well as the Fresnel equations. They are also simple enough for us to analyze what happens to rays that enter them.

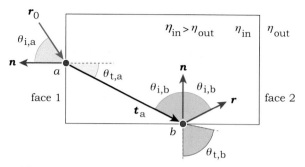

Figure 28.17. Incident and transmitted rays for a rectangular box.

28.5.1 Theory

Consider Figure 28.17, where a ray r_0 hits a box from the outside at point a on face 1, and the transmitted ray t_a hits the inside of the box on an *adjacent* face at point b. Each face has four adjacent faces, which touch it.

When $\eta > 1$, we are going to work out when total internal reflection will occur at b. As Figure 28.17 shows, the incident angle $\theta_{i,b}$ at b is related to the transmitted angle $\theta_{t,a}$ at a by

$$\theta_{i,b} = \pi/2 - \theta_{t,a},$$

which gives

$$\cos\theta_{i,b} = \sin\theta_{t,a}. \tag{28.14}$$

In turn, the transmitted angle $\theta_{t,b}$ at b is given by Equation (27.4) with $\eta \leftarrow 1/\eta = \eta_{out}/\eta_{in}$:

$$\cos\theta_{t,b} = \left[1 - \eta^2\left(1 - \cos^2\theta_{i,b}\right)\right]^{1/2},$$
$$= \left[1 - \eta^2\cos^2\theta_{t,a}\right]^{1/2}, \tag{28.15}$$

by using Equation (28.14). Equation (27.4) also expresses $\theta_{t,a}$ in terms of $\theta_{i,a}$:

$$\cos\theta_{t,a} = \left[1 - \frac{1}{\eta^2}(1 - \cos^2\theta_{i,a})\right]^{1/2}.$$

Substituting this expression for $\cos\theta_{t,a}$ into Equation (28.15) gives the following relationship between $\theta_{i,a}$ and $\theta_{t,b}$:

$$\cos\theta_{t,b} = (2 - \eta^2 - \cos^2\theta_{i,a})^{1/2}. \tag{28.16}$$

From Equation (28.16), total internal reflection will occur at point b when

$$2 - \eta^2 - \cos^2 \theta_{i,a} < 0. \tag{28.17}$$

This inequality is satisfied for all $\theta_{i,a} \in [0, 2\pi]$ when

$$\eta > \sqrt{2} \approx 1.414. \tag{28.18}$$

What does this mean? The inequalities (28.17) and (28.18) tell us that when the relative index of refraction of a rectangular box is greater than $\sqrt{2}$ and the transmitted ray t_a hits an adjacent face, total internal reflection *will always occur*. If you look at a transparent glass or plastic box, the four faces that touch the face you look in will appear as perfect mirrors due to this total internal reflection. The same thing happens with a transparent cylinder.

What happens to the internally reflected ray at b? This will hit face 2, the face opposite face 1, either directly or after it has bounced one or more times off of other faces adjacent to face 1 (see Figure 28.18). When it eventually hits the opposite face, there's no total internal reflection, and the transmitted angle is the same as $\theta_{i,a}$ (see Exercise 28.11). This means that transmitted rays exiting the opposite face travel in the same direction as the incident rays.

Figure 28.18 could also be the cross section of a solid cylinder. In terms of the rays traveling from face 1 to face 2, a real-world example is fiber-optic cables, at least the thick ones used in decorative lamps. Here, the light is piped along them by total internal reflection.[2]

After reflection off of face 2, the rays can then travel back and forth between the two opposite faces. Because of total internal reflection along the adjacent faces, there's no loss of energy at those hit points, but the rays are split into reflected and transmitted rays when they hit the opposite faces. Figure 28.19

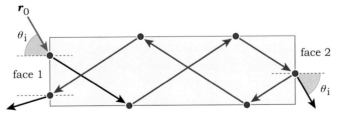

Figure 28.18. When rays hit face 1, they eventually exit face 2 in the same direction.

---

2. Fiber optic cables used for communications are so thin that their behavior has to be described by the wave theory of light instead of geometric optics.

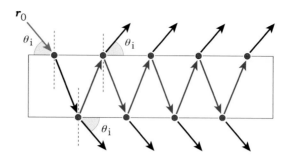

Figure 28.19. A transparent box with multiple reflected and transmitted rays.

shows a box with rays bouncing directly between opposite faces. None of the rays shown here hit the adjacent faces.

I should point out here that Figures (28.17)–(28.19), being drawn in two dimensions, can be somewhat misleading. Since boxes are 3D objects, the incident ray can be oriented anywhere in the hemisphere above the hit point on face 1; the hit point can also be anywhere on face 1. Consequently, the internal rays can hit any or all of the four adjacent faces during their journeys between faces 1 and 2.

The above analysis leads to the following conclusions about transparent rectangular boxes whose relative index of refraction is greater than $\sqrt{2}$: all rays that enter a given face of a rectangular box with $\eta > \sqrt{2}$ eventually exit from the opposite face or come back out the same face, due to total internal reflection on adjacent faces. For boxes in the real world: All light that comes out a given face of a rectangular box with $\eta > \sqrt{2}$ came in from the opposite face or from the same face, due to total internal reflection on the adjacent faces.

Figure 28.20 shows a transparent cube with $\eta = 1.5$, where the camera is close to the box and is looking directly through the middle. In Figure 28.20(a), `max_depth` = 2, and rays that don't hit any of the faces adjacent to the face nearest the camera go through the box. The dark areas are where the rays do hit the adjacent faces and undergo total internal reflection but don't get out of the box because of the extra bounce or bounces. In Figure 28.20(b), where `max_depth` = 3, most of these rays do get out the opposite face and bring back the color of either the background or the plane. I'll leave it as a question for you to explain the four dark squares at the corners of the box (see Question 28.3). In Figure 28.20(c), where `max_depth` = 4, all of the rays get out. Because of total internal reflection, the background color is reflected from the bottom surface and the checker plane from the top surface.

To demonstrate the effects of total internal reflection in more detail, Figure 28.21 shows the cube with a sphere that's partly inside it. This cre-

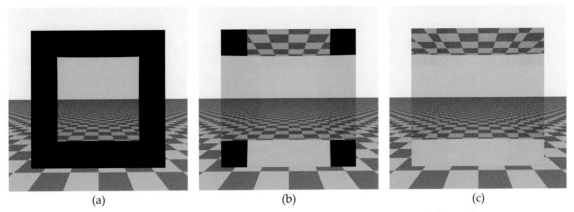

(a)   (b)   (c)

Figure 28.20. Transparent cube ray traced with `max_depth` = 2 (a), `max_depth` = 3 (b), and `max_depth` = 4 (c).

ates a dilemma for shading the sphere. Technically, the sphere has no direct illumination; radiance from the light source has been refracted through the cube before it hits the sphere and has been color filtered. This means that the sphere's illumination is a caustic. To shade the sphere in Figure 28.21, I've just turned shadows off for the point light that illuminates this scene. As a result, the shading is incorrect but still looks OK.[3] Later in this chapter, I'll discuss another technique (also incorrect) for shading opaque objects inside transpar-

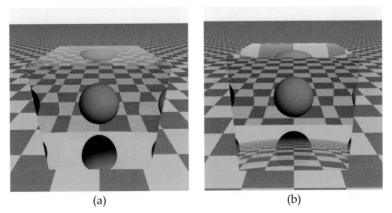

(a)   (b)

Figure 28.21. The cube in Figure 28.20 with a sphere with $\eta = 1.5$ (a) and $\eta = 1.13$ (b).

---

3. The fact that part of the sphere sticks out of the back of the cube creates a sharp transition in its shading in Figure 28.21.

ent objects. In Figure 28.21(a), where $\eta = 1.5$, the reflections of the sphere and background color are clearly visible off of the bottom face and the lower parts of the sides. The effect of the Fresnel equations is visible on the top.

In Figure 28.21(b), the index of refraction is 1.13, which is less than 1.414, and, consequently, total internal reflection only occurs over a part of the bottom and side faces.[4] You can see the plane and background color refracted through the lower part of the cube. Here are some things to notice: the line where total internal reflection begins is curved; there's a faint image of the sphere below the line of total internal reflection; color filtering increases on the refracted image of the plane, from zero on the bottom edge of the cube to a maximum along the line of total internal reflection. The animations `Eta=1.5.mov` and `Eta=1.13.mov` show these cubes rotating about the x-axis, which goes through their centers. By stepping through the $\eta = 1.13$ animation frame by frame, you can see in detail what's happening at the bottom of the cube.

Figure 28.22 shows a number of thin transparent glass blocks ray traced with `max_depth` = 15. Notice how the blocks are lightest when viewed through their thinnest dimension. Also notice that all of the tops have the same darker color and that their ends get darker as the blocks get longer. These variations in color are due to the different path lengths that the rays have to travel through the blocks. In the real world, panes of glass might look completely transparent when we look through them, but ordinary window glass is actually a green color, which is seen when you look at the edges. These are usually dark green, like the ends of the blocks, because the light traverses the whole width of the pane before it comes out. For a given block, the total path length of the light depends on the viewing angle at the end (see Question 28.11).

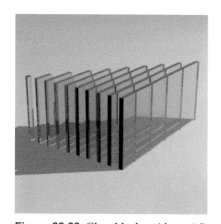

Figure 28.22. Glass blocks with $\eta = 1.5$.

28.5.2 Transmission of Light through a Pane of Glass

Suppose you are looking through a window that has a single pane of glass. How much of the light from the outside gets through the glass? We can compute this using Figure 28.23, which is a *radiance transfer diagram* for a transparent box near an emissive surface.

---

4. The value $\eta = 1.13$ is not arbitrary (see Question 28.7).

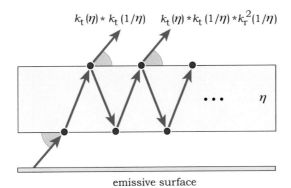

$$k_t(\eta) * k_t(1/\eta) \qquad k_t(\eta) * k_t(1/\eta) * k_r^2(1/\eta)$$

$$\eta$$

emissive surface

Figure 28.23. Radiance transfer through a pane of glass.

Figure 8.23 shows a single ray of light that is emitted from the surface, hits the pane, bounces around inside, and exits from multiple points. These are on both sides of the pane, but only rays that exit from the top contribute to the transmitted radiance. Figure 28.23 indicates the fractions of radiance transmitted by the first two exiting rays, assuming the glass is completely clear.[5] These two fractions are enough to see the pattern. The general expression is

$$f_n = k_t(\eta)\,k_t(1/\eta)\left[1 + k_r^2(1/\eta) + k_r^4(1/\eta) + L\ \right] = k_t(\eta)\,k_t(1/\eta)\sum_{j=0}^{\infty} k_r^{2j}(1/\eta)$$

$$= \frac{k_t(\eta)\,k_t(1/\eta)}{1 - k_r^2(1/\eta)}, \tag{28.19}$$

using Equation (2.18) for the sum of an infinite geometric series. At normal incidence, where Equation (28.6) applies, the expression (28.19) becomes

$$f_n = \frac{1 - k_r}{1 + k_r} = \frac{2\eta}{1 + \eta^2}. \tag{28.20}$$

For $\eta = 1.5$, $f_n \approx 0.923077$, so that a pane of glass transmits about 92.3% of the light at normal incidence.

When we ray trace a pane of glass in front of the emissive surface, with a black background, the situation is different. The rays are shown in Figure 28.24, where a single incident ray r_0 results in multiple transmitted rays that hit the emissive surface and contribute to the exitant radiance along r_0.

---

5. I've ignored the η factors for the transmitted rays, as these cancel.

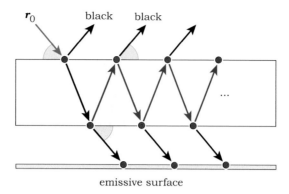

r_0 black   black

...

emissive surface

Figure 28.24. Ray tracing a pane of glass in front of an emissive surface.

Since the background is black, the rays that exit from the top of the pane don't contribute any radiance. However, the total fraction of radiance returned along r_0 is the same as the expression (28.19). Ray tracing therefore gives the right answer!

Figure 28.25, another strong contender for the most boring image in the book, is actually quite instructive. This shows a thin clear glass box, ray traced in front of an emissive object whose emitted radiance is (1.0, 1.0, 1.0). The background color is black, and there are no light sources. The gray area is the box, where the radiance returned from each ray is (0.923077, 0.923077, 0.923077), in agreement with Equation (28.20) to six decimal places for $\eta = 1.5$. It's therefore a good test for the transparency code.

Figure 28.25. Thin box with no color filtering and $\eta = 1.5$ ray traced with `max_depth = 10`.

Finally, consider ray tracing a pane of glass with no other objects in the scene with a background color that's not black. The appropriate figure for this is Figure 28.19, where all rays that exit the pane bring back the background color. In this case, the total fraction of the background color returned along r_0 must be 1.0 by conservation of energy. This applies to all transparent objects, provided that $k_r + k_t = 1.0$ and that there's no color filtering. It explains why the cylinder and thick ring in Figure 27.19 don't change the background color when it passes through them, why sections of the thick ring in Figure 27.32(c) are invisible, and why the sphere in Figure 28.6 will disappear when you ray trace it with a high enough value of `max_depth`.

28.6 Transparent Spheres

What, not more transparent spheres? Yes. This time, short sections on reflections, objects inside spheres, and the camera inside spheres. As these topics are actually more interesting than those in Chapter 27, please read on.

28.6.1 Where Are the Reflections?

I'll consider here a transparent sphere and an emissive sphere, both with grid lines. The scene is similar to the one discussed in Section 24.7.1, but this time, the emissive sphere has white and gray checkers, the transparent sphere has a pale blue-green filter color with orange grid lines, and there's no rectangle. The stereo pair of the transparent sphere in Figure 28.26 shows the reflections of the emissive sphere. The reflection on the outside surface is faint, because of the Fresnel equations, and is inside the sphere. There's no color filtering here because the rays that generate this reflection don't enter the sphere. The large blue-green area is the reflection on the inside surface of the sphere. The stereo pair demonstrates that this reflection is not inside the sphere; part of it is behind the sphere. This is difficult to see without stereoscopy and grid lines on both spheres. Notice that this reflection goes all the way around the transparent sphere. Question 28.13 asks you to think about these images.

28.6.2 Sphere Inside a Transparent Sphere

If you look at a completely clear transparent glass sphere, there is something about it that's not apparent—part of the inside is invisible. The reason

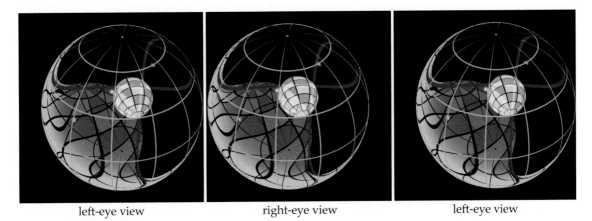

left-eye view   right-eye view   left-eye view

Figure 28.26. Stereo pair of a transparent sphere and an emissive sphere.

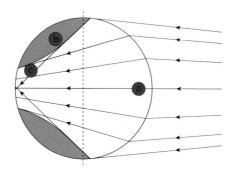

Figure 28.27. No transmitted rays inside a glass sphere go through the dark areas. The red circles correspond to the red sphere locations in Figure 28.28.

is refraction, as demonstrated in Figure 28.27. This shows several internal transmitted rays for $\eta = 1.5$, with the camera located 10 radii from the sphere center. No rays go through the cyan areas, which form a volume of revolution in 3D about the central viewing axis.[6] This is the invisible region. As the camera moves closer to the sphere, this region will change, and in the limit that the camera is just outside the surface, the region will be completely different.

To visualize this, we can ray trace a transparent sphere with a small red sphere inside that's near the surface. To demonstrate some additional optical effects, the red sphere is reflective. Its direct illumination will again result from having the lights not cast shadows. In Figure 28.28, the transparent sphere is a unit sphere with its center at the origin, the red sphere inside has radius 0.1 with its center at (0, 0, 0.8), and the camera's location is (0, 0, 10), consistent with Figure 28.27. Figure 28.28(a) shows a perspective view of the spheres in their orginal locations, as indicated in Figure 28.27. In Figure 28.28(b), the spheres have been rotated 120° about the y-axis, which places the red sphere in the invisible region. In Figure 28.28(c), the rotation angle is 162°, and in Figure 28.28(d) it's 164°. These are also indicated in Figure 28.27. Because the appearance of the red sphere changes rapidly as it moves into and out of the invisible region, the best way to appreciate this is to watch the animation **SphereInGlass.avi** on the book's website. This was rendered with max_depth = 3 and without the Fresnel equations. In this animation, the spheres are rotated by one degree for each frame. You may

6. As some of the rays in this figure are sketched, the region shown is only approximate.

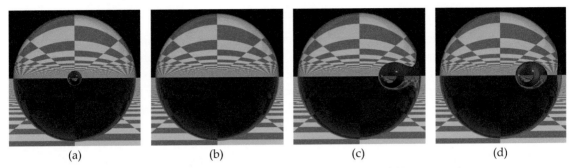

(a)   (b)   (c)   (d)

Figure 28.28. Small red sphere inside a glass sphere rotated through the following angles: (a) 0°; (b) 120°; (c) 162°; (d) 164°. These were rendered with `max_depth = 6`.

be able to see some of these effects if you can look at a sphere with small air bubbles in it, such as a paperweight.

Figure 28.29 shows a transparent diamond sphere with the same red sphere inside, rotated through the indicated angles. Because of the larger value of η, the appearance of the red sphere changes even more rapidly with angle than it does in the glass sphere. Notice that Figure 28.29(a) and (b) only differ by half a degree. Also note that although the rotation angles are less than 180°, so that the red sphere is physically on the right-hand side of the diamond sphere, most of its image is on the left-hand side. The corresponding animation is **SphereInDiamond.avi**.

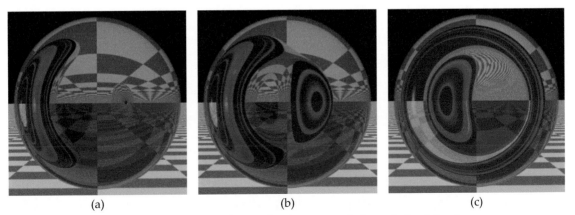

(a)   (b)   (c)

Figure 28.29. Small red sphere inside a diamond sphere rotated through the following angles: (a) 172.5°; (b) 173°; (c) 178°. The hole in (b) only appears for about half a degree of rotation.

28.6.3 Camera Inside a Transparent Sphere

Although we can't put a real camera inside a real glass sphere, we can certainly put a ray-tracing camera inside a transparent sphere and find out what the world would look like from the inside. As you'll see, the resulting images are much more interesting than when it's outside. But first, we can use some simple mathematical analysis to give us an understanding of what the views will look like.

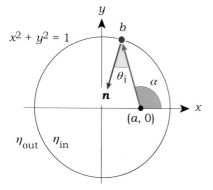

Figure 28.30 shows a cross section of a unit sphere with the camera on the x-axis at distance a from the origin, where $a \in [0, 1)$. The primary ray makes an angle α with the positive x-axis, where $\alpha \in [0, \pi]$, and hits the sphere at point b with coordinates (x, y). We have three parameters: a, α, and η, and the following analysis is to find out if the primary ray can undergo total internal reflection when it hits the inside surface of the sphere.

Figure 28.30. Camera inside a transparent sphere at distance a along the x-axis.

We first need to calculate $\cos \theta_i$, where θ_i is the angle of incidence at a. To do this, note that the 2D (x, y) unit direction of the primary ray is

$$d = (\cos \alpha, \sin \alpha),$$

which gives the following expression for the primary ray in the (x, y) plane:

$$p = (a, 0) + t(\cos \alpha, \sin \alpha). \tag{28.21}$$

If we substitute Equation (28.21) into the equation $x^2 + y^2 = 1$ for the sphere in the (x, y) plane, we get the following quadratic equation for t:

$$t^2 + 2a(\cos \alpha)t + a^2 - 1 = 0,$$

which is easily solved to give

$$t = -a \cos \alpha \pm (a^2\cos^2\alpha - a^2 + 1)^{1/2}. \tag{28.22}$$

It follows from Equations (28.21) and (28.22) that the coordinates of the point b are

$$\begin{aligned}
x &= a \sin^2\alpha \pm \cos \alpha \, (a^2\cos^2\alpha - a^2 + 1)^{1/2}, \\
y &= -a \sin a \cos \alpha \pm \sin \alpha \, (a^2\cos^2\alpha - a^2 + 1)^{1/2}.
\end{aligned} \tag{28.23}$$

Taking the positive root of Equation (28.23) and using the fact that $\cos \theta_i = -n \cdot d$, where $n = (-x, -y)$, we get

$$\cos \theta_i = (a^2\cos^2\alpha - a^2 + 1)^{1/2}. \tag{28.24}$$

Substituting Equation (28.24) into Equation (27.4) gives the following simple condition for total internal reflection:

$$\sin \alpha > \eta/a, \qquad (28.25)$$

where $\eta = \eta_{out}/\eta_{in}$.

The case $\eta \geq 1$ (sphere has a smaller η than the surrounding medium). In this case, it's impossible to satisfy the inequality (28.25) because $a < 1$ and the maximum value of $\sin \alpha$ is 1. For example, if the camera is inside an air bubble in water, or a hollow glass or plastic sphere, total internal reflection will not occur for any primary rays.

The case $\eta < 1$ (sphere has a larger η than the surrounding medium). This is the more interesting case because, here, it *is* possible to satisfy (28.25). Because the inequality is so simple, the analysis is easy. First, from the right-hand side of (28.25), we see that when $a < \eta$, $\eta/a > 1$. Therefore, total internal reflection cannot occur for camera locations with $a < \eta$.

When $a > \eta$, we have $\eta/a < 1$, and, hence, $\sin \alpha > \eta/a$ can be satisfied for some values of α. Figure 28.31 shows a plot of $\sin \alpha$, for $\alpha \in [0, \pi]$, and a sample value of $\eta/a = 0.6$. This figure shows that there's a critical angle α_c such that $\sin \alpha > \eta/a$ for all $\alpha \in (\alpha_c, \pi - \alpha_c)$. Now, what is α_c? This is just the value of α for which $\sin \alpha = \eta/a$:

$$\alpha_c = \sin^{-1}(\eta/a). \qquad (28.26)$$

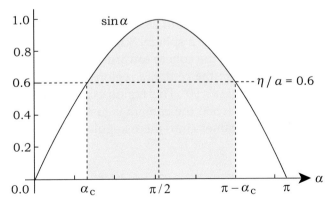

Figure 28.31. Plot of $\sin \alpha$ for $\alpha \in [0, \pi]$, where, for $\eta/a = 0.6$, total internal reflection occurs in the gray shaded interval $\alpha \in (\alpha_c, \pi - \alpha_c)$.

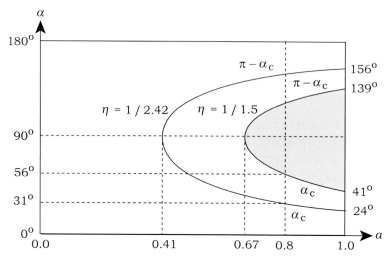

Figure 28.32. Critical angle curves for total internal reflection for η = 1/1.5 and η = 1/2.42. Total internal reflection occurs in the shaded regions.

Figure 28.32 displays curves of α_c and $\pi - \alpha_c$ as a function of a for two values of η. These are η = 1/1.5 ≈ 0.67 for glass and η = 1/2.42 ≈ 0.41 for diamond. In this figure, the angular region of total internal reflection is between the upper and lower curves. These curves meet at $\alpha_c = \pi$, where $a = \eta$. The numbers on the right are the values of $\alpha_c = \sin^{-1}(\eta)$ in degrees at the surface of the sphere.

Figure 28.33 shows another way of visualizing the angular regions of total internal reflection for these values of η, for $a = 0.8$. Rays shot into the gray regions undergo total internal reflection.

With the help of Figures 28.32 and 28.33, we can now describe how total internal reflection happens inside a sphere. Suppose the camera moves along a radial line from the center of the sphere towards the surface. When the camera is at distance $a = 1/\eta$ from the center, a region of total internal reflection appears, centered on the angle $a = 90°$. This region expands rapidly and reaches a maximum angular width when the camera is just inside the surface of the sphere. Rays shot from the camera into these angular regions never get out of the sphere.[7]

---

7. Provided there are no objects in the sphere. If there's a reflective object inside, as in Section 28.6.2, the rays can get out by hitting it and being reflected from its surface.

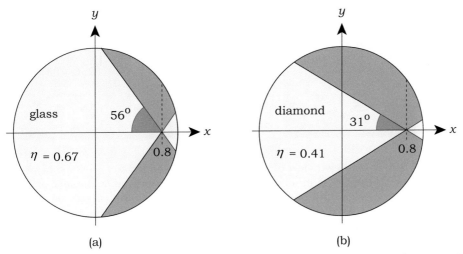

Figure 28.33. Angular regions (gray) of total internal reflection at $a = 0.8$: (a) $\eta = 1/1.5, \alpha_c = 56°$, in (b) $\eta = 1/2.42, \alpha_c = 31°$. These angles are indicated on the left-hand side of Figure 28.32.

Conversely, when $a > \eta$, rays can only get out in two circular cones of directions centered on the line through the camera location and the center of the sphere. Both cones have the same half angle $\alpha_c = \sin^{-1}(\eta/a)$.

We can now look at some ray-traced images. The scene in Figure 28.34 consists of a transparent diamond sphere with radius 4, a ring of spheres surrounding it, and a checker plane. To help the visualization, the spheres are constructed with two hemispheres, the top one orange and the bottom one faintly reflective cyan. A top-down view is in Figure 28.34(a). In Figure 28.34(b) and (c), the camera is inside the transparent sphere at $(0, 0, 2)$. In Figure 28.34(b), it's looking along the positive z-axis. The black area is where total internal reflection occurs. Question 28.16 asks you a number of things about this image. In Figure 28.34(c), the camera is looking in the positive x-direction ($\alpha = \pi/2$), and some rays get out in both cones. In Figure 28.34(d), the camera is looking along the negative z-axis through the center of the sphere. The view in this direction is quite different from the view in the positive z-direction. As you can see, there's a rich optical environment inside a solid diamond sphere that you can explore (see Exercises 28.21–28.24).

There is, however, an aspect of this scene that's not apparent from just looking at these images. The radiance brought back along each primary ray that gets out is increased by a factor of $(\eta_{in}/\eta_{out})^2 = 2.42^2 \approx 5.86$ as it crosses the sphere surface. This means that Figure 28.34(a) and (b) can't both be correct unless some-

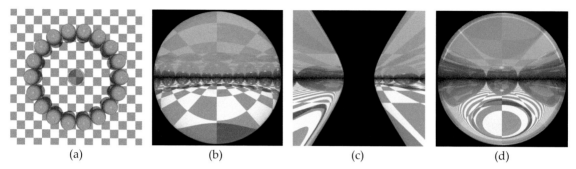

(a)   (b)   (c)   (d)

Figure 28.34. (a) Top-down view of a transparent diamond sphere, ring of spheres, and checker plane; (b) view from inside the transparent sphere centered on the cone of exiting directions around the positive z-axis; (c) view with the camera looking at right angles to the cones of exiting directions; (d) view centered on the cone of exiting directions around the negative z-axis. The interior images were rendered with max_depth = 4.

thing has changed. If Figure 28.34(a) is correct, views inside the sphere will be washed out, or if these are not washed out, views outside will be too dim.

This situation reflects many real-world photography situations where you take photographs under a variety of lighting conditions: bright sunlight, sunset, indoors, outdoors, daytime, and nighttime. Your camera will make adjustments to its exposure time and/or its aperture width to achieve the correct exposure of the film or CCD. All we have to do here is change the exposure time of our camera. That's why the Camera base class has a data member exposure_time. When the camera is inside the transparent sphere, we set the exposure time to $1.0/(2.42^2) \approx 0.17$, and when it's outside, we use the default value of 1.0, as we have used for all images up to this point.

In the animation **FlyThrough.avi**, the camera flies through the transparent sphere with $\eta = 2.24$, but the scene outside is slightly different, the Transparent material is used instead of Dielectric, and there is no η^2 factor. When the camera is inside the sphere, the image sometimes changes so quickly that it's best to step through the animation one frame at a time.

28.7 A Glass of Water

It's worthwhile modeling and rendering a glass of water, because it's a common object and a fairly complex example of an object that consists of different transparent media. Figure 28.35 shows the dimensions of a basic glass of water that has its base on the (x, z) plane and is centered on the y-axis.

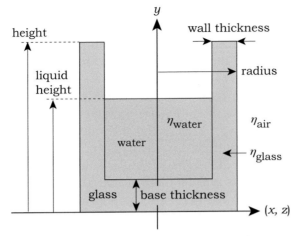

Figure 28.35. Specification of a basic glass of water.

Figure 28.36 shows the objects that are required to model this glass of water, which is defined by the boundaries between pairs of dielectrics. These are as follows:

- glass-air boundary: annulus, concave cylinder, convex cylinder, disk;
- water-glass boundary: convex cylinder, disk;
- water-air boundary: disk.

In particular, we don't define the water with a solid cylinder that just fits inside a tall thick ring for the glass walls; that won't work. There must be a single boundary between each pair of dielectrics. The dimensions and locations of the objects also have to be defined so that the whole object fits together.

A more sophisticated glass of water has a rounded rim modeled with a half torus (easier on the lips!), rounded inside and outside corners at the bottom modeled by quarter tori, and a *meniscus* for the water, also modeled with a quarter torus (see Figure 28.37). A meniscus is formed because water makes tangent contact with surfaces. This causes the water surface to curve upwards around the inside of the glass. Although a quarter torus is not based on physical principles, it still makes a good meniscus and adds an extra touch of realism to the model.

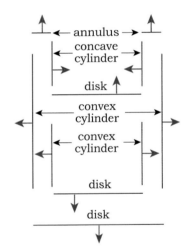

Figure 28.36. Objects required to define a basic glass of water. The red arrows are normals. As far as the water and glass are concerned, the water is inside the glass; that's why the normal to the disk at the bottom of the water points down and the normal to the water's curved surface points outwards. Similarly, the water and glass are inside the air.

Figure 28.37. A more sophisticated glass of water has a curved top, rounded edges, and a meniscus for the water.

I've only implemented the basic glass of water, but with a meniscus. You can implement the other model as an exercise. The meniscus radius is an extra physical parameter that requires the dimensions of the water-air disk and inner glass-air cylinder to be adjusted.

The other parts of the definition are the dielectric materials, of which there are *three*—one for each type of boundary. The glass-air boundary has $\eta_{in} = 1.5$, $\eta_{out} = 1.0$; the water-air boundary has $\eta_{in} = 1.33$, $\eta_{out} = 1.0$; the water-glass boundary has $\eta_{in} = 1.33$, $\eta_{out} = 1.5$. The filter colors are $c_f = (0.65, 1.0, 0.75)$ for the glass and $c_f = (1.0, 0.25, 1.0)$ (magenta) for the water, to make it more visible. The glass of water is built as a compound object where each component is assigned the appropriate material. The class GlassOfWater is on the book's website.

Figure 28.38 shows three views of the glass where I've added a straw. In Figure 28.38(a), the light doesn't cast shadows so that the straw receives direct illumination. The meniscus is clearly visible in both images, but since it's small and its thickness rapidly approaches zero at the top, there's no visible color filtering in it. There's also no meniscus on the straw. Notice how the straw appears to bend as it enters the water as a result of refraction. In Figure 28.38(b), the camera is near the base of the glass, and you can see the total internal reflection on the top surface of the water. In Figure 28.38(c), the glass of water casts shadows, which improves the image, and the part of the straw that's in the water still receives direct illumination because the Matte material that's used for the straw does not have shadows cast on it (see Section 16.7).

(a)   (b)   (c)

Figure 28.38. Glass of water and straw rendered with: (a) no shadows; (b) camera looking up; (c) shadows and direct illumination on the straw.

The images in Figure 28.38 took a long while to render, with just nine samples per pixel for antialiasing, because they use `max_depth = 10` and the internal surfaces result in many extensive ray trees.

28.8 Fishbowls

Spherical fishbowls are another interesting set of objects to render because they involve more modeling with part objects, we have the primitives to put them together, and the images look good.

Figure 28.39(a) shows a basic fishbowl that can be modeled with a part torus for the rim, a convex part sphere for the outer surface, a concave part sphere for the glass surface above the water, a convex part sphere for the water-glass boundary, and a disk for the water-air boundary. Figure 28.39(b) shows a more realistic bowl with flat bottoms for the glass and water and a meniscus for the water. I'll discuss how to construct a round-bottomed bowl with a meniscus. The bowl in Figure 28.39(b) is left as an exercise.

Exercise 21.7 covered how to construct the outer part sphere of a spherical bowl, but the rim in that exercise was a whole torus because the bowl was opaque. Although the generic torus parameters a and b will be the same, as will the vertical translation distance, we now need a convex part torus. Figure 28.40(a) shows part of the cross section of a bowl with a thick wall that's centered on the world origin. Here, α is half the opening angle, as defined in Figure 21.16(a). For the rim half torus, $\theta_{min} = \pi/2 - \alpha$ and $\theta_{max} = \theta_{min} + \pi$. Recall from Figure 19.19(b) that for a generic torus, these angles are measured counterclockwise from the (x, z) plane.

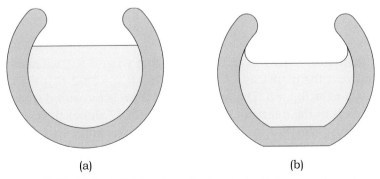

(a)   (b)

Figure 28.39. (a) Basic fishbowl; (b) fishbowl with flat base and meniscus.

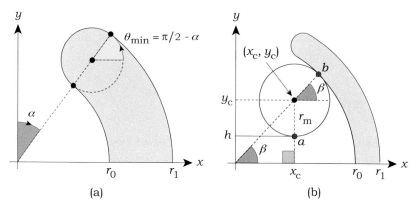

Figure 28.40. (a) Construction of the rim; (b) construction of the meniscus.

Figure 28.40(b) illustrates how the meniscus is constructed, where the buff-colored disk is the cross section of a torus that makes tangent contact with the top of the water at height h above the (x, z) plane. This is the point a. The torus also makes tangent contact with the inner surface of the bowl at point b. The meniscus will be the section of the torus between a and b. Because a part torus is specified by its angular ranges, all we have to do is calculate the angle β, a simple task. The relevant parameters are the inner radius of the bowl r_0, the water height h, and the meniscus radius r_m. These uniquely define β.

We start with expressions for the disk center coordinates (x_c, y_c). From Figure 28.40(b),

$$y_c = h + r_m.$$

Since the radial distance of (x_c, y_c) from the center of the bowl is $r_0 - r_m$,

$$x_c = [(r_0 - r_m)^2 - (h + r_m)^2]^2.$$

Then,

$$\beta = \tan^{-1}(y_c/x_c).$$

That's all there is to it. However, the trick is that when $h > 0$, we need *two* part tori to construct the meniscus surface. One has $\theta_{min} = 3\pi/2$, $\theta_{max} = 2\pi$, and the other has $\theta_{min} = 2\pi$, $\theta_{max} = \beta$. The reason is that the θ is measured from the (x, z) plane, which is in the interval $[3\pi/2, \beta]$. Figure 21.17 shows the consequences of ignoring this. Why not measure θ from the y-axis and avoid the problem? We would then have to use two part tori to define the rim. The point is that we have to measure θ from somewhere, and we always have to use two part tori when the angular range passes through $\theta = 0$.

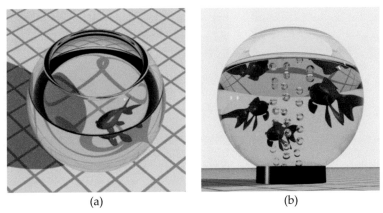

(a)   (b)

Figure 28.41. (a) View looking down on a fishbowl with a fish. The fish model is courtesy of James McNess. (b) View looking up.

When the bowl is less than half full of water ($h < 0$), we only need a single part torus (see Exercise 28.33).

With the meniscus, the concave part sphere that forms the inner glass-air boundary has $\theta_{min} = \alpha$, $\theta_{max} = \beta$; the water-glass boundary has $\theta_{min} = \beta$, $\theta_{max} = \pi$; the radius of the disk that forms the water-air boundary is x_c.

The FishBowl class is also on the book's website, so that you can just enjoy ray tracing it. Figure 28.41 shows two images with fish; after all, a fishbowl isn't much use without them. Figure 28.41(a) was rendered with max_depth = 10 and took a long time to render because of the number of boundaries. *Adaptive depth control*, as explained in Exercise 28.40, would improve the rendering times.

 ## 28.9 Caustics

Caustics are formed in two ways from transparent objects. First, the light can be reflected from the object before hitting another object, as for purely reflective materials. Second, the light can be refracted through the object before hitting another object. The caustics created by refraction are usually the brightest because the light can be concentrated, and they are affected by any color filtering.

Caustics add an essential element of realism to ray-traced images, but we can only render them using path tracing. Photon mapping is again a much more efficient technique for rendering purposes. Figure 28.42(a) shows a path-traced image of a red transparent sphere and a rectangle illuminated by a

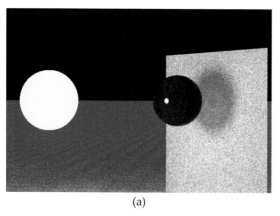 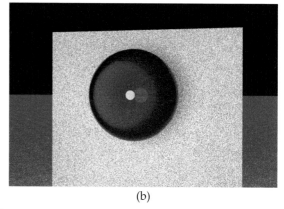

(a)   (b)

Figure 28.42. Path-traced images of a transparent sphere and a caustic. These were rendered with 256 samples per pixel and are therefore quite noisy.

spherical light, where a caustic is on the rectangle. Figure 28.42(b) is a close-up view that shows the light's reflection on the outside of the sphere, on the inside of the sphere, and a magnified view of the caustic seen through the sphere.

Further Reading

The Fresnel equations are derived and discussed in great detail in a number of classic optics textbooks such as Hecht (1997) and Born and Wolf (1999).[8] They are also covered in Hall (1988). There are separate Fresnel equations for conductors (metals) (see Hall (1988), Born and Wolf (1999)).

Pharr and Humphreys (2004) discusses a material that's similar to the Dielectric material presented here and also quotes the Fresnel equations for conductors.

Lee and Uselton (1991) discusses the model of color filtering presented here and the derivation of Equation (28.9). See http://en.wikipedia.org/wiki/Beer-Lambert_law for information about the Beer-Lambert law.

Wang et al. (2005) presents an interesting model for water drops on surfaces. This could provide a more physically based technique for modeling the meniscus in the glass of water and the fishbowls.

Some transparent objects have an index of refraction that varies with position. These can be ray traced with a *ray-marching* algorithm (Suffern and Getto, 1991).

---

8. The first edition of Hecht was published in 1987; the first edition of Born and Wolf was published in 1959.

Jensen's 2001 book and his papers, cited in previous chapters, discuss the use of photon mapping for ray tracing caustics with transparent materials.

There are a number of optical effects that are not incorporated in the transparency model presented here. These include polarization and *dispersion*, where the index of refraction depends on the wavelength of light. Guy and Soler (2004) discusses these and other effects in the real-time rendering of gemstones. This paper also cites earlier references on rendering a variety of optical effects.

Rainbows are the most spectacular result of dispersion, and, in fact, René Descartes used the theory of ray tracing to explain the rainbow and published the results in 1637. He couldn't, however, explain the colors because it wasn't until 30 years later that Sir Isaac Newton discovered that white light consists of light of different wavelengths and that the index of refraction of glass depends on the wavelength. Watt (2000) has a nice discussion of this.

Robert Greenler's wonderful book *Rainbows, Halos, and Glories* (Greenler, 1990) discusses atmospheric optical phenomena, many of which are the result of refraction. Greenler's book *Chasing the Rainbow* (Greenler, 2000) is also wonderful. A classic book on atmospheric optics is *Light and Color in the Outdoors* (Minnaert, 1993).

Questions

28.1. Figure 28.43 shows the three cylinders in Figure 28.8 rendered with the RGB primary colors. Can you explain what has happened here? In particular, why aren't the results the same as those in Figure 3.10, which, incidentally, wasn't ray traced.

28.2. Recall from Figure 28.18 that when rays exit a rectangular box from the face opposite of the face they entered from, they travel in the same direction as the incident rays. Suppose you are looking at a scene through a transparent box, such as a pane of glass. How does this affect the image that you can see?

28.3. Can you explain the four black squares in Figure 28.20(b)?

28.4. If you look carefully at Figure 28.20(c), you will see two vertical lines of discontinuity in the image of the checker plane at the top of the cube. What causes these? Are there any other discontinuities in this image?

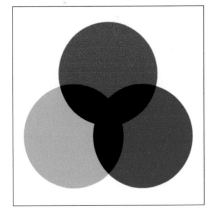

Figure 28.43. Three cylinders rendered with pure red, green, and blue filters and a white background.

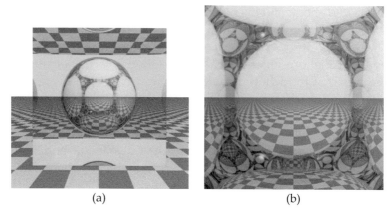

(a)   (b)

Figure 28.44. Reflective sphere inside a transparent cube: (a) rendered with max_depth = 5;
(b) zoomed-in view rendered with max_depth = 9.

28.5. In Figure 28.21(b), total internal reflection begins on a curve, and the
plane, as seen refracted through the bottom face, is also curved. Since
perspective projection preserves straight lines and the cube consists of
planar faces, what causes the curvature?

28.6. In Figure 28.21(b), what causes the faint image of the sphere below the
region of total internal reflection?

28.7. According to Table 27.1, common transparent media such as glasses and
plastics have indices of refraction greater than the critical value $\sqrt{2}$ discussed in Section 28.5. You might think, therefore, that it's impossible to
see a transparent rectangular box with a relative index of refraction less
than $\sqrt{2}$, but that's not true. If you had a such box, how can you look at
it with a relative index of refraction less than $\sqrt{2}$? What would be the
value of η?

28.8. Figure 28.44 shows two views of the transparent cube in Figure 28.20
with a reflective sphere inside. Can you explain the appearance of the
sphere in these images?

28.9. Although the direct illumination of the sphere in Figure 28.44 is incorrect, the reflections of the plane and background color are correct.
Why?

28.10. Figure 28.45 shows the boxes in Figure 28.22 ray traced with max_depth
= 4. Can you explain the appearance of this image?

28.11. If you look at the edge of a pane of glass, the path length of the light that
you see coming out depends on your viewing angle of the edge. Why
does it depend on this? Is there a maximum path length through a given
pane?

28.12. Suppose you had 50 perfectly clear panes of glass, stacked face-to-face, like a vertical deck of cards, and you tried to look through them. What do you think you would see? Here's the answer—at normal incidence, you should see an almost perfect mirror. See if you can work out why. Hecht (1997, p. 103) shows a photograph of 50 microscope slides (thin blocks of glass) where you can see the reflection of the camera. Unfortunately, we can't ray trace even a single ray through 50 panes of glass. Why is this?

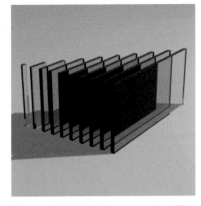

Figure 28.45. The scene in Figure 28.22 traced with max_depth = 4.

28.13. Figure 28.46 shows a view of the two spheres in Figure 28.26, where the camera is too near the line joining their centers.

What are the thick green bands in Figures 28.26 and 28.45? If you look at the reflection of the emissive sphere on the outside surface of the transparent sphere, you can see that the reflection on the inside surface shows through it. Why does this happen? In Figure 28.45, why is the reflection on the inside surface in two parts? How does each part form? Why is the "annular" part that's just inside the silhouette brighter than the part that's near the middle of the sphere? What value of max_depth do you need to see each part?

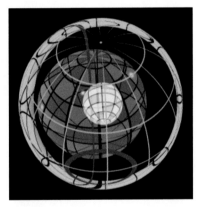

Figure 28.46. Another view of the spheres in Figure 28.26.

28.14. Figure 28.47 shows zoomed-in views of the red sphere in Figure 28.28(d), rendered with the indicated values of max_depth. In Figure 28.47(a), what is the red band on the lower part of the sphere, and why is it not visible on the top part? In Figure 28.47(b),

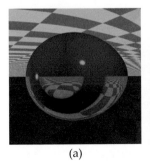   

(a) (b) (c) (d)

Figure 28.47. Zoomed-in views of the red sphere in Figure 28.28(d), rendered with the following values of max_depth: (a) 3; (b) 4; (c) 6; (d) 8.

why is this band now visible on the top part? In other words, why is the rest of the sphere brighter? Why is most of the band brighter in Figure 28.47(c)? Why are there dark rings on its inner and outer edges? In Figure 28.47(d), why can you see reflections of the checker plane in the band? Hint: An arbitrary ray that's reflected inside a sphere will bounce around on the surface of a *disk* that bisects the sphere. Given enough bounces, the ray will eventually hit any object that's inside the sphere and crosses the disk.

28.15. If you rendered a stereo pair of Figures 28.28(c) and (d) or the images in Figure 28.29, do you think it would be successful? If not, why not?

28.16. Here are some questions about Figure 28.34(b). To start with something easy, what is the dark area at the bottom of the image? The top halves of the spheres are yellow, and the bottom halves are cyan, but these look brown and green, respectively, although the transparent sphere is completely clear. You can see some of the true colors on the far-left and far-right spheres. The cause seems to be a faint secondary image of the spheres that overlaps their direct images but is inverted top to bottom. How are these secondary images formed, and why do they change the colors of the direct images? How is the image of the checkers in the sky formed? Is this related to the sphere images? If you look closely at the checkers in the sky, you will see another faint checker image that looks like the bottom part of Figure 28.34(d). How is this formed?

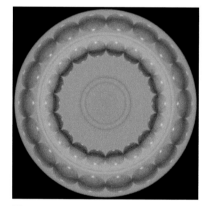

Figure 28.48. Looking out the bottom of the transparent sphere at a reflective plane. This was rendered with `max_depth = 8`.

28.17. What can you explain about Figure 28.34(d)?

28.18. In Figure 28.48 I've replaced the checker plane in Figure 28.34 with a mirror. This is a view looking vertically down at the plane with the camera at $(0, -2, 0)$. Can you explain this image?

28.19. Notice the large dark area on the water in Figure 28.41(a). What causes this?

28.20. Imagine that you're a small fish in a large spherical fishbowl, and that your owners have a cat. Can you hide from the cat? Does it matter how close the cat is? And let's face it, the cat's going to be close. Does it matter how thick the glass is?

Exercises

28.1. Derive Equation (28.5).

28.2. Prove that the relations in Equation (28.6) are correct.

28.3. Add the `FresnelReflector`, `FresnelTransmitter`, and `Dielectric` classes to your ray tracer and make sure that they compile.

28.4. Derive the expression (28.13) for the minimum path length of a ray through a transparent sphere. What is the maximum path length?

28.5. Reproduce the images in Figure 28.5.

28.6. Re-render the transparent ellipsoid in Figure 27.24(a) with a dielectric material. What has happened to the black strip?

28.7. Render the sphere in Figure 28.6 with all values of `max_depth` from 1 to 7. Experiment with different values of η. For example, find out what value of `max_depth` you need to make a diamond sphere disappear.

28.8. Figure 28.49 is an image of two spheres, where the left sphere is a generic sphere that has been uniformly scaled with a factor of 4.0 and the right sphere has a radius of 4.0. Since the filter color and rendered color of both spheres are identical, this demonstrates that color filtering works correctly for scaled objects. Scaling, of course, changes the length of rays that hit the generic sphere. Use this image to test that color filtering works in this situation in your ray tracer.

28.9. Reproduce the figures in Sections 28.4.2–28.4.5.

28.10. Derive Equation (28.16) and the inequalities (28.17) and (28.18).

28.11. In Figure 28.18, prove that the transmitted angle on face 2 is the same as the incident angle on face 1.

28.12. Reproduce Figures 28.20–28.22.

28.13. Derive expressions (28.19) and (28.20) for the fraction of radiance transmitted through a pane of glass.

Figure 28.49. Color filtering with a scaled generic sphere on the left and a sphere of radius 4.0 on the right.

28.14. Prove that ray tracing a pane of glass gives the same result as Equation (28.19).

28.15. Render the scenes displayed in Figures 28.26 and 28.46 and experiment with different values of max_depth and η, different camera angles, and the size and distance of the emissive sphere. Also experiment with other filter colors, including white.

28.16. See if you can sketch the invisible region inside a transparent sphere when the eye point is just outside the sphere and at infinity (parallel viewing). How does changing the value of η affect the regions?

28.17. Reproduce Figures 28.28 and 28.29. Experiment with different parameters such as the index of refraction, rotation angles, maximum recursion depth, location and radius of the red sphere, and viewing parameters.

28.18. Render a glass sphere with many small random air bubbles in it.

28.19. Derive Equations (28.23) and (28.24).

28.20. Derive the inequality (28.25).

28.21. Implement the scene in Figure 28.34 and reproduce these images. By varying max_depth, find out how many bounces are required for the various optical effects to occur. Experiment with different values of η and the viewing parameters. Change the objects outside the sphere; for example, make the sphere's radius and the ring radius larger or smaller. My original scene had a torus instead of a ring of spheres, and it looked good. In particular, find out what the world looks like from inside a spherical rain drop.

28.22. Put some reflective objects inside the transparent sphere with the camera in Figure 28.34.

28.23. Experiment with fisheye, panoramic, and stereo cameras inside the transparent sphere in Figure 28.34.

28.24. Replace the transparent sphere in Figure 28.34 with a triaxial ellipsoid. This will completely break the symmetry, let most rays get out after enough bounces, and provide a much more complex optical environment than a sphere. Figure 28.50 is an example image produced by placing the ellipsoid inside a sphere with a 2D spherical checker texture on it.

Figure 28.50. Camera inside a transparent ellipsoid.

28.25. Find out what things look like from inside the nested spheres in Figure 28.15. Be careful with the exposure time.

28.26. Allow objects rendered with Matte or Phong materials to optionally not have shadows cast on them.

28.27. Add the glass of water described in Section 28.7 to your ray tracer and use it to reproduce the images in Figure 28.38. Experiment with different values of max_depth, filter colors, and dimensions. Compare your images with a real glass of colored water.

28.28. Implement a glass of water with rounded edges at the bottom of the glass and water.

28.29. Add the Fishbowl class to your ray tracer with the meniscus, as described in Section 28.8, and use Figure 28.41 for testing (with or without the fish).

28.30. Figure 28.51 shows three rays that traverse a fishbowl, ignoring refraction. Two rays cross an odd number of boundaries, and one crosses an even number. For each ray, write down the formula for the product of all the η^2 factors. What implications do these have for ray-traced images of the bowl when the camera is outside it? How do they affect the appearance of the fish? See also Exercise 28.32, which covers the case when the camera is in the water.

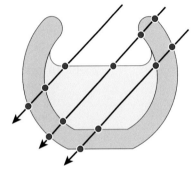

Figure 28.51. Rays that traverse a fishbowl with water in it can intersect an odd or an even number of boundaries.

28.31. The images in Figure 28.41 use a fishbowl where the physical dimensions are initialized in the default constructor. Modify the Fishbowl class so that these can be specified in the build functions. Experiment with different physical bowl parameters, filter colors, viewing parameters, and values of max_depth.

28.32. Find out what the fish can see, particularly when they can see another fish or are looking up at the top of the water (refer to Figure 27.27). How would you set the exposure time when the camera is inside the water?

28.33. Modify the fishbowl so that it uses a single part torus for the meniscus when it's less than half full of water. You will also have to modify the member functions that set the materials.

28.34. Implement a fishbowl with flat bottoms as illustrated in Figure 28.39(b).

28.35. Implement a fishbowl with flat bottoms and rounded edges, instead of the sharp edges in Figure 28.39(b). It will help to have completed Exercise 28.34.

28.36. Spherical glass bowls often have flat horizontal tops. Implement this variety

28.37. Model and render a common bathroom mirror.

28.38. Model and render the object shown in Figure 28.52. This is a transparent cube with spherical caps cut out of four faces. There's also a reflective sphere inside.

28.39. Render some gemstones that are convex polyhedra. By using an area light, reflections of the light off of the inside surface will happen automatically, and with the Fresnel equations, color filtering, and the grid acceleration scheme, you have the tools to produce nice images. You can find gemstone models on the Web. See Guy and Stoler (2004) for state-of-the-art images rendered using additional optical effects.

Figure 28.52. Cube with part spheres cut from four faces.

28.40. In adaptive depth control, a ray tracer stops tracing secondary rays when they stop making a contribution to the image. This is also called *ray culling*. In our ray tracer, this will be when their maximum RGB component is less than 1/255. We can estimate this by keeping track of the product of all the k_rs, k_ts, η^2s, and filter amounts that multiply the radiance returned to a hit point, and stop when each (r, g, b) component is less than 1/255. Implement this and find out how much it reduces your rendering times for the panes of glass and the fishbowl images. As my current rendering time is 18 hours for Figure 28.22 at 300 × 300 pixels, 16 samples per pixel, and max_depth = 15, this is definitely worth implementing. To prevent it from slowing down the ray tracer when it's not required, try to keep all of the code in the Dielectric class.

28.41. A Fresnel reflector material would be an improvement on the Reflective material in Chapter 24. Implement a reflective material where k_r is determined by the Fresnel equations. You can use $\eta = 1.5$.

28.42. Implement a glossy transmitter material using a similar approach to the one adopted in Chapter 25 for glossy reflection. Additional complications will arise from the fact that reflected and transmitted rays can be inside or outside the object. Consequently, reflected rays can be above the tangent plane when the direction of mirror reflection is inside the object, and transmitted rays can also be above the tangent plane when the direction of perfect transmission is inside the object. A simple approach would be to only evaluate the Fresnel equations for the perfect specular reflection and transmission directions. This will avoid problems with total internal reflection.

28.43. If you have implemented a Fresnel reflector and a glossy transmitter material, you will have a number of BRDFs and BTDFs that need to evaluate the Fresnel equations. You could just reproduce the code, as I've done for the `Dielectric` material, but a better design would be to use objects that perform the evaluations. Implement a `Fresnel` class for this purpose.

29 Texture Mapping

Image courtesy of Adeel Khan

Objectives

By the end of this chapter, you should:

- appreciate how textures add interest to images;
- understand some simple texture-mapping techniques;
- have added textured materials to your ray tracer.

29.1 Introduction

Although the old saying "a picture is worth a thousand words" is overused, it's quite appropriate here, and in fact, I'm going to start with two pictures. Figure 29.1 shows a scene rendered without using any textures, not even a checker pattern. Although there's some interesting geometry here, it's a fairly bland image. In contrast, Figure 29.2 is the same scene rendered with a variety of *texturing techniques*, and the difference is striking. No extra geometry has been added; only the shading of the objects in Figure 29.1 has been altered. In computer graphics, a texture is a color that varies with location. Texturing is a general term for applying textures to objects, a process that can add visual

643

Figure 29.1. Interior scene rendered with no textures.

Figure 29.2. Same scene as in Figure 29.1 but rendered with a variety of textures. The water surface is Ken Musgrave's water bump map, as described in Musgrave (2003b).

complexity and interest to scenes and do this inexpensively. Textures also make scenes look more natural because most surfaces in the real world are textured. Indeed, the world would look very boring without textures.

Textures can be either stored or procedurally generated, and each can be one-, two-, or three-dimensional. In this chapter, I'll only discuss 2D textures that are stored in images and applied to the surface of objects through various *mapping techniques*.

We can use textures to modulate any aspect of a material's interaction with light: its reflection, scattering, transmission, emission, or absorption. In addition, textures can be used to modulate the surface normal, a process known as *bump mapping*, and the surface location, which is called *displacement mapping*. There's also a technique called *clip mapping*, where textures can be used to cut away parts of an object's surface. Chapter 16.15 is an example.

Figure 29.2 illustrates the following texture-mapping techniques: rectangular (the picture on the wall), cylindrical (the checkered cylinder's curved surface), and spherical (the Earth sphere). It also illustrates a 2D procedural texture for the top of the checker cylinder and 3D procedural textures for simulating wood (the floor and picture frame), marble (the bunny), and sandstone (the bath sides). The reflective color c_r of the wall tiles has been modulated with a turbulence function, and finally, the water surface is a bump map. The details are in the build function for Figure 29.2 on the book's website, with the texture images.

 ## 29.2 Implementing Textures

Once you have implemented textures, they are simple to use, because the only thing they do is return an RGBColor given a ray-object hit point. They all define a get_color function for this purpose. A 2D stored texture returns the color from an image, and a procedural texture computes it on the fly. Because textures return colors, I only use them to modulate material colors: c_d, c_s, c_r, and c_e, but of course, they can also be used to modulate the reflection coefficients k_a, k_d, k_s, and k_r or k_t (see Exercise 29.9). In this chapter, I'll only discuss textures that modulate the diffuse color c_d. Listing 29.1 shows the declaration of the Texture base class, which has no data members. The get_color function has a ShadeRec reference as a parameter because the ImageTexture::get_color

```
class Texture {
    public:

        // constructors, etc.

        virtual RGBColor
        get_color(const ShadeRec& sr) const = 0;
};
```

Listing 29.1. The Texture base class declaration.

```
class ConstantColor: public Texture {
    public:

        // constructors, etc.

        void
        set_color(const RGBColor& c);

        virtual RGBColor&
        get_color(const ShadeRec& sr) const;

    private:

        RGBColor color;           // the color
};


RGBColor
ConstantColor::get_color(const ShadeRec& sr) const {
    return (color);
}
```

Listing 29.2. Code from the class `ConstantColor`.

function in Listing 29.7 uses the (u, v) texture coordinates at a hit point, and these are stored in the `ShadeRec` object (see Listing 29.12). I'll only use these to render textured triangle meshes, but in commercial applications, that's the most important use of textures.

The simplest texture returns a specified color, independent of the hit point. This texture can be useful when you want some components of a texture-based material to be the same color at all points. For example, if you want the Earth sphere in Figure 29.2 to have a white specular highlight, you could use a constant color texture for c_s. Listing 29.2 shows part of the code for the `ConstantColor` texture. The `ConstantColor::get_color` function doesn't demonstrate how the texture is always evaluated in the local coordinate system of the object, as I'll explain in Section 29.4.

We incorporate textures into materials with spatially varying BRDFs, whose properties depend on position through storing textures instead of RGB colors. The names of the BRDFs and the materials start with `sv_`. Listing 29.3 shows code from the `sv_Lambertian` BRDF. The difference between the `Lambertian` and `sv_Lambertian` BRDFs is that the latter stores the diffuse color as a texture pointer and defines spatially varying versions of rho, f,

```
class SV_Lambertian: public BRDF {
    public:

            // constructors, etc.

            virtual RGBColor
            rho(const ShadeRec& sr, const Vector3D& wo) const;

            virtual RGBColor
            f(const ShadeRec& sr, const Vector3D& wo, const Vector3D& wi) const;

            virtual RGBColor
            sample_f(const ShadeRec& sr, const Vector3D& wo, const Vector3D& wi)
                    const;

    private:

            float kd;
            Texture* cd;
};

RGBColor
SV_Lambertian::rho(const ShadeRec& sr, const Vector3D& wo) const {
    return (kd * cd->get_color(sr));
}

RGBColor
SV_Lambertian::f(const ShadeRec& sr, const Vector3D& wo, const Vector3D& wi)
    const { return (kd * cd->get_color(sr) * invPI);
}
```

Listing 29.3. Code from the class SV_Lambertian.

and sample_f, which have a ShadeRec reference as an additional parameter. I haven't reproduced the code for sample_f.

A simple textured material is SV_Matte in Listing 29.4. Note that the function SV_Matte::set_cd sets the same texture in the ambient and diffuse BRDFs, consistent with the shading model in Chapter 14 where the ambient and diffuse shading components share a single diffuse color.

Listing 29.5 shows the SV_Matte::shade function. The only difference between this and the Matte::shade function in Listing 14.14 is that this version calls the spatially varying versions of rho and f.

```
class SV_Matte: public Material {
    public:

        // consructors, etc.

        void
        set_cd(const Texture* t_ptr);

        virtual RGBColor
        shade(ShadeRec& s);

    private:

        SV_Lambertian* ambient_brdf;
        SV_Lambertian* diffuse_brdf;
};

inline void
SV_Matte::set_cd(const Texture* t_ptr) {
    ambient_brdf->set_cd(t_ptr);
    diffuse_brdf->set_cd(t_ptr);
}
```

Listing 29.4. Partial declaration of the class SV_Matte.

```
RGBColor
SV_Matte::shade(ShadeRec& sr) {
    Vector3D wo = -sr.ray.d;
    RGBColor L = ambient_brdf->rho(sr, wo) * sr.w.ambient_ptr->L(sr);
    int num_lights = sr.w.lights.size();

    for (int j = 0; j < num_lights; j++) {
        Light* light_ptr = sr.w.lights[j];
        Vector3D wi = light_ptr->compute_direction(sr);
        wi.normalize();
        float ndotwi = sr.normal * wi;
        float ndotwo = sr.normal * wo;

        if (ndotwi > 0.0 && ndotwo > 0.0) {
            bool in_shadow = false;

            if (sr.w.lights[j]->casts_shadows()) {
                Ray shadow_ray(sr.hitPoint, wi);
                in_shadow = light_ptr->in_shadow(shadow_ray, sr.w.objects);
```

Listing 29.5. The function SV_Matte::shade.

```
            }

                if (!in_shadow)
                        L += diffuse_brdf->f(sr, wo, wi) * light_ptr->L(sr) *
                                light_ptr->G(sr) * ndotwi;
                }
            }

        return (L);
    }
```

Listing 29.5 (continued). The function `SV_Matte::shade`.

 29.3 Mapping Techniques

29.3.1 General Procedures

In texture mapping, we take a 2D image and map it onto the surface of a 3D object, but there's a fundamental problem with this procedure. Unless the surface of the object is *mathematically flat*, distortion will occur during the mapping process. Although the definition of a mathematically flat surface is rather complex, you can just think of a sheet of paper. Any shape that you can bend it into without stretching or tearing it is mathematically flat. An example is a circular cylinder. Images can be mapped onto such surfaces without distortion. We can still map images onto surfaces that are not flat, but the images are usually pre-distorted to counteract the resulting distortion.

The great advantage of texture-mapping techniques lies in the sources of the images. They can come from anywhere: photographs, spacecraft and satellite imagery, computer images from a variety of software including ray tracers, and painting and drawing programs. There's no limit to the variety of images that can be used.

The mapping process is different for each type of surface and involves mapping the ray-object hit point to a pixel in the 2D image. To keep the mapping architecture as simple as possible, I'll only map textures onto generic objects, and I'll only discuss default mappings where the image covers the entire surface of the object. I also do a preliminary mapping of the 3D ray-object hit point to 2D *normalized texture coordinates* $(u, v) \in [0, 1] \times [0, 1]$. This is standard practice in computer graphics, where it's known as (u, v) mapping. If the image has resolution (h_{res}, v_{res}), we can then use the following simple expressions for the *texel coordinates* $(x_p, y_p) \in [0, h_{res} - 1] \in [0, v_{res} - 1]$:

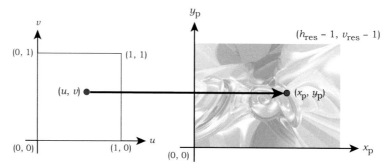

Figure 29.3. (a) (u, v) texture coordinates; (b) corresponding texel coordinates (x_p, y_p) in a texture image.

$$x_p = (h_{\text{res}} - 1)u,$$
$$y_p = (v_{\text{res}} - 1)v, \qquad\qquad (29.1)$$

for all mappings.[1] Here, x_p and y_p will be stored as integers. Figure 29.3 illustrates the relationship between (u, v) and (x_p, y_p). Because of this common procedure, I can concentrate below on the calculation of u and v in the various mappings.

After we compute the pixel coordinates for a given hit point, we can extract the pixel color from the image and use it for shading the point. A useful debugging technique is to return pure red (1, 0, 0) for the image color if the pixel coordinates in expressions (29.1) are not valid, that is, if $(x_p, y_p) \notin [0, h_{\text{res}} - 1] \times [0, v_{\text{res}} - 1]$. This technique revealed several errors I had made while implementing the following mappings.

29.3.2 Rectangular Mapping

We first map the rectangular texture image to a generic rectangle $(x, z) \in [-1, +1] \times [-1, +1]$ in the (x, z) plane (see Section 19.5.2). The mapping discussed here maps the entire texture image onto the rectangle, regardless of its aspect ratio. Given a hit point $(x, 0, z)$ in this rectangle, the expressions for u and v are

$$u = (z + 1)/2,$$
$$v = (x + 1)/2.$$

---

1. A texel is another name for a texture pixel.

Figure 29.4 shows an image mapped to a rectangle. Since the generic rectangle is a square, we have to scale this so that its shape is the same as the image. In this case, the image has an aspect ratio of 1.5, requiring the generic rectangle to be scaled by a factor of 1.5 in the z-direction before it's displayed. We usually have to apply further transformations to the rectangle to scale, rotate, and translate it.

29.3.3 Cylindrical Mapping

Figure 29.5 shows a hit point p on a generic cylinder and an image to be mapped onto the cylinder. This also shows the corresponding point on the image, as determined by the cylindrical coordinates $\phi \in [0, 2\pi)$ and $y \in [-1, +1]$ of the hit point.

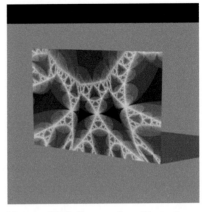

Figure 29.4. Rectangle with texture-mapped image *LightLace*, by Kevin Suffern, 1994.

If the hit point has coordinates (x, y, z), the formula for the azimuth angle ϕ is given by Equation (2.10):

$$\phi = \tan^{-1}(x/z)$$

and can be computed with the code in Listing 2.1. The (u, v) parameters are then

$$u = \phi/2\pi,$$
$$v = (y + 1)/2.$$

The only cylindrical mapping I'll consider here maps the left side of the image $(u = 0, \phi = 0, x_p = 0)$ onto the line where the generic cylinder intersects the (y, z)

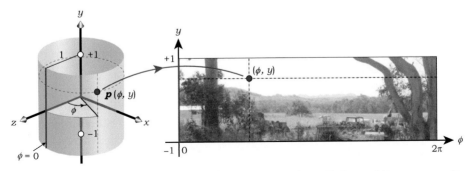

Figure 29.5. A hit point on the surface of a generic circular cylinder and its corresponding point on an image. Photograph by Kevin Suffern.

Figure 29.6. Cylinder with texture-mapped image.

coordinate plane with $x = 0$ and $z = 1$. This is indicated by the two vertical red lines in Figure 29.5. Figure 29.6 is a rendered version of the image in Figure 29.5. Note the discontinuity across the $\phi = 0$ line (in the middle of a tree trunk).

If we want to map an image onto a cylinder without any visual discontinuity along this line, it must *tile horizontally*. This means that the left and right boundaries of the image join seamlessly, like strips of wallpaper. Although the image used here doesn't tile horizontally, the checker image mapped onto the cylinder in Figure 29.2 does.

29.3.4 Spherical Mapping

We can also map images onto the surface of a sphere, but unfortunately, spheres are not mathematically flat. Just try wrapping a sheet of paper around a sphere! If we therefore take an image and map it onto a sphere, it becomes distorted.

Given a hit point on a generic sphere with coordinates (x, y, z), we need to find the values of ϕ and θ from Equations (2.3) with $r = 1$. Because the azimuth angle ϕ is the same as for the cylindric mapping, this only leaves θ to discuss. Solving the second equation in (2.3) gives

$$\theta = \cos^{-1}(y),$$

where $\cos^{-1}(y)$ can be coded as acos(y). This is what we want because acos(y) $\in [0, \pi]$, but we do have to take into account the fact that $\theta = 0$ when $v = 1$.

The (u, v) parameters are therefore

$$u = \phi/2\pi,$$
$$v = 1 - \theta/\pi.$$

Figure 29.7 illustrates the spherical coordinates (θ, ϕ) for a hit point on the surface of a generic sphere.

Since $\phi \in [0, 2\pi]$ and $\theta \in [0, \pi]$, the parameter space in the (ϕ, θ) plane has a 2:1 aspect ratio, as shown in Figure 29.7. This means that an image that just covers the surface of a sphere must also have this aspect ratio. Images with other aspect ratios can be used by scaling them appropriately or by adjusting the mapping equations.

Figure 29.8 shows a grid that's mapped onto a sphere in Figure 29.9 to illustrate the distortion. This figure shows how the distortion increases towards

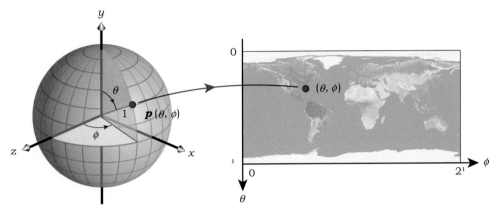

Figure 29.7. A hit point on the surface of a generic sphere and its corresponding point on an image. Note that the polar angle axis points down because $\theta = 0$ is at the top of the sphere.

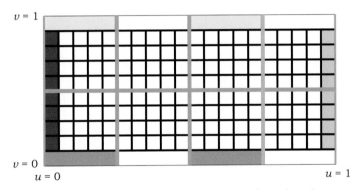

Figure 29.8. Grid to be mapped onto the surface of a sphere.

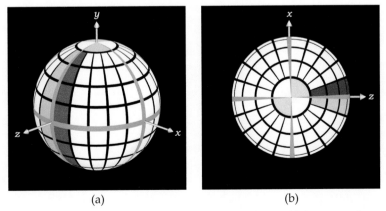

Figure 29.9. The results of mapping the grid in Figure 29.8 onto a sphere.

(a)   (b)

Figure 29.10. (a) Sarah. Photograph by Kevin Suffern; (b) distortion at the south pole.

the north and south poles ($y = \pm 1$) where the lines $v = 0$ and $v = 1$ in Figure 29.8 are compressed to points. Notice how the yellow rectangles have been compressed to small circular quadrants near the north pole ($y = +1$). The columns of red and green squares show how the left and right boundaries of the image are mapped onto the curve where the sphere intersects the (y, z) plane with $z > 0$. If this sphere were the Earth, the horizontal black lines in Figure 29.8 would be mapped onto the parallels of latitude, the vertical lines would be mapped onto the meridians of longitude, and the middle horizontal blue line would straddle the equator.

When we apply the spherical mapping to an ordinary image such as Figure 29.10(a), the distortion is apparent, as Figure 29.10(b) demonstrates,

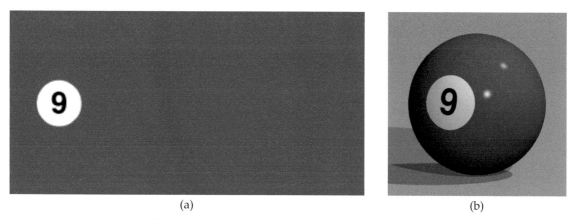

(a)   (b)

Figure 29.11. A billiard ball rendered with the texture image on the left.

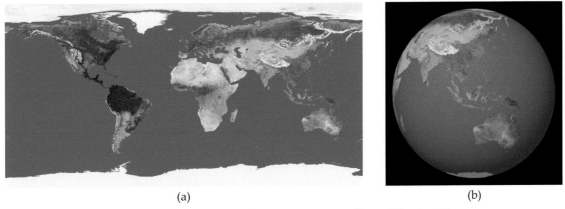

(a) (b)

Figure 29.12. (a) Mercator projection of the Earth. Image courtesy of James Hastings-Trew; (b) the image mapped onto a sphere.

where we have a painfully distorted dog. Also, since Figure 29.10 doesn't tile horizontally, the discontinuity at $\phi = 0$ is obvious.

Since the distortion has reasonable limits within latitude ±30° of the equator, we can map images that contain visual information in this region onto spheres with little apparent distortion. Figure 29.11 shows an example.

29.3.5 The Mercator Projection

The above discussion may give you the impression that spherical projections aren't much use, but that isn't the case. It's possible to deliberately distort an image so that when it's mapped onto a sphere, it appears undistorted. The mathematical technique, called the *Mercator projection*, was invented by the Belgian cartographer Gerardus Mercator, 1512–1594. It has been used for navigation and maps of the world for hundreds of years. Figure 29.12(a) is a Mercator projection of the Earth's surface. Notice how large and distorted Antarctica, the Arctic ice sheet, and Greenland appear. Figure 29.12(b) shows this image projected onto a sphere; Figure 29.13 shows the north polar region, which, like the rest of the image, is undistorted.

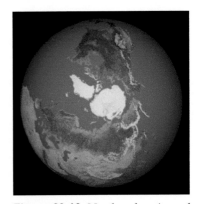

Figure 29.13. North polar view of the Earth.

29.3.6 Light-Probe Mapping

In some ways, the light-probe mapping is the most interesting. These are produced by placing a reflective sphere in an

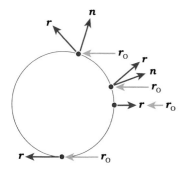

Figure 29.14. Parallel rays that are reflected from a sphere sample the whole environment that surrounds the sphere, except the part that's directly behind the sphere.

environment and taking one or more photographs of it. The whole environment, except for the part directly behind the sphere, will be seen in the reflections. Figure 29.14 illustrates how this happens with a number of parallel rays. A ray that hits the middle of the sphere is reflected straight back; rays that hit the sphere tangentially are "reflected" in the same direction.

For a hit point with coordinates $(x, y, z) \in [-1, 1]^3$ on a unit sphere at the world origin, we can define two angles α and β as shown in Figure 29.15.

The expressions we need are

$$\alpha = \cos^{-1}(z),$$
$$\sin \beta = y/(x^2 + y^2)^{1/2}, \tag{29.2}$$
$$\cos \beta = x/(x^2 + y^2)^{1/2},$$

where $\alpha \in [0, \pi]$, and $\beta \in [0, 2\pi]$. The (u, v) coordinates are

$$u = [1.0 + (\alpha/\pi) \cos \beta]/2.0, \tag{29.3}$$
$$v = [1.0 + (\alpha/\pi) \sin \beta]/2.0.$$

Figure 29.16 shows the type of image that can result from photographing a reflective sphere in the center of the Uffizi Gallery buildings. To use this as a background texture, we apply it to a large sphere that surrounds the scene and use a light-probe mapping that implements Equations (29.2) and (29.3) (see Section 29.4). Although it's not apparent, Figure 29.16 is a mirror image of the environment and is therefore mirror "reversed." For example, notice that

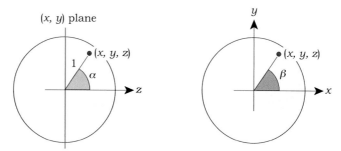

Figure 29.15. The angle α is the angle between the positive z-axis and the line joining the hit point on the unit sphere. The angle β is the projected angle on the (x, y) plane.

the tower is on the left side of the road. When we use the light-probe mapping, the buildings are rendered the right way around, as in Figures 11.8 and 11.13. Notice that the tower is on the right side of the road in those images.

Paul Debevec's Uffizi Gallery image, which is the source of all these figures, is reproduced in Figure 29.17. Notice that this is not mirror reversed as it's not a light-probe image. Instead, this was created from 18 photographs of the buildings (see the Further Reading section).

To use this image with the light-probe map, all we have to do is use

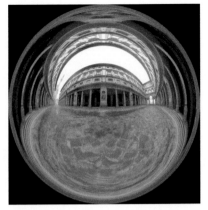

Figure 29.16. The Uffizi buildings reflected on a light-probe sphere.

$$\alpha = \cos^{-1}(-z) \qquad (29.4)$$

instead of the expression in Equation (29.2). This is an option in the light-probe mapping (Listing 29.11) and is how Figures 11.8 and 11.13 were rendered. Figure 29.16 is a 360° fisheye camera image of Figure 29.17 but using the original expression (29.2) for α in the light-probe mapping. The reflective sphere in Figure 25.8(f) shows the Uffizi Gallery buildings reversed, as it must.

 ## 29.4 Implementing the Mappings

I've implemented the above mapping techniques with an `ImageTexture` texture class, derived from `Texture`, and a separate `Mapping` inheritance hierarchy that implements the individual mappings in separate classes. The image is stored in an `Image` object by calling the `Image::read_`

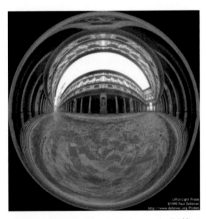

Figure 29.17. Paul Debevec's Uffizi Gallery image.

`ppm_file` function. The `ImageTexture` class declaration in Listing 29.6 contains pointers to both an image and a mapping.

Listing 29.7 shows the function `ImageTexture::get_color`. Note that the code checks the mapping pointer before it gets the pixel coordinates. This is because triangle meshes with textures don't need a mapping, as I'll explain in the following section. In this case, the mapping pointer will be null, as it's set to null in the `ImageTexture` constructor. Something else to notice is that this is where we finally use the local hit point, after computing it in all of the hit functions starting from Chapter 3. In this context, the local hit point is where the ray hits the generic object that's being textured.

```
class ImageTexture: public Texture {
    public:

        ...

        virtual RGBColor
        get_color(const ShadeRec& sr) const;

    private:

        int hres;              // horizontal image resolution
        int vres;              // vertical image resolution
        Image* image_ptr;      // the image
        Mapping* mapping_ptr;  // mapping technique used, if any
};
```

Listing 29.6. The class `ImageTexture` declaration.

```
RGBColor
ImageTexture::get_color(const ShadeRec& sr) const {

    int row, column;

    if (mapping_ptr)
        mapping_ptr->get_texel_coordinates(sr.local_hit_point, hres,
            vres, row, column);
    else {
        row = (int)(sr.v * (vres - 1));
        column = (int)(sr.u * (hres - 1));
    }

    return (image_ptr->get_color(row, column));
}
```

Listing 29.7. The function `ImageTexture::get_color`.

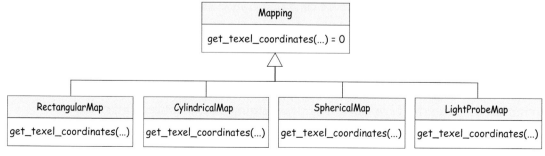

Figure 29.18. The `Mapping` inheritance chart.

The mapping classes are simple because they have no data members and they only have to define the single function get_texel_coordinates. Figure 29.18 shows their inheritance chart.

Listing 29.8 shows the declaration of the Mapping base class, which has no data members.

As an example of how a mapping is implemented, Listing 29.9 shows the get_texel_coordinates function for the spherical mapping.

```
class Mapping {
    public:
            ...

            virtual void
            get_pixel_coordinates (const Point3D& local_hit_point,
                        const int hres,
                        const int vres,
                        int& row,
                        int& column) const = 0;
};
```

Listing 29.8. The Mapping base class.

```
void
SphericalMap::get_texel_coordinates(const Point3D& local_hit_point,
        const int hres,
        const int vres,
        int& row,
        int& column) const {

    // first, compute theta and phi

    float theta = acos(local_hit_point.y);
    float phi = atan2(local_hit_point.x, local_hit_point.z);
    if (phi < 0.0)
        phi += TWO_PI;

    // next, map theta and phi to (u, v) in [0, 1] x [0, 1]

    float u = phi * invTWO_PI;
    float v = 1 - theta * invPI;

    // finally, map u and v to the texel coordinates

    column = (int) ((hres - 1) * u);        // column is across
    row = (int)   ((vres - 1) * v);        // row is up
}
```

Listing 29.9. The function SphericalMap::get_texel_coordinates.

```
void
World::build(void) {

    // construct view plane, tracer, camera, light

    // image:

    Image* image_ptr = new Image;
    image_ptr->read_ppm_file("Earth.ppm");

    // mapping:

    SphericalMap* spherical_map_ptr = new SphericalMap;

    // image based texture:

    ImageTexture* image_texture_ptr = new ImageTexture;
    image_texture_ptr->set_image(spherical_map_ptr);
    image_texture_ptr->set_mapping(spherical_map_ptr);

    // textured material:

    SV_Matte* sv_matte_ptr  = new SV_Matte;
    sv_matte_ptr ->set_ka(0.45);
    sv_matte_ptr ->set_kd(0.65);
    sv_matte_ptr ->set_cd(image_texture_ptr);

    // generic sphere:

    Sphere* sphere_ptr = new Sphere;
    sphere_ptr->set_material(sv_matte_ptr );

    // transformed sphere:

    Instance* earth_ptr = new Instance(sphere_ptr);
    earth_ptr->set_material(sv_matte_ptr );
    earth_ptr->rotate_y(60);
    add_object(earth_ptr);
}
```

Listing 29.10. The build function for Figure 29.12(b).

Listing 29.10 shows part of the build function for Figure 29.12(b). This illustrates the various things you have to do to set up a spatially varying matte material that can be used to render a textured sphere.

Listing 29.11 shows the function LightProbe::get_texel_coordinates, which implements Equations (29.2)–(29.4). This code works for all camera locations and viewing directions.

```
void
LightProbe::get_texel_coordinates(const Point3D& hit_point,
        const int hres,
        const int vres,
        int& row,
        int& column) const {

    float x = hit_point.x; float y = hit_point.y; float z = hit_point.z;

    float d = sqrt(x * x + y * y);
    float sin_beta = y / d;
    float cos_beta = x / d;
    float alpha;

    if (map_type == light_probe)          // the default
        alpha = acos(z);

    if (map_type == panoramic)
        alpha = acos(-z);

    float r = alpha * invPI;
    float u = (1.0 + r * cos_beta) * 0.5;
    float v = (1.0 + r * sin_beta) * 0.5;
    column = (int) ((hres - 1) * u);
    row = (int) ((vres - 1) * v);
}
```

Listing 29.11. The function `LightProbe::get_texel_coordinates`.

29.5 Antialiasing

Strictly speaking, a ray-traced image of an image-based texture will suffer aliasing unless the pixels and texels exactly match, a situation that rarely occurs. The culprit here is the fixed resolution of the images. A given pixel can cover many texels or a fraction of a texel. In the former case, a lower-resolution filtered version of the texture results, and the resulting figures generally look good (see Figure 29.19(a) and previous figures in this chapter).

In the latter case, the rendered textures look pixelated, as Figure 29.19(b) and (c) demonstrate. When this happens, we could perform *intrinsic* antialiasing, where the texture antialiases itself by averaging the returned color over neighboring pixels in the image. Shirley and Morley (2003) discusses this with uniform and weighted averaging. Alternatively, we could just use standard antialiasing techniques as discussed in Chapters 4 and 5. I've used this in

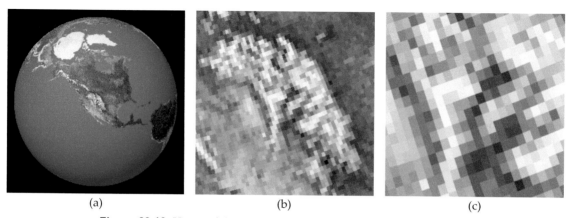

(a)   (b)   (c)

Figure 29.19. Views of the Earth with magnification factors of 1 (a), 8 (b), and 16 (c), anti-aliased with multi-jittered sampling. These are 300×300 pixel images, with one ray per pixel in (a) and (b) and 25 rays per pixel in (c).

Figure 29.19(c), but it's not as effective as intrinsic antialiasing because it only antialiases the edges of the image pixels.

Aliasing of textures with fine detail can be a serious problem, particularly in animation sequences. As a result, a lot of research has been done on the intrinsic antialiasing of textures, both image-based and procedural (see the Further Reading section). To keep things as simple as possible, I'll just use standard antialiasing techniques.

If you want to avoid pixelation effects, here are some tips. Use texture images with resolutions that are as high as practical, avoid zooming in close to objects with image-based textures, and avoid placing the camera close to such objects. A disadvantage of high-resolution images is that they can use a lot of memory. The Earth image in Figure 29.12(a) is 1024×512 pixels and hence can be rendered up to this resolution (as a flat image) without becoming pixelated.

29.6 Triangle Meshes

For commercial ray tracing, triangle meshes are the most commonly textured objects. I'll discuss here how to apply image-based textures to triangle meshes that are read from PLY files. To do this, I'll add two new mesh triangles to the inheritance chart in Figure 23.5. These triangles, called `FlatUVMeshTriangle` and `SmoothUVMeshTriangle`, are shown in Figure 29.20. I've also added functions to the base class mesh `MeshTriangle` to interpolate u and v. This is the

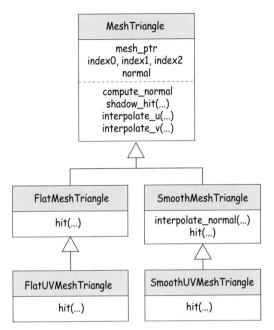

Figure 29.20. Mesh triangle inheritance chart that includes (u, v) mapped triangles.

appropriate place for these functions because the interpolation is independent of whether the shading is flat or smooth.

In a triangle mesh with (u, v) mapping, each vertex stores the (u, v) texture coordinates, as indicated in the Mesh class code in Listing 23.2. These are interpolated in a (u, v) mapped triangle's hit function, and their values at the hit point are stored in the ShadeRec object. The SmoothUVMeshTriangle hit-function code in Listing 29.12 illustrates this, where the relevant code is in blue. Because we interpolate u and v in the same way as the normal, I won't reproduce the code for this here. What's missing from this hit function is the statement that stores the local hit point in the ShadeRec object. That's not required here because the function ImageTexture::get_color in Listing 29.7 doesn't use the local hit point when it uses u and v. The hit functions for FlatUVMeshTriangle and SmoothUVMeshTriangle are the ones that don't store the local hit-point coordinates.

The first example I'll discuss is the two triangles from Section 23.4 with (u, v) mapping added. Figure 29.21 is the top-down view of the triangles from Figure 23.6(a) with the (u, v) coordinates indicated at each vertex.

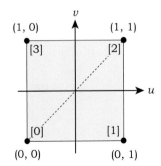

Figure 29.21. The triangles in Figure 23.6 showing the (u, v) coordinates.

```
bool
SmoothUVMeshTriangle::hit(const Ray& ray, float& tmin, ShadeRec& sr) const {

    Point3D v0(mesh_ptr->vertices[index0]);
    Point3D v1(mesh_ptr->vertices[index1]);
    Point3D v2(mesh_ptr->vertices[index2]);

    double a = v0.x - v1.x, b = v0.x - v2.x, c = ray.d.x, d = v0.x - ray.o.x;
    double e = v0.y - v1.y, f = v0.y - v2.y, g = ray.d.y, h = v0.y - ray.o.y;
    double i = v0.z - v1.z, j = v0.z - v2.z, k = ray.d.z, l = v0.z - ray.o.z;

    double m = f * k - g * j, n = h * k - g * l, p = f * l - h * j;
    double q = g * i - e * k, r = e * l - h * i, s = e * j - f * i;

    double invDenom = 1.0 / (a * m + b * q + c * s);

    double e1= d * m - b * n - c * p;
    double beta = e1 * invDenom;

    if (beta < 0.0 || beta > 1.0)
        return (false);

    double e2 = a * n + d * q + c * r;
    double gamma = e2 * invDenom;

    if (gamma < 0.0 || gamma > 1.0)
        return (false);

    if (beta + gamma > 1.0)
        return (false);

    double e3 = a * p - b * r + d * s;
    double t = e3 * invDenom;

    if (t < kEpsilon)
        return (false);

    tmin = t;
    sr.normal = interpolate_normal(beta, gamma);
    sr.u = interpolate_u(beta, gamma);
    sr.v = interpolate_v(beta, gamma);

    return(true);
}
```

Listing 29.12. The function SmoothUVMeshTriangle::hit.

```
ply
format ascii 1.0
comment (u, v) texture coordinates are included with each vertex
comment this file contains two triangles
element vertex 4
property float x
property float y
property float z
property float u
property float v
element face 2
property list int int vertex_indices
end_header
-1.0 0.0 -1.0 0.0 0.0
-1.0 -1.0 1.0 1.0 0.0
1.0 0.0 1.0 1.0 1.0
1.0 -1.0 -1.0 0.0 1.0
3 0 1 2
3 0 2 3
```

Listing 29.13. PLY file that defines two (u, v) mapped triangles. The (u, v) parts are in blue.

Listing 29.13 is a PLY file that includes the (u, v) coordinates with each vertex. The (u, v) relevant parts are in blue. The Grid code for reading (u, v) mapped triangles is analogous to the code for reading triangles without (u, v) mapping: there are two short top-level functions called read_flat_uv_triangles and read_smooth_uv_triangles that call the same function read_uv_ply_file.

The following is an important point. I don't use a mapping to render (u, v) mapped triangles because we don't need one; the (u, v) coordinates at each vertex are all that we require. These can be set by the software that's used to construct the mesh, or in case of the file in Listing 29.13, set manually. If we use an ImageTexture with a null mapping pointer, the code in Listing 29.7 will return the interpolated texture image color at each hit point on a triangle mesh.[2] Figure 29.22 shows the triangles in Figure 23.7 rendered using flat and smooth shading with the image from the back wall in Figure 29.2. Because of the texture, the difference in shading is not as obvious as it is in Figure 23.7.

The final example is the penguin from Section 23.4 with textures. There are two textures involved—one for the body and one for the eyes, as shown

---

2. The code in Listing 29.7 does have one adverse consequence (see Exercise 30.11).

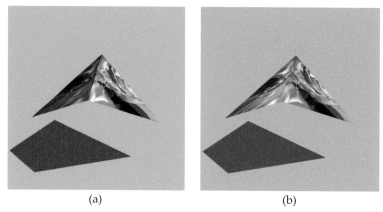

Figure 29.22. Two (u, v) mapped triangles rendered with flat shading (a) and smooth shading (b).

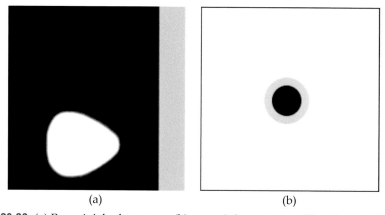

Figure 29.23. (a) Penguin's body texture; (b) penguin's eye texture. The black outline in (b) is simply to create a border; it's not part of the texture.

in Figure 29.23. It's common for complex objects to use multiple textures. Figure 29.24 shows the textured penguin rendered with smooth shading.

Notes and Discussion

The PPM file format stores images as raw data, and PPM files are therefore simple to parse. The ray tracer reads texture images from PPM files using code in the Image class. This class is on the book's website. A major improvement would be to get the ray tracer to read texture images from other file formats such as JPEG and TIFF. The skeleton ray tracer can already read files in these formats, but only for displaying the images on screen (See Exercise 29.10).

 Further Reading

The first paper on texturing was Blinn and Newell (1976). The most comprehensive book on texturing is *Texturing & Modeling: A Procedural Approach*, by Ebert et al. (2003), now in its third edition. This book is written by many of the people who invented the techniques, and it contains a lot of wonderful information and images. Peachey (2003), Worley (2003a), Apodaca and Gritz (2000), and Pharr and

Figure 29.24. Textured penguin rendered with smooth shading.

Humpheys (2004) discuss antialiasing strategies and techniques for textures.

The rectangular, cylindrical, and spherical mappings were devised by Haines (1989). The idea of using a mapping-class inheritance hierarchy comes from Wilt (1994).

The image *LightLace* in Figure 29.4 was first published in Suffern (1994).

The Earth cloud image used in figure on the first page of this chapter and the specular map in Figure 29.25(a) are on the website http://planetpixelempo-rium.com/planets.html, by James Hastings-Trew. The Earth image used in the figure on the first page of this chapter, and in Figures 29.2, 29.7, 29.12, 29.13, and 29.19, was on this website but has now been replaced by the image shown in Figure 29.25(b) rendered with transparent oceans. This wonderful site contains high-resolution maps of the Earth, the other planets, and the moon.

Debevec (1998) discusses the light-probe map. The website http://www.debevec.org/Probes contains a wealth of information about light probes, the history of reflection mapping (of which the light probe is an example), and the formulae for the light-probe mapping. Equations (29.2) and (29.3) and Listing 29.11 are based on information on this website. Akenine-Möller and Haines (2002) also discusses the light-probe map and its history. They use the original name of sphere map.

 Questions

29.1. If an image just covers the curved surface of a generic cylinder without scaling, what is its aspect ratio?

29.2. How can you render a cube that has a different material on each face?

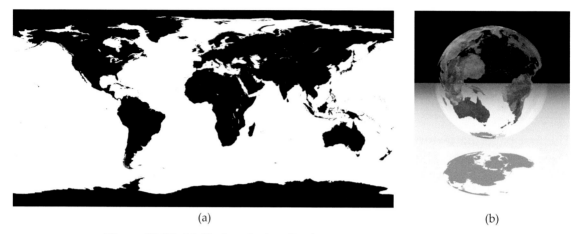

(a)   (b)

Figure 29.25. (a) Black-and-white Earth map. Image courtesy of James Hastings-Trew; (b) transparent Earth with shadows. Image courtesy of Adeel Khan.

Exercises

29.1. Implement the texture classes, the sv_Matte material, and the mappings described in Section 29.3. Use these to reproduce Figures 29.4, 29.6, 29.12(b), and 29.13. There are JPG and PPM versions of the texture images on the book's website.

29.2. Implement mappings with parameters to allow you to cover a section of a rectangle, a cylinder, or a sphere with an image, or alternatively, tile these surfaces with multiple copies of an image.

29.3. Implement a toroidal mapping that will allow you to map a rectangular image onto the surface of a torus. For a torus with parameters a and b,

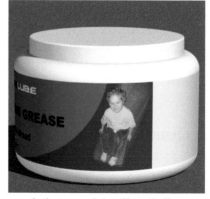

Figure 29.26. A product jar. Graphics design and photograph by Chris Suffern.

(a)   (b)

Figure 29.27. A scene rendered with two different environment lights. The sky images are courtesy of Lopez-Fabrega Design, http://www.lgrafix.com.

what aspect ratio must the image have to completely cover the surface of the torus without gaps or overlaps? If you want to avoid visual discontinuities, what tiling conditions must the image satisfy?

29.4. Implement the light-probe map and use it to render Figures 11.8, 11.13, and 29.16.

29.5. Render the textured triangles in Figure 29.22.

29.6. Render the penguin in Figure 29.24.

29.7. Figure 29.25(a) shows a black-and-white Earth map. Use this to render a transparent Earth sphere like that in Figure 29.25(b) (see Exercise 31.17). There are JPG and PPM versions of Figure 29.25(a) on the book's website.

29.8. Implement a parameterized product jar (or bottle), as illustrated in Figure 29.26, and put a texture on it.

29.9. Implement a spatially varying emissive material and use it to render scenes with an environment light that has a texture on it. Figure 29.27 shows two examples.

29.10. Add the ability for the ray tracer to read texture image files from JPEG, TIFF, and other file formats. A possible approach would be to implement an inheritance hierarchy of image classes, with one derived class for each file type. Each derived class would define its own version of the function get_color.

30 Procedural Textures

Image courtesy of Riley Perry

 Objectives

By the end of this chapter, you should:

- understand the advantages and disadvantages of procedural textures;
- know how to implement 2D and 3D checker textures;
- know how to transform textures;
- know how to attach textures to transformed objects.

30.1 Introduction

Texture mapping and proceduralism are the two major texturing techniques used in computer graphics. Procedural textures use code to generate colors, instead of extracting them from images. A procedural texture's `get_color` function uses the coordinates of a hit point and algorithms to generate the color. This approach has a number of advantages and disadvantages compared with stored textures. The following lists are based on Peachey (2003).

671

Advantages.

- No mapping is required. Procedural textures can be defined for all points in world space, a property that allows objects to appear to be carved out of the texture material.
- Procedural textures are compact, with many requiring little or no storage of data.
- Many procedural textures take a number of parameters, a feature that allows a single algorithm or set of related algorithms to generate a variety of related textures.
- Procedural textures don't suffer the same aliasing problems as stored textures because they don't have a fixed resolution.

Disadvantages.

- Although the number of procedural textures is vast, they have all been written by programmers, and the programming has often been difficult.
- Because code has to be executed every time a procedural texture returns a color, they can be slower than stored textures.

Procedural textures were invented independently by Darwyn Peachey and Ken Perlin in 1985 and have since become an indispensable tool for image synthesis. In 1997, Perlin was awarded a Technical Achievement Award from the Academy of Motion Picture Arts and Sciences for his pioneering work on procedural textures. Figure 30.1 shows three examples of noise-based procedural textures. I'll discuss the wrapped noise and marble textures in Chapter 31.

In general, 3D procedural textures can be applied to non-generic objects, for example, arbitrary spheres and axis-aligned boxes. They can also be applied

(a)   (b)   (c)

Figure 30.1. Procedural textures: (a) wrapped noise; (b) marble; (c) Larry Gritz wood.

to transformed objects, but the relationship between affine transformations and textures has to be examined carefully (see Section 30.3).

30.2 Checker Textures

The only procedural textures I'll discuss in this chapter are 2D and 3D checker textures. There are a number of reasons for this. Checkers are a relatively simple example of a procedural texture. I've used 2D and 3D checker textures extensively in previous chapters to add interest to images and convey information about them. Its regular structure makes the 3D checker the best texture for illustrating textures and transformations in Section 30.3. Finally, the 3D checker is the most iconic texture in computer graphics. I'll start with the 3D version because the 2D versions to be discussed are actually more complex.

30.2.1 3D Checker Textures

The basic idea is to fill world space with axis-aligned cubes of two different colors, with the cubes in face contact and the colors alternating across the faces. Figure 30.2 shows a number of simple objects rendered with 3D checkers.

There are a number of ways we can define a 3D checker texture, but one of the simplest involves the Standard C Library function floor. As this returns a double, we can cast this to an int and use the code in Listing 30.1. Here, the Checker3D class stores the checker size and two checker colors.

There is, however, a problem with this implementation. When we use it to render the scene in Figure 30.2, the result in Figure 30.3 obviously leaves a

Figure 30.2. 3D checker textures.

```
RGBColor
Checker3D::get_color(const ShadeRec& sr) const {

    float x = sr.local_hit_point.x;
    float y = sr.local_hit_point.y;
    float z = sr.local_hit_point.z;

    if (((int)floor(x / size) + (int)floor(y / size) + (int)floor(z /
        size)) % 2 == 0) return (color1);
    else
        return (color2);
}
```

Listing 30.1. The function `Checker3D::get_color`.

lot to be desired. Although the curved surfaces are fine, there are no checkers on the flat surfaces. The reason is that these lie on checker boundaries, and as a result, the color returned by `Checker3D::get_color` depends on which way the hit-point coordinates are rounded.

Fortunately, there are numerous solutions, some more general than others. One solution is to avoid placing planar checkered surfaces on checker boundaries. For example, place a checkered ground plane at $y = \pm0.001$ instead of $y = 0.0$. This works, but it's inconvenient. It's better to have the solution built into the texture. We could use 2D checkers, but they only apply to certain surfaces. The simplest technique is to just jitter the hit-point coordinates by a small (negative) amount eps, as in Listing 30.2. This is the code I've used for Figure 30.2, but see Exercise 30.2, as there are still some problems.

Figure 30.3. The scene in Figure 30.2 rendered with the code in Listing 30.1 and one ray per pixel.

```
RGBColor
Checker3D::get_color(const ShadeRec& sr) const {

    float eps = -0.000187453738;  // small random number
    float x = sr.local_hit_point.x + eps;
    float y = sr.local_hit_point.y + eps;
    float z = sr.local_hit_point.z + eps;

    if (((int)floor(x / size) + (int)floor(y / size) + (int)floor(z /
        size)) % 2 == 0) return (color1);
    else
        return (color2);
}
```

Listing 30.2. Revised Checker3D::get_color function.

```
Checker3D* checker_ptr1 = new Checker3D;
checker_ptr1->set_size(1.0);
checker_ptr1->set_color1(black);
checker_ptr1->set_color2(white);

SV_Matte* sv_matte_ptr1 = new SV_Matte;
sv_matte_ptr1->set_ka(0.75);
sv_matte_ptr1->set_kd(0.75);
sv_matte_ptr1->set_cd(checker_ptr1);

Sphere* sphere_ptr = new Sphere(Point3D(-9.5, -1, 0), 2.5);
sphere_ptr->set_material(sv_matte_ptr1);
add_object(sphere_ptr);
```

Listing 30.3. Code fragment from the Figure 30.2 build function.

Like all 3D procedural textures, the 3D checker is simple to use once you have implemented the algorithm. As an example, Listing 30.3 shows how to set up the sphere in Figure 30.2. Because there's no mapping, the texture can be applied to an arbitrary sphere; the code in Listing 30.2 will return the checker color regardless of where the local hit point is in world space.

30.2.2 2D Checker Textures

In previous chapters, I've used a variety of 2D checker textures for illustration purposes. One complicating factor is that the 2D checkers have to be designed for each type of surface to which they are applied. In spite of the extra effort required, the results are worth it, as Figure 30.4 shows. If you compare this with Figure 30.2, you'll notice how much better the checkers look on the sphere, cone, and cylinder. That's because each surface has its own type of checker. For example, the sphere has checkers designed for a spherical surface, the curved surface of the cylinder has checkers designed for a cylindrical surface, and the top and bottom of the cylinder have checkers designed for a disk. I've called the 2D checkers in Figure 30.4 ConeChecker, CylinderChecker, DiskChecker, PlaneChecker, RectangleChecker, and SphereChecker.

I'll illustrate how to write 2D checkers with a texture that's designed for planes, as this is the simplest. Of course, all you really have to do is write a texture that uses a 2D version of the Checker3D::get_color function in Listing 30.2; a simple task. But 2D checkers allow us to do something that's quite useful in 2D but not all that useful in 3D. We can render checkers with outlines. I've used this in a number of places, such as the part objects in Chapter 19 and for illustrating reflections in Chapter 24.

Figure 30.5(a) shows a single checker of size s in the x- and z-directions, to be rendered with outlines of width w. To accomplish this, the code has to determine if a hit point p is in the outline or in the "interior" of the checker. We therefore need a distance measure across each checker in the x- and z-directions. Although the floor function can't provide this by itself, the function $f_x = p_x/s - \text{floor}(p_x/s)$ provides a linear measure of the distance in the x-direction. A plot of this function appears in Figure 30.5(b).

The function f_x has a maximum value of 1.0, and x is inside the outline when $f_x < w/(2s)$ or $f_x > 1 - w/(2s)$. This works for positive and negative values of x. The function PlaneChecker::get_color in Listing 30.4 is designed for the user to specify the outline width as an absolute value; that is, it's not specified as a fraction of the checker size.

Figure 30.4. The objects in Figure 30.2 rendered with a variety of 2D checkers.

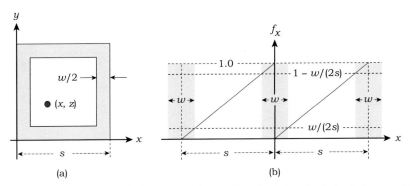

Figure 30.5. (a) A checker with the part of the outline that's inside it shaded gray; (b) plot of the function f_x across two adjacent checkers with the x extents that are inside the outline shaded gray.

```
RGBColor
PlaneChecker::get_color(const ShadeRec& sr) const {

    float x = sr.local_hit_point.x;
    float z = sr.local_hit_point.z;
    int ix = floor(x / size);
    int iz = floor(z / size);
    float fx = x / size - ix;
    float fz = z / size - iz;
    float width = 0.5 * outline_width / size;
    bool in_outline = (fx < width || fx > 1.0 - width) || (fz < width ||
    fz > 1.0 - width);

    if ((ix + iz) % 2 == 0) {
        if (!in_outline)
            return (color1);
    }
    else {
        if (!in_outline)
            return (color2);
    }

    return (outline_color);
}
```

Listing 30.4. The function `PlaneChecker::get_color`.

When all of the checkers are the same color, the outlines can help convey information about the shape of objects. See the figures in Section 19.7 and Exercise 30.5.

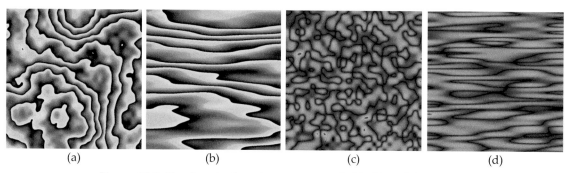

(a)   (b)   (c)   (d)

Figure 30.6. Simple noise-based textures unscaled in (a) and (c) and with nonuniform scaling in (b) and (d).

 ## 30.3 Textures and Transformations

We often need to apply affine transformations to textures, for the same reasons that we need to apply them to objects. For example, we may have to scale or orient a texture so that it looks appropriate when used to render a particular object. Also, scaling or shearing an original texture can transform it into something that looks quite different. To illustrate this, Figure 30.6 shows two simple noise-based procedural textures from Chapter 31 with and without nonuniform scaling. I'll call transformations that are applied directly to textures *intrinsic transformations*.

Another reason for transforming textures is to attach them to transformed objects. We can achieve this by transforming the textures with the same transformations as the objects.

30.3.1 Intrinsic Texture Transformations

Figure 30.7 illustrates why scaling a texture may be necessary. Scene designers must be able to adjust the scale of a texture to match the size of the object to which it's applied, and here we see spheres of different sizes rendered with the same 3D checker texture. Any of these spheres and checkers could be sensible combinations, except possibly the far-right sphere, which is completely inside a black checker. In contrast, the 3D checkers in Figure 30.8 have been scaled so that their size relative to the spheres remain the same.[1]

---

1. Of course, you can more easily achieve the same effect by making the checkers smaller.

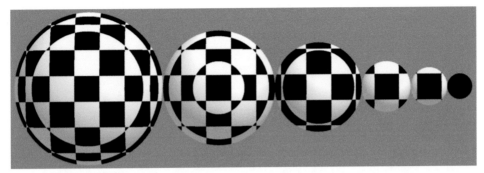

Figure 30.7. Spheres of different sizes with the same 3D checker texture.

Figure 30.8. Spheres of different sizes with 3D checker textures scaled with the size of the spheres.

How do we transform textures? The simple answer is that we don't. Instead, we inverse transform the hit point. Yes, that's similar to the process we use to intersect transformed objects, but here we only have to inverse transform a point, not a ray. Let me illustrate texture scaling with the help of Figure 30.9. Figure 30.9(a) shows a section of a checker texture with a hit point with coordinates (x, y), located in a yellow checker. Suppose we want to render the checkers twice as large, that is, scale them by a factor of 2 in the x-and y-directions. If we do this, as in Figure 30.9(b), the hit point in Figure 30.9(a) will now be in a white checker, as indicated. Now, let's scale the hit-point coordinates by 0.5 before we return the original checker texture color, as in Figure 30.9(c). Notice how this shifts the hit point to the same position in the texture as in Figure 30.9(b), with the result that the checkers will be rendered twice as large—exactly the result we want.

This process also works in 3D, of course, and for arbitrary sequences of affine transformations. To implement texture transformations, I'll use *texture*

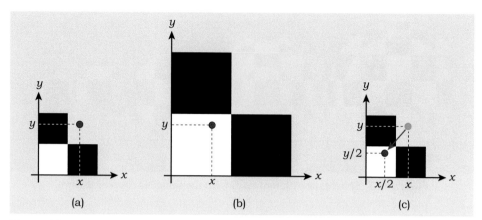

Figure 30.9. (a) Hit point on a checker texture; (b) checkers scaled by a factor of 2; (c) hit-point coordinates scaled by a factor of 0.5.

instances with the class TInstance, as declared in Listing 30.5. Note that TInstance inherits from Texture, in the same way that Instance inherits from GeometricObject.

```
class TInstance: public Texture {
        public:

                        // constructors, etc.

                        void
                        set_texture(Texture* t_ptr);

                        virtual RGBColor&
                        get_color(const shadeRec& sr) const;

                        // affine tranformation functions:

                        void
                        scale(const float sx, const float sy, const float sz);

                        // other affine transformations

        private:

                        Texture* texture_ptr;   // texture being transformed
                        Matrix inv_matrix;      // inverse transformation matrix
};
```

Listing 30.5. The class declaration TInstance.

```
void
TInstance::scale(const float sx, const float sy, const float sz) {

    Matrix inv_scaling_matrix;    // temporary inverse scaling matrix

    inv_scaling_matrix.m [0][0] = 1.0 / sx;
    inv_scaling_matrix.m [1][1] = 1.0 / sy;
    inv_scaling_matrix.m [2][2] = 1.0 / sz;

    inv_matrix = inv_matrix * inv_scaling_matrix;
}
```

Listing 30.6. The function TInstance::translate.

```
RGBColor
TInstance::get_color(const ShadeRec& sr) const {

    ShadeRec local_sr(sr);
    local_sr.local_hit_point *= inv_matrix;

    return (texture_ptr->get_color(local_sr));
}
```

Listing 30.7. The function TInstance::get_color.

Listing 30.6 shows the function TInstance::scale. Listing 30.7 shows the code for TInstance::get_color, but see Exercise 30.10.

Listing 30.8 shows an example of creating a checker instance and scaling it in a build function.

30.3.2 Object Transformations and Textures

To attach a texture to an object, we must apply the same transforms to the object and the texture. For example, if we translate an object 3 units to the right along the x-axis, we must also translate the texture 3 units to the right. How do we do this? The simplest way is to only apply textures to generic objects and always evaluate the texture in the local coordinate system of the generic object.

Figure 30.10 illustrates this process, where we translate a generic box three units to the right along the x-axis with a checker texture attached. Consider a ray that hits the translated box in the middle of the yellow checker at the red

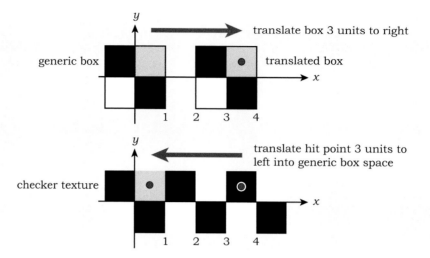

Figure 30.10. The box at the top is translated 3 units to the right, while the hit point on the texture is translated 3 units to the left.

dot, with coordinate $x = 3.5$. In the untranslated checker texture in the lower half of the figure, the center of the yellow checker is at $x = 0.5$, while the hit point at $x = 3.5$ is in the middle of a black checker. In this case, we have to translate the hit point three units to the left to get it into the middle of the yellow square. For translation, this is exactly what we do when we inverse transform the ray and intersect it with the generic object. This also applies for an arbitrary sequence of affine transformations.

It looks like we have to inverse transform the ray, but fortunately, we don't. The simplest way to implement this is to compute the local hit point in the object's hit function and return it in the ShadeRec object, a process we have always carried out. As I explained in Section 21.4, each ray ultimately hits an untransformed object, and it's the hit-point coordinates on the untransformed object that the function Texture::get_color uses to compute the color. Therefore, you don't have to do anything new to attach textures to transformed objects.

Figure 30.11 demonstrates how texture and object transformations interact. Figure 30.11(a) shows a face of a generic box with a checker texture. In Figure 30.11(b), the checker has been scaled by a factor of 2 in the horizontal direction, and in Figure 30.11(c), the box has also been scaled by a factor of 2 in the horizontal direction. Notice how the texture has been scaled by another

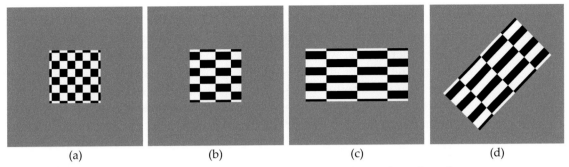

<table>
<tr><td>(a)</td><td>(b)</td><td>(c)</td><td>(d)</td></tr>
</table>

Figure 30.11. (a) Generic box and checker; (b) checker scaled by a factor of 2 in the *x*-direction; (c) box scaled by a factor of 2 in the *x*-direction, (d) box rotated 45° about the *z*-axis.

```
void
World::build(void) {

    // construct view plane, etc.

    Checker3D* checker_ptr = new Checker3D;
    checker_ptr->set_size(0.3);
    checker_ptr->set_color1(white);
    checker_ptr->set_color2(black);

    TInstance* checker_ptr2 = new TInstance(checker_ptr);
    checker_ptr2->scale(2, 1, 1);

    SV_Matte* sv_matte_ptr = new SV_Matte;
    sv_matte_ptr->set_ka(0.8);
    sv_matte_ptr->set_kd(0.4);
    sv_matte_ptr->set_cd(checker_ptr2);

    Box* box_ptr1 = new Box(Point3D(-1.0), Point3D(1.0));
    box_ptr1->set_material(sv_matte_ptr);

    Instance* box_ptr = new Instance(box_ptr1);
    box_ptr->scale(2, 1, 1);
    box_ptr->rotate_z(45);
    add_object(box_ptr);
}
```

Listing 30.8. Part of the build function for Figure 30.11.

factor of 2 with the box. In Figure 30.11(d), the box has been rotated, and so has the texture. Part of the build function for this figure is in Listing 30.8.

30.3.3 Excluding Object Transformations

Sometimes, we don't want to apply all of an object's transformations to a texture. In other words, we want the object to *slide through* the texture instead of having the texture attached. Scaling an object is an example. Suppose we wanted to model a round checkered tabletop as in the left of Figure 30.12. We start with a generic cylinder, shown in the middle, scale it by (10, 0.5, 10), and translate it into position. The problem is that if we apply the cylinder's scaling to the checker, we end up with the result on the right, which, in this case, is not what we want.

We therefore need a way to *exclude* some object transformations from the texture. I do this by including a boolean `transform_the_texture` data member in the (geometric object) `Instance` class, which is set to true by default (see Listing 21.5). Build functions can set it to false, in which case the statement

```
if (!transform_the_texture)            // for textures
    sr.local_hit_point = ray.o + t * ray.d;
```

from the `Instance::hit` function in Listing 21.6 results in the hit point on the *transformed* object being returned, instead of the untransformed object hit point. For nested instances, the assignment `sr.local_hit_point = ray.o + t * ray.d;` will be executed multiple times as the recursion stack unwinds, but the final assignment will be made with the original, untransformed ray. Because this mechanism only allows us to exclude a single transformation at a time, we have to construct a separate instance for each transformation that we wanted to exclude.

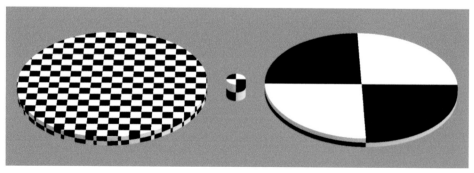

Figure 30.12. Generic circular cylinder in the middle, with scaled and translated versions to the left and right.

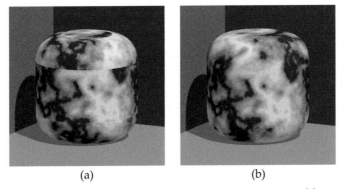

(a)   (b)

Figure 30.13. (a) Beveled cylinder rendered with a discontinuous marble texture; (b) rendered with a continuous marble texture.

As a further example, Figure 30.13(a) shows a beveled cylinder rendered with a marble texture from Chapter 31, where the marble is discontinuous across the bevel edges. This problem is caused by the fact that the bevels are tori and have been translated vertically from their generic locations to the bevel locations. By default, the texture is translated with these. In contrast, the vertical curved surface (an open cylinder) and the disks at the top and bottom are not translated.

The following is a code fragment from the BeveledCylinder constructor that constructs the top bevel:

```
Instance* top_bevel_ptr = new Instance(new Torus(radius - bevel_radius,
                                   bevel_radius));
top_bevel_ptr->translate(0, top  - bevel_radius, 0);
objects.push_back(top_bevel_ptr);          // objects is Compound::objects
```

We need to add the statement

```
top_bevel_ptr->transform_texture(false);
```

before the torus is added to the list of objects, and we need to add a corresponding statement for the bottom bevel. The result appears in Figure 30.13(b), where the marble is now continuous. The animation **Attached.mov** shows a moving disk with a 3D checker attached; in contrast, the animation **NotAttached.mov** shows the weird effects that result when the disk moves through a stationary 3D checker texture.

Further Reading

The classic papers on procedural texturing are Peachey (1985) and Perlin (1985). The book *Texturing and Modeling: A Procedural Approach* (Ebert et al., 2003) is a great source of information on procedural textures. For example, it has chapters by Peachey (2003) and Perlin (2003).

Ferguson (2001) presents a nice collection of procedural textures. Apodaca and Gritz (2000) also discusses procedural textures. Shirley and Morley (2003) and Shirley et al. (2005) discuss a stripe texture that renders stripes of alternating colors, instead of checkers. Pharr and Humpheys (2004) discusses 2D and 3D checker textures.

 Questions

30.1. What are two ways that you can render a vertical plane with 2D checkers?

30.2. The following code fragment shows another way of implementing 2D and 3D checker textures:

```
if (sin(PI * x / size) * sin(PI * z / size)  * sin(PI * z / size) > 0.0)
     return (color1);
else
     return (color2);
```

What are its advantages and disadvantages compared with using the floor function?

30.3. How could you construct the left cylinder in Figure 30.12 without excluding any texture transformations?

 Exercises

30.1. Implement a 3D checker texture as described in Section 30.2 and use Figure 30.2 to test your implementation.

30.2. Make eps positive in Listing 30.2 and render the scene in Figure 30.2. Can you explain the differences in the checkers?

30.3. Figure 30.14 shows an open cylinder of radius 1.5 rendered with a 3D checker texture that has the indicated checker sizes. I have not applied any transforms to the checkers, and all images are correct. What has

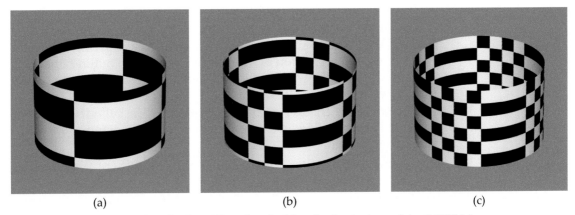

(a)   (b)   (c)

Figure 30.14. Open cylinder of radius 1.5 rendered with a checker texture of size 0.6708 (a), 0.416 (b), and 0.3 (c).

caused the wide strips of solid color? Prove that the formula between the cylinder radius and the checker size that creates this situation is $s = r/(2n^2 + 2n + 1)^{1/2}$, where s is the checker size, r is the cylinder radius, and $n \in [1, \infty)$. In Figure 30.14, $n = 1, 2, 3$ in Figure 30.14(a), (b), and (c), respectively.

30.4. Study the build functions for Figures 30.2 and 30.4 and note in particular how the cylinder and box are constructed in Figure 30.4. Implement the six types of 2D checker textures required for this figure.

30.5. Figure 30.15(a) shows a beveled cylinder rendered with three types of 2D outlined checkers: disk checkers for the top and bottom, torus check-

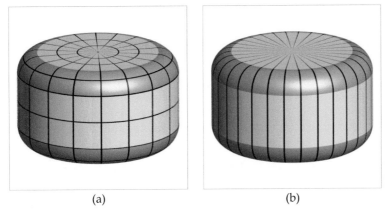

(a)   (b)

Figure 30.15. Objects rendered with outlined 2D checkers.

ers for the bevels, and cylinder checkers for the side. Notice how the radial outlines on the top and the bevels and the vertical outlines on the side surface all join smoothly. Implement this object, giving particular care to the implementation of the checkers so that the outlines match.

Figure 30.15(b) shows a variation where only a single set of outlines is rendered. Implement this as well.

30.6. Implement a 3D checker texture that's defined in cylindrical coordinates. This would allow you to render the cylinder in Figure 30.4 with a single solid texture.

30.7. Implement a 3D checker texture that's defined in spherical coordinates and test it with the sphere in Figure 30.4.

30.8. Implement the TInstance class as described in Section 30.3 and use Figure 30.11 to test it.

30.9. It's not difficult to write a version of any of the checker textures that renders the checkers with different *textures* instead of different *colors*. Figure 30.16 shows a sphere rendered with a marble and a wood texture. I've used a new version of the 2D sphere checkers to do this. It stores two texture pointers but doesn't include outlines. Notice how the specular highlight is on the wood and marble checkers, because the sphere is still rendered with a single material.

Figure 30.16. Sphere rendered with an SV_Phong material where the diffuse color texture contains a wood and a marble texture.

Write versions of one or more of the checker textures that incorporate two textures.

Exercises 31.16 and 31.17 extend this basic procedure into techniques that are far more practically useful.

30.10. The function TInstance::get_color in Listing 30.7 is inefficient because it copy-constructs the whole ShadeRec object each time it's called, but it only needs the local hit-point coordinates. We can make it more efficient by using a class derived from ShadeRec that only stores these coordinates and the world reference.[2] The get_color function would then look like the following:

---

2. It needs the world reference to construct the base class ShadeRec object in its constructor.

```
RGBColor
TInstance::get_color(const ShadeRec& sr) const {

    ShortShadeRec short_sr(sr.w, sr.local_hit_point);
    short_sr.local_hit_point *= inv_matrix;

    return (texture_ptr->get_color(short_sr));
}
```

Implement this and test how much time it saves.

30.11. Apply a series of affine transformations to the textured triangle meshes in Figures 29.22 and 29.24 and make sure that everything is transformed correctly. Then, try to exclude the transformations as discussed in Section 30.3.3. Can you explain the results?

31 Noise-Based Textures

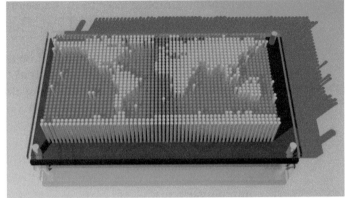

Image courtesy of Mark Langsworth

Objectives

By the end of this chapter, you should:

- understand the desirable properties of noise functions for texture synthesis;
- understand how to construct and interpolate 3D lattice noises;
- understand how sums of lattice noises can be used to construct the fractal sum, turbulence, and fractional Brownian motion functions;
- have implemented a variety of noise-based textures, including marble and sandstone.

A characteristic of natural textures is their randomness. They may contain structures or colors that repeat, but the exact details are always different. Stones, woods, and clouds are examples. We can simulate many of these textures with functions built from pseudorandom numbers. These are known as *noise functions*, or just noises. The original functions were invented by Ken Perlin in 1985 and have been used extensively for image synthesis ever since. Noises are different from *noise* used in previous chapters as the name for the random pixel colors that arise from undersampling. The texture colors in this chapter will be random, but deliberately so, and in a controlled manner.

31.1 Noise Functions

31.1.1 Desirable Properties

Here is the simplest way to make a noise function. Just make the color of a texture proportional to `rand_float`. Figure 31.1(a) shows the result of doing this with a grayscale image.

This is called *white noise*, and it has a major problem as far as image synthesis is concerned. The problem is that there's no correlation between its values at adjacent points, no matter how close together they are in world space. Figure 31.1(b) demonstrates this with a plot of the pixel values along the center row in Figure 31.1(a). This lack of correlation gives white noise an infinite amount of detail, and as such, it will always result in aliasing, no matter how high a resolution we use to render it. If we render an object with this texture, it will look roughly the same, regardless of how far we zoom into it, because hit points from adjacent pixels will always use different values of `rand_float`. In animation sequences, the surfaces of moving objects will flicker (see the animation **WhiteNoise.mov** on the book's website). Another problem is the boring appearance, as Figure 31.1(a) demonstrates.

Now, if `rand_float` by itself isn't suitable for texture synthesis, what sort of random function is? The following list of desirable properties is based on a list in Peachey (2003):

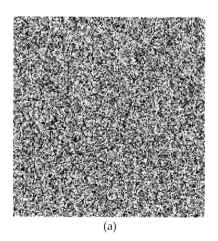
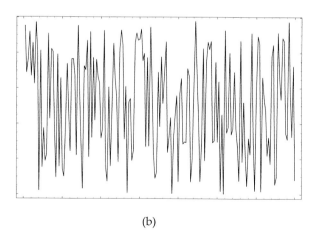

(a)   (b)

Figure 31.1. White noise: (a) 2D grayscale image; (b) 1D plot along center row of pixels in (a). Pixels are numbered along the bottom.

- it's a repeatable pseudorandom function;
- it has a known range, say, from −1 to +1;
- it's *band-limited*, which means that the rate at which it varies with position is limited;
- it doesn't exhibit obvious periodicities or regular patterns;
- it's *stationary*, which means that its statistical characteristics don't vary with position;
- it's *isotropic*, which means that its statistical characteristics are the same in all directions.

As it turns out, we can't construct a function that satisfies all of the above properties exactly, but we can construct a variety of functions that are close enough for texture-synthesis purposes.

31.1.2 Lattice Noise Functions

One of the oldest techniques for generating noise functions is based on uniformly distributed pseudorandom numbers (PRNs) at the vertices of an *integer lattice* that extends over all of world space. In an integer lattice, the coordinates of the lattice points are the integers: $(x, y, z) = Z^3$. As a result, the noise values are equally spaced and one unit apart in each coordinate direction. Noise values at points that are not on the lattice points are obtained by interpolation from the lattice-point PRNs. These are known as *lattice noise functions* and were devised by Perlin (1985). They have remained a popular way to implement noise functions for procedural texturing because they are efficient, come close to satisfying the above properties, and produce excellent textures.

If a single PRN is stored at each lattice point, we can use them to construct *value* lattice noise functions; if three PRNs are stored, we can use them to construct *vector* noise functions. I'll only discuss value noises in this chapter. Vector noises are used for bump mapping. Figure 31.2 is a schematic diagram of part of the integer lattice, which divides texture space into unit cubes.

The construction of a lattice noise function involves the following three steps:

1. Place noise values at the lattice points.
2. Use a hashing technique to find the cell in which a noise value is required.
3. Use interpolation to find noise values at points inside the cells.

Step 1 only has to be performed once, but Steps 2 and 3 have to be performed every time a noise value is required by the ray tracer. I'll discuss these steps in turn, using the techniques described by Peachey (2003), but first, we need to

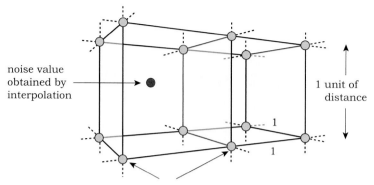

noise value
obtained by
interpolation

1 unit of
distance

noise values specified on integer lattice

Figure 31.2. Noise values on the integer lattice (blue) drawn in perspective and a value inside one of the cubic cells (red) to be computed by interpolation.

look at the lattice noise classes whose inheritance chart appears in Figure 31.3. For simplicity, I've left out a number of data members and have only listed the value noise functions.

The base class LatticeNoise stores the integer lattice and contains the code for setting it up. The two derived classes implement the interpolation techniques. As their names imply, LinearNoise implements linear interpolation, and CubicNoise implements cubic interpolation. The function that does this is value_noise, which is pure virtual in LatticeNoise and defined in each derived class. Listing 31.1 shows the relevant parts of the LatticeNoise class declaration, including class-specific constants that are defined in the file **LatticeNoise.h**.

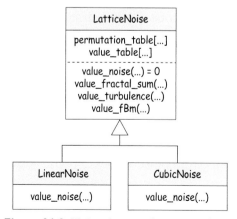

Figure 31.3. Noise classes inheritance chart.

```
const int kTableSize = 256;
const int kTableMask = kTableSize - 1;
const int seed_value = 253;

class LatticeNoise {
    public:

        // constructors, etc.

        virtual float
        value_noise(const Point3D& p) const = 0;

    protected:

        static const unsigned char permutation_table[kTableSize];
        float value_table[kTableSize];

    private:

        void
        init_value_table(int seed);
};
```

Listing 31.1. Declaration of the base class `LatticeNoise`.

The function `init_value_table` stores 256 pseudorandom numbers in the 1D array `value_table`, where `rand_float` is seeded with `seed_value`. Although the seed value is arbitrary, the seeding is critical for constructing the same noise functions each time we run the ray tracer. As it turns out, these 256 PRNs are all we need to simulate an infinite 3D lattice of PRNs. The code for `init_value_table` in Listing 31.2 uniformly distributes the PRNs in the range [−1, +1]. It's similar to the `valueTabInit` function in Peachey (2003). This function is executed in each `LatticeNoise` constructor.

```
void
LatticeNoise::init_value_table(int seed_value) {
    set_rand_seed(seed_value);
    for (int i = 0; i < kTableSize; i++)
        // in the range [-1, +1]
        value_table[i] = 1.0 - 2.0 * rand_float();
}
```

Listing 31.2. The `LatticeNoise::init_value_table` function.

We want any hit point p with world coordinates $(x, y, z) \in (-\infty, +\infty)^3$ to appear to be somewhere in the lattice. The illusion that we have an infinite 3D lattice is due to the following clever programming by Perlin and Peachey. The first step is to find the integer parts of the hit point's coordinates, but here, we can get the integer coordinates (ix, iy, iz) by using the same technique that we used for the 3D checker in Section 30.2.1. We then hash (ix, iy, iz) into the range (ix, iy, iz) $\in [0, \mathsf{kTableSize} - 1]^3$ using the C bitwise-and operator &.[1] A simple approach would be to use

```
x_index = ix & kTableMask;, y_index = iy & kTableMask;,
z_index = iz & kTableMask;
```

but to reduce the aliasing effects due to the regular spacing of the lattice points, it's better to randomize the indices. Peachey does this by using an auxiliary array of kTableSize random integers in the range [0, kTableSize − 1]. This is the permutation_table array in Listing 31.1, which is initialized to the values in Peachey (2003, p. 70). The code is on the book's website at the start of the **LatticeNoise.cpp** file. Perlin uses a similar hashing technique.

Peachey then uses the two macros PERM and INDEX to access the value_table array:

$$\#define\ PERM(x)\ perm[(x)\&kTableMask] \tag{31.1}$$

$$\#define\ INDEX(ix,iy,iz)\ PERM((ix)+PERM((iy)+PERM(iz))) \tag{31.2}$$

Notice how the array index returned by INDEX has been hashed three times, once for each of the ix, iy, and iz values. You may be wondering why I haven't written the macros (31.1) and (31.2) as inline C++ functions. When I experimented with this, PERM ran about 10% slower, and the performance of INDEX was hopeless, probably because the recursive calls to PERM in INDEX prevented it from being inlined. I've therefore left them as macros, for reasons of efficiency and because they are part of the history of texturing. INDEX is called from LinearNoise::value_noise and CubicNoise::value_noise in Listings 31.3 and 31.6, respectively.

---

1. I use & instead of the mod operator %, because i % j can be negative when i < 0, but i & j is always non-negative (Peachey, 2003).

31.2 Interpolation Techniques

The technique we use to interpolate the lattice noise values determines, more than anything else, the quality of the resulting noise functions. I'll discuss two techniques here: trilinear interpolation and tricubic interpolation. Linear interpolation is simple and executes quickly but doesn't give good results; cubic interpolation is more complex, slower to execute, but gives better results. For each technique, I'll discuss interpolation in 1D, 2D, and 3D, in that order.

31.2.1 Linear Interpolation

Given two quantities, for example, the numbers a and b, a function that *linearly interpolates* these numbers is

$$f(x, a, b) = a + (b - a)\, x.$$

We have $f(0, a, b) = a$, and $f(1, a, b) = b$, with the numbers joined by a straight line segment as in Figure 31.4. As linear interpolation is a common operation, the function $f(x, a, b)$ has the popular name $lerp(x, a, b)$.

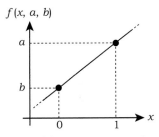

Figure 31.4. Linear interpolation.

We can use *lerp* to interpolate a 1D sequence of PRNs as shown in Figure 31.5, where the blue dots are the PRNs, equally spaced along

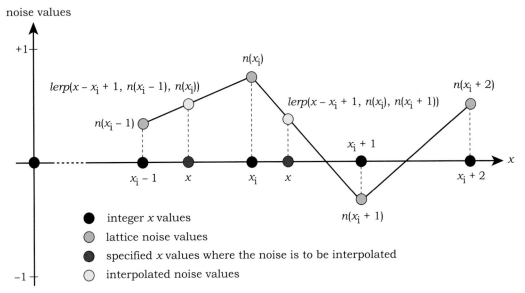

Figure 31.5. Piecewise linear interpolation of 1D noise values.

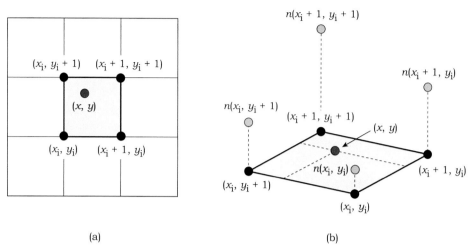

(a)   (b)

Figure 31.6. (a) Unit cell in the (x, y) plane with indicated corner coordinates and a point (x, y) to be interpolated; (b) 3D view of the PRNs at the corners, with heights above the (x, y) plane proportional to their values (all positive here for purposes of illustration).

the x-axis. The noise values between each successive pair of PRNs are interpolated with separate *lerp* functions. For example, the values between $n(x_i)$ and $n(x_i + 1)$, where $x \in [x_i, x_i + 1]$, are given by

$$lerp(x - x_i, n(x_i), n(x_i + 1)).$$

Note that the interpolated noise values only depend on the two PRNs on either side of the interpolated point x. The sequence of straight line segments is known as a *piecewise linear* interpolation of the noise values. Although the individual line segments are continuous at the noise values, their gradients are discontinuous.

This 1D linear-interpolation technique can be easily extended to higher dimensions. I'll discuss next the bilinear interpolation of a 2D grid of PRNs because this should make it easier for you to understand 3D interpolation. Figure 31.6(a) shows a unit cell in the (x, y) plane, shaded green, over which we'll interpolate the noise values. We only need these values at the four corners, as shown in Figure 31.6(b).

We compute the interpolated value in two steps. First, we interpolate *twice* in the x-direction, between the noise values $n(x_i, y_i)$, and $n(x_i + 1, y_i)$ and between $n(x_i, y_i + 1)$ and $n(x_i + 1, y_i + 1)$. This is shown in Figure 31.7(a) with the blue lines and orange dots. The interpolated values are

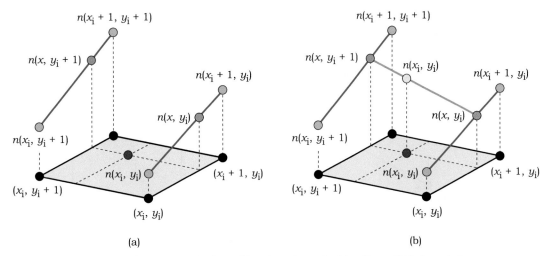

Figure 31.7. (a) Interpolation twice in the x-direction along the blue lines; (b) interpolation once in the y-direction along the orange line.

$$n(x, y_i) = lerp(x - x_i, n(x_i, y_i), n(x_i + 1, y_i)),$$
$$n(x, y_i + 1) = lerp(x - x_i, n(x_i, y_i + 1), n(x_i + 1, y_i + 1)).$$

Next, we interpolate these values *once* in the y-direction along the orange line, as shown in Figure 31.7(b), to give the final interpolated noise value $n(x, y)$ at the yellow dot. Its value is

$$n(x, y) = lerp(y - y_i, n(x_i, y_i), n(x, y_i + 1)). \qquad (31.3)$$

If you have understood the processes leading to Equation (31.3), you should be well placed to understand trilinear interpolation. Unfortunately, you will have to try to make do without the aid of diagrams analogous to Figures 31.6(b) and 31.7. The problem is that there are simply not enough dimensions to draw them. Figures 31.6(b) and 31.7 are 3D diagrams that show the PRNs and interpolated noise values for a 2D lattice of PRNs. We would need 4D diagrams to show the analogous information for a 3D lattice of PRNs. I can, however, show the *locations* of the PRNs at the vertices of a 3D cell, as in Figure 31.8(a), along with the location of a 3D interpolation point (red dot). I can also show the locations in 3D of the interpolated noise values in the x- and y-directions, as in Figures 31.8(b) and 31.9, and describe the interpolation process. What I can't show are the *values* of the PRNs.

We first interpolate *four times* in the x-direction, along the four edges of the cell that are parallel to the x-axis. These are drawn in blue in Figure 31.8(b),

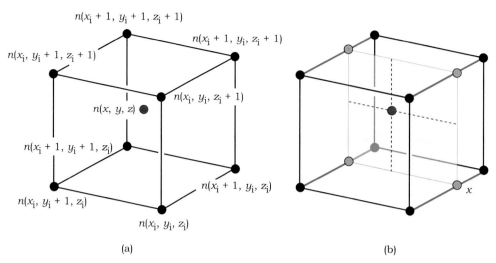

Figure 31.8. (a) Vertices of a cubic cell with lattice coordinates indicated and an interpolation point inside the cell; (b) locations of the four interpolated noise values in the x-direction.

and the locations of the interpolated noise values are indicated by the orange dots.

We next interpolate *twice* in the y-direction along the lines joining the top two and bottom two x-interpolated values. These are the orange lines in Figure 31.9(a), and the locations of the resulting y-interpolated noise values are indicated by the yellow dots. Finally, we interpolate *once* in the z-direction along the red line joining the two y-interpolated values (see Figure 31.9(b)).

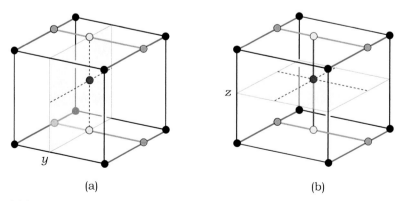

Figure 31.9. (a) Locations (yellow dots) of the two interpolated noise values in the y-direction; (b) location (red dot) of the single interpolated noise value in the z-direction.

```
float
LinearNoise::value_noise(const Point3D& p) const {
    int ix, iy, iz;
    float fx, fy, fz;
    float d[2][2][2];
    float x0, x1, x2, x3, y0, y1, z0;

    ix = floor(p.x);
    fx = p.x - ix;

    iy = floor(p.y);
    fy = p.y - iy;

    iz = floor(p.z);
    fz = p.z - iz;

    for (int k = 0; k <= 1; k++)
        for (int j = 0; j <= 1; j++)
            for (int i = 0; i <= 1; i++)
                d[k][j][i] = value_table[INDEX(ix + i, iy + j, iz + k)];

    x0 = lerp(fx, d[0][0][0], d[0][0][1]);
    x1 = lerp(fx, d[0][1][0], d[0][1][1]);
    x2 = lerp(fx, d[1][0][0], d[1][0][1]);
    x3 = lerp(fx, d[1][1][0], d[1][1][1]);
    y0 = lerp(fy, x0, x1);
    y1 = lerp(fy, x2, x3);
    z0 = lerp(fz, y0, y1);

    return (z0);
}
```

Listing 31.3. 3D trilinear interpolation of PRNs.

The above trilinear interpolation process can be coded as in Listing 31.3. This is based on C code from Hill and Kelley (2006).

I use a templated version of the lerp function so that I can use it to interpolate value and vector PRNs (see Listing 31.4). This is defined in the file **LinearNoise.h**, but it's not a member function of the LinearNoise class.

Figure 31.10(a) shows a grayscale image of LinearNoise::value_noise at a resolution of 150×150 pixels. Note the blocky, rectangular look, which is caused by the regular grid of lattice noise values and the linear interpolation. Figure 31.10(b) shows a 1D plot based on the pixels along the center row in

```
template<class T> T
lerp(const float f, const T& a, const T& b) {
    return (a + f * (b - a));
}
```

Listing 31.4. Templated `lerp` function.

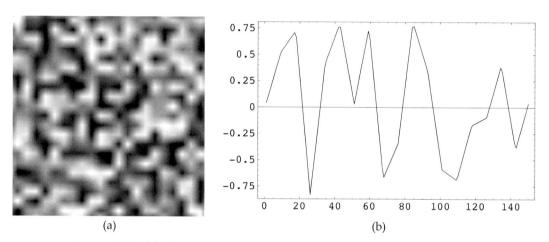

(a)   (b)

Figure 31.10. (a) 2D slice of linearly interpolated lattice noise; (b) 1D plot of linearly interpolated lattice noise.

Figure 31.10(a). As you would expect, the graph consists of a number of connected straight line segments.

31.2.2 Cubic Interpolation

With the preceding discussion of linear interpolation, you should be in a good position to understand the more complex processes of cubic interpolation. One-dimensional cubic interpolation involves constructing a curve that passes through the noise values and has a continuous slope everywhere. This is illustrated in Figure 31.11. Unfortunately, we pay a price in terms of algorithm complexity and computational cost for the smooth curve in Figure 31.11. To interpolate between the noise values $n(x_i)$ and $n(x_i + 1)$ *and* have continuous slopes at $n(x_i)$ and $n(x_i + 1)$, we not only have to use $n(x_i)$ and $n(x_i + 1)$, but also the neighboring noise values $n(x_i - 1)$ and $n(x_i + 2)$. That is, to smoothly interpolate noise values in the green interval $x \in [x_i, x_i + 1]$, we have to use noise values that span the light-gray interval $x \in [x_i - 1, x_i + 2]$.

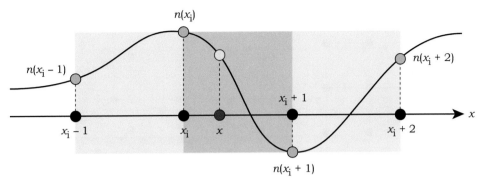

Figure 31.11. Cubic interpolation of 1D noise values.

How do we do the interpolation? There are a number of suitable mathematical curves that go under the collective name of *splines*. I'll use cubic Catmull-Rom splines (Catmull and Rom, 1974) because these go through the noise values and because we need splines of at least degree three (cubic) to give continuous slopes at the noise values. Although splines may sound mysterious, they are simply polynomial functions (Rogers, 2001). The curve in Figure 31.11 for the interval $x \in [x_i - 1, x_i + 2]$ is of the form

$$ax^3 + bx^2 + cx + d = 0,$$

where the coefficients are determined by the noise values $n(x_i - 1)$, $n(x_i)$, $n(x_i + 1)$, and $n(x_i + 2)$. I won't go into the details of how we derive the coefficient expressions; Hill and Kelley (2006), Rogers (2001), and other references cited in the Further Reading section cover that. Listing 31.5 shows the code for the function `four_knot_spline`, which is templated so that it can return

```
template<class T> T
four_knot_spline(const float x, const T knots[]) {
    T c3 = -0.5 * knots[0] + 1.5 * knots[1] - 1.5 * knots[2] + 0.5 * knots[3];
    T c2 = knots[0] - 2.5 * knots[1] + 2.0 * knots[2] - 0.5 * knots[3];
    T c1 = 0.5 * (-knots[0] + knots [2]);
    T c0 = knots[1];

    return (T((c3*x + c2)*x + c1)*x + c0);
}
```

Listing 31.5. The function `four_knot_spline`.

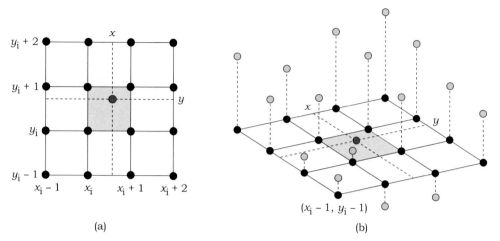

Figure 31.12. (a) A unit square and its eight neighbors with an interpolation point (x, y); (b) 3D view showing the 16 PRNs required for the interpolation.

a float or a vector. The value of the x parameter is where we want to evaluate the noise, and the lattice noise values are stored in the knots array. In spline theory, knots are a common name for the points that define the curve. This function is in the file **CubicNoise.h**.

Bicubic interpolation of noise values in 2D proceeds as follows. To interpolate in the green unit square $(x, y) \in [x_i, x_i + 1] \times [y_i, y_i + 1]$, in Figure 31.12(a), we need to use the noise values at the corners of this square and the corners of its eight neighboring squares. Figure 31.12(b) shows sample noise values (some negative) to illustrate the interpolation process. The red dot with coordinates (x, y) in the green square is where we wish to interpolate the noise values.

We first interpolate four times in the x-direction using noise values from $x_i - 1$ to $x_i + 2$. These are 1D interpolations with the y values $y_i - 1$, y_i, $y_i + 1$, and $y_i + 2$ and result in the four cyan spline curves in Figure 31.13(a). We then perform a single interpolation in the y-direction, using the interpolated noise values on the cyan curves at the required value of x. These are the orange dots in Figure 31.13(a), and the resulting spline is the orange curve shown in Figure 3.13(b). Finally, we obtain the required noise value at (x, y) (the yellow dot) by evaluating this curve at y.

Now we can tackle 3D tricubic interpolation. To interpolate the PRNs in a cubic cell, we need the PRNs at the vertices of the cell and its 26 neighboring cells in 3D, some of which are shown in Figure 31.14(a). A cubic cell has six face neighbors (mauve), 12 edge neighbors (yellow), and eight vertex

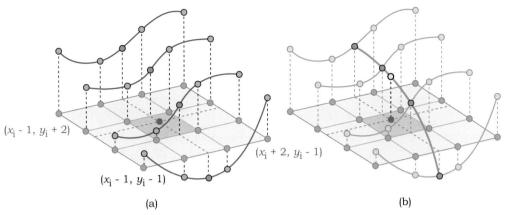

(a)   (b)

Figure 31.13. (a) Interpolation four times in the x-direction along the cyan spline curves; (b) interpolation once in the y-direction along the orange spline curve.

neighbors (gray). We can still draw the interpolation lines and the location of the interpolated noise values, but there are a lot more of these than there are for trilinear interpolation. We first interpolate 16 times in the x-direction along the cyan lines in Figure 31.14(b). These run from $x_i - 1$ to $x_i + 2$, with their

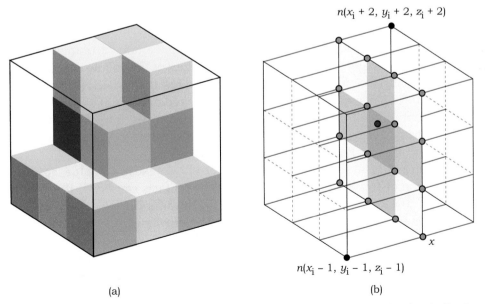

(a)   (b)

Figure 31.14. (a) Some of the neighbors of a cubic cell (green): face (mauve), edge (yellow), and vertex (gray); (b) interpolation in the x-direction 16 times (cyan lines).

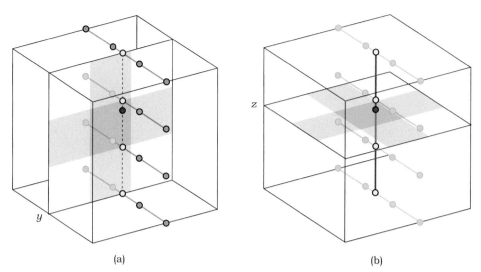

Figure 31.15. (a) Interpolation four times in the y-direction along the orange lines; (b) interpolation in the z-direction along the red line.

ends distributed from $y_i - 1$ to $y_i + 2$ and from $z_i - 1$ to $z_i + 2$. From these, we obtain 16 interpolated noise values at the required value of x: the orange dots in Figure 31.14(b).

We next interpolate four times in the y-direction along the orange lines in Figure 31.15(a) to get the four interpolated y values at the yellow dots. Finally, we interpolate once in the z-direction along the red line in 31.15(b) to get the noise value at the specified (x, y, z) location (the red dot again).

It's not difficult to translate this interpolation process into code. The algorithm `CubicNoise::value_noise` in Listing 31.6 is essentially the same as the function `vnoise` by Peachey (1998), translated to C++.

Figure 31.16(a) shows a grayscale image of `CubicNoise::value_noise` at a resolution of 150 × 150 pixels. Although the artifacts caused by the integer lattice are just as apparent as they are with the linear noise, the cubic noise has a softer, more rounded appearance. Figure 31.16(b) shows a 1D plot based on the pixels along the center row in Figure 31.16(a).

Because cubic noise looks better than linear noise, I'll use it for all of the texture images in the remainder of this chapter. The structure of the noise-based textures that I'll discuss in Sections 31.4–31.7 will make it simple for you to specify the type of interpolation in the build functions (see Listing 31.13 for an example).

```
float
CubicNoise::value_noise(const Point3D& p) const {
    int ix, iy, iz;
    float fx, fy, fz;
    float xknots[4], yknots[4], zknots[4];

    ix = floor(p.x);
    fx = p.x - ix;

    iy = floor(p.y);
    fy = p.y - iy;

    iz = floor(p.z);
    fz = p.z - iz;

    for (int k = -1; k <= 2; k++) {
        for (int j = -1; j <= 2; j++) {
            for (int i = -1; i <= 2; i++) {
                xknots[i+1] = value_table[INDEX(ix + i, iy + j, iz + k)];
            }
            yknots[j+1] = four_knot_spline(fx, xknots);
        }
        zknots[k+1] = four_knot_spline(fy, yknots);
    }

    return (four_knot_spline(fz, zknots));
}
```

Listing 31.6. The `CubicNoise::value_noise` function.

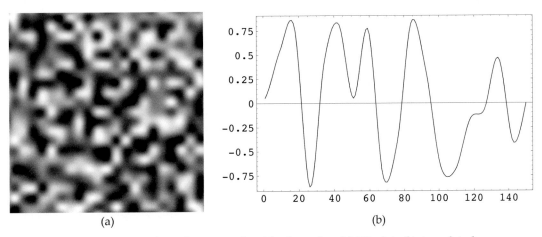

(a)   (b)

Figure 31.16. (a) 2D slice of tricubic interpolated lattice noise; (b) 1D plot of interpolated lattice noise.

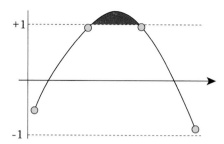

Figure 31.17. Overshooting of cubically interpolated noise values.

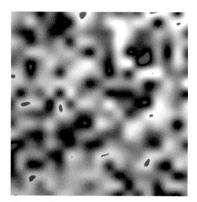

Figure 31.18. Cubic noise with out-of-range values rendered in red.

31.2.3 Overshooting

Here's a minor problem with cubic noise: it can overshoot the range [−1, +1] defined by the lattice noise values. Figure 31.17 shows how this can happen when two successive lattice noise values are close to +1 and the curve goes above the +1 value. This is a natural part of cubic interpolation. Figure 31.18 shows a 2D slice of cubic noise where values outside the range [−1, +1] are colored red.

Because overshooting can create rendering artifacts, it needs to be addressed. I've done this by clamping the final spline value in `CubicNoise::value_noise` to the range [−1, +1]. The `return` statement in Listing 31.6 then becomes

```
return (clamp(four_knot_spline(fz, zknots), -1.0, 1.0));
```

where `clamp` is the simple utility function in Listing 31.7.

This is a fairly crude approach because any of the 21 splines executed in Listing 31.6 can be out of range, but it works.

```
inline float
clamp(const float x, const float min, const float max) {
        return (x < min ? min : (x > max ? max : x));
}
```

Listing 31.7. The `clamp` function from `Maths.h`.

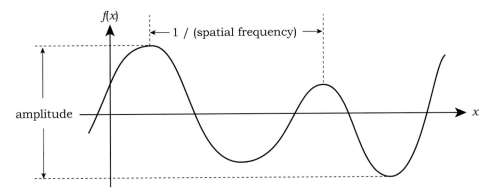

Figure 31.19. Definitions of amplitude and spatial frequency.

31.3 Sums of Noise Functions

We could implement textures that only use the basic linear and cubic noise functions, but as Figures 31.10(a) and 31.16(a) indicate, the textures aren't particularly interesting. The real utility of the noise functions for texture generation comes from summing them with different *amplitudes* and *spatial frequencies*, a technique known as *spectral synthesis*. This gives us much more visually interesting textures, but first, we need some definitions. Figure 31.19 shows part of a noise function where the amplitude is the vertical distance between the top and bottom, and the spatial frequency is the inverse horizontal distance between the crests.[2] Smoothly varying functions have a range of spatial frequencies up to some maximum frequency, which measures how closely spaced the crests are. In other words, the maximum frequency specifies how quickly the function varies with position. Functions that have a finite maximum spatial frequency are *band-limited*. Functions that don't have continuous slopes, such as the piecewise linear noise function in Figure 31.5, have infinite spatial frequencies. This can result in aliasing. White noise also has infinite spatial frequencies. The above discussion is very informal; spatial frequencies are part of *Fourier analysis* (see the Further Reading section).

A lattice noise function has an amplitude of about 2 and a maximum spatial frequency of about 2 (twice the lattice cell size).

---

2. The usual name for the amplitude of a function is the *range*.

31.3.1 Fractal Sum

The formula for the fractal sum function is

$$fractal\_sum(p) = \sum_{j=0}^{n-1} \frac{noise(2^j * p)}{2^j},$$ (31.4)

where p is a hit point that needs to be shaded and n is the number of terms. Here are the first three terms written out explicitly:

$$fractal\_sum = noise(p) + \frac{1}{2} noise(2 * p) + \frac{1}{4} noise(4 * p) + \dots.$$

This shows that the first term is just the noise function itself, while each successive term has half the amplitude of the previous term and twice the spatial frequency. Figure 31.20 illustrates how a fractal sum forms in 1D. Here, the top-left curve is the first term, and the curves in the middle, from top to bottom, are the second, third, and fourth terms. The curves on the right are a fractal sum with two terms at the top and eight at the bottom. This figure is based on Apodaca and Gritz (2000), p. 252, and is reproduced here with permission.

Because we multiply the spatial frequency in successive terms by the same factor that we divide the amplitude by (2.0 in this case), the terms are *statistically self-similar*. This is just a fancy way of saying that each term is a uniformly scaled version of the preceding term, but because the noise functions are random, each curve is different, and the similarity is only true in a statistical sense. If the functions were periodic, like sine functions, the terms

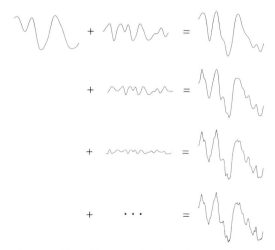

Figure 31.20. Terms in the *fractal_sum* function.

would be exact scaled copies of each other and therefore exactly self-similar. The fractal sum curve is also statistically self-similar in the sense that if we zoom into any section of it, the resulting curve will look similar. Of course, how far we can zoom in before the curves flatten out depends on how many terms we use, but we can keep it looking the same by adding more terms. This property extends to two and three dimensions.

Self-similarity is a key property of many fractals (see Mandelbrot (1972)). This is why the sum in Equation (31.4) is called a fractal sum; it's actually a fractal curve.[3] In 2D, it would be a fractal like a mountain range is a fractal.

In music, sounds whose frequencies differ by a factor of two are known as *octaves*. Because the spatial frequency of each successive term in a fractal sum is twice that of the preceding term, these are also commonly called octaves. I'll use this notation from now on and in the code.

As a fractal sum is a sum of noise functions, its value can be outside the range [−1, +1]. Although we can't compute the exact range, we can easily compute its bounds. From Equation (31.4), the minimum or maximum possible values would occur if all the noise functions happened to line up so that their minimum or maximum values occurred at the same point in space. The bounds can then be written as geometric series, and it follows from Equations (31.4) and (2.17) that

$$fractal\_sum \in \left[-\sum_{j=0}^{n-1} \frac{1}{2^j}, \sum_{j=0}^{n-1} \frac{1}{2^j} \right] = \left[-2\left[1 - \left(\frac{1}{2}\right)^{n-1} \right], 2\left[1 - \left(\frac{1}{2}\right)^{n-1} \right] \right]. \quad (31.5)$$

For example, when $n = 1$, $fractal\_sum \in [-1.0, 1.0]$, and when $n = 2$, $fractal\_sum \in [-1.5, 1.5]$. In practice, the range of values will be smaller than these bounds because it would be a fluke if all of the terms actually lined up. The code that computes $fractal\_sum$ scales the values to lie inside the interval [0, 1] because this allows us to keep the texture code as simple as possible. By clamping cubic noise to [0, 1], the values of $fractal\_sum$ are guaranteed to lie within the bounds.

Although I'll use the closed interval notation [0, 1] to specify the range of values returned by all of the noise function sums, it's a bit misleading in this context. The actual values returned will generally by a subset of this interval, for example, [0.25, 0.75], which I'll just refer to as being inside [0, 1].

Listing 31.8 shows the function `value_fractal_sum`. Note that this is a member function of `LatticeNoise` because the code is independent of how

---

3. Technically, it's called a band-limited fractal because the maximum spatial frequency, as determined by the highest term, is finite. True fractals are only mathematical concepts with infinite amounts of detail and are therefore not band-limited.

```
float
LatticeNoise::value_fractal_sum(const Point3D& p) const {
      float amplitude = 1.0;
      float frequency = 1.0;
      float fractal_sum = 0.0;

      for (int j = 0; j < num_octaves; j++) {
            fractal_sum += amplitude * value_noise(frequency * p);
            amplitude *= 0.5;
            frequency *= 2.0;
      }

      fractal_sum = (fractal_sum - fs_min) / (fs_max - fs_min);

      return (fractal_sum);
}
```

Listing 31.8. The function `LatticeNoise::value_fractal_sum`, where `fs_min` and `fs_max` are the fractal sum bounds.

`value_noise` is interpolated. The variables `num_octaves`, `fs_min`, and `fs_max` are data members of `LatticeNoise`.

How many octaves should you use? That depends on the scene and the effects you want. Often, you'll want the smallest details, which belong to the highest octave, to be about one pixel in size, but `num_octaves` can be difficult to estimate. In practice, I've found that between 1 and 8 octaves are enough for most scenes.

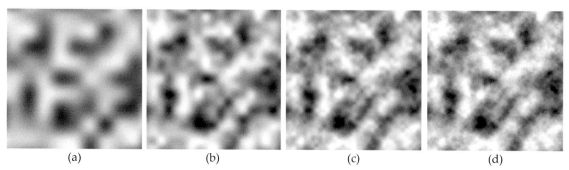

(a)   (b)   (c)   (d)

Figure 31.21. 2D cross sections of the *fractal_sum* function with 1 (a), 2 (b), 3 (c), and 8 (d) octaves.

Figure 31.21 shows 2D slices of *fractal_sum* rendered using the indicated number of octaves. A nice feature of *fractal_sum* is that the small-scale features that appear as the number of octaves increases help to disguise the regular lattice structure that's apparent in the pure cubic noise in Figure 31.21(a).

31.3.2 Turbulence

Ken Perlin's famous turbulence function from Perlin (1985) differs from the fractal sum function in only one aspect: it uses the absolute value of the noise functions. The formula is

$$turbulence = \sum_{j=0}^{n-1} \frac{abs(noise(2^j * p))}{2^j}. \tag{31.6}$$

Using the absolute value folds the noise functions across their zero values, which creates gradient discontinuities, which in turn create infinite spatial frequencies. To illustrate the folding, Figure 31.22 shows a plot of the absolute value of the cubic noise function in Figure 31.16(b). Compared with *fractal_sum* using the same number of octaves, the spatial frequency associated with the crests is essentially doubled.

The code for `LatticeNoise::value_turbulence` appears in Listing 31.9. Although *turbulence* and *fractal_sum* have the same maximum bound, the minimum value of turbulence is zero.

Figure 31.23 shows 2D slices of turbulence where the black lines in Figure 31.23(a) are the zero folds. As the number of octaves increases, these become wispy filaments that give turbulence a markedly different appearance from a fractal sum. Notice how the lattice structure is completely disguised.

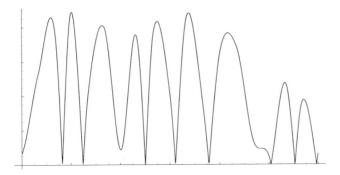

Figure 31.22. The absolute value of a cubic noise function.

```
float
LatticeNoise::value_turbulence(const Point3D& p) const {
    float amplitude = 1.0;
    float frequency = 1.0;
    float turbulence = 0.0;

    for (int j = 0 ; j < num_octaves; j++) {
        turbulence += amplitude * fabs(value_noise(frequency * p));
        amplitude *= 0.5;
        frequency *= 2.0;
    }

    turbulence /= fs_max;

    return (turbulence);
}
```

Listing 31.9. The `LatticeNoise::value_turbulence` function.

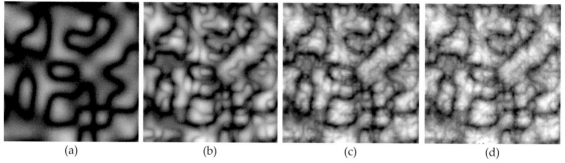

(a)   (b)   (c)   (d)

Figure 31.23. 2D cross sections of the *turbulence* function with 1 (a), 2 (b), 3 (c), and 8 (d) octaves.

31.3.3 Fractional Brownian Motion

We can generalize the fractal sum formula (31.4) by allowing the ratios of amplitudes and spatial frequencies in successive terms to have arbitrary values. The ratio of amplitudes is called the *gain*, and the ratio of spatial frequencies is called the *lacunarity*.[4] The resulting noise function is called *fractional Brownian motion*, or *fBm* for short. Its formula is

$$fBm = \sum_{j=0}^{n-1} gain^j * noise(lacunarity^j * p). \qquad (31.7)$$

---

4. As lacunarity is Latin for "gap" and represents, in this case, the gap between spatial frequencies, gap would be a simpler name, but lacunarity is commonly used.

When *gain* = 0.5 and *lacunarity* = 2, *fBm* is the same as *fractal_sum*, but *fBm* allows us to construct statistically self-similar noise functions with the more general relation of *gain* = 1/*lacunarity*. In addition, we can use any independent values of gain and lacunarity to get the texturing effects that we want. For arbitrary values of these parameters, *fBm* isn't self-similar.

It follows from Equations (31.7) and (2.17) that

$$fBm \in \left[-\sum_{j=0}^{n-1} gain^j, \sum_{j=0}^{n-1} gain^j \right] = \left[-\frac{1-gain^{n-1}}{1-gain}, \frac{1-gain^{n-1}}{1-gain} \right]. \qquad (31.8)$$

The closed-form bounds in Equation (31.8) are only valid for *gain* ≠ 1. When *gain* = 1, it follows from Equations (31.7) and (2.16) that

$$fBm \in [-n, n].$$

The code for *fBm* appears in Listing 31.10, where gain, lacunarity, fBm_min, and fBm_max are all data members of LatticeNoise. I've also kept the variable name num_octaves, although technically, the terms aren't octaves unless lacunarity = 2.

```
float
LatticeNoise::value_fBm(const Point3D& p) const {
        float amplitude = 1.0;
        float frequency = 1.0;
        float fBm = 0.0;

        for (int j = 0; j < num_octaves; j++) {
                fBm += amplitude * value_noise(frequency * p);
                amplitude *= gain;
                frequency *= lacunarity;
        }

        fBm = (fBm - fBm_min) / (fBm_max - fBm_min);

        return (fBm);
}
```

Listing 31.10. The function LatticeNoise::value_fBm.

The parameter space of *fractal_sum* and *turbulence* are simple to explore with a few figures because their single parameter num_octaves is discrete. In contrast, *fBm* has a far richer 3D parameter space with the addition of *lacunarity* and *gain*, which are floating-point numbers. I can therefore only show a few sample images.

Varying the gain has a dramatic affect on the behavior of *fBm*. Small values result in smoothly varying *fBm*s where the low-frequency terms dominate. If *gain* = 0, *fBm* is the same as *noise*(p) because there's only a single non-zero term. In Figure 31.24(a), with six octaves, the gain is 0.25, and the result is similar to *noise*(p), although there is some evidence of the high-frequency terms. Large values of gain result in rapidly varying *fBm*s where the high-frequency terms dominate. When *gain* = 1.0, there's no attenuation of the terms in Equation (31.7), and the result is a spiky function, as shown in Figure 31.24(b). Note that the vertical scales in Figures 31.24(a) and (b) are quite different. Figure 31.25 shows 2D plots of *fBm* for various values of *gain*.

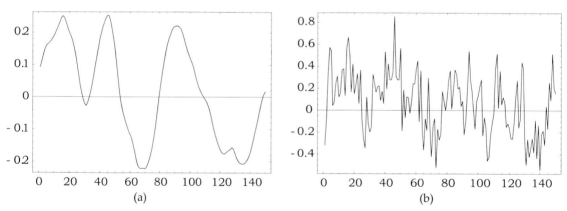

Figure 31.24. 1D plots of *fBm* with six octaves and *lacunarity* = 2: (a) *gain* = 0.25; (b) *gain* = 1.0.

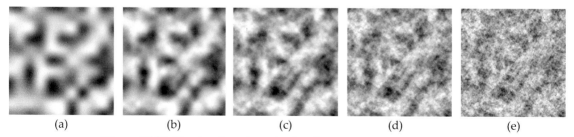

Figure 31.25. Varying the *gain* in the *fBm* function with six octaves and *lacunarity* = 2. From (a) to (e), *gain* = 0.0; 0.25; 0.5; 0.75; 1.0.

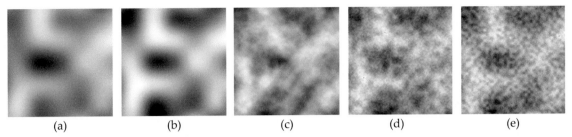

(a)   (b)   (c)   (d)   (e)

Figure 31.26. Varying the *lacunarity* in the *fBm* function with six octaves and *gain* = 0.5.
From (a) to (e), *lacunarity* = 0.5; 1; 2; 4; 8.

Figure 31.26 shows the results of varying the *lacunarity*. Note the interesting mottled appearance in Figure 31.26(e), which results from using *lacunarity* = 8. Figure 10.6 in Apodaca and Gritz (2000) shows similar sequences of images to those in Figures 31.25 and 31.26, although the parameters and image details are different.

 ## 31.4 Basic Noise Textures

To render the noise images in the previous sections in this chapter, you only have to implement two textures: *fBm* and *turbulence*. That's because *fractal_sum* is a subset of *fBm*, and both *fBm* and *turbulence* reduce to pure noise when there's a single term. The texture classes are simple because most of the code is in the noise classes. I'll discuss here how to implement an *fBm* texture called FBmTexture whose class declaration is in Listing 31.11. Build functions can assign a LinearNoise or a CubicNoise pointer to the noise_ptr data member. Adding a color to the texture allows it to produce much more interesting images than grayscale can produce. The data members min_value and max_value allow the texture to scale the value returned by the noise's value_fBm function.

Other than the usual functions such as constructors and access functions, we only have to write get_color, a simple function, as Listing 31.12 indicates.

It's useful to be able to expand or contract the range of values returned by value_fBm, as this allows us to increase or decrease the dynamic range of the texture colors. This is where min_value and max_value come in. The get_color function maps value = 0 to min_value and value = 1 to max_value, but since the values returned by value_fBm will usually be inside [0, 1], the scaled values will be inside [min_value, max_value]. We can use min_value < 0 and max_value > 1 to increase the range or use min_value > 0 and max_value < 1 to decrease it.

```
class FBmTexture: public Texture {
    public:

        // constructors, etc.

        virtual RGBColor
        get_color(const ShadeRec& sr) const;

    private:

        LatticeNoise* noise_ptr;
        RGBColor color;
        float min_value, max_value;    // scaling factors
};
```

Listing 31.11. Partial class declaration for FBmTexture.

```
RGBColor
FBmTexture::get_color(const ShadeRec& sr) const {

    float value = noise_ptr->value_fBm(sr.local_hit_point);
    value = min_value + (max_value - min_value) * value;

    return (value * color);
}
```

Listing 31.12. The function FBmTexture::get_color.

Figure 31.27 shows a number of spheres rendered with *fBm* textures. Figure 31.27(a) shows cubic noise again, still not particularly interesting, but arguably better than the grayscale images in Section 31.3. Figure 31.27(b) is *fractal_sum* with six octaves. Figure 31.27(c) shows the mottled *fBm* from Figure 31.26(e). A section of the build function for Figure 31.27(c) is in Listing 31.13. This shows how to construct the noise, texture, and material and how to expand the range with min_value and max_value.

Figure 31.28 shows the sphere rendered with a turbulence texture using eight octaves. In Figure 31.28(a), min_value = 0.0, and max_value = 1.2. In Figure(b), min_value = 0.25, and max_value = 0.75, which results in a reduced-contrast texture.

Setting values for min_value and max_value is a matter of trial and error. If you want to increase the dynamic range, overflow can easily occur, and it's

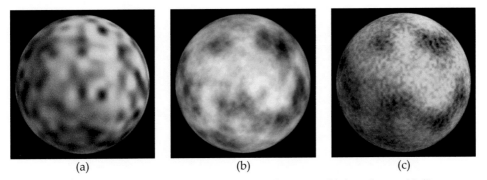

Figure 31.27. Colored noise functions: (a) cubic noise; (b) *fractal_sum*; (c) *fBm*.

```
void
World::build(void) {

    // build view plane, etc.

    // the noise:

    CubicNoise* noise_ptr = new CubicNoise;
    noise_ptr->set_num_octaves(6);
    noise_ptr->set_gain(0.5);
    noise_ptr->set_lacunarity(8);

    // the texture:

    FBmTexture* fBm_texture_ptr = new FBmTexture(noise_ptr);
    fBm_texture_ptr->set_color(0.7, 1.0, 0.5);    // light green
    fBm_texture_ptr->set_min_value(-0.1);
    fBm_texture_ptr->set_max_value(1.1);

    // the material:

    SV_Matte* sv_matte_ptr = new SV_Matte;
    sv_matte_ptr->set_ka(0.25);
    sv_matte_ptr->set_kd(0.85);
    sv_matte_ptr->set_cd(fBm_texture_ptr);

    // the object

    Sphere* sphere_ptr1 = new Sphere(Point3D(0.0), 3);
    sphere_ptr1->set_material(sv_matte_ptr);
    add_object(sphere_ptr1);
}
```

Listing 31.13. Build function fragment for Figure 31.27(c).

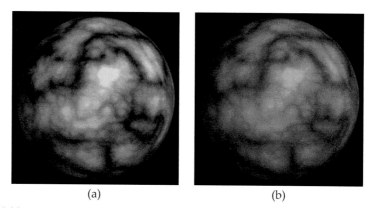

(a)   (b)

Figure 31.28. Turbulence texture rendered on a sphere with different values for min_value and max_value.

useful to be able to detect this. Fortunately, all you have to do is replace the return (value * color); statement in Listing 31.12 with

```
if (value < 0.0 || value > 1.0)
        return (RGBColor(1, 0, 0));
else
        return (value * color);
```

to return red when overflow occurs. This is independent of any shading or lighting. I used this code to render Figure 31.18.

 ## 31.5 Wrapped Noise Textures

We can produce another set of interesting textures by making two simple modifications to the FBmTexture::get_color function. First, we expand the amplitude of the noise function by multiplying it by a number that's greater than one. Then, we wrap the values back into the range $\in [0, 1]$ with the floor function, in exactly the same way that we computed fx, fy, and fz in the value_noise functions in Listings 31.3 and 31.6. This results in the noise value range [0, 1] being traversed multiple times and produces ridges of color in the textures when the value drops from 1 to 0. If this is hard to follow, don't worry, as it can all be done in two lines of code. Listing 31.14 shows the get_color function for a texture called WrappedFBmTexture. Here, value $\in [0, 1]$ exactly, provided the expansion_number is large enough, and there's no need to scale it with min_value and max_value.

```
RGBColor
WrappedFBmTexture::get_color(const ShadeRec& sr) const {

    float noise = expansion_number * noise_ptr ->value_fBm(sr.local_hit_point);
    float value = noise - floor(noise);

    return (value * color);
}
```

Listing 31.14. The function `WrappedFBmTexture::get_color`.

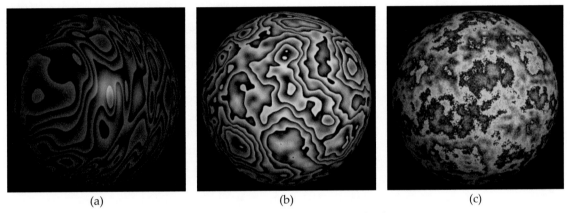

(a)   (b)   (c)

Figure 31.29. Various *fBm*-based textures with wrapped colors.

Figure 31.29 shows three examples. Figure 31.29(a) has two octaves, *lacunarity* = 4, *gain* = 0.25, and `expansion_number` = 2.0. Figure 31.29(b) has six octaves, *lacunarity* = 2, *gain* = 0.5 (so it's a *fractal_sum* function), and `expansion_number` = 5.0. Figure 31.29(c) shows a wrapped version of the flowery *fBm* texture from Figure 31.27(c) with six octaves, *lacunarity* = 6, *gain* = 0.5, and `expansion_number` = 3.0 (see also Exercises 31.6, 31.7, and 31.13).

 ## 31.6 Marble

We can use noise-based textures to simulate the appearance of a number of types of rock. I'll discuss marble here because it's a classic procedural texture. Natural marble is an igneous rock, because it was originally a sedimentary rock that was melted and had its colored layers undergo turbulent mixing. The marble texture simulates this mixing process by using the *turbulence* or *fractal_sum* functions.

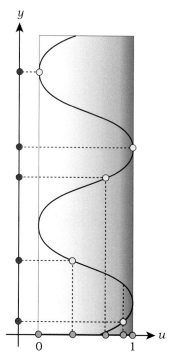

Figure 31.30. The y-coordinate of the hit point periodically cycles through the color ramp. The red dots on the y-axis are hit points, the yellow dots are the corresponding points in the ramp, and the orange dots are the resulting u texture coordinates.

Marble texture was developed by Perlin (1985) who used the *turbulence* function, but I'll use *fractal_sum* here because I've found that it produces better marble textures than *turbulence*. You should, of course, experiment with both.

To render a marble texture, we first need to create a color ramp that represents marble colors. There are a number of ways to do this: create a ramp image with a paint or image-processing program, or from a photograph, and use it in an image-based texture; use an interpolating spline whose knot values are of type RGBColor, or define the ramp algorithmically in the marble code. I'll use the first technique because it's the most flexible, and you can see the colors before you render the marble. Figure 31.30 shows a simple ramp that varies from white at the left to blue at the right.

Suppose we want to apply a marble texture to a particular object. We need a way to repeatedly cycle through the ramp as the object's hit points traverse the object. I do this by passing the y-coordinate of the hit point to a periodic function whose values are mapped onto the ramp. A curve that illustrates this is superimposed on the ramp in Figure 31.30. Although we could use a spline for the function, a sine function, as originally used by Perlin (1985), is quite adequate. The values of the sine curve are mapped to the texture coordinate $u \in [0, 1]$ and are used to compute the pixel coordinates in the ramp image. The mapping is

$$u = [1 + \sin(y)]/2. \tag{31.9}$$

Since the ramp is one-dimensional, the image that stores it only has to be one pixel high, but if you are like me, you'll need it high enough to be able to see the colors while you are working on it. Figure 31.31 shows the color ramps for the blue and gray marble textures that I've used in previous chapters.

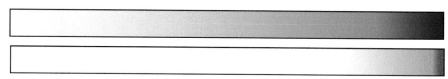

Figure 31.31. Two ramps that can be used to generate marble textures. The black outlines are only here to help visualize the ramps.

```
class RampFBmTexture: public Texture {

    public:

        // constructors, etc.

        virtual RGBColor
        get_color(const ShadeRec& sr) const;

    private:

        Image* ramp_ptr;        // stores the ramp image
        LatticeNoise* noise_ptr; // supplies the value_fBm noise function
        float a;                // the amount of fBm

};
```

Listing 31.15. Partial declaration of the class `RampFBmTexture`.

Listing 31.15 shows part of the declaration of the class `RampFBmTexture` that I'll use to implement marble. Because this texture will use the `value_fBm` function, it can be used to simulate other ramp-based textures in addition to marble, without changing the code.

Listing 31.16 shows a preliminary version of the function `RampFBmTexture::get_color` that just reproduces the ramp. The class `RampFBmTexture` doesn't need a mapping pointer because the mapping is built in with Equation (31.9). The vertical ramp image resolution doesn't matter, because the code only uses the top row.


```
RGBColor
RampFBmTexture::get_color(const ShadeRec& sr) const {

    float y = sr.local_hit_point.y;
    float u = (1.0 + sin(y)) / 2.0;
    int row = 0;            // use top row of ramp image
    int column = u * (ramp_ptr ->hres - 1);

    return (ramp_ptr->get_color(row, column));
}
```

Listing 31.16. Preliminary version of the function `RampFBmTexture::get_color`.

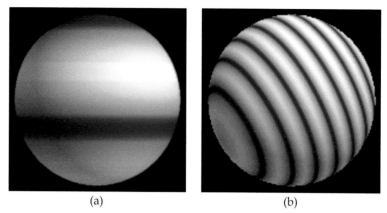

(a)   (b)

Figure 31.32. (a) The top ramp in Figure 31.31 applied to a sphere; (b) after scaling and rotation.

Figure 31.32(a) shows the results of mapping the top ramp in Figure 31.31 to a sphere. You can also apply affine transformations to the texture to adjust it to the sphere or to any other object. In Figure 31.32(b), I've scaled the texture in the y-direction and rotated it.

Of course, the ramp by itself is not marble. To render marble we have to add some fractal sum noise to the texture, in the following way:

$$p.y \leftarrow p.y + a * fractal\_sum(p). \tag{31.10}$$

Here, p is the ray-object hit point, and a is a number that specifies the amount of fractal sum noise that we add. Note that although the noise is added to the y-component of p, it's the full hit point p that is passed to *fractal_sum*. That's critical. If we consider a series of hit points where only the x- and z-components change, the y-component on the left-hand side of Equation (31.10) will still change. This fact, combined with the nature of the *fractal_sum* function, simulates the turbulent mixing of the layers. It was Perlin's original insight that led to his turbulence function and the first marble texture.

Listing 31.17 shows the final version of RampFBmTexture::get_color, which incorporates Equation (31.10). To generate marble, we use the fractal sum parameters (*gain* = 0.5, *lacunarity* = 2.0) in the value_fBm function.

Figure 31.33 shows the effects of increasing the amount of perturbation while keeping the number of octaves fixed at six. Notice how the veins get thinner and more tangled as a is increased. The only way to

```
RGBColor
RampFBmTexture::get_color(const ShadeRec& sr) const {

    float noise = noise_ptr->value_fBm(sr.local_hit_point);
    float y = sr.local_hit_point.y + a * noise;
    float u = 0.5 * (1.0 + sin (y));
    int row = 0;
    int column = u * (ramp_ptr->hres - 1);

    return (ramp_ptr->get_color(row, column));
}
```

Listing 31.17. Final version of the function `RampFBmTexture::get_color`.

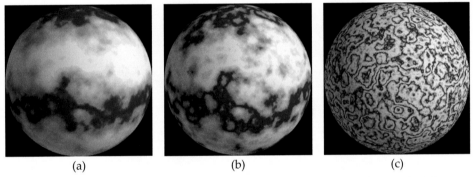

      (a)   (b)   (c)

Figure 31.33. Marble with different amounts of noise a: (a) 1.0; (b) 2.0; (c) 10.0.

really appreciate how the turbulent mixing is simulated is to watch the **MarbleForming.mov** animation on the book's website. In this animation, a is increased with each frame.

Figure 31.34 shows the effects of applying affine transformations to marble. The small-scale marble in Figure 31.34(a) is not particularly effective; marble is better seen in small sections. The nonuniform scaling in Figure 31.34(d) completely changes the appearance.

With the ramps in Figure 31.31, I normally use a = 2.5–3.5 and six octaves because this seems to produce the most realistic images. You could well argue, however, that none of the above images really look like marble, particularly when you compare them to a photograph of real marble in Figure 31.35.

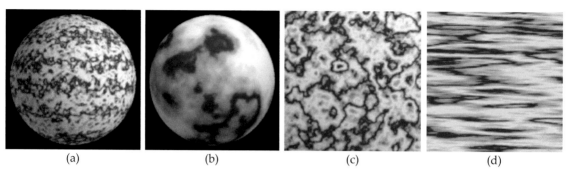

(a)   (b)   (c)   (d)

Figure 31.34. Marble with four octaves and different amounts of scaling: (a) uniformly scaled with (0.3, 0.3. 0.3) and a = 2.5; (b) uniformly scaling with (3.0, 3.0, 3.0) and a = 2.5; (c) close-up view with a = 10.0; (d) the texture in (a) nonuniformly scaled with (0.2, 2.0, 0.2).

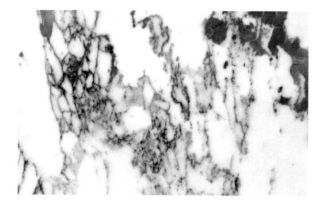

Figure 31.35. Real marble. Photograph by Chris Suffern.

31.7 Sandstone

Let me add an Australian flavor to this chapter by simulating some of the Hawkesbury River sandstone that underlies Sydney. Figure 31.36 shows photographs of four different sandstones, which do not do justice to this beautiful rock. Sandstone is sedimentary rock formed from layers of different-colored sands.

With `RampFBmTexture` implemented, it's a simple process to simulate sandstone because all we have to do is change the ramp and use appropriate parameters. I got the ramps by taking a thin section through each of the photographs in Figure 31.36, approximately perpendicular to the layers. These are shown in Figure 31.37.

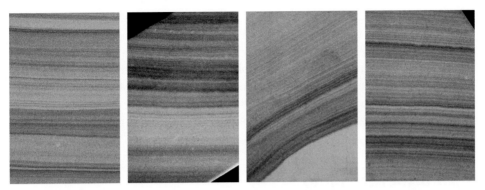

Figure 31.36. Hawkesbury River sandstone. Photographs by Kevin Suffern.

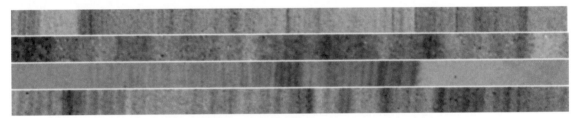

Figure 31.37. Sandstone ramps.

Figure 31.38. Sandstone cylinders created with the four ramps in Figure 31.37.

The difference between the marble and sandstone simulations is the amount of perturbation, which is much smaller for sandstone. The sandstone cylinders in Figure 31.38 use four octaves and $a = 0.1$. They are more realistic-looking than the marble because they are based on photographs. Because of the complexity of the ramps in Figure 31.37, an image-based technique is the only practical way to render sandstone.

But wait, how can we get away with this and create a 3D sandstone texture from a 1D sample in a photograph? The answer, in this case, lies in the nature of sandstone, the most attractive of which consists of parallel 2D layers of distinctive and contrasting colors, with *small* amounts of distortion. As long as we only render small chunks, the results can closely mimic real sandstone.

 ## Further Reading

A lot of Section 31.1 comes from Peachey (2003). Perlin's original paper (Perlin, 1985) introduced lattice noise, turbulence, marble, and other textures. You can find his implementation of lattice noise in Perlin (2003). It's instructive to compare this with Peachey's implementation presented here, as there are significant differences.

Peachey (2003) also presents the code for evaluating Catmull-Rom splines for any number of knots. Hill and Kelley (2006) and Rogers (2001) discuss the theory and application of spline curves and surfaces.

The version of *fBm* defined by Equation (31.7) is the same as RenderMan's *fBm* (Apodaca and Gritz, 2000). Musgrave's version, as described in Musgrave (2003), is expressed differently but does the same job.

The theoretical underpinnings of much of the material in Sections 31.1–31.3 lie in Fourier analysis. See, for example, Bracewell (2000) and Kreyszig (2005), Chapter 10.

Apodaca and Gritz (2000) contains RenderMan code for the Larry Gritz wood texture, along with an extensive discussion of it and images. This is a beautiful and insightful piece of noise-based modeling by Larry Gritz.

You should also check out the wonderful cellular textures in Worley (2006).

 ## Questions

31.1   Can overshooting happen with linearly interpolated lattice noise?

31.2.   From Equation (31.5), what are the bounds of *fractal_sum* in the limit $n \to \infty$?

31.3.   From Equation (31.8), what are the bounds of *fBm* in the limit $n \to \infty$? You will need to consider the cases *gain* < 1.0 and *gain* > 1.0 separately.

31.4.   Why doesn't the lacunarity affect the *fBm* bounds?

31.5. Is turbulence self-similar?

31.6. The main deficiency in the sandstone textures are that they are too "clean." If you look carefully at the photographs in Figure 31.36 and the ramps in Figure 31.37, you will see that real sandstone has a myriad of grains whose colors are darker than the surrounding material. These are pits on the surface created when sand grains have been dislodged during the smoothing process. The dark colors are due to shadowing. What has happened to the grains in the sandstone textures in Figure 31.38?

 Exercises

31.1. Add the noise classes to your project and make sure you get a clean compile.

31.2. Add the FBmTexture and TurbulenceTexture classes and use the images in Sections 31.3 and 31.4 to test them.

31.3. Use linear interpolation with the *fBm* and *turbulence* textures and see what difference it makes to the images in Sections 31.3 and 31.4. What difference does it make to the timings?

31.4. Implement the WrappedFBmTexture class and render the images in Figure 31.29 for testing purposes.

31.5. Experiment with a wrapped turbulence texture.

31.6. We can increase the visual interest of the wrapped *fBm* texture by using multiple colors. A simple way to do this is to have the get_color function return a color that depends on the value of noise, as Listing 31.18 demonstrates for two colors. This uses expansion_number = 2. For *n* colors, you can use expansion_number = *n*, but that's only a guideline. Figure 31.39 shows examples using one and three colors.

```
RGBColor
WrappedTwoColors::get_color(const ShadeRec& sr) const {
        float noise = expansion_number * noise_ptr->value_fBm(sr.local_hit_point);
        float value = noise - floor(noise);

        if (noise < 1.0)
                return (value * color1);
        else
                return (value * color2);
}
```

Listing 31.18. The get_color function for a two-color wrapped *fBm* texture.

Figure 31.39. Wrapped *fBm* texture with two colors in the left image and three colors in the right image.

31.7. Implement a *nested noises* texture. This is a texture that contains a pointer to another texture and whose `get_color` function calls `get_color` on the nested texture with the return statement `return (value * texture_ptr->get_color(sr));`. Figure 31.40 shows an example that involves nested multicolored wrapped *fBm* textures. You can, of course, nest the noises arbitrarily deep.

Figure 31.40. Nested multicolored wrapped *fBm* textures.

31.8. Implement the `RampFBmTexture` as described in Section 31.6 and use it to simulate marble by using the ramps in Figure 31.31.

31.9. Use *turbulence* instead of *fBm* to simulate marble. Compare the results.

31.10. Watch the **MarbleForming.mov** animation on the book's website and see if you can spot any differences between the simulated turbulent mixing and how layers of real rock would mix.

31.11. Use the ramps in Figure 31.37 to simulate sandstone.

31.12. Explore the *fBm* parameter space with the marble and sandstone ramps and design you own ramps. Figure 31.41(a) and (b) are images using the top ramp in Figure 31.37. Figure 31.41(c) uses a different ramp.

31.13. A limitation of the wrapped textures in Figure 31.29 is that each texture only contains a single color that's rendered from light to dark. The multicolored versions in Figures 31.39 and 31.40 still only have 2 or 3 colors rendered in the same way. The wrapped textures would be more flexible

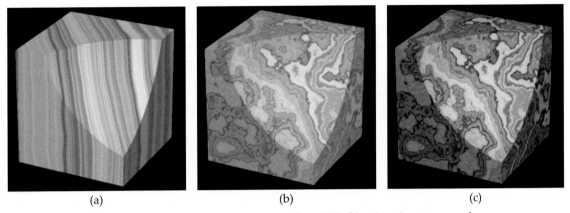

(a)   (b)   (c)

Figure 31.41. (a) Sandstone texture with one octave and $a = 0.05$; (b) using six octaves and $a = 1.0$ produces a texture that doesn't look like sandstone; (c) same parameters as in (b) but with a different ramp.

if they were based on color ramps, like the `RampFBmTexture`. Implement a wrapped ramp-based *fBm* texture as illustrated in Figure 31.42.

31.14. Implement a version of the `Reflective` material in Chapter 24 where the reflective color c_r is a texture pointer. You can then use any texture to modulate c_r. As an example, the wall tiles in Figure 29.2 use a turbulence texture for this purpose. See if you can replicate these. Also experiment with other textures. This exercise will require the spatially varying version of the `PerfectSpecular` BRDF.

Figure 31.42. Three examples of a wrapped ramp *fBm* texture.

31.15. Implement a texture that contains two texture pointers and returns the color of their product. That is, the get_color function will return texture_ptr1->get_color(sr) * texture_ptr2->get_color(sr).[5]

31.16. Implement a texture that contains two texture pointers and decides, for each hit point, which texture to use. The only difficulty with this would be making the decision, for which you would want maximum flexibility. Here is a suggestion. Write a set of classes organized in an inheritance hierarchy with the base class called, say, ChooseTexture. Each derived class would only have to define a single Boolean function called, for want of a better name, use_texture_1. The code inside the get_color function would then be simple, as the following code fragment shows:

```
if (use_texture_1(sr))
    return (texture_ptr1->get_color(sr));
else
    return (texture_ptr2->get_color(sr));
```

This approach solves a couple of potential problems. The function use_texture_1 may need a number of parameters, but these can't be function parameters because it needs the same interface for all applications. It may also need resources, such as an image or another texture. By using classes, any parameters and resources can be data members of the classes and available to the function use_texture_1 without using function parameters.

31.17. Repeat Exercises 31.15 and 31.16 for materials. This would provide one way to do Exercise 29.7, where the "material chooser" class stores the specularity map shown in Figure 29.25(a) and queries it to decide whether to use a glass material or the Earth texture material at each hit point.

31.18. On the book's website, you will find my implementation of Larry Gritz's wood texture, as illustrated in Figures 29.2 and 30.1(c). Add this to your ray tracer and use it to produce nice wood images. As this is a sophisticated texture, with many parameters, you will need to consult Apodaca and Gritz (2000).

30.19. Overlapping random spheres like those in Figure 22.17 can be used to create a 3D texture that mimics random crystals, but it's not trivial to implement. It has a lot in common with the lattice noises (Ferguson, 2001). See if you can implement this.

31.20. Implement some of Steven Worley's cellular textures.

---

5. The idea for this exercise comes from Pharr and Humphreys (2004).

Bibliography

Akenine-Möller, T., and E. Haines (2002). *Real-time rendering*, Second edition. Natick, MA: A K Peters.

Amanatides, J., and A. Woo (1987). A fast voxel traversal algorithm for ray tracing. In *Proceedings of Eurographics '87*, pp. 3–10. Amsterdam: Elsevier.

Anton, H. (2004). *Elementary linear algebra*, Ninth edition. New York: Wiley.

Apodaca, A. A., and L. Gritz (2000). *Advanced RenderMan: Creating CGI for motion pictures*. San Francisco: Morgan Kaufmann.

Arvo, J. (1995). Applications of irradiance tensors to the simulation of non-Lambertian phenomena. In *Proceedings of SIGGRAPH '95, Computer Graphics Proceedings, Annual Conference Series*, pp. 335–342. Reading, MA: Addison Wesley.

Arvo, J. and D. Kirk (1989). A survey of ray tracing acceleration techniques. In *An introduction to ray tracing*, edited by A. Glassner, pp. 201–262. San Francisco: Morgan Kaufmann.

Arvo, J. and D. Kirk (1990). Particle transport and image synthesis. *Computer Graphics (Proceedings of SIGGRAPH '90)*, 24(4), 63–66.

Ashikhmin, M., S. Premoze, and P. Shirley (2000). A microfacet-based BRDF generator. *Proceedings of SIGGRAPH 2000, Computer Graphics Proceedings, Annual Conference Series*, pp. 65–74. Reading, MA: Addison-Wesley.

Ashikhmin, M., and P. Shirley (2000). An anisotropic Phong light reflection model. Technical Report UUCS-00-014, University of Utah.

Ashikhmin, M., and P. Shirley (2002). An anisotropic Phong BRDF model. *journal of graphics tools*, 5(2), 25–32.

733

Beck, K. (2004). *Extreme programming explained: Embrace change*, Second edition. Boston: Addison-Wesley.

Birn, J. (2006). *Digital lighting & rendering*, Second edition. Indianapolis, IN: New Riders Press.

Blinn, J. F. (1977). Models of light reflection for computer synthesized pictures. *Computer Graphics (Proceedings of SIGGRAPH '77)*, 11(3), 192–198.

Blinn, J. F. (1989a), What we need around here is more aliasing. *IEEE Computer Graphics and Applications*, 9(1), 75–79.

Blinn, J. F. (1989b). Return of the jaggy. *IEEE Computer Graphics and Applications*, 9(2), 82–89.

Blinn, J. F. (1998). *Jim Blinn's corner: Dirty pixels*. San Francisco: Morgan Kaufmann.

Blinn, J. F., and M. E. Newell (1976). Texture and reflection in computer generated images. *Communications of the ACM*, 19(10), 542–547.

Bloomenthal, J. (Ed.) (1997). *Introduction to implicit surfaces*. San Francisco: Morgan Kaufmann.

Born, M., and E. Wolf (1999). *Principles of optics: Electromagmetic theory of propagation, interference and diffraction of light*, Seventh edition. Cambridge, UK: Cambridge University Press.

Bracewell, R. N. (2000). *The Fourier transform and its applications*, Third edition. New York: McGraw-Hill.

Bresenham, J. E. (1965). Algorithm for computer control of a digital plotter. *IBM Systems Journal*, 4(1), 25–30.

Bui, P. T. (1975). Illumination for computer generated pictures. *Communications of the ACM*, 18(6), 311–317.

Bulka, D., and D. Mayhew (2000). *Efficient C++: Performance programming techniques*. Boston: Addison-Wesley.

Catmull, E. and R. Rom (1974). A class of local interpolating splines. In *Computer Aided Geometric Design*, edited by R. Barnhill and R. Riesenfeld, pp. 317–326. New York: Academic Press.

Chiu, K., P. Shirley, and C. Wang (1994). Multi-jittered sampling. In *Graphics gems IV*, edited by P. S. Heckbert, pp. 370–374. San Diego, CA: Academic Press.

Cook, R. L. (1984). Shade trees. *Computer Graphics (Proceedings of SIGGRAPH '84)*, 18(3), 223–231.

Cook, R. L., T. Porter, and L. Carpenter (1984). Distributed ray tracing. *Computer Graphics (Proceedings of SIGGRAPH '84)*, 18(3), 137–145.

Cook, R. L., and K. E. Torrance (1981). A reflectance model for computer graphics. *Computer Graphics (Proceedings of SIGGRAPH '81)*, 15(3), 307–316.

Cook, R. L., and K. E. Torrance (1982). A reflectance model for computer graphics. *ACM Transactions on Graphics*, 1(1), 7–24.

Curless, B., and M. Levoy (1996). A volumetric method for building complex models from range images. *Proceedings of SIGGRAPH '96, Computer Graphics Proceedings, Annual Conference Series*, pp. 303–312. Reading, MA: Addison Wesley.

Debevec, P. (1998). Rendering synthetic objects into real scenes: Bridging traditional and image-based graphics with global illumination and high dynamic range photography. *Proceedings of SIGGRAPH '98, Computer Graphics Proceedings, Annual Conference Series*, pp. 189–198. Reading, MA: Addison Wesley.

Dutré, P. (2003). *Global illumination compendium*. Available online (http://www.cs.kuleuven.ac.be/~phil/GI/).

Dutré, P., P. Bekaert, and K. Bala (2006). *Advanced global illumination*, Second edition. Wellesley, MA: A K Peters.

Ebert, D. S., F. K. Musgrave, D. Peachey, K. Perlin, and S. Worley (2003). *Texturing & modeling: A procedural approach*, Third edition. San Francisco: Morgan Kaufmann.

Ferguson, R. S. (2001). *Practical algorithms for 3D computer graphics*. Natick, MA: A K Peters.

Fisher, F., and A. Woo (1994). R.E versus N.H specular highlights. In *Graphics gems IV*, edited by P. S. Heckbert, pp. 388–400. San Diego, CA: Academic Press.

Foley, J. D., A. van Dam, S. K. Feiner, and J. F. Hughes (1995). *Computer graphics: Principles and practice in C*, Second edition. Boston: Addison-Wesley.

Ford, W., and W. Topp (2001). *Data structures with C++ using STL*, Second edition. Upper Saddle River, NJ: Prentice Hall.

Fujimoto, A., T. Tanaka, and K. Iwata (1986). ARTS: Accelerated ray-tracing system. *IEEE Computer Graphics and Applications*, 6(4), 16–25.

Gardner, G. Y. (1984). Simulation of natural scenes using textured quadric surfaces. *Computer Graphics (Proceedings of SIGGRAPH '84)*, 18(3), 11–20.

Glassner, A. S. (1984). Space subdivison for fast ray tracing. *IEEE Computer Graphics and Applications*, 4(10), 15–22.

Glassner, A. S. (Ed.) (1989). *An introduction to ray tracing*. San Francisco: Morgan Kaufmann.

Glassner, A. S. (1995). *Principles of digital image synthesis*, Volumes 1 & 2. San Francisco: Morgan Kaufmann.

Goldsmith, J., and J. Salmon (1987). Automatic creation of object hierarchies for ray tracing. *IEEE Computer Graphics and Applications*, 7(5), 14–20.

Goral, C. M., K. E. Torrance, D. P. Greenberg, and B. Battaile (1984). Modeling the interaction of light between diffuse surfaces. *Computer Graphics (Proceedings of SIGGRAPH '84)*, 18(3), 213–222.

Greenler, R. (1994). *Rainbows, halos, and glories*. Cambridge, UK: Cambridge University Press.

Greenler, R. (2000). *Chasing the rainbow: Recurrences in the life of a scientist*. Milwaukee, WI: Elton-Wolf Publishing.

Guy, S. and C. Soler (2004). Graphics gems revisited: Fast and physically-based rendering of gemstones. *ACM Transactions on Graphics, Proceedings of ACM SIGGRAPH 2004*, 23(3), 231–238.

Haines, E. (1989). Essential ray tracing algorithms. In *An Introduction to Ray Tracing*, edited by A. S. Glassner, pp. 33–77. San Francisco: Morgan Kaufmann.

Haines, E. (2001). Triangles per vertex. *Ray Tracing News*, 14(1). Available online (http://www.acm.org/tog/resources/RTNews/html/).

Hall, R. (1989). *Illumination and color in computer generated imagery*. New York: Springer-Verlag.

Halton, J., and G. Weller (1964). Algorithm 247: Radical-inverse quasi-random point sequence. *Communications of the ACM*, 7(12), 701–702.

Hammersley, J. M., and D. C. Hanscomb (1964). *Monte Carlo methods*. London: Chapman and Hall.

Hanrahan, P. (1989). A survey of ray-surface intersection algorithms. In *An introduction to ray tracing*, edited by A. S. Glassner, pp. 79–119. San Francisco: Morgan Kaufmann.

Hanrahan, P., and J. Lawson (1990). A language for shading and lighting calculations. *Computer Graphics (Proceedings of SIGGRAPH '90)*, 24(4), 289–298.

He, D. X., K. E. Torrance, F. X. Sillion, and D. P. Greenberg (1991). A comprehensive physical model for light reflection. *Computer Graphics (Proceedings of SIGGRAPH '91)*, 25(4), 175–186.

Hearn, H., and M. P. Baker (2004). *Computer graphics with OpenGL*, Third edition. Upper Saddle River, NJ: Prentice Hall.

Hecht, E. (1997). *Optics*, Third edition. Boston: Addison-Wesley.

Heinrich, S., and A. Keller (1994a). *Quasi-Monte Carlo methods in computer graphics part I: The qmc buffer*. Technical Report 242/94, University of Kaiserslautern.

Heinrich, S., and A. Keller (1994b). *Quasi-Monte Carlo methods in computer graphics part II: The radiance equation*. Technical Report 243/94, University of Kaiserslautern.

Herbison-Evans, D. (1995). Solving quartics and cubics for graphics. In *Graphics gems V*, edited by A. W. Paeth, pp. 3–15. San Diego: Academic Press.

Hill, F. S., Jr. (1990). *Computer graphics*. New York: Macmillan Publishing Company.

Hill, F. S., Jr. (1994). Pleasures of "perp dot" products. In *Graphics gems IV*, edited by P. S. Heckbert, pp. 138–148. San Diego: Academic Press.

Hill, F. S., Jr., and S. M. Kelley (2006). *Computer graphics using OpenGL*, Third edition. Upper Saddle River, NJ: Prentice Hall.

Hodges, L. F., and D. F. McAllister (1985). Stereo and alternating pair techniques for the display of computer generated images. *IEEE Computer Graphics and Applications*, 5(9), 38–45.

Hunter, R. S. (1937). Methods of determining gloss. *Journal of Research of the National Bureau of Standards*, 17, 77–281. NBS Research Paper, RP 958.

Jensen, H. W. (1995). Importance driven path tracing using the photon map. In *Proceedings of the 6th Eurographics Workshop on Rendering*, edited by P. Hanrahan and W. Purgathofer, pp. 326–335. New York: Springer-Verlag.

Jensen, H. W. (1996a). Global illumination using photon maps. In *Proceedings of the 7th Eurographics Workshop on Rendering*, edited by X. Pueyo and P. Schröder, pp. 21–30. New York: Springer-Verlag.

Jensen, H. W. (1996b). The photon map in global illumination. PhD thesis, Technical University of Denmark.

Jensen, H. W. (2001). *Realistic image synthesis using photon mapping*. Natick, MA: A K Peters.

Johnsonbaugh, R., and M. Kalin (2000). *Object-oriented programming in C++*, Second edition. Upper Saddle River, NJ: Prentice Hall.

Kajiya, J. T. (1986). The rendering equation. *Computer Graphics (Proceedings of SIGGRAPH '86)*, 20(4), 143–150.

Kaplan, M. R. (1985). Space-tracing: A constant time ray tracer. *SIGGRAPH '85 State of the Art in Image Synthesis Seminar Notes*. New York: ACM Press.

Kato, T. (2002). The "Kilauea" massively parallel ray tracer. In *Practical parallel rendering*, edited by A. Chalmers, T. Davis, and E. Reinhard, pp. 249–327. Natick, MA: A K Peters.

Kato, T., H. Nishimura, T. Endo, T. Maruyama, J. Saito, and P. H. Christensen (2001). Parallel rendering and the quest for realism: The "Kilauea" massively parallel ray tracer. *SIGGRAPH 2001 Course Notes 40*. New York: ACM Press.

Kay, T. L., and J. T. Kajiya (1986). Ray tracing complex scenes. *Computer Graphics (Proceedings of SIGGRAPH '86)*, 20(4), 269–278.

Keller, A. (1995). A quasi-Monte Carlo method for the global illumination problem in the radiosity setting. In *Proceedings of Monte Carlo and Quasi-Monte Carlo Methods in Scientific Computing*, pp. 239–251. Berlin: Springer-Verlag.

Keller, A. (1997). Instant radiosity. In *Proceedings of SIGGRAPH '97, Computer Graphics Proceedings, Annual Conference Series*, pp. 49–56. Reading, MA: Addison Wesley.

Kernighan, B. W., and R. Pike (1984). *The UNIX programming environment*. Upper Saddle River, NJ: Prentice Hall.

Kernighan, B. W., and R. Pike (1999). *The practice of programming*. Boston: Addison-Wesley.

Kernighan, B. W., and D. Ritchie (1988). *The C programming language*, Second edition. Upper Saddle River, NJ: Prentice Hall.

Kirk, D., and J. Arvo (1988). The ray tracing kernel. In *Proceedings of Ausgraph 88*, edited by M. Gigante, pp. 75–82. New York: ACM Press.

Kolb, C., D. Mitchell, and P. Hanrahan (1995). A realistic camera model for computer graphics. In *Proceedings of SIGGRAPH '95, Computer Graphics Proceedings, Annual Conference Series*, pp. 317–324. Reading, MA: Addison Wesley.

Kollig, T., and A. Keller (2002). Efficient multidimensional sampling. In *Computer Graphics Forum (Proceedings of Eurographics 2002)*, 21(3), 557–563.

Korsch, H. J., and A. Wagner (1991). Fractal mirror images and chaotic scattering. *Computers in Physics*, 5(5), 497–504.

Kreyszig, E. (2005), *Advanced engineering mathematics*, Ninth edition. New York: John Wiley & Sons.

Lafortune, E. P., and Y. D. Willems (1993). Bi-directional path tracing. *Proceedings of Compugraphics '93*, pp. 145–153. Sintra, Portugal: Graphic Science Promotions & Publications.

Lafortune, E. P., and Y. D. Willems (1994). A theoretical framework for physically based rendering. *Computer Graphics Forum*, Special Issue on Rendering, 13(2), 97–107.

Lambert, J. H. (1760), *Photometry, or, on the measure and graduations of light, color, and shade*, translated by D. L. DiLaura (2001). New York, The Illuminating Engineering Society of North America.

Langetepe, E., and G. Zachmann (2006). *Geometric data structures for computer graphics*. Wellesley, MA: A K Peters.

Lee, M. E., and S. P. Uselton (1991). A body color model: Absorption of light through translucent media. In *Graphics gems II*, edited by J. Arvo, pp. 277–282. San Diego: Academic Press.

Levine, J. R., T. Mason, and D. Brown (1992). *lex & yacc*, Second edition. Sebastopol, CA: O'Reilly & Associates.

Lewis, J. P. (1984). Texture synthesis for digital painting. *Computer Graphics (Proceedings of SIGGRAPH '84)*, 18(3), 245–252.

Lewis, J. P. (1989). Algorithms for solid noise synthesis. *Computer Graphics (Proceedings of SIGGRAPH '89)*, 23(3), 263–270.

Lewis, R. R. (1994). Making shaders more physically plausible. *Computer Graphics Forum*, 13(2), 109–120.

Lippman, S. B., J. Lajoie, and B. E. Moo (2005). *C++ primer*, Fourth edition. Boston: Addison-Wesley.

Lord Kelvin (1901). Nineteenth century clouds over the dynamical theory of heat and light. *Philosophical Magazine*, 6(2), 1–40.

Mandelbrot, B. B. (1983). *The fractal geometry of nature*. New York: W. H. Freeman and Company.

Metropolis, N., A. W. Rosenbluth, M. N. Rosenbluth, A. H. Teller, and E. Teller (1953). Equations of state calculations by fast computing machines. *Journal of Chemical Physics*, 21(6), 1087–1091.

Meyers, S. (1996). *More effective C++: 35 new ways to improve your programs and designs*. Boston: Addison-Wesley.

Meyers, S. (2001). *Effective STL: 50 specific ways to improve your use of the standard template library*. Boston: Addison-Wesley.

Meyers, S. (2005). *Effective C++: 55 specific ways to improve your programs and designs*, Third edition. Boston: Addison-Wesley.

Möller, T., and B. Trumbore (1997). Fast, minimum storage ray-triangle intersection. *journal of graphics tools*, 2(1), 21–28.

Morrison, D., S. Wolff, and A. Fraknoi (1995). *Abell's exploration of the universe*. Philadelphia: Saunders College Publishing. The first edition of *Exploration of the universe*, by G. Abell, was published in 1964.

Mortenson, M. E. (1999). *Mathematics for computer graphics applications*, Second edition. New York: Industrial Press.

Musgrave, F. K. (2003a). A brief introduction to fractals. In *Texturing & modeling: A procedural approach*, Third edition, edited by D. S. Ebert, F. K. Musgrave, D. Peachey, K. Perlin, and S. Worley, p. 429–445. San Francisco: Morgan Kaufmann.

Musgrave, F. K. (2003b). Fractal solid textures: Some examples. In *Texturing & modeling: A procedural approach*, Third edition, edited by D. S. Ebert, F. K. Musgrave, D. Peachey, K. Perlin, and S. Worley, p. 447–487. San Francisco: Morgan Kaufmann.

Nicodemus, F. E., J. C. Richmond, J. J. Hsia, I. W. Ginsberg, and T. Limperis (1977). Geometric considerations and nomenclature for reflectance. Monograph 161, US Department of Commerce, National Bureau of Standards. Available online (http://units.nist.gov/Divisions/Div844/facilities/specphoto/pdf/geoConsid.pdf).

Niederreiter, H. (1992). *Random number generation and quasi-Monte Carlo methods*. Philadelphia: Society for Industrial and Applied Mathematics.

Oren, M., and S. K. Nayar (1994). Generalization of Lambert's reflectance model. In *Proceedings of SIGGRAPH '94, Computer Graphics Proceedings, Annual Conference Series*, pp. 239–246. New York: ACM Press.

Peachey, D. R. (1985). Solid texturing of complex surfaces. *Computer Graphics (Proceedings of SIGGRAPH '85)*, 19(3), 279–286.

Peachey, D. (2003). Building procedural textures. In *Texturing & modeling: A procedural approach*, Third edition, edited by D. S. Ebert, F. K. Musgrave, D. Peachey, K. Perlin, and S. Worley, p. 7–94. San Francisco: Morgan Kaufmann.

Perlin, K. (1985). An image synthesizer. *Computer Graphics (Proceedings of SIGGRAPH '85)*, 19(3), 287–296.

Perlin, K. (2003). Noise, hypertexture, antialiasing, and gesture. In *Texturing & modeling: A procedural approach*, Third edition, edited by D. S. Ebert, F. K. Musgrave, D. Peachey, K. Perlin, and S. Worley, p. 337–410. San Francisco: Morgan Kaufmann.

Pharr, M., and G. Humphreys (2004). *Physically based rendering: From theory to implementation*. San Francisco: Morgan Kaufmann.

Phong (1975), see Bui, P. T. (1975).

Reinhard, E., G. Ward, S. Pattanaik, and P. Debevec (2005). *High dynamic range imaging: Acquisition, display, and image-based lighting*. San Francisco: Morgan Kaufmann.

Rogers, D. F. (2001). *An introduction to NURBS: With historical perspective*. San Francisco: Morgan Kaufmann.

Rubin, S. M., and T. A. Whitted (1980). A 3-dimensional representation for fast rendering of complex scenes. *Computer Graphics (Proceedings of SIGGRAPH '80),* 14(3), 110–116.

Rubenstein, R. Y. (1981). *Simulation and the Monte Carlo method.* New York: John Wiley & Sons.

Samet, H. (1989a). *The design and analysis of spatial data structures.* Boston: Addison-Wesley.

Samet, H. (1989b). *Applications of spatial data structures.* Boston: Addison-Wesley.

Schlick, C. (1994). A survey of shading and reflectance models. *Computer Graphics Forum,* 13(2) 121–132.

Schreider, Y. A. (1966). *The Monte Carlo method.* New York: Pergamon Press.

Schwarze, J. (1990). Cubic and quartic roots. In *Graphics gems,* edited by A. S. Glassner, pp. 404–407. San Diego: Academic Press.

Shirley, P. (1991). Discrepancy as a quality measure for sample distributions. In *Proceedings of Eurographics '91,* edited by F. H. Post and W. Barth, pp. 183–193. Amsterdam: Elsevier.

Shirley, P. (1992). Nonuniform random point sets via warping. In *Graphics gems III,* edited by D. Kirk, pp. 80–83. San Diego: Academic Press.

Shirley, P. (2000). *Realistic ray tracing.* Natick, MA: A K Peters.

Shirley, P., M. Ashikhmin, M. Gleicher, S. R. Marschner, E. Reinhard, K. Sung, W. B. Thompson, and P. Willemsen (2005). *Fundamentals of computer graphics,* Second edition. Wellesley, MA: A K Peters.

Shirley, P., and K. Chiu (1997). A low distortion map between disk and square. *journal of graphics tools,* 2(3), 45–52.

Shirley, P., and R. K. Morley (2003). *Realistic ray tracing,* Second edition. Natick, MA: A K Peters.

Shirley, P., P. C. Y. Wang, and K. Zimmerman (1996). Monte Carlo techniques for direct lighting calculations. *ACM Transactions on Graphics,* 15(1), 1–36.

Shreiner, D., M. Woo, J. Neider, and T. Davis (2005). *OpenGL programming guide: The official guide to learning OpenGL, Version 2,* Fifth edition. Boston: Addison-Wesley.

Sierpinski, W. (1915). Sur une courbe dont tout point est un point de ramification. *Les Computes rendus de l'Académie des Sciences,* 160, 302–305.

Smith, A. R. (1995). A pixel is not a little square, a pixel is not a little square, a pixel is not a little square! (And a voxel is not a little cube). Technical Memo 6, Microsoft. Available online (ftp://ftp.alvyray.com/Acrobat/6_Pixel.pdf).

Smits, B. (1998). Efficiency issues for ray tracing. *journal of graphics tools*, 3(2), 1–14.

Suffern, K. G. (1993). *Blue glass*. SIGGRAPH '93 Electronic Art Exhibition.

Suffern, K. G. (1994). *LightLace*. In *Fractals: A 1994 calendar*, edited by F. K. Musgrave. New York: Universe Publishing.

Suffern, K. G. (1996). *Anemones*. In *Fractals: A 1996 calendar*, edited by D. H. Hepting. New York: Universe Publishing.

Suffern, K. G. (2000). Ray tracing four spheres at the vertices of a regular tetrahedron. *The Visual Computer*, 16(7), pp. 379–385.

Suffern, K. G., and P. H. Getto (1991). Ray tracing gradient index lenses. *Computer Graphics International '90 Proceedings*, pp. 317–331. New York: Springer-Verlag.

Suffern, K. G., S. Hopwood, and I. Sinclair (1993). Reflections in a spherical cavity. In *Models and techniques in computer animation*, edited by N. M. Thalmann and D. Thalmann, pp. 206–214. Tokyo: Springer-Verlag.

Sweet, D., E. Ott, and J. A. Yorke (1999). Topology in chaotic scattering. *Nature*, 399, 315–316.

Sweet, D., B. W. Zeff, E. Ott, and D. P. Lathrop (2001). Three-dimensional optical billiard chaotic scattering, *Physica D*, 154(3), 207–218.

Thomas, G. B., Jr., and R. L. Finney (1996). *Calculus and analytic geometry*, Ninth edition. Boston: Addison-Wesley.

Turk, G., and M. Levoy (1994). Zippered polygon meshes from range images. In *Proceedings of SIGGRAPH '94, Computer Graphics Proceedings, Annual Conference Series*, pp. 311–318. New York: ACM Press.

Veach, E. (1997). Robust Monte Carlo methods for light transport simulation. PhD thesis, Stanford University. Available online (http://graphics.stanford.edu/papers/veach_thesis/).

Veach, E., and L. J. Guibas (1994). Bidirectional estimators for light transport. In *Proceedings of the 5th Eurographics Workshop on Rendering*, pp. 147–162. New York: Springer-Verlag.

Veach, E., and L. J. Guibas (1995). Optimally combining sampling techniques for Monte Carlo rendering. In *Proceedings of SIGGRAPH '95, Computer Graphics Proceedings, Annual Conference Series*, pp. 419–428. Reading, MA: Addison Wesley.

Veach, E., and L. J. Guibas (1997). Metropolis light transport. In *Proceedings of SIGGRAPH '97, Computer Graphics Proceedings, Annual Conference Series*, pp. 65–76. Reading, MA: Addison Wesley.

Vince, A. J., and C. A. N. Morris (1990). *Discrete mathematics for computing*. West Sussex, UK: Ellis Horwood.

Wald, I., P. Slusallek, C. Benthin, and M. Wagner (2001). Interactive rendering with coherent ray tracing, *Computer Graphics Forum (Proceedings of Eurographics 2001)*, 20(3), 153–164.

Wallace, J. R., M. F. Cohen, and D. P. Greenberg (1987). A two-pass solution to the rendering equation: A synthesis of ray tracing and radiosity methods. *Computer Graphics (Proceedings of SIGGRAPH '87)*, 21(4), 311–320.

Wang, H., P. J. Mucha, and G. Turk (2005). Water drops on surfaces. In *Proceedings of SIGGRAPH 2005, Computer Graphics Proceedings, Annual Conference Series*, pp. 921–929. New York: ACM Press.

Warren, J., and H. Weimer (2002). *Subdivision methods for geometric design: A constructive approach*. San Francisco: Morgan Kaufmann.

Watt, A. (2000). *3D computer graphics*, Third edition. Boston: Addison-Wesley.

Weghorst, H., G. Hooper, and D. P. Greenberg (1984). Improved computational methods for ray tracing. *ACM Transactions on Graphics*, 3(1), 52–69.

Westlund, H. B., and G. W. Meyer (2001). Applying appearance standards to light reflection models. *ACM Transactions on Graphics, Proceedings of ACM SIGGRAPH 2001*, 20(3), 501–510.

Whitted, J. T. (1980). An improved illumination model for shaded display. *Communications of the ACM*, 23(6), 342–349.

Williams, A., S. Barrus, R. K. Morley, and P. Shirley, (2005). An efficient and robust ray-box intersection algorithm. *journal of graphics tools*, 10(1), 55–60.

Wilt, N. (1994). *Object-oriented ray tracing in C++*. New York: John Wiley & Sons.

Wong, T. T., W. S. Luk, and P. A. Heng (1997). Sampling with Hammersley and Halton points. *journal of graphics tools*, 2(2), 9–24.

Worley, S. (2003a). Advanced antialiasing. In *Texturing & modeling: A procedural approach*, Third edition, edited by D. S. Ebert, F. K. Musgrave, D. Peachey, K. Perlin, and S. Worley, pp. 157–176. San Francisco: Morgan Kaufmann.

Worley, S. (2003b). Cellular texturing. In *Texturing & modeling: A procedural approach*, Third edition, edited by D. S. Ebert, F. K. Musgrave, D. Peachey, K. Perlin, and S. Worley, pp. 135–155. San Francisco: Morgan Kaufmann.

Woo, A. (1990). Fast ray-box intersection. In *Graphics gems*, edited by A. S. Glassner, pp. 395–396. San Diego: Academic Press.

Index

O